THE COMPUTER IN THE VISUAL ARTS

Anne Morgan Spalter

Brown University

THE COMPUTER IN THE VISUAL ARTS

Addison-Wesley

AN IMPRINT OF ADDISON WESLEY LONGMAN, INC.

Reading, Massachusetts • Harlow, England • Menlo Park, California • Berkeley, California
Don Mills, Ontario • Sydney • Bonn • Amsterdam • Tokyo • Mexico City

Publishing Partner:	Peter Gordon
Senior Production Editor:	Amy Rose
Associate Editor:	Helen Goldstein
Production Coordinator:	Brooke Albright
Composition:	Michael and Sigrid Wile
Text Designer:	Melinda Grosser for *silk*
Copyeditor:	Jerrold Moore
Proofreader:	Jennifer Brownlow Bagdigian
Cover Designer:	Diana Coe

Access the latest information about Addison-Wesley books from our World Wide Web site: http://www.awl.com/cseng

Many of the designations used by manufacturers and sellers to distinguish their products are claimed as trademarks. Where those designations appear in this book, and Addison-Wesley was aware of a trademark claim, the designations have been printed in initial caps or all caps.

PANTONE MATCHING SYSTEM® and PANTONE® are registered trademarks of Pantone, Inc.

The programs and applications presented in this book have been included for their instructional value. They have been tested with care, but are not guaranteed for any particular purpose. The publisher does not offer any warranties or representations, nor does it accept any liabilities with respect to the programs or applications.

Library of Congress Cataloging-in-Publication Data

Spalter, Anne Morgan.
    The computer in the visual arts / Anne Morgan Spalter.
       p.   cm.
    Includes bibliographical references and index.
    ISBN 0-201-38600-3
    1. Art and electronics.   2. Computer art.   I. Title.
N72.E53S65   1999
702'.85—dc21   98-8294
                                       CIP

This book was typeset in FrameMaker 5.5 on a Power Macintosh G3. The insert was typeset in Quark 3.3. The fonts used were Bembo and Optima. It was printed on Rolland, a recycled paper.

1 2 3 4 5 6 7 8 9 10-MA-0201009998

This book is dedicated to my husband Michael, my parents Dane and Alice Morgan, my brother Dane Morgan III, my mother-in-law Josie Spalter, in memoriam, and to Andries van Dam.

PREFACE

Zither, chess, book, painting, sword.

These symbolize classical skill.

There was once a wanderer who cared nothing for fame. Although he had many chances for position, he continued to search for teachers who could help him master five things: zither, chess, book, painting, and sword.

The zither gave him music, which expressed the soul. Chess cultivated strategy and a response to the actions of another. Books gave him academic education. Painting was the exercise of beauty and sensitivity. Sword was a means for health and defense.

One day a little boy asked the wanderer what he would do if he lost these five things. At first the wanderer was frightened, but he soon realized that his zither could not play itself, the chess board was nothing without players, a book needed a reader, brush and ink could not move of their own accord, and a sword could not be unsheathed without a hand. He realized that his cultivation was not merely for the acquisition of skills. It was a path to the innermost part of his being. Skills Meditation (#21) from *365 Tao Daily Meditations* by Deng Ming-Dao *(Copyright © 1992 by Deng Ming-Dao. Reprinted by permission of HarperCollins Publishers, Inc.)*

The Computer in the Visual Arts is the book I wished I had when I began to use a computer to create art work. Although I was able to teach myself various software packages, I had no sense of the general concepts underlying them and knew of few other artists who made the computer their chief medium of expression. When I started to teach the use of computers in the visual arts, I realized even more acutely how hard it was to grasp the field as a whole—its history, the relevant art theory, the breadth of work of current practitioners, and the relationships between different types of software.

I wrote *The Computer in the Visual Arts* to answer my questions and those of countless other artists and designers: Why doesn't my color printout match the image on my screen? What is a spline, and why should I care? Who were the first artists to explore this field? How have other artists used the incredible capabilities of the computer in expressive ways? How does Postmodern theory apply to computer works? What does a "3D" program do?

Since I began to use a computer in my art over a decade ago, computer art and design courses have evolved from isolated electives in art schools to become standard offerings in colleges and universities around the world. At the same time, knowledge of the computer has become a prerequisite for many traditional jobs in design, illustration, and photography, as well as for entirely new types of jobs, such as multimedia and Web development. This book can help practicing artists learn new skills and provides curricular and reference material for a wide range of courses.

The Computer in the Visual Arts differs from program manuals and other books on computer graphics and computer art because it integrates history, theory, art examples, and explanations of the concepts underlying all of the major types of computer graphics software. Features of the book include:

- Hundreds of art works by leaders in the field of computer art.
- An abundance of diagrams and illustrations explaining visual concepts.
- Quotes from personal interviews with dozens of artists and pioneering computer scientists to help illuminate the origins of this dynamic field and suggest future directions.
- Descriptions of all the main program types: digital painting and photoediting, digital design and layout, the building and rendering of 3D worlds, animation, multimedia, and the Web, each presented as part of a larger picture.
- Chapters on input (such as scanning) and output (such as printing) that address the wide range of tools and techniques for working with art software and creating screen-based and hard-copy works.
- A chapter on electronic color that explains the color concepts affecting all types of visual software packages.
- Exercises at the end of each chapter designed for use by individual readers or in a classroom setting. Application-specific versions of the exercises help users get started right away with popular software.
- Annotated suggested readings at the end of each chapter to provide jumping off points for further exploration.
- A supporting Web site at http://www.awl.com/cseng/spalter

The Computer in the Visual Arts can be used by the amateur artist at home and by professional visual artists, including fine artists, graphic designers, photographers, videographers, illustrators, architects, industrial designers, animators, and multimedia and Web developers. It is appropriate for artists and designers just beginning to use a computer as well as those who have already embraced it, and for teachers and students in a classroom. It will also be useful for museum and gallery professionals, art critics, and art enthusiasts who wish to better understand the impact of the computer on visual art and design. The content is presented independently of specific computer platforms and software applications. Beyond basic computer proficiency, the only prerequisite is a desire to explore this important and inspiring new medium.

To contact the author please send email to ams@awl.com

ACKNOWLEDGMENTS

This book could not have been written without the invaluable assistance of numerous colleagues, students, friends, and family, as well as the talented staff at Addison Wesley Longman.

Of all the people who played a role in this project, Andy van Dam contributed the most time and energy, an extraordinary feat given his schedule! His first-hand knowledge of the field of computer graphics, both technical and historical, were important influences, and his passion for the material brought the concepts alive to me. In addition to teaching me most of the technical concepts in these pages, he gave detailed critiques of nearly every draft of the entire text and provided constant support and encouragement as mentor and friend. I am also enormously grateful to Alvy Ray Smith, who responded to an E-mail request for historical information about painting programs by asking to see the rest of the manuscript. He then read several drafts of the text and provided detailed critiques that were a graphics education in and of themselves. It was an honor to have access to his technical insights and many original ideas about the use of the computer in art and design.

I have been honored to have the intellectual and moral support of several influential individuals whose encouragement and belief in me has at times made all the difference. I would like to thank again Andy van Dam and Alvy Ray Smith, as well as Thomas Banchoff, Phil Davis, Carl Gustin, Roger Mandle, William J. Mitchell, and John Sculley.

Many subject-matter experts read sections of the manuscript; their feedback was instrumental in improving its accuracy and depth (any omissions or remaining errors are my own). A big thank-you to David Barkan, William Buxton III, Jonathan Corson-Rikert, Phil Davis, Joseph DeLappe, David Durand, Robert Duvall, David Elliott, Barbara Hoffman, John Hughes, Dane and Alice Morgan, Dane Morgan III, Paul Kahn, David and Tina Reville, Cynthia Beth Rubin, Mark Safire, Scott Sona Snibbe, Morey Stettner and Margie Wachtel, Peter Wegner, Brian Wallace, and William Wooten. Many others contributed imagery and quotations. A special thanks goes to David Reville for his photography, as seen in Figures 1.5, 2.16, 3.1, 3.3-3.6, 3.8, 3.12, 3.22, 9.2, 9.6, 9.7, and 9.14.

I taught my first computer art course in 1992 at the Rhode Island School of Design (RISD) and would like to thank Roger Mayer at Brown University and Christina Bertoni at RISD as well as others at RISD who supported my efforts to establish the joint Brown and RISD course "The Computer and the Visual Arts." In 1993, I began to work with The Brown University Computer Graphics Group, which has provided a wonderful home base for me over the past five years. I would like to thank all the staff, students, and faculty involved with the Graphics Group who answered my late-night questions and provided support throughout the long writing process. I am also grateful to Eugene Charniak, former Chair of the Computer Science Department, who saw fit to give me, then an adjunct lecturer in a different department, office space and, with the rest of the Computer Science Department at Brown, made me feel so welcome.

The Brown Graphics Group is part of a five-university consortium, the National Science Foundation Science and Technology Center for Computer Graphics and Scientific Visualization. My experiences with people from all five universities (Brown, Caltech, Cornell, the University of North Carolina at Chapel Hill, and the University of Utah) gave me a breadth of understanding and access to ideas that influenced the structure and choice of topics presented in this book. Images from these labs appear throughout the book, thanks in particular to innumerable folks at Brown and to David Breen (Caltech), Jonathan Corson-Rikert (Cornell), Sam Drake (Utah), and David Harrison (UNC).

One of the most enjoyable parts of writing this book has been the opportunity to meet (whether in person, online, or by phone) the artists featured herein. Many began to use the computer when doing so was considered quite radical, and I am especially indebted to all the pioneers who struggled against enormous odds to tame this new medium. Space precludes listing here all the artists whose work appears in the book, but I would like to thank each of them for letting me reproduce their work and for sharing their motivations and experiences with me. Some spent considerable additional time educating me on various aspects of the field and putting me in touch with their colleagues. In particular, I would like to thank Laurel Paley, Cynthia Beth Rubin, Michael Rees, Kathleen Ruíz, Roman Verostko, James Faure Walker, and curator Brian Wallace.

I have had the pleasure of working with a number of extraordinary students at Brown, many of whom provided significant assistance in the writing and illustration of this book. I would like to thank Jeff Beall for his 3D scenes in Figure 8.16; Steven Cuellar (a high school student who worked in the Brown computer grapics lab) for his lighthouse model, used in Figures 7.2, 8.21, and 8.37; Suzanne Hader for her research assistance; Scott Klemmer for Figures 1.4, 4.26, 6.2–6.4, 6.6–6.8, and 7.16; Jesse Kocher for the color mixing applets shown in Color Plate 1 and for Figure 7.27; Sara Langseth for various modeling projects; Michael Legrand for Figures 7.12, 7.19, 7.28, 8.5, 8.14, 8.34, 10.3, 10.13, 10.24, 10.37, and the 3D models used in Figures 11.6, 11.7, and 11.9d; Alex Slawsby for the Bryce landscapes appearing in Figures 7.31, 8.37, and 11.6; Jacob Tonski for his model of Narragansett Electric used in Figure 8.19; Diego Velasco for Figure 10.38; and all the students who worked with me as Summer Workshop TAs and as part of other Graphics Group projects.

Many companies provided tangible support in the form of software. I would like to thank Sara Allen and Norm Meyrowitz at Macromedia, Leslie Bixel and Martin Newell at Adobe, Roman Ormandy at Caligari, Tad Trueblood at Strata, Inc., John Wilczak at MetaCreations, and the folks at mFactory (purchased by Quark, Inc.), Lightscape, Inc., FutureWave (purchased by Macromedia), and Fractal Design (purchased by MetaCreations). I am also deeply indebted to Carl Gustin, who while at Apple Computer and then at Kodak, gave both psychological support and extremely generous donations of hardware, including the computers on which most of this book was written.

My family and friends have been enormously patient and understanding as I worked through countless evenings, weekends, and holidays. I would like to thank all of you and apologize here for my absence or too-brief presence at gatherings and various events during which I was struggling to meet deadlines. In particular, I would like to thank Paul and Amy Blavin, David Elliott, Misha and Jane Joukowsky, Steven Perelman, Andy and Debbie van Dam, and David and Beth Shaw for their moral support and unwavering confidence. Thanks also to Jack Aber for giving me a copy of the Cybernetic Serendipity catalog. My mother and father, Dane and Alice Morgan, provided tremendous psychological support as well as reading numerous chapters. My father contributed the inspirational video footage from the Galápagos. In addition, "Paddy" provided a perfect place for concentrated writing sessions.

No one has born the brunt of my workaholism more than Michael Spalter, my husband and best friend, who has been convinced from the beginning of the growing importance of the field of computer art and design. His belief in my ability to create this book kept me from giving up when the task seemed impossible. He has provided encouragement and guidance even while making many sacrifices in his schedule and our lives together. Without his support, this book would not have been completed.

I had no idea how many people were involved in the publishing of a book and am extremely grateful for the amazing team at Addison Wesley Longman. There is only space here to mention some of the key players. Peter Gordon took this project on even though I am a new author in a new field; I hope that his belief in this book and his willingness to risk publishing it will be amply rewarded! Helen Goldstein helped shepherd the writing and orchestrated seemingly endless permissions requests. Amy Rose and her assistant Brooke Albright oversaw the incredibly complex production process, with which my last-minute changes often interfered. The beautiful interior design was done by Melinda Grosser and the cover by Diana Coe. The manuscript went through numerous editing passes. Most notably, here at Brown, Katrina Avery marked up many drafts, fixing both grammar and muddled thinking; I doubt that there is a sentence untouched by her skilled hand. Also here at Brown, Rosemary Simpson created the incredibly complete index. Jerry Moore did an exemplary job in copyediting the final manuscript as did Jenny Bagdigian in proofreading the ever-changing page proofs. A big thanks is also due to Sigrid and Mike Wile, whose lightning-fast compositing efforts served to accelerate the schedule after I had slowed it down. The work continues even after publication and Michael Hirsch has probably played a key role in getting this book into your hands.

Finally, welcome to the world, Amelia!

Contents

CHAPTER 2

Digital Painting and Photoediting—
2D Raster Graphics 37

CHAPTER 3

Keyboards, Mice, Tablets, Scanners, and Displays 87

CHAPTER 4

Digital Design and Layout— 2D Geometric Graphics 117

Chapter 5

Electronic Color 159

CHAPTER 6

Printing 181

CHAPTER 7

Building 3D Worlds—3D Geometric Graphics I 211

Chapter 8

Rendering 3D Worlds—3D Geometric Graphics II 257

CHAPTER 9

3D Input and Output 297

Chapter 10

2D and 3D Animation and Video 323

CONCLUSION 439

APPENDIX A
Modern Art Periods 447

APPENDIX B
Computing Theory 453

URL List 457

References/Bibliography 461

Index 471

CHAPTER 1

Computers and Computer Art: A Brief History

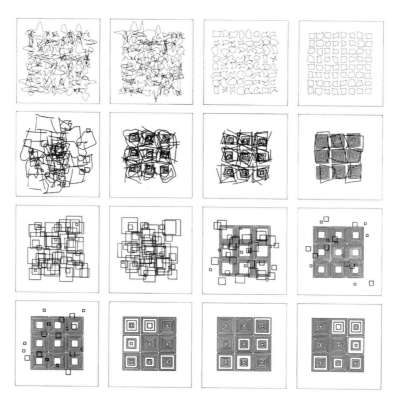

Figure 1.1 Vera Molnar, *Squares*, **Series 4, 1974.** As a traditional painter, Molnar worked in a geometric style, developing pictures in "a series of small, probing steps, altering the dimensions, the proportions and number of elements, their density and their form, one by one in a systematic way." She noted that "making a series of pictures that were alike except for the variation of one parameter is not uncommon in the history of art (haystacks and the Rouen Cathedral by Monet, for instance).... Art at its inception is essentially intuitive, it is in its elaboration that intuition needs control and aid by cognition." For her, a "computer-assisted procedure is only a systemization of the traditional-classic approach" [Leavitt, 1976, pp. 35, 36]. *(Courtesy of Vera Molnar)*

1.1 INTRODUCTION

Computers in the future may have only 1,000 vacuum tubes and weigh no more than 1.5 tons.
Popular Mechanics, *March 1949.*

When I began there was no software for artists. My first software experience was with punchcards in a course I followed at the Control Data Institute back in the spring of 1970. I never dreamed then that I would be able to have computing power in my own studio [Verostko, 1997].
Roman Verostko, *computer artist.*

If, over the past 30 years, transportation technology had improved at the same rate as information technology with respect to size, cost, performance, and energy efficiency, then an automobile would . . .

> *be the size of a toaster*
> *cost $200*
> *go 100,000 miles per hour, and*
> *travel 150,000 miles on a gallon of fuel [Lazowska, 1996].*

Ed Lazowska, Professor and Chair of the Department of Computer Science and Engineering, University of Washington.

No other art medium is bound to a technology that changes as rapidly as the computer. In fact, the rapid advance of computer technology is unlike almost anything else in human history. As recently as thirty years ago, the few computers that existed were esoteric devices used only by governments, large corporations, and universities. Today, more than one of every three American families has a personal computer, and a digital wristwatch can contain more computing power than machines that a few decades ago took up entire rooms and cost millions of dollars. Hand-held computer games that currently sell for less than $200 have more advanced graphics capabilities than high-end graphics workstations of the 1980s or even the early 1990s. The pace of technological change must be taken into account when you look at art created with computers: The computers used by artists in the 1960s were dramatically different from those used now.

The rapid pace of technological change creates an atmosphere in which many artists and designers are waiting impatiently for better, faster equipment. The feeling that, if only you had a faster computer or better software or a higher-end printer, you would be able to do better work is a trap to be avoided. Although advances in technology expand the visual languages available to artists, the quality of artwork is determined by the artist. Artist James Faure Walker put it well: "With so much delightful and affordable hardware around I have to remind myself that in the British Museum, the Greek vase section, there are several outright masterpieces produced in two colors and with rudimentary technology, but with an artistry we can only dream about. It's a quiet power. A few lines drawn, apparently casually, two and a half thousand years ago" [Walker, 1995].

An understanding of the leaps in computer technology is important not only for looking backward and critiquing the computer art work of the 1960s–1990s in context, but also for better understanding the present and anticipating the future. The limits that artists and designers currently face will be much different a decade from now.

1.1.1 Three Periods of Computer Art

The changes in the computers available to artists divide the history of computer art into three loosely demarcated periods. The **first period,** to the mid 1970s, was full of the excitement of breaking entirely new ground and was defined in part by the need to learn programming and the difficulty of gaining access to equipment. Margot Lovejoy, author of the survey text *Postmodern Currents,* called this pioneering phase the "first wave" and placed it from 1965–1975 [Lovejoy, 1997]. Herbert W. Franke, author of *Computer Graphics—Computer Art,* also distinguishes between a first period, an "isolated" beginning of computer art, and an "expansive period" that he places from the late 1960s onward [Franke, 1985].

A noticeable change occurred during a **second period,** which started sometime during the 1970s and stretched into the 1980s. (Exact dates for the beginning and end of each period cannot be given because some artists gained access to new types of computers long before others did.) This second period featured the increased use of minicomputers, the advent of the personal computer, the commodification of interactive graphics software (requiring no programming by the artist), the widespread adoption of computers by design firms, and the expansion of the computer art community. Designers and photographers were able to digitize photographic material and experiment with a wide range of styles. Toward the end of the 1980s, personal computers became powerful enough to run software products formerly available only on dedicated systems and affordable chiefly to the media and entertainment industries. The computer became a valuable Postmodern art tool: Artists could work directly with images and the image-making methods of the sources they were critiquing. Although not "high art," the fake sitcoms and advertisements of "Saturday Night Live" during the 1970s and early 1980s provide a good example. When Gilda Radner, in a housedress, smiled and said, "Shimmer! A floor wax or a dessert topping. It's both! The greatest shine you ever tasted," everyone laughed but no one thought it was a real ad. Since production teams began using the same types of graphics programs as network television, however, audiences have had to pay close attention to the words and product names to recognize that they are still watching the show and need not head to the kitchen for the ad break.

In the 1990s, a **third period** began, characterized by the integration of computer graphics into countless aspects of work and home life, including most areas of business, science, and entertainment. The barriers to entry are low: More and more artists and freelance designers, illustrators, and photographers can buy their own computers and begin experimenting with a wide range of software. Artists are still taming digital frontiers, but the computer is also becoming a standard tool for visual thinking and design, either on its own or as part of traditional art and design processes. A vigorous computer art community still exists, but many artists entirely outside it are beginning to use computers in high-profile ways. Shows are still curated with "computer art" themes, but work done with computers is now commonly included in shows with themes having nothing to do with computers or even technology. In commercial design, computer knowledge is a prerequisite for most jobs.

1.2 Landmarks in Computer Technology— 1890 to the Early 1960s

The uninitiated artist asks: what can this machine do for me? Really, the question should be: what can I do with this machine? [Leavitt, 1976]
Ruth Leavitt, artist and editor of Artist and Computer.

There it sits, the ultimate shape-shifter. What does one do with a shimmering blob of unlimited potential? [Laurel, 1980, p. 80]

Brenda Laurel, *researcher, writer, and artist, editor of* The Art of Human–Computer Interaction *and author of* Computers as Theatre.

Studying the history of the computer is different from studying the history of any other technology used for art, such as casting or photography, or of machines in general. The computer is not a machine like a toaster or a tractor or a camera. These devices are built for predetermined purposes. A computer has no specific purpose and has therefore been dubbed the first (and only) **general-purpose machine.** Fundamentally, all it is built to do is manipulate symbols. The purpose or functionality of the computer depends on the software stored within it—new software provides endless new functionality. A computer can help you do your income taxes, write an interactive novel, play an adventure game, compose a symphony, make a visual art piece, and much more. It is because of software that computers will do things in the future that we cannot anticipate today. Thus human creativity remains the driving force behind this technology.

Legend has it that in the early 1950s, IBM assessed the U.S. market for computers and concluded that only five would be needed. In the 1970s IBM underestimated the importance of Digital Equipment Corporation (DEC) and its smaller computers; these **minis** then took away substantial market share from IBM's mainframes. When the idea of a "personal" computer was broached in the 1970s, two of the most frequently asked questions were: Why would anyone want to own one? What would you do with it? The capabilities of computers are not predefined, however, and constantly expand to take advantage of progress in the underlying technology. The history of computer art is thus interwoven with the history of computer technology and its uses.

1.2.1 A Digression: The Printing Press

The history of the printing press, described in this brief digression from the main subject of this chapter, sheds light on concepts that were important in the creation of computer images and issues that are central to recent art theory.

Mediaeval monks produced manuscripts by drawing each letter and each picture by hand. For both image and text, eye-hand coordination and the skill of the hand were paramount, and the contact of pen or brush to parchment defined the entire process of writing or painting (see Fig. 1.2).

In the 1450s, however, Johannes Gutenberg invented movable metallic type (see Fig. 1.3). The impact of the printing press highlights an intrinsic difference between text and images. Text is already an abstract encoding composed of a limited number of symbols; as long as these symbols can be recognized, the meaning is intact. For images, however, there was no equivalent, until recently, of the alphabet. Copying a visual art work always changed it because the meaning of an image and its physical realization could not be separated. A cheap paperback can have the same content as an original manuscript, but a printed reproduction of an oil painting involves changes in scale, color, texture, medium, and context, all of which affect the perceived content of the work. In addition, despite the invention of photography and lithography, print-based

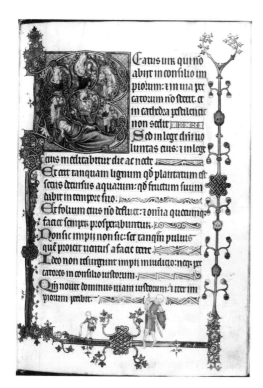

Figure 1.2 Illuminated manuscripts combine word and image. Image and word are created with the same hand-controlled processes and their visual integration is important to the feeling of the work. This page, from a collection of Psalms c. 1310–1320, shows the tree of Jesse in the initial B and David and Goliath in the borders. *(Courtesy of The Pierpont Morgan Library/Art Resource, NY)*

Figure 1.3 A printing workshop from Leipzig, Germany in 1740. Choosing metal type (left) and printing (right). *(Courtesy of Image Select/Art Resource, NY)*

image reproduction technologies remain relatively inefficient and expensive (which is why most of this book is in black and white).

Now, for the first time since the Middle Ages, the technology of image creation and distribution is again close to that of text (which is why a Web site accompanies this book). Text and music have had abstract symbolic notational systems for thousands of years; the visual arts have just achieved such a system for the first time.

A computer artist still sees a physical image drawn on a screen or paper or other medium, but that image is generated from textual and numerical instructions or **code** (see Fig. 1.4). If the image is stored as a series of color values, as in a paint program, the artist can change these values individually to make new pictures, for instance combining different photographs together to create scenes that never really existed. See Chapter 2, Digital Painting and Photoediting—2D Raster Graphics, for a discussion of this

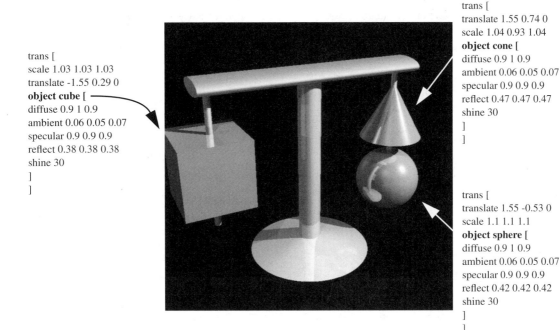

trans [
scale 1.03 1.03 1.03
translate -1.55 0.29 0
object cube [
diffuse 0.9 1 0.9
ambient 0.06 0.05 0.07
specular 0.9 0.9 0.9
reflect 0.38 0.38 0.38
shine 30
]
]

trans [
translate 1.55 0.74 0
scale 1.04 0.93 1.04
object cone [
diffuse 0.9 1 0.9
ambient 0.06 0.05 0.07
specular 0.9 0.9 0.9
reflect 0.47 0.47 0.47
shine 30
]
]

trans [
translate 1.55 -0.53 0
scale 1.1 1.1 1.1
object sphere [
diffuse 0.9 1 0.9
ambient 0.06 0.05 0.07
specular 0.9 0.9 0.9
reflect 0.42 0.42 0.42
shine 30
]
]

Figure 1.4 **Images on the screen are drawn according to textual and numerical instructions.** This entire scene was designed with a single page of text and numeric instructions. Instructions for placing the cube, cone, and sphere ("scale" and "translate") and determining how light will affect them ("ambient," "specular," "reflect," and "shine") are shown. The creator of this program can edit the image by changing the code, say by replacing "sphere" with "cube" in the text on the lower right to make a cube appear under the cone instead of the sphere or by changing the number after "scale" to make an object larger or smaller.

approach. If the image is stored as geometric descriptions, as indicated in Fig. 1.4, the artist can edit and reorganize shapes in two dimensions (2D) and three dimensions (3D), creating a brochure, for example, with text and crisp graphics or making a 3D model of the Taj Mahal. See Chapter 4, Digital Design and Layout—2D Geometric Graphics, and Chapter 7, Building 3D Worlds—3D Geometric Graphics I, for coverage of these methods.

1.2.2 FROM TEXTILES TO TABULATION

The name *computer* puts off many artists because it implies mathematical calculation, but this implication is an accident of history, not an inherent characteristic. Computers could have been developed in a different context, such as fabric design; in fact, an experiment in automated weaving led to several innovations that later were used with computers.

In 1806, Joseph-Marie Jacquard put into use the first **Jacquard loom,** which could weave patterns according to encoded instructions (see Fig. 1.5). "The device was fiercely opposed by weavers, who feared that this labor-saving machine would ultimately deprive them of their livelihood. The advantages of Jacquard's machine, however, could not be denied, and by 1812 there were over 11,000 of them in use throughout France" [Blum, 1966, p. 25]. Although it was a mechanical device, not a computer, it used two ideas that would later affect computers and computer art: the translation of images into arrays of discrete color values (based on the same principle as digitizing a photograph with a scanner) and the use of punched cards to convey instructions (storing an image as a sequence of instructions). Designers drew their fabric patterns onto gridded paper and then assigned numeric values to each of the grid's squares, based on the pattern colors. These numbers were used to determine the location of small holes punched into cardboard cards—which in turn controlled the yarn

Figure 1.5 **A working Jacquard loom at the Rhode Island School of Design.** (a) The long chain of stitched-together punched cards can be seen folded at the upper left of the loom and entering the loom. Until quite recently, textile students were required to take a one-semester course in the use of this machine. (b) An example of student fabric; the complexity of this design makes it virtually impossible to weave by hand.

Folded chain of cards ➡

(a)

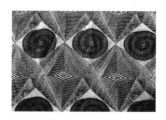

(b)

colors used by the loom. (This innovation was built on the earlier technology of music boxes, player pianos, and even a similar weaving prototype, which used perforations in paper or metal rolls.)

Because computers manipulate symbols, the first computers could have been designed as artists' tools, following in the steps of the Jacquard loom. But it was the need for fast, accurate numeric calculations that inspired Charles Babbage in 1823 to start building his **difference engine,** a complex mechanical machine for calculating logarithms and trigonometric functions that were important to the military for the construction of tables for ballistics calculations. In 1833, in the midst of numerous financial and technical difficulties preventing the complete construction of the machine, Babbage conceived and started to design a much more flexible and powerful invention, a general-purpose, steam-powered computer that he called the **analytic engine.** His design incorporated the four main components of modern computers: input, processing, storage, and output. Instructions were to be input with **punched cards** like the ones that Jacquard had pioneered for his loom.

The writings of Lady Augusta Ada King Lovelace (née Byron), Lord Byron's daughter, are our chief source of information about Babbage's efforts. She worked closely with Babbage on many aspects of his design and used her mathematical and literary skills to promote the analytical engine. She is often called the first programmer because she wrote a program for the analytical engine to calculate Bernoulli numbers. The U.S. Department of Defense named its current programming language Ada in her honor.

Women in Computing and Computer Art

Women have been involved in computers and their uses from the earliest days (see Fig. 1.6). In fact, computers were literally named after the women who aided the World War II effort by computing firing trajectories (by hand): Their job title was *computer,* and the machine later built to perform this same task was also called a computer. Women worked with teletypes and punched cards in government projects such as the census and also programmed early computers by rewiring them, a job that was considered menial but actually required a great deal of knowledge and skill. In addition to Lady Ada Lovelace, pioneers of computer science include U.S. Navy Commodore Grace Murray Hopper, a mathematician who worked on early computers, wrote the first paper on compilers (programs that translate textual and numerical instructions into the 1s and 0s necessary to control the computer), and helped to create the first programming language that could be used on more than one machine, the COmmon Business-Oriented Language (COBOL).

Unfortunately, role models for women in computer science are currently few and far between, and the situation seems to be getting worse, not better. The percentage of women earning bachelor's degrees in computer science has steadily declined from 37% of the total in 1985 to 30% in 1990 and 29% in 1995 [National Science Foundation (NSF), 1997]. Because only a few computer scientists and programmers are women, most of the commercial tools used by computer artists are created by men. I hope that some of you will help reverse this disturbing trend!

Figure 1.6 Women and the early days of computers. Women creating punched cards with the Type II keypunch for an IBM 163. *(Courtesy of The Computer Museum History Center)*

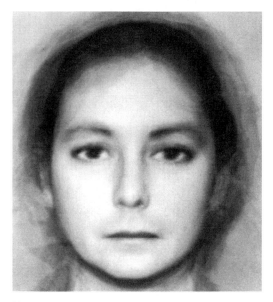

Figure 1.7 Nancy Burson with David Kramlich and Richard Carling, *Androgyny (six men and six women)*, **1982** (Simulated photograph, 8" × 10"). The faces of six men and six women were composited to create a single image. *(Courtesy of Nancy Burson)*

Although men dominate the field of computer science, computer art has had significant numbers of female artists from the very beginning and today seems to have at least as many women as men, if not more. Even when the creation of computer art was intimately tied to math and science, women were visible participants. One of the first computer artists, Lillian Schwartz, is still pursuing her work. Other early practitioners who continue to inspire the next generation of artists include Colette Bangert, Nancy Burson (see Fig. 1.7), Darcy Gerbarg, Ruth Leavitt, Margot Lovejoy, Vera Molnar, Barbara Nessim, Sonia Landy Sheridan, Vibeke Sorensen, Nicole Stenger, Joan Truckenbrod, and many others. Jasia Reichardt was the curator for one of the first important shows of computer work, the 1968 "Cybernetic Serendipity." Cynthia Goodman was the curator for the "Computers and Art" show in 1986 and wrote an accompanying text that included a history of computer art.

To the best of my knowledge, no studies have been conducted on gender issues in computer art, but women may be attracted to this new field for the same reason that they were attracted to photography and video: "In the early 1980s many women artists chose to address the fact that creativity has traditionally been founded upon not only talent but privilege. Many of them chose photography as their medium—perhaps because it is an alternative to the absolute domain men have had in paint" [Staniszewski, 1995]. Thus the computer may attract female artists precisely because it is new and, unlike traditional fine art media, does not have a history of primarily male practitioners. Examples of computer art work done by women in the 1980s and 1990s appear throughout this book.

Babbage was unable to obtain the funding needed to complete his vision, and an unsuccessful gambling scheme for statistical handicapping of horses left both Babbage and Lovelace deeply in debt. A working difference engine was finally constructed much later in Sweden and worked as intended, but the analytic engine was never fully realized. Had the analytic engine been successful, the first programmable computer would have emerged in the late nineteenth century, not at the end of World War II [Bunch, 1993].

Complex calculating machines were eventually constructed with great success. In 1890, the results of the U.S. census were counted with the help of a "tabulating machine" developed by Herman Hollerith. The practicality of his machine was proven when the census was calculated in a matter of months—calculating the previous census had taken almost 10 years. Hollerith's company grew quickly and was later merged with several other firms and renamed the Computing-Tabulating-Recording Company. In 1924, to reflect its expanding and successful role in the business world, it was renamed again to become the International Business Machines Corporation, or IBM.

1.2.3 World War II and Its Aftermath

Although keeping track of people and processes became more and more essential to government and large corporations, most of the significant advances in computing did not come until World War II. Recognizing the merits of the computer in calculating missile trajectories, breaking enemy codes, and building new types of weapons, the U.S. government's defense and intelligence agencies strongly supported computing research. Allied developments in computer technology (e.g., Britain's code-breaking Colossus machines) and Germany's insistence that computers were an unnecessary and distracting avenue of research were essential to the outcome of the war. During the Cold War that followed, the advantages that computer technologies could provide (e.g., giving early warning of missiles and determining their targets) continued to push the technology forward (see Fig. 1.8).

Funding from the Ballistics Research Laboratory of the United States supported work on the first large-scale, general-purpose electronic digital computer, the Electronic Numerical Integrator and Computer, or **ENIAC** (see Fig. 1.9).[1] (The Harvard Mark I, an electromechanical computer that used phone relays, containing more than

---

[1] The first electronic digital computers (designed for special purposes, not for general computing use) were built from 1937 to 1942 by John V. Atanasoff, an American theoretical physicist at Iowa State College (now Iowa State University). The code-breaking electronic digital computer, the Colossus, was built in Great Britain in 1943.

Figure 1.8 Air Force SAGE, 1958. The Semi-Automatic Ground Environment, or SAGE, computer occupied 40,000 square feet for each two-system installation and had 30,000 vacuum tubes per system. It was used for tracking aircraft with radar from 1958 to 1983, first for defense purposes and later as part of an air traffic control system. A computer light "gun" was used to select planes (represented as bright dots on the display). *(Courtesy of The Computer Museum History Center)*

Figure 1.9 ENIAC, the world's first large-scale electronic computer. At a speech given on Valentine's Day, 1996 for the fiftieth anniversary of ENIAC, Vice President Al Gore held up a Valentine's Day card and pointed out that the ENIAC, despite its enormous bulk (more than 80 feet wide and 30 tons), had less computing power than his card's simple voice chip [Gore, 1996]. *(Courtesy of The Computer Museum History Center)*

500 miles of wire and weighing more than 35 tons, had already been created by Howard Aiken in 1944.) Completed in 1946 at the University of Pennsylvania by John W. Mauchly and J. Presper Eckert, ENIAC contained 18,000 vacuum tubes (the forerunners of transistors). Many experts were skeptical of the project because vacuum tubes were notoriously unreliable, but ENIAC was an immediate success and ran productively for almost 10 years. In addition to performing ballistics calculations, ENIAC played a vital role in the design of the hydrogen bomb.

The military and corporate origins of the computer influenced people's perceptions of computer art. As computers become more and more a part of everyday life, however, this initial characterization is finally fading. How different people's views would have been had the computer evolved as a weaving machine and visual production tool rather than as a mammoth calculator!

1.3 Computer Art Through the Early 1970s

With the commercialization of computer-driven pen **plotters** in the early 1960s, the computer became capable of drawing as well as typing, but artists frequently worked "blind," unable to see their work until it was printed. These early printing devices worked like big Etch-a-Sketch machines: The computer controlled the rotation of two motors that positioned a drawing pen. Such plotters could draw only lines, not curves.

Computer art at first centered on producing computer-generated images by using **algorithms,** or instructions for completing a specific task, in this case drawing programmed lines and shapes and varying them systematically. This focus reflected both the computer's strength (its ability to handle symbolic instructions) and its limitations (the whole piece had to be planned in advance because the artist could not see the image until it was printed). The commercialization of display screens and computer monitors in the mid- to late-1960s let artists see their creations in a new way.

Early computer art was a celebration of both the power of the computer and its limitations. Artists and scientists were inspired by the ability to create images automatically, to program something with aesthetic qualities, and to make a machine identified with text and numbers produce pictures. The "look" of the early artwork was dictated in large part by limitations: Works were composed almost exclusively of lines and simple curves and were almost always black and white. The visual language was dominated by geometric shapes and compositions were often made up of rotated and scaled copies.

Primitive output options such as the first pen plotters were one reason that the art world shunned early computer work: It did not have the physical look and feel that most people associated with fine art. Similarly, although computers were used from the mid 1960s onward for technical drawings, the results provided little temptation for most designers and illustrators to forgo their traditional tools.

To enliven potentially boring, too predictable compositions, random number generators were used to add variation that lent a kind of human character to many pieces. In one informal but telling experiment, programmer, engineer, and soon-to-be artist A. Michael Noll created a computer-generated Mondrian drawing and showed it, side by side with a real Mondrian drawing, to a number of people and asked them to guess which was the real Mondrian (see Fig. 1.10). More people chose the fake one than the real one, saying that it looked more handmade and less automated. Such experiments were of interest to artists, scientists, psychologists, and philosophers who wanted to use computers as analytic tools for studying perception and aesthetics [Noll, 1966]. The original experiment raised questions about the lack of artistic training of the participants (they were all technical or administrative staff at Bell Labs). Noll devised a subsequent experiment in which participants were shown a series of computer-generated compositions with varying degrees of randomness, designed to more closely approximate the real Mondrian. There were no statistically meaningful differences between the preferences of participants with artistic training and those without such training [Noll, 1972].

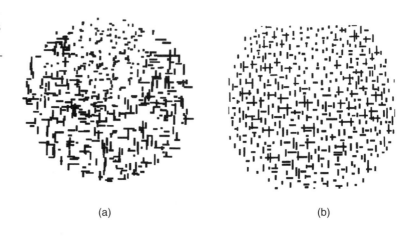

Figure 1.10 Which one is the Mondrian? Noll asked viewers to identify the computer picture and to say which composition they preferred. Only 28% were able to identify the computer-generated picture (a) *Computer composition with Lines, A. Michael Noll, 1965 (© 1965 A. Michael Noll)* and 59% preferred the computer-generated image to the real Mondrian (b) Piet Mondrian, *Composition with Lines, 1917. (Collection of the Kröller-Müller Museum, Otterlo, The Netherlands)*

(a)   (b)

The First Computer Images

Ben F. Laposky is credited with creating the first computer art, beginning in 1950. It consisted of analog wave patterns photographed off the screen of an oscilloscope, which was an analog, rather than a digital, machine. (See Chapter 2; Digital Painting and Photoediting—2D Raster Graphics, for a discussion of the important distinction between digital and analog.) He called these works oscillons. In 1960 the Boeing Computer Graphics Group coined the term *computer graphics*. The Group's leader, William Fetter, had a background in graphic design and believed strongly in the potential of computer graphics. Figure 1.11 shows an image from a project that involved the use of computer graphics to determine the best configuration for an airplane cockpit. The designer could animate the articulated human figure to assess whether instruments would be within easy reach of the pilot and whether the pilot would have adequate visibility [Fetter, c. 1971].

Like the experiment based on the Mondrian piece, much visual computer work from this early period does not fall neatly into the standard categories of fine or applied art or scientific or aesthetic research. Scientists such as Noll, Ken Knowlton, and Leon Harmon, all of whom worked at the Bell Labs in Murray Hill, New Jersey, used computers to study perception and scientific theories of representation. The image shown in Fig. 1.12 is part of a series by Harmon and Knowlton designed "to develop new computer languages which can easily manipulate graphical data, to explore new forms of computer-produced art, and to examine some aspects of human pattern-recognition" [Reichardt, 1968, p. 87]. The distinction between artist and programmer was not particularly meaningful to them. "In some art exhibits we were supposed to be artist and programmer in collaboration. So we flipped a coin, and thus Leon became the artist and I the programmer" [Knowlton, 1998]. Their work appeared in many

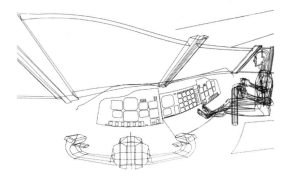

Figure 1.11 Early graphics used for cockpit design, 1968. *(The Boeing Company Archives)*

Figure 1.12 Leon Harmon and Kenneth C. Knowlton, *Mural*, 1966 (originally printed at up to 5′ × 12′). This image was created by scanning a photograph and calculating gray values for each of 4000 small patches of the image. Instead of printing with traditional halftones, each patch is represented by a small iconic symbol whose proportion of black to white ink produces the desired gray value. The traditional female nude pose, an icon in itself, dissolves into the tiny symbols, which represent elements of the modern, electronic, computerized world, including (from light to dark) multiplication and division signs, transistors, zener diodes, vacuum triodes, resistors, tape reels, and a wiring crossover. All of these symbols are in turn composed of the character α. There are three viewing levels: Very close up one sees αs; from a middle distance sets of these form the electronic symbols; far away one sees the overall image. *(Courtesy of Ken Knowlton)*

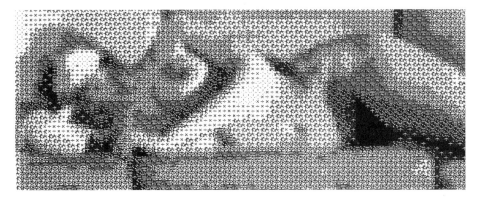

art shows and inspired other scientists and artists to experiment on their own. Lillian Schwartz, an artist who had worked in media ranging from Japanese brush painting to molten acrylic, began working with Knowlton in 1969 and experimented widely with still, motion, and sculptural pieces made with computers.

Controversy about the artistic status of early computer images stemmed in part from the fact that only people associated with institutions having suitable computers could even use digital image-making technology. Many of these people were scientists who were also artists or simply had an interest in art. Traditional artists and designers who did manage to get access to the equipment either had to work closely with someone who could program or, more frequently, had to learn how to program—no art applications could be purchased off the shelf. Because the field was so new, experimentation was essential and often combined artistic and scientific goals.

For some, programming was an intriguing part of the creative process. Vera Molnar, whose traditional work was based on variations of geometric figures, said that "the computer-aided approach is only a systemization of the traditional-classic approach. . . . I am in favor of the introduction of computer science in the Art School curriculum" [Leavitt, 1976, p. 36]. Manfred Mohr, who also came from a traditional art background, has said that "through detailed programming analysis, one is able to visualize logical and abstract models of human thinking, which lead deep into the understanding of creative processing" [Leavitt, 1976, p. 94]. For others, the programming aspect of computer use was a necessary evil. Lillian Schwartz reminds readers in her *Computer Artist's Handbook* that in the early days "to perform the simple act of drawing a line over a page, exerting pressure on the pencil, charcoal, or other instrument to change the thickness of the line, becomes a major task in programming" [Schwartz, 1992, p. 107]. Cynthia Beth Rubin waited to become involved with computers until she could use them without having to program: "I am deeply engaged in the research of my source materials, so there's only so much time to make art—I realized that if I were programming as well, I would not have the time I need to work on the content" [Rubin, 1997].

The first show of digital graphics in the United States was in 1965 at the Howard Wise Gallery in New York City. The show included works by A. Michael Noll and Bela Julesz (also at Bell Labs). Other early exhibitions included a large show in 1967 at the Museum of Modern Art in New York, curated by K. G. Pontus Hultén, called "The Machine as Seen at the End of the Mechanical Age." A concurrent show at the Brooklyn Museum entitled "Some More Beginnings: Experiments in Art and Technology" featured additional computer art works. In 1968, "Cybernetic Serendipity," curated by Jasia Reichardt, contained computer-generated artwork, music, poetry, film, and sculpture, as well as 2D images. The experimental nature of the works was clearly acknowledged. In the introduction to the accompanying catalog Reichardt wrote, "The idea behind this venture . . . is to show some of the creative forms engendered by technology. . . . Cybernetic Serendipity deals with possibilities rather than achievements . . . [and] there are no heroic claims to be made because computers have so far neither revolutionized music, nor art, nor poetry, in the same way that they have revolutionized science" [Reichardt, 1968, p. 5].

As more and more artists became involved, computer art began to be taken seriously. Robert Rauschenberg and his partner Billy Kluver, a physicist at Bell Labs, helped give credibility to this new field by forming Experiments in Art and Technology (EAT) in 1967. In 1968, EAT organized an important lecture series by scientists, including Leon Harmon and Ken Knowlton, who were pioneering visual uses of computers. Further acceptance was demonstrated by the inclusion of computer art works in the 1970 Venice Biennale, where they were displayed next to Constructivist works by Joseph Albers and Max Bill.

The mixing of art work, design work, scientific visualization, and perceptual studies common in early computer art shows made it difficult to assess the potential of the computer as a fine art medium. The computer's ties to the scientific and military worlds made the concept of a computer-based art that used algorithms and mathematical formulas seem foreign indeed. Many art critics felt that the message was not as advanced as the medium and that most early computer works failed to address issues of concern to the art world, focusing instead on a formalistic approach to image making.

Part of the combination of often intense criticism and total lack of interest in computer art by the mainstream art world undoubtedly arose because the scientists creating the tools and the artists and critics spoke different languages (and still do). Critics frequently attacked the use of automated image creation and randomness, when expressed in terms of algorithms and performed on computers, either as a meaningless exercise, much as art photography had been criticized half a century before, or as a self-reflexive approach to art that ignored the issues arising in the Postmodern art world. But early computer art can be viewed as a direct descendant of modernist concerns with form and as a continuation of Dada and Surrealist work that grows out of both choice among materials, such as Dadaist assemblages, and chance.

Artistic decisions based on chance, and approaches such as Jean Arp's use of random shapes challenged conventional notions of art by suggesting that the will and conscious mind were not as different from chance as people might hope. Computer artists also used chance, although their goal usually was not that of the Avant-Garde but a more Modernist systematic exploration of marks and form. Roman Verostko, a pioneering computer artist, writes:

> I was familiar with "automatic painting" and interested in the origins of abstract expressionism, especially during my New York period (1959–63). So when I tried to create a computer simulation of automatic painting procedures, I was after a simulation that would truly place the form-generating initiators within the computer—this would make the "computer's computing procedures" the medium. I wanted to get beyond the use of a computer as a tool and get to a point where the "computing" became the form-generating agent [Verostko, 1997b].

Verostko has achieved this goal, even developing his own term for this art-making approach, **epigenetic,** to indicate a process of growth through algorithms analogous to the biological development of simple or unorganized forms into larger, complex entities—for example, a plant growing from a seed. In the mural shown in Fig. 1.13, "thousands of lines cluster and mirror themselves with improvisations derived from a

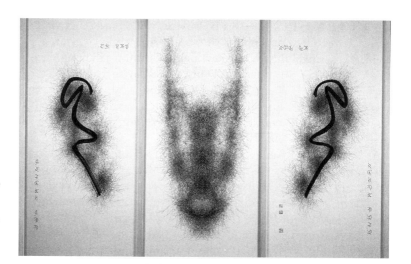

Figure 1.13 Roman Verostko, *Epigenesis: The Growth of Form*, **1997** (right triptych, 9' × 6'). Installed at the Frey Science and Engineering Center, University of St. Thomas (St. Paul Campus). *(Courtesy of Roman Verostko)*

single initiating form" [Verostko, 1977a]. The artist painted a full-scale version of the initial stroke shape onto the left and right panels of Fig. 1.13 by using a large brush in the plotter.

Photocopier Art

Many of the issues that arose with the advent of computer art were foreshadowed not only by photography, with its scientific beginnings and inherent reproducibility, but also by photocopier art. In the 1960s and 1970s, artists began to work with Xerox machines and other types of photocopiers. Sonia Landy Sheridan was a pioneer in this area, working as an artist in residence in the late 1960s at the 3M Corporation on the first full-color copier. She founded the Generative Systems Department at The Art Institute of Chicago in 1970, which has since evolved to encompass computer art. Like early computer artists, photocopier artists "directly derived their experience with the machine, with no art historical precedents to draw from, [and] began to discover a new repertoire of methods, a new hierarchy of imagery, and new categories of artwork within the discipline imposed by the small office format (8.5" × 11"; 11" × 14"; 11" × 17") of the machine" [Lovejoy, 1997, p. 121].

The photocopier brought the issue of reproducibility to the fore and presented a Postmodern challenge to the Modernist concepts of originality, the aura of a work, and the often elitist spaces of galleries and museums in which most art work had to be seen. With their low cost and gratifying copying speed, photocopiers encouraged the production of artists' books and engendered mail art. They offered artists many options that also are important in much of computer art, such as creating seamless collages, changing scale and rotation of collage elements, easily reconfiguring and systematically varying compositions, and rapidly reducing and enlarging entire works. Like computer art, copier art grew in popularity and found support (David Hockney became a prominent user of the machines) but was often both criticized and ignored by the art world because of its machine-based nature and the corporate origins of the equipment.

The photocopier and the computer began separately but are merging in powerful, integrated machines that can scan images from paper or transparencies and make high-quality copies (often rivaling traditional offset printing) on a variety of media. Built-in computer systems let the operator work with color balance and a range of special effects similar to those in image-editing software.

Both art and science in the twentieth century are still based on investigation and exploration of new terrains, but the areas of interest, the thought processes, and the concepts and vocabulary specific to each field are so markedly different that they make artist–programmer collaborations notoriously difficult. "Hybrid" artists versed in both science and art have been key figures in computer art. Charles Csuri, Herbert Franke, Ruth Leavitt, Frieder Nake, Lillian Schwartz, and many others from this early period moved back and forth between science and art and provided communication between those worlds. Sometimes they were accepted more in one realm than the other, and sometimes they were fully appreciated in neither.

1.3.1 Two Early Computer Artists

The works shown and described in this section are typical of early computer art work.[2] Note the use of rectangles and other easily specified shapes, repeated motifs, and controlled order/decay-of-order using random variations.

FRIEDER NAKE   Nake is a mathematician who arranged one of the earliest computer art shows in the former West Germany, at the Technische Hochschule in Stuttgart in 1965. For *Rectangular Hatchings,* shown in "Cybernetic Serendipity," Nake exhausted an entire class of drawings by running through a specific pattern in all its variations (see Fig. 1.14). He found this process to be in some ways analogous to pursuing a visual theme in any art form, with intuition replaced by the use of variation based on random number generation. It can be thought of as an abstract, reductionist attempt to produce a vocabulary of marks that are then combined into compositions via random but constrained variation. After the process is completed, the artist chooses the

---

[2]A great number of talented artists have contributed to the artistic use of computer technology—space permits mentioning only a few here, along with a limited number of examples. Because this text focuses on visual works produced with computers, examples from the nonvisual arts, such as musical and conceptual works and visual works involving the use of computers but not produced by them (such as sculptures made of physical computer components), are not covered.

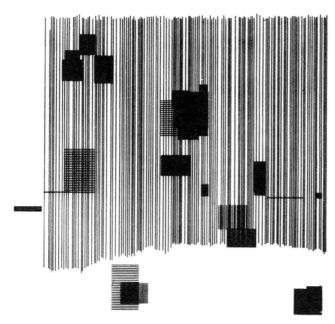

Figure 1.14 Frieder Nake, *Rectangular Hatchings,* 1965.
(Courtesy of Frieder Nake)

pieces that he or she deems most successful.

Although many aspects of Nake's work are "generated" and his hand is not directly involved, his pieces have an aesthetic consistency. In most early computer art, the programming controlled every aspect of the work's creation, from the definition of the medium—the type and range of marks—to the final compositional strategies. But the choice in the first place to produce the works by this remote method, the type of mark chosen, the way the program (written by the artist) gathers and varies the mark, and the pieces finally selected to represent the concepts intended are just as much artistic decisions as a photographer's judgment about what to photograph, which point of view to use to create the image, and how to crop the scene. In both cases the hand does not make marks on a surface, but the mind is directly involved and a personal view of the world is revealed.

The combination of systematic, mathematically driven experimentation and the limitations of the plotters often yielded a geometric look. Curves could be defined mathematically on the computer, but because plotters could only draw straight-line segments, curves were approximated with many short lines and the result often was not very effective. Early computer art work has a Constructivist quality in its programmatic depiction of space within an intentionally limited vocabulary. Like Mondrian and Malevich (although without Malevich's political philosophy), computer artists worked with the basic elements of visual spatial construction.

Nake's early computer works met with success, but he has not continued to create such works. Currently a professor of computer science and lecturer in the art department of the University of Bremen, he has, however, remained intrigued by the possibilities and implication of the computer as an art medium.

MANFRED MOHR   Manfred Mohr's computer work from 1969 onward has explored 2D, 3D, 4D, and higher-dimensional cubes as a source of powerful, chiefly linear, and exclusively black and white 2D compositions (see Fig. 1.15). He puts this one class of form through its paces, seeking within it the letters and syntax of an entire expressive language.

The goals, processes, and philosophy at work in Mohr's ongoing artistic research predate his computer use. For example, he was already working in black and white (with occasional gray), using simple, often linear forms, and exploring compositions based on systematic variation. It is not surprising, therefore, that his use of the computer has not been influenced by the emergence of new technological capabilities. He still programs his work himself, printing it on a plotter. The computer remains an invaluable tool, enabling him to mine a much greater geometric territory and more fully explore his ideas than he could otherwise. "One of the best compliments I ever received on my work," says Mohr, "was when a viewer came up to me at a show and said, gee you're crazy not to be using a computer to do this!" [Mohr, 1997]

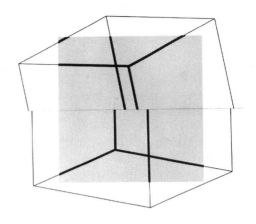

Figure 1.15 **Manfred Mohr, P-196-EE, 1977–1979** (from the *Cubic Limit* series, acrylic on canvas, 136 cm × 136 cm, collection of Dr. Friedrich Mautsch, Köln). *(Courtesy of Manfred Mohr)*

1.3.2 THE SEARCH FOR THE LAWS OF AESTHETICS

Algorithmic, computer-generated, plotter-printed art pieces such as those discussed here did not compete directly with traditional methods and processes; they were new ways of conceptualizing and producing imagery. This new approach was influenced by Max Bense, a German philosopher and mathematician, who had proposed a theory of "exact aesthetics" that postulated definable laws of aesthetics for which the computer would be the perfect production tool [Bense, 1965]. The goal of uncovering natural geometric relationships associated with beauty was not new—the Greeks had used the golden rectangle thousands of years earlier—but the computer offered powerful tools for investigating rules of composition and isolating aesthetically pleasing factors. The exact aesthetics, once discovered, could be used by the computer to create any number of aesthetically correct visual pieces, and could also be used to assess all past works and all works created for any purpose in the future. The systematic processes pursued by artists such as Mohr belong, according to Bense, to "that class of processes that begin with equal probabilities, and thus purely stochastically, but in the course of which the probability of certain signs being chosen and appearing becomes progressively greater, while the probability for certain others . . . progressively decreases and finally vanishes" [Bense, 1965, p. 215].

Figure 1.16 Charles Csuri, Still Frames from *Chaos to Order*, 1967. *(Courtesy of Charles Csuri)*

1.3.3 REPRESENTATIONAL IMAGERY

Although most early computer art work was abstract, representational images were also made with methods such as that used in Knowlton and Harmon's perception studies (illustrated previously in Fig. 1.12) or by hand plotting all points of the image and connecting them with lines. Charles Csuri, a pioneering artist who is still exploring the computer's potential, created the computer-animated film *Chaos to Order* in 1967 (see Fig. 1.16). Lines making up the bird are moved over time to random locations and then recomposed to return to the final, ordered image.

1.3.4 COMPUTER FILM

A film actually is just a sequence of still images, so the computer's ability to generate images automatically makes it a natural candidate for producing animated films. Both abstract work based on geometric transformations such as Nake's and representational work based on preplotted points such as Csuri's could be drawn with incremental changes on separate frames to create the illusion of motion in computer-generated animations. Many early artists used these animation techniques and some of the most important come from a single family, the Whitneys: Brothers John and James and John's three sons all worked with computer-based film ideas, from modulations of waveforms to abstract geometric shapes.

As with many early computer graphics experiments, the first experiments in computer-generated film were carried out at Bell Labs and combined artistic and scientific endeavor. As early as 1963, E. E. Zajac created a film simulating the motion of a communications satellite, represented by a box, orbiting the earth (a sphere). A. Michael Noll's research included pioneering work in stereoscopic movies, computer-generated holography, and computer-simulated dance [Noll, 1994]. Other experiments involved letters and colors and ways of moving them over time. Knowlton created an animation system called BELFLIX (from "Bell Flicks") for scientific purposes and modified it, working with artists including Lillian Schwartz and experimental filmmaker Stan Van Der Beek.

Canadian filmmaker Peter Foldes creatively metamorphosed people and objects in the film *Hunger*, which was nominated for an Academy Award in 1974 in the Animated

Figure 1.17 A sequence from *Hunger/La Faim*, a film by Peter Foldes, 1974 (National Film Board of Canada). Computer animation system, Nestor Burtnyk and Marceli Wein, National Research Council of Canada. *(Courtesy of the National Research Council of Canada)*

Shorts category. The film also received the Prix de Jury at the Cannes Film Festival that year and won several other awards, including one from the Berlin Film Festival. The film portrays a slim business man who begins to eat voraciously. He becomes increasingly overweight in a series of scenes, all of which use the slow changing of lines from one shape to another, as in Figure 1.17. Many of the scenes are sexually charged, with scantily clad women who change back and forth into food products. In a final, nightmare scene, the now obese protagonist is devoured by a starving community.

1.3.5 COMPUTER SCULPTURE

Most early computer work was 2D, but several artists, including Vera Molnar and Georg Nees, used the computer either to plan or provide instructions for manufacturing 3D objects. Figure 1.18 shows two computer sculptures that Georg Nees created with a computer-driven machine tool.

Figure 1.18 Georg Nees, computer sculptures, 1969. The artist created the designs for these sculptural pieces on a computer and then output to punched tape, which was used to control an automatic machine tool. *(Courtesy of Georg Nees)*

1.4 LANDMARKS OF COMPUTER TECHNOLOGY—AFTER 1960

Radical changes have taken place since 1960 in the circuitry of computers—from delicate glass vacuum tubes to transistors and from miniaturization of transistors to integrated circuit chips containing millions of transistors on a wafer the size of a thumbnail.

1.4.1 BETTER, FASTER, CHEAPER

Dramatic technological changes have led in turn to different ways of using computers, in particular enabling new methods of visual interaction and communication. The changes in computer circuitry have contributed to the fastest price drop and performance improvement ever in the history of technology. Gordon Moore (cofounder of Intel) predicted in 1965 that the transistor density of semiconductor chips would double roughly every 18 months. Thus, along with decreasing prices for hard disks and other components, about every year and a half you can buy, for the same money, a computer that is twice as fast as the one you bought 18 months ago. The gigantic mainframe computer shown in Fig. 1.19, which would have been shared by all the employees of an entire company, was less powerful than the original personal computers. The IBM mainframe System/370 Model 168 was priced at $3.4 million in 1970, but IBM's personal computer PS/2 Model 80, with comparable computing power, was priced at only $11,000 when introduced in 1987.

1.4.2 INTERACTIVE GRAPHICS

Interactive graphics is the reason that the computer is now a household item and that people with no training in math or science can use it to create complex visual images. In 1963, a Ph.D. student at MIT, Ivan Sutherland, demonstrated the first interactive geometric graphics system—one in which users could actually see what they

Figure 1.19 IBM 704 mainframe computer, mid-1950s. *(Courtesy of The Computer Museum History Center)*

Figure 1.20 Ivan Sutherland using Sketchpad, c. 1955. On the display is part of a bridge, with numbers calculated by Sketchpad that show the forces in the structural members. Sutherland is holding the light pen, which was used directly on the screen, in his right hand; his left hand is resting near a box of push buttons programmed to perform such operations as erasing, moving, locking, and constraining elements on the screen. The four black knobs below the display control zooming and panning. *(Courtesy of MIT Lincoln Laboratory, Lexington, Mass.)*

were drawing and change it on the screen. Although visual feedback was not a new discovery (the SAGE computer used a screen for showing the locations of planes, for instance, as shown in Fig. 1.8), Sutherland created the first complete system for working interactively with geometric forms. His program, called **Sketchpad,** allowed users to draw lines and shapes on a screen and manipulate them with a light pen (see Fig. 1.20). Interactive graphics quickly became a flourishing area of computer science research because, as Sutherland described it:

> The Sketchpad system makes it possible for a man and a computer to converse rapidly through the medium of line drawings. Heretofore, most interaction between men and computers has been slowed down by the need to reduce all communication to written statements that can be typed; in the past, we have been writing letters to rather than conferring with our computer. . . . The Sketchpad system, by eliminating typed statements (except for legends) in favor of line drawings, opens up a new area of manmachine communication [Sutherland, 1963].

1.4.3 RASTER GRAPHICS

The technologies necessary to make interactive graphics affordable and visually realistic were brought together in the 1970s at Xerox Corporation's Palo Alto Research Center (Xerox PARC). Its mission was to create an office machine of the future that nonscientists could use productively.

In a decision that would be of great importance to artists, Xerox PARC researchers resolved to base their systems on a different type of computer screen technology from the one most commonly used at the time. Computer screens in the early 1970s worked in much the same way as a plotter: The user guided an electron beam from one point on the screen to the next to trace out the edges of objects—a high-tech version of connect-the-dots, illuminating screen phosphors between each point (see the screen shown previously in Fig. 1.20). This deflected beam could trace out only lines. It had limited speed and was for all practical purposes incapable of filling in areas with solid colors or patterns, just like the early plotters. Also like early plotters, it used, in general, only one or two colors. The researchers at Xerox PARC replaced this process for drawing images on a monitor with a process much like that used for television. They divided the screen into a mosaic of phosphor dots that were turned on or off by a beam that swept the screen methodically row by row. They called these rows *rasters,*[3] and images made on this new type of screen came to be called **raster graphics.** Raster graphics allowed users to fill in selected areas of the screen and thus to create realistic-looking computer images for the first time.

Moore's law was especially important for raster graphics. Raster images require the storage and manipulation of many color values, often as many as a million or more per image. The user creates and places a raster image in a temporary storage area called a **frame buffer** before drawing it on the screen. Faster, cheaper memory chips for frame buffers made higher-resolution images feasible by speeding up the rate at which changes to an image could be calculated and drawn on the monitor. Faster, cheaper memory also made it feasible to work with full-color images, which require three separate frame buffers, one each for red, green, and blue color values. Without the effect of Moore's law on memory chips and processor speeds, raster graphics would have remained prohibitively expensive (in terms of both money and time) for casual use.

The Xerox PARC researchers took advantage of raster graphics in the creation of a new type of interface that used image icons to suggest visual metaphors, centered on the idea of a virtual desktop. This new type of interface, dubbed a **graphical user interface** (GUI), was a forerunner of Apple's interface for the Macintosh and Microsoft's Windows. The graphic interface worked best with a new type of input device called a **mouse.** Douglas Engelbart had invented the mouse at Stanford Research Institute (SRI), now SRI International, in the mid 1960s for his pioneering wordprocessing and hypertext system, Augment/NLS, but it had not caught on in the computer community (and had no obvious use with computers that worked with

---

[3]*Raster* originally designated the metal shelf for a line of type in a mechanical press.

stacks of punched cards). In the 1970s the Xerox PARC researchers used the mouse, in conjunction with the visual interface, to point, click, and drag in order to perform operations that previously required typing many commands.

Xerox eventually developed a commercial computer for use with a GUI and a mouse (see Fig. 1.21), but it never marketed the product. In the end a young company called Apple Computer brought the fruits of this research to the rest of the world (see Fig. 1.22). In 1984 Apple released a small, inexpensive, appliancelike computer called the Macintosh, or Mac. The release of the Mac was heralded as not only a technical accomplishment, but also a political one. For decades, large corporations had offered employees only limited access to centrally controlled computers. People not affiliated with institutions that had computers were mostly out of luck. The idea of a personal computer that was easy to use was truly revolutionary. Steve Jobs, who had cofounded Apple and led the Macintosh team, evangelized the Mac as a tool for personal empowerment. In a now famous 1984 Super Bowl ad introducing the Mac, an athletic woman wielding an ax runs through a meeting of IBM-style clone workers transfixed by a Big Brother–type spokesperson. She smashes the large screen with his image to smithereens. The ad concluded with a deep voice-over: "On January 24, Apple Computer will introduce the Macintosh and you'll see why 1984 won't be like *1984*." The Macintosh's easy-to-use technology and personal empowerment philosophy appealed to artists and designers and was the first type of computer that many used.

In addition to using a desktop metaphor like Xerox PARC's, the Macintosh also ran a piece of software called MacPaint®, created by Bill Atkinson. MacPaint was an affordable but simple, strictly black and white painting program. Although much more powerful, full-color painting programs were already in use in academia and industry (Alvy Ray Smith created the first full-color paint program in the late 1970s at the New York Institute of Technology [Smith, 1978]), it was MacPaint that introduced many computer users to the possibility of making

Figure 1.21 Xerox's Alto computer, 1973. The Alto was the first personal workstation, offering raster graphics, local-area networking, and laser printing. *(Courtesy of Xerox Palo Alto Research Center and Brian Tramontana)*

Figure 1.22 The original 128k Macintosh released in 1984. The first Mac had a small, built-in black and white screen and could be plugged in and used by people with little if any prior computing experience. It ran at 8Mhz (the recent Apple G3 series runs at 300Mhz). *(Courtesy of Apple Computer, Inc.)*

images on their home machines. Now, without any knowledge of programming or engineering, artists and designers could turn on their computers, grab the mouse, and start making pictures.

1.5 COMPUTER ART IN THE LATE 1970s AND 1980s

The history of computer art took a turn after the introduction of the personal computer and interactive graphics software. The initial thrill of computer image generation had worn off somewhat, and the new tool had not been widely adopted by artists or accepted by the art world. However, the number of people who had begun using the computer for purposes other than scientific research—and no longer needed to study computer science or work closely with programmers—was growing. Schools and small companies could afford computers, and the use of computer graphics began to spread to all areas of design and architecture.

The 1970s were a quiet time in the computer art world, a lull that reflects a shift in its creators and audiences. Despite the hope that artists and scientists would begin to work together as a matter of course and that an artist's education would include information technology and programming, the artists who continued or started to use computers during the 1970s fell more and more into two separate camps. On the one hand were artist–programmers who used the computer to write their own programs as well as produce their own images. These artists often felt that the creation of the software tools for making art set the computer apart from all previous art-making media. Ruth Leavitt stated, "It is the option to create one's own work tools that, in my mind, makes the computer unique" [Leavitt, 1976, p. 101]. Many artists followed the path laid down by the earliest computer artists and developed more complex approaches to programming artwork. They include Harold Cohen's artificially intelligent drawing and painting software and William Latham's "genetically grown" 3D creatures (discussed further in Chapter 7, Building 3D Worlds—3D Geometric Graphics I). On the other hand, for many artists who were newcomers to the field, interactive graphics were making computers artistically accessible for the first time. Commercial programs originally developed in research labs or for military needs became mainstream products in professional applications (e.g., Autodesk's AutoCAD®) and easy-to-use programs (e.g., Apple's MacPaint and MacDraw).

This new way of using computers to make art would eventually become more common than the artist–programmer paradigm, but in the 1970s and much of the 1980s computers were still expensive and difficult to use and had limited graphic capabilities. For example, until 1987 the Mac had only a tiny (9″) black and white screen and limited memory capacity but still cost several thousand dollars. Dot matrix printers were the only affordable kind (aside from character printers). Laser printers became more common in the late 1980s but cost between $5000 and $10,000; plotters were also expensive and couldn't handle raster graphics. In addition, art made with computers was still stigmatized and associated with scientific approaches to image making, even though many serious artists had been working with the medium for some time.

Figure 1.23 Joan Truckenbrod, *Syllogism,* **1986** (digital photograph, 24″ × 26″). The artist splintered photographic images of herself and her daughter to express the complex, multifaceted, interwoven nature of the roles played by a parent and child. *(Courtesy of Joan Truckenbrod)*

The artists who were programming their own works continued to do so and gained new adherents steadily from the 1960s into the 1990s. Artists who started to learn how to use commercial packages and buy their own equipment appeared in the art world in the late 1980s and early 1990s. Several changes drove a new perception of computer graphics: Adobe Postscript® and off-the-shelf design and layout programs based on it (see Chapter 4, Digital Design and Layout—2D Geometric Graphics) helped create the desktop publishing revolution, and improved color paint programs and scanning let artists more easily work with photographic material (see Chapter 3, Keyboards, Mice, Tablets, Scanners, and Displays).

Artists such as Nancy Burson, Carol Flax, and Joan Truckenbrod (see Fig. 1.23) found that the ability to bring photographic imagery into their work let them deal directly with content and issues current in the art world, such as gender, identity, and family structures. In 1988, Marnie Gillett and Jim Pomeroy were curators of "Digital Photography: Captured Images, Volatile Memory, and New Montage" at SF Camerawork in San Francisco. The show caught the attention of many artists and demonstrated the potential of uniting the capabilities of the computer with those of the camera. Some artists well known for their traditional work found the computer a valuable tool. David Hockney, for instance, uses a computer to construct photocollage works, Andy Warhol bought an Amiga to experiment with color combinations for his silk screens, and Nam June Paik uses digital video effects in his TV and video sculptures. The early period of computer art has been relatively well documented by now, and its participants are known through books such as Herbert W. Franke's *Computer*

Graphics—Computer Art [Franke, 1985], first published in 1971 and the first comprehensive integration of the aesthetic and the technical in computer art. In 1976, Ruth Leavitt put together *Artist and Computer,* a collection of statements and examples of work by thirty-five artists [Leavitt, 1976], and in 1986 Cynthia Goodman included a history of computer art in *Digital Visions: Computers and Art* [Goodman, 1987] (written to accompany the traveling 1987 show "Computers and Art").

In the introduction to *Digital Visions,* Goodman writes, "Until recently, most artists who used computer technology considered themselves part of a relatively small and closed community. Today, a computer art community still exists, but its mandate is broad and its membership vast" [Goodman, 1987, p. 14]. She noted that organizations such as the Association for Computing Machinery's Special Interest Group on Computer Graphics (ACM SIGGRAPH) provided an early meeting place for artists using the computer. "In 1967, it took almost a year to get thirty signatures to start the Special Interest Committee for Computer Graphics, the precursor to the Special Interest Group," says Andries van Dam, cofounder of SIGGRAPH. "Now the annual SIGGRAPH convention is more than ten times as large as its parent organization's convention—over 40,000 people attended in 1997" [van Dam, 1997]. SIGGRAPH and other conferences, such as ARS ELECTRONICA, started in 1979, the Inter Society for the Electronic Arts (ISEA), founded in 1990 but based on international symposia that began in 1988, and the more recent ACM Multimedia and World Wide Web conferences continue to provide needed forums. In addition, traditional organizations such as the College Art Association (CAA), are also becoming more involved. I started the Special Interest Group for Computers in the Visual Arts (CAA SIGCIVA) in 1996. Examples of artwork from this recent period are presented throughout this book.

1.5.1 Synergy Between Literary Theory and Computer Graphics Technology

As the computer matured throughout the 1970s and 1980s, art theories inspired by literary theorists become of interest to computer artists. The theoretical codification of visual and textual "codes" created by media and the cultural assumptions that were (and still are) the subject of much critical writing seemed particularly appropriate for theorizing about an art form that depended on breaking images into a symbolic notation. Postmodern literary theory has held that the artist dictates the meaning of the work far less than the reader, who can deconstruct the work in terms of political and social codes to reveal meanings of which the author may have been unaware.

The process of reading images by deconstructing them into codes is facilitated by the computer, which also creates images by breaking them into (symbolic, mathematical) codes. The technical encoding complements the analytic/critical one, suddenly making it much easier to search for, gather, isolate, and arrange visual material. The new medium is inherently multiauthored, can claim appropriation and montage among its most natural abilities, is directly responsible for much of the visual language of modern mass media, and, with the advent of worldwide networks such as the Internet, is global in its reach.

1.6 Computer Art in the 1990s and Beyond

In 1993, for the first time ever, people in this country bought more PCs than VCRs.
Carol Bartz, Chair of Autodesk, remarks from the Millennium Conference, 1995.

Dramatic changes have taken place in the last five years that once again are in large part the result of technical advances in both hardware and software. Computers have become powerful enough and inexpensive enough to make them enticing for large numbers of artists and self-supporting designers, in addition to companies involved with visual communication of all kinds. A personal computer suitable for a range of artistic uses, including working with photographic material and video, multimedia and 3D graphics, now costs about $2000–3000, which is comparable to studio requirements for other equipment-intensive art fields (e.g., a professional-quality video camera or a small etching press). Service bureaus can pick up where personal or school equipment leaves off, offering a range of scanning and production services on high-end machines.

The site of creation has always been the mind. The computer emphasizes this fact and yet, somewhat ironically, as a medium and craft it is still extraordinarily demanding of its users. Although in the future you may use computers without even realizing it (just as you can drive a car, use a watch, set your alarm clock, and use a Walkman without thinking about the dozens of computer chips involved), this technology and its uses are still in the early stages of development.

One of the most talked-about applications of this ever-improving technology has been so-called virtual reality (see Fig. 1.24). Although the basic software and hardware have been in use since the late 1960s, advances in both areas can now bring us visually rich worlds that give the user a feeling of being immersed in and interacting

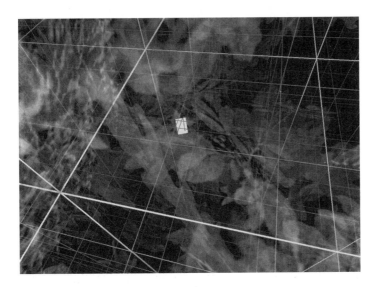

Figure 1.24 Char Davies, *Cartesian Grid and Forest,* real-time frame capture from the immersive virtual environment, *Osmose,* 1995 (entrance grid to the forest world). This landmark virtual-reality work was created with sophisticated equipment that is not yet affordable for most artists. If Moore's law continues to hold, however, virtual environments will become a common form of artistic creation. *(Courtesy of Char Davies and Softimage, Inc.)*

(a)

(b)

(c)

(d)

Figure 1.25 Christine Tamblyn, *Mistaken Identities*, **1995** (CD-ROM). (a) An introductory screen. (b) The user can click on the bookcase items to navigate to a timeline, scrapbook, portrait gallery, and other options. (c) A view of the timeline. (d) An image from a sequence about Josephine Baker. *(Courtesy of the Estate of Christine Tamblyn)*

with, virtual spaces and their inhabitants. Virtual reality is discussed further in Chapter 9, 3D Input and Output.

The current period is especially marked by the use of 3D graphics, multimedia, interactivity, and the advent of the Internet and the World Wide Web. Formerly restricted to high-end graphics workstations using the UNIX® operating system, serious 3D graphics applications with advanced modeling tools and realistic rendering can now be used on Macs and PCs (as well as the Amiga, an excellent early low-end 3D platform). Multimedia or hypermedia has been an aspect of computer art from the beginning, but only recently could someone buy a personal computer designed for multimedia production. Artists can now produce their own multimedia work and make their own CD-ROMs.

As shown in Fig. 1.25 and described by its creator:

Mistaken Identities is an interactive CD-ROM inspired by the lives of 10 famous women . . . chosen for their emblematic status as female role models. However, the

CD-ROM examines them as complex figures whose identities are not essential or fixed, but contingent and mutable. . . . The project combines aspects of an academic essay or documentary film with intuitive associations between graphics, films, texts and sounds . . . [and] alternative narrative strategies permit viewers to access the information in the project according to their own proclivities [Tamblyn, 1997].

Interactive art pieces, whether designed for CD-ROMs, diskettes, kiosks, or the Web, are a meeting place for artists concerned with programming and those concerned more with the implications of the computer for art theory. Simplified programming languages and visual programming environments can serve to reunite tool builders and tool users. The Web is increasingly accessible and promises to play a major role in future art creation and distribution. Examples of artwork created with computers in the 1990s are presented throughout this book.

Conclusion

The term *computer art* still has clear meaning for many images and animations generated with customized programming, in interactive or networked formats, or based on virtual environments and complex behavioral simulations: A viewer is confronted with the tool as it delivers its message. For many other types of art that involve the use of computers, however, the term no longer applies because the fact of the computer's use is not of primary importance. As practitioners of more and more traditional art forms begin to utilize digital processes, almost all art and design will be computer art and design. Digital processes are already an integral part of most mass-media image production. Photography, architecture, and many aspects of design and illustration have absorbed the computer into their practice.

Artists routinely submit works to shows with no indication that any digital processes have been used. A piece that simply lists "photograph" as the medium may well have been color balanced, edited, or entirely created with a computer. In many art shows with a computer art theme, the artists' statements are directly tied to concerns of the art world and are more concerned with art theory than any technical achievements. In the catalog for the 1994 show "The Computer in the Studio," Nicholas Capasso wrote, "Today, computer-assisted art is not necessarily about computers. Owing to increased artist access to computers and their technological kin, art made with the help of computers is about anything and everything deemed viable in the aesthetic climate of pluralism that has prevailed since the early 1970s" [Capasso and Wallace, 1995, p.4].

The ubiquity of the computer in all aspects of modern culture is often the subject, if not the technical rationale, for computer-based works. In the catalog accompanying "Iterations: The New Image," Timothy Druckrey wrote, "Today computer technology has departed from its first uses—political, military, and scientific—and, like photography, has assumed a multitude of functions that are now distant relations to the medium's initial purpose" [Druckrey, 1993, p. 11]. One of these functions has come to be artistic creation that critiques the ongoing development of computer technology and its ever-expanding roles. According to Druckrey, "The convergence of disciplines—science, communication, medicine, entertainment, the space industry, computing, biology, engineering, video, and the arts—represents a watershed of linked ideas, mostly associated with the issue of representation, which are increasingly 'enframed,' to use a term of Martin Heidegger, by technology" [Druckrey, 1993, p. 17].

For this Renaissance-style convergence to take place in a meaningful way, however, the connection between art and science established in the early years of computer art must not be abandoned. As the computer becomes more of an art appliance there is a danger that artists will take it for granted, much as people take for granted the camera's magical ability to make photographs. Unlike technologies such as photography, however, the computer's uses and the tools that can be created for it will continue to change, often dramatically. Although some graphics programs can be used without extensive training and much information can be derived from accompanying manuals, artists must also delve more deeply into the underlying concepts of this medium if they are to understand its nature and comment on its interdisciplinary use from a position of true interdisciplinary knowledge.

Suggested Readings

ACM SIGGRAPH. *Visual Proceedings.* Show catalogs, essays, slides, CD-ROMs, and videotapes. The Association for Computing Machinery's Special Interest Group on Computer Graphics produces visual proceedings from every annual conference. Many important computer artists have participated in the annual art shows.

Druckrey, Timothy (ed.). *Electronic Culture: Technology and Visual Representation.* Aperture Foundation, 1996. Includes a valuable historical essay section in addition to many recent probing essays. Requires some fortitude to make sense of both the theory and science vocabulary and references. Not for beginners in either field. Good bibliography included.

Franke, Herbert W. *Computer Graphics—Computer Art,* 2d ed. Springer-Verlag, 1985. The first edition in 1971 was the first comprehensive book on the integration of the aesthetic and the technical in computer art.

Goodman, Cynthia. *Digital Visions, Computers and Art.* Harry N. Abrams, 1987. A catalog and book published in conjunction with the 1987 traveling show "Computers and Art." Includes a history of computer art and discussions of issues raised by the show and its artists.

ISEA. *Visual Proceedings.* Show catalogs and essays and video tapes. The Inter Society for the Electronic Arts publishes proceedings from its annual symposia. Many important computer artists have participated in the annual symposia art shows.

Jennings, Karla. *The Devouring Fungus: Tales of the Computer Age.* W.W. Norton, 1990. Entertaining coverage of the history of computing.

Leavitt, Ruth (ed.). *Artist and Computer.* Harmony Books, 1976. Personal statements and visual examples by thirty-five artists working with computers.

Lovejoy, Margot. *Postmodern Currents: Art and Artists in the Age of Electronic Media,* 2d ed. UMI Research Press, 1997. An important survey of electronic media that integrates history and theory. Inspired by Walter Benjamin's essay "Art in the Age of Mechanical Reproduction," the book covers a range of media in addition to computers and includes examples of diverse artworks.

Palfreman, Jon and Doron Swade. *The Dream Machine: Exploring the Computer Age.* Boston: WGBH Television; and London: BBC Books, 1991. An in-depth look at the history of computers and their impact on the modern world. A PBS Television series in five parts and the companion book *The Machine That Changed the World.* Amazing footage and interviews bring the history of computers to life.

Reichardt, Jasia (ed.). *Cybernetic Serendipity.* A Studio International special issue, 1968. A catalog (and essays) for one of the first large, internationally prominent computer art shows. Includes work by many early computer artists in a variety of fields.

Exercises

1. *Is the method the message—I?* Choose an artist who used computers in the 1960s or 1970s or who currently uses algorithmic methods. (Some good sources for finding such artists are given in the Suggested Readings for this chapter.) Before reading about the artist, critique one piece as if you had no knowledge of how it was made. Then find out as much as you can about the artist and the techniques used—the technology available and the artist's goals. Critique the piece again. Summarize your results by discussing the differences and similarities in the two critiques.

2. *Is the method the message—II?* Is it important to know how and when a work was created? Under what circumstances? Think of an example in which a work's meaning changes when such information is known and one in which it stays the same. For example, it may or may not be relevant that Monet was nearly blind near the end of his life, but it is probably important to know that aesthetic decisions in many Dadaist pieces were determined by randomness and chance. How is such knowledge important in looking at computer art works? Do you think it is always, sometimes, or never important? Explain your answer.

3. *Procedural image making.* Create a work in the style of early computer artists by drawing a simple shape and developing a set of rules for changing it (all this can be done with pencil and graph paper or in a draw program; if you know how to program, you can code this exercise). For example, you could start with a square. A simple procedure would be to move the square over one unit and rotate it 45°. If you repeat this procedure, the square will look as if it is tumbling across the page. A more complex procedure could involve scaling the square as it rotates or moving it up or down, as well as sideways. You may want to use random numbers to position your shape or control the transformations.

4. *Moore's law and you.* Use Moore's law (that computers will double in power about every 18 months with no rise in price) to estimate how much faster your favorite graphics program will be in five years and how much more memory you will have available. How would these changes affect the way in which you are creating work?

5. *Technology's influence on art.* What other art media aside from computers have been dramatically affected by technology? Choose one to discuss. How have technological innovations changed the ways that art is made with this medium? For example, the invention of canvas and stretchers made it possible for painters to work outdoors, carrying all their equipment with them. Give examples of art works created before and after the technological invention you choose.

6. *Perception of computers influences on computer art.* How have the computer's origins and development in the military and academia influenced the ways in which artists have used it? What is the relationship, if any, between the roots of computer image creation technology and current graphics programs?

CHAPTER 2

Digital Painting and Photoediting— 2D Raster Graphics

Figure 2.1 **Richard Rosenblum,** ***Black Ryder,*** **1994** (dimensions vary). Richard Rosenblum's images look photographic but clearly are created with a computer: The laws of physics are reinvented, objects are impossibly rearranged, and relative scale is dramatically altered. A successful sculptor, Rosenblum found that he could make 2D images on the computer by using the same visual ideas he had been investigating in his 3D sculpture. In both, forms and textures become separated from their original physical sources and, although retaining representational identity, metamorphose into something shaped in every way by the artist. His sculptural pieces, cast from natural forms, draw on analog likenesses; the computer has let him use the analog light-cast of photography in a digital context to compose sampled materials with previously unimaginable flexibility. The photographic skin, separated from its physical ties, becomes a type of mark, evocative of the physical forms and light that created it but no longer subservient to them. Rosenblum intentionally sets limits on the computer medium by using only a small subset of paint-type program features. He uses simple strategies based on techniques discussed in this chapter, including selection, copying and pasting, and brush-type work. The difficulty of the process lies in long hours of experimentation, not in any high-end special effects. *(Courtesy of Richard Rosenblum)*

2.1 Introduction

Many artists and designers are seduced by the computer during their first encounter with digital painting and photoediting programs, perhaps because the tools and techniques resemble those of traditional drawing, painting, and darkroom operations. The concepts underlying these programs are the basis of computer applications in many areas—from fine art to weather analysis and from medical imaging to broadcast TV.

Popular examples of these programs include Adobe Photoshop®, MetaCreations Painter®, Microsoft Image Composer®, and Broderbund Kid Pix®. Paint and photo programs also include features without traditional counterparts, such as the ability to rotate and resize regions within a piece and to warp and "process" areas, often in dramatic ways, increasing the visual language available for 2D art and design.

The basic concepts and capabilities used in painting and photoediting programs are essential parts of the artist's computer vocabulary and play a role in all types of computer-based image creation, from digital painting to computer-based graphic design to 3D, animation, digital video, and multimedia. Painting and photoediting programs are variously called *raster, bitmapped,* or *sample-based graphics* (terms defined and explained later in this chapter). *Image-processing* and *image-editing* programs also rely chiefly on raster graphics. Virtually all computer-based images, no matter how they are originally created, become raster images before they are displayed on a screen or printed by a computer-driven printer.

Most painting and photoediting programs offer a combination of raster graphics and an approach that uses geometry. Because these combinations are best understood after you have learned about both raster and geometric graphics and the differences between them, I discuss combined approaches at the end of Chapter 4, Digital Design and Layout—2D Geometric Graphics.

2.1.1 Entering a Postphotographic Era

As photography has historically come to mediate, if not wholly represent, the empirical world for most of the inhabitants of industrialized societies (indeed, the production and consumption of images serves as one of the distinguishing characteristics of advanced societies), it has become the privileged agent and conduit of culture and ideology [Solomon-Godeau, 1984, p. 76].

Abigail Solomon-Godeau, photographic historian, contemporary art critic, and Professor of the History of Art & Architecture at the University of California, Santa Barbara.

The most dramatic impact of raster graphics on art, design, and photography has been the digital editing and processing of photographic information, because it calls into question the very concept of photographic realism and the philosophical assumptions behind photographic truth (see Fig. 2.2).

Photography is challenged from two directions by computer graphics. On the one hand, the camera captures the world in perspective, automatically, and brings it to the computer artist to reshape as desired. On the other hand, 3D graphics provides automatically correct perspective, as well as lighting and textures that can seem extraordinarily realistic. Thus an image that appears to be a photograph may have been altered in a raster-type program, or it may be entirely synthetic—created in a 3D graphics program (discussed in Chapter 7, Building 3D Worlds—3D Geometric Graphics I; and Chapter 8, Rendering 3D Worlds—3D Geometric Graphics II). The work of MANUAL takes advantage of both of these capabilities (see Fig. 2.3). In their ongoing project, "The Trouble with Arcadia," Ed Hill and Suzanne Bloom are trying to "loosen the concept (and reality) of 'Arcadia' from its unexamined niche in history" [MANUAL, 1998]. Because

Figure 2.2 Michele Turre, *Me, My Mom & My Girl at Three,* 1992. The artist is interested in the effect of technologies on image making. In this one piece she was able to showcase four distinct phases of image-making history: The picture of her mother came from a high-quality 1920s studio portrait and has the soft lighting, grainy film base, and soft printing style of that era. The picture of herself came from the 1950s and has the sharp focus of a 4 × 5 camera. The picture of her daughter was captured from video and still has scan lines running through it. She then combined these three photographic technologies in an image that speaks clearly of the computer age. *(Courtesy of Michele Turre)*

of the encroachment of technology into formerly bucolic settings, Arcadia, an idealized, paradiselike natural landscape, has become more wishful thinking than reality. "It is from the deliberate perspective of electronic culture that we are attempting to revisualize and reconstruct ancient Arcady" [MANUAL, 1998].

The integration of photomanipulation and realistic 3D graphics into everyday visual discourse is bound to change our assumptions about the reality of "the photograph." Our concept of visual truth may come full circle as new technologies come into play: When the technique of linear perspective was first used in large paintings, people deemed it miraculous, a kind of sixteenth-century virtual reality (see Fig. 2.4).

Figure 2.3 MANUAL (Ed Hill and Suzanne Bloom), *Arcadian Landscapes: The Red Grove,* 1998. The collaborative duo MANUAL uses the computer to manipulate photographic information and to create 3D forms. Scenes that at first glance seem like examples of nature photography are actually "highly constructed landscapes meant to have disarmingly seamless appearances" [MANUAL, 1998]. *(Courtesy of Ed Hill and Suzanne Bloom)*

The technology of the photograph reduced the level of realism accorded to the technology of perspective alone, providing an even more direct connection with light reaching the eye of an observer. But in a postphotographic world, the strength of that connection is again uncertain. Every photograph becomes a painting.

The demise of the truth value of photography will be slow and may never be complete. The power of photographic-style images to represent, even create, reality cannot be overestimated. For example, when *Time* magazine released its June 27, 1994, issue with O. J. Simpson on the cover, readers couldn't help but notice that the "same" photograph, used on the cover of *Newsweek* and within the same issue of *Time,* looked markedly different. *Time* had darkened O. J.'s skin tone on the cover and slightly blurred the image to, they claim, create a more dramatic and tragic effect. The result was a mixture of documentary photography and illustration, but the impact was more powerful than a drawing because of people's belief in the veracity of apparently photographic images. (The author was not able to secure permission to reproduce this cover image.)

Although sophisticated observers of visual communication may know intellectually that all images are subjective, no one can be on guard all the time. In fact, already we are constantly influenced by media images that have no computer component—the president gives a speech with the flag waving in the background; a smiling woman, having nothing at all to do with the production of a car, convinces audiences of its desirability. "[Photography] is easily accepted as a window on the world rather than as a highly selective filter, placed there by a specific hand and mind. . . . 'This is Peter Jennings' is a culturally accepted statement whether one is presenting the person or pointing at a shape on a television screen" [Legrady, 1995, p. 190].

Fine-art photographers instantly say "we know it's not real" and "although there is a sense in which the camera does indeed capture reality, not just interpret it, photographs are as much an interpretation of the world as paintings and drawings are" [Sontag, 1973, pp. 6–7]. But art photography is a very small portion of most people's visual diet, and even well-educated consumers of visual media tend to take images on faith. For example, who would have guessed that the 1989 cover of *TV Guide* purporting to show Oprah Winfrey was actually Oprah's head on actress Ann-Margret's body. (The author was not able to secure permission to reproduce this cover image.)

The repercussions of a technology that absorbs the language of the photograph are only just beginning to be felt and are bound to be dramatic. In many industries, the photograph's claim to concrete representation is as important as the government's backing of a nation's currency. "The camera, in all its manifestations, is our god, dispensing

Figure 2.4 Masaccio, *Trinity with the Virgin, St. John and Donors,* **1427** (fresco painting, Florence, Sta. Maria Novella). Fifteenth-century viewers of Masaccio's *Trinity* (the first painting to use proper linear perspective) must have been struck by a sense of reality that is lost to us now. *(Courtesy of Alinari/Art Resource, NY)*

(a)　　　　　　　　　(b)　　　　　　　　　(c)

Figure 2.5 Michele Turre, *You Wish . . .* from the project *Tree Fix,* 1997 (each panel 11″ × 13.75″, quad-toned inkjet prints, transferred onto watercolor paper in an etching press). The *Tree Fix* series makes the viewer more aware of the interactions between technological and natural aspects of modern landscapes. (a) The unnatural shape of a tree that has been pruned to keep it away from overhead power or telephone lines is suddenly emphasized by (b) the elimination of wires. (c) Finally Turre heals the tree, returning it to its ideal natural shape. *(Courtesy of Michele Turre)*

what we mistakenly believe to be the truth. The photograph is the modern world" [Lawson, 1984, p. 162]. Artists can manipulate the truth-value of photograph-like images to fool viewers, present paradoxical and impossible situations, or guide viewers to a new or enhanced understanding by combining documentary implications with the painterly options made available on the computer. Just as MANUAL used technology to create the image in Fig. 2.3 as a means to envision a nontechnological ideal, so Michele Turre, in Fig. 2.5, used the computer to reveal the impact of technology on a landscape. For artists, the advent of the postphotographic period is as important as the invention of photography itself and surely one of the defining events in twentieth-century art.

2.2 Concepts

Painting and photoediting programs are intuitive and fun to use right away, but the joy of using a medium is tainted if artists or designers are frequently mystified by the effects of their actions. Knowledge of the fundamental concepts used in these programs helps artists and designers take full advantage of often complex features and clarifies the roles of raster images in other types of graphics programs.

If you have never used a paint or photoediting program before, I suggest that you experiment with one before reading this section (or at least skip ahead to read about some of the capabilities of these programs). After you have used a painting or photo-editing program for a while, come back and read about the important concepts involved in this type of computer graphics.

2.2.1 Continuous and Analog Versus Discrete and Digital

Digital technologies have become an important part of late twentieth-century culture: Once information is encoded numerically, it can be examined, distributed, and merged in ways impossible with analog media. If the colors in an image are **discrete,** or easily separable into individual pieces as in a mosaic or needlepoint, you can assign numbers to each color element, thus encoding the information in a **digital** format. Figure 2.6 shows a simplified digitization process that can be done by hand, reminiscent of the hand process used to create patterns for the punch cards of a Jacquard loom (see Chapter 1).

If the colors in an image are **continuous,** however, as with traditional photography and painting, there is always another color between any two points of color. Reproducing the information in a digital image is as easy as copying numbers, but what about reproducing an image created in a continuous medium, such as oil paint? The most common approaches historically have been **analog** methods, in which some continuous physical process translates changes in one medium into changes in another. For example, making a photographic reproduction of a painting involves the response of a film emulsion to continuously changing frequencies of light reflecting off the painting's surface. In analog musical reproduction, sound waves continuously alter physical characteristics of a medium.

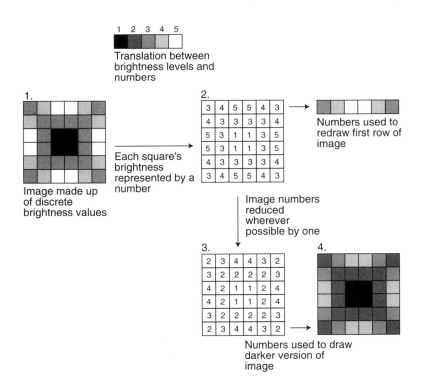

Figure 2.6 Digitizing by hand. The mosaic-style image (1) is made up of thirty-six squares, each with a single shade of darkness. The image was then expressed as a collection of numbers (2) that indicate the relative darkness of each square. It is easy to translate this digital representation back into a visual image by using the numbers to select the right shades of gray. The artist can easily change the values represented in the digitized version by changing the numbers, raising them to make them lighter or lowering them to make them darker (3) and (4).

The distinction between discrete and continuous is often useful only at certain levels of detail. For instance, a photograph is, for most practical purposes, continuous, even though under a microscope the image consists of many individual, discrete grains.

SAMPLING   Analog images are **digitized** by reducing their continuously varying values and colors to discrete quantities based on measurements, or **samples**, taken at equal spatial intervals. Think about the difference between walking up a flight of stairs or walking up a ramp. A ramp essentially rises continuously, whereas a staircase has discrete steps. To design a staircase based on a ramp, you could mark off the height of the ramp at equal intervals and then make stairs accordingly (see Fig. 2.7). When an image is digitized, its continuously varying values and colors are sampled at equal spatial intervals, just as the height of the ramp was sampled to determine the height of the stairs (see Fig. 2.8).

Note that the digitized image in Fig. 2.8 looks striped rather than smoothly graduated like the original. Although a digital version of an image is dramatically easier to change, store, and distribute than an analog version, information is always lost in the translation from analog to digital form (although sometimes the original analog form can be fully reconstructed from the digital information). The science of sampling well depends on the **frequency** of the samples (how many are taken per inch), the way the samples are calculated, and the way the sample information is used to recreate the image. See Section 3.4.1 for a discussion of how frequently an image should be sampled for good results. Some troublesome effects caused by the use of discrete samples rather than continuous data, such as aliasing ("the jaggies") and Mach banding, are covered in Chapter 4, Digital Design and Layout—2D Geometric Graphics; and Chapter 8, Rendering 3D Worlds—3D Geometric Graphics II.

Samples can be generated by hand (moving a mouse or stylus) or can come from digitizing photographs or traditional art work. Many computer artists feel that digital work, especially marks made with a mouse or through menu choices, lack the "messiness" of analog media. When he began using the computer a decade ago, artist James Faure Walker felt that "it was like being let loose in the play-room with a new set of paints—the paint program." But the world of digital data had an unexpected anonymity to it. Initially, he says, "I couldn't bridge the gap between the clean digital image

Figure 2.7 Sampling a ramp's height to make stairs.

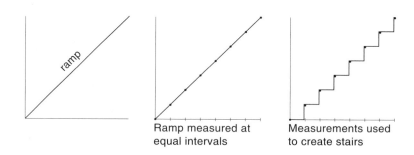

Ramp measured at equal intervals

Measurements used to create stairs

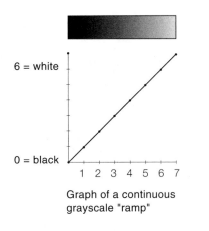

Graph of a continuous grayscale "ramp"	Graph of discrete samples of the grayscale ramp taken at equal intervals

Figure 2.8 Sampling a continuous image.

and the messy atmospherics of painting. . . . Most of the computer work I was seeing, including my own, told me far too little, it could have been made anywhere, in the desert, in the arctic, on the moon" [Walker, 1996]. His solution has been to integrate digital mark making (samples of his hand motion) with images captured from concrete objects in his home and neighborhood. He works them into computer paintings, and the computer work in turn feeds his rendering of traditional oil paintings done at the same time (see Fig. 2.9).

2.2.2 THE PIXEL

What I am about to say is so fundamental that I wish I could shout it from the treetops and have people remember! A pixel is a point sample—that is, the value of a continuous thing at a single point (with zero dimensions). If only this were understood, we might be able to rid the world forever of the misconception that a pixel is a little square [Smith, 1995].

Alvy Ray Smith, creator of Paint, the first full-color paint program

Each of an image's sample locations, together with its sampled values, is called an **image pixel** (short for *picture element*). For color images, three samples are usually used for each image pixel, one for red, one for green, and one for blue; this choice of samples gives RGB color images their name. Computer images based on pixels are thus sometimes referred to as **sample-based graphics.** Image pixel information is stored in a rectangular array and translated into screen or printer images in a series of horizontal rows called rasters, hence the name *raster graphics.*

Studio view, November 1996

Figure 2.9 James Faure Walker, *Self-Portrait in Leicester Square*, 1995 (composite inkjet, 35″ × 30″). The studio view shows the messy atmospherics that help to inspire Walker's work. *(Courtesy of James Faure Walker)*

Confusingly, screen and printer images are also described in terms of pixels. In general, however, there is not a one-to-one correspondence between image pixels and screen or printer pixels. A **screen pixel** is the smallest area that a particular combination of software and hardware can illuminate on a monitor. This roundish area is usually composed of several groups of red, green, and blue phosphors, and there are anywhere from 72 to 85 screen pixels per linear inch. When a document is viewed at 100% scale, each image pixel is represented by a screen pixel. When a document is viewed at a scale larger than 100%, each image pixel is represented by several screen pixels. On "multiresolution" monitors, the user can change the number of screen pixels per inch. The same situation applies to printers; an individual image pixel can be represented by a single **printer pixel,** or dot, but different printers produce slightly different dot shapes and different numbers of dots per inch. In many types of computer printing, a single image pixel is represented by a group of printer dots in a process called **halftoning.** To eliminate any confusion, in this text I always distinguish between image pixels, screen pixels, and printer pixels or dots (see Fig. 2.10).

All raster graphics operations—whether performed by drawing with a mouse, making a menu choice, or other means—alter the sample values of the image pixels. The pixel value–changing paradigm holds for even the most sophisticated program features and is often a more useful way to think about this type of image making than as a simulated painting or photographic experience.

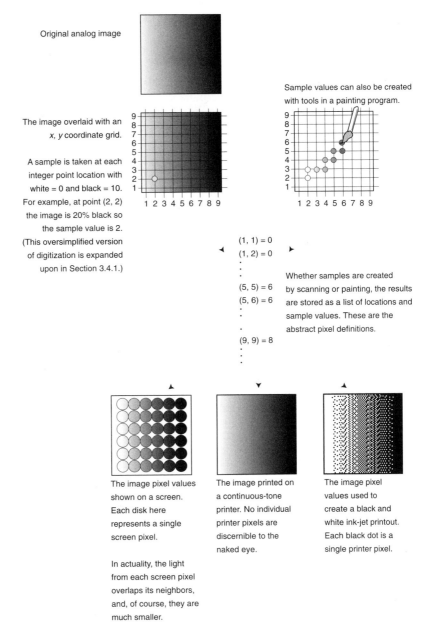

Original analog image

The image overlaid with an *x, y* coordinate grid.

A sample is taken at each integer point location with white = 0 and black = 10. For example, at point (2, 2) the image is 20% black so the sample value is 2. (This oversimplified version of digitization is expanded upon in Section 3.4.1.)

Sample values can also be created with tools in a painting program.

(1, 1) = 0
(1, 2) = 0
⋮
(5, 5) = 6
(5, 6) = 6
⋮
(9, 9) = 8
⋮

Whether samples are created by scanning or painting, the results are stored as a list of locations and sample values. These are the abstract pixel definitions.

The image pixel values shown on a screen. Each disk here represents a single screen pixel.

In actuality, the light from each screen pixel overlaps its neighbors, and, of course, they are much smaller.

The image printed on a continuous-tone printer. No individual printer pixels are discernible to the naked eye.

The image pixel values used to create a black and white ink-jet printout. Each black dot is a single printer pixel.

Fιgυre 2.10 The relationship between image pixels and screen and printer pixels.

Pixels are often described as little mosaic squares that make up digital images, but image pixels are only samples of color at specified locations, just like the height samples taken from the ramp in Fig. 2.7. Sometimes screen pixels appear to be squares because of the way that computer hardware scales images for "zooming in" (see Section 2.6.4). Early computer screens also made images look like they were made up of little squares or rectangles because their screen resolution was so low. This effect is caused by *aliasing* (see Chapter 4, Digital Design and Layout—2D Geometric Graphics).

Interestingly, well before computers were invented, the pioneering abstract painter Wassily Kandinsky thought about how an abstract geometric concept could be translated into a mark in a visible physical medium. Posing the problem of bringing an abstract, zero-dimensional entity, the point, to life on a canvas as a fundamental issue of art theory, he wrote, "The invisible geometric point must assume a certain proportion when materialized, so as to occupy a certain area of the basic plane." This materialization of the point is "the result of the initial collision of the tool with the material plane. . . . Paper, wood, canvas, stucco, metal—may all serve as this basic plane. The tool may be the pencil, burin, brush, pen, etching-point, etc." [Kandinsky, 1947, p. 28]. In a similar way, the computer makes the numeric geometric and color information of an image's pixels visible through the use of phosphor on a screen, iron oxides and plastic (laser printer toner), and many other materials.

2.3 ANATOMY OF A PAINTING OR PHOTOEDITING PROGRAM

Painting and photoediting programs build on many familiar metaphors from traditional painting, drawing, and photography. Some common painting and photoediting program tools include paint brushes, airbrushes, pencils, erasers, and photographic processes such as lightening or darkening an image, changing the color balance, enhancing contrast, and cropping. Although many program features do not have traditional counterparts, the basic components of today's raster graphics programs still resemble the first mass-market paint metaphor interface, that of Apple's MacPaint, released in 1984. Figure 2.11 shows the basic components of a painting and photoediting program.

Drawing Area or Canvas. The screen area is the drawing area in which the tools of the painting program work. Almost all of today's programs can open more than one drawing area for a single image file, but do not let different files share a common drawing area. This capability is not a necessity, though; some programs, such as Microsoft's Image Composer, let users open more than one image file into a single drawing area.

Tools. Different modes of "painting" (laying down and changing marks), selecting, and navigating are displayed in and selected from a collection of icons known as the main **tool palette** or **tool bar.**

Palettes. In addition to the main tool palette, subsidiary palettes exist for tool customization, such as changing the brush size, shape, and opacity. Palettes are

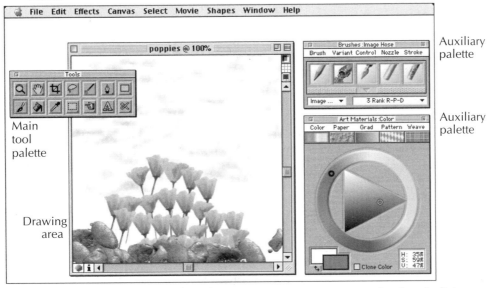

Figure 2.11 Basic components of a paint program. *(Painter is a registered trademark of Meta-Creations. These materials are copyrighted 1998.)*

often provided for choosing colors, line widths, and patterns and for arranging elements used in image creation.

Menus. Many processes in painting and photoediting programs are available only through menu choices. Common menu items are the standard cut, copy, and paste under the Edit menu, and such operations as flipping an image across its horizontal or vertical axis. In general, menus are used to perform operations that change selected portions of an image or even the entire image, while tools are most often associated with work based on motions of the hand.

2.4 LOCAL TOUCH

Touch is the artist's experience of making a mark in the process of creation. In traditional artwork, the sense of touch is based largely on the physical sensation of using an implement, say chiseling a stone or drawing with charcoal (as shown in Fig. 2.12); in contrast, touch on the computer refers mostly to emotional and aesthetic sensations, since the feedback is primarily visual, not tactile.

Figure 2.12

2.4.1 The Concept of Touch

The sense of touch varies dramatically among the different types of image-creation programs and affects what and how artists create with them. The kinds of touch available are determined by the concepts that underlie the program. For each type of computer graphics paradigm in this text, I give an overview of the essential concepts, followed by discussions of the types of touch available.

The sense of touch in painting and photoediting programs is sometimes hand-based and gestural, as in drawing and painting. However, the sense of touch often depends more on choosing processes and applying them to particular areas of the image—for instance rotating an area of an image. Debates spurred by the invention of photography about the role of the hand continue in the realm of digital image making. How does someone interpret a piece in which the involvement of the hand is unclear—for instance, a digital image that looks like an unaltered photograph but has in fact been skillfully altered by hand? Under what circumstances does this distinction matter?

In this text I introduce a new term, **local-touch** mark making, meaning a mark controlled by the hand in a process involving the accumulation over time of relatively small marks to create a larger image (see Fig. 2.13). This type of mark making is seen in most traditional drawing and painting techniques—the artist's use of a piece of char-

Figure 2.13 Local-touch image creation. The local-touch marks making up this bird image were controlled by hand, using a simple brush tool (see sample stroke and cross-hatching at top). As marks accumulate, the image changes and each new mark is a reaction to the constantly changing appearance. The sum of many relatively small marks and many separate decisions contribute to the "hand-drawn" feeling of the image.

coal, for instance, to sketch a portrait by layering a variety of marks made with different pressures and speeds and different parts of the charcoal. The artist simultaneously observes and records and makes new marks based on the appearance of all the marks accumulated up to that time. In addition to 2D work, such as drawing with a pencil, painting with a brush or making a mural with fingerpaint, local touch processes are used in a number of sculptural methods, including chiseling stone and sculpting clay.

I introduce the terms *local touch* (here) and *global touch* (in Section 2.5) because existing terms do not adequately convey the different types of mark making available to the computer artist. In his thought-provoking book *The Reconfigured Eye,* William Mitchell refers to hand-based marks as "intentional," meaning that they are not part of an automated, mechanical, optical, or digital process [Mitchell, 1992]. Local touch and global touch are different ends of a continuum, rather than mutually exclusive options, however, and the hand is often used to guide processes that affect large portions of a work all at once but still evidence obvious intentionality. See Section 2.5.4 for a description of such global, but still often hand-based, processes.

2.4.2 TRANSPARENCY, TOOL SHAPE, AND MIXING BEHAVIOR

Most interesting local-touch options involve some degree of transparency so that a history of marks can evolve and complex color mixtures can be created. This feature is especially common in tool modes that attempt to imitate traditional media. For example, in MetaCreation's "natural media" program Painter, virtually all the different brush tools, from simulations of colored pencils to watercolor, are designed to be somewhat transparent. Other variables include the tools' shapes and mixing behaviors. A magic-marker brush, for instance, not only builds up a more opaque and saturated color when used to draw over the same area repeatedly, but it also mixes with other colors already on the drawing area (see Fig. 2.14). In many programs, brushes can paint with isolated

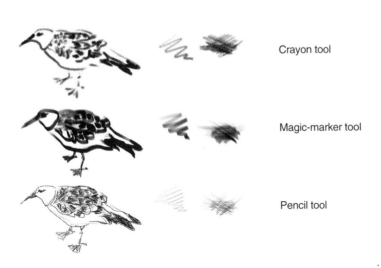

Crayon tool

Magic-marker tool

Pencil tool

Figure 2.14 Local-touch simulating traditional media. All mark-making variations are determined by different transparency levels, mixing behaviors, brush shapes and other factors that give character to individual marks and sequences of marks.

Figure 2.15 Joan Truckenbrod, *Seize Steering,* 1995 (watercolor print on Arches paper, 32″ × 36″). Truckenbrod uses a paint program's local-touch drawing methods, as well as scanned imagery, to create her Ecotextures, multilayered images that weave together iconography of the family and natural and technological environments. The space and marks speak simultaneously of primitive image making, as on cave walls, and of high-tech visual tools. *(Courtesy of Joan Truckenbrod)*

properties of a color, increasing its intensity, for instance, without changing its grayscale value (how bright or dark it is). Such choices let artists create unique styles of local-touch mark making that may or may not resemble the results of working with traditional media.

In general, the options available for brush tools depend largely on the software package used, although a great variety of effects can be achieved in almost any paint program if you simply experiment with the shape, size, and transparency of the brush. Just as a printmaker must spend time working with different etching tools or a sculptor with implements to model clay, so you must become acquainted with a paint or photoediting program's tools and experiment with the variations available to you. Learning to use a program's brush tools and creating and saving personalized versions of their use is a process of defining a new medium as well as learning. Artist Joan Truckenbrod integrates old and new image-making vocabularies in a dialectic between what she calls "artificial templates" and the natural world to create Ecotextures (see Fig. 2.15). She says, "Ecotextures are constructs for absorbing natural rhythms into our schedules. . . . There is a different resonance to one's life if there is a constant interplay between contemporary business, organization, and educational forms and the natural environment" [Truckenbrod, 1997].

2.5 GLOBAL TOUCH

Global-touch tools change an entire image area simultaneously, performing operations such as scaling or rotating an area or replacing one color with another. The hand may be involved in selecting the area to change and sometimes even in changing it, but the feeling is different from the local-touch process of accumulating marks over time.

The artist can sit back (or go out for coffee, depending on the complexity of the operation) while the computer "processes" that region. Because of the difference in approach, such methods are often called **image processing,** rather than painting or image editing.

Global processes, like what Mitchell calls "algorithmic" processes [Mitchell, 1992, p. 30], are common on the computer but comparatively rare in traditional art work. An obvious and again important exception is photography: Almost all photographic processes, from the taking of the picture to development and further darkroom work, are global processes (see Fig. 2.16). The hand plays almost no role, and changes made to the image usually affect either the whole piece or a predetermined region of it. Enlargement, image reversal, and color balance alteration are all globally implemented decisions.

Figure 2.16

2.5.1 Tonal Mapping

In a darkroom, an artist can change an image's exposure time or the chemicals used in processing it to make it lighter, darker, or higher contrast. On the computer, the artist makes these and related changes by taking a pixel's sample color value and **mapping** it to a new sample value by performing some preset operation on it, for instance raising its value to make it lighter. If a grayscale image has a value of 0 for black pixels and 10 for white pixels, a mapping operation that added 2 to each pixel would make the whole image lighter—for instance, mapping a sample value of 5 to a sample value of 7. Typical mapping options include lightening and darkening an image, raising or lowering the contrast, and inverting the values (exchanging white for black and dark grays for light grays). Remapping values can also help reveal detail by making light colors a bit darker in highlights or by making dark colors a bit lighter in shadows. Tools available for tonal mapping have a variety of names, including brightness/contrast, curves, histograms, and levels.

Figure 2.17 shows a generalized mapping option and the effect of several tonal mappings. To read this type of diagram, place your finger on a gray value along the horizontal, or *x,* axis of the graph area, which represents a gray value in the original image. Now move your finger up until it meets the line, which represents the action of the mapping operation. To find the pixel's new value, move your finger over to the vertical, or *y,* axis; the position on the *y* axis is the new value. If you have studied math you will recognize the graph as a function, an operation that takes an *x* value (the pixel's original gray value) and delivers a *y* value (the pixel's new gray value).

Image as scanned

(a)

Original image grays

Effect of mapping
on a simple
black-to-white gradient

Figure 2.17 Tonal mapping.
(Detail, Rembrandt Harmenszoon van Rijn, *Self-Portrait*, 1652, Kunsthistorisches Museum, Vienna, Austria). (a) A not-so-hot scan. (b) The lightest gray values were mapped to white and the darkest grays to black. Contrast was also increased by slightly lightening middle light grays and darkening middle dark grays. *(Courtesy of Foto Marburg/Art Resource, NY)*

(b)

Original image grays

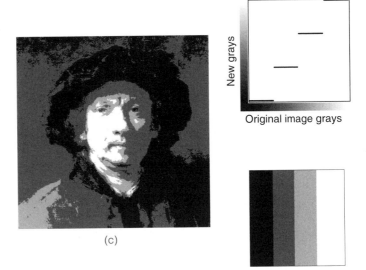

Figure 2.17 (continued).
(c) The image posterized to four grays.

(c)

The same techniques can be used to remap values for the individual color components (e.g., red, green, and blue or cyan, magenta, yellow, and black) of a piece. Making a color component lighter or darker shifts the color balance. Different aspects of color can also be remapped—for instance, increasing saturation without changing color value or hue. (For further discussion of these color terms and operations, see Chapter 5, Electronic Color.)

2.5.2 FILTERING

Filtering is a good example of how understanding the concepts behind a visual tool can clarify its current and potential uses. At first glance, filtering options in painting and photoediting programs can appear to be a complex set of different, unrelated tools. These options include filters for blurring an image, sharpening it, and finding edges of shapes within it, and for creating special effects such as embossing and making images glow. These final effects are all noticeably different but all are achieved by a single method.

The mapping technique discussed in Section 2.5.1 mapped a single pixel's brightness to a new brightness, producing the same results regardless of the pixel's location or the values of its neighboring pixels. **Filtering,** however, changes a pixel's value by tak-

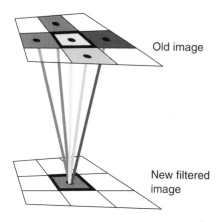

Old image

New filtered
image

Figure 2.18 Filters work by averaging the brightnesses of neighborhoods of pixels.

ing into account not only its original brightness but also the brightness of its neighbors (see Fig. 2.18). All the effects mentioned in this section are obtained by the use of techniques for averaging each pixel in the image with its neighbors.

Origins of Filtering Vocabulary in Signal Processing

The vocabulary of filtering comes from **signal processing,** which deals with electrical or sound waves over time. The relationship between signal processing and image filtering is highly mathematical and filtering is described here only qualitatively. However, some of the signal processing vocabulary is used throughout the computer graphics literature and knowing it can be helpful. Perhaps most important, images often are analyzed in terms of frequencies, which correspond to how rapidly values change in the image. **High-frequency** areas have adjacent color values that are very different from one another, say, black right next to white or even dark gray next to light gray. Artists and designers usually think of them as **high-contrast areas** or **edges.** High frequencies often are found in areas of fine detail and along boundaries of objects; for example, a black and white line drawing has almost nothing but high frequencies. **Low-frequency** or **low-contrast** transitions have slowly changing color values, say from a midgray to a slightly darker one over several inches, and are found in gradients and soft forms, such as cloud banks. A **high-pass filter** removes low frequencies, making the image look sharper, and a **low-pass filter** removes high frequencies, making an image look blurred. Just as musicians use filters to improve or distort a sound recording, so the filters discussed here are used to filter unwanted frequencies out of an image or to accentuate some frequencies over others. These distinctions are also important in the discussion of scanning in Chapter 3, Keyboards, Mice, Tablets, Scanners, and Displays.

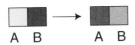

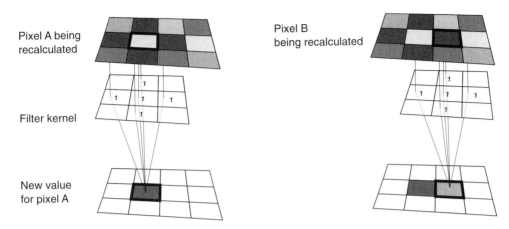

Figure 2.19 A simple blurring filter. The blur filter moves over the image, calculating each new pixel value based on an even mixture of its old value and the values of four surrounding pixels. The 1s in the filter kernel indicate that each pixel value is given equal weight in the averaging process.

Figure 2.20 A less simple blurring filter. Here the central pixel has a weight of 3 instead of 1. Note that the resulting final pixel is lighter than that shown at the left in Fig. 2.19.

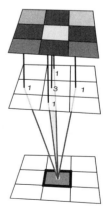

Figure 2.19 shows a grid of pixel values and a filter; the pixel over the center of the filter is being averaged with four of its neighbors. This blend becomes the center pixel's new value and the filter moves on, making the pixel to the right of the former one the new center pixel. Again, the average of that pixel with its neighbors is calculated and becomes the new value. This process of sequentially averaging whole neighborhoods in order to get new pixel values is called **convolution.** The matrix of values that defines the filter is called the **convolution kernel** or **filter kernel.** For color images, the process is repeated three times, once each for the red, green, and blue brightnesses of each pixel. The simple averaging described **blurs** the image because the new pixel values become more like the pixels nearby, filtering out high frequencies or sharp changes from one level of brightness to another (see Fig. 2.19).

The results of this filter can be improved by varying the influence of each pixel in the averaging process, that is, by using a **weighted average** (see Fig. 2.20). One of the best weighting functions for this purpose is a **Gaussian curve,** a shape that resembles a hat or bell, named after its inventor, mathematician Carl Friedrich Gauss. It weights the central pixel (the one being assigned a new value) most strongly and neighboring pixels more and more weakly with distance from the center. A simple triangular-shaped filter does the same thing, but the Gaussian filter usually produces more convincing, smoother looking results (see Fig. 2.21). All high-end image-processing programs offer Gaussian blurring. For any particular blurring filter, the greater the number of neighbors considered, that is, the greater the **filter radius** or **support,** the more pronounced the effect will be. If an image is blurred repeatedly, the pixel values eventually merge into a single value (not usually very enlightening).

Blurring can be used to give an image a softer feel or make it seem out of focus. Blurring filters can also help remove "noise" from an image, such as random specks from a scan of a grainy or dirty photograph or even small patterns such as halftones and

Figure 2.21 Averages weighted according to different shapes.

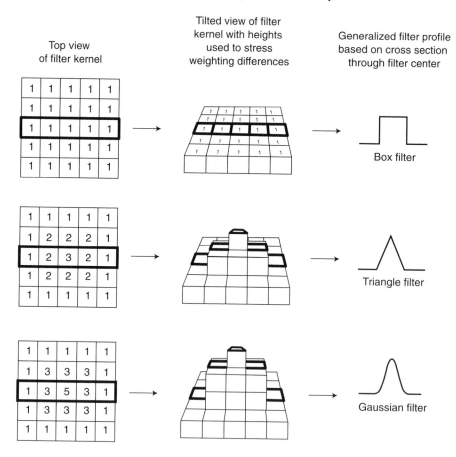

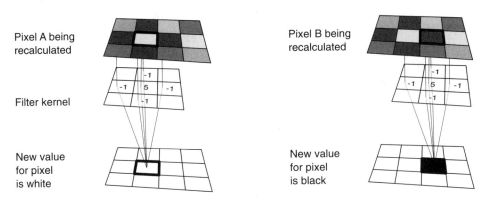

Figure 2.22 A sharpening filter.

moirés. Variations on blurring include directional blurs, in which the blurring takes place along a single angle, and motion blur (discussed in Chapter 10, 2D and 3D Animation and Video).

Blurring combines positive weights of the neighboring pixels, but **sharpening** filters weight neighboring pixels negatively, accentuating the differences between pixels rather than making them more similar (see Fig. 2.22). Sharpening is perceptually the opposite of blurring, filtering out low-frequency areas by increasing the value differences between pixels instead of decreasing them. Note, however, that, although the operations may seem opposite in nature, sharpening does not "undo" the effect of blurring; repeated applications of both types of filtering merely cause the quality of the image to deteriorate. When sharpening is taken to the extreme, the image disintegrates into an often staticlike mixture of high-contrast pixel areas.

Variations on sharpening include restricting sharpening effects to areas with large value differences (very high-frequency areas). Such filters *sharpen edges* while leaving the rest of the image untouched. **Edge detection** identifies high-frequency areas or contrast changes in pixel values, often erasing other parts of the image to provide outlines of shapes and forms.

Because filtering takes into account pixels' relationships to one another, filters often can be used to explore the formal structure of a piece, changing or revealing desired aspects of the piece and suppressing others. Blurring, for example, eliminates small detail and reveals large-scale value and color masses, often giving insight into a piece's overall composition. Sharpening accentuates small details and can be used to reveal linear structures and color and value transitions. Figure 2.23 shows the results

(a)

(b)

	-1		-1
		5	
	-1		-1

(c)

(d)

		1		
		2		
1	2	3	2	1
		2		
		1		

-5	4	-5	
3	6	3	
-5	4	-5	

Figure 2.23 Filtering examples. The filter kernels are shown below each example.   (a) Original image. (b) Sharpened. (c) Blurred. (d) Edges found.

obtained by using blurring and sharpening techniques, as well as a number of variations on a photograph of an electrical plant.

Artists and designers can experiment with a wide range of filters in today's photo-editing programs and try out their own filter designs by using custom filter-making options such as Adobe Photoshop's Filter Factory® and MetaCreations KPT Convolver®.

2.5.3   SIMPLE TRANSFORMATIONS

Both tonal mapping and filtering map old pixel values to new ones. **Transformations** map pixel values to new locations within the image.

Three basic transformations can reposition an object in an astonishingly wide variety of ways. These essential transformations are **translation** (moving), **rotation** (turning), and **scale** (making something larger or smaller). You will find these transformations useful in paint-type programs and will rely on them in draw-type programs; without them 3D graphics would be all but impossible. (I discuss moving images and portions of an image in the context of composition in Section 2.6.) Rotation is used to turn an object around its center or some other point. Scaling can make an object uniformly larger or smaller, changing its size but not its proportions. **Nonuniform scaling** alters an image non-uniformly, making it, for instance, smaller horizontally but not vertically and thus notice-ably distorting most realistic imagery.

In addition to these basic transformations, images can be **flipped** across a horizon-tal or vertical axis to create mirror images and **distorted** by squashing or stretching them within a rectangular scaffold.[1] In Fig. 2.24 these transformations were used to create a number of different-looking birds from a single original image. See if you can spot the transformations before reading the caption.

Artist Nancy Buchanan used simple transformations to create a work about mod-ern housing developments (see Fig. 2.25).

2.5.4   ALGORITHMIC TOUCH AND SPECIAL EFFECTS

The tonal mapping, filtering, and transformation operations discussed previously are part of the basic vocabulary of global touches that an artist or designer working with a computer soon learns. Other more complex effects can combine different mapping, filtering, and transformation operations to create dramatic results that would not only be impossible to create with local touch tools, but would also be difficult even to imag-ine. These algorithmic operations leave their own stylistic mark. Their aesthetic use has in common with photography their independence of the hand and their contribu-tion to a style of image or mark that usually has little to do with the individual artist, but rather with the algorithm used—whether a fancy "swirl" or a recording of light.

---

[1] Flipping across a horizontal or vertical axis can also be thought of as negative scaling by 100% in either the *x* or *y* direction, respectively. Although this method is not at first intuitive, I mention it here because a number of pro-grams take advantage of it.

Original (untransformed) bird

Figure 2.24 Transformations. The original bird is at the upper left; (1) distorted; (2) distorted; (3) scaled down (uniformly) and rotated; (4) flipped across *x* or *y* axis, scaled up in *y* but not *x*; (5) original; (6) flipped across *x* or *y* axis, scaled down (uniformly) and rotated; (7) distorted; (8) scaled up in *x* but not *y*; (9) flipped across *x* or *y* axis, scaled down (uniformly) and rotated; (10) scaled down (uniformly); (11) scaled down (uniformly) and flipped horizontally (across *y* axis); (12) scaled down (uniformly) and rotated; (13) scaled up (uniformly) and flipped horizontally (across *y* axis).

Some processes are so involved—and introduce so much of their designer's aesthetic decisions into the marks they leave—that thinking of them as a separate category of touch is helpful. Thus I use **algorithmic touch** here to describe a type of complex global touch that creates or changes visual information in a distinctive fashion with its own "personality."[2] For example, photography is an algorithmic touch that uses a chemical process to create an image based on light. Because the process is the same no matter who takes the picture, a photograph is usually easily recognized as such.

Examples of algorithmic touch include the familiar swirling colored spaces created by the mathematics of fractals and tools such as automated texture creation. For exam-

---

[2]Technically speaking, almost all the marks made in a computer graphics program depend at some point on automated processes or algorithms.

Figure 2.25 Nancy Buchanan, *Developing*, 1995 (screen from interactive art work). This image, based on a photograph of a housing development, was created with a rectangular selection tool and simple global operations such as flipping and rotation. These tools help create an image that emphasizes the sameness of housing developments, the technology involved in their construction, and their systematic spread. *(Courtesy of the artist)*

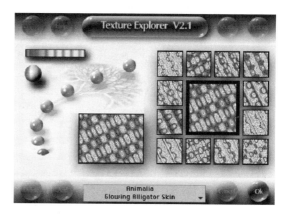

Figure 2.26 Algorithmic texture. Meta-Creations Kai's Power Tools Texture Explorer lets the user influence the texture design by choosing one of the current texture's mutations (shown in the small texture blocks). The chosen mutation then becomes the current texture and new mutations based on it fill the surrounding squares. The user can influence the degree of mutation in each iteration as well as colors and other variables. The user continues to select among the new mutations until a desired texture is achieved. *(KPT is a registered trademark of MetaCreations. These materials are copyrighted 1998.)*

ple, KPT Texture Explorer (see Fig. 2.26) uses a combination of preset procedures and choices made by the artist to generate a texture. Instead of creating marks by hand, artists influence how existing textures are "mutated" to create new ones, exercising their visual judgment rather than hand-based skill to arrive at a texture that fills their aesthetic needs.

Many algorithmic and special effects options, such as Texture Explorer, are available as **plug-ins,** or small pieces of software that can be added to an application after purchase to provide extra functionality. Because algorithmic touches generally have noticeable effects, they are sometimes presented in a special-effects menu or options area. These options often not only recalculate pixel values, but also move pixel values to new locations, using spatial transformations much more complex than flipping an image or rotating it. For example, different plug-ins allow the user to change from rectangular to polar coordinates, make an image look as though it were under water, and even twirl an image around a center point as through it were swirling down a drain (see Fig. 2.27). Other effects include options such as automatically redrawing a work in the style of van Gogh or an Impressionist or Pointillist painting.

(a)

(b)

Figure 2.27 Examples of algorithmic touch. (a) Original unretouched photograph. (b) Water was swirled. (In addition, some of the boats have been erased and the remaining boat and child have been moved, scaled, and rotated.) (c) Water was pinched inward toward center and a page-turning effect applied to the lower right corner. (Again, boy and boat have been scaled and rotated.)

(c)

These global-touch options are seductive, and artists should be prepared to spend time experimenting with such effects to learn when and where they actually are useful. In general, applying an elaborate algorithmic special effect to an entire image produces gimmicky looking results. Applying such effects in moderation or to small portions of an image can add interesting aesthetic variation and a range of touch that would be difficult or impossible to achieve with the basic local-touch or global-touch tools.

The use of algorithmic touch raises many issues. For instance, if you produce a picture algorithmically (entirely or in large part), should you include the author(s) of the algorithm on your piece? In what sense are they your collaborators? Can someone else distinguish how much of the piece's effect is due to your decisions and how much to the programmers of the relevant algorithm(s)? Under what circumstances is this distinction important?

2.5.5 SELECTION AND MASKING

When using global-touch tools, the artist must first differentiate a selected region from other areas to remain unchanged. **Selection** is the opposite of the traditional process of **masking,** which protects an area from being changed, as when an artist paints through a stencil or uses a mask in traditional filmmaking or animation. Selection tools are used to indicate which parts of the image are available for alteration and which parts are to be masked off. Selections by themselves do not produce any kind of permanent mark.

Increasingly sophisticated selection techniques have made selection and masking as flexible as most mark-making tools and just as important in creating and editing images. Many paint programs let users add and subtract selection areas in order to arrive at complex and even discontinuous areas. In Fig. 2.28, the Ferris wheel silhouette was selected and then the background areas within the spokes were removed from the selection.

Some paint programs let artists create numerous selected areas that act as separate **sprites,** or **paint objects,** that can be reselected and repositioned at any time. Another approach offers **layers,** each of which can be worked in without affecting the others. For further discussion of paint objects and layers, see Chapter 4, Digital Design and Layout—2D Geometric Graphics; and Chapter 10, 2D and 3D Animation and Video.

Selection plays an important role in the work of Richard Rosenblum, letting him bring together selected portions of images from different places and times into a single composition (see Fig. 2.29).

2.5.6 THE LOCAL-GLOBAL CONTINUUM

As mentioned in the initial discussion of touch, the distinction between local and global touch is not always clear. Some selection tools certainly involve a local-touch way of working, even though the operation does not make a mark. A local tool that is made very large could be used as a stamp to sharpen or color a large area, like a global tool. Also, imagine tools that would let an artist control global processes with gestural hand motions. In some ways this approach is already possible with tools sometimes

(a)

(b)

Fiɡure 2.28 Using multiple selection techniques. (a) Various methods were used to select portions of the three photographs taken by the author from the New Jersey Turnpike. (b) Selected components were composed with other selections from the same photographs, merging the structural elements of industrial and amusement-park apparatus. *(Anne Morgan Spalter,* A Modern Landscape, *1993, collection of Beth and David Shaw.)*

Figure 2.29 **Richard Rosenblum,** **_Sarajevo,_ 1994** (dimensions vary). *(Courtesy of Richard Rosenblum)*

called **cloning tools,** which use as a source a reference point on one image and copy pixels to another area in the same or a different image. Such an approach can transform a global operation such as copy and paste into a combination of global- and local-touch processes (see Fig. 2.30).

Unlike photography or painting, in which local or global touches are often obvious, it is frequently impossible to know where the hand has touched a piece in a computer work (see Fig. 2.31). A "brush stroke," a piece of captured light, a mark generated entirely by computer code—any of these may masquerade as any other. Thus:

> The distinction between the causal process of the camera and the intentional process of the artist can no longer be drawn so confidently and categorically. Potentially, a digital "photograph" stands at any point along the spectrum from algorithmic to intentional. The traditional origin narrative by which automatically captured shaded perspective images are made to seem causal things of nature rather than products of human artifice—recited in support of their various projects by Bazin, Barthes and Berger, Sontag and Scruton—no longer has the power to convince us. The referent has become unstuck [Mitchell, 1992, p. 31].

Figure 2.30 Cloning tools offer both local- and global-touches. The clone tool picks up pixel value information from the location designated by the crosshair and lets the artist paint it in another location, designated by a circle, combining local-touch motion and feel with the global-touch operations of copy and paste. (a) The boat in the corner was replaced by water from elsewhere in the image. (b) The girl was cloned into the empty boat. (c) The girl was scaled to fill the new boat and cloning was used to fill in the missing parts of her original boat's interior.

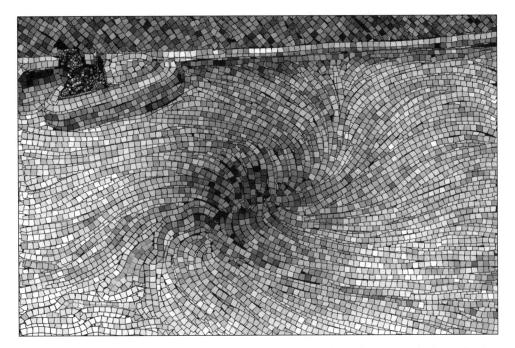

Figure 2.31 Cloning tools offer both local and global touches. This mosaic look, applied to the image in 2.27b, was produced by a combination of local- and global- (algorithmic) touches. The tiles are generated automatically in MetaCreations Painter mosaic mode (although tile size and other parameters can be selected) as the user draws with a brush-type tool. The tool can respond to pressure (when the artist is using a pressure-sensitive tablet), say by making tiles larger when more pressure is applied. Such local-touch options are combined with global, algorithmic options such as greater randomization of tile size and color.

2.6 COMPOSITION

The **composition** of a piece is its structure, the overall arrangement of form and color in the creation of space (see Fig. 2.32). This space may be representational or abstract, illusionistic or iconographic; whatever the logic or artistic inspiration, there are compositional strategies for arriving at a satisfactory structure. The composition guides the viewer's eye through the design and controls the work's visual unfolding. Composition functions at all levels of detail, including the size and proportions of a piece, its major groupings and general tonal structure, and overall color themes and tensions. The act of composing is thus not strictly a formal one, but takes into account the content to be conveyed.

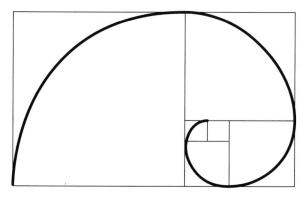

Figure 2.32 A rectangle constructed according to the Golden Mean (a proportion used as a compositional tool in architecture and design).

2.6.1 MOVING THE EDGES

One assumption in most compositional strategies is that the work has defined edges: Visible, usually linear, transitions (e.g., frames and canvas edges) demarcate the artwork from the wall or the rest of a printed page or determine the part of a larger scene visible in a photograph. Placing a form very close to an edge is different, aesthetically, from placing it in the middle of an image. What happens to composition when edges can be expanded indefinitely or the image cropped at any time during the creation of the piece? These operations are possible without the computer but usually leave visible traces and are rarely reversible, especially if part of an image is cropped away. With a paint-type computer program, the artist can simply set boundaries at the start and decide not to change them (i.e., force the computer to simulate the compositional limitations of physical media). However, such a decision, made quite frequently, ignores a new compositional tool.[3]

2.6.2 PLACEMENT OF ELEMENTS

The location of an element within a piece is, of course, important in any medium. On the computer, changing position is a global-touch operation, and thus location is much more flexible than ever before. The placement of an image can be easily experimented with and, even more important, detailed areas can be moved without having to be re-created. The compositional strategies of collage are thus always available—and the collage elements can be constantly redefined with selection tools. In a traditional art or design piece, creating a very detailed area without having thought through its place in the overall structure is usually problematic. On the computer, however, the artist can develop the internal details of an object before completing an overall composition. Freedom from having to erase and re-create and then rearrange and reattach physical elements flattens the usual hierarchy of compositional steps.

When an artist uses parts of previous work or other digitized images, compositional information is present from the beginning, whether in isolated pieces to be moved around as collage-like elements or for the whole piece. For example, an artist may scan in a photograph (or use a digital camera) and begin with a document consist-

---

[3]Although the computer does makes edges easy to move, most commercial software restricts compositional innovation by constraining canvas shapes to rectangles. This is a convention, not a necessity.

Figure 2.33 Annette Weintraub, *Inferno,* 1994 (tiled and laminated thermal wax prints, 31" X 47"). The artist combined images from slides and stills on the computer. She then superimposed over these fragments transparent linear pattern elements that imply the grid of the city, architectural plans, and cloth patterns, which she calls "the fabric of the city." *(Courtesy of Annette Weintraub)*

ing solely of that image. Element placement then involves either the alteration of existing elements or the insertion of new ones (see Fig. 2.33).

Annette Weintraub began her art career as a traditionally trained painter but became interested in the computer in part because the plasticity of the digital image appealed to her as a fitting metaphor for the cycles of disintegration and reconstruction represented in her work. Use of the computer caused a radical shift in her art making: The hand-drawn, personalized, imaginary architectural forms of her paintings did not function as expected on the computer. Instead she began to compose images in a different way, using photographic fragments, and her work shifted from private imagery to the depiction of public spaces.

Weintraub's work features the vernacular of photography and modern urban industrial architecture in spatial compositions created with computer compositing methods, seamlessly blending photographic fragments into at times dizzying spaces that capture the psychological experience of a modern city. The images are unified by the time of day—night—and the artificial light penetrating the darkness. Although the light captures the illumination of media, movies, and other entertainment, the audience is absent and fragments of illuminated signage appear like messages sent out into an uninhabited world (see Fig. 2.33).

2.6.3 IMAGE SIZE: FILE SIZE, RESOLUTION, AND COLOR DEPTH

How "big" is a computer paint program image? What aesthetic decisions are intertwined with the physical dimensions of a digital image and the amount of information represented within them? How does the concept of size contribute to the new art-making vocabulary made possible by the computer?

The size of much traditional visual work is usually determined at the beginning of the creation process: Stretcher bars for a canvas are made to be a certain size, for example, and without a lot of work that's the size they stay. Photographs can be printed at different sizes, offering more flexibility, but the computer offers still greater flexibility. On the computer, an artist can make decisions about size at any time before, during, and after a piece is created. Size thus becomes an integral part of the working process, an aesthetic decision that, like the ability to move the edges of the image and endlessly reposition its elements, gives an unprecedented fluidity to the act of composition.

The powerful concept of size in a computer image is not always related to the sense of size and scale that an artist has developed from a lifetime of interaction with the physical world. Artists working with computers must develop an intuitive sense of the new size parameters relevant to the digital realm. Manfred Mohr, who has been creating art with computers for almost 30 years, finds the option of easily varying size exciting. In his experience, the optimal size for a piece depends both on the context in which it is being displayed and the piece itself. He prints his images in different dimensions for different venues but believes that each piece has its own range of sizes in which it functions effectively.

In this text, the *size* of a raster graphics image is its **file size,** or the amount of information needed to describe the image. File size can also be thought of as the amount of disk space necessary to store the file. This definition does not take into account compression—a way of making the file size smaller for storage purposes (discussed in Chapter 12, The World Wide Web). File size is determined by a combination of the image's **dimensions** (height and width), its **resolution,** the number of image pixels per inch (or other unit of measurement), and **color depth,** the number of different color choices available for each pixel.[4]

The concept of image dimensions, the image's height and width, is the same as in traditional media. The concept of resolution, unique to the computer, is always given in terms of linear inches (i.e., how many pixels are representing a line 1 inch long or other unit of measure). Because resolution does not indicate what portion of the visual field that the pixels cover, you should always consider viewing distance when making decisions about resolution. For example, an image printed for a billboard does not need anywhere near the resolution per linear inch that an image printed for a magazine does.

To find out how many pixels are contained in an image, first square the number of pixels in a linear inch (the resolution), giving you pixels per square inch. Then multiply by the number of square inches in the image (its width multiplied by its height). More succinctly:

Number of pixels in image = (height $\times$ width) $\times$ resolution^2.

When you know the dimension and resolution, you can get a sense of the traditional, physical size of the piece and the density of information, but there is one more

---

[4]The addition of an alpha channel (discussed in Section 2.6.5) and other layers or paint objects will make the file larger. File size is also influenced, although only slightly, by a computer's operating system and hardware. For example, the current Apple Macintosh system increments file size in units of 32K.

factor to consider: The color depth of the pixels, which is the number of color choices available for each pixel location. The minimum number of choices for coloring an image is two, usually black and white. Such an image, in which each pixel is described by a "color or no color" decision, is called a 1-bit image or a **bitmap.** A **bit,** for BInary digiT, represents one of two choices (e.g., on or off, 0 or 1, black or white, etc.). Because of this terminology, the term **bitmapped images** is sometimes used to refer to raster graphics imagery. Adding another bit gives four possible combinations of choices and thus four possible colors for the 2-bit image. How many color choices are there in a 3-bit image?

You may have noticed a pattern in this process—each additional bit creates twice as many choices as before. Thus 8-bit color would have $2 \times 2 \times 2 \times 2 \times 2 \times 2 \times 2 \times 2$ (more conveniently written as 2^8) or 256 colors. Although 256 colors is a lot, it is not enough to represent color photographic images very well. Images in 8-bit color often have bands or patterns of color instead of smooth gradations. Grainy effects or outright patterns can appear because of a process called *dithering* which, like Impressionist paintings, alternates available colors in a variety of small patterns or random sprinklings to simulate colors that cannot be shown directly. (See Chapter 6, Printing, for a further discussion of dithering and a special type of dithering called *halftoning*.) **True** or **full-color** images, which are equivalent to photographic quality, are usually 24-bit images and thus have 2^{24}, or approximately 16.7 million, different possible colors for each pixel (see Fig. 2.34).

The number of pixels in the image multiplied by the image's color depth is the file size, a measure of "how much information" you are dealing with and thus the type of image quality that can be expected, how the image will react to different types of editing and processing, and what output choices make sense. In equation format,

File size = (height $\times$ width) $\times$ resolution^2 $\times$ color depth.

For example, a 300 pixel per inch (ppi), 8.5″ $\times$ 11″ full-color image probably has clear detail and no harsh color transitions and may look photographic. A 1-bit 8.5″ $\times$ 11″ image at 100 ppi, however, is only two colors, probably black and white, and somewhat blocky. The more you work with the computer, the more you will think in terms of file size and develop intuition about what it implies.

Because the concept of file size is confusing at first, many artists slow down their system unnecessarily by creating very large files. For instance, white space in a paint-type image contributes just as much to the file size as colored areas do—you can make your file size smaller by cropping the extra white space. The file size depends on the square of the resolution, so raising the resolution increases the file size dramatically (or exponentially, to be more mathematically precise).

Aesthetically, an information-rich image has a different appeal from an information-poor image; the first may look like a high-quality photograph or seamless hand-drawn or abstract work, and the latter may look blocky and jagged, grainy, and banded. Understanding and working with all the aspects of size—dimensions, resolution, and color depth—lets you avoid frustration and unwanted effects and take better control of the powerful visual language of the computer.

One bit
0 = off
1 = on

1-bit (each bit can be
either on or off)
can describe
two different colors.

Bit 1	bit 2
0	0
0	1
1	0
1	1

2-bits can describe
four different colors.

Bit 1	Bit 2	Bit 3
0	0	0
0	0	1
0	1	0
0	1	1
1	0	0
1	1	0
1	0	1
1	1	1

3-bits can describe
eight different colors.

Figure 2.34 1-, 2-, 3- and 8-bit color depth. Detail from Jan Vermeer, *Young Girl Reading a Letter,* Staatliche Kunstsammlungen, Dresden, 1657. *(Courtesy of Alinari/Art Resource, NY)*

8-bits can describe
256 different colors.

Calculating File Size

Storage space is measured in terms of bytes, usually thousands of them, called **kilobytes** (KB or K), sometimes thousands of kilobytes, called **megabytes** (MB), and even thousands of MB, or **gigabytes** (GB). For digital movies, **terabytes** (1000 GB) and **pedabytes** (1000 terabytes) become useful. The file size in KB can be calculated because each color choice takes 1 bit of memory and a byte is equal to 8 bits.

How big is a 1-bit image that is 10″ × 10″ and has a resolution of 100 ppi? How many bits does it take to describe this picture? Each pixel needs 1 bit, and there are 100 pixels in each linear inch. Thus in a square inch there are 100 × 100, or 10,000 pixels. The image is 10″ × 10″, or 100 square inches, and thus the total number of pixels is 100 × 10,000, or 1 million pixels. Each pixel takes 1 bit of storage space, so the file size is 1 million bits. To get KB, divide by 8 (to get bytes) and then by 1000 (to get KB). Dividing by 8000 gives 1,000,000/8000 = 125, so the file size is 125KB.[5]

ZOOMING IN AND OUT   When traditional painters need to see a part of their work in greater detail, they merely put their eyes nearer to the canvas; when they want to see the entire picture, they can walk away and view it from a distance. Because of the constraints of computer screens, however, you will often find it difficult to view a complete image while working on it. Your perception of the parameters determining file size (height and width, pixel resolution, and pixel depth) is influenced by how you view the file. Although you can usually check these components numerically, they are not always obvious from visual inspection.

Your view of the file is dependent on the device through which you see it. If a high-resolution file is printed on a low-resolution printer, much of the information may be missing from the final output. The constraints of computer screens will also affect your sense of an image's dimensions, resolution, and color depth. If you view a color file on a black and white monitor, the pixel depth appears less than it actually is. You cannot, at one time, view all the information in even a 5″ × 5″, 300-ppi image on a standard-sized screen because most screens are under 21″ diagonally and have only 72 to 85 screen pixels per inch. With 72 screen pixels per inch, slightly more than 4″ of screen space are needed to show all the information contained in one inch of a 300-ppi image. The 5″ × 5″, 300-ppi image would require a 20″ × 20″ screen (greater than 28″ diagonally).

---

[5]There are actually 1024 bytes in a kilobyte, 1024 kilobytes in a megabyte, and so on, but approximation is often used to make size calculations easier.

As a response to this serious problem, all painting and photoediting programs offer ways of **zooming into** and **zooming out of** an image. These controls do not permanently change any of the numerical parameters of the image size, but they do change the way in which these parameters are made visible. You can usually view images in paint programs at several zoom settings at once by opening additional windows into the same file, thus simultaneously receiving the traditionally mutually exclusive benefits of standing close to a work and stepping away from it.

When an image is zoomed out, you cannot see all the information available: There are more image pixels per inch than there are screen pixels to represent them. The software can use only every other image pixel (or every third or fourth one, depending on the zoom ratio) to create the screen image. Because all the pixel information is not being shown, details can seem to disappear completely; a 1-pixel–thick line may blip out of existence (of course it's still there, you just can't see it). For this reason, it is difficult to do detailed work or make precise selections in a zoomed-out mode.

What about the appearance of "big pixels" when you "zoom into" a paint-type image? This effect might well lead you to believe that pixels are not abstract but have a square shape that is revealed by magnification in the zooming process; this is not the case, however. The information stored in a single pixel makes a very small, roundish shape on most types of computer screens. The mechanics of the monitor and the nature of the screen phosphor both serve to blend the pixel information into an image that appears to be continuous. During zooming, however, video hardware uses **pixel replication** to make image detail easier to work with; each image pixel is replicated to create, say, a 2×2 or 4×4 grid of identical values. The grids of identically colored screen pixels appear on the screen as solid color squares (see Fig. 2.35).[6]

2.6.4 SCALE

Unlike zooming in and out, which temporarily displays the image at larger or smaller size, scaling an image up or down either adds or deletes pixels, permanently increasing or decreasing the file size. Scaling is often referred to as **resampling** because the number of samples (pixels) changes. When an image is scaled or otherwise transformed, it usually deteriorates somewhat. New pixels based on guesswork are introduced when the user scales up, and some information is always discarded when the user scale down.

The most primitive method of scaling up resembles zooming in: Pixel brightnesses are simply replicated to create the necessary additional pixels. More sophisticated methods for creating new pixels also guess at the new values, but instead of basing their guesses on information from a single pixel they average over entire neighborhoods of sample values to create new values. Does this sound familiar? It turns out that the weighted averages used in the low-pass, blurring type of filters discussed in Section

---

[6]Aliasing can also make images appear to be composed of little squares, as discussed in Chapter 4, Digital Design and Layout—2D Geometric Graphics.

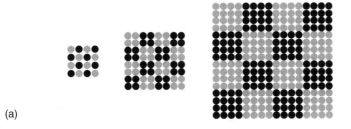

(a)

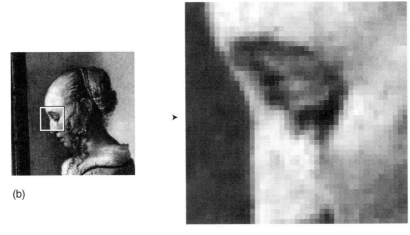

(b)

Figure 2.35 Little squares created by a fast video hardware scaling method. (a) Video hardware scales images by pixel replication, giving the impression that pixels are really very small squares that the user simply wasn't seeing clearly before. Here, each original screen pixel on the left becomes a group of 4 in the middle and 16 on the right. The groups of pixels look like squares of solid colors, but they do not represent the shape of an image pixel (which has no shape) or of a screen pixel—they are merely an artifact of this fast method of temporarily blowing up the image. (b) Zooming in. Detail from Jan Vermeer, *Young Girl Reading a Letter,* Staatliche Kunstsammlungen, Dresden, 1657. *(Courtesy of Alinari/Art Resource, NY)*

2.5.2 are exactly what's needed. Although for images with many high frequencies (e.g., those with fine detail or text, or those consisting mostly of black and white line work) such filters cannot do as good a job as resampling from the original continuous image, the results usually are satisfactory. With slow-changing images like a gradient, scaling

(a)

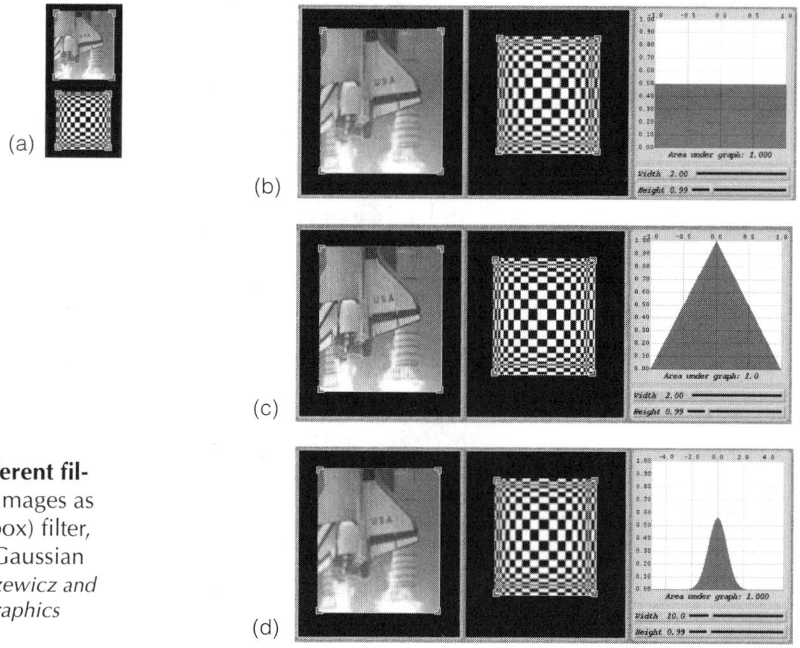

(b)

(c)

(d)

Figure 2.36 Scaling with different filters. (a) Original images. Both images as scaled up with (b) a constant (box) filter, (c) a triangular filter, and (d) a Gaussian filter. *(Courtesy of Marcin Romaszewicz and the Brown University Computer Graphics Group)*

up or down has few if any deleterious effects. Figure 2.36 shows two images—a high-contrast black and white grid image and a more typical photograph—scaled with the same basic filters, as previously illustrated in Fig. 2.18.

RELATIVE SCALE   As an aspect of composition, the scale of elements (representational or abstract) defines the depth of space created, the balance of color, and the dramatic configuration of the work. Like many global-touch processes, scale changes can be made in traditional artwork, but usually they are prohibitively difficult; in a paint-type program resizing any selectable region and reintegrating it into the image is relatively simple.

Changes in relative scale in photography-based computer works can be particularly dramatic and often disconcerting. In an unaltered photograph, scale is automatically coherent and immediately related to recognizable objects: The viewer usually is locked into a fixed relationship with the scale of the depicted space.

In Michele Turre's work, scale frequently plays a key role. The visual association between the dolls and real people in Fig. 2.37 is created principally with scale. With this simple technique Turre is able to evoke issues of gender roles, cultural implications, and the family. The doll in panel (b) is "an austere, matronly classical dancer, associated

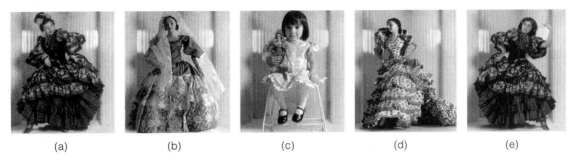

Figure 2.37 Michele Turre, *The Spanish Dance, My Mother, My Dolls, My Daughter, Myself,* 1993 (Iris print on BFK Rives paper, 9.5" × 43"). (a) A promotional photograph of Turre's mother, a professional Spanish dancer. (b) and (d) Dolls that the artist's grandmother brought her from Spain. (c) The artist's daughter, seemingly enormous among the dolls, representing the future. (e) The artist inserted into the photograph of her mother. *(Courtesy of Michele Turre)*

with aristocracy and strict Catholicism. [The doll in panel (d) is] a Flamenco dancer in a polka-dot dress, in a more sexualized pose, glancing over her shoulder, more associated with Romany tradition." Turre notes the many differences between herself and her mother in panel (e): "I wear no jewelry, my hair is wrong, I've left on my eyeglasses. I can't succeed in the masquerade, as much as I think I might like to." In panel (c), Turre's daughter "is dressed in the sort of frilly party dress some three-year-olds are partial to—the ruffles echo the ruffles of the dance costumes. She innocently holds one of the dolls pictured in another panel. She is unaware of the social and cultural implications surrounding her. . . . She loves her doll for superficial reasons. What will womanhood be for her?" [Turre, 1998]

2.6.5 THE ALPHA, OR TRANSPARENCY, CHANNEL

Ed Catmull and I invented the integral alpha channel in late 1977 at the New York Institute of Technology. I remember the moment very clearly. Ed was working on his sub-pixel hidden surface algorithm for SIGGRAPH paper submission. He was rendering images over different backgrounds using the new technique. I was working with him since I knew where all the interesting background images lay in our file system. We had six of the rare 8-bit frame buffers at NYIT at this time. I would position a background in three of them (equivalently one RGB frame buffer) over which he would render a foreground element. A different background required a new rendering, a very slow process then.

Ed mentioned that life would certainly be easier if, instead of re-rendering the same image over different backgrounds, he rendered the opacity information with the color information once at each pixel into a file. Then the image could be composited over different backgrounds, without re-rendering, as it was read pixel-by-pixel from the file. . . . [B]y the next morning [I] had the full package . . . ready for use. All Ed had to do was write the alpha information into a fourth frame buffer [Smith, 1996a].

Alvy Ray Smith, winner with Ed Catmull and Tom Porter of a 1996 Technical Academy Award for "pioneering inventions in digital compositing."

Transparency (also referred to by its reverse, opacity) is a powerful tool for creating a sense of space in 2D art. Examples abound, from Rembrandt's transparent glazes that build up rich and evocative canvases to the formal teaching exercises designed by Joseph Albers in which students mix colors that create a sense of transparency. In time-based art, such as animation, transparent celluloid is used as a drawing surface in order to layer, and thus move separately, the different parts of a character (see Chapter 10, 2D and 3D Animation and Video, for discussion of more time-based uses of transparency). Transparency is vital in computer graphics because it lets artists vary opacity for aesthetic effects and combine images easily.

In paint-type programs, different samples associated with a single pixel are stored in different frame buffers (see Chapter 1), or **channels,** each of which can be manipulated separately. For instance, an RGB image has a red, a green, and a blue channel. As described in the preceding Smith quotation, Smith and Catmull added a fourth frame buffer to store information about how much of each color should contribute to the final image—in other words, how transparent each color in the image would be. They called this fourth channel the **alpha channel** because the equation used to calculate transparency used the Greek letter alpha (α) for the fraction of the color that would show through in the final image. An alpha value of 0.5 makes a pixel's color 50% transparent; an alpha value of 1 leaves the color untouched. In programs that use an alpha channel, artists can precisely control transparency and save their settings with the image. Alpha values customarily affect all the color channels equally.

Different programs offer different methods of working with transparency values. Some offer an eraser tool that creates complete or partial transparency. Many offer a separate view of the alpha channel as a grayscale image in which black indicates areas of the image that remain at 100% of their color value (alpha value of 1) and lighter values indicate areas of increasingly transparency (or vice versa). An alpha channel overlay is a useful feature that shows the alpha values as a transparent color on top of the image.

Gray values in an alpha channel represent partial transparency or malleability—for example, a selection that fades out around the edges. Alpha channels are vital in **compositing,** or the merging of two (or more) images with varying levels of transparency (see Fig. 2.38).

Artist Emily Cheng uses digital compositing to integrate images from different time periods into a single composition, intermingling different styles, periods, and artistic goals by interactively adjusting transparency values. Her work comments on the computer's ability to change all visual information into a homogeneous electronic format, at the same time letting the viewer consider diverse visual information in a new way (see Fig. 2.39).

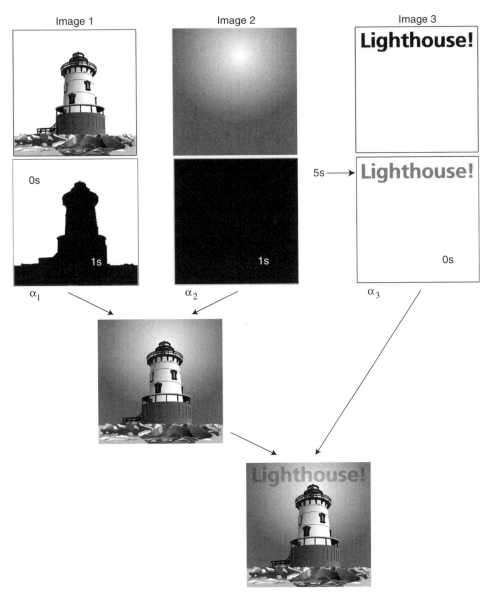

Figure 2.38 Using an alpha channel. The lighthouse in Image 1 has an alpha channel (shown below it) that masks the white background. The masked lighthouse is composited with Image 2, the gradient (its alpha channel, shown below it, has no masked areas). The composited lighthouse/gradient image is then composited with the "Lighthouse!" text in Image 3. The text's alpha channel (shown below it) makes the text semitransparent and masks everything else in that image.

Figure 2.39 Emily Cheng, *1993EC0012,*
1993 (from a series of forty-one monoprints, 30″ × 20″). The complex images
that result from the artist's use of paint-
type computer graphics speak not only of
times past and their interrelationships, but
of the current era and the role of technology in visual thinking. *(Courtesy of
Emily Cheng)*

Cheng uses formal aesthetic choices, here
with the aid of transparency and digital compositing methods and hand-painted gouache areas,
to create compositions that intermingle cultural
contexts. She combines different pictorial traditions into single works that speak of the complex
relationships among cultures of different places
and times—from the art of Byzantium and the
early Renaissance to Magao cave paintings in
Dunhuang, China. Explicitly narrative aspects of
the works are masked and the viewer is forced to
draw meaning from the varied schematics and
methods for creating visual form. With a background in painting, Cheng worked in an abstract
style during the early 1980s, but toward the end
of the decade she began incorporating imagery
from print advertisements and other sources into
her work, using photocopiers and collage. The
computer's collage and transparency capabilities
were a perfect starting point for further investigations into Eastern and Western visual styles and
their associations.

Conclusion

Painting and photoediting programs bring to artists both the freedom and the tyranny of the
pixel. All parts of the pointillist pixel array are
equal, with each color unconnected to its neighbors. There are no privileged shapes and no mark
has integrity beyond the artist's mind. This paradigm offers unprecedented flexibility for defining
and using local-touch tools, whether simulations
of traditional marks or the creation of new marks.
Local and global processes are combined in ways
impossible with other media, and one can switch
between local and global processes with ease.
The types of global and algorithmic pixel-changing processes offered by painting and
photoediting programs have few if any traditional counterparts—and the full potential
of their use is just beginning to be explored.

The freedom of the pixel is vividly illustrated in the reduction of photographic
information to pixels. Light captured on film is difficult to play with after the fact, but
light translated into pixel information becomes the same "substance" as every other

type of mark in a paint program. Painting and photography are now joined in a way that is certain to change the creation and interpretation of both media.

The tyranny of the pixel comes from the same qualities that offer such exciting new freedoms. Every pixel stands alone and the artist always comes back to a mosaic of discrete sample information, never a series of overlapping strokes as in a painting or of related shapes as in a collage. In Chapter 4, Digital Design and Layout—2D Geometric Graphics, I introduce the other fundamental paradigm of computer graphics, which is based not on discrete pixels but on continuous geometry. An understanding of both raster- and geometry-based graphics is important for all other types of graphics programs, from 3D to multimedia.

Suggested Readings

Foley, James, Andries van Dam, Steven Feiner, and John Hughes. *Computer Graphics, Principles and Practice.* Addison-Wesley, 1990. The standard reference. Although tough going for beginners, this book is comprehensive and almost always has the most thorough, correct, and detailed explanations of the principles underlying computer graphics.

Kerlow, Isaac Victor, and Judson Rosebush. *Computer Graphics for Designers and Artists,* 2d edition. Van Nostrand Reinhold, 1996. Clearly presented technical information, suitable for nontechnical readers, with diagrams and examples.

Mitchell, William J. *The Reconfigured Eye, Visual Truth in the Post-Photographic Era.* MIT Press, 1992. Theory and technical concepts, artfully interwoven. A must-have for any computer artist's library.

Negroponte, Nicholas. *Being Digital.* Vintage Books, 1996. A book for the general public that can be read painlessly in an afternoon. Full of fascinating ideas by someone who knows what he's talking about. Based on Negroponte's comparison of atoms and bits and on his WIRED columns, this book can give artists an idea of the changes that the computer may bring to people's everyday lives. Even after correcting for the hype factor, the reader is still left with a great deal to think about.

Smith, Alvy Ray. "A Pixel is *Not* a Little Square! A Pixel is *Not* a Little Square! A Pixel is *Not* a Little Square!" Microsoft Technical Memo No. 6, 1995. The title speaks for itself. Accessible to both technical and nontechnical readers. Available via his Web site at http://www.research.microsoft.com/research/graphics/Alvy/default.htm

Sontag, Susan. *On Photography.* Dell, Inc., 1977. A must-read for all interested in photography and the issues it raises. Although not the most current of books and not explicitly about computers, many of the issues so thoughtfully and clearly presented here carry over naturally to them.

Exercises

1. *Hand drawing.* Using only one of the brush-type tools in your paint program, make a realistic drawing of your hand. The goal of this exercise is for you to become familiar with whichever brush-like tool you have chosen. Experiment with its parameters and try to push its limits to achieve a straightforward observation-based drawing. Experiment with different brush sizes and other options available in your program (e.g., brush shape, opacity, color-mixing methods, and fade-out rate). How do these tools compare with their traditional counterparts? How is observational drawing on a computer different from drawing with traditional media such as charcoal and paper? How do you think computer graphics technology will affect the perceived importance of directly observing and drawing images?

> With Adobe Photoshop 5.0: Use Photoshop's Paintbrush Tool from the main tool palette. Experiment first with different brush sizes from the Brush palette (Window:Show Brushes) and then try altering the opacity settings (double-click on the Paintbrush icon to bring up the Paintbrush Options palette). The Options . . . choice from the pop-up menu in the Brushes palette lets you change the shape and softness of the brush. Draw with variations on size, shape, and opacity and see what range of marks you can create. Check out the Fade (and Fade to) and Wet Edges options in the Paintbrush Options palette but for now leave the numerous mode options alone. Finally, make a custom brush: Select a small portion of your image with the Rectangular Marquee Tool and choose Define Brush from the Brushes palette pop-up menu.

> If you have a pressure-sensitive tablet, take advantage of the Style Pressure options on the Paintbrush Options palette.

2. *Selection tools.* Most computer graphics programs work on the select-then-perform-action paradigm. How do selection tools influence the creative process? Create three pieces in a paint-type program, starting from scratch or using a digitized image. In each piece, use only one different selection tool. How does the means of selection affect what you are inspired to do? What you are able to do? If you could create your own selection tool, what would it enable you to do?

> With Adobe Photoshop 5.0: For the first piece use only the Rectangular Marquee Tool. Work on creating marks and structuring composition, using the rectangular areas selectable with this tool. Leave its shape rectangular for now but try some of the other options in the Marquee Options palette. For the Marquee Tool and other selection tools described next experiment with Selection:Transform Selection. You will see small handles appear at the corners and midsections of the selection. Place the cursor on the handles to scale and in between handles to rotate. Try using the Control key (Windows) or Command key (Mac) to freely distort the selection. For the next piece, use the Lasso Tool, which lets you draw with a selection line and thus achieve a local-touch feeling.

> For the final piece try the Magic Wand Tool. This tool is more complex than the previous two and can give markedly different results; its power is best seen when working with a photographic image. Use the Magic Wand Tool to select and relocate identifiable objects and also to work with color masses that span several objects.

> Remember that selection areas can be added to with the Shift key, subtracted from with the Option key (Mac) or Alt key (Windows), and moved without affecting the underlying image by leaving the tool choice on the selection tool rather than switching to the Move Tool.

3. *Moving edges.* Create a piece or start with a previously completed work. Now resize the canvas area around it, adding at least an inch on all its sides. Rework your piece until it fills the new area. Repeat this process at least three times, saving each version as you go. What happens when elements near an edge move away from it? How is the tension in your composition affected? Does the additional space inspire you to create new aspects of the piece or enlarge existing elements? How do the color relationships change?

> With Adobe Photoshop 5.0: Resize the working area or canvas using Image:Canvas Size.... Add at least an inch to the width and height each time.

4. *Scale*. How does scale influence the creative process when you're using a computer? Will an image output in Persian-miniature size also function as a billboard? Make an image that means two different things at two very different scales, say, smaller than 5″ × 5″ and larger than 30″ × 30″. You may use tiling or photocopier enlarging to make the larger image.

> With Adobe Photoshop 5.0: Make a medium-sized image and then use Image: Image Size ... to resample it to create both a larger and smaller version (make sure that "resample image" is checked). This method will help you avoid the potential pitfalls of either creating a small image with insufficient information to scale up well or a large image with too much detail to scale down well. With this method, you can make adjustments to each image. Alternatively, you can simply use the Scale option in File:Page SetUp ... to print the image larger or smaller. Keep in mind, however, that Photoshop prints only one piece of paper per file (it shows the center of the image). To tile the image you must break it into separate files or print it from a different program.

5. *The new family photo album*. The tools of selection, scaling, and cutting and pasting or cloning are changing how artists and designers think about photography. Soon they will also directly affect the personal use of photography by nonartists. Today, photography is the single most common means of visual creation practiced by people who do not consider themselves artists or designers; for example, virtually every family in developed countries has a photo album somewhere in their house. Susan Sontag writes:

> Photography is not practiced by most people as an art. It is mainly a social rite, a defense against anxiety, and a tool of power.... Not to take pictures of one's children, particularly when they are small, is a sign of parental indifference, just as not turning up for one's graduation picture is a gesture of adolescent rebellion.... [T]hrough photographs, each family constructs a portrait-chronicle of itself [Sontag, 1973, p. 8].

What will the family portrait of the future—one that incorporates digital technology—look like? How might it reflect modern changes to the nuclear family? Gather several photos from your own album and scan them into the computer. What changes are you tempted to make? Make them. Changes can range from touching up images to removing or adding people, changing the scenery, and so on.

> With Adobe Photoshop 5.0: In this exercise and the next, try using Photoshop's Rubber Stamp Tool. In this case, the Rubber Stamp Tool can make erasing people, moving people between photographs and changing background scenery a breeze. Start with its default settings of Clone Aligned, Normal Mode, and 100% opacity. Option-click (Mac) or Alt-click (Windows) to set a point to clone from, then draw elsewhere. Try different brush sizes for

different tasks and experiment with the Hardness setting of the brushes—softer settings can make blending new family members easier.

6. ***Change the world.*** You may not be able to change the world, but you can change a picture of it. Make a completely believable image created from actual photographs. The piece should obey all the laws of physics as evidenced in photographs, such as light angle and consistent color, shading, proper perspective, and realistic relative scaling. Material can come from your own photos, magazines, the Web, and other sources. Examine the results and see if the collage is obvious and why. Surprisingly, many images that look somehow fake turn out to be real photographs, raising questions about how people interpret and decode photographic conventions in the first place.

With Adobe Photoshop 5.0: As in the previous exercise, try the Rubber Stamp Tool, but now experiment with opacity settings and the Clone Non-Aligned option. To correct for different color casts of different images, use Image:Adjust:Variations. Try using simple transformation, such as flipping the image horizontally, to make all the lighting come from the same general direction. The Edit:Transform:Distort and Perspective options can help you rearrange portions of an image to fit into a single perspective view. Filtering, in particular blurring, sharpening, and noise, may be helpful in giving all your images the same texture.

7. ***Nonrealistic scanning.*** Create a piece by using scans of textures. Do not include any photographic or otherwise realistic or representational imagery. Suggested texture sources include clothes, books, leaves, and found objects.

With Adobe Photoshop 5.0: In addition to cutting and pasting and cloning to combine portions of your scans, try using different layers (Windows:Show Layers) and varying the opacity setting of each one to help integrate parts of the materials.

CHAPTER 3

Keyboards, Mice, Tablets, Scanners, and Displays

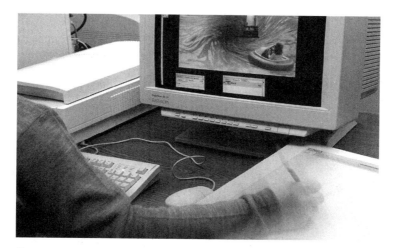

Figure 3.1 A typical setup with keyboard, mouse, tablet, and scanner. Keyboards, mice, tablets, scanners, and displays are the most standard visible components of a computer graphics setup. (Printers are usually essential, too, and are covered in Chapter 6, Printing.) The types of touch and composition tools offered by a piece of software are always modulated by this array of devices: the feeling of a brush tool is greatly enhanced by a pressure-sensitive tablet, for instance, and the scanner opens up a multitude of options for gathering ready-made compositions and colors.

3.1 INTRODUCTION

Consider for a moment a thought experiment designed by William Buxton, a pioneering researcher in human–computer interaction: "Imagine a time far into the future, when all knowledge about our civilization has been lost. Imagine, further, that in the course of planting a garden, a fully stocked computer store from the 1980s was unearthed, and that all of the equipment and software was in working order. Now, based on this find, consider what a physical anthropologist might conclude about the physiology of the humans of our era? My best guess is that we would be pictured as having a well-developed eye, a long right arm, uniform-length fingers and a "low-fi" ear. But the dominating characteristic would be the prevalence of our visual system over our poorly developed manual dexterity." [Buxton, 1986, p. 319]

William Buxton, Chief Scientist, Alias | Wavefront and Silicon Graphics, Inc. (SGI), and a professor at the University of Toronto.

Lack of input sophistication and "feel" is one of the chief complaints of traditionally trained artists and illustrators who use computers. The feeling of distance, lack of control, and lack of physical feedback strongly affect the experience of making computer–based art.

Why have input tools remained so anemic while other aspects of software and hardware have undergone dramatic and revolutionary changes? The answer lies in a combination of issues in technology and marketing, as well as sociology. Most early computers had virtually no input devices. Instead, instructions were coded on punched cards and fed to the computer by a card-reading machine. By the 1960s, monitors became available for use as output devices, and keyboards (mimicking the typewriter) were introduced. This setup has remained the standard during the decades since and has been altered only by the widespread commercial introduction of the mouse in the 1980s. Tablets and styli (which have existed since the 1960s) have recently become affordable and practical for artists and designers.

The introduction of the mouse and the use of tablets are both cases in point. Douglas Engelbart invented the mouse in the early 1960s (see Fig. 3.2) and demonstrated it to large numbers of people in 1968, but it was more than a decade before its utility was widely acknowledged. Only when Apple began selling computers with a graphical interface in the late 1980s did the average computer user meet a mouse. Why was there such resistance? Most obviously, the then-standard textual command-line interfaces did not benefit very much from the use of a mouse. The advent of graphical user interfaces, described in Chapter 1, made the use of a mouse more compelling and, in the case of the Mac, essential for use of the computer. For fast typists, however, having to switch back and forth between the keyboard and a mouse can still be annoying. Although tablets have been in use by artists and scientists since the early days of computing, it was not until the late 1980s that they became practical and affordable. In particular, pressure-sensitive tablets finally came into their own when a small company, Wacom, convinced large graphics software companies to support their tablets by adding new code to their products. Today, all major art programs support pressure-sensitive tablets, and the effect on the type of marks that can be made has been profound.

Despite this slowness of innovation, a wide range of input devices has been created, many of which are useful for artists, illustrators, and designers. In this text I cover both the low and high ends to give artists and designers a sense of what the field can offer, even when particular devices are not yet readily available or easy to use with personal computers and off-the-shelf software.

These devices fall into two categories: those that *sample motion* (usually by tracking the hand or body) and those that *sample other data* such as light, color, pressure, or position (e.g., scanning). In the first category are such familiar devices as mice and tablets, as well as less familiar ones such as motion trackers for virtual environments. The second includes desktop scanners and digital cameras as well as more esoteric devices, such as those that can scan for position and color value at the same time. Here,

Figure 3.2 The original mouse prototype, 1963–1964. (*Courtesy of Douglas Engelbart*)

I discuss only 2D hand motion–sampling and color–sampling devices. See Chapter 6, Printing, and Chapter 9, 3D Input and Output, for coverage of printing and 3D input and output.

3.2 SAMPLING HAND MOTION

Keyboards, mice, and tablets are the most common devices used to translate hand motion into marks and motion seen on the screen. The keyboard is most often associated with inputting text, but can also be used to move a cursor, play a video game, and type in coordinates to place or define an object in an art program. The mouse and the tablet and stylus bring the muscles of the hand into play in a more direct fashion, linking the traditional art skills of the hand more directly to results on the computer.

3.2.1 KEYBOARDS

The keyboard remains an essential input device; it is necessary for inputting textual and numerical characters and useful for switching modes and issuing commands. For some types of visual work, such as 3D computer-aided design (CAD), numerical accuracy is paramount, often making that the keyboard the chief input tool. Variations on basic keyboard design include extended keyboards with a row of command keys and built-in number pad and arrows and split keyboards that better accommodate the natural resting position of the hands (see Fig. 3.3). For most visual artists, however, the keyboard fails to fulfill a basic need—interpreting the motion of the hand.

Figure 3.3 Different types of keyboards. (a) An ergonomic and extended keyboard has a built-in number pad and arrow key area, as well as function keys along the top. (b) A split keyboard adjusts to accommodate the natural angles of the wrists; a numerical keypad can be attached.

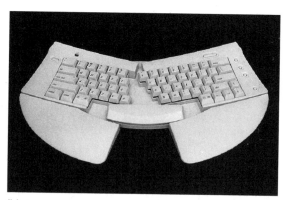

(a)　　　　　　　　　　　　　　　(b)

Figure 3.4 Different types and styles of mice. (a) and (b) Two friction-based mice, one with two buttons and one with one. (c) An optical mouse with three buttons on its gridded and reflective pad.

3.2.2 The Mouse and Its Variations

Mice excel at tracking and selection; even more important to artists and designers, the mouse and other input devices that track hand motion make possible the local, hand-based types of touch described previously in Chapter 2. The numerous mice available (see Fig. 3.4) are more similar than different but do have variants such as different numbers of buttons (one, two, and three are all common), balls made of different types of plastic, and optical systems instead of balls. Different shapes offer slight variations of hand grip and some styles may feel more comfortable than others. Most mice use a simple friction-based mechanism: The movement of the ball turns small rollers that register the horizontal and vertical components of the movement.

Many people prefer an upside-down mouse called a **trackball.** The trackball base stays in place, and the user rolls the exposed ball with the fingertips (see Fig. 3.5).

Figure 3.5 Trackballs. (a) A trackball with large button "wings" on either side. (b) A trackball with wrist pad and front and side buttons.

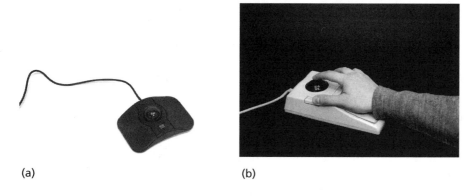

(a)   (b)

Although useful for navigation, the use of trackballs for drawing is virtually impossible. Trackballs take up less desk space than regular mice and thus are particularly useful with portable computers.

The condition of the mouse or trackball is important when it is your primary input tool. A mouse gives so little tactile feedback compared with traditional tools that every nuance has a profound effect. Mice of all types quickly become dirty and begin to work poorly; they must be cleaned regularly.

Categorizing input devices by type, such as "mice," may suggest that all input devices in a single category are interchangeable. Unfortunately, input devices are most frequently designed for specific computer platforms and even specific applications. Knowing that a device is a mouse does not guarantee that it will work with your particular machine or software, even though other mice may have functioned without difficulty.

3.2.3 TABLETS AND STYLI

Mice and their variants are great for positioning a cursor on screen (pointing), selecting objects, using menus, and clicking and double-clicking. For drawing—using the motion of the hand to create line and form—a tablet–stylus combination is usually unbeatable. As previously noted, a mouse requires the use of only a few of the muscles of the wrist and fingers and a small amount of arm motion. In contrast, a stylus requires the use of many of the same muscles that drawing with a pen or pencil does and offers a similar range of movement.

Most tablets sold for art creation have cordless styli because the pull of a cord reduces the effectiveness of the stylus as a drawing device. Tablets can also be used with a mouselike device called a **puck**; the puck resembles a traditional mouse, but its precise location on a surface is shown through a cross-hair in a transparent viewfinder. Pucks are useful for precisely digitizing various types of layouts and engineering or architectural drawings and often have four or more buttons that can be programmed for specific tasks. Figure 3.6 shows several types of tablets, styli, and a puck.

Most tablets determine the position of the stylus or puck by passing electrical signals back and forth between it and the tablet. When an artist draws with a stylus, electrical impulses sent through a fine wire mesh inside the tablet induce a current in the stylus that sends an electrical signal from the stylus to the tablet. The tablet software determines the stylus's location from the strength of this signal and adjusts the on-screen cursor accordingly. A puck sends signals in the same way.

With some tablets, the signal can also be varied with pressure, an important feature that gives another dimension or channel to the input. In many art software programs the pressure component can be set to represent one or more factors such as line thickness or opacity, color change, brush wetness, and brush angle (see Fig. 3.7).

The range of motion, in particular of the arm, depends on the size of the tablet. With a 4″ × 5″ tablet, mostly the hand, fingers, and wrist are used; if the tablet is 12″ × 12,″ much more of the arm must be used. A desk-sized tablet, often used for architectural

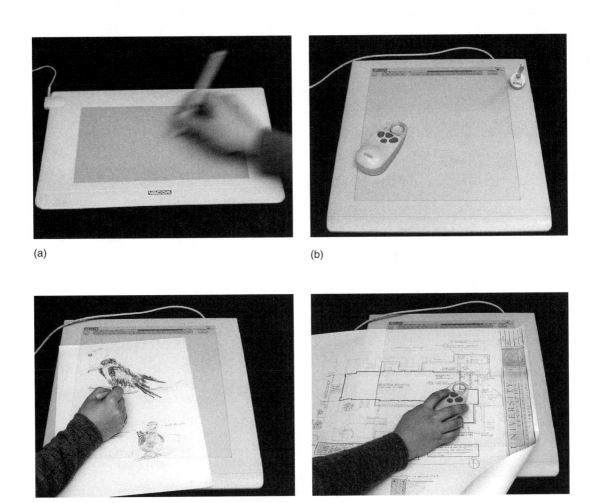

(a)

(b)

(c)

(d)

Figure 3.6 Tablets with different styli and a puck. (a) A small (5″ × 7″) tablet with cordless pen. (b) A large (12″ × 12″) tablet, pen, and four-button puck with button areas at its top. (c) A pen being used to trace a drawing. (d) A puck in use to digitize an architectural drawing.

and mechanical drafting, offers a range of muscle movement and body involvement closer to that of traditional media. A larger tablet is also useful for tracing large images. Tablet resolutions vary, so you should experiment before purchasing a tablet.

Try signing your name and doodling an image with all the input devices available to you. Compare their quality and ease of use. Now perform the same experiment under time pressure. What do the results tell you about which devices to use when?

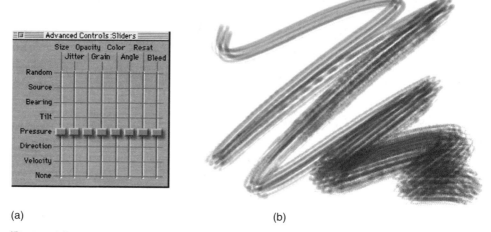

(a)

(b)

Figure 3.7 Customizing the use of a pressure-sensitive tablet. (a) Artists can link many factors to stylus pressure in MetaCreations Painter creating (b) highly varied lines. *(Painter is a registered trademark of MetaCreations. These materials copyrighted 1998.)*

Relative Versus Absolute Motion

Although nearly all available input devices offer the basic actions of tracking, selecting, and dragging, there is an important conceptual distinction between absolute and relative modes of operation. In an **absolute mode,** the position of the pointing device, such as a stylus on a tablet, corresponds directly to the cursor's position on the screen: If the stylus is in the upper right corner of the tablet, the cursor is in the upper right corner of the screen. In an absolute mode, when the user lifts the stylus and sets it down somewhere else, the position of the cursor changes. In a **relative mode,** the user can lift the stylus and set it down somewhere else without moving the cursor. Some input devices, such as mice, are inherently relative and some, such as touch screens, are inherently absolute. Others, such as tablets, can be set to absolute or relative modes.

Absolute modes of operation are essential in tracing a drawing to digitize it or working with other hard-copy references such as architectural drawings. Absolute motion is required for an input device such as a light pen that draws directly "on" the screen rather than on a remote surface. For many artists and designers, the action of moving the hand on the desktop to control a cursor on the computer screen adds to the sense of physical disconnection from the work, and engaging with absolute physical references can create a stronger sensation of working with a tangible medium. Relative input is useful, however, when desk space is limited or one-to-one correspondence is not important.

3.3 Reconceiving Computer Input

Researchers exploring multimedia input design focus on user skills and needs rather than on the logic of the computer. For example, people frequently use both hands in daily life and in art (from tying their shoes to chiseling marble), yet two-handed input for the computer (except for the keyboard) is almost nonexistent. If you challenge yourself to go through half a day without using your nondominant hand (try putting a rubber band around it to remind yourself not to use it), the significance of this restriction becomes even clearer.

Input mechanisms could also take advantage of a user's feet, providing pedals similar to those in automobiles or organs. More varied input devices were common in the early days of graphic computing (e.g., light pens, foot pedals, dials, and chording keypads). However, many of them proved impractical for general use and only keyboards and simple mouse variants have emerged commercially. William Buxton, integrating the historical uses of input devices with his own theoretical and practical approaches, has designed a two-handed input system that can be used with SGI's Alias|Wavefront® software to let artists and designers manipulate features such as color and tool palettes, rulers, stencils or masks, and even the page itself with one hand while painting with the other. This and other innovative input setups may well become standard options for 3D and other types of art programs in the future.

3.4 Sampling Colors

Sampling hand or body motion is important in controlling the virtual tools of the computer program. However, the digitization of existing imagery or of light coming from real-world 3D objects is equally important to many computer artists.

3.4.1 Scanning

Scanners sample light intensity and color and translate the information into pixels. A **desktop scanner** is a standard peripheral in a computer artist's or designer's studio. Until recently, most models cost $1000 or more, but now are priced as low as $100. Desktop scanners can be used to scan photographs, hand drawings, found objects—anything that can be laid on its glass digitization area—into computers. The scanner is a vital link between traditional touch and composition techniques and the computer's powers of manipulation. A hand-drawn image or other work created with traditional methods can be scanned into a computer for subsequent creative work. After computer manipulation, if more traditional work is desired, the image can be printed, worked on some more, and scanned back into the computer again.

Transparency scanners, sold primarily in 35-mm slide format, have higher resolution than scanners designed to handle reflective materials and usually cost more, starting at about $500. Some reflective image scanners have transparency attachments that

Figure 3.8 A desktop scanner with transparency option. As with a photocopier, papers (or other objects) are laid face down on the glass scanner bed. A moving light source in the scanner lid can illuminate transparencies.

can scan a variety of image sizes (see Fig. 3.8). These attachments cost less than separate transparency scanners but are not often suitable for professional-quality work.

Unlike mice and tablets, which have relatively few user-controlled settings, a scanner can deliver quite different results depending on a user's knowledge and skill. Getting the most from a scanner involves understanding the concepts of image sampling. In Chapter 2 (Sections 2.2.1 and 2.2.2), I discuss the basic theory of sampling: taking a series of measurements of a continuous or analog source to create discrete data values. In scanners, sampling is done by shining a light on (or through, in the case of transparencies) a material and averaging the reflection or transmission over small areas of the image at regular intervals. The number of samples taken per inch (dpi, or dots per inch) is the resolution of the scanner. Today's typical desktop scanners range anywhere from 300 to 1200 dpi; some go even higher. The number of colors the scanner can record (the color depth) ranges from gray scale (256 gray levels) to full color (24-bit color) to 32-bits. Most programs can't handle more than 24-bit color, and higher-depth images usually are mapped to 24-bit programs, resulting in better looking color scans with more detail and more clarity in subtle light and dark areas.

The resolutions claimed by some scanner manufacturers are achieved not by using high hardware sampling rates, but instead by resampling the scanned data to create a higher-resolution file. The two processes do not lead to the same results; in any case, resampling usually gives better results if used with a paint or photoediting-type program where the user has more control over the process.

The largest image that most desktop scanners can scan is approximately $10'' \times 14''$, and larger format scanners are significantly more expensive. Unless you need to scan large documents frequently, scanning the occasional large image in sections and recombining the sections in an image-editing program is easier and cheaper.

Scanned images must often be corrected, either to look more like the original source or to fill specific image-editing needs, such as color balance and contrast. Virtually all scans need to be sharpened. Most of the filters described in Chapter 2 are designed for the purpose of correcting and improving scanned materials. In addition to the requisite sharpening, variations on the basic blur filters can help offset moiré patterns and stray marks, and edge-sharpening filters can improve image legibility. Remapping of pixel values lets artists alter the overall lightness, darkness, and contrast and also work within individual color channels to alter mapping within them and perform common operations such as shifting the color balance. Although many good filters exist to aid in the correction process, keep in mind that every filtering process eliminates some image information; getting a good scan to begin with is much better than touching up a bad one. Also, you should keep a copy of the unretouched file until you are completely satisfied with your filtering results.

Service bureaus have faster and higher-resolution scanners than can be purchased in the standard desktop format. Some scanners, for instance, achieve very fast scan rates by using an array of light-sensitive charge-coupled devices (CCDs) instead of one strip that must move across the entire image. Very high–resolution scanners usually are **drum scanners,** which rotate the image on a drum past a fixed light and sensor assembly. Drum scanners can scan 4000 to almost 20,000 pixels per inch and use photomultiplier tubes instead of CCDs to capture 10–14 bits/pixel. Many drum scanners also offer productivity features, such as the ability to scan images in batches, each with individual settings.

CHOOSING A SCANNING RESOLUTION   Because a scanner can record only a limited number of discrete samples of the continuous image placed on it, some information is always lost and the scanned image is never exactly the same as the original. If too little information is recorded, the resulting image will not be a good approximation of the original and may contain annoying aliasing artifacts. But recording more information than can be used wastes storage space and slows work unnecessarily. (Large files can also lead to higher service bureau charges.)

Choosing an optimal resolution depends on the intended use for the image, the nature of the image, and the limitations of your computer setup. Practical issues such as storage space and scanning and manipulation time are important because scanning can easily produce very large files. For instance, a $4'' \times 6''$ photo scanned in 24-bit color at 1200 dpi yields a file larger than 103 MB.

For images that will be printed on a printer with the use of halftone screens, a general rule of thumb is that the image should have a resolution 1.5 to 2 times the number of *halftone cells per inch* or *line frequency* at which the image will be printed (assuming that the image is being printed at its original size). In practice, you can often get by with even less (see Chapter 6, Printing, for further discussion of image resolution choices).

For images to be used on the Web or for other screen-based displays, you will usually need less information than for printing; a 75-ppi file is all that most screens can show. You may also find yourself scanning an image without knowing exactly the use to which it will be put or at what sizes; in that case you probably should use the highest resolution practical for your computer setup to preserve your options.

The nature of the image itself can also be an important consideration. Theoretically, you could reconstruct a continuous image from discrete pixels exactly (using a reconstruction filter, as discussed in Sections 2.5.2 and 2.6.4) if the image has been sampled above the **Nyquist rate,** which is twice the image's highest frequency (frequency is a measure of the abruptness and degree of brightness changes). What this part of sampling theory means in practice is that accurately representing an abrupt, high-contrast value change requires a higher resolution than does sampling slow-value transitions. Thus scanning an airbrush of a gradient or a photograph of softly changing colors in ocean waves requires less resolution for an aesthetically satisfying result than does scanning in text or line drawings.

MOIRÉ PATTERNS   Scanning resolution can also affect the creation of unwanted pattern effects. When two small patterns such as lines or even a grid of dots interact with one another, a larger-scale pattern called a **moiré pattern** can result. Moiré patterns can be caused by interactions between multiple patterns in a photograph or an image halftone and the scanner's sampling grid. They can often be avoided by increasing the sample rate (see Fig. 3.9).

ALIASING   When the sampling rate is too low, noticeable and often distracting **aliasing** occurs. As described in more detail in Chapter 4, Digital Design and Layout—2D Geometric Graphics, aliasing occurs when something appears to be something that it is not, as when a straight line looks like a jagged staircase on the screen. Problems with aliasing are accentuated in areas containing many brightness changes over a short distance (see Fig. 3.10) and for shapes with thin lines and important small details, such as text (see Fig. 3.11).

Figure 3.9 Sampling rate and moiré effects. If a halftone image is scanned at a resolution similar to the halftone spacing, a distracting moiré pattern may well occur. (a) The moiré interaction is similar to that shown between the two equal-scale dot grids. (b) Scanning at a higher resolution can often prevent this result, with a smaller-scale grid not causing a noticeable moiré pattern.

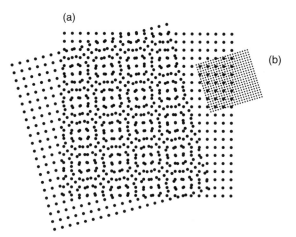

(a)

(b)

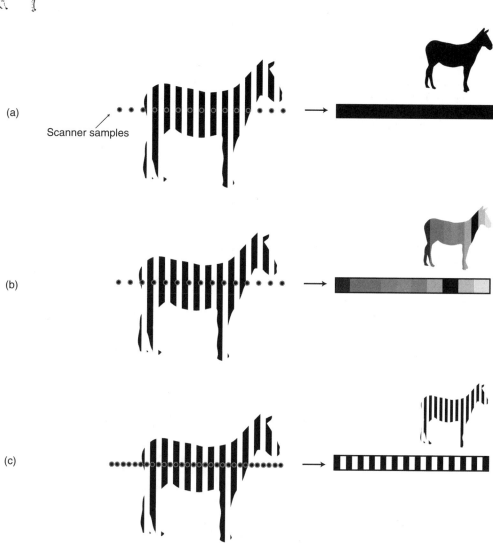

Figure 3.10 Scanning resolution and aliasing. (a) The number of samples per inch is the same as the spacing of the black lines in the stylized zebra. In addition, in this case, they are perfectly aligned. The resulting zebra is entirely black. (b) The number of samples per inch is the same, but they are not aligned with the stripes. The areas contributing to each sample often include both black and white, resulting in a grayish final pixel value and an oddly striped zebra. (c) The number of samples is twice the number of stripes per inch and captures the striping. Even if it were offset somewhat, the striping would still be pretty good.

| 300 dpi | 150 dpi | 72 dpi | 15 dpi | 10 dpi |

Figure 3.11 Scanning finely detailed images such as text. At 300 dpi, this 60-point "T" looks good. At 10 dpi it is scarcely recognizable. Well-defined object edges benefit from higher-resolution scanning, as do objects that are so small that aliasing can affect both their interior colors and edges.

Copyright Protection

The computer offers new ways to copy, distribute, display, and perform creative works. But in creating works from digitally captured images, sounds, or text—and especially in displaying, performing, or distributing works over networks such as the Internet—copyright law can easily be inadvertently infringed. Computer artists must therefore, even while students, become at least somewhat familiar with the often esoteric area of intellectual property rights.

The copyright law is based on the power of Congress, given in the U.S. Constitution, to "promote the Progress of Science and useful Arts, by securing for limited Times to their Authors and Inventors the exclusive Right to their respective Writings and Discoveries" [US, 1787]. It is with this goal in mind that copyright law is interpreted by the courts and periodically updated by Congress. (The most recent complete revision was in 1976.) The law's intent is not to ensure remuneration for artists but, by providing economic and other incentives made possible by control over their own work, to "stimulate artistic creativity for the general public good" [US, 1975].

Copyright protects not facts or ideas or discoveries but only the original expression of ideas as fixed in a tangible medium (i.e., something that can be physically copied). Thus a great idea for a painting cannot be copyrighted, nor can a law of physics such as $e = mc^2$. **Fixation** in a tangible medium is considered to be fulfilled for files stored on a hard drive, diskette, or other digital medium, or possibly even for data stored in RAM. A work that appears on the screen momentarily as part of a live digital transmission is not considered fixed, but an image completely downloaded and written to disk or RAM may be so considered [US, 1995, p. 27]. By this definition almost any image appearing on a computer screen could be copyrighted material. It remains to be seen how courts will interpret fixation in the context of digital creation and networks.

As creator or "author" of a work you can easily attain basic copyright protection. Any work of art that you create is automatically copyrighted as soon as it exists in a tangible form, even as data on a hard drive. To strengthen your case should you ever need to contest a copyright infringement, however, you should affix a copyright notice to any published copies of your work. In the case of visually perceived works, the notice is simply the copyright symbol, ©, or the word Copyright (or Copr.), the year of first publication, and your name. If you believe that you may need to defend your copyright in the future, you should also register it with the Copyright Office by mail or electronically at http://lcweb.loc.gov/copyright/.

Many works are in the **public domain** (i.e., their copyrights have expired or were never established). If a work was copyrighted in the United States more than 75 years ago (from January 1 of the current year), its copyright has expired; thus works published before January 1, 1924 are now in the public domain.

The consequences of infringing upon copyrights can include an injunction to halt any activity involving the copyrighted materials, impoundment of relevant materials and products, statutory damages (not less than $500 and not more than $20,000, as the court considers just), or actual damages arising from the illegal use of copyrighted material and any profits made. A knowing infringer is treated differently from an innocent infringer, especially one who, after due diligence, was led to conclude that the proposed use would not be an infringement. If the copyright is infringed upon willfully for commercial advantage or private gain, a criminal suit can be brought against the infringer.

For the most part, copyrighted material that happens to be in digital form is treated as though it were in an analog form. Distributing copyrighted digital material, such as software or images, over a Web server or bulletin board is just as illegal as physically copying disks and distributing them by mail. An action that infringes upon a copyright for an analog art work is almost certain to infringe upon the copyright of a digital counterpart.

The computer artist's main rights ensured by the law are the following.

Reproduction. When a work is stored on a computer, even for a brief time, a copy has been made. Copies are made in the process of digitizing work or copying a file to or from another machine.

Derivative works. A derivative work is one based on one or more preexisting works. In other words, you can't take someone's book and make it into a multimedia project without permission.

Distribution. If a copyrighted work is displayed, without permission of the copyright holder, on a publicly accessible network server, the copyrights of display (and possibly performance) and potentially of distribution are probably being infringed upon.

Public performance and display. A work must be seen or heard or otherwise rendered to constitute a performance. To be public, a performance does not require that the viewers be in the same place or experience it at the same time. Likewise, a work is displayed whenever it is publicly accessible for viewing, whether through downloading a file or browsing.

So, for example, if you scan in an image from a magazine, you have almost certainly infringed upon the reproduction copyright. If you use the image in a class assignment and it is seen by your twenty-five or so classmates, the chances are slight that anyone will care. If you put your art work, including the scanned image, on the Web, you are probably infringing upon the public display copyright. As others can easily copy the image, you have probably also infringed upon the distribution copyright. Whether or not you are likely to get caught and prosecuted, you should respect the copyright: Someday the images stolen or misused may be your own!

Fair Use

Copyright law includes provisions of crucial importance to artists and other users of copyrighted material who are seeking not to make a profit but instead to educate, study, or criticize. The set of limitations on the copyright law contained in the **doctrine of fair use** enables teachers, students, and researchers to use copyrighted work under a number of conditions without requesting permission or paying licensing fees. There are four main considerations in determining fair use.

1. ***The purpose and nature of use.*** Study and nonprofit educational uses are usually permitted, particularly if the copies are made spontaneously. The latter criterion distinguishes photocopying for class an article that appears the day before from photocopying a book that the teacher knows well in advance will be used. Commercial uses generally are not permitted.
2. ***The nature of the copyrighted work.*** The nature of the work involves distinctions such as whether the work is published or unpublished (published works are more likely to be fair use than unpublished works), fact or fiction (factual works are more likely to be fair use than fiction), and possibly also whether it is in digital or analog form [US, p. 78]. This last consideration is usually of less importance than the purpose and nature of use.
3. ***Nature and substantiality of the material used.*** Is an entire image or only a small portion used? Is the portion used an important or insignificant aspect of the work? In general, if the entire work is reproduced, the use is less likely to be considered fair. However, even a small portion of a work can be considered vital to the meaning of the piece and thus protected from reproduction. Because the physical portion used cannot alone determine infringement, this criterion is often considered to be the least important of the four.
4. ***Effect of use on potential market for the work.*** Will the new work or material copied directly from it compete with the original? Works parodying an original usually do not compete because the two serve different markets, but copying of a work that affects the market for the original is probably not a fair use. The economic effect is often the chief consideration in determining fair use.

However, predicting how a court will view these factors in any particular case is difficult.

Protecting digital images, citing them, and locating copyright holders is made easier by **steganographic** or **digital fingerprint** or **digital watermarking** software that embeds hidden labels within images. With such systems, an artist can effectively "sign" the work in a way that will make it identifiable even if it is cropped, compressed, or printed and rescanned. With the watermarking filter from Digimarc, for example, a user can register to receive an ID and become part of Digimarc's database (see http://www.digimarc.com/). After the filter has been installed, any software that can recognize Digimarc's watermark automatically indicates that the file is copyrighted.

(a) (b)

Figure 3.12 Digital cameras. (a) Mid- and low-range digital still cameras are integrated units that offer a range of options, such as zoom, exposure settings, focus, and digital previews. The price usually corresponds directly with the resolution offered. (b) Digital camcorders are becoming practical and popular consumer products.

3.4.2 Digital Still Cameras

The need to scan photographs can be eliminated by using a digital camera to take the original pictures (see Fig. 3.12). Like a rapid scanner, a digital camera uses an array of stationary CCDs to scan an entire view at the same time through its lens. (If a moving CCD were used, as in most desktop scanners, any motion in the scene or of the camera would cause blurring.) Digital cameras range in price from a few hundred dollars to $10,000–$20,000. With low-end models, the user has little control over the resolution used, and often there is no preview.

3.4.3 Digital Video Cameras

Video can be shot onto analog film and digitized afterward, but digital video cameras are becoming practical alternatives. Now available for about $1500, digital camcorders can help artists and designers, as well as home video users, integrate video, still images, and computing technology.

Digitizing video from analog tape can be accomplished with some digital video cameras or through a computer with an NTSC conversion card (often just called a **video card**). Depending on the card or computer used, the user may be able to grab both individual video frames and sequences. Video frame grabs are a flexible way to capture still images with a quality comparable to low-end digital cameras (sometimes called **still video cameras**).

Digital video-editing systems are becoming more affordable. However, there are still many barriers to their use by individuals, not the least of which are the massive storage requirements for high quality: A few minutes of full-color, full-sized digital video can require several gigabytes of disk space. A full digital system might include a digital camera, analog video decks, and related equipment, and a **nonlinear editor** (NLE). An NLE includes software designed for editing digital video, a computer, many gigabytes of hard drive space, and often a backup device as well, such as a tape drive. Such systems are not yet practical for casual use, but when compared to the cost of renting time in a video studio, this option is becoming increasingly attractive to professional video producers and serious video artists.

3.5 The Art of Input

Ways of using the input devices, like ways of using output devices and like the programs themselves, are suggested by the manufacturer and the context for which the device was originally built. Because these tools are built for business or to imitate traditional aspects of the commercial design process, visually creative people need to explore ways of making input devices their own, testing their limits and capabilities on the basis of their physical scope, not on assumptions about how they should be used. For example, it can be interesting to use the mouse on a surface other than a desk, to move an image while it being scanned, to place 3D objects on a scanner bed, or to reconfigure a monitor/mouse/chair relationship.

Lane Hall and Lisa Moline are computer artists who often work collaboratively and are known for utilizing innovative and low-budget input and output techniques. Although their final work is usually a 2D combination of printing techniques, many of their input methods involve the creation of large, organic and often messy, sharp, or heavy sculptural forms that cannot be safely placed on a scanner bed (see Fig. 3.13).

Figure 3.13 Input sculptures. These four sculptural objects are incorporated into the pieces shown in Fig. 3.14. The carved solid wood model is more than a foot in diameter. Hall and Moline also use video digitization to capture images of moss and tubers from their garden. *(Courtesy of Lane Hall and Lisa Moline)*

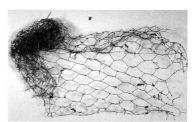

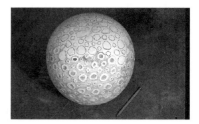

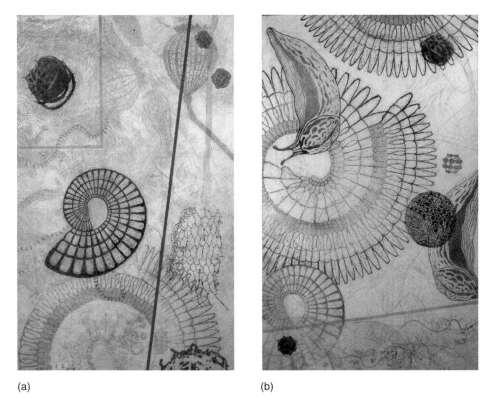

(a)   (b)

Figure 3.14 Woodland Goiter Series. (a) *Night Bait* and (b) *Wire Broom,* Lane Hall and Lisa Moline, 1995, 65″ × 40″. *(Courtesy of Lane Hall and Lisa Moline)*

Hall and Moline bring such elements into their computer art through inexpensive video digitization (a video camera running DCTV digitization software, hooked up to their Amiga computer). For higher-resolution images, they take photographs of 3D objects and then scan the photos on a flatbed scanner. Try to identify in Fig. 3.14 the objects shown in Fig. 3.13.

Many artists and designers find that placing 3D objects directly on the scanner, rather than scanning a photograph, provides a more engaging result. Hall and Moline even utilized this technique with their six-month-old daughter (see Fig. 3.15).

> We like to approach digital technology with a fairly open mind, and really have no preferred methods for input, although we have worked to create our own "style" with the equipment we have available. Generally, we first let the technology help shape our ideas, then we bend the technology to suit our interests. As the technology gets more sophisticated and "artist-friendly" we take advantage, but still like to use the now "outmoded" technology we have, like our dot-matrix printer and fairly old software. A good example of this process is demonstrated in my "Insecto-Theology" series. [Figure 3.16] shows the detail of a hand-drawn bee, done using an ancient IBM package called

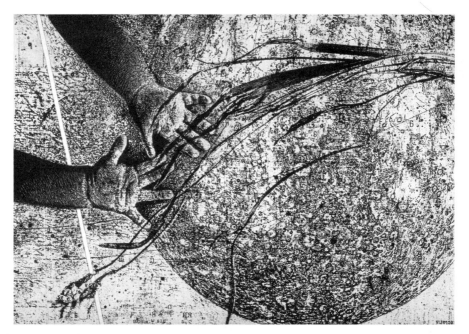

Figure 3.15 Lane Hall, *Grabby,* **1994** (17″ × 11″). This image was created with scanner input from an actual baby and real plant materials (scanned separately). *(Courtesy of Lane Hall)*

"Drawing Assistant®" and a very awkward electrostatic (rather than ball) mouse. Even though it is rigid and geometric, there is an interesting grace to the drawing which is built up using only circles, ellipses, squares, rectangles and straight lines. Exploiting technical limitations is always interesting! [Moline, 1996]

3.6 Found Data

Nowadays, more and more information is created or stored digitally, and current input options include much that the artist has not personally digitized—vast amounts of visual data can be found on the Web and in image databases or encountered on the job. Artist Kathleen Ruiz worked in a university medical school and found the data produced by various body-scanning techniques fascinating, both aesthetically and conceptually. Gathering such data was not a mechanical process, like scanning a photograph, but involved the use of film obtained from the diagnosis and treatment of real patients who often had ingested dyes or were intubated (see Fig. 3.17).

Figure 3.16 Lisa Moline, *Female Monarchy,* **1989** (from the Insecto-Theology Series, intaglio, letterpress, and computer graphics on Rives, 28″ × 14″). *(Courtesy of Lisa Moline)*

Through the input techniques of medical imaging and VR, artist Diane Gromala brings her body literally into her art work. She uses her own experiences with pain and medical visualizations (X-rays, MRI data, and 3D models based on these) as the primary materials (see Fig. 3.18).

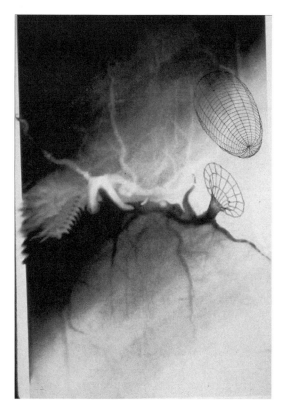

Figure 3.17 Kathleen Ruíz, *Cardiac Arrest,*
1991. *(Courtesy of Kathleen Ruíz and The Sandra
Gering Gallery)*

Figure 3.18 Diane Gromala, *Dancing With
Virtual Dervish: Virtual Bodies,* 1996. The artist
in VR gear, composited with a view from within
this virtual reality piece. *(Courtesy of Diane
Gromala)*

3.7 Dangers of Input

Long-term repetitive use of muscles in the hands and wrists is associated with musculo-skeletal problems such as repetitive strain injury, tendinitis, and carpal tunnel syndrome (see Fig. 3.19). Although the exact cause-and-effect relationships have not been determined, enough evidence exists of the dangers of input devices to make them a concern for anyone who spends large portions of the day using a computer. The typical desktop setup can also lead to back pain, eye fatigue, and other ailments. Ergonomists suggest taking frequent breaks and arranging the keyboard and mousing area to avoid awkward positions. Although guidelines have been developed (see the U.S. National Library of Medicine monograph at http://wwwetb.nlm.nih.gov/monograp/ergo/hazards.html), the best arrangements differ among individuals and their effectiveness is influenced by other factors such as posture and stress level. Lighting also seems to affect many computer users, and they should experiment with adjustable lamps (especially good for avoiding glare) and different lighting levels.

Artists and designers can avoid musculoskeletal injuries by paying attention to the comfort and convenience of their computer setups and listening and reacting to any messages of pain or discomfort from the body. Straightforward adjustments, such as a better chair, a lower keyboard rest, or an input device with differently situated buttons, can remedy potentially harmful situations. Repetitive motions themselves can be lessened if you use several different input devices to reduce the motions made with a single muscle group. Also, function keys can be used for operations such as cut and paste and for automation of tedious sequences, either within a software package or through an external **macro program** (which can record a sequence of mouse or keyboard operations).

In addition to harmful effects of input devices, a great deal of concern has been voiced about very low-frequency (VLF) and extremely low-frequency (ELF) electromagnetic fields from CRTs. Until scientific research and surveys reach a definite conclusion on the possible dangers of CRTs, computer users should avoid sitting unnecessarily close to the front of a CRT (although the 29 inches advised makes viewing detailed work difficult) or within four feet of the back or sides. Electromagnetic fields are not blocked by walls, so the people working nearby and their CRT use, if any, must also be considered.

Figure 3.19 Repetitive input motions can contribute to pain and injury. A computer scientist wears a cast as part of recovery from carpal tunnel surgery. His assistant (hand visible in back) is wearing a rollerblading wrist guard to keep his wrists straight while using a mouse.

3.8 Introduction to Output

Images created with a computer are usually exhibited in a medium different from the one the artist or designer sees while creating them. Unlike a traditional art work, one electronic file can be realized with many different output media, at different sizes, and at different times and places. This unprecedented separation between *design space* and *display space* (see Chapter 10, 2D and 3D Animation and Video) provides new freedom for artists using the computer. But it also demands attention not only to one, but in principle to an unlimited number of output decisions, from 2D printouts to wall-sized projections and video and virtual reality.

3.9 Computer Displays

Almost all computer-based art and design is created on-screen and much is also shown that way, particularly multimedia and Web-based pieces. In addition, screen images can be projected onto other surfaces for installations and public showings.

The common goal of all **display systems** is to take pixel data and draw an image with light, using materials such as phosphors, liquid crystals, LEDs, or light projected through colored filters onto a screen. (Vector-based displays draw images directly from geometric data but are not discussed here because they are not used with personal computers.)

Because screen images are created by adding different colors of light rather than by selectively absorbing them, they have a physical quality that is different from pigment-based imagery. The screen surface glows and, although its resolution is almost always far below that of printed output, screen images seem more continuous because the phosphors (or other materials) show colors of varying intensity and are not as clearly delineated as dots on a page.

Screens are an inherently time-based medium. Their fleeting images must usually be refreshed more than sixty times a second to remain visible and flicker-free, requiring continuous electrical currents along with complex mechanics and optics. Because displays are expensive, they are rarely used to display a single image for a long period of time. Rather, the screen is used as a portal into the computer, offering the viewer temporary visualizations of information, like drawings in the sand that are easily and regularly washed away.

The relationship of the screen to the viewer is an important aspect of screen-based computer art. The personal computer screen, usually on someone's desk, is an intimate viewing option, and a laptop screen can be even more so. A large-screen or multi-screen display such as a video wall is geared toward public showings. Usually the screen itself is an obvious part of the piece—even if its bulk is hidden in a kiosk or incorporated into an installation, the light of the screen and its slick glass surface create a window into some other place.

3.9.1 Screen Types

Desktop computer monitors and TV screens are both usually based on **cathode ray tubes** (CRTs), which are glass tubes in which an electron gun fires a stream of electrons that is deflected toward phosphors coating the inside of a glass screen (see Fig. 3.20). The electrons excite the phosphors, which relieve themselves of extra energy by

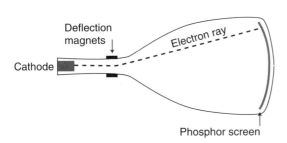

Figure 3.20 **Picture tube of a monochrome CRT.** The electron ray, or beam, is systematically deflected to illuminate the entire screen in less than 1/60 of a second.

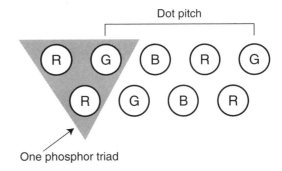

Figure 3.21 **Color phosphor groupings.** Here the phosphors are arrayed in triads, but many other configurations, such as vertical strips, may be used. The dot pitch—the distance between green phosphors—is a good indicator of the screen's resolution.

emitting light. Because the light is emitted rapidly and the phosphor soon returns to its darkened state, each phosphor on the screen must be refreshed by new electrons.

In a color screen, groups of red, green, and blue phosphors are arrayed in groups of three (or some other configuration) and are stimulated in varying intensities by three different electron guns, one for each color of phosphor (see Fig. 3.21). The phosphors in each group are close enough to each other that their combined light is perceived by the eye, as in a pointillist painting, to be a single color. Part of the success of this illusion depends on the CRT's **resolution**—the smallest discernible dot size that the display can show—which depends closely on the spacing, or dot pitch, of the red, green, and blue phosphor groups. **Dot pitch** is the distance from the center of one green phosphor to the next and ranges from 0.44 to 0.47 mm for low-resolution displays to 0.28 to 0.31 mm for high-resolution displays. Ultrahigh-resolution displays are manufactured with dot pitches of 0.21 mm or less to 0.27 mm [Whitaker, 1994, p. 262].

All color CRTs have essentially the same phosphor colors and are thus capable of displaying full color, but not all computers come with the necessary video memory (VRAM) to handle full-color information for each image pixel. In the recent past, personal computers supported chiefly 8-bit color—only 256 different colors could be used on the screen at once. An illusion of more colors can be created, however, with **dithering,** a process that groups combinations of two or more available colors in pointillist fashion to simulate a color that cannot be displayed (see Chapter 6, Printing, for further discussion of dithering). Most programs automatically dither a full-color document in order to display it on a 16- or 8-bit monitor; in such cases the changed appearance is only temporary and does not affect the document when it is later viewed in full color.

Today most personal computers are capable of at least 16-bit color—more than 65,000 colors—and can be easily upgraded to show 24-bit full color, or almost 17 million colors, created with combinations of 256 intensity levels of red, green, and blue. With only about a million pixels on most computer screens, displaying almost 17 million colors at once usually is not even a consideration.

Color CRTs contain a **shadow mask,** a metal sheet with tiny holes in it, to ensure that each gun's electron stream reaches its intended colored phosphor. High-resolution screens require shadow masks with smaller holes, and fewer electrons get through to strike each phosphor, dimming the image. Technical challenges in shadow-mask technology and the need for more accurate electron guns make high-resolution monitors much more expensive than standard monitors. Their cost also increases with size.

Today's color CRTs are bright and crisp, having richly colored phosphors—and are visible from almost any angle. But a large CRT weighs well over 50 lb, is delicate, and does not fit under an airline seat. For laptop computers and portable projection systems, different screen technologies, **flat panel displays,** are used.

Most flat panels are **liquid-crystal displays** (LCDs) or use plasma. In an LCD display, the crystals are sandwiched between sheets of glass containing polarized coatings and metal grid lines. The grids are used to send electrical impulses to specific liquid crystal units. The polarized coating blocks light from crystals that are stimulated by the electric field of the grid, making them appear dark. Because of the polarization, LCD flat panel displays are often hard to see from an angle. Today's LCD displays usually are **active-matrix LCDs,** which use transistors for each crystal instead of wire grids. The transistors allow faster response times (resulting in more clarity and less ghosting from the cursor or other moving objects) and brighter colors when viewed from an angle. **Plasma displays** use neon gas trapped in tiny "bulbs," small pockets between layers of horizontal and vertical conducting strips, that are used to stimulate phosphors at specific locations on the screen.

Both LCD and plasma displays have low power requirements and are sturdier than CRTs, making them desirable for use with laptops and computers that may be treated roughly. Flat panel displays do not have the same highly reflective thick glass facing as CRTs, and their small size and weight call less attention to their mechanical, electric, and optical composition. Large flat panel displays have proved difficult to manufacture reliably at a reasonable cost but, like other components of computing, are rapidly dropping in price. Low-cost flat panel displays will likely become available in the next decade. They may eventually replace CRTs and could also be used to hang static images or time-based computer artwork on a wall.

3.9.2 PROJECTION

Both CRTs and flat panel displays are used in **projection systems.** Images can be projected with LCD panels by shining a bright light through a display and using a lens to focus the image on a wall or screen. LCD-based flat panel projection systems that use an overhead projector as a light source now sell for less than $1000. Some more expensive models have a built-in bright light source and projector. In large rooms or rooms that cannot be blackened, however, a fixed, high-quality projector with a strong light source is necessary. **Three-gun projectors** developed for this purpose contain their own light source and use grayscale CRTs to display the red, green, and blue channels of the image separately. The three grayscale displays are projected through red, green, and blue filters and merged with lenses on the projection screen. (Grayscale displays can be manufactured with higher resolution than color displays because they do not require shadow masks or triads of phosphors. In addition, shadow-mask CRTs do not let enough light through for large-scale projection needs.) This type of projection unit still costs at least several thousand dollars. The computer's red, green, and blue signals can be converted to NTSC, the standard U.S. video format, for viewing with a video projector or television set. However, NTSC has lower resolution (approximately 500 × 700 pixels) than much computer work and can distort the proportions and colors of the computer image. Figure 3.22 shows several computer projection systems. Expensive (about $10,000), the CRT full-color system must be permanently installed; it is good for use in large spaces. Much less expensive (about $1000), the LCD panel projector offers many thousands of colors (degradation of image color and contrast are quite noticeable, however); it is lightweight, good for traveling, and good for use in small rooms that can be darkened completely.

Artists have used a wide range of projection methods for displaying computer-based work, from direct computer projectors such as those just described to slides, video projection, and laser disc, a digital storage format that is similar to a CD-ROM. For example, artist Jennifer Steinkamp uses a computer and 3D modeling software to design her large-scale animated installation pieces. After working out the details of each installation in a computer model of the actual space, Steinkamp records her abstract animations on laser disc and projects them with a video projector onto walls and other spaces. By using projection, Steinkamp is able to realize her computer art work at a scale impossible with present screen-based display technologies. Instead of

Figure 3.22 Computer projection systems. (a) CRT projection system. (b) LCD panel projector. Light source is a standard overhead projector.

(a)   (b)

(a)

(b)

Figure 3.23 Projection pieces by Jennifer Steinkamp. (a) *Inney* (simulation shot), Huntington Beach Art Center, Huntington Beach, CA, 16′ × 15′, 1995. (b) *Untitled,* from the show "Photography and the Photographic" at the California Museum of Photography, Riverside, CA, 1994. (c) *Gender Specific,* Bliss House, Pasadena, CA, 8′ × 10′ and 8′ × 10′, 1989. *(Courtesy of Jennifer Steinkamp and ACME Gallery, Los Angeles)*

(c)

existing within traditional frames or within the familiar frame of a television or computer monitor, Steinkamp's pieces take over and transform large physical spaces, involving the viewers' full bodies as they move about in the space (see Fig. 3.23). Steinkamp uses a computer monitor to work on models of her installations, which gives her complete control over the basic design as well as subtle effects of angle and lighting. In Fig. 3.23(a) the animated work is based on measurements of the building's architecture. The 3D animations are rendered and output to laser disk for use in the physical space. Sound for her works is done in collaboration with "techno" composers such as the musical group Grain. Steinkamp describes the intent of her pieces in words to the musicians—who sometimes compose without having seen the visuals. Steinkamp's background in video led her to experiment with a language of flickering abstract patterns that, when projected, both combine with and defy physical spaces, as shown in Fig. 3.23(b). As in immersive virtual reality, the works are seen as part of a continuous environment. Instead of seeing inside the house in Fig. 3.23(c), a passerby sees swirling, rhythmically fluctuating patterns of colored light.

Conclusion

The experience of using the computer for art and design is mediated by its basic input and output devices: keyboards, mice, tablets, scanners, and displays. The choice of input tool and type of display influences essential tasks such as selecting software painting tools, drawing lines, making gestures, and viewing changes interactively. Research into new and more exotic interaction devices will certainly affect creative visual computer use in the future.

Although few artists and designers are in a position to create their own input devices or substantially modify existing devices, awareness of the issues surrounding input and display, the options available, and the limitations of existing tools can help artists make informed choices among devices and take full advantage of their capacities and capabilities.

Suggested Readings

Buxton, William A. S., http://www.dgp.toronto.edu/people/BillBuxton/billbuxton.html Buxton maintains a complete cross-indexed listing of his books and research papers on human–computer interaction on his Web pages.

Circular 22: How to Investigate the Copyright Status of a Work. Washington, D.C., U.S. Government Printing Office; and **Circular 1: Copyright Basics,** Washington, D.C., U.S. Government Printing Office. Both publications are available also through the Copyright Office, Library of Congress (http://lcweb.loc.gov/copyright/).

Kerlow, Isaac Victor, and Judson Rosebush. *Computer Graphics for Designers and Artists.* This book is a general book on computer graphics that includes sections on input devices.

Sherr, Sol (ed.). *Input Devices.* Academic Press, 1988. For those who want to understand the gory technical details, this book contains detailed information about input devices and how they work.

Strong, William S. *The Copyright Book,* 3d edition. MIT Press, 1990. Clearly written, practical description of copyright law.

U.S. Code, Title 17, *Copyright Act.* Read the law yourself from the source! An online hypertext version is available at http://www.law.cornell.edu/uscode/17)

Whitaker, Jerry. *Electronic Displays, Technology, Design, and Applications.* McGraw-Hill, 1994. Another technical book, this text describes the inner workings of different types of monitor and projection technology. Artists and designers interested in input theory and use should also consult the interface design readings in Chapter 11, Multimedia and Interactivity.

Exercises

1. Input device pros and cons: Choose two or three different input devices and try the following experiments.

Sign your name.
Draw or trace over a simple line drawing made beforehand on a piece of paper.
Draw or trace over a more tonal image, trying to fill in the necessary areas.

Can someone tell which input device you have used for each task? Now spend some time using each device to do standard menuing tasks (clicking, dragging, selecting, etc.). Which input device is best for which type(s) of task?

2. Absolutely relative: With a tablet and stylus create a simple drawing in an absolute and then a relative mode. Does the relative mode affect your drawing abilities? If so, how?

3. Sublime images: Using a digital or still camera, explore your living space and neighborhood. Take pictures of things that you find sublime. Document them (they could be objects or more abstract features, such as a certain type of lighting) with multiple views and angles. Store these images on a removable medium (e.g., a Zip disk) or, if you used a real camera, have the images put on a Kodak PhotoCD. (Many photo and drug stores now provide this option.) Use these images throughout the rest of this book in other exercises.

4. Creative input: Drawing inspiration from Lane Hall and Lisa Moline's approach to input, try to stretch the effects possible with flatbed or video scanning. Suggestions: Scan interesting textures and shapes of found objects and fabrics, create 2D or 3D forms with traditional materials, creating colors and textures difficult or impossible to generate easily on the computer. Add to this input repository weekly and use the results in exercises in subsequent chapters.

5. One projection at a time: Create a computer art work to be displayed on a timer-controlled slide projector. How does this approach suggest narrative and rhythm for a work?

6. Installation space-projection: Use a computer projector to project a static image or an animation onto a specific place with the goal of warping or changing the experience of that space for viewers.

7. Screen saver art: Create an art work to be used as part of a screen saver or as wallpaper for your screen. Does viewing a work in either of these modes trivialize it? How does this forum change your perception of the work's purpose?

CHAPTER 4

Digital Design and Layout— 2D Geometric Graphics

Figure 4.1 Michael Holcomb, *Self-Portrait,* 1994.
Michael Holcomb creates portraits and environments with the basic types of marks—lines, curves,
and fills—available in 2D geometry-based programs. He explores abstract geometric mark-making
in a context of traditional visual conventions (e.g.,
portraiture) and the impact of this new language on
graphic communication and culture. *(Courtesy of
Michael Holcomb)*

4.1 Introduction

Digital design and layout programs are an elusive art medium. Also called **vector-
based** programs because of their similarities to early vector graphics, or **draw
programs** because of the first mass-market success, Apple's MacDraw, they are a

standard component of any modern design studio but are almost completely ignored by fine artists. The reasons are largely historical: Digital design and layout programs have evolved chiefly to serve design professionals and illustrators by translating virtually all traditional design and paste-up processes into the digital realm, eliminating the need for rub-on letters, ruling pens, gouache, and rubber cement. The same strengths that make these programs useful for designers and illustrators, however—an extraordinary level of control over line, form, and placement—are valuable for many types of artistic endeavors. For example, the ability to create polished illustrations and designs, complete with proper typography, is useful not only for applied artists, but also for fine artists who desire to critique mass media graphics by using the same visual language as commercial art professionals. Thus Douglas Kornfeld describes his piece shown in Fig. 4.2 in the following way:

> This installation is made up of a grid of 48 generic tree symbol/signs on eight foot steel posts around one of the large trees in Deering Oaks Park. Each sign, fabricated to highway standards, has a black silhouette tree image silkscreened onto a fluorescent yellow background. In this work I use these symbol/signs to address issues of: the singular vs. the multiple, natural vs. machine made, the pastoral vs. the planned, the generic vs. the unique. This work serves to warn us, in bright warning sign color, that the use of signs and symbols can flatten our awareness as well as illuminate it [Kornfeld, 1997].

In this chapter I present the elegant visual language of digital design and layout programs. This material should be valuable to graphic designers, illustrators, and fine artists alike.

So, what is the difference between a raster-based program and a geometry-based program? A raster image is based on pixels (see Chapter 2). A **geometry-based** program is built up of abstract geometric forms, not lists of color samples, but geometric descriptions of lines and curves and shapes such as squares and circles. (These forms are sometimes referred to as **objects** and geometry-based programs as **object-oriented** programs, but they should not be confused with object-oriented programming methods and languages, which

Figure 4.2 Douglas Kornfeld, *Forest City Sculpture Festival,* 1997 (Deering Oaks Park, Portland, Me.). Kornfeld drew the tree images in a draw program and then pasted them as decals into a 3D program in which he had modeled the sign structures. He then composited the signs into an image of the park. *(Courtesy of Douglas Kornfeld)*

are unrelated.) Two-dimensional geometry-based programs take computer graphics, as Kandinsky would have appreciated, from point and line to plane.[1]

Even if you never use a 2D geometry-based program, understanding the basic concepts and components is essential for many other types of graphics programs, including:

- geometry-based features of paint programs, such as Bezier selection paths, layers, and paint objects or sprites (covered at the end of this chapter);
- fundamental ideas used in 3D modeling and 2D and 3D animation programs, such as the paradigm of geometry-based graphics, a type of curve called a spline, anti-aliasing, and more; and
- the visual capabilities of desktop publishing programs.

Today's professional mass-market design and layout applications such as Adobe Illustrator®, Macromedia Freehand®, and CorelDRAW® emphasize extensive control over line, curve, shape definition and composition, professional typesetting capabilities, and color tools for prepress production. Some programs, such as Claris MacDraw®, are aimed at users with less formal composition and printing needs. Although not as powerful, such programs are less expensive and often significantly easier to use than the professional prepress packages.

Other 2D geometry-based applications include 2D **computer-aided design** (CAD) programs that offer even more advanced tools for line, curve, and shape definition and composition. These programs are used to produce complex, highly accurate drawings and plans in engineering, industrial design, architecture, and other technical fields. They typically require more powerful computers and more RAM than standard digital design programs. Many features formerly unique to CAD software, such as the intelligent snapping together of lines and shapes to make them join precisely and the automated display of dimensions (e.g., the exact length of a line that the user has drawn) have been adopted in digital design and layout programs, offering artists greater accuracy and new types of control over spatial relationships.

Early 2D computer art was almost all geometry-based and used the same elements (lines and curves and closed shapes) now available interactively to artists and illustrators through design and layout programs. Many inspiring artists still work in this style. Although these artists usually write their own programs, examples of their work in this chapter help shed light on potential artistic uses of this type of software.

And finally, digital design and layout programs often are based on the assumption that the user will be designing primarily for print, not the screen. In this chapter I present digital design and layout programs as ways to create images, and consider printing features in greater depth in Chapter 6, Printing.

4.1.1 A New Level of Flexibility

Both digital painting and design bring the computer's extraordinary flexibility to the act of creation. The near absence of penalty for experimentation is, however, both a

---

[1] *Point and Line to Plane* is the title of Kandinsky's best known book.

blessing and a curse. Although the unprecedented flexibility of the computer encourages exploration of artistic ideas, it also reduces the structure that a physical medium often enforces. In using a physical medium, an artist makes many decisions that are essentially irreversible. When a piece of stone is carved away, a black mark is made with charcoal, or a line is drawn with a ruling pen, the process and the medium keep a work moving in a single direction, and choices tend to become more and more limited as the piece nears completion. And, as in a science fiction story in which immortality changes the meaning of the protagonist's life, an infinitely malleable and flexible image-making tool may remove a process of struggle against the limitations of a medium that is important in fueling a work of art. In using a computer, an artist's decisions have no inherent permanence; especially in geometry-based programs, no mark cannot be undone or replaced. Practical factors, such as workable limits on file size and image complexity, do constrain computer artists, but the ease with which changes can be made and choices reversed directly affect the art-making process.

The challenge is to take advantage of the computer's unprecedented flexibility without becoming distracted by the endless options available. This freedom can make finishing visual projects difficult because closure and completeness associated with art work are dictated at least in part by the media and the processes used. A computer artist can limit his or her use of digital tools to approximate traditional progressions more closely or restrict courses of action by saving only a few versions or not using the Undo command. The artist can also choose to abandon, at least in part, the concept of a completed work and try instead to create new forms that exploit the nearly infinite flexibility of this new medium.

The computer medium does not dry up, become brittle, or fade away, so the life cycle of computer-based works is open-ended.[2] Real-world aesthetic and time constraints remain, but time- and process-related constraints of the medium often do not. Many computer artists are experimenting with open-ended, often collaborative interactive works that have no inherent point of closure (see Chapter 11, Multimedia and Interactivity, and Chapter 12, The World Wide Web).

4.2 Concepts

Every part of a digital design and layout program image is made up of **linear elements**—lines and curves—and colors applied both to the linear elements and the spaces they enclose.

---

[2]Note, however, that computer files and media have lifetimes like any other medium, although their effects can be minimized with effort. Problems such as "code rot" (the tendency of programs to stop working because of changes in infrastructure, such as operating system code), programs written for machines or operating systems that are no longer available, information stored in formats that are no longer easy to read, and the physical deterioration of storage media are all real concerns.

4.2.1 Geometric Shapes

Artists can create and manipulate shapes interactively on the screen without thinking about numbers or equations. However, within the program every line and curve and shape is described geometrically in terms of a Cartesian coordinate system with a horizontal x axis and a vertical y axis. Point locations are given in the form (x, y). For example, the essence of the code for a solid black line could be "a line from point $(1, 1)$ to point $(6, 6)$, with a thickness of one point, to be drawn in black" (see Fig. 4.3). It is this type of geometric object description that is acted upon when an artist selects an object on the screen and changes it.

4.2.2 Geometry and the Nature of Selection

Geometric descriptions make the selection process different from selection in a raster program. In Fig. 4.4(a), for example, a rectangular selection is made and moved in a raster version of a lighthouse image. Although a precise area can be delineated and altered in this way, there is no inherent relationship between any of the parts of the image: They are all just pixel values. Compare this situation with selection in a design and layout program, shown in Fig. 4.4(b). Here, the objects making up the lighthouse light and top-level balcony are selected together and dragged to a new location. The background, which was not selected, remains untouched. The choices available for selection depend entirely on the objects used to create the image. If the contour of the

Figure 4.3 Continuous geometric shape definitions. (a) In a raster-based program, a line is simply a series of discrete pixels. Here, a line was drawn from (1, 1) to (6, 6). Changes to the line can be made only by changing the individual pixel values. (b) In a geometry-based program, a line is a continuous mathematical description. This line is defined for every location between (1, 1) and (6, 6), not just at integer locations. Changes to the line cause rewriting of its underlying description.

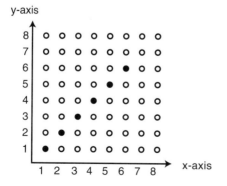

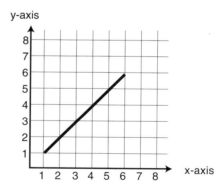

lighthouse had all been drawn as one shape, the top could not have been selected individually.

The user can select any graphic element in a design and layout program at any time, either by clicking on its screen image or by choosing among named objects in a list. The user can then transform selected objects by translating, rotating, or scaling them and can also distort, recolor, and otherwise alter and edit them.

The digital design and layout approach makes selection much easier for the most part. However, it forces the artist to think of images as collections of objects rather than as a fluid surface defined only by pixel values. The complexity of object shapes and colors is limited by the vocabulary available for describing them and precludes many paint-type touches, such as creating complex shading by smudging colors (see Fig. 4.5).

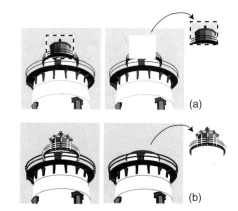

Figure 4.4 Selecting shapes in digital design and layout vs. paint programs. (a) In a paint program, possible selections depend on the capabilities of the selection tool. (b) In a digital design and layout program, available selections depend on which lines and curves were used to create the image.

Figure 4.5 Digital design and layout program shapes cannot be smeared or smudged. (a) Smoke is drawn in a digital design and layout program with three geometric shapes filled with gradients. The effect is of hard-edged forms that only vaguely resemble smoke. (b) The image is rasterized (a process described in Section 4.2.3) and moved into a paint program where the simple smoke shapes are smudged into more expressive smoky patterns. This type of smudging between shapes, blending adjacent pixel values, is not possible in geometric programs. (c) The smoke composition created in the paint program would probably not occur to an artist using a digital design and layout program, but even if it did, it is still almost impossible to avoid the hard edges or surmount the lack of means for creating complex gradients such as those made by smudging.

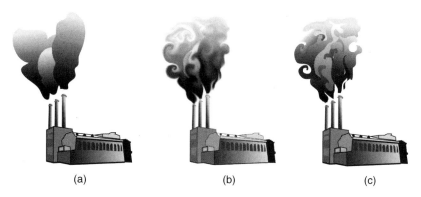

(a)　　　　　　　(b)　　　　　　　(c)

4.2.3 Drawing Geometric Shapes by Sampling

The geometric description in a digital design and layout program is not directly visible (except as text and numbers); it must be translated into a raster-type image by a process called **rasterization** before it can be shown on a raster-based screen. Recall from Chapter 2 that a pixel is simply a point location with associated sample values, usually of color. The challenge in converting a geometry-based object description into a raster image is to calculate the necessary pixel color values by sampling the underlying geometric form. This process raises the same issues of accuracy and resolution as in the Chapter 3 discussion of sampling an analog artwork by scanning it.

The method used to create sample values can dramatically affect the image quality. The simplest approach, **point sampling,** involves calculating the brightness of the geometric shape at each pixel location, but it can produce misleading results. For example, in Fig. 4.6 (as in the ramp shown previously in Fig. 2.7) a geometric description of a sloping line ends up looking like a staircase.

Aliasing, and a Partial Solution—Antialiasing   The jagged "stairs" in Fig 4.6 are an example of **aliasing**. An alias is a name that is in some way fictitious. Here, the fiction is uneven, stairlike changes in direction in what is supposed to be a smooth line. Unfortunately, as infinitely many samples are needed to represent a continuous geometric shape description, there is always some aliasing, whether it is noticeable or not.

The effects of aliasing are accentuated by low sampling rates and low resolution screens (again, see the discussion of scanning in Chapter 3). With a very high sampling rate (about 1200 to 2400 samples per inch) and a printer that can represent such a large number of samples per inch, you can bypass the problem of jaggies—the eye simply can't discern them anymore. But standard computer screens will not have this level of resolution anytime in the near future.

To counteract the effects of aliasing, sampling methods more sophisticated than the point sampling illustrated in Fig. 4.6 are used. In Fig. 4.7, for instance, a system of proportional weighting is used to assign pixel values so that the line appears relatively smooth, although sometimes a bit blurry. This method of counteracting the unpleasant effects of aliasing is an example of **antialiasing.**

Even better methods weight the values nearest the pixel location more strongly than those near the edge of the surrounding area. The weighting is accomplished with the types of filters previously discussed in Section 2.5.2. The method used in Fig. 4.7 corresponds to a box filter; more advanced methods utilize triangular or Gaussian filters.

Artists can use aliasing to create marks that suggest the digital state of the image or a

Figure 4.6 Simple sampling of a geometrically defined line. Here, all pixel locations covered by the line were set to black and the rest were set to white. The result is "stairs" or "jaggies" of same-height pixels.

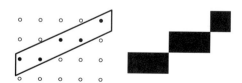

conversion from analog to digital. In Fig. 4.8, for instance, artist Rita DeWitt contrasts the old-fashioned pose and proper dress of the woman in the photograph with the blocky digital marks into which her image disintegrates. These marks give a sense of decomposition of the image that also speaks to the passage of years between the availability of the two technologies involved. The aliased-looking mark reveals the structure of the now-digital image and is a formal counterpart to the discrete, somewhat crazed needlework stitches.

4.2.4 ADOBE POSTSCRIPT

Most professional design and layout programs are designed around a geometric page description language called Adobe **PostScript.**

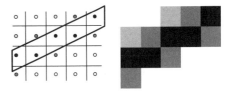

Figure 4.7 A more complex sampling of a geometric line. This sampling method considers not merely the value at each precise pixel location but also in the area around each pixel: The pixel's value reflects the proportion of that area covered by the line. If the entire area is covered, the pixel is set to black; otherwise, it is set to some shade of gray. For example, if the line covers half the pixel's surrounding area, the pixel's value would be 50% gray.

Figure 4.8 Rita DeWitt, *Class of '97: Lily Alexander,* **1991** (Canon Color Laser Copier 500 heat transfer, digitally manipulated, on silk and velvet with hand embroidery and hand-applied color, 34″ × 28″ × 2″). (a) Full picture. (b) Detail. *(Courtesy of Rita DeWitt)*

(a)

(b)

Digital design and layout programs that do not use PostScript usually offer some subset of its capabilities. The focus in this chapter is primarily on PostScript-based programs, but most of the material also applies to digital design and layout programs based on other geometric languages, such as Apple's QuickDraw® or Hewlett-Packard's HP GL® (Graphics Language).

One of the most important aspects of the PostScript language is its device-independence. Shape descriptions in PostScript are independent of the specific type of computer or printer. They can be used in the same way on a Macintosh, a PC, or a Unix machine and can be transferred to any printer having a PostScript interpreter. Another important property of PostScript is that it integrates text and graphics: The same types of lines, curves, and fills are used to form both. Consequently, both text and graphics can be altered in the same ways.

PostScript was essential to the desktop publishing revolution in the late 1980s because it let designers work on-screen with resolution-independent forms and text that could then be printed on a laser printer or high-end typesetter. The reason that printed PostScript images look so crisp and clean is that a PostScript printer resamples the underlying geometry of the image by using the printer resolution (anywhere from 300 to 2400 printer pixels, or dots per inch) instead of the raster file created during sampling for the screen (usually 72 to 85 image pixels per inch). Obviously a boon to designers, desktop publishing also inspired other types of artists to work in the book format (for an example, see Craig Hickman's work later in this chapter).

4.3 ANATOMY OF A DIGITAL DESIGN AND LAYOUT PROGRAM

Figure 4.9 is a screen grab of some typical digital design and layout program features. They include the drawing area, main tool palette, a number of auxiliary palettes, and the main menu bar and are described as follows.

Canvas, or drawing area. The drawing area is a screen area in which the drawing program tools work. Only the demarcated section of the drawing area, called the **page,** can be printed. Although the drawing area is 2D, every object (graphic element or text block) is considered either "in front of" or "behind" any other object and the objects are overlapped accordingly when displayed on a screen or printed. The user can usually open more than one drawing area for a single file.

Main tool palette, or tool bar. A typical main tool palette contains at least one type of selection tool, uniformly depicted as a short arrow, and tools for creating and editing vertices, lines, curves, and closed shapes. Color choices and common global-touch options such as scaling and rotation are on the main tool palette in some programs; in others the user can access them via menus and dialog boxes or auxiliary palette choices.

Auxiliary palettes. Digital design and layout programs, like other graphics applications, increasingly use auxiliary palettes to organize tools and control their dif-

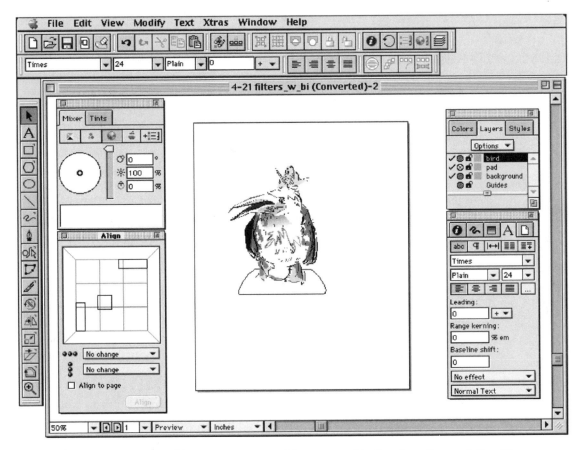

Figure 4.9 Digital design and layout program working area and tool and auxiliary palettes (Macromedia Freehand). The drawing area is a rectangular area with a small drop shadow and the main tool palette is on the far left. The toolbar below the menus provides direct access to many menu functions. *(Portions copyright 1998 Macromedia, Inc. Used with permission.)*

ferent settings. Both the main palette and menu choices can be used to call up auxiliary palettes. For instance, the user can often customize line- and curve-making tools in a main tool palette with line widths, colors and patterns chosen from an auxiliary palette.

Menus. Most tool-oriented functionality is accessed through palettes to keep menus uncrowded. Palettes often contain choices for specific global transformations, such as rotation and scaling, and for "plug-ins," or modular functions stored separately from the main program. The user can access type tools such as font and style choices from menus, as in many word processors, or may collect them in an auxiliary palette.

4.4 Touch

The sense of touch in digital design and layout programs is always mediated by the geometric methods used to describe object shapes. Gestural drawing is usually impractical. The artist can draw a curve, for instance, and receive visual feedback from the screen, as in a paint program, but the digital design and layout program must then create a mathematical description of the curve that the artist has drawn. This approximation can eliminate many subtleties not conveniently described by the types of mathematical functions used, and further editing is almost always required. In addition, changing the curve in current digital design and layout programs is nothing like redrawing a curve in a paint program. Although this process makes digital design and layout programs lack the direct, intuitive sense of touch of paint programs, it also makes available many new ways of "touching" that can lead to new ways of thinking about creating and compositing forms.

4.4.1 Local-Touch Tools

The visual vocabulary of digital design and layout programs is entirely composed of line and curve elements and ways of treating the spaces they enclose. Artists can create straight lines and certain types of curves. Areas enclosed by lines or curves can be filled with solid colors, color gradients, or patterns, or can be used to mask or clip other elements.

Vertices **Vertices** are selectable points on linear elements (straight and curved lines), like the dots in a connect-the-dots game. The artist can create them as part of forming new elements or add them to an existing line or curve between existing vertices. Each vertex in a PostScript shape can join only one ingoing and one outgoing curve or line.

Paths (Lines and Curves) A **path** is any linear element in a PostScript program that runs through an unbroken sequence of vertices (see Fig. 4.10). Paths are not visible until they are assigned a color, or, in PostScript terminology, are **stroked.** Paths in most PostScript-based programs can be stroked only with a single-weight line and a single color, although sometimes a pattern, typically dashes, can be used. This severe limitation mimics the effects of a ruling pen and other graphic design tools, but may make artists trained in the use of more variable media feel deprived. Ideally, paths could be stroked with any type of line defined by the programmer—a line that starts off thick and tapers off, for instance, or has fluctuating edges. Although such stroking is not currently available, its effect can be simulated in many programs with tools that draw a closed, filled shape resembling a paint-type brush stroke in appearance. Some programs create other effects by using paths as guides for tiled patterns, but such patterns are themselves made up of paths with a single width and single color. Figure 4.11 shows a range of path-stroking options. The interior region of a path can be filled with a single color, gradient, or pattern, as discussed in Section 4.4.3. (In some programs open paths

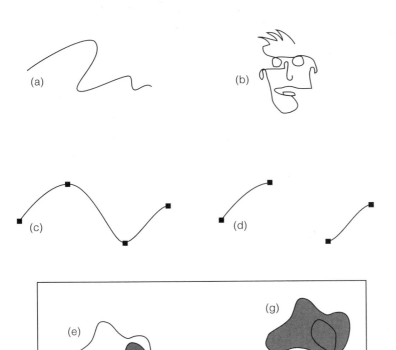

Figure 4.10 Open, closed, and filled paths. Vertices are shown as small black squares. In most digital design and layout programs, a shape's vertices become visible only when the shape is selected. (a) An open path. (b) Another open path. (c) A path with four vertices. (d) The same vertices used to make two separate paths. (e) A closed, unfilled path. (f) A closed, filled path. (g) Also a closed, filled path. (h) An open, filled path.

can also be filled.) Paths can also be used to mask or clip areas of a drawing. When a path is used in this way, only the graphics visible inside the path remain—the rest of the drawing is clipped away (see Fig. 4.12).

SPLINE CURVES   Both 2D and 3D image creation and animation programs make frequent use of a special class of curves called **splines** that are created by a mathematical technique that fits a curve to a set of given points called **control points.** Often the artist places the points, and then the program creates a curve based on them. A series of

(a)

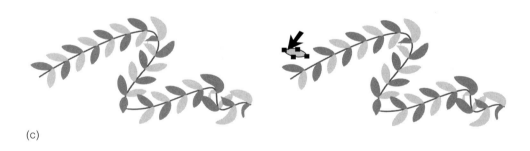

(b)

(c)

Figure 4.11 Stroking paths. (a) A path stroked with black, gray, and a dashed line. (b) A path drawn with a pressure-sensitive tablet that appears to have varying width. In fact, as can be seen on the right, this "path" is a filled shape. (c) The path on the left was used to guide a laurel pattern. Unlike real stroking, however, the pattern itself is made up of stroked paths, as shown at the right.

Figure 4.12 Using paths as clipping regions. An elliptical path was used as a mask or clipping region to change the framing of a lighthouse image.

straight lines through the points, a **polyline,** can be thought of as an unimaginative spline.

Some types of splines go near each control point but not through any of them (see Fig. 4.13a). **B-splines** blend positions of control points without passing through any of them and hence do not provide anchor points for precise location. Although difficult to use for sketching (if the interface merely allows the user to place the control points), this type of curve can be useful for tasks such as creating an animation or camera path among a number of objects. A particular variety of B-splines is sometimes referred to as a **nonuniform rational B-spline** (NURB). These curves are among the most frequently used curves in computer graphics. Others pass through some but not all the

Figure 4.13 Different types of splines. (a) B-spline. (b) Bezier curves. (c) Catmull–Rom spline.

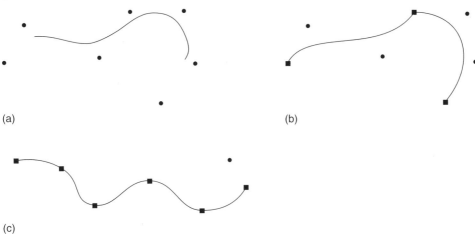

(a)

(b)

(c)

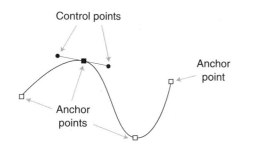

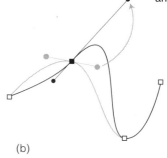

Control points

Anchor point

Anchor points

A control point moved further away from its anchor vertex

(a)

(b)

Figure 4.14 Use of control points to influence changes in curvature. (a) The lines between a vertex and a control point indicate the direction of the curve as it enters and then exits the anchor vertex. The distance from a vertex to a control point shows the proportional emphasis of the curve's direction. (b) Greater vertex-to-control-point distance makes the curve swing upward more dramatically. (Note that all anchor vertices remain unchanged.)

control points (see Fig. 4.13b). **Bezier curves,** named after French engineer Pierre Bezier, offer direct control over the location of the curve with anchor points (depicted as squares) and over the curvature between the points with two off-the-curve control points (depicted as disks). Bezier curves are particularly useful and flexible but require artists to work with off-path control points, which can be confusing. They are the curves most commonly used in digital design and layout programs. Still others pass through all their control points (see Fig. 4.13c). The Catmull–Rom spline restricts the curvature choices but puts all points on the curve itself, which can make drawing and editing more straightforward. Thus the same set of control points can produce different curves, depending on the type of spline used.

The off-the-curve control points of a Bezier curve represent the ends of lines that start from each anchor vertex and extend in the direction of the curve at that spot (see Fig. 4.14a). The direction of the line represents the direction of the curve; its length gives an indication of how far the curve continues in its present direction before heading toward the next vertex (see Fig. 4.14b).[3]

Graceful curves are the basis of many images by artist Jean-Pierre Hebert. He writes his own software to create beautiful compositions out of simple elements (see Fig. 4.15). These pieces are made not by placing vertices by hand but by designing algorithms that control the vertices and how the curves are drawn.

[3]For those of you who have had some calculus, the control points are the ends of tangent vectors and are used to change the slope of the curve, or the curve's first derivative. The length of the tangent line is often used to indicate the size of the second derivative, or how fast the slope is changing.

Figure 4.15 Jean-Pierre Hébert, detail of *N'a pas Dit Son Premier Mot,* 1993
(India ink on paper, HP plotter, 35.5" × 25.5"). *(Courtesy of Jean-Pierre Hébert)*

4.4.2 Working with Local-Touch Tools

Drawing with Paths

Both straight lines and curves depend on series of vertices, so path-drawing techniques are based on different strategies for placing those vertices (both anchor points and control points). Some path-drawing tools guarantee a certain type of vertex; others let you choose the vertex type while designing the path. (All vertices can, of course, be edited afterward.) Clicking and dragging methods include clicking and releasing the mouse button at each desired vertex location or clicking to place a vertex and dragging to adjust the path curvature before placing the next vertex (see Fig. 4.16a and b). You must judge whether the path-creation method should emphasize rapid vertex placement, curve adjustment while drawing, or other features.

Often a desire to draw without frequent starts and stops outweighs the desire to place each vertex individually. Freehand tools let you draw as though you are using a painting program. When you release the mouse, a curve approximating the hand-drawn line appears (see Fig. 4.16c). You can usually adjust the sensitivity or "tightness" of the curve approximation: the more sensitive the curve fitting, the more vertices are placed. Although this method yields a more exact interpretation of the curve, the frequent vertices create a bumpier path that often requires more editing than a looser but smoother version.

Figure 4.16 Creating paths. (a) Repeated clicking can be used to create a polyline. (b) By clicking and dragging control points, the user can shape a curved path at each new vertex. (A combination of clicking and click-dragging can be used to create paths composed of lines and curves.) (c) Freehand paths can be drawn with dragging, as in a paint program, freeing the artist from stop-and-go methods (top). Here, vertex location and control point positions are chosen automatically (bottom).

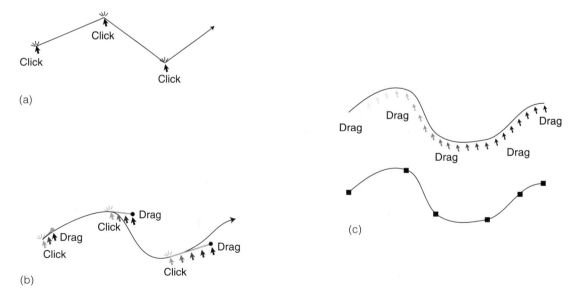

Painterly Brush Strokes with Paths   Currently, you can stroke the results of path-making tools only with a single line width and opaque color, and as a result all digital design and layout program lines have a similar character. One solution is a pressure-sensitive freehand tool, sometimes called a **brush tool,** that modulates mark width according to signals from a pressure-sensitive input device (see Fig. 4.17). This tool creates what looks like a line that varies in width but is actually a closed path stroked and filled with the same color. Although brushlike tools introduce intuitive mark-making vocabulary, editing the resulting shapes can be tedious.

Numeric Input   Another type of touch is available through the keyboard. You can type in numbers to define and alter objects numerically, to define and change their attributes textually, and (in some programs) to name the objects and record information about them. This last capability is vital in creating architectural plans or designing objects that will later be manufactured. Using numerical input yields a different kind of local touch. You can indicate all objects' positions, sizes, and relationships precisely. Such an approach facilitates drawing when measurement is important and lets you explore aesthetic ideas involving exactitude and numerically calculated, complex spatial relationships.

Editing as Touch   In the local-touch mark-making methods just described, skill in adjusting and editing paths is often as important as their initial creation. This editing-as-touch process is encouraged by the ease of changing aspects of the lines and fills and the difficulty of creating them exactly as desired the first time. The dynamic nature of paths offers great opportunities for accuracy in linear form. You can further edit paths by removing and adding vertices and by cutting them apart and joining them. You can also rearrange and recombine linear elements like elements of a construction set to create infinitely many combinations. Rearranging paths and tweaking linear objects' positions and curvatures are fundamentals of touch in 2D geometric programs.

4.4.3 Global-Touch Tools

After creating linear elements, you can work with attributes of the paths and any interior space they enclose including stroking lines with a color. A path enclosing an area can have a **fill**: a solid color, gradient, or pattern drawn

Figure 4.17 Pressure-sensitive path option. (a) Waves drawn with standard path options. (b) Waves drawn with a pressure-sensitive path option.

(a)

(b)

in the enclosed area (see Fig. 4.18). A fill is the only way to create a solid area of color. As with global-touch tools in a paint program, the entire area is colored at the same time—there are no local-touch coloring tools. Touch and color are therefore almost completely separate in digital design and layout programs. You must create areas of complex color with gradients and patterns or build them up as overlapping sequences of filled but unstroked shapes.

GRADIENTS You can use a separate **gradient tool** to blend colors (see Fig. 4.19). Most programs offer a choice of linear or radial gradients and many let you select not just beginning and end colors but intermediate ones as well.

Figure 4.18 Filling paths. (a) Bird wings were filled with white. The branch path was stroked with black. (b) Bird wings were filled with diamond pattern. The branch path was stroked with dashes. (c) Bird wings were filled with transparent stripe pattern. The branch path was stroked with gray. (d) Bird wings were filled with custom feather pattern. The branch path was stroked with rope pattern. (e) Bird wings were filled with a star pattern, the head was filled with a polka-dot pattern and back-filled with a confetti pattern, and the beak was filled with a black-to-white gradient. The branch path was stroked with a laurel pattern.

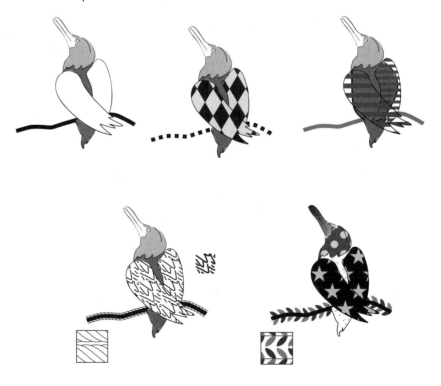

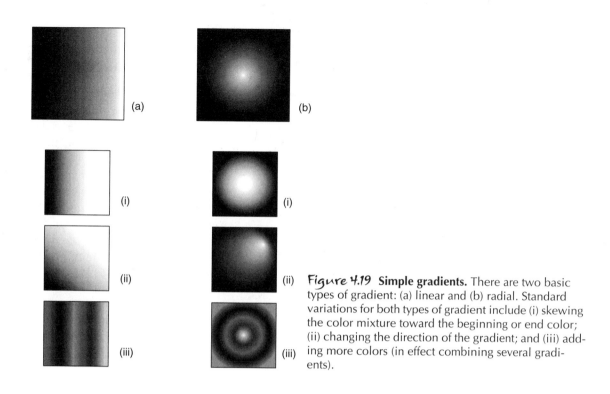

(a)   (b)

(i)   (i)

(ii)   (ii)

(iii)   (iii)

Figure 4.19 Simple gradients. There are two basic types of gradient: (a) linear and (b) radial. Standard variations for both types of gradient include (i) skewing the color mixture toward the beginning or end color; (ii) changing the direction of the gradient; and (iii) adding more colors (in effect combining several gradients).

BLENDING OR INTERPOLATION Many digital design and layout programs can implement global touches in incremental steps so as to make one object slowly change into another. This process, called **blending** or **interpolation** (guessing at new values between two or more known values), automatically calculates intermediate forms or colors. This blending technique, also sometimes called **morphing** (related to but not the same as the morphing described in Chapter 10, 2D and 3D Animation and Video), can be used to create subtle, highly controlled color blends (see Fig. 4.20) and to change one shape into another (see Fig. 4.21).

Figure 4.20 Blending colored shapes to create complex gradients. In Fig. 4.5, smoke from a factory chimney was enhanced in a paint program by smudging colors. Sometimes similar complex gradient effects can be produced in a digital design and layout program by using blends of differently colored shapes.

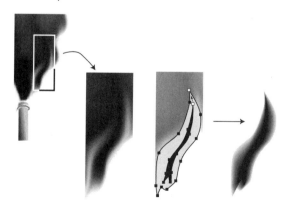

Figure 4.21 Blending shapes to create "morphs." The sitting bird on the left morphs into the flying bird in the middle and then into the airplane on the right.

ALGORITHMIC TOUCH Global transformations have not been as prevalent in digital design and layout programs as in paint programs, but are now being incorporated into them. The basic geometric transformations of translation, scaling, rotating, flipping, and sometimes distortion comprise the standard vocabulary of global image change. Many more elaborate algorithmic transformations (such as twirling the image around a center point or deforming it to give the impression of pinching) are offered by today's digital design and layout programs.

Just as a paint program's algorithmic processing options change pixels, design and layout programs often have options to process a selected group of vertices and paths. For example, certain options make the placement of vertices more erratic or allow rotation of a selected object by preset or random amounts. Figure 4.22 shows

Figure 4.22 Algorithmic touches used to change the feeling of a drawing. (a) Initial bird drawing. This same drawing was altered in each of (b)–(e) by applying only a single filter effect. (b) Adobe Illustrator's Twirl filter at 60°. (c) Adobe Illustrator's Ink Pen filter (with one combination of the many settings available). (d) MetaCreations KPT Vector Effects'® Sketch filter with a small sketch effect. (e) MetaCreations KPT Vector Effects' Warp frame filter.

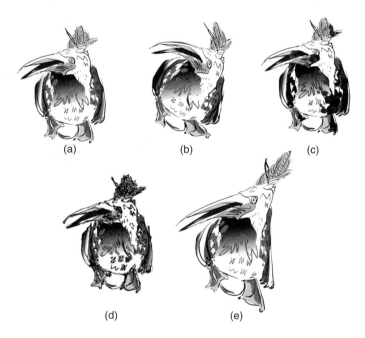

(a) (b) (c)

(d) (e)

how these effects can be used to change the feeling of a drawing algorithmically. Most often such effects are applied to a portion of a drawing or image, not the entire work.

An algorithmic process in a paint program takes in pixels and, no matter how complex it is, spits out pixels. In a 2D geometric graphics program, algorithmic effects can automatically change the geometry of an image in ways that make it impossible to change back. Paths can be broken up and often large numbers of new objects and vertices are produced, making the image difficult if not impossible to edit further. Automated variations are the basis of much early computer art (see Fig. 4.23 and also Chapter 1) and continue to be used by many artists.

4.4.4 BOOLEAN OPERATIONS (ADDING AND SUBTRACTING SHAPES)

Combining object definitions to create new forms is also a global operation. Such combinations, called **Boolean operations** after mathematician George Boole,[4] include **union** (adding objects together), **intersection** (preserving only the area common to both objects), **difference** (subtracting objects from one another), and **exclusion** (creating a shape that includes everything but the area of intersection) (see Fig. 4.24).

In digital design and layout programs, Boolean operations can subtract one path from another (letting you form complex negative spaces), create a single path based on an outline of a number of objects, or create new objects from areas where objects overlap (see Fig. 4.25).

Figure 4.23 Georg Nees, *Gravel Stones*, c. 1965. In this early piece, Nees repeated a square across a row and varied its rotation by random, increasingly large amounts. *(Courtesy of Georg Nees)*

---

[4]George Boole (1815–1864) invented an algebra of logic consisting of two classes of objects and the basic operators AND, OR, and NOT. This symbolic algebra is crucial to the working of much modern technology, from telephone switching to digital computers. Boolean algebra also provides a natural way to work with the union and intersection of sets of elements. Here, the sets are shapes.

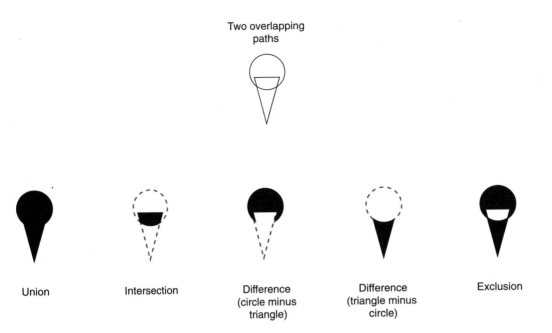

Two overlapping
paths

Union   Intersection   Difference
(circle minus
triangle)   Difference
(triangle minus
circle)   Exclusion

Figure 4.24 Some basic Boolean operations.

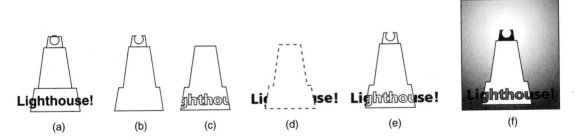

(a)   (b)   (c)   (d)   (e)   (f)

Figure 4.25 Example of the use of Boolean operations. (a) Components of a lighthouse: a base, tower, top, circle for the light, and letters spelling out "Lighthouse!". (b) Base and tower were joined into one path with *union*. The top and circle created a new path with *difference* (the top minus the circle). (c) The Lighthouse! text was translated into paths and subtracted from the form created in (b) with *difference*. (d) With the reverse *difference* process, the new tower of (b) was subtracted from the text paths to create the ends of the Lighthouse! text. (e) The text pieces were arranged to recreate the word Lighthouse! (f) The various combinations were all used to create a sense of light in the final piece. A radial gradient was centered in the middle of the top piece (which was filled with a dark gray). The gradient shows through the text that crosses the body of the lighthouse but does not affect the text on the ends. The unioned tower and base form was filled with white and stroked with black.

4.4.5 TYPOGRAPHY

Although letters have more specific predefined cultural meanings than the lines and curves of which they are made, the ease with which text can be worked with and incorporated into imagery encourages its use in digital design and layout programs. For designers laying out an ad or designing a brochure, typography is obviously essential. The same professional quality control that attracts designers to digital design and layout programs is a wonderful tool for any artist incorporating text with other visual elements in a work. Many digital design and layout programs include standard text-control features such as tabs and margin settings, spell checking, word wrap, and text flow from one area to another, as well as typographic controls over kerning, horizontal spacing, and ligatures. Type can be placed anywhere on a page and rotated, scaled, and deformed, just like any other digital design and layout object. Text can flow inside or around irregular shapes and can follow the path of any curve. In addition, typographic forms can be translated into collections of geometric curves and lines and worked with like any other object. For example, in Fig. 4.26 (from left to right) the letters K 8 were set in Futura; the 8 was scaled 90%; the 8 was rotated so that its axis is parallel with the K's upstroke; the 8 was translated leftward to overlap with the K, and the text was converted to outlines; using the Boolean *exclusion* operation, the overlapping sections were reversed out; the altered text was used in conjunction with other items to create the logo.

The ability to combine text and images is the basis of a whole class of programs not discussed here—**desktop publishing** applications. Instead of using a single-page paradigm like the programs discussed here, they include controls for handling multiple pages of text, such as automatic page numbering, headings, and style sheets, and controls for multiple text flows. Images usually are imported into a desktop publishing document and cannot be edited. The image creation tools offered in page layout programs, such as Adobe PageMaker®, Quark Express®, and Adobe Framemaker®, are only subsets of design and layout-type programs.

Artist Craig Hickman (creator of Broderbund's innovative Kid Pix program) uses digital design and layout programs, as well as image-editing programs, to create images, work with text, and combine the two in artists' books that comment on the

Figure 4.26 Text can be altered like any other geometric object. Altered letters were used to create a logo (based on the business founder's apartment number in New York City).

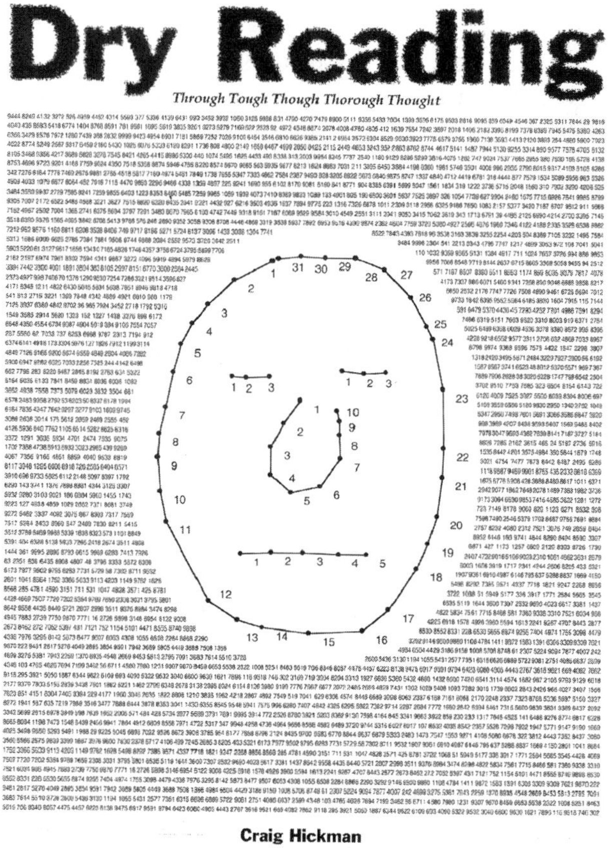

Figure 4.27 Craig Hickman, *Dry Reading,* **1991** (cover, artist book, 8.5″ × 11″, 24 pages). The connect-the-dots face and background of seemingly random multidigit numbers suggest some sort of scientific analysis, but the expression of the face (dozing) and the furry letters in the title immediately eliminate this possibility. *(Courtesy of Craig Hickman)*

use of such technologies. In *Dry Reading* (see Fig. 4.27), a play on the look of desktop publishing (it is made with the same computer tools) and scholarly journals, Hickman used text and images within the context of conventional format (8.5″ × 11″) off-white, staple-bound pages to comment on visual and textual conventions. Throughout the book, the formal visual structures—text in columns, nicely arranged images with a variety of halftone effects, bulleted lists, and the like—suggest some sort of scholarly quasi-scientific newsletter, but the content (or lack thereof) provides a humorous and telling commentary on such works. In a spread called Frame of Reference from *Dry Reading* (see Fig. 4.28), Hickman filled the text columns with words whose only relationship to one another is that they all begin with either "e" or "f." Drop caps, introductory and in-text quotes, footnotes, and occasional italics as well as a bullet-point list give these pages a sense of authority that is aided by the processed-looking images.

Figure 4.28 Craig Hickman, *Dry Reading,* 1991 (pages 6 and 7, artist book, 8.5″ × 11″, 24 pages). *(Courtesy of Craig Hickman)*

4.4.6 Importing Raster Images

Another aspect of a digital design and layout program's touch is the ability to include raster images. In the piece shown in Fig. 4.29, Michael Holcomb combined curves and gradations made with a digital design and layout program and paint-type images, created elsewhere and arranged within the composition. He combined the two types of mark making to extend the range of textures and visual interest of the work. Holcomb views the formal layering and nature of the different types of marks as a metaphor for a "conceptual layering of sense and nonsense, a composite of visual puns, bitmaps, and objects, photographic realism and 3D computer cartoons in an 'apparent' image" [Holcomb, 1996].

Although a raster image cannot be edited pixel by pixel in most of today's design and layout programs, it can be imported, displayed, moved, scaled, and rotated. These two types of computer graphics are fundamentally distinct: One is based on pixels and the other on geometry. Bringing a paint image into a digital design and layout program

Figure 4.29 Michael Holcomb, *Professor of Bee Attitude,* **1994.** *(Courtesy of Michael Holcomb)*

does not make it an editable geometric composition, and bringing a geometric image into a paint program rasterizes the geometry. There is no reason, however, not to build a program that allows both types of editing in the same document. Some programs already combine a mix of raster- and vector-based features (see Section 4.6).

4.5 COMPOSITION

Geometry-based programs offer unique compositional tools inspired by traditional graphic design needs, CAD, and sometimes the computer itself. Artists who program their own 2D geometric work often use compositional tactics that are radically different from the Western, Renaissance notion of arrangements of objects as seen from a single point of view in a perspective space. Early computer artists more often explored "spaces" of permutations and composed with aesthetic statistical variations that were only later represented by visible forms (see Chapter 1). Refer to Chapter 7, Building 3D Worlds—3D Geometric Graphics I for a discussion of additional algorithmic compositional strategies.

4.5.1 THE PAGE

The drawing area in a design and layout program has two distinct regions, a rectangular **page,** or printable area, and a **scratch area** around the page. Tools function identically in both regions, but only information on the page is sent to the printer. Page dimensions are easily changed, and reducing the page size does not eliminate any part of the image—it is still visible in the scratch area. The page–scratch area relationship is an intuitive compositional support, letting the artist easily see the effects of moving the edges of a piece. Because the edges are visualized within a larger area, the aesthetic interactions of object images and the spatial limits of the piece are easy to explore.

4.5.2 Placement

Many guides exist to help with object placement, including tools and methods that work with numeric measurements and ensure orderly part-to-part connection. Most CAD programs, and many digital design and layout programs, measure and produce text labels for line lengths and angle degrees (see Fig. 4.30). Most digital design and layout programs also provide nonprinting customizable grids and movable guidelines.

Objects can also be organized into preset arrangements through menu and dialog choices of align and distribute. **Align** arranges selected objects relative to one another along horizontal and vertical axes. **Distribute** equalizes the distance between objects, as measured from their centers or most extreme points. By using align and distribute in concert, you can place objects in predictable horizontal and vertical formations (see Fig. 4.31). In many forms of design, such control is invaluable.

Precise positioning along axes and the even distribution of objects are used by Manfred Mohr in Fig. 4.32 to create a composition from random paths through hypercubes (four-dimensional cubes). Mohr favors the computer because it lets him explore variations of form in an exhaustive, statistical manner. His custom software, which principally uses lines, has in common with commercial digital design and layout programs the ability to make "precision [a] part of aesthetical expression" and aid in "high-speed execution and therefore multiplicity and comparativity of the works" [Mohr in Leavitt, 1976, p. 96].

4.5.3 Composing with Objects: Groups and Layers

Every object in a digital design and layout program has a **stacking order**: It is either behind or in front of every other object. When two objects are in the same place, one overlaps the other, often creating the illusion of depth. Because all objects overlap in exactly the same way, however, the result all too frequently suggests a very flat,

Figure 4.30 Anne Morgan Spalter, *Rate × Time = Distance,* **1991** (laserwriter printout photocopied onto 18″ × 24″ paper). Here, the artist used the automatic line- and angle-measuring capabilities of a CAD program to investigate an emotional, potentially dramatic scene—a multiple-car crash—analytically and quantitatively. The geometry-based tools allow one to focus almost exclusively on deconstructing the scene according to formal visual relationships.

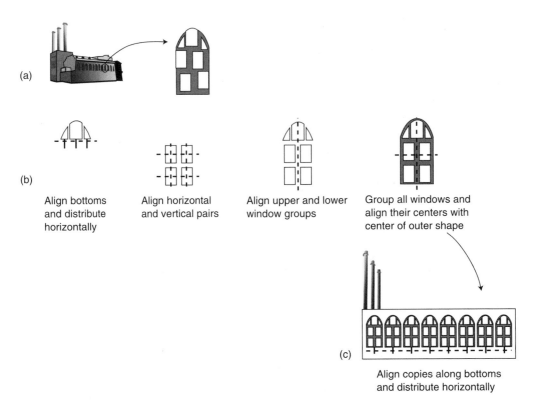

(a)

(b)

Align bottoms
and distribute
horizontally

Align horizontal
and vertical pairs

Align upper and lower
window groups

Group all windows and
align their centers with
center of outer shape

(c)

Align copies along bottoms
and distribute horizontally

Figure 4.31 Align and distribute example. Windows and other repetitive, symmetric forms are perfect candidates for automated composition tools such as align and distribute. (a) The pieces of the window were created and moved into approximate positions. (b) The pieces then were composed in groups and finally with one another to form the window object. (c) The windows themselves were then arrayed on the side of the building by using alignment and distribution.

uniformly lit shallow trough in which the entire image lies. As illustrated in Fig. 4.33, filled objects cover objects "below" them and unfilled objects, like the triangle, allow others to show through. A feeling of deeper space can be evoked by traditional spatial cues such as perspective and shadows and coloring that support illusionistic space.

MANAGING OBJECTS FOR COMPOSITION   Methods for managing objects are extremely important in design and layout programs. Detailed images are almost always composed of many smaller objects because each shape can have only one interior fill and one exterior line description.

All digital design and layout programs offer **grouping**: the ability to make a number of objects act as one in order to change them all in the same way at the same time. Grouping objects does not, however, join their paths and fills. By grouping selected objects together, the artist can move, rotate, and perform other operations while retaining the objects' spatial interrelationships.

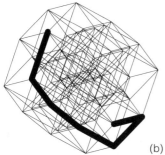

Figure 4.32 Manfred Mohr, *P-480/101011*, 1992 (ink on paper, 30 cm × 30 cm; collection of Catherine and Françoise Treves, Paris). (a) Each of the lines making up this work is a path traversing (b) a six-dimensional hypercube along its edges. *(Courtesy of Manfred Mohr)*

Objects that are grouped retain their relative stacking order, but the group as a whole is treated as a single object that must exist in front of or behind all other objects on the page. Thus objects not in the group cannot be interwoven with any grouped objects.

Often the artist may want to change the position of collections of objects in the stacking order without forcing them to act as a single object. Most digital design and

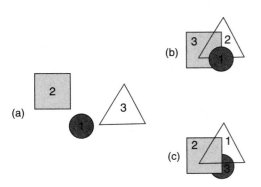

Figure 4.33 Stacking order. (a) Stacking order is not obvious when objects do not overlap, but each object has its own place in the stacking order and is in front of or behind every other object. (b) and (c) Objects can be moved up and down in the stacking order.

layout programs offer user-defined **layers** for this purpose. Each layer can be viewed (and printed) separately and layer order can be easily changed. Objects can be grouped within a layer, but usually not across layers.

Layers can be "turned off" (not drawn on the screen) to keep the composition process fluid and reactive—because rasterizing many geometric object descriptions can take considerable time, removing unnecessary layers from view improves response time. Hiding layers also helps the artist see objects in other layers more clearly. "Locking" a layer prevents unintended changes.

Layers are particularly helpful for organizing drawings containing many logically or visually distinct object collections, such as a detailed anatomical study or a house plan with wiring and plumbing layout overlays. In Fig. 4.34, for instance, the artist used layers to isolate the different, often overlapping carousel horses during the drawing process and to change and hide the background photo and the foreground text. Because each horse is composed of many individual shapes and grouped areas of detail, layers were important to prevent the inadvertent selection of details of one horse while working on another. And, because the horses were originally traced from the background photograph, it was essential to be able to view each horse and the background separately, without other horses intervening. Layers were also useful in making print tests of the different aspects of the piece.

4.5.4   Size and Scale

In many ways the concept of the size of a geometric description is not very meaningful. The rulers along horizontal and vertical axes in digital design and layout programs are relevant only as a reference in printing. The objects that comprise the image can be rerasterized at any scale and resolution without degrading the image or changing the file size. Because digital design and layout images usually are not created to be viewed on the screen, however, their size is often defined as the intended printing dimensions.

File size in a geometry-based program has a relationship to the visual status of the image but not necessarily to its dimensions. It can be more usefully thought of as a measure of complexity of the piece: As each object is added in the piece, the file size becomes larger. Descriptions of objects that are simple and have no fills take less room to store than descriptions of the same number of complicated, filled shapes.

Two-dimensional geometry-based programs distinguish between changing a shape's definition by moving individual vertices and changing its scale. In the first case, the line

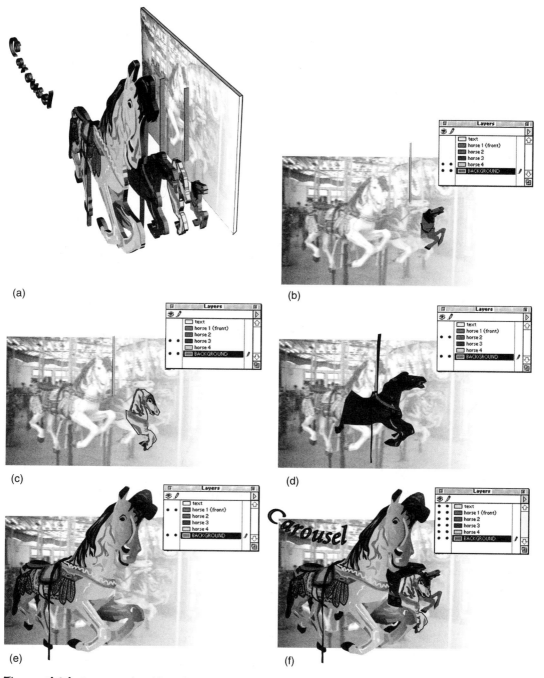

Figure 4.34 An example of layering. (a) This diagram shows the concept of layering and depicts each horse, the background image, and the text in separate layers (real layers do not have any 3D properties). (b) The background photo and the first horse layer. (c), (d), and (e) show the second, third, and fourth horses. (f) All the layers.

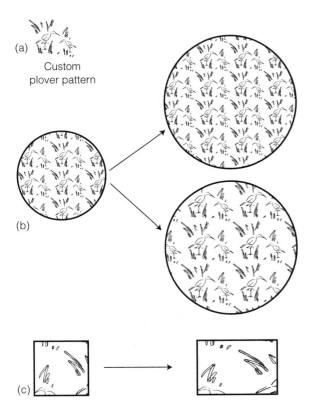

(a) Custom plover pattern

(b)

(c)

Figure 4.35 Subtleties of scaling. The visual effect of scaling depends in part on how object outlines and patterned fills are handled. (a) A custom plover pattern. (b) First, a circle was scaled uniformly by 150%, as shown on the top, without scaling of the line weight or the patterned fill, and then, as shown on the bottom, with both line weight and pattern scaled. (c) When a shape is scaled nonuniformly, the line remains a single weight but the interior pattern can be distorted.

width stays the same; in the second, the line width can change in proportion to the scale factor. Patterned fills can also be scaled with the image or set to remain the same size and increase in number (see Fig. 4.35). In current programs, the line always has a constant width around the entire object perimeter, even if the scaling affects the object nonuniformly, say, by squashing it vertically while expanding it greatly horizontally. Patterns, however, if changed with scaling, can become distorted if nonuniform scaling is used.

Compositional aesthetics in digital design and layout programs can change noticeably with changes in scaling. Complexity and detail are affected immediately. Geometry-based images do not become blurry or grainy or develop artifacts when scaled, but rather remain sharp and clear. The new relationships among linear and color-filled areas emphasize disproportionate increases in surface area (fills) over the increased width of linear elements. Often line width must be adjusted after scaling to maintain the desired balance between the linear and filled components of a piece. Colored fills may also need adjusting: an image that has pictorial depth and linear variety at a small size may appear flat and oversimplified when scaled up.

4.5.5 ACCURACY AS A COMPOSITIONAL TOOL

The accessibility of numeric calculation and physical measurement in computer-based art provides useful new ways for artists to conceptualize and compose their work. Digital design and layout programs, evolving along with more industry-specific CAD programs, often let artists create and position objects with numeric input. Relationships among objects—the essence of composition—can thus be considered visually and empirically and implemented quantitatively (as illustrated previously in Fig. 4.30).

Computer artists who program their own work often use numeric input to describe objects or parameters.

4.5.6 COLOR

Color selection in design and layout programs is often tedious. Although names and swatches are available for color systems such as PANTONE®, color pickers that provide views of a number of color-space slices are rare. The emphasis in color choice and management, as in other aspects of design and layout programs, is on printing. Palettes can be used to collect colors, but the process of color definition (if the artist does not want to use a preset list of swatches) is often time-consuming. Once custom palettes have been designed, however, they can be stored with a template document for later use.

Colors can be applied only to paths or areas enclosed by paths. In programs currently available, each object can have only a single path color and a single fill. Fills can be solid colors, gradients, and preset or customized patterns and tiles. Under these rather severe restrictions, modulated color can be difficult to achieve. Gradients offer a way to create transitions between colors, letting artists create a sense of spatial depth and of light falling on objects. Color issues in digital design and layout and other programs are discussed further in Chapter 5, Electronic Color.

4.6 COMBINING RASTER AND GEOMETRY-BASED GRAPHICS

Increasingly, applications are combining the various object-definition and composition concepts from 2D geometry-based programs with the direct, often more intuitive and varied pixel-changing methods of paint and photoediting programs. For example, the geometry-based concepts of discrete objects can be combined with raster images by letting users define a selected area of a paint image as a **paint object,** or **sprite,** that can be clicked on, dragged and put in front of or behind other objects in a stacking order. MetaCreations Painter and Microsoft ImageComposer both offer such paint-type objects. Adobe Photoshop involves a different approach, offering a stack of layers in which one can work. A **layer** is merely a paint object that is the same size as the canvas area. Whatever they are called, sprites or layers or paint objects combine visually to create an integrated 2D image but remain separate for editing purposes.

In addition to aiding in composition, geometry-based tools are often used with paint and photoediting programs to aid in the selection process. A **path tool** that lets the artist create a Bezier curve or spline is commonly used to define selection areas. Unlike a freehand or lasso tool, a path tool creates fully editable lines and curves that can be saved and changed at any time. Such selection tools are extremely valuable for selecting complex objects and objects with curves. Figure 4.36 shows the use of object-based selection and composition to define and arrange paint objects.

Figure 4.36 Geometry-based selection tools and paint-type objects. (a) Original image. (b) An outline was created of the leftmost boat and child with geometry-based path tools; the path was converted to a selection. (c) This and other selections were defined as discrete paint objects or sprites. Paint objects can be stored for easy reuse. Here, for instance, a lighthouse from elsewhere was added. Partially transparent drop shadows were added to the boats and lighthouse, and the water was touched up to remove the boats.

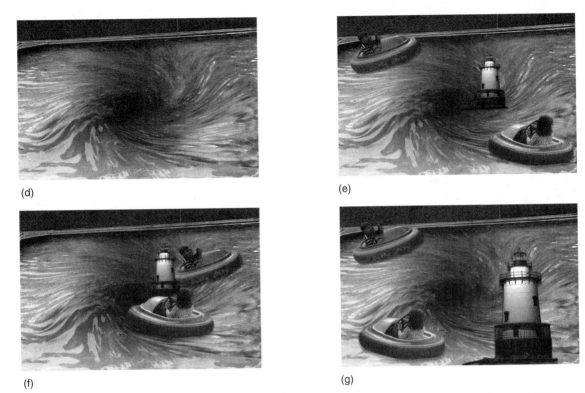

(d)   (e)

(f)   (g)

Figure 4.36 (continued) (d) The water was distorted with various algorithmic raster-based tools. (e) The paint objects can be dragged to different locations to experiment with different compositions. (f) Like geometry-based objects, paint objects have a stacking order that can be changed. Here the stacking order was used to overlap images, emphasizing spatial relationships. (g) Paint objects can be individually scaled, as well as rotated or otherwise distorted. Here the lighthouse was scaled up.

The act of moving paint objects around immediately suggests animation possibilities. The use of paint objects or sprites is indeed important in computer animation (see Chapter 10, 2D and 3D Animation and Video).

Another approach, the one taken by MetaCreations Expression® and FutureWave SmartSketch®, uses tools that behave similarly to paint tools but create geometric lines, curves, and fills. Brush and eraser tools are used to create and alter paths, for instance, a more intuitive alternative to the techniques required in most design and layout programs (see Fig. 4.37). As in the standard digital design and layout programs, a tool can be used to create shapes that give the impression of variable-width paths. Unlike other digital design and layout programs, however, the number and position of vertices are modified to create more simple shapes. The desired balance of objects and geometry-versus sample-based imagery depends on the artist's specific needs.

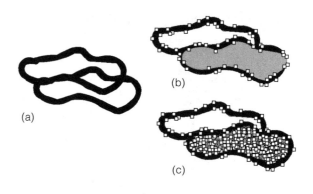

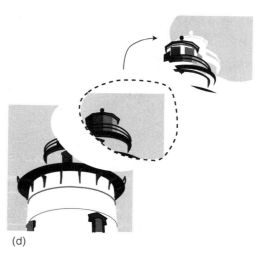

Figure 4.37 FutureWave SmartSketch, a
geometry-based program with paintlike tools.
Compare the number of vertices created by filling in a cloud (a) by sketching with the brush
tool in FutureWave SmartSketch (b) to that in a
more standard digital design and layout program
(c). (d) Paintlike selection tools divide paths to
make a clean separation. All of the components
that result remain selectable as geometric
objects (right top). (e) Similarly, erasing removes
paths, splitting and closing off shapes to form
new pieces in the image. The eraser is used on
the lighthouse (left). The resulting paths are
shown without fills at right.

Hybrid approaches often inherit constraints as well as create new features. For
example, although using sprites aids in composition, it also usually means that multiple objects cannot be painted across, portions of several objects cannot be selected
together, and every object must be in front of or behind every other object. Simi-

larly, although using paint-type tools to make and edit geometry-based marks is intriguing and in some cases useful, at other times the sheer number of small objects created when differently colored lines overlap or pieces of a shape are erased can make editing difficult.

There is no doubt that the features of 2D raster and geometry-based programs will continue to merge into applications offering useful blends of the two, combining digital painting, photoediting, and image processing with more geometric compositional tools, movable geometric and raster-based objects and typographical control.

Conclusion

This chapter introduced a new paradigm for image creation: the use of continuous geometric object descriptions versus images based on arrays of pixels. Design and layout programs are only one type of 2D geometry-based application and are targeted chiefly to the needs of graphic designers and illustrators working with print media. Historically, however, artists used geometry-based methods long before raster-based methods, and many noteworthy artists continue to work with object-creation and composition strategies based on geometric object descriptions.

Virtually every concept and method discussed in this chapter, including continuous geometric object definitions, selection methods, antialiasing, fills, interpolated shapes, algorithms that change shapes, Boolean operations, spline curves, and automated compositional tools such as grouping, aligning, and distributing, is essential not only in all 2D geometry-based programs but also in both 3D and animation programs. Three-dimensional modeling programs take geometric object descriptions to the next physical dimension; animation and video programs let artists use splines, interpolation, and object-based composition tools to control both 2D and 3D raster- and geometry-based elements over time.

Suggested Readings

Kerlow, Isaac Victor, and Judson Rosebush. *Computer Graphics for Designers and Artists,* 2d ed., Van Nostrand Reinhold, 1996. Kerlow is a long-time computer artist, teacher (founder of Pratt Institute's computer graphics program) and force in the computer art community, Rosebush is well respected in the computer science world. Their book was written for artists but is technically sophisticated. The style is like hypertext "lexia," little tidbits and self-contained units of knowledge. Although it has an overall structure, the book is more a reference than a narrative or high-level "how to," with explanations of most of the key terms used in computer graphics and illustrated with plenty of color images.

Mitchell, William J. *The Reconfigured Eye, Visual Truth in the Post-Photographic Era.* MIT Press, 1992. This treatment of 2D and 3D imaging topics (but not the 2D geometric part) is less technical and more theory-oriented than in Mitchell and McCullough's *Digital Design Media.*

Mitchell, William J., and Malcolm McCullough. *Digital Design Media,* 2d ed., Van Nostrand Reinhold, 1995. Originally entitled *Digital Design Media, A Handbook for Architects and Design Professionals,* this book covers, from a practical viewpoint, a wide range of technical subjects, from basic graphics principles in 2D and 3D design to various aspects of production. The theme is computer-aided design (CAD), especially as applied to architecture. Although much of the book is devoted to 3D, the chapter on "Drafted Lines" is a non-PostScript–based presentation of 2D geometry-based graphics. The next chapter, "Polygons, Plans, and Maps," provides an approach to 2D different from the one used in the present book and in most books aimed at designers.

Tufte, Edward R. *The Visual Display of Quantitative Information.* Graphics Press, 1983; Tufte, Edward R. *Envisioning Information.* Graphics Press, 1990; Tufte, Edward R. *Visual Explanations: Images and Quantities, Evidence and Narrative,* Graphics Press, 1997. These three books by Tufte are lush, self-published volumes full of engaging and enlightening examples of both good and bad information design, from maps of Napoleon's armies to diagrams for the space shuttle. *The Visual Display of Quantitative Information* and *Envisioning Information* deal with static graphics; *Visual Explanations* leaps into the world of change and motion and the computer. The flexibility and precision of line and color offered by draw-type programs make them perfect for experimenting with the ideas presented in all three texts.

Exercises

1. *Self-Portrait in Two Graphics Paradigms.* Create a self-portrait in a digital design and layout program. Now rasterize it and work with it in a paint program. Note at least three substantial differences between the two approaches. How do they relate to the concepts underlying the two program types? How do the different graphics paradigms used affect your presentation and the aspects of yourself that you focus on and are able to communicate?

> With Adobe Illustrator 7.0 and Adobe Photoshop 5.0: Create a self-portrait in Illustrator, using the Pen tool and freehand Pencil tools to create linear elements and boundaries of shapes. (If you have a pressure-sensitive tablet, try the Brush tool as well.) Experiment with solid fills and gradients to fill areas with flat and modulated colors. Save your image in the Illustrator format. Now open Photoshop and open your Illustrator file from within Photoshop. Photoshop's Image Size ... dialog box will come up, with the dimensions of your image and a suggested resolution. Set the resolution to 200–300 dpi (or within practical limits of your machine). Choose Anti-aliased by clicking on its check box. Work with the image in Photoshop, using drawing tools such as the Brush and Airbrush as well as options like the Blur and Smudge tools. Some filters may be useful too.

2. *Moody Gradients.* Create a piece depicting a specific place and mood, using shapes with no outlines, filled with different customized gradients. Create atmosphere and space by layering gradients and using shape-blending to create complex gradients.

> With Adobe Illustrator 7.0: Turn off outlines by choosing the "none" in the stroke option of the main tool palette. Create several custom gradients by using the gradient palette, giving them descriptive names. Put all of them in the swatches palette for easy access. Choose one of your gradient fills and begin drawing the shapes for your image. Experiment with

more complex gradient creations, using the Blend tool. (Use the Direct-selection tool to select a single vertex on each of two objects. Choose the Blend tool and click on one vertex and then the other. Choose a number of in-between shapes and click on OK.)

3. *Interpolation Creatures.* Make several simple drawings of recognizable animals. Choose sets of two and use shape interpolation or blending to create new, intermediate animals.

> With Adobe Illustrator 7.0: Explore the Blend tool in more detail. Experiment with changing the percentage contributions of the shapes and with blending colors and shapes at the same time.

4. *Designing with Type.* Make a personal business card (go wild with the profession). Use type, directly or converted to outlines and modified, to convey your professional expertise and to design a simple graphic.

> With Adobe Illustrator 7.0: Use the Type tool to type the needed words. Type in your name, address, and company as separate text items so that you can move them around easily. Draw a box to represent a 3.5″ × 2″ business card and arrange the text within it. In addition to the basic textual information, use textual elements of the company name to create a logo or in some way add a graphical element to the card. Note: You may need to change the text to outlines to achieve the desired effects.

5. *Your Own Composition Tool.* Write a one-page design for a new digital design and layout program composition feature that you would find useful. Start by considering the compositional tools available in your digital design and layout program. What probably inspired the programmers to add these particular options? What audience are they intended for? Would your tool address a different audience? Explain.

6. *Fix-It-Yourself.* Use the desktop publishing capabilities of digital design and layout programs (or a real desktop publishing program), such as making polished diagrams, importing paint images, and working with type, to create an instructional booklet on a fix-it-yourself project of your choice (real or imaginary).

> With Adobe Illustrator 7.0: As Illustrator is geared to single-page projects, make this a one-page instructional handout. Use lines to create rules and click and drag with the Text tool to create text areas. For an interesting effect, create a shape and position the Text tool on the edge of the shape and then click to make the text flow within the shape. You can also make text flow along a path in this way. Use simple and complex shapes to create technical-looking diagrams (the Stylize:Add Arrowheads filter can be helpful). Create a banner headline and text headings to guide a novice through the steps necessary to fix your product.

CHAPTER 5

Electronic Color

Figure 5.1 Brightness contrast, one example of the relative nature of color. Two identical grays appear different, depending on their background: a lighter background makes the gray look darker; a darker background makes the gray look lighter. This effect, called **brightness contrast**, is one of the many phenomena reinforcing the relative nature of color. On the screen, as on paper or canvas, the instability of color and its variable psychic effects have not succumbed to scientific explanation. However, an understanding of some concepts in color science and color theory can greatly enhance the scope of an artist or designer's work on the computer.

5.1 INTRODUCTION

Just as the knowledge of acoustics does not make one musical—neither on the productive nor on the appreciative side—so no color system by itself can develop one's sensitivity for color. This is parallel to the recognition that no theory of composition by itself leads to the production of music, or of art [Albers, 1987, p. 2].

Joseph Albers, color theorist, teacher, and painter.

The computer lets artists experiment with color to an unprecedented degree, often completely changing the process of making, applying, and revising color decisions. Colors can be chosen from geometric "color spaces" (see Section 5.8), compared numerically, applied, reapplied, erased without repercussions, and altered in powerful and subtle ways. The extraordinary flexibility of electronic color makes it a much more dynamic and independent part of image creation and composition than it is in any traditional medium.

Although effective use of color on the computer depends more than anything else on a general understanding of color and experience with it, several concepts are unique to the computer. A working knowledge of these concepts lets artists and designers take full advantage of the potential of color in all aspects of computer-based work, from scanning and on-screen design to display and printing.

5.1.1 Visible Light

Visible light occurs in but one small part of the full electromagnetic spectrum—the part with wavelengths from about 400 to 700 nm (a nanometer is a billionth of a meter). Longer wavelengths are invisible infrared or heat radiation; even longer wavelengths (up to several feet long) are microwave and FM radio waves (AM radio waves can be more than 300 m long!). Shorter wavelengths include X rays and gamma rays (see Fig. 5.2).[1] In the mid 1600s, Isaac Newton passed white light through a glass prism and saw a rainbow emerge from the other side: The prism was refracting the light at different angles, according to its wavelength. (He also noted that this rainbow of light could be passed through a second prism to reconstitute white light.) The 400–500 nm waves appeared reddish and orangish to him, and the higher-frequency/shorter-wavelength light, at the other end of the rainbow or spectrum, appeared blue. He deduced that white light was composed of all the colors of the spectrum (see Fig. 5.3).

5.2 Subtractive Versus Additive Color Mixing

The colors of the spectrum are limited because each one comprises only one wavelength of light. However, many more colors can be created by mixing different spectral wavelengths of light. Purple, for instance, is a mixture of low (reddish)- and high (bluish)-frequency light. In general, adding new colors of light to a mixture increases the number of frequencies present, and the mixture becomes closer to white. If enough different colors of light are added, white light results. When more light energy of any wavelength is added, the mixture becomes brighter. Thus mixing light is called an **additive** color mixing system. This is the type of color mixing used in a theater to illuminate the actors and sets, or on the screen of a computer monitor.[2]

The type of color mixing familiar to most artists is that done not with lights but with paints or pigments. Each color of paint can be thought of as a filter that removes all the light frequencies except the one meeting the eye. For example, a red paint reflects back only the wavelengths that create a sensation of red; the rest are absorbed. Mixing in more and more different colors leads to darker and darker results as more

---

[1]Energy can be described in terms of wavelength or frequency. These are different ways of looking at the same phenomena: Longer wavelengths mean lower frequencies, and shorter wavelengths mean higher frequencies.

[2]Computer screens actually use **partitive mixing**, in which the eye averages different colored lights (screen phosphors), as opposed to true additive mixing in which light colors have already been combined. The distinction between partitive and additive is not used here, however, because there is little practical difference for computer artists.

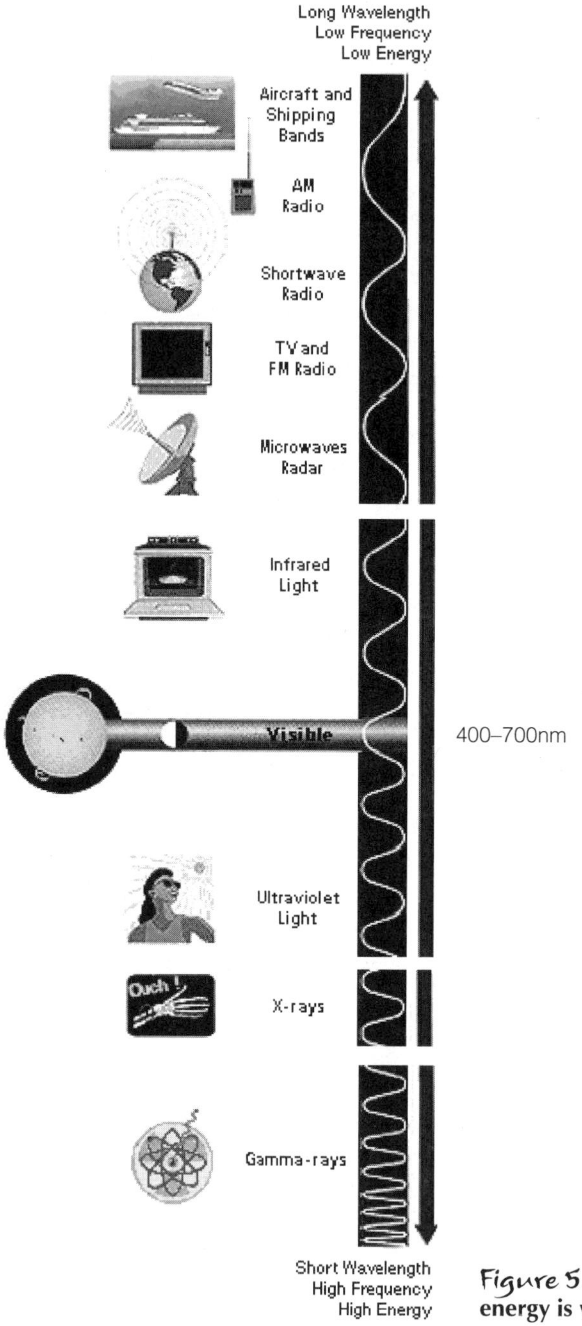

Long Wavelength
Low Frequency
Low Energy

Aircraft and
Shipping
Bands

AM
Radio

Shortwave
Radio

TV and
FM Radio

Microwaves
Radar

Infrared
Light

Visible   400–700nm

Ultraviolet
Light

X-rays

Gamma-rays

Short Wavelength
High Frequency
High Energy

Figure 5.2 Only a tiny portion of electromagnetic energy is visible. *(Courtesy of Ronald J. White)*

and more of the light energy is absorbed. (The absorbed energy becomes heat, which is why white cars, for instance, are cooler than black ones.) This method of mixing colors is called **subtractive** because each color, when mixed with others, acts as a filter, subtracting some set of light frequencies from the total mixture.

In either case, the color perceived depends only on which wavelengths of light reach the eye (and how much total light energy is present), not on whether those wavelengths were determined by adding wavelengths or filtering them out. The wavelengths themselves do not have a color; color is a sensation created by the eye and brain. For instance, the same wavelengths may look very different to different viewers for reasons ranging from color blindness to having just stared at a bright color or having spent time in a darkened room.

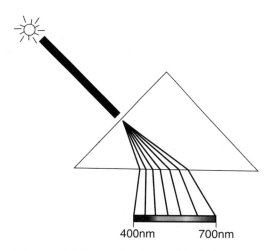

Figure 5.3 Spectral colors. White light emerges from a prism at different angles, each representing a different wavelength.

5.3 Primary Colors

Although the different individual spectral frequencies can be mixed to produce colors not found in the rainbow, there is no way to re-create exactly any of the pure colors of the rainbow (single-frequency, or monospectral, lights) from combinations of the others. These colors are thus considered to be the **primary colors** of visible light. More generally, in any system of colors, those that cannot be mixed from any of the others are called **primaries.**

There are infinitely many different spectral wavelengths. Thus to re-create accurately on a computer monitor in their purest forms all the colors that people can see would require mixing infinitely many different colored phosphors. Interestingly (and very conveniently), however, a large and rich **color-mixing space** can be created by mixing a small number of colors; usually only three are used. The trick is to pick the right ones.

5.3.1 Primary Colors for Subtractive and Additive Mixing

The primaries used for printing, cyan, magenta, and yellow (CMY), often are called the **subtractive primaries** because they usually are the best choices for creating the largest color-mixing space for light-absorbing pigments, in particular for inks.[3] A different set of primaries, the **additive primaries,** is used for mixing lights, as on a color display. These light primaries are usually called red, green, and blue (RGB). Aside from the variation between red and magenta and between blue and cyan, pigment colors are much less bright than colored light. Color Plate 1 shows subtractive CMY primaries and additive RGB primaries.

The subtractive mixture of cyan, magenta, and yellow pigments does not usually produce a rich black. A fourth, truly black, ink is used in printing to replace equal mixtures of cyan, magenta, and yellow. (Using a black ink this way also makes financial sense because only about a third as much is needed for black regions.) **Four-color printing,** or **process printing,** is the printing of images with cyan, magenta, yellow, and black (CMYK) inks. Most computer printers use either CMY or CMYK inks, but some ink-jet printers use six ink colors that include lighter versions of magenta and cyan as well as the usual four colors. Other combinations and numbers of inks may well become common in the near future.

5.4 Mixing Colors

The computer screen always uses additive mixing to create the final image, but computer art programs simulate a wide range of mixing techniques. Usually, the mixing options only partially resemble real-world additive or subtractive color mixing. Additive painting modes in paint programs would be frustrating because colors so rapidly become white and then cannot be changed by adding more color. (In the physical world, adding red light to white light, for instance, would create pink light. On the computer, once white has been reached, more color cannot be added.) True subtractive painting modes that work like filters would quickly lead to black areas. Many programs offer opacity settings for applying color with a brush tool or other means that average the new and the underlying colors. It is worth taking the time to experiment with the default and optional modes in your favorite programs to figure out the mixing rules that are being used. Some programs (e.g., MetaCreations Painter) simulate the mixing behaviors of traditional media. In the felt-tip-pen mode in Painter, for instance, colors bleed into one another in a way that is very similar to the way that inks from real pens do. Moreover, putting a partially transparent yellow on top of a dark blue does not lighten the blue, as it would in most painting programs' default "averaging" settings (see Color Plate 2).

Impressionist and Pointillist paintings involve the use of both additive and subtractive mixing effects. When they are viewed up close, only the subtractive mixing effects are noticeable—paint colors mixed on the palette or laid on top of one another. From a slight distance, however, the individual dabs are not discernible and, to the eye, their

---

[3]Cyan and magenta pigments were unknown when the red, blue, and yellow primaries were first established. They are used now because they can create a larger mixing space than traditional blue and red [Gerritsen, 1988].

colors blend additively. The effect of process printing with halftones is also part subtractive and part additive. Sometimes the dots overlap and mix subtractively, and sometimes they are distinct and from a distance are bright enough to mix additively.

5.5 GAMMA CORRECTION

Have you ever worked hard to create an image, only to view it on another type of computer and discover that it is washed out or that detail is gone from the shadows? These effects can be caused by differences in the way various computer platforms, such as Macs, PCs and Unix machines, handle a process called **gamma correction.**

Gamma is a measure of the nonlinearity of an RGB monitor. If the voltage driving the electron gun is doubled, the phosphor brightness does not generally double as a result (see Chapter 3 for a discussion of basic CRT components). The actual relationship involves an exponent, gamma (γ), that is usually 2.5. **Gamma correction** adjusts pixel data for a monitor's nonlinearity.

Unfortunately, there is no standard way to handle gamma correction, so an image that looks fine on one platform may well look washed out or muddy on another. The end-goal of gamma correction, and other corrections made to image data in different stages of software and hardware, is to distribute a limited number of values (of gray or of a color), usually 256, in an optimal fashion. This allows the reproduction of continuous photographic-type images without banding and other types of noticeable discontinuities.

In general, images made on PCs, which often have no gamma correction, will look too bright and even washed out on a Mac or Unix machine (see Fig. 5.4). The reverse is also true: Images made on a Mac, for instance, look darker and lose detail in the shadows when displayed on a PC. Differences in gamma correction cause problems whenever work is displayed on different types of computers and monitors—for example, with Web pieces or CD-ROMs.[4] Artists and designers creating work for more than one platform need to test their images on all of them.

The problem of gamma-correction differences on different computer platforms can be compounded in collaborative work when individual artists and designers correct for gamma differences on their own machines by changing the image data, using tonal mappings (see Chapter 2). Such mappings may make an image look better on a particular machine, but they don't solve the problem of creating an image that will appear the same on different machines and across platforms (in fact, such alterations make this problem worse).

---

[4]The difference in gamma is often overshadowed by the problem of badly adjusted monitors. Before worrying about gamma, artists and designers need to adjust correctly their displays: First adjust the black level control (often confusingly called "brightness") until the black elements of your image appear completely black (but no further). Then set the light intensity produced for white (often confusingly called "picture" or "contrast") to a comfortable level [Poynton, 1998].

(a)

(b)

(c)

Ideally, gamma–correction information is stored separately from image data, as in the Portable Network Graphics (PNG) image file format. With the PNG format, which now is supported by most major Web browsers, artists can create a single image that will look great on any properly adjusted monitor.

5.6 Color Consistency

Color consistency is of concern to many computer artists, especially those doing pre-press work. Sometimes the problem can seem overwhelming. Each monitor (even if of the same brand) is likely to show slightly different colors for the same image file, owing to differences in settings, the quality of the optics and mechanics, gamma correction, and age. The color is also significantly affected by the lighting in the room. Moreover, different scanners can produce quite different colors for the same image, and the output of color printers can vary dramatically. Finally, a conversion from RGB to CMYK either before or during printing often eliminates many of the most highly saturated, brightest colors.

Ideally, you want to scan an image, display it correctly on the monitor, work with it, and create a print that closely resembles the colors of the original. Approaching this ideal usually requires your active participation in adjusting the gamma correction for the monitor, the scanner, and possibly the printer too. In addition to the gamma correction provided by your computer's basic hardware and low-level software, you can fine-tune the display by using a software program that provides a grayscale (or other test patterns) to help you adjust how images are shown (see Fig. 5.5).

Devices such as printers or scanners often have precomputed gamma profiles that can be used by color-matching software to make adjustments and predict results better.

Figure 5.5 Gamma correcting in software. (a) Badly corrected gamma: The first two gray swatches are indistinguishable, and jumps in value are erratic in the lighter swatches. (b) Better corrected gamma: The gamma has been adjusted so that the change in value from one swatch to the next is more even. *(Portions courtesy of Thomas Knoll)*

(a)

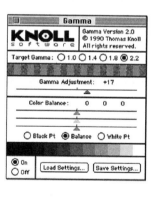

(b)

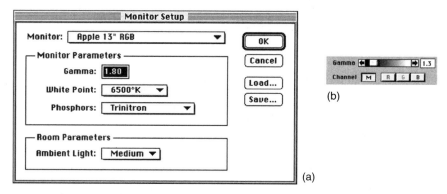

(a)

(b)

Figure 5.6 Many devices have preset gamma profiles or can be adjusted by the user. (a) Dialog box for gamma adjustment based on monitor characteristics. (b) Gamma slider in a scanning package that affects how the image is scanned.

A scanner may offer a choice of monitors to scan for, or an image-processing program may offer a choice of printer settings for specific machines to predict ink spreading (dot gain) better.

Calibrating a scanner to work with your monitor requires scanning in a test page, viewing it on the screen, and then adjusting the way that the scanner scans both gray-scale and RGB images (see Fig. 5.6). Once you have set up the monitor correctly by choosing the right black level and picture setting, a dialog box like the one shown, from Adobe Photoshop, can help optimize the color display for images used in a specific program. (The 6500°K temperature setting for white is meant to approximate the whiteness of sunlight.) With the monitor and image-editing program correctly adjusted, you can use a gamma slider in the scanning software to adjust the scanner. Adjusting these controls on the scanner is better than changing the image's color balance and brightness afterward in an image-processing program (which usually causes an overall loss of color information and may make future image computations less predictable). Because judging the accuracy of each device depends in part on the accuracy of the others, you should use outside reference material, such as PANTONE® swatches, premade test documents, or other color-matching tools.

Some printers offer gamma controls, either in software or through selections made by the printer itself. The goal is to obtain printouts that resemble the screen image. Be sure that your image is in a CMYK mode first—many RGB colors cannot be printed, regardless of the gamma settings (see Section 5.9). If the printer's gamma cannot be changed, use gamma software to alter the monitor's displayed colors to make them look as much as possible like the printout. (Often a standard color-calibration image is provided, either as part of your printer software or part of a color management kit.) You can also use gamma-adjustment utilities to vary the color balance and set the white of the monitor to resemble the paper stock you're using.

5.7 Color-Matching Systems

One simple way in which people communicate about color and discuss color interaction is by naming colors. Common names include standards such as red, green, blue, purple, and orange (or, in industries such as interior decoration, mauve, persimmon, beige, forest green, moonseed, etc.). Although these names are imprecise and often culturally dependent, they do serve useful functions, such as identifying specific colors for reuse. Many early graphics programs used a palette of textual names for color picking and some still offer named lists (see Fig. 5.7).

More sophisticated naming systems include numbers for clearer identification and provide reference swatches of printed colors. In the **PANTONE MATCHING SYSTEM®**, PANTONE® colors (identified by numbers rather than descriptive names) are used in conjunction with reference books of carefully printed PANTONE color swatches, and final images are printed with PANTONE Color Inks. Such systems use naming and tangible reference materials to bypass the color-consistency problems of computer setups. Thus you can choose a PANTONE color in an art program on the basis of the precisely created swatch color rather than the screen color (which may or may not be correct). **Spot color separations** (separate images for each color used) are sent to a printer who makes plates and prints the image with the appropriate PANTONE Color Inks (see Color Plate 3).

Professional-level digital design and layout programs have color pickers that are based on PANTONE Color Systems and other naming systems. Although such systems offer accuracy of final color quality, the problem of judging color relationships accurately on the screen remains. Digital painting and photoediting programs, especially those used for prepress work, also offer similar lists. However, identifying each color by name and creating a separate printing plate for each one is best used for designs with only a few colors and, in any event, cannot be used with photographic imagery.

5.8 Color Spaces

Choosing colors for a visual work requires more than just naming them or determining their wavelengths. It is essential in color composition to be able to consider colors in context, not just as isolated definitions. A **color space** is a way of ordering colors in one, two, or three dimensions to help the artist choose and work with color.

For more than 2000 years (from about 600 B.C. to A.D. 1600), artists believed that color was the result of the "struggle

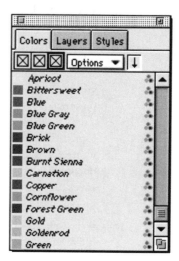

Figure 5.7 A palette of named colors. Macromedia Freehand's list of names and swatches can be used to select colors. New colors can be defined and named by the user. *(Portions copyright 1998 Macromedia, Inc. Used with permission.)*

between light and darkness" and so reordered the colors by their brightness, with black followed by blue, then red and green, then yellow, and ending in white [Gerritsen, 1988]. Newton, in addition to defining a 1D space based on the order of the spectrum, created a new type of color space: He arranged the spectral colors in a circle, adding purple to connect red and blue. An advantage of a circular color space is that the colors can be arranged in many ways by changing the amount of space allotted to each. Artists often put contrasting colors on opposite sides of the circle. Several of the computer color spaces discussed here are based on circles, with an added dimension to show changing lightness and darkness.

5.8.1   The RGB Cube

The most fundamental color space for the computer is based on the way that the screen must be programmed, as combinations of red, green, and blue light. This is a color-mixing space based on the three phosphor colors of RGB monitors. It usually is represented as a cube with red, green, and blue values forming the three axes. Fully 3D color pickers (rarely used) and slices of the RGB cube and other color spaces are used for color selection in some programs (see Color Plate 4).

Although RGB space is convenient for programmers, its use is not intuitive for traditionally trained artists and designers. Not only is additive mixing difficult to predict for those not accustomed to it, but a simple decision such as lightening or darkening a color can also take several steps.

5.8.2   The HSV and HSL Spaces

The hue, saturation, value, or lightness spaces (HSV and HSL) have immediate intuitive appeal and more closely resemble traditional color-picking decisions and color-mixing techniques than RGB spaces. In these spaces **hue** (H) refers to the different distinct color sensations, such as red, green, blue, yellow, and so on, **saturation** to the amount of white light (equal amounts of red, green, and blue) mixed with a hue, and **value** (V) or **lightness** (L) to the intensity of light (how much red, green or blue is present).

The HSV space is often represented by some sort of cone with hues around the top in the familiar circle form (see Fig. 5.8). Changes in value, also called brightness or lightness,[5] are represented along the vertical axis of the cone as the total amount of light decreases (by using less than 100% of red, green, or blue). At the bottom of the cone,

---

[5]In traditional color theory, **lightness** describes value changes of reflective objects and **brightness** describes value changes of light-generating or luminous objects. The terms are often used interchangeably, however, in popular computer graphics applications.

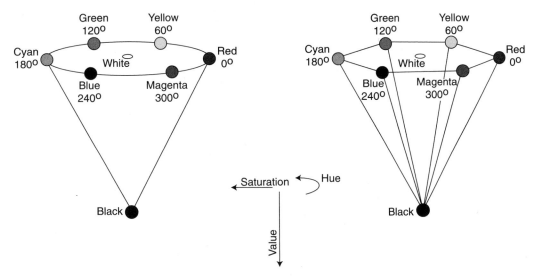

Figure 5.8 HSV cone and hexcone. (a) A true cone. (b) A hexcone, a six-sided cone, which is easier to program than a real cone. Hues are arrayed around the space with red at 0° and cyan at 180°. Saturation is highest around the edges and decreases toward the center axis. Value or brightness changes along the vertical axis, with black at the cone's tip.

no red, green, or blue is used and black results. The path from the black tip of the cone to the white center of the top circle shows all the grays—completely desaturated or achromatic colors with varying levels of brightness. An HSV space can also be shown as a cube (see Color Plate 5), like the RGB space, or a cylinder.

The HSL space is a variation of the HSV cone or hexcone. Instead of white being at the center of the topmost circle, it is pulled up into a cone that mirrors the cone formed with the top circle and the black vertex (see Color Plate 6a). The center of the widest circle (or hexagon) thus becomes gray instead of white.

In some programs, HSV or HSB or HSL spaces are used as color pickers, with slices through the spaces shown for context (see Color Plate 6b). A moment spent figuring out the type and shape of the space used will help you make sense of any program's color system.

5.8.3 THE HWB SPACE

Although HSV, HSB, and HSL spaces are more intuitive than RGB, they still can be confusing. For example, artists tend naturally to think of reducing value as adding black and of desaturating a color as adding white. But, in an HSL space, fully saturated hues have a lightness of 0.5 and thus desaturate toward middle gray, not white. Although full hues in HSV space desaturate to white, any colors with values of less than 1 desaturate toward some level of gray. To make a color whiter, as if adding white pigment, the artist must not only desaturate it but also fully brighten it.

The hue, whiteness, blackness space (HWB) solves these problems. Following Alvy Ray Smith's admonition to "Choose a hue. Lighten it with white. Darken it with black" [Smith, 1996b][6] makes the HWB space intuitive for artists and designers. Unfortunately it is not yet widely used. In HWB space, hue has the same meaning as in HSV and HSL spaces. Whiteness, like saturation, varies from 0 to 1, but a color with a whiteness value of 1 is always full white, not a shade of gray. A whiteness value of 0 produces the color **shade,** a mixture of pure hue with black. Blackness, like value or lightness, varies from 0 to 1. A color with a blackness value of 1 is always completely black, and a color with blackness value of 0 produces the color **tint,** a mixture of pure hue with white. As in paint mixing, the two actions are not opposite: Adding some white and then some black does not bring the user back to the original color. Color Plate 7 shows a comparison of color picking with HWB and HSV spaces. The same color is chosen in both pickers, but to make the color whiter in the HSV space, the user must both desaturate and brighten it. In the HWB space, the user simply slides toward white with the whiteness slider.

5.8.4 Perceptually Based Spaces and the Munsell System

The RGB, HSV, and HWB spaces have convenient geometries that let artists work directly with the RGB screen colors or with more intuitive arrangements. These spaces are designed for simplicity and ease of programming. However, they do not take into account perceptual phenomena such as the fact that a bright yellow is much lighter than a bright blue and that many more levels of saturation of blue can be distinguished than of yellow. In **perceptually based space,** the perceived difference between a color and its neighbor is the same in any direction.[7]

For any 20° movement around the circle of hues in a perceptual color space, for instance, the degree of perceptual change is the same. For any step inward toward white, a step of a certain distance always translates to the same amount of perceptual change. Accurate representation of the perceptual differences results in much more chaotic-looking color spaces than those discussed so far.

The **Munsell system** is a perceptually based color-picking system that uses numbers, a standardized color description vocabulary, and a 3D space (see Color Plate 8). The system combines the numbering and print-matching accuracy of the Pantone approach with the conceptual guidance of a geometric space and psychological data on perception.

---

[6]Note that Alvy Ray Smith also implemented the first HSV space.

[7]The perceived color differences are determined by averaging the results obtained from many viewers.

5.8.5 USING COLOR SPACES

The elements that define the spaces discussed here, such as the RGB components of an image or the hue, saturation, and value of a color, become ways of thinking about and changing color on the computer. Things impossible in traditional media become commonplace. For example, you can select a color in your image and then change its saturation without changing its hue or value. If you reduce saturation to nothing, you can create a grayscale image from a full color image. Conversely, you can add hue and saturation to grayscale images to colorize them. Some programs offer features that invert colors (exchanging them for colors with opposite RGB values), and, using color balance sliders, you can tip the image (or a selected portion of it) toward red or cyan.

Color spaces can also guide the selection of colors. For example, you can easily choose several hues with the same saturation or several shades or tints of the same hue. The precision available is unlike anything from the world of painting, letting you reuse exactly the same colors elsewhere if you want to (either by recording their numerical values or by copying and pasting). Each color space has its own personality, and there are many unexplored potentials of even simple spaces such as RGB. For instance, selecting a range of colors from a single slice along one of the RGB axes can create an aesthetically pleasing palette. You can structure color compositions by contrasting certain colors with their inverse or by using colors from only one portion of a color space. Exploring the color spaces in your favorite programs can make them even more powerful tools for your use.

5.8.6 YOUR OWN COLOR SPACE

Unfortunately, the color spaces in today's programs do not contain many of the basic features of color orderings used by artists for hundreds, even thousands, of years. They are not ordered correctly by brightness because they are not perceptually based, and HSV cones don't oppose contrasting or complementary colors or offer any guidance on how sets of colors should be combined. Some of the limitations of existing color space–picking options can be overcome by designing your own space in a separate file that you keep open while working. A circle that reflects red–green, yellow–blue dualities with shades and tints can become a strong basis for color composition decisions. You may choose several colors and then literally mix them to simulate a traditional painting palette from which you can select colors. Simply becoming aware of the somewhat odd constructions and limitations presented by current ways of choosing and manipulating color can help inspire you to think creatively about computer-based color use.

5.8.7 THE CIE SPACE

The final space discussed here, the CIE space, was developed in 1931 by the *Commission Internationale de l'Eclairage* (International Lighting Committee). Its purpose was to represent all visible wavelengths and their combinations in a geometric space with useful conceptual properties in which all other color spaces can be shown and compared.

The CIE space provides color definitions that are independent of devices but does not predict what specific combinations of wavelengths will look like; in any case, no printing or standard display process can accurately display all the visible colors. In addition, because the perceived color of a combination of wavelengths changes with the physiology of the viewer, ambient light, and other factors, the CIE space cannot be used effectively as a color-naming tool.

The CIE space (see Fig. 5.9) resembles the HSV cone in that fully saturated hues are arrayed around a horseshoe-shaped form, something like the top of a deformed HSV cone, and mix to form white. Unlike the computer's HSV space, which is based on the same red, green and blue primaries as the RGB space, the CIE space contains infinitely many distinct visible hues—in fact, the entire spectrum. Colors grow darker (or have less **luminance,** in CIE parlance) as they near the tip of this conelike form.

In paint programs that use a CIE space, a version of the flat part of the form, called the **chromaticity diagram** (chromaticity is hue and saturation), can be represented by red–green and yellow–blue color axes; a third control changes the value or luminance (see Color Plate 9). One of the benefits of some versions of the CIE space and HSV-type spaces is that artists can work with brightness without changing hue or satu-

Figure 5.9 CIE space. (a) A 3D plot of the CIE space, capped at an arbitrary level of light energy. A projection of the $X + Y + Z = 1$ plane shown here is used to create (b) the 2D chromaticity diagram, which shows hue and saturation, but not value. *(Courtesy of Gary Meyers)*

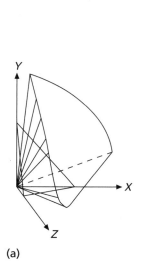

(a)

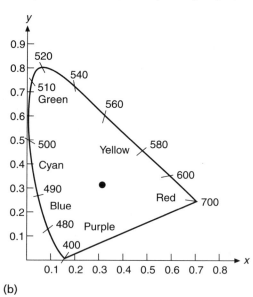

(b)

ration (i.e., without changing the color). The user can always switch into CIE space without losing color data because that space contains all other color spaces. Also, although screen colors are limited to the RGB color space, the wider range of colors definable in the CIE space sometimes produces better printing results (in particular with Postscript level-two printers).

5.9 COLOR GAMUTS

Because the CIE space shows all visible colors, it is ideal for comparing color **gamuts,** or the range of possible colors that can be created with different color-mixing choices and different media. Although it does not provide luminance differences, the 2D chromaticity diagram (a projection of the "face" of the CIE space) is more convenient for this purpose than the full, 3D space (see Fig. 5.9b). The CRT color gamut is much larger than the NTSC or PAL broadcast gamuts or the CMYK gamut of process printing, for instance (although some colors cannot be created on a monitor but can still be printed). Color Plate 11 compares the gamuts of an RGB monitor, slide film, and process printing.

Because some colors that can be created on the CRT cannot be reproduced with cyan, magenta, and yellow inks, designing print work on a computer requires care. Many programs provide a visual preview of the printable colors or give some sort of warning when a color is used that is "out of gamut."

5.10 COLOR CHANNELS

Geometric representations of color spaces such as RGB, CMY, and CIE are useful. Sometimes, though, separating the different pixel samples, such as the three needed for an RGB image, into separate files for viewing and editing is more practical. Many programs handle this with features called **channels**. An RGB image would have three channels (i.e., red, green, and blue), and a CMYK image would have four channels (i.e., cyan, magenta, yellow, and black), also called **color separations** (see Color Plate 11). In each channel, the image appears in grayscale, with the gray values representing the amount of the channel's color used in the composite image. For example, a black area in the magenta channel indicates a full-intensity magenta contribution to the image; a white area indicates that no magenta is used in that area in the image. An artist can work in a single color channel without affecting the other channels. This flexibility is useful for color correction, especially in the use of CMYK channels for printing process color plates and for creating special effects—the channels can be swapped, for instance. Different color spaces imply different channels.

5.11 Palettes

Once you have chosen colors, you should keep a collection of them for reuse. Color *palettes* or *colormaps*, like traditional paint palettes, can hold custom-mixed colors arranged in any order you want. Unlike a color space that you design yourself, a palette of swatches can be saved and used inside other images. Another benefit of the palette is that the colors are drawn in discrete squares instead of continuous gradations so that each color can be rechosen easily, without your having to keep track of numeric color descriptions. These smaller palettes commonly contain sliders or miniviews of a color space, allowing you to change and add colors without recourse to a comprehensive color picker that shows a section of an entire color space.

Most applications start up with an empty palette or fill the palette with a default set of colors that frequently bear no resemblance to the color scheme used in the displayed image. Customizing the palette to display colors appropriate to the image, and in an order that best reflects their intended use, pays off. A customized color space can be used to generate palette swatches. Palettes can provide an intermediate level of control over color choice and, when used thoughtfully, can be a great help in organizing color composition.

5.11.1 Eye-Dropper Tool (Image as Palette)

Design and use of the palette are most important during the initial stages of color composition. When a sound color structure is in place, another color-choosing approach—the **eye-dropper** tool—becomes easier to use than either pickers or palettes. With an eye-dropper tool, you can click anywhere in an image to choose the color at that location. The color sucked up by the eye-dropper tool becomes the active painting color and can also be released by the eye-dropper tool into a palette color square. The eye-dropper tool thus makes the image itself into a palette. If you begin with digitized materials or other image sources, all the necessary colors may well already exist in the working document. The palette is still a useful intermediary, however: It keeps track of important colors economically (you don't need to have an extra image file open) and the colors are easier to select. When you use an image file as a palette, accurately choosing and rechoosing a desired color from often complex areas is difficult.

The eye-dropper tool can also help you create customized palettes. First, bring up an image with a color structure that appeals to you or scan in colored objects (e.g., leaves or magazine clippings). Then use the eye-dropper tool to select colors and place them in a palette. You can also leave open an image with desirable colors and color relationships and use that image's color (via selection by the eye-dropper tool) in a new piece.

5.11.2 Eight-bit Palettes

In images of lower color depth, the term **palette** often refers to the specific colors allowed in the image. An 8-bit palette, for instance is made up of 256 specific color choices out of the almost 17 million RGB colors available on the monitor. Each entry in the reduced color palette is indexed to a specific RGB value. When color number 3 is used, for example, its RGB value is contained in an index, called a **color look-up table, clut,** or **colormap**. This indexing arrangement makes possible the storage and utilization of many different palettes of 256 colors.

Cluts can be important whenever you are working with less than full color depth, but most programs let you work only with cluts of 256 or fewer colors. Because many computer users still have only 8-bit displays, 8-bit color palettes and cluts are frequently used in onscreen projects created for wide distribution, including Web graphics, animations, and especially multimedia works. Such works usually are created in full color and then reduced to the best palette possible. Images with low color depths, such as 8-bit and below, also take up less space, making their transmission over a network and display on a screen faster.

Choosing the best clut for an image or image sequence is often painstaking work. You can handpick color choices or use software that chooses optimal palettes automatically. Some programs, such as Equilibrium's DeBabelizer, can create a "superpalette," a clut optimized for several images at once. Also, the system software for different platforms use different cluts, so that an image optimized for a PC's system may look terrible on a Mac and vice versa. This problem is particularly acute for cross-platform multimedia CD-ROMs and World Wide Web graphics because many viewers have 8-bit screens and files need to be kept as small as possible. Predicting how your image will look to a wide range of viewers is often difficult. You can ensure color consistency by reducing images to a clut with colors that are contained in the system cluts of the main computing platforms (Macs, PCs, and Unix machines). Although this overlapping set of colors has fewer than 256 colors, it can make your graphics reliably attractive to many more viewers. Color Plate 12 shows a single image displayed with several different cluts.

Conclusion

A strong advantage of computer color is the ability to isolate specific aspects of color, such as RGB components, CMYK components, and hue, saturation, and brightness. Visualizations of these factors in color spaces provide mental models of color structures and often are used as the basis for color pickers within art programs.

Color consistency and color matching still present challenges. Printing an image that looks like the picture on the artist's screen, or even sharing images among different computer setups, often is fraught with difficulties. However, great progress has been made in color matching in recent years, and the situation continues to improve. Because many of the computer's color capabilities are not found in traditional media, many aspects of color have not yet been exploited either in program interfaces or by artists.

To take full advantage of the color potential of computers, software designers must work with artists to create color-editing and analysis tools. In addition, color education, which often is neglected, will have to take into account the new design possibilities and methods made possible by the computer. Theory and tools to assist in learning are nothing, however, without the practice and experience of hands-on work with color, and thus the practice and experimentation made possible by the computer's extraordinary flexibility may contribute the most to its value as a learning and production tool for artists.

Suggested Readings

Albers, Josef. *Interaction of Color.* New Haven: Yale University Press, 1987. First published in 1963, this small paperback contains an affordable subset of the text and images in Albers's original tomes of hand–silk screened examples. It guides the reader through Albers's systematic exercises to increase sensitivity to color and develop intuition in its use.

Gerritsen, Frans. *Evolution of Color.* Shiffer, 1988. An enlightening history of the evolution of color that helps put approaches to color theory in perspective.

Itten, Johannes. *The Art of Color: The Subjective Experience and Objective Rationale of Color.* (trans. Ernst van Haagen). Van Nostrand Reinhold, 1974. First published in 1961, this book (and its smaller version, *The Elements of Color: A Treatise on the Color System of Johannes Itten Based on His Book the Art of Color,* Van Nostrand Reinhold, 1970) addresses many of the same color principles that Albers did but is geared more toward a philosophy of color and research into its subjective interpretation.

Norman, Richard B. *Electronic Color, The Art of Color Applied to Graphic Computing.* Van Nostrand Reinhold, 1990. An overview of basic color theory, especially that relevant to the computer; includes expanded coverage of many of the topics in this chapter and contains exercises.

Swirnoff, Lois. *Dimensional Color.* Van Nostrand Reinhold, 1992. A wonderful, lushly illustrated book that explores the relationship between color and form, using examples from architecture, painting, and nature. Controlled experiments, which can be reproduced by the reader, show how color can make a shape appear to recede or advance in space.

Exercises

1. Create your own color space. Analyze the way you currently choose colors. What are you really looking for? Groups of similar hue? Or brightness? Or perhaps sets of complementary colors? Design a color space, on paper, that is optimal for your personal color needs. Create several slices through this space (if it is 3D) in a painting or drawing program. Use this set as an alternative or in addition to the color pickers provided in your software. Sometimes simply having a strong mental model of a color space can make choosing and using color easier.

2. Mix your own. With some real paints, choose three colors with different hues and arrange them on a palette at three points of an imaginary triangle. Fill in the mixing space enclosed by the triangle by mixing the colors—the center should have an equal mixture of all the colors, and, as the mixture reaches each vertex, it should approach that single color. Now try to replicate this color space on the computer. Can you achieve the same colors? Can you make them mix in the same ways? (*Hint:* Try scanning in the finished color space painting as a guide.)

3. Mixing options. Different types of software offer different ways of mixing colors. Explore your favorite piece of painting or drawing software and create examples of each type of mixing available. Print them out as a catalog to keep nearby and remind you of the options available.

4. Personal color names. Many programs that provide color naming have an option to edit the color names. Customize a set of color names with names that draw on your emotional reactions to the colors. "Angry red," perhaps, or "sleepy blue" or "super-happy yellow." Try using these named colors over the next few weeks. How do they influence your use of color and attitude toward it?

5. Channeling. In a paint-type program, open a full-color RGB image (or create a new one) and then view only the individual channels. Work in each one, changing back to the multichannel view between each session. Soon you will start to gain an intuitive sense of the RGB components of your piece. Try the same thing with CMYK channels. (Note that altering the K channel is a convenient way to change the values in your work.) Try printing the work on a color printer, as well as viewing the changes on the screen.

6. Creating custom palettes. Go outdoors and collect natural, mostly organic objects such as leaves, flowers, and grasses. Arrange them together or one at time on a scanner and digitize them. Create a document in a paint program with all your objects in it. Create a custom palette by choosing individual colors (or ranges of colors) from this piece. Save the palette. Now use it to create an entirely different work or to recolor a piece that you have already completed. The new work could be a representational drawing of the objects themselves or something completely unrelated.

CHAPTER 6

Printing

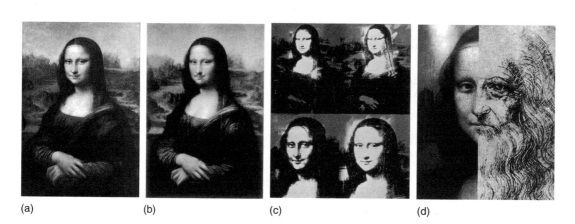

(a)   (b)   (c)   (d)

Figure 6.1 **Mona Lisa, from the Renaissance to Dada, Pop, and computer art.** (a) **Leonardo da Vinci** (*Mona Lisa* (La Gioconda), oil paint, 1503–06): "Most scholars believe that da Vinci, the quintessential Renaissance man, began the portrait in Florence in 1502 or 1503 and, apparently obsessed with it, carried it with him for many years. But who was his model. . . ?" [Reit, 1981, p. 176]. *(Courtesy of Giraudon/Art Resource, NY)* (b) **Marcel Duchamp** (*L.H.O.O.Q,* pencil over color reproduction, 1919): Using the recognition power of the image, Duchamp graffitied it by painting on a moustache and beard. His gesture went beyond that of a Dada attack on high art, however; he was commenting as well on Leonardo's sexual orientation [Rubin, 1968, p. 19]. *(Courtesy of Cameraphoto/Art Resource, NY,* © 1999 Artists Rights Society (ARS) New York/ADAGP, Paris/Estate of Marcel Duchamp) (c) **Andy Warhol** (*Four Mona Lisas,* silkscreen, 1963): In his reproductions of four different "original" Leonardo Mona Lisas, Warhol's work calls into question the uniqueness of the most commonly reproduced Mona Lisa (from the Louvre in Paris) and at the same time takes advantage of the famed status of the original. *(Courtesy of Art Resource, NY* © 1999 Andy Warhol Foundation for the Visual Arts/ARS, NY) (d) **Lillian Schwartz** ("*It is I*" (Mona/Leo), digital image, copyright Lillian Schwartz 1987, printed with permission from *The Computer Artist's Handbook,* W.W. Norton, 1992): "While she was juxtaposing images on the screen, Schwartz was astonished by the physiognomic similarities between a self-portrait of Leonardo and his famous painting of the Mona Lisa" [C. Goodman, 1986, p. 82]. She became convinced after further study and historical research that the famous painting was a female self-portrait of Leonardo himself, thus echoing through visual research with computer technology Duchamp's earlier impulses. *(Courtesy of Lillian Schwartz)*

6.1 Introduction

The concept of an original work is rendered obsolete by digital image making and computer printing. A "print" has no "original" visual image from which it is printed, such as a stone or film negative, and the original digital file can be duplicated many times. The print is therefore both original and reproduction. Yet discussions of the ease with which images can be multiplied might lead someone to think that printing is simply a matter of pressing a button. Nothing could be further from the truth. Making digital information tangible with printing can demand just as much attention as creating the imagery in the first place.

In this chapter I address some of the theoretical implications of computer printing and then describe basic printing concepts, types of printers, and techniques that combine computer work with traditional processes.

6.1.1 ORIGINALITY AND THE ORIGINAL

Even the most perfect reproduction of a work of art is lacking in one element: its presence in time and space, its unique existence at the place where it happens to be. . . . The presence of the original is the prerequisite to the concept of authenticity [Benjamin, 1968, p. 220].
Walter Benjamin, critic and philosopher.

The dynamic between original works of art and reproductions makes certain images, such as Leonardo da Vinci's Mona Lisa, extraordinarily well known. The Mona Lisa is so widely reproduced and the original so highly praised that it has become an icon for all of fine art. But what if Leonardo had created the Mona Lisa on a computer? Would it still be "in a large bay off the main picture gallery called the Salle des États, [hanging] in a specially built alcove, humidity-regulated, temperature-controlled, electronically guarded, and shielded by bullet-proof glass" ? [Reit, 1981, p. 220.] Would the millions of reproductions now in circulation even exist? Or would everyone be able to purchase an "original" print? Perhaps because of the tension between the Mona Lisa's status as a unique image and its ubiquity in reproduction, it has inspired visual commentary by many artists, appeared in countless art works, advertisements, and animations, and become a cult image in computer graphics (see Fig. 6.1).

Modernism flaunted the uniqueness of both its artists and their artworks. Postmodernism, with its concerns about media and venues outside traditional art institutions, has focused more on work in which the "aura" (Walter Benjamin's term) of the original is itself critiqued. For example, artist Sherry Levine created a series of photographs that were themselves photographs of the work of other photographers, such as Edward Weston and Eliot Porter, in violation of their copyrights. The point was to show that the photographers' works were themselves copies—of nature in Weston's and Porter's cases. Observing the rephotographed work makes the viewer aware that the "original" is merely a copy of nature and that nature itself is being viewed within cultural codes. "Levine's act of theft . . . opens the print from behind to the series of models from which it, in turn, has stolen, of which it is itself the reproduction" [Krauss, 1984, p. 87]. The Dadaists, with their found objects and development of collage, began this investigation decades earlier: "What [the Dadaists] intended and achieved was a relentless destruction of the aura of their creations, which they branded as reproductions by the very means of production" [Benjamin, 1968, p. 238].

The lack of an "original" in photography was a much debated point while photography was first struggling for acceptance as an art medium. Many saw it as a drawback. Benjamin saw it as a political freedom: "The unique value of the 'authentic' work of art has its basis in ritual, the location of its original use value [such as images worshipped as part of religion]. For the first time in world history, mechanical reproduction emancipates the work of art from its parasitical dependence on ritual" [Benjamin, 1968,

p. 224]. Mechanical reproduction did not revolutionize the art world as Benjamin had anticipated, but electronic reproduction may.

Benjamin also pointed out the lack of discussion on how photography, with its inherent multiplicity, was changing traditional forms of art. Photography's magical ability to capture details of reality freed painters from the role of documentors and lessened artistic concerns with realism, but the ability to make multiple copies was largely suppressed, as in fine-art printmaking, by artificially limiting the number of prints made. "In so far as contemporary art photography has become as much a creation of the market place as an engine of it, it comes as no surprise to encounter the ultimate denial of photography as a mechanically reproducible technology in such phenomena as Emmet Gowin's recent production of 'monoprints'—editions of a single print from a negative" [Solomon-Godeau, 1984, p. 77]. Similar approaches have been taken with computer-printed pieces: Richard Rosenblum (see Figs. 2.1 and 2.29) creates limited editions of each of his images in a variety of sizes, and Manfred Mohr (see Figs. 1.15 and 4.32) considers each plotter printing of his work a drawing and makes only one.

Although images certainly have been copied before, from photography to the industrialized spirit of the Bauhaus, the computer offers an accuracy and ease of replication and distribution that bring this issue to a new level. Benjamin said of film: "Mechanical reproduction is inherent in the very technique of film production. This technique not only permits in the most direct way but virtually causes mass distribution" [Benjamin, 1968, p. 224]. He attributed this forced reproduction to the sheer cost of film creation: Individuals could not support it as an art form.[1] Today, seeing a movie is much easier than seeing an original painting or sculpture and is about on par with finding and purchasing a book or music CD. But VHS tape is very much a second- or third-generation copy, rather than an exact replica. (In addition, TV's aspect ratio is different from that of many film formats so that much of each original frame is cropped.)

For a computer art piece, however, the term "original" may truly have no meaning, challenging the notion of a copy or reproduction. Each print or viewing on a screen is as original as the next. A file does not change when duplicated and, unlike a photographic negative or printing plate, does not suffer any degradation from copying or printing.[2]

Not only is computer art work easy to replicate, but it is so easy that people are prompted to do so—the medium itself seems to encourage it. Once an image is reduced to "information" (bits, 0s, and 1s), it takes on a different nature from physically based art work. Ease of replication is further encouraged by ease of printing and electronic distribution. The Internet and World Wide Web let an artist make any type of digital information available to tens of millions of people. Interesting images are interlinked and passed around like ideas in a conversation. As many Internet users have proclaimed, they feel when working with this medium that it encourages replication and distribution, that "information wants to be free."

---

[1]His prediction did not materialize immediately because films, although reproduced, could not for all practical purposes be owned until the advent of video and home VCRs.

[2]This ease of reproduction can be offset, however, by the deterioration of digital storage media and the introduction of error in copying and transferring processes. The ease with which digital files can be lost or destroyed means that backup and archival systems play an important role in preserving digital art works.

An artist can still enforce a more Modernist, market-oriented approach by limiting prints, ensuring high prices for a rare commodity. Other alternatives include new paradigms for art markets that resemble those of the music or publishing industry, with low unit prices or licensing fees and much larger distribution than is customary in the visual arts. The pleasure of listening to a new CD is not diminished by knowing that others have purchased the identical thing, for example, and it is conceivable that in the future dozens, hundreds, or even thousands of people will pay a small price for the same piece of "original" visual artwork.

6.2 Concepts

The quality of most computer printing techniques is a combination of the printer's physical media and software-based processes. Software options of rasterization and halftoning are discussed first, because the basic concepts of these processes apply to almost all types of printing (see Chapter 5 for a discussion of color matching and overall color management).

6.2.1 Rasterization

Two preparation stages performed by software are of particular importance to artists and designers: *rasterizing,* or *ripping the image,* and creating a *halftone.* The artist can influence both of these stages, the results of which can determine, sometimes even more than the printing device used, the final appearance and feeling of the work.

Except for vector-based plotters that draw by moving a pen from one coordinate to the next, computer printers can print only rasterized images (i.e., arrays of pixel values, usually printed row by row, just as they are displayed on the screen). If the image in question is already a pixel-based image, it need not be rasterized. However, if the image is in a geometry-based program, such as a 2D digital design and layout program, continuous geometric shape descriptions must be translated into a raster format.

Rasterizing, or **ripping an image,** can be done within the printer, in software on a computer, or with a separate peripheral, all called **raster image processors** (RIPs). PostScript printers have built-in software, memory, and a RIP. Built-in PostScript capabilities can raise the price of a laser printer by several hundred dollars, but ripping an image in software can be very time-consuming. For PostScript output requiring very large, high-resolution files, such as those sent to professional typesetters, a separate hardware RIP costing tens of thousands of dollars is used.

6.2.2 Halftoning

Seeing the difference between a glowing, continuous-looking screen image and a duller, grainy-looking printout is often a profoundly disappointing moment for novice computer artists. Printouts are generally less realistic and vibrant than screen images for a variety of reasons. Most obviously, the screen creates images with light, whereas the

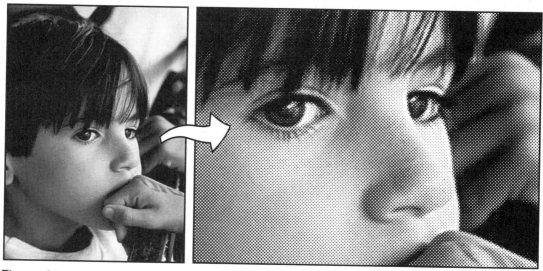

Figure 6.2 A grayscale image simulated with traditional halftones.

paper merely reflects light. Moreover, CRT phosphors can have as many as 265 brightness levels, and, at only a short distance, the red, green, and blue phosphors blend seamlessly to create almost 17 million different colors.

A printer has only one intensity of each color ink and yet must somehow create the illusion of different grays and different color brightnesses. How can a laser printer with only black toner create the illusion of a grayscale image? The trick used in most printing technologies is to print patterns of different-sized dots, or **halftones,** that, when viewed at a distance, blend with each other and the paper color to give the appearance of a wide range of gray values or colors (see Fig. 6.2). This technique can be imitated by computer printers. As most computer printers can print only one dot size, however, each halftone shape is composed of many printer dots (see Fig. 6.3).

The halftone shapes are sometimes called printer **spots** to differentiate them from the printer dots that compose them. Each printer spot is drawn in a **halftone cell** that is several printer dots high and wide. If a halftone cell of, say, 2 × 2 printer dots is used, a full black area would be created by printing a spot of all four black printer dots in the 2 × 2 cell (see Fig. 6.4), and a 50% gray area would be created by printing a smaller spot using only half the printer dots in the cell. In general, the

Figure 6.3 Close-up of the printer dots simulating round halftones.

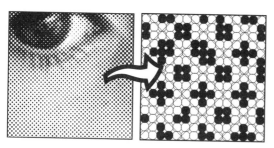

number of gray levels that can be simulated in any halftone cell is equal to the height and width of the halftone area plus 1 (to take into account an all-white area). Similarly, the width or height of the halftone area can be found by dividing the printer resolution by the halftone, or **screen frequency,** also referred to as **lines per inch** (lpi).

In addition to the screen frequency, the angle of the screen affects the appearance of the printed image. In Figs. 6.2 and 6.3, the screen is at a 45° angle; if it were at a 90° angle, say, the effect would be markedly different. A 45° angle typically is used for single-color printing, but in process color printing four-color halftone plates must be printed in such as way as to bring the CMYK dots close together, but not too close, and to avoid the effects of moirés or other obvious patterns (see Color Plate 13). In general, it is best to use the default process color screens set by your program or printer.

Halftoning can inspire creative solutions, and many programs allow artists to design their own halftones shapes. Consider again the mural piece in Fig. 1.12. It is composed of tiny icons, each selected to represent different gray levels. Ken Knowlton has continued to explore the concept of halftone identity and the relationship of picture elements

Figure 6.4 Computer printer halftone spots. (a) With a single printer dot size, a 2 × 2 halftone cell can contain spots corresponding to five different gray levels. (b) A 3 × 3 halftone cell can contain spots corresponding to 10 different gray levels.

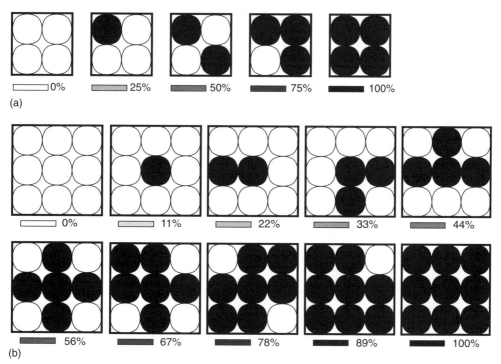

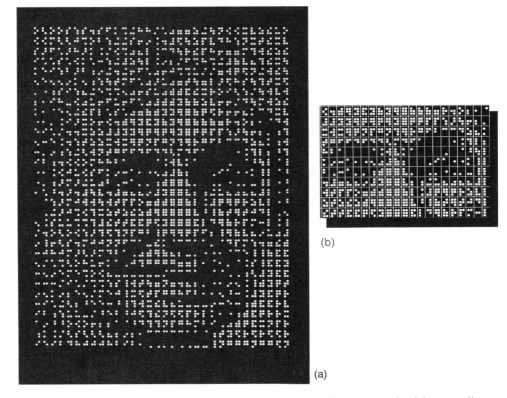

(b)

(a)

Figure 6.5 Ken Knowlton, *Helen Keller in Simulated Braille,* **1998.** Each of the 64 cells is used 16 times. Based on a photograph courtesy of the American Federation for the Blind, Helen Keller Archives. *(Copyright 1998 Ken Knowlton, Merrimack, NH.)*

to the whole in his more recent work. For example, Knowlton used a computer to help him analyze a photograph of Helen Keller (courtesy of the American Foundation for the Blind). He then created the image shown in Fig. 6.5(a) with simulated braille in which every one of the 64 cells is used 16 times. The division into cells is shown in the detail of the eye area in Fig. 6.5(b).

6.2.3 DITHERING

Simulated halftones are a subset of a more general display and printing technique called **dithering,** which involves creating a pattern of screen pixels or printer dots to simulate colors or gray levels that cannot otherwise be displayed. Halftoning is a special case of dithering called a **clustered dot dither** because the dots are clustered to form larger shapes. This method is also referred to as **amplitude modulated** (AM) **dithering,** or **screening,** because the factor being changed is the amplitude or size of the spot.

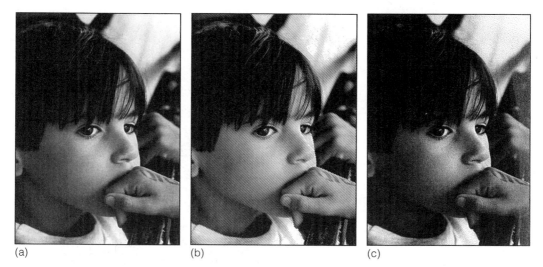

(a)   (b)   (c)

Figure 6.6 Halftoning and FM screening examples. (a) Typical computer halftone image. (b) Halftone shaped into a line pattern instead of simulating round dots. (c) Diffusion dithering, a type of FM screening.

Frequency modulated (FM) **dithering,** or **screening,** does not use cells and screens but instead distributes dots with more complex algorithmic methods. The frequency, rather than the amplitude, of dots needed to simulate the grays of halftones is affected (see Fig. 6.6c). Because FM screening does not use screen angles, it virtually eliminates visual artifacts such as repeating dither and moiré patterns, especially in multiplate color printing. In the **error diffusion** method of FM printing, the choice of dot locations is based on fixed variables, making each printing of an image identical. An alternative method is called **stochastic printing** because it contains a random variable.

Although primarily used for screen display, some printers, including almost all inkjet printers, use FM techniques instead of simulating traditional halftones with clustered dot dithers. The need for small but discernible dots in FM methods makes them impractical for most laser printers and a challenge for traditional printing processes. Although FM techniques currently are more costly, increasing research and a demand for the results they offer may make this a more widespread and affordable alternative in the near future.

PRINTED IMAGE RESOLUTION VERSUS GRAY LEVELS.   An image with only fully black marks requires no halftoning and can always be printed at the printer's full resolution. Black text from a word processor, for instance, is not halftoned. But when images are halftoned, the choice of screen frequency always involves a trade-off between the number of gray levels the artist seeks to represent and printed image resolution. Figure 6.7 shows three different screen frequencies used for a single 600-dpi printer. Because there is no reason to retain the high resolution of the image shown in part (a) in the other two, image resolution was adjusted to follow the 2X rule (that image resolution

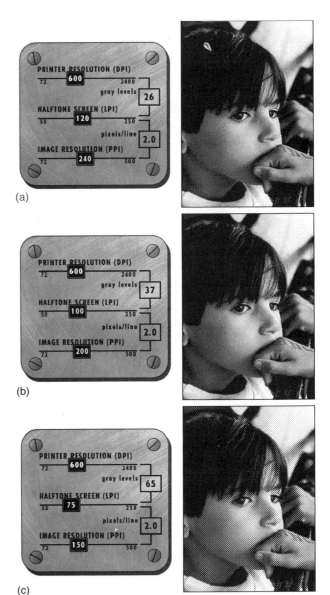

Figure 6.7 Trade-offs between resolution and gray levels. (a) Spatial resolution is relatively high, so the image looks sharp and "in focus." Halftone dots are not very noticeable, but gray levels are limited, emphasizing contrast and eliminating subtle gray changes. Banding is evident in areas with gradients. (b) Spatial resolution is high enough to produce a clear image at reading distance and halftone dots are noticeable but not distracting. With almost twice as many possible grays as in (a), many subtle changes are restored and banding has disappeared. (c) Spatial resolution is compromised, and at reading distance the halftone pattern is distracting. However, at a distance the additional gray levels become noticeable.

does not usually need to be higher than about 2X the screen frequency). In order to create an image with 256 gray levels (more than enough to make most images look realistic and as many as PostScript can describe), halftone cells would have to be 16 × 16 printer dots, or approximately 37 lpi on a 600-dpi printer. This requirement would reduce the spatial resolution so greatly that the result probably would not be satisfactory; most laser printer output has only a few more than 100 gray levels (e.g., 53 lpi on a 600-dpi printer).

For PostScript printers, the best-compromise halftone settings recommended by the manufacturer are stored in ROM and can be selected by choosing the printer's default in a program's print dialog box. As an artist, at times you will want to control this balance yourself. If printing camera-ready copy for a newspaper image, for example, 85 lpi is standard. If a piece is to be tiled and viewed from a distance, you may decide to spread the image data over a larger area and use a looser halftone screen to represent more of the grays in the image data. Some laser printers can literally produce halftones (i.e., vary the size of the dots). Although this variation is slight, it can significantly enhance images (especially photographic ones) by increasing the gray levels simulated by a halftone cell area. This capability is called resolution-enhancement technology (RET) on HP printers and PhotoGrade on Apple printers.

FILE RESOLUTION AND PRINTING. Your laser printer may be able to print 600 dpi, but if you are halftoning an image, far fewer image pixel values can be represented per inch. As a result, sending very high–resolution files to a printer can be waste of time (and money in the case of service bureaus). The 2X rule often can be used to reduce an image's resolution, avoiding unnecessary waiting times (see Fig. 6.8).

72ppi
(monitor resolution)

133ppi
(1X screen frequency)

Figure 6.8 Image resolution should be adjusted for a given screen frequency: 1.5 to 2 times the screen frequency usually is sufficient. The screen frequency in this book is 133 lpi.

200ppi
(1.5X screen frequency)

266ppi
(2X screen frequency)

333ppi
(2.5X screen frequency)

6.3 THE PSYCHOLOGY OF THE PRINT BUTTON

The psychology of the print button is often difficult to resist: You might easily feel that clicking the button is a final step, after which you need only go out for coffee and return when the printer has completed its task. This attitude is not surprising because a single click of the mouse causes your work to be realized all at once, without any intervention on your part. You cannot stop the computer printer and then have it continue to print in a different manner, retrace a line, or switch a halftone shape in the middle of the work. In a process that is almost the opposite of what occurs in most traditional work, the image is realized in a physical medium without your influence. Often printers are located on a network at some distance from the user's machine, perhaps in another room and run by a technician. Each printout may also cost money, discouraging too much experimentation.

The ease of pressing the print button also belies the subtlety and difficulty of getting good prints, especially from color printers. An artist who works for many days on a piece and then sends it with two minutes' consideration to a printer is omitting an essential part of the computer art-making process. Time, patience, and persistence are needed to master even one color printer's quirks and capabilities.

The Beyond the Print Button side boxes accompanying the printer-type descriptions in Section 6.4 offer suggestions for creative experimentation that can enhance the effects a printer has to offer. You can also expand your output options by combining computer printing with traditional art-making methods, from drawing and painting to printmaking and photography.

6.4 PRINTER TYPES

The basic printer types can be described in terms of their mechanisms, medium, average costs, and the software concepts previously described. Over the past 10 years, the price of printers has dropped consistently. Black and white PostScript laser printers cost nearly $10,000 in the late 1980s; today, faster models with higher resolution and better-quality printing cost less than $2000. Color computer printers have come down in price from more than $20,000 to anywhere from $1000 to $10,000, with some that utilize technologies such as ink-jet dropping below $200. Although the price ranges given in the following printer descriptions will almost certainly be somewhat high by the time this book is published, they are included to give you a sense of the relative costs of computer printing technologies.

Media costs are also indicated, especially when they are an appreciable part of the overall printer cost. They are an important consideration when you purchase a printer. They are also directly reflected in service bureau charges for printing and often are more than the printer cost (although maintenance, repair, and operator time can figure in too).

Knowledge of printing concepts, printer types, and their cost is important in making informed decisions about the technology to choose for your art work. But, as with input devices, no amount of written information can substitute for testing the printer in person with the type of jobs that you plan to run on it.

6.4.1 Laser Printers

Black and White. **Laser printers** are known for their high-quality text and graphics printing. Even at the low end, they boast crisp, clear lines, relatively solid blacks, high printing speeds (usually 10 to 20 pages per minute), and reasonable purchase prices (some cost less than $400 without PostScript); they cost only pennies per page to use, produce little noise, and are reliable. Not surprisingly, black and white PostScript laser printers are a mainstay of most computer setups and are used for everything from correspondence to camera-ready newsletter layout and visual art work.

A laser printer, black and white or color, works much like a Xerox machine. A laser beam transfers the image to a cylindrical roller as an electrostatic charge. When this charged roller is dusted with toner, the toner sticks only to the charged areas and creates the desired image on the roller. The toner is transferred by contact to a sheet of paper and a high-heat process then fuses the toner to the page, literally melting it into the fibers of the paper.

Toner is a powder made up of iron oxide (rust), which is easily given a magnetic charge, and plastic, which is easily melted. Other ingredients, such as sand and wax, help give toner the right properties to flow from the reservoir onto the roller.

The fusing process requires a high temperature (about 300°F); therefore nothing that melts easily, such as Scotch tape, should be attached to paper put through a laser printer. In particular, whereas transparencies for laser printers are designed to withstand high temperatures, transparencies intended for a copier may melt and damage the printer. Also, thermographically printed letterheads or other designs may not be able to withstand the heat and can also damage the printer.

Many types of paper can be fed through a laser printer, including medium-weight drawing papers such as Canson's charcoal paper or Strathmore 400 drawing series (specific capacities are listed in each printer's manual). If a paper is too thin it may tear. Rice paper is thin but strong and often works. Linty papers should be avoided because the lint can clog the printer. Also, toner may not fuse well to some absorbent rag papers or very slick materials. In such cases, clear spray fixative or spray shellac can be applied after printing. These sprays will also create deeper, more consistent black areas.

Beyond the Print Button—I

Experiment with different papers! This advice applies to any printer that does not require special paper.

As with any small-format printer, creative solutions to size restrictions should be considered. Books can be made with many small pages (see Craig Hickman's book in Figs. 4.27 and 4.28) or pages can be tiled together in interesting ways.

Run the image through twice or more to create a more textured surface and darker blacks (be forewarned, however, that registration is not perfect, so this approach is not recommended for work requiring great accuracy). Increased texture and pictorial space also can be achieved by printing different images on top of one another, rather than by compositing them in the computer.

Color toner cartridges can be swapped in and out of a single-color laser printer to print different colored images on top of one another. Because of the mechanics of the printer, toner is not left over when the colors are switched.

Figure 3.15 shows a toner drawing by Lane Hall and Lisa Moline. They created this one-of-a-kind piece by printing the image on a laser printer onto bond paper and then photocopying it onto stiff 11″ × 17″ Japanese paper. The print was sent through the photocopier many times so that images are superimposed. After each photocopying, they removed toner with a sharp knife, scratching back to the surface of the paper (hence the term "toner drawing"). The print is finished only after repeated photocopying and scratching. The surface has an interesting texture of built-up toner and meticulous hand work. A similar process can be used for smaller works with a laser printer alone.

COLOR **Color laser printers** use the same technology as single-color printers, but have cyan, magenta, yellow, and black toner cartridges. Color laser printing has recently increased in quality and availability and decreased dramatically in price (almost every major printer company offers a color laser printer at prices generally in the $3000 to $6000 range). Although color laser printers vary in quality, the overall results obtained from them are very good. Because of their speed (about 5 to 15 pages per minute), reliability, and low media costs (only about 20¢ per page for text with a graphic; more for page-sized photos), they are becoming favorites of copy centers and service bureaus, as well as businesses.

Thin films of dry toner do not make a lush surface, however, and many service bureaus and copy shops do not let customers use their own paper with the printer. Also, as with most color printers, visible halftone patterns can make a printout look grainy.

Beyond the Print Button—II

Color copying can make an image look smoother because the dots merge somewhat. Most color copiers also have digital adjustments for color balance or even special effects.

6.4.2 DOT-MATRIX IMPACT PRINTERS

Low-cost **dot-matrix impact printers** no longer compete in cost or quality with other printing technologies, but they still can be surprisingly useful. Many cost less than $500, though large-format and higher resolution models are more expensive. Their lack of popularity can also be attributed to their poor print quality and the loud noise they make while printing.

The dot-matrix impact printer works like a typewriter: Instead of letters, metal wire ends (the dots) are arranged in a matrix and smacked against a ribbon in different combinations, transferring ink onto the paper. Impact printers can print on many different types of paper and many models were designed with wide carriages, so that they can handle relatively large images. In addition, the impact printer has a simple open mechanism and paper path, making experimenting with different papers and techniques easier. The resolution usually is quite low.

The artistic potential of this type of printer has been explored in depth by artists Lisa Moline and Lane Hall. The works shown in Fig. 3.14 are part of a series printed on a 16-inch wide dot-matrix printer with a four-color ribbon. The images were printed directly onto Japanese paper. To get around the size limitation of the printer, the artists tore the paper into strips and then taped them back together, often with colored tape for emphasis. The rich surfaces are built by repeated computer and wood-block printings and are often worked on by hand as well.

Beyond the Print Button—III

Hall and Moline, who work with impact printers by choice, give the following suggestions [Hall and Moline, 1996].

- There is no complex paper path or high heat in an impact printer, so the possible range of papers is greater than with many other types of printer. Traditional art papers work well, as do already existing papers such as maps and book pages and gold- and silver-leafed paper.
- Custom "carbon paper" can be created by coating the back of ordinary paper with colored pastels. Place the carbon paper against a fresh sheet of printing paper. The physical impact of a dot-matrix printer transfers the pastel and produces subtle colors not available in printer ribbons.
- Paper stencils can be used to mask out portions of the page before printing.
- Many impact printers take pin-feed paper that comes in a stack of perforated sheets. This and other pin-feed paper products can be used to overcome the usually severe size constraints of computer-printed output and create long scrolls or banners.

6.4.3 Ink-Jet Printers

Ink-jet printers are many computer artists' and designers' favorite type of printer. They are economically priced (prices have fallen to less than $200 at the low end; better quality ink-jet printers range from $500 to thousands of dollars), and the colors are often deeply saturated and pleasing. Instead of dry toner and a heat-fusing process, ink jets use aqueous (water-based) inks that are sprayed or otherwise dispensed from disposable ink reservoirs through small jets onto the paper surface. Although many media, such as different types of paper and even cloth, can be used, clay-coated glossy paper made especially for ink-jet printers usually yields the best results because more ink remains near the surface of the paper instead of being absorbed into it. The unreliability of the color—it can change dramatically, depending on the paper, for instance—makes them generally inappropriate for professional color proofing. In addition, ink-jet printers usually are much slower than laser printers and have less consistent and reliable image quality. The cost per page generally is higher than for toner-based printing, mostly because of the cost of ink-jet paper. (The media cost of ink alone for a midrange four-color printer is about 7¢ a page, and the cost of paper ranges from pennies a page for plain paper to about a dime for matte ink-jet paper to more than a dollar for premium glossy ink-jet paper.)

For inexpensive color printing, ink-jet printers offer more capabilities and flexibility than comparably priced color printers based on other technologies (at the low end of color printing, no other technologies currently compete in price). Figure 6.9 shows a self-portrait by artist Michael Wright printed with a low-end ink-jet printer. Wright uses a video capture board, Amiga computer, and low-end ink-jet printer to create

Figure 6.9 Michael Wright, *Shaken*, 1995 (ink-jet print, 4′ × 5′). *(Courtesy of Michael Wright)*

large-scale tiled portraits. The artifacts introduced by the printing technique, as well as those from the video-capture and image-manipulation processes, are an integral part of his work.

Beyond the Print Button—IV

Like impact printers, ink-jet printers do not use heat and have a simple paper path, allowing many types of paper and even collaged work to be used. Paper can be run through repeatedly to build up textures and patterns and create a sense of overlapping forms and pictorial depth.

HIGH-END INK-JET PRINTERS   Ink-jet printers dominate both the low end and the high end of color computer printing. Among artists, the most popular high-end ink-jet printers are produced by Iris Graphics (now owned by Scitex Corporation). Iris printers can print up to 32 different-sized dots (real halftones) and, as a result, have effective resolutions comparable to an 1800-dpi printer. The color quality is truly marvelous, and prints can be matte or glossy. Iris printers can print on a range of materials, papers, and fabrics from canvas to silk and mylar, creating breathtaking results. These high-end printers cost $20,000 to as much as $85,000 for Iris's fine-arts printer; service bureaus charge between $200 and $300 for a large-size (46″ × 33.5″) Iris print.

Unfortunately, the standard inks fade with exposure to light within a period of about five years. Prints exposed to sunlight without a UV laminate or UV-protective plexiglas become noticeably lighter and less saturated after only a few months. Some colors fade faster than others—black is the most stable and magenta the least. New inks and print drivers can produce more richly saturated and archival prints. Some printers have taken matters into their own hands: Jon Cone of Cone Editions in East Topsham, Vermont, has been instrumental in creating archival options for artists using ink-jet technology. Cone's modifications of both the software and hardware of Iris Graphics ink-jet printers enable him to make prints of extraordinary quality that are archival for 20–24 years (about as good as Cibachrome, now Ilfochrome) [Cone, 1996]. Many artists use his printing facilities or one of the more than a dozen printing shops that he has set up featuring his customized printers. Figure 6.10 shows a work by Richard Rosenblum printed at Cone Editions. The deep blacks and archival properties of this print would be impossible with standard Iris printer setups. Continually improved archival measures and lower prices will make high-end ink-jet printing an ever more attractive alternative for computer art work.

Figure 6.10 Richard Rosenblum, *Pirate Crab,* 1994. *(Courtesy of Richard Rosenblum)*

6.4.4 THERMAL WAX PRINTERS

Although they are now not so popular, **thermal wax printers** once dominated the business market for color printers and, until dye sublimation printers became more affordable, were the printer of choice for rapid color proofing. For many artists they were also the first personally controllable color printers that provided decent-quality results. Thermal wax printers have continued to evolve and can turn out accurate and compelling images, often at high speed. Costs are generally in the $1000 to $5000 range, with media costs at $0.50 to $1.50 per letter-sized page.

There are two main types of thermal wax printers. One uses a ribbon consisting of sequential panels of cyan, magenta, yellow, and often black wax-based colors that are melted onto the paper by a heated dot-matrix print head. A full section of the four color swatches is rolled through the printer for each print no matter what is printed: A single word in black uses the same amount of media as a full-page, full-color image. The second type of thermal wax printer, **solid-ink printers,** uses solid wax crayons that are melted and sprayed onto the paper, where they then cool and adhere. Because the wax goes from a solid to a liquid and back to a solid, this type of printer is sometimes called a **phase-change printer.**

As in the other low-end color printing technologies discussed so far, colored dots are still plainly visible, preventing the output from attaining a truly photographic look. Wax-based color often is not as saturated as that produced by aqueous inks, and the wax has its own identifiable look and feel. However, multiple passes can build up an otherwise thin texture and produce interesting colors and a sense of depth, somewhat like the traditional paint process of glazing. Thermal-wax prints can fade rapidly in sunlight and should be protected with UV plexiglas.

Annette Weintraub has made thermal wax her output medium of choice for hard-copy color works (see Fig. 6.11). Her *Night Light* series depicts urban environments and is constructed from pieces of photographs of industrial enclaves, highways, and commercial strips. The scenes are uninhabited, and the exaggerated and unnatural colors of cities at night are emphasized. "The cyan, magenta, yellow and black screened dots of process color and the clearly artificial surface of the cold-wax print are consistent with the qualities of artificial light and color in the nocturnal commercial environment. The grid of tiled pages laminated onto a single sheet reintroduces an element of the patterning grid and repetition of the urban environment" [Weintraub, 1995].

Figure 6.11 Annette Weintraub, *Holiday Night,* 1994 (from the *Night Light* series). *(Courtesy of Annette Weintraub)*

6.4.5 Dye Sublimation Printers

Dye-sublimation printers, or *dye subs* as they are called, produce images that look like glossy photographs. No dots are visible to the naked eye, so dye subs are the ideal printers for many computer artists, especially those working in a photographic tradition. Figure 6.12 shows an image by Ken Golden, who relies on the dye-sub print's photographic look to arouse specific associations in the viewer's mind. In the *Family Inqueeries* series, Golden scanned in family photos and then added visual elements that challenge the notion of family and speak to the artist's experiences of growing up gay. The pieces are printed on a dye sub to give them the look and surface quality of real photographs (even though the digital compositions are not meant to be photorealistic). The white borders resembling those of early photographs complete the snapshot effect.

Most dye subs cost between $5000 and 10,000 (more for large-format, high-quality machines), but several companies now offer dye subs for less than $1000. Printing time is 2 to 3 minutes and up, depending on file size and complexity. Because most dye subs require a special type of paper that accepts and diffuses the dye, many types of experimentation are impossible. (No interesting effects are obtained by printing on plain paper.) Also, media costs are higher than for almost any other type of printer in this price range: An 8.5″ × 11″ page costs about $2 to $3 to print, and a 12″ × 12″ or tabloid page can cost $5 to $6 or more.

The dye-sublimation printer mechanism is similar to that of a thermal wax printer: The ribbon is a roll with cyan, magenta, yellow, and sometimes black sheets in a sequence. Unlike thermal wax, however, the dye from the ribbon is sublimated (changed into a gas) and absorbed by the paper; it spreads with a soft edge instead of forming a hard dot. The saturation of the color created by the dye's interaction with the special paper can be controlled by varying the temperature of the heating elements, eliminating the need for halftoning. The sublimation process can also be used to mix colors directly, eliminating the need for groups of cyan, magenta, yellow, and black dots. Thus the resolution of a dye sub (as with high-end

Figure 6.12 Ken Golden, *James & Flo w/Friend,* 1994 (2.5″ × 2.5″). From the series *Family Inqueeries. (Courtesy of Kenneth Sean Golden)*

ink-jet printers) is not as important a factor as with other printing technologies: a 300-dpi dye sub produces much more photorealistic-looking images than even a 600-dpi ink-jet or laser printer.

Dye-sub prints fade in ultraviolet light. Some ribbons, however, have an extra laminating sheet that can significantly enhance the life of a print and, as with most color computer-printing technologies, images should be framed with UV-protective plexiglas. Although the properties of dye-sub prints are constantly improving, if archival prints are needed, dye-sub printing should be used only for proofing. A traditional photographic process, such as Cibachrome or archival digital image printing, should be used for final production.

6.5 LARGE-SCALE PRINTING

One of the most frustrating aspects of printing for many artists is the small size of the output. Originally designed for business letters, most laser printers print 8.5″ × 11″ paper from one tray and legal-sized documents (8.5″ × 14″) from another and allow smaller sheets to be fed manually (or through an envelope tray). Printers capable of printing tabloid-sized sheets (11″ × 17″) cost significantly more than the standard sizes. Large-scale, high-end ink-jet printers and many plotters can print large images (several feet wide and of almost unlimited length) because the paper is on a roll, but other color printers are limited to a size of 8.5″ × 11″ or sometimes 12″ × 12″. For many artists, these size constraints alone are a reason not to pursue most of the available low-cost printing solutions.

6.5.1 PLOTTERS

Ironically, printing size options were better in the early days of computer graphics when artists used vector-based **plotters,** which usually are quite large and give more room for experimentation in both the size of the printed work and media used. Plotters such as the one shown in Fig. 6.13 use a set of pens or other mark-making implements that are controlled by instructions from the computer. Unlike the printers discussed so far, this type of plotter accepts geometric instructions about vertices and the lines between them, not pixel values. Thus the pens move around the page from point to point instead of creating an image in a sequence of horizontal lines. Although this process makes printing photographic imagery difficult (if not impossible), it does offer features unavailable in other types of computer printers. There are no halftoning or aliasing artifacts such as jaggies, and lines can physically cross over one another, creating a sense of layered depth. In addition, the user can change the mark-making medium by substituting different drawing implements. The large ink-jet printers that have replaced most vector-based plotters are also called plotters but accept only raster image data.

Figure 6.13 **A pen plotter executing Roman Verostko's drawing instructions.** This type of plotter rolls the paper back and forth vertically while a pen moves horizontally. Some plotters have movable pens that traverse a fixed sheet of paper.

Artist Roman Verostko started his artistic career as a painter but has been creating art with computers and plotters for more than 15 years. He now makes his own plotter inks with acrylic pigments and replaces the ink pens with Chinese brushes and other tools. Verostko writes programs that feed pen selection and coordinate choices to the plotter to create his imagery.

Printing technology can become obsolete, just like software packages. For example, although Verostko and Jean-Pierre Hebert depend on vector-based plotters to create their work, most companies have stopped making these plotters. Both artists have purchased several plotters and are always on the lookout for extra machines to cannibalize for spare parts. What will happen when these last plotters break down? How will the "signature" of this machine be interpreted years from now when it becomes associated with a particular time period or even particular people?

6.5.2 Large Raster-Based Printers

Large-scale printers that work with raster images are becoming more affordable. Service bureaus (see Section 6.8) are providing more options in this area, driven by the demand for fast color proofing, very small color runs, outdoor signage, trade shows, and large-scale images. Most such printers are based on ink-jet or electrostatic technology (similar to laser printers). Plastic-based inks printed onto vinyl and laminated can be used outdoors in direct sunlight without rapid fading. The quality is often geared toward displays to be seen at a distance and may not be satisfactory close up.

High-resolution large-scale printers such as those made by Scitex, Linotronic-Hell, and Agfa are called **typesetters** and are used by professional graphic designers and production personnel to create very high-resolution output for commercial printing. Typesetters typically print at 1200 to 2400 dpi and instead of toner use a photographic process that develops the image onto a resin-coated paper or transparent film. Typesetter output is not usually the final product but is used to shoot printing plates. Anyone interested in the output from such high-end printers should consult a local service bureau. More and more printing houses are using digital prepress, and the artist often can deliver material on disk directly to the printer, rather than printing and delivering camera-ready copy.

6.5.3 Tiling

Between the single letter-sized page and an expensive large-scale print is another option—**tiling.** By tiling an image, that is, spreading it over any number of individual pages, an artist can assemble a very large work from standard printer output. Douglas Kornfeld describes a major tiled work, shown in Fig. 6.14, as follows:

> The entire installation was made up of more than 10,000 individual images. Each was printed on a laser printer, hand-cut, and then individually stapled to the gallery walls. It took 400 hours to install. [The front wall is based on an image from a twelfth-century Psalter entitled the *Entrance to Hell*.] It was scanned and extensively altered using the computer. In the foreground you see hundreds of symbolic figures; these appear to be spilling out of the walls behind you and then marching across the floor into the mouth of hell.

> The maze design [on the right wall] was originally from the floor of a medieval cathedral in France. Its purpose was to serve as a substitute for a pilgrimage to the Holy Land, its circuitous path a metaphor for the long journey to Jerusalem as well as the path to spiritual enlightenment. I placed the standard boy icon in the center of one of these mazes and the girl icon in the center of the other. In the steps leading to the center I placed the many variations of these icons that spill out of the air conditioning slots. This is a celebration of diversity and depicts how symbols can be used for "good" purposes—a pathway to redemption. Around the mazes are more than 3000 individual slips of paper each with a boy or girl icon stapled to the wall [Kornfeld, 1995].

Figure 6.14 Douglas Kornfeld, *Pathways to Damnation or Redemption,* **1995** (installation at the Fuller Museum of Art in Brockton, MA). Kornfeld developed the piece by creating images in a draw-type program, exporting them to a 3D program in which he had built a model of the space, and then applying the images as textures. When the virtual results were satisfactory, the adventure of creating the physical work began. The images were tiled in Adobe Illustrator, printed on a 300 dpi laser printer (eight toner cartridges were used), and then the white margins of each piece of paper were cut off by hand with a ruler and X-acto knife. One the biggest challenges was marking off accurate grids on the walls of the museum. For the monster on the front wall there was only one inch leeway [Kornfeld, 1998]. *(Courtesy of Douglas Kornfeld)*

Front wall

Right wall

The visible seams that tiling leaves can be either minimized or made a part of the work. The tiling option in most graphics software distributes the image evenly over a range of pages, but tiling by hand or with flexible tiling software can let the artist use different-sized tiles and thus break up the regular grid structure that otherwise results. When tiling, be sure to use archival materials such as wheat paste or framer's tape; adhesives such as rubber cement, spray mount and Scotch tape will eventually yellow and eat away at the paper. Paper changes shape with temperature and humidity, so tiling inevitably leads to some wrinkling and waves. Tiled (and other) works can be mounted with dry mounting or archival adhesive to a board or foam core to fix the paper and keep it from deforming. (However, mounting to a substrate drastically reduces the resale value of an art work.)

6.6 TRADITIONAL PRINTMAKING AND PHOTOGRAPHY

Although today's computer printers continue to advance in quality and fall in price, they generally leave a great deal to be desired as an art medium. The printing process is still largely aimed at producing short-lived color proofs, and this intention strongly influences artists who are using that equipment. For instance, generating texture of any kind is almost impossible and any interactive control over the printing process is rare.

Computer artwork need not have its final tangible 2D form in a computer print-out, however. Through photography and photoprinting techniques, the world of traditional art can be productively integrated with computer printing to offer an exciting interface between new and old art-making processes. Photography, photosilkscreen, photoetching, and photolithography all are options. Color separations and registration marks can be printed directly from most high-end graphics programs.

6.6.1 FILM-BASED IMAGES

Sometimes photographing an image directly from the screen or using a film recorder is effective and efficient. Relatively slow daylight film (anything under 200-speed) should be used. (Many artists choose 64-speed slide film.) If you choose to use this method, set your camera on a tripod and block out the computer screen edges with black fabric. Be sure to turn off or lower the lights in the room and do not use a flash (both cause glare). Expose the film for at least 1/30 second to avoid catching the screen redrawing. You can simulate a gray card by creating an entirely gray image in a graphics program. In any case, always bracket, because fluctuating screen light can cause erratic light-meter readings.

For higher-quality images, use a **film recorder** (service bureaus have them if you don't have access to one directly). A film recorder contains a small, very high–resolution black and white CRT that projects through red, green, and blue colored gels. The image is created slowly on the film, one raster line at a time. High-end film recorders can output 35 mm slides at 4000 dpi and can also make 4 × 5s and other transparencies. Expect to pay anywhere from $0.50 to several dollars per image, depending on quality, whether the image is already rasterized, and how quickly you need it.

6.6.2 Photoprintmaking

Photoprintmaking for all types of printing requires a plate maker, essentially a light box with a vacuum seal and strong UV lights. The printing plate is covered with a photosensitive emulsion and the positive or negative transparency (depending on the printing process) is placed between the plate and the surface of the plate maker. Air is removed to bring the transparency and plate together and the lights are turned on, hardening the light-sensitive emulsion.

Laser printouts or photocopies can also be used directly as lithographic transfers. Artists Lane Hall and Lisa Moline suggest the following [Hall and Moline, 1996]: Dampen the print with gum arabic and roll it up with ink and a brayer. The toner on the paper repels the gum arabic; the paper, saturated with gum arabic, repels the printer's ink. The toner attracts the ink and fills with whatever color ink you use. You can then print this onto any surface you desire, directly to paper or to an etching or lithographic plate.

The interplay between different types of traditional printing and computer output varies. For lithographic plates that can be etched only once, the computer image transfer is a one-time process. If a stone is used, further hand-drawn or computer-based work can be added, but regrinding photoetched stones can be time-consuming. With silkscreen, the screen can be exposed only once. Unlike lithography, different-colored inks can be wiped in different areas of a silk screen or an etching with a high level of control. Gradient rolls and other printing techniques can be used with all three methods. Etching is perhaps the most flexible overall. Parts of the image can be removed with a burnisher, and the image can be worked on almost indefinitely with repeated hand-drawn or photoetched additions. An etching press is also more economical for individual use than lithography. Silkscreen is perhaps the most economical and practical for many artists because a press is not needed.

The transparencies used for photoprintmaking and as output of film recorders can also, of course, be used in traditional photographic processes. (To create a negative instead of a positive, even with slide film, simply invert your screen image.) Developing prints yourself instead of pressing a print button or sending a file to a service bureau lets you control the printing process interactively by adjusting exposure, color balance, and scale in the physical realm. Doing so also lets you utilize hands-on photographic techniques mimicked in Adobe Photoshop and similar programs (e.g., dodging, burning, and even more dramatic image-manipulation methods).

Photographic printing can be done on much larger paper than most computer printing and can also be archival. In fact, the most archival computer printing processes actually are forms of pigment-transfer photography. The UltraStable process, for instance, developed by Charles Berger, uses pigments instead of dyes and requires a

Figure 6.15 Ken Golden, KSG.70 McDonald's Bag, Inside, 1992. From *Cardboard Story*, a series of cyanotype prints of hands on cardboard (each meant to be seen as one of many elements). Every piece has an accession number, noting the source of the cardboard and highlighting the artist's concerns with recycling, availability, and accessibility of materials. *(Courtesy of Kenneth Sean Golden)*

color separation to work from (no problem for a computer-based piece). UltraStable prints are expected to last more than 500 years, or longer than even the most archival of photographs such as Ilfochrome. A 23″ × 36″ print costs about $500.

When concern for archival properties is not paramount, artists can make simple contact prints or use photochemicals such as Liquid Light to print images onto a variety of materials. Figure 6.15 shows the work of Ken Golden (see also Fig. 6.12), an artist who uses the computer for image capture and processing but chooses extremely low-cost and equipment-free output techniques.

6.7 COMBINING DIGITAL AND TRADITIONAL TECHNIQUES

Output need not consist solely of one medium or technique or even a fixed sequence of techniques. Collage and montage can let artists integrate the computer into more familiar ways of working and make the most of the strengths of the computer and of traditional art approaches and materials. Printouts can be incorporated into drawings, paintings, and collages; computer animations can become part of live-action movies. In short, an interchange and mingling of techniques can be fruitful, letting artists take advantage of the best of all worlds and mix the aesthetics of computer-generated work with traditional efforts. For example, in the work shown in Fig. 6.16 Michael O'Rourke used a computer plotter to create a structural wireframe image and then used pastels to add color and a wide range of line and form not then available with a computer printing method. For O'Rourke, the combination of media was not just a formal solution but part of an ongoing investigation into the ways that different

Figure 6.16 Michael O'Rourke, Icon #1, 1987. (Courtesy of Michael O'Rourke)

mark-making techniques define and fill space (see also Fig. 7.13). The computer may also be used simply as a visualization tool, with final work rendered in traditional media.

6.8 Service Bureaus

A **service bureau** provides input and output services such as high-resolution scanning and high-quality printing. Many service bureaus grew naturally as shops offering typesetting, printing, or photographic processing that began to incorporate more digital options. Designers, illustrators, and photographers are their largest client base, but a few, such as Cone Press and Nash Editions, focus on fine-art needs.

With the rapid growth of computer prepress tools, service bureaus have become more used to dealing with people who have less technical knowledge than graphics professionals and are offering an ever wider range of services and assistance. If you are interested in trying a new printing technique or need high-end services such as high-resolution drum scanning or typesetter printouts, a service bureau is the place to go. However, copy stores now usually offer some computer-based services that overlap with those formerly provided only by professional service bureaus, such as low-end color computer printing, scanning stations, and workstation rental time. In addition to local establishments, which can be found in the yellow pages, digital files can be mailed

Conclusion

Computer printing is still in its infancy and is fraught with problems. Most computer printers are developed for business needs such as letter writing or for short-term design and illustration purposes. Artists must consciously assess the advantages and disadvantages of different print output choices and become aware of alternative ways to use a printer that its manuals would not suggest. The expectations that they have of a "print," based on experience creating and viewing traditional prints and the expectations inherent in the technology (pushing a button and receiving a printout), affect how artists and designers use and view computer printouts. Developing a sense of a printer as a physical medium in which the artist is working takes time and experimentation. Like software, new printers are created every day, and artists often must decide whether to stay with an older, more familiar printing technology or begin experimenting with new and different machines.

Artists immediately notice that most computer printing looks terrible by traditional standards. The few exceptions include high-end typesetters used to create mass-printed works and the expensive high-end ink-jet technologies such as the Iris printer. Many computer artists address this problem by using traditional photography and printmaking or integrating computer prints with traditional printmaking and collage. Others seek to master the nature of their printer as they would any other artistic tool, learning its strengths and weaknesses and integrating them into the meaning and message of their artwork.

Suggested Readings

Blatner, David, and Steve Roth. *Real World Scanning and Halftones.* Peachpit Press, 1993. Thoroughly covers all the basic and some more advanced concepts important for optimizing the process of scanning images and printing them. Although the information is inherently technical, the writing style makes it appropriate even for beginners. For artists and designers who are already familiar with the basics, this book clarifies more advanced points and also provides a handy reference.

Bruno, Michael H. (ed.). 16th edition. International Paper Company, 1995. *Pocket Pal, A Graphics Arts Production Handbook.* What can be said about a book in its sixteenth edition? Graphic designers have come to know and trust this source of information on graphic arts printing. It is mostly concerned with traditional processes but includes digital printing information.

Cost, Frank. *Pocket Guide to Digital Printing* (Pocket Guide Series). Delmar, 1996. An easy-to-use practical guide that covers printing concepts, analog and digital printing processes, type, halftoning, color management, and digital printing applications.

Durbeck, Robert C., and Sol Sherr (eds.). *Output Hardcopy Devices.* Academic Press, 1988. A technical book on hardcopy output that describes how different types of printers work.

The editors of *Flash* magazine. *Underground Guide to Laser Printers.* Peachpit Press, 1993. Everything you wanted to know about laser printers and more. Written for nontechies and full of truly amazing ideas and tips about getting the most out of laser printing.

Saff, Donald, and Deli Sacilotto. *Printmaking, History and Process.* Holt, Rinehart, and Winston, 1978. An invaluable reference for printmakers, whether entirely traditional or incorporating the computer through photoprintmaking processes.

Exercises

The key to successful printing involves systematic, sometimes tedious, experimentation. In general, don't accept your first few printouts as the final word on how your image can look.

1. Finishing the photo album. Continue Exercise 5, Chapter 2, "The new family photo album." Now use a dye sub to produce the actual album. Experiment with simulating traditional photo formats—for example, the standard 4″ × 6″ or 3″ × 5″ sizes or the Polaroid-type borders (as in Ken Golden's piece in Fig. 6.12).

2. Creative halftones. Create your own halftone shape in the spirit of Ken Knowlton's *Mural* in Fig. 1.12. Use the choice of shape either to reinforce the image or to present a new interpretation of it.

3. Laser layers. Using a draw-type program, create an image that is either abstract with strong spatial qualities or represents a real 3D space. Use several layers. Print the image one layer at a time, reinserting the same piece of paper to build the layers on top of each other. Continue to work on the image, adding several more layers by using the printout as feedback when creating the next layer (rather than just looking at the screen).

4. Aliens in your home town—integrating the hand. Imagine that your home town has been destroyed by aliens who think you've stolen their missing ballpoint pens. They find nothing and leave without saying goodby. Use the computer to draw portions of the landscape that they left behind, which should include the remnants of their advanced blasting and digging machinery. Print out your work. Now draw into the image (use color if you have a color scanner and printer). Scan it in, work on it on the computer, and then reprint it. Repeat three times. The end result should demonstrate the different types of marks that the hand and computer can make to add visual interest to the landscape.

5. Tile city. Don't let the small paper size of most printers keep you from creating large-scale works. You can always arbitrarily tile an image, but you can also design works with tiling in mind. Create a piece based either on a simple, page-sized grid or on any random rectangular portions (with none larger than your printer can print). Suggestions: a city grid, a series of variations, an abstract work, or closeups and far-away views of the same scene. If the sections are regular enough, you may be able to tile the image automatically; otherwise make each section a separate file and print it out. Assemble the finished project. Suggestions: Rather then segmenting a coherent image that must be reconstructed in the right order, experiment with works that can be combined at the tiling stage in many different ways.

CHAPTER 7

Building 3D Worlds— 3D Geometric Graphics I

Figure 7.1 Kathleen Ruíz, *Random Mummy,* **1991** (digital photograph, 4.5″ × 6″). Kathleen Ruíz works with 3D programs to create spatial constructions that "monumentalize the invisible or visually unknown." Although her work is realized with geometric modeling programs and in real 3D materials such as granite, it remains conceptual. The evocative, abstract forms become sites for the expression of her ideas about "belief structures." For example, in this piece a simple but mysterious 3D object is covered with random numbers. For her "the idea of randomness in a conceptual space relates to the physical states of genetic causality and the seeming randomness in accidental situations in everyday life (the statistics of who is born when and where)" [Ruíz, 1996].

Her meditative 3D objects refer directly to the artifice of 3D geometry and the desire to construct systems and beliefs. Ruíz has been working with computers and electronic multimedia for more than 15 years, producing work with a variety of media combinations, including a virtual set design for playwright Neil Simon. Her work in many media is united by the conceptual theme of borders between "physical objective space and incorporeal subjective space" [Ruíz, 1996]. *(Courtesy of Kathleen Ruíz and The Sandra Gering Gallery)*

7.1 INTRODUCTION

Do we represent the construction, or construct the representation? This question lies at the heart of debates concerning the new alliance of the sciences, arts, and technologies, as well as debates about the role of computers in conception and construction [Virilio, 1991, p. 103].

Paul Virilio, cultural theorist

Three-dimensional programs are entirely new and unprecedented types of tools for visual artists. With 3D graphics, artists and designers can for the first time in human history rapidly create, view, and change 3D forms without using physical 3D materials. With 3D graphics, they can construct abstract 3D spaces—building and combining objects, giving them different "material properties" such as reflectiveness, transparency, and textures, and controlling lighting effects.

Three-dimensional graphics have revolutionized the working methods of many professions, including everything from theoretical mathematics, aviation design, flight simulation, and precision manufacturing to architecture, advertising, video games, and Hollywood entertainment. Imagine trying to convey your designs for a new lighthouse, for instance, to a maritime agency. Plan and elevation drawings offer accuracy but do not give most people an intuitive sense of a structure's form. Architectural renderings could depict the lighthouse from different perspectives, but each different rendering would involve literally going back to the drawing board. A physical scale model would let a viewer quickly take in many views, but would be laborious to make, difficult to change, too small to explore, and could be in only one place at a time. In contrast, a 3D computer program enables designers to create 3D models and look at them from any point of view (see Fig. 7.2). These models can also be shared among interested parties in different geographic locations at the same or different times.

Michael Rees, a traditional sculptor turned computer user (see Section 9.5), enjoys the flexibility that 3D programs afford him:

> If I'm spending a little time making something with my hands and I've got two forms,
> I can't put one inside the other. I can't shrink one down to 1/10th the size and drop it
> into the other.... Realizing the potential of the computer was like falling into a pit
> that happened to have a bunch of gold in it. You've fallen, but in some sense you're
> richer for it [Rees, 1998a].

Making and viewing 3D computer work can be alternately unbelievably frustrating and deeply rewarding. Part of the problem lies in the inherent complexity of 3D graphics and in the difficulty of working with 3D information on a 2D screen with a 2D input device (e.g., a mouse). Many obstacles can be overcome, however, by learning some of the vocabulary specific to 3D programs and understanding some of the basic concepts that make them work. Unfamiliar technical terms and phrases common in 3D programs, such as *primitives, polygonal meshes, sweeping a profile, Gouraud shading,*

Figure 7.2 Views of a 3D lighthouse model. With this computer-based 3D model, designers and others can explore the proposed structure from any point of view—even from inside.

Figure 7.3 **Douglas Kornfeld, *Who Are You?*, 1995.** The artist built the project three times: in Providence, RI, in Boston, MA in the midst of the construction site for the Central Artery Project (acting as a construction fence), and at the Forest City Development in Cambridge, Massachusetts. Viewers are led to compare the appearance of passersby with the cutouts, calling attention to the dynamic relationship between symbols and actual instances of the stereotypes they represent. *(Courtesy of Douglas Kornfeld)*

and *ray tracing,* will become clear as you study this chapter and Chapter 8, Rendering 3D Worlds—3D Geometric Graphics II. The more you learn of the underlying principles, the easier it will be for you to become comfortable with any 3D program, even one that you have never used before.

A 3D artist is at once a sculptor, painter, and conceptual artist, frequently an animator or filmmaker, and until recently, often a computer scientist as well. Douglas Kornfeld uses 3D programs and image-editing software to envision commissioned projects and to create virtual sculptures that may never be realized. These works involve sculptural skills, photographic decisions, and 2D composition of the type associated with painting and drawing. He created the *Who Are You?* project, shown in Fig. 7.3, to be viewed on-screen over the Web or in a gallery as photographs, but exhibition of the 2D image led to commissions to create actual sculptures.

7.2 CONCEPTS

Three-dimensional programs involve the use of virtually all the concepts and methods discussed in the previous chapters on 2D image creation, as well as new ideas peculiar to the third dimension. The conceptual and technical issues thus span several fields of artistic endeavor (and numerous other professions) and include most of the issues raised in other types of image-creation software. Only a few of these topics can be touched on here. (See Chapter 10, 2D and 3D Animation and Video, for coverage of 3D animation.)

7.2.1 MODELING AND RENDERING

In digital design and layout programs, 2D geometry is used to define 2D shapes and continuous 2D geometric descriptions are rasterized to create images for raster-based screens and printers. In 3D programs, **3D geometry** is used to define 2D and 3D shapes, and continuous 2D and 3D geometric descriptions are rasterized to create images for raster-based screens and printers.

So why are 3D programs so much more complex than 2D programs? What new concepts are involved? The challenges lie primarily in representing the added dimension and describing the effects of light on object surfaces. These challenges divide the field into two distinct areas, modeling and rendering (the topic of Chapter 8). In **modeling,** you create 3D objects, just as you create 2D objects in a digital design and layout program. In **rendering,** you rasterize the models, but the process is more complex than in 2D; the computer must project the 3D information onto a 2D plane for display and calculate lighting effects on object surfaces. Although new graphics hardware available in most PCs has greatly accelerated rendering times, a complex scene might still require minutes—even hours or days—to render.

7.2.2 WHAT IS A MODEL?

Modeling is coping with complexity [van Dam, 1994].
Andries van Dam, co-author of Computer Graphics, Principles and Practice

A **model** is a version of an object, concept, or phenomenon that represents some of its important features. For instance, an architectural model shows the shape of a building and its parts, as well as its overall visual appearance. It is not the same size as the real building, probably doesn't depict the wiring and plumbing or have the characteristics of real building material, and quite often is completely empty inside. The builder of a model must decide which features of the real object or other entity to incorporate in it. The use of models is crucial in fields as varied as particle physics and Hollywood stage set design.

All art work involves modeling, that is, representing some part of a scene, a feeling, or an experience, while leaving other parts out. For example, when Matisse painted a woman's face with a few deft brush strokes, he was extracting the "salient features," the important information that he felt modeled the face. At the same time he was ignoring thousands of details that would not have contributed to his painting. The examples of art works shown in this chapter use 3D modeling to depict everything from realistic objects to abstract concepts and from visualizations of information to emotions and states of mind.

A good model captures information and relationships vital for a specific purpose, whether that purpose is functional or aesthetic. A good model lets its creator conceive ideas that would be difficult, if not impossible, to come up with when faced with a real phenomenon in all its complexity. For example, in war movies, the general may conceive a battle strategy by using salt and pepper shakers on a tablecloth; scientists were able to think about atoms in new ways after physicist Niels Bohr created his geometric model of the atom.

Geometric models need not be based on physical geometric forms. Information about a company's reporting hierarchy can be represented in an organization chart, and data from the stock market or a scientific experiment or opinion poll can be plotted as bar graphs or pie charts in two or three (or more) dimensions. **Scientific visualization** usually refers to the creation of images based on very large sets of data (some

Figure 7.4 Visualizing and exploring wind flow over the space shuttle. The "rake" with streamlines (positioned near the shuttle nose) and the cutting plane (positioned across the wing) are both 3D interaction devices created to help scientists explore or "mine" the data in different ways. Darker grays indicate faster wind flow [Herndon, 1994]. *(Courtesy of The Brown University Computer Graphics Group)*

geometric and some not), such as wind flow speeds and directions over the hull of the space shuttle (see Fig. 7.4). Wind flow over the space shuttle is measured in a wind tunnel and the data are visualized with 3D graphics. The data set used here was gathered to help NASA decide where to place an escape hatch. Visualizing such data frequently reveals information that would be near-impossible to gather from looking at towering piles of numerical printouts.

7.2.3 What's 3D About 3D Modelers?

If it looks like a duck and quacks like a duck, it must be a duck.
Proverbial

A 3D program shows an image on a 2D screen, so what's 3D about it? One way to think about it is that 3D modelers model both 3D geometry (object shapes) and 3D light interactions. You can move an object in a 3D space and rotate and scale it in 3D. When you render it, the object can have reflections, shadows, and other 3D lighting effects. These effects depend on a different space from that of a 2D geometric program: The space has *depth*. In 3D programs, a new axis is added to the x, y Cartesian coordinate system used in 2D graphics. The third dimension or depth is created by adding a z *axis*, a new axis perpendicular (at a right, or 90°, angle) to the x and y axes (see Fig. 7.5).

In addition to modeling the geometry of 3D space, 3D programs can model other aspects of the 3D world. **Behavioral modeling** models an object's behavior, such as a stone falling to the ground if dropped, moving in an arc through the air when thrown, or colliding with other objects. Behaviors are also used to animate articulated characters, determining facial expressions and realistic skin folds.

The primary research goal in 3D graphics for the last several decades has been to model the real 3D world accurately. This pursuit is interdisciplinary, requiring scientific understanding of phenomena such as the nature of light and its interaction with various materials, and mathematical understanding of the shape and structure of complex forms of human-made and natural objects. When is a model accurate enough? is a question for both scientists and artists. For both, the question might be rephrased, How much and what type of detail is needed to build the image or system desired? Sometimes all that is needed is a still picture. At other times, an animated walkthrough of a synthetic environment such as a building, a maze, or a space vehicle, or an interactive world in which objects have meaningful behaviors, is needed. Three-dimensional spatial information—depth—almost always is needed, but behavioral modeling and the modeling of other aspects of 3D reality, such as sound and physical feedback, also can be important.

7.2.4 Making a 3D Geometric Model

Although 3D geometric modeling programs can seem overwhelmingly complex, virtually all modeling is based on the six tasks shown in Fig. 7.6. These stages in creating a model are a useful way of understanding any 3D program and supply the organization for this chapter and Chapter 8, Rendering 3D Worlds—3D Geometric Graphics II. In practice, the tasks often are performed in parallel. For example, you might choose a material during the process of assembling components because the material's

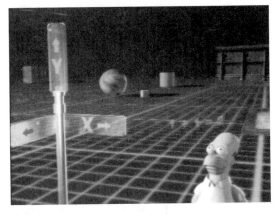

Figure 7.5 Homer Simpson in 3D space. More than 3 ½ minutes of computer-generated character animation were created by PDI for The Simpsons' "Tree House of Horror VI," the first time a traditional 2D character has been re-created in 3D form for television. *(Courtesy of Twentieth Century Fox and Pacific Data Images)*

Figure 7.6 The artist's tasks in 3D modeling. 1. Create simple model elements. 2. Assemble them into more complex objects. 3. Arrange objects in a 3D scene. 4. Choose materials. 5. Set up lights. 6. Choose viewpoint(s) and rendering methods.

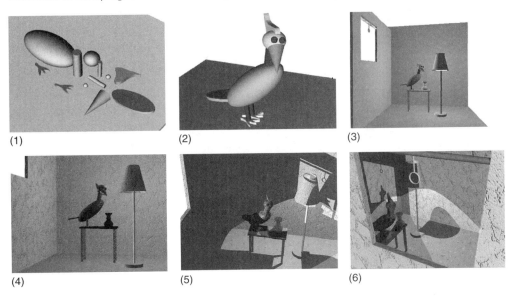

(1) (2) (3)

(4) (5) (6)

appearance affects your choice of components. Similarly, you may find it useful to do a full rendering of your model well before it is completed in order to better assess the results of modeling and choice of materials.

Volume Visualization and 3D Sample-Based Programs

Just as 2D programs can be divided into geometry-based applications (e.g., digital design and layout programs) and raster- or sample-based applications (e.g., digital painting and photoediting programs), so 3D programs can be divided into geometry-based applications (the type described in this chapter) and sample-based programs. Raster-based 3D graphics is based on a 3D equivalent of a pixel, a point in 3D space with associated values called a **voxel** (for *volume element*). Three-dimensional sample-based graphics require tremendous computational support, and today's PCs do not have enough processing power to handle such graphics in real time. In the near future, however, this type of program should become available to artists.

Today, 3D sample-based graphics are used primarily in medicine, engineering, and other fields for **volume visualization,** the modeling of object's interiors (not usually an option with geometry-based modeling programs). In medicine, for example, the interior of the body is visualized by using sample-based data from medical imaging equipment such as CAT (computer-aided tomography) or MRI (magnetic resonance imaging) scanners.[1] Object interiors are also of interest to engineers and designers who want to understand the effects of stress or temperature on their materials.

Volumetric sculpting, or the sculpting of voxel-based models, was pioneered at Brown University [Galyean, 1991] and further developed at the Massachusetts Institute of Technology and the State University of New York at Stony Brook. Sculpting tools act like 3D paintbrushes and erasers to build up and sculpt away material (see Fig. 7.7).

Although they are not currently available to most artists, 3D sample-based options such as volumetric sculpting, painting in 3D, and artistic use of 3D imaging techniques will certainly be a part of future commercial 3D programs.

> Voxel-based modeling will open up new worlds for 3D artists, but before it can become a commercial reality, three things must happen:
>
> First, personal computers will need more memory (just as they needed additional memory in order to do 2D sample-based graphics in the '70s).
>
> Second, we will need faster algorithms for drawing voxel-based models on the screen (we're almost there).
>
> Third, better input and output devices are required. The feel of the "material" is essential in voxel-based modeling, so force-feedback devices are critical.

---

[1] For an example of volume visualization, use the Web to view the Visible Human Project—complete, anatomically detailed, 3D representations of the male and female human body based on transverse CAT, MRI, and cryosection images of representative male and female cadavers at one-millimeter intervals. This project's Web sit may be accessed at http://www.nlm.nih.gov/research/visible/visible_human.html

Figure 7.7 Volumetric modeling. *The Thinker,* a piece created with a custom-made interactive voxel-based sculpting system. *(Courtesy of Daniel C. Robbins)*

Just as digital design and layout and digital painting and photoediting programs are merging now, by the time voxel-based modelers become common, you will find them integrated with geometry-based 3D modeling [Hughes, 1997].

John F. Hughes, coauthor of "Sculpting: An Interactive Volumetric Modeling Technique" [Galyean, 1991] and also of *Computer Graphics, Principles and Practice* [Foley, 1996].

7.3 ANATOMY OF A 3D PROGRAM

Three-dimensional program interfaces lack the standardization that has occurred in 2D. An understanding of the basic modeling tasks described in Section 7.2 provides guidance when you face unfamiliar setups. Sometimes tasks are broken into separate modules or even entirely separate applications. A 3D application may use one program module to create models and a different module to render them. Some programs provide separate applications for making simple shapes, assembling them, rendering a scene, and creating an animation.

Menu bar

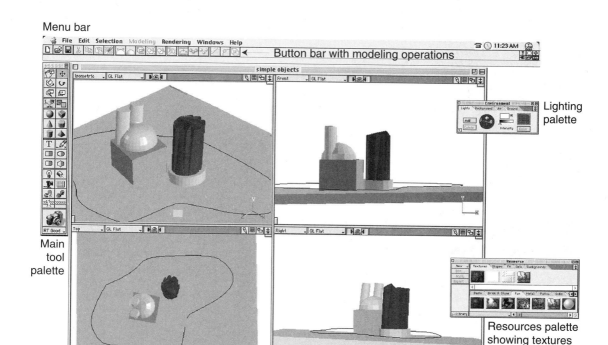

Four views into the 3D world

Figure 7.8 The interface of a 3D program (Strata StudioPro).

With these cautions in mind, the following are some common interface features used in 3D modeling programs, many of which are illustrated in Fig. 7.8.

The world. Like the drawing area in digital painting and photoediting programs, the world is the space in which objects are created and moved about. The world is a 3D Cartesian coordinate system with three axes conventionally called x, y, and z. In most 3D programs, multiple views into the world can be opened on the screen simultaneously; 3D programs allow separately stored 3D objects to be brought into a world at any time.

Tool palette or tool bar. Tools for moving, rotating, and scaling objects and viewpoints usually are present on a tool palette. Icons for basic object creation—choosing premade shapes or constructing simple objects—also are usually available directly from the main tool palette. Often the user can switch between different modes, such as modeling or rendering with tool bar buttons. The user often can access additional features by clicking tool bar buttons to bring up dialog boxes.

Auxiliary palettes. Because a 3D program has so many features, a large number of auxiliary palettes may be available. Managing the palettes can be important to conserve screen space for your art work (a second monitor helps!). Tools for controlling lighting, cameras, object materials, and color picking often are found on auxiliary palettes.

Menus and dialog boxes. Basic file functions (e.g., saving and copying) and ways to switch between program modules usually are accessed through menus and dialog boxes. Menus frequently provide an easy-to-browse list of main program functions; choosing the function from a menu then brings up either a dialog box or an auxiliary palette.

Feedback area. Because 3D modelers have so many features and few standard ways of presenting them, 3D programs frequently offer context-sensitive textual help on-screen. A feedback area may prompt the user to complete steps in sequence for an operation, or it may simply indicate the name and functionality of a selected tool. Full online manuals also are often available.

Other. To accommodate the complexity of 3D, some programs have interfaces that use objects or techniques not usually integral to 2D software. Examples include

- the use of different *modes* (e.g., modeling versus rendering) to change choices available in menu and tool bars, and
- in-scene 3D controls or **3D widgets** used as guides or to change objects (e.g., movable "construction planes" for aligning objects and controls, and handles that surround an object, letting the user rotate, scale, or deform it).

7.4 3D Touch–Creating Building Blocks

7.4.1 Primitives

In large part, the primary building blocks of a computer graphics application are responsible for the sense of touch offered. The use of pixels defines the types of touch available in digital painting and photoediting programs, and the use of 2D geometric object descriptions characterizes 2D digital design and layout programs. For 3D programs, the primary building blocks are 3D **primitives**—3D shapes that are not composed of any subsidiary 3D forms (and thus usually are quite simple). Although simple 3D shapes can be constructed from 2D shapes (with processes described in Section 7.4.2), 3D primitives are conveniently premade and are defined in concise ways that take up less storage space. Figure 7.9 shows some typical and not so typical 3D primitives: a sphere, cube, cone, cylinder, torus (a donutlike shape), a dodecahedron, and a banana. Software programmers choose certain primitive shapes as useful starting points for creating components of more complex objects. Thus these shapes usually are quite general, but any shape can be used as a primitive; for example, a banana could be a useful primitive in a 3D program to model South American plant life. Rita DeWitt chose to work with primitives in their own right in an animation entitled *Platonic Solids* (see

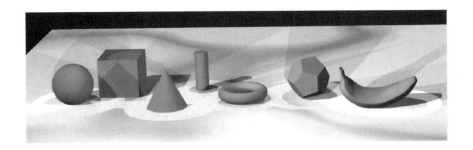

Figure 7.9
3D primitives.

Fig. 7.10). The sphere, as an analog for the universe, contains the Platonic solids (tetrahedron, cube, octahedron, dodecahedron, and icosahedron), which German astronomer Johannes Kepler believed were the building blocks of all matter.

7.4.2   Sweeps

Basic 3D forms can also be created by drawing a 2D geometric shape, referred to as a **profile,** and then **sweeping** it through space to describe a 3D form (see Fig. 7.11). A profile can be swept along a straight line or curved path in a process called *extrusion* or around an axis to make a *revolved* (or *lathed*) form. A *scaling extrusion* uses scaled profiles. The concept of extrusion can be extended to include more than one profile in a process called *lofting* (or *skinning*).

Like a playdough machine or cookie press, **extrusion** moves a 2D profile along a straight or curved path to make a 3D form. Short extrusions along a straight line are

Figure 7.10   Rita DeWitt, score by Rodney Thomaston, *Platonic Relationships,* **Computer Animations, 1993.** *Platonic Relationships* is a theatrical treatment of the ideal Platonic relationships as elements in a three-part play—(a) Platonic Relationships, (b) Non-Platonic Relationships, and (c) Freudian Relationships. The creative element, embodied in the pencil, is the instrument of ideas. Animation gives life to the simple shapes, and they dance around one another in ways appropriate to each part's title. *(Courtesy of Rita DeWitt)*

(a)   (b)   (c)

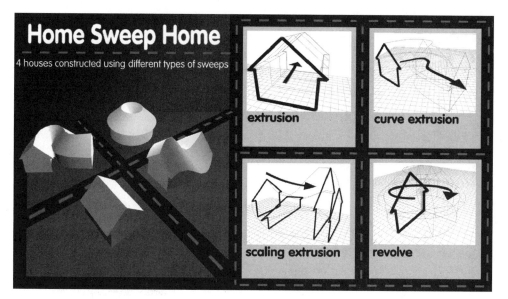

Home Sweep Home

4 houses constructed using different types of sweeps

extrusion

curve extrusion

scaling extrusion

revolve

Figure 7.11 Basic examples of sweeps.

often used to create **surface detail polygons,** which are low-relief details for larger, more complex forms such as windows and doors on the side of a building.

Revolves produce symmetrical results similar to pieces produced on a lathe or potter's wheel (note the vase shown in Fig. 7.6). A single profile can create any number of revolve forms, depending on the position of the axis of rotation. Although natural objects rarely are absolutely symmetric around an axis of rotation, many human-made 3D objects are created in this way.

Lofting expands the designer's object vocabulary from symmetric shapes and single cross sections to include any object that can be envisioned as a series of cross sections—from human-made forms such as airplane wings to natural 3D forms that are hard to approximate with sweeps and simple extrusions. An arm, for instance, can be created as a series of varying ellipses and then skinned over. Figure 7.12 shows a lizard created entirely by lofting.

Figure 7.12 A lofted lizard.

These methods of extending 2D forms into a third dimension raise many questions about the nature of dimensionality in 3D computer art. Sometimes the artist works like a sculptor and sometimes like a painter, and the final piece often has a blend of 2D and 3D characteristics. In the 3D work shown in Fig. 7.13, Michael O'Rourke used simple 3D graphics object-creation methods, such as primitives and sweeps. This piece asks the aesthetic and philosophical question, What is depth? and explores how people perceive and interpret 3D representations on a picture plane.

The image's 3D objects range from volumetric-looking forms, such as the cylinders and cone on the left, to a 3D form that has volume but begins to take on decidedly linear qualities—the calligraphic tube extrusion that wends its way through most of the image. O'Rourke combined the rendering of these 3D models with a 2D image designed with shadows and a tubular-looking form that seems related to the 3D tube, as well as strictly linear cross-hatchings.

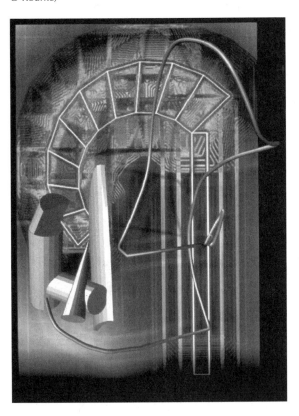

Figure 7.13 Michael O'Rourke, *Slucid via Ghana*, 1985 (Cibachrome print, 37″ × 47″). *Slucid via Ghana* is one of a series of works in which the artist explores technical, perceptual, and theoretical differences between 2D and 3D space. (*Courtesy of Michael O'Rourke*)

It is not clear where the 3D structures end and the 2D structures begin. When viewed in person, the work is obviously 2D—it hangs on a wall—but it can be mistaken for a photograph of a real 3D object. That calls into question the need to determine the status of each element and the entire work as either a picture of something outside itself or as a self-contained object. The interplay between dimensions is further emphasized by the framing of the work. The tubular 3D modeled element juts beyond the frame of the 2D image, and the bottom fades into black—ambiguities that make the viewer question where the work begins and ends.

O'Rourke was trained as a sculptor but has been using computers to create art for almost 20 years. From his first virtual wireframe sculptures through his current work with high-end 3D software, he has been concerned with exploring emotional states and spatial experiences. For him, the visual languages of traditional and computer-based art work easily intermingle.

Object Representations

When creating objects, your 3D modeling software must choose a method of describing the object's geometry. The most common method uses **polygons,** or closed 2D shapes such as rectangles and triangles comprising straight lines that do not intersect each other. A **polygonal mesh** is essentially a description of an object in terms of flat, polygonal pieces that are joined (see Fig. 7.14). A **polyhedron** is a closed polygonal mesh.

All 3D programs understand polygons, and most 3D file-exchange formats are based on polygonal descriptions. For cubelike forms or even more complex forms with flat surfaces, a polygonal representation describes the desired shapes quite accurately. For curved forms, however, such as spheres and cylinders, a polygonal representation can only approximate the desired surface.

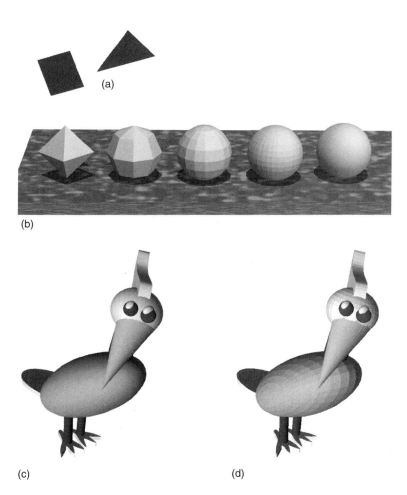

(a)

(b)

(c)   (d)

Figure 7.14 Polygonal and curve- or spline-based models.
(a) Two polygons. (b) Increasing resolution of a polygonal representation of a curved model. (c) Spline-based bird. (d) Polygonal-mesh bird.

You can render polygonal models of curved objects to look smooth, but to model a curved surface more accurately you need real curved shapes, not linear approximations. **Curve- or spline- or NURBS-based models** create more realistic-looking, accurately detailed renderings of curved forms. Because they are based on real curves, not lines, they can be edited and deformed in ways not possible with a polygonal mesh. Curve-based representations are much more succinct than polygonal ones but require more complex mathematics and thus more processing time, making them slower to work with. In addition, a curve-based representation may still only approximate the desired form.

A program that lets you create and store curve-based forms often uses a polygonal representation in draft rendering modes in order to keep the program responsive. If so, you can often adjust polygonal resolution to trade off rendering time for quality of appearance. Figure 7.14 shows different polygonal resolutions for a sphere and compares spline and polygonal models.

Some operations, such as Boolean operations, cannot be performed easily unless the objects affected are defined as closed polygon meshes. Most 3D programs that offer such features require that you "simplify" or convert a spline-based object's representation to a polygonal mesh before such operations can take place, in order to simplify the math and make the program run faster. Once you have treated a spline-based object in this way, however, it usually cannot be changed back to the more accurate curved representation.

7.4.3   BOOLEAN OPERATIONS

Many real–life 3D objects can be modeled with compositions of simple shapes. Not all forms, however, can be made by assembling primitive shapes and increasingly more complex subobjects. For instance, how would you model a drinking glass? A cylinder is a good start, but what can be added to a cylinder to make it into a glass? For a simple glass, a volume of revolution might work, but for a glass with, say, a rectangular exterior and a cylindrical interior that is not sufficient.

The drinking-glass challenge and related form–creation problems can be solved by subtracting one object from another, rather than assembling different objects (see Fig. 7.15). For a glass, you can subtract a narrow cylinder from a slightly wider one, or from a cuboid to get a rectangular exterior. Adding and subtracting shapes are part of a set of Boolean operations that can be performed with solid objects (see the discussion of Boolean operations in 2D in Chapter 4). This approach allows you to use the Boolean operations of union, difference, and intersection on solid 3D objects. Figure 7.16 illustrates the Boolean modeling process.

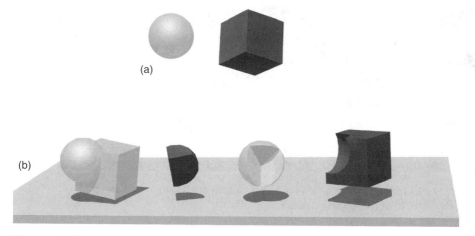

Figure 7.15 Boolean operations on solids. (a) The two original shapes. (b) From left to right: union, intersection, sphere minus cube, and cube minus sphere.

Figure 7.16 A modern-style table base created by subtracting spheres from a cube. This shape would be difficult, if not impossible, to create in any other way. (a) Four spheres are positioned around a cube. (b) One by one the spheres are subtracted from the cube, leaving (c). (d) Metallic material settings are defined for the base and a glass table top is added.

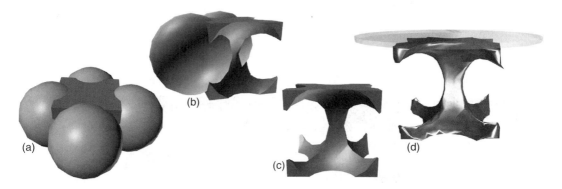

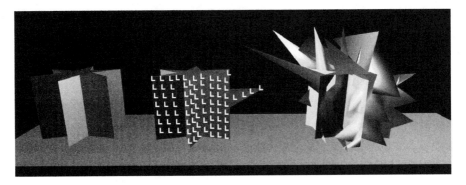

Figure 7.17 Sculpting with "digital clay." This simple 3D star (left) is deformed by moving the vertices of its polygonal mesh.

7.4.4 DIGITAL CLAY AND 3D SCULPTING

What happens when you get tired of cubes and spheres? Of course, you can make your simple shapes larger and smaller by scaling, but most real-world objects, especially those in nature, do not look like collections of geometric primitives or even sweeps. You can create complex forms by lofting images, but often you will need something much like a cube or cone, but not *exactly* like one.

An approach to modifying simple objects called **digital clay,** or **3D sculpting** (not related to volumetric sculpting), lets you click and drag on polygon vertices. By pushing and pulling on the vertices and connecting lines of the object's polygonal mesh, you can warp any polyhedral object into various bent, twisted, and distorted new shapes (see Fig. 7.17). Common deformations that are time-consuming to perform vertex by vertex are often offered separately. These can include operations such as tapering, bending, and twisting (see Fig. 7.18).

You can also use digital-clay approaches with spline-based models. Just as you can make complex linear contours (e.g., those used in digital design and layout programs)

Figure 7.18 Standard deformations of tapering, bending, and twisting.

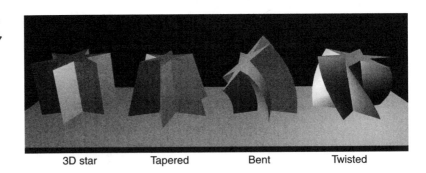

3D star   Tapered   Bent   Twisted

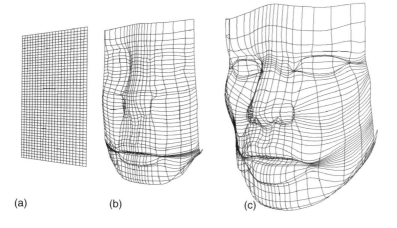

Figure 7.19 **Using a spline patch.** (a) A spline patch formed by a boundary of four splines. (b) Increased resolution and manipulation of some vertices. (c) Completed spline-patch face.

(a)   (b)   (c)

with spline curves, you can describe complex surfaces with **spline patches,** or 2D surfaces bounded by four splines (see Fig. 7.19a). You can move vertices on the edges and interior of the patch to deform the surface to create varied contours difficult to approximate with polygonal deformations or assemblages of basic geometric shapes (see Fig. 7.19b and c). By increasing the "resolution" of the patch (creating more vertices), you can model very detailed surfaces. You can use patches to create clouds, water, or irregular surfaces such as a piece of draped fabric. Patches are used often in car and airplane design and in designing surfaces for computer-aided manufacturing (CAM). You can even join spline patches to model more complex surfaces and create solid 3D forms. In the future, you will be able to create more complex topologies, such as those shown in Fig. 7.20, by using this approach [Grimm, 1995].

Figure 7.20 **Spline-based solid modeling examples.** These models were created in a custom modeling system. Complicated smooth objects can be made, including forms with multiple holes. (These models started out as single bloblike surfaces.) *(Courtesy of Cindy Grimm and The Brown University Computer Graphics Group)*

Similar Forms Created in Different Ways

There is no "correct" method for making a particular shape. The method you choose depends on a number of factors, including the strengths of your software and how you want to edit the shape in the future. Figure 7.21 shows three approaches to creating a simple bucketlike shape that could be used as a vase, a drinking glass, or a component of a more complex object. On the top stair is a cylinder sculpted by moving vertices of its polygonal mesh. This method yields a nonsymmetric, hand-made look, and the shape can be re-sculpted at any time. After the final shape is created, the interior is hollowed out by subtracting a scaled copy of the solid form from itself. The middle stair shows a similar shape created by rotating a 2D profile around an axis. This method ensures symmetry, and the profile can be edited and rerotated at any time around a different axis to adjust the 3D shape. On the bottom stair, a similar shape is created by lofting several circular cross sections. This method permits changes such as editing the original cross sections or adding new cross sections (as here). (Note that a base or cap would have to be added on the bottom to make this a realistic-looking container.)

For a vase with a profile that might change, rotation is probably best. For a somewhat symmetric shape that may need fine tuning, say, to create a natural-looking form, the sculpting approach may be better. For a shape that can easily be approximated in varying detail with cross sections, the lofting approach allows easily made changes.

Figure 7.21 **Different methods used to create a simple bucket shape.**
(a) moving vertices, (b) rotation, (c) lofting.

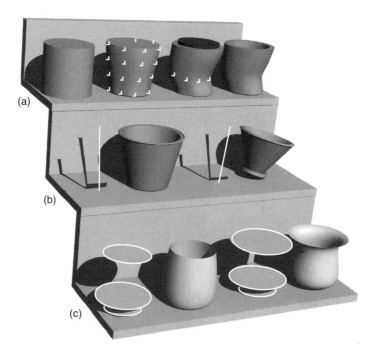

(a)

(b)

(c)

7.5 Assembling the Building Blocks

Artists can create complex and varied 3D surfaces from single polygonal or spline-based forms, but most 3D modeling is done by assembling relatively simple objects into a more complex whole.

7.5.1 Decomposition

Unless an object is unusually simple (e.g., a single block of wood), it contains subcomponents that need to be distinguished. Deciding which components are needed is called **decomposition.**

For artists used to materials such as clay or those who come from a primarily 2D background, decomposition requires a completely new way of thinking about objects. Instead of drawing one view of a 3D object or sculpting away clay to reveal a final form, the artist doing 3D computer modeling must learn how to make a complex form from simple components, ultimately constructed from primitive geometric pieces (e.g., the elements of the simple bird model previously shown in Fig. 7.6).

A single complex form can be modeled in innumerable ways, and the choice depends on the intended appearance and functionality of the digital model being created. Extensive detail doesn't guarantee a better model, any more than a detailed, complicated style implies a better painting. The process of object creation both in computer art and in traditional drawing, painting, and sculpture requires the artist to choose which aspects of objects and environments to represent and which to ignore.

7.5.2 Composition

Object **composition** is the action-filled opposite of the mostly conceptual decomposition process. After breaking down the object to be modeled conceptually and constructing the necessary elements, the artist must assemble the individual components. For a complex object, subparts are assembled first and then combined into more complex parts until the object is complete.

The most essential and basic operations provided for assembling objects are *translation* (moving), *rotation* (turning), and *scaling* (changing the object's size). The functionality of all 3D graphics programs is based on these transformations, and to a 3D modeler they soon become second nature.

Positioning 3D objects intuitively and accurately with a 2D screen and 2D input devices such as the mouse remains challenging. A mouse moves only in a 2D plane, and yet it must reposition and otherwise alter objects in a 3D space. In addition, the view of these objects is restricted to a 2D screen, so depth is hard to judge (see Fig. 7.22). (For alternatives, see Chapter 9, 3D Input and Output.)

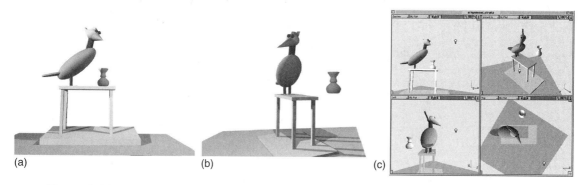

(a)　　　(b)　　　(c)

Figure 7.22 Misleading 2D views of a 3D composition. (a) The bird and vase seem to be properly aligned with the top of the table. (b) A view from an angle, however, reveals, that they are not. (c) Because of this problem, artists working in 3D usually look at several views at once.

When you manipulate real objects, their relative positions usually are obvious. In real life you can grasp objects, move your head slightly, reposition your body, see reflected light, and hear sounds. These multiple sources of feedback provide an extraordinary amount of information from which you can deduce an object's position and motion. In present 3D modeling programs, most of those cues do not exist.

Sketch

Although 3D modelers are powerful tools, they are often difficult to use and are far from intuitive. The interfaces of most 3D programs are better used for assembling a planned model than for experimenting. For example, the 3D computer graphics dinosaurs in *Jurassic Park* were modeled only after elaborate, detailed drawings and sometimes even physical models had been developed.

Robert Zeleznik, of The Brown University Computer Graphics Group, was inspired to create a different type of 3D program after he tried to teach some middle-school children how to use a 3D modeler:

> I saw them making simple shapes like cubes and spheres and using a text editor to make their names in 3D. I thought I'd impress them and show them how real modeling was done. I sat down to make something more complicated and suddenly I realized how hard it was to make anything other than primitives. I thought, "there's got to be a better way" [Zeleznik, 1997].

Zeleznik's better way is a research tool called SKETCH that is designed to bridge the gap between hand sketches and computer-based modeling programs. Using SKETCH is like drawing with pencil and paper because only gestures are used (no menus, dialog boxes, or

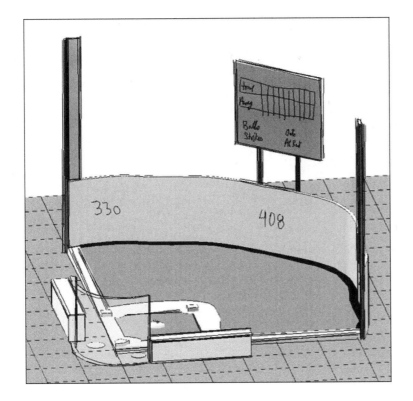

Figure 7.23 A 3D scene made with **SKETCH.** *(Courtesy of Bob Zeleznik and The Brown University Computer Graphics Group)*

buttons), but the user's hand motions produce 3D polygonal models rather than 2D images. Users sketch an object using familiar graphic conventions for representing 3D forms, such as three connecting lines to show the corner of a cube. Components of an object are grouped automatically, making object assembly much easier than in most of today's 3D modelers. "The idea is to build on things people already know how to do, like draw; artists don't have to interrupt the creative process to look through lists and call up dialog boxes, they can just make the type of gestures that come naturally" [Zeleznik, 1996, p. 163].

Because objects in SKETCH are defined gesturally, not with numeric input, they may be only approximate models of a final idea. To convey the sense of informality, SKETCH uses a nonphotorealistic rendering method (see Section 8.4.1) that makes models look as if they were drawn by hand instead of a computer. The model shown in Fig. 7.23 took Zeleznik, who is not an artist, only a few minutes to create. He began by making a curtain rod and the scene evolved, like a doodle, into a baseball field. The nonrealistic rendering lets viewers know that they are looking at a sketch, not an accurate scale model.

7.5.3 Hierarchy

The components in a 3D model usually have structural relationships. Suppose, for instance, that you are building a model of a bird. How do you connect the components so that you don't have to move each one separately to reposition the bird? And how can you let some parts move independently of others—for instance, making the beak open and close? The answer is hierarchy.

A **hierarchy** in 3D computer graphics is a structure that organizes model components by their ability to control each other. Hierarchies can be visualized as tree diagrams.

Tree Diagrams

Hierarchies are often depicted as **tree diagrams,** which are structured like upside-down trees (see Fig. 7.24). At the top of a tree is the **root.** Each **node,** including the root, is a **parent** of the nodes directly beneath it, called descendants or **children.** Components with no children are called **leaves.**

Figure 7.24 A tree diagram.

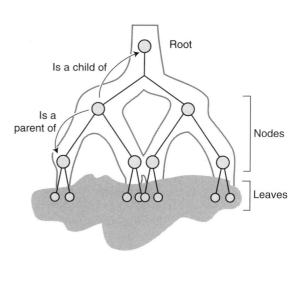

A hierarchy can be designed for almost any type of part-to-part relationship. One popular type of hierarchy is a **connected-to** hierarchy that shows how the components of a model are connected. Figure 7.25 shows a connected-to hierarchy for a simple bird model. Changes to an object affect an object's children but not its parent,

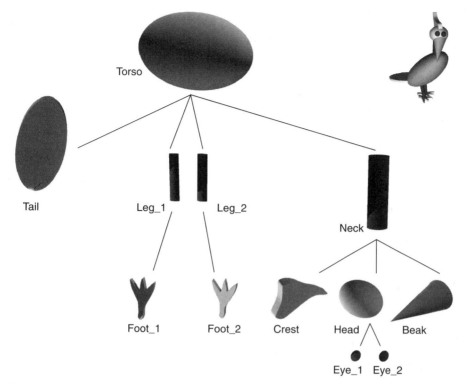

Figure 7.25 **A connected-to hierarchy of the simple bird model.** The torso is the root. The tail, legs and neck are connected directly to the torso. The feet are connected to their respective legs, and the crest, head, and beak are all connected to the neck. The eyes are connected to the head.

whereas changes to a root object affect all the other objects in the hierarchy. Thus moving the torso moves the entire bird, but moving the beak, which is a leaf, does not affect anything else (i.e., the beak moves or is otherwise transformed separately from the bird's head).

The usefulness of a model can depend on hierarchy decisions. If the bird's feet were connected directly to the torso in Fig. 7.25, for instance, they would not stay attached to the legs if they were repositioned. For simple models the repercussions of poor hierarchy design usually can be handled, but when models are made up of dozens of parts, the ways in which they are connected become crucial.

The implementation of hierarchy varies from program to program. The main conceptual difference is that some applications let users include only actual components drawn on the screen in their hierarchy (as in Fig. 7.25), whereas others allow **abstract objects** that are collections of other objects to be named and used. In Fig. 7.26, the root node Bird is not a polygonal form but is a *composed-of* collection of other components (some of which are themselves abstract composed-of collections). A **composed-of**

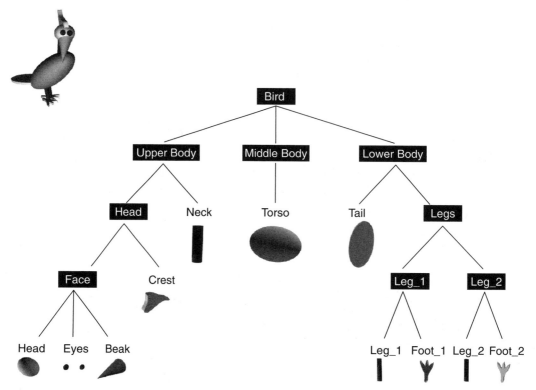

Figure 7.26 Composed-of hierarchy of the simple bird model, using abstract nodes. The *bird,* an abstract object, is composed of an *upper body,* a *middle body,* and a *lower body,* all also abstract collection objects. The *middle body* is composed of a geometric object, the torso. Both the *upper body* and *lower body* are made up of more composed-of objects and finally the geometric components of the bird. (All abstract objects are in reverse type.)

hierarchy ends in leaves that are the actual geometric objects drawn on the screen. In other words, only abstract objects are allowed to have children.

Each approach has advantages and disadvantages, and some applications provide combinations of features. Advantages of the connected-to organization include simplicity and the fact that it often reflects the actions that a modeler takes to establish linkages between parts of a model. The lack of abstract objects can be a disadvantage, however, when an artist is conceptualizing, editing, and animating complicated models. For example, imagine modeling a car; conceptual groupings for complex geometries, such as the engine and the drive train and their important subcomponents, would let artists easily identify and select parts of this complex model, as well as keep track of the overall structure.

Abstract objects can be selected and transformed—the effects of the transformations are passed down the hierarchy to the leaves (the geometric objects). For instance, if the root bird object in Fig. 7.26 were scaled, the entire bird model would be scaled. If the upper body were rotated, the neck, head, beak, eyes, and crest would all be rotated together. As in the connected-to hierarchy, transforming any object affects only its children, not its parent. For example, if the eyes were moved, no other part of the bird would be affected.

7.5.4 JOINTS

Hierarchy becomes part of the aesthetic of the object because it guides the object's creation, that is the modeling of its geometric form. The hierarchy structure is also the basis for defining **joints,** which are the relationships among the model parts that determine precisely how one part can move relative to another.

For example, in modeling a human being, the body parts should stay connected when the figure is moved but should not be completely immobile. The head should be able to turn through about an 180° arc but not spin around 360°, like the child's head in *The Exorcist*. And when the head turns, the body should stay still, not turn with it. The more detailed and realistic the joints, the easier it is to pose or animate the model realistically.

Joints are defined by constraining translation and rotation of one object in relation to another. An extreme form of a joint is grouping or locking, which binds two (or more) objects together so that they move and change as one. Figure 7.27 depicts several familiar types of joints. A **slider** can move along one axis but not others, and it

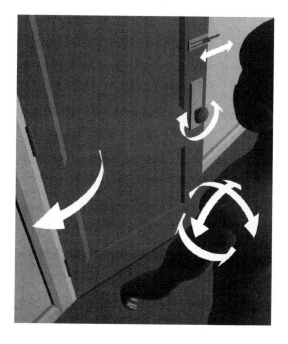

Figure 7.27 Familiar types of joints. The safety lock is a slider and the doorknob is a pin joint; the door rotates on a hinge and the shoulder is a ball and socket joint.

Figure 7.28 Masked booby with neck skeleton. A skeleton (shown in gray) runs through the bird's neck and is used to control animation.

cannot rotate at all. A **pin joint** permits rotation around a single axis but not translation. A **ball and socket joint** permits rotation around all three axes but not translation (in the case of a real arm the degree of rotation is limited, of course). As the old spiritual goes, "the hip bone's connected to the thigh bone, and the thigh bone's connected to the knee bone."

Specifying each part-to-part relationship is one way to model joints. Another method views the joints less as part of an object connection hierarchy and more as a skeleton within the model that causes the model to move and bend. With skeleton joints, an interior **skeleton structure** is created inside the model and constraints are associated with the skeleton, rather than with each piece of model geometry (see Fig. 7.28). One immediate advantage is that a skeleton from one model can be duplicated and used in another model. (See Chapter 10, 2D and 3D Animation and Video, for further discussion of the uses of skeletons and joints.)

7.5.5 MASTER–INSTANCE RELATIONSHIPS

In the **master–instance** hierarchy relationship, one object is used to create any number of identical copies of itself, called **instances.** Like copying and pasting, creating an instance makes a new object that looks like the original. Also like copying and pasting, changes to the new versions of the object do not affect the original. Unlike copying and pasting, however, in a master-instance hierarchy the master object still affects the shape, scale, and rotation of its instances (see Fig. 7.29). The master can also be used to redefine surface attributes such as color and transparency.

Interestingly, master-instance hierarchies were features of the first model-based drawing program ever created: Ivan Sutherland's Sketchpad [Sutherland, 1963]. Today, they usually are included only in high-end modeling and CAD packages.

Master–instance hierarchies are especially useful in designing complex scenes in which identically shaped items are used repeatedly but may need to be redesigned globally. Master–instance hierarchies give artists a powerful type of touch and an approach to composition that have no analogy in traditional art-making processes. Although developed and refined in the context of technical design, hierarchies can provide exciting but, so far, underutilized ways to work with abstract pieces or to introduce different ways of thinking about the components of a model.

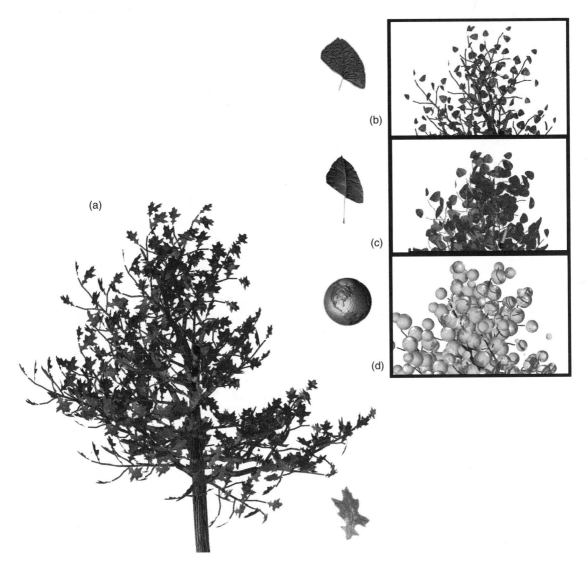

Figure 7.29 **The power of a master-instance hierarchy.** (a) The oak leaf is a master shape that is used to create every leaf in the full tree to its left. (b) Changing the leaf shape to a pear leaf changes the entire tree into a pear tree, (c) a red bud leaf makes a red bud tree. (d) The master can be edited to make any shape, not only realistic leaves but fanciful objects such as the earth model used here. *(Trees created with Ransom Interactive Tree Pak Volume 1 (courtesy of Troyan Turner.)*

7.6 ALGORITHMIC FORM GENERATION

The mark of the hand's motion and a sense of style based on gesture play almost no part in 3D modelers. There are still important differences, however, between creating a model by hand (designing each component individually and determining its position and constraint relationships) and using global, algorithmic 3D processes.

7.6.1 MODELING NATURE

The realistic depiction of natural landscapes has been a driving force throughout much of art history. In the Renaissance, art was described as a "mirror of nature" and the nineteenth-century Romantic landscape painters, such as Corot, discovered the joy of nature for its own sake. In the twentieth century, photographers such as Ansel Adams used their cameras to capture images of the wilderness that would not only become documents of historical and artistic value but also help to create an awareness of the necessity of preserving the ecology of the planet.

Until the late 1970s and early 1980s, nature was almost entirely beyond the grasp of 3D graphics because natural forms, such as trees, plants, flowers, mountains, and water, are prohibitively difficult to model realistically with a building-block or sculptural approach. A tree might conceivably be modeled by placing hundreds or thousands of branch and leaf forms on a trunk structure, as in Fig. 7.29 but such an approach requires a major time commitment. Even creating a detailed line drawing of a tree in which hundreds of leaves are individually drawn is simple compared with positioning hundreds of 3D leaf objects in a modeling program.

Algorithmic and procedural form-generation techniques now enable artists to create 3D objects and scenes that would be impractical, if not impossible, to model in any other way. At the beginning of this chapter I noted that 3D graphics let artists create abstract and yet realistic geometric forms. The implications of this capability are great even when you consider only geometric-looking objects. However, when the computer, tended by an artist creator or "gardener," grows abstract and yet visually realistic natural landscapes, the results can easily conjure up thoughts more of science fiction than art history.

FRACTALS   Many natural forms could not be described geometrically until the invention of *fractals*.

> Fractal objects mimic natural structures in a nonspecific way. For example, fractal techniques in general cannot be used to build a copy of any particular real mountain that you have seen; rather, they describe how to create a shape that looks like some mountain. So if you want to model Mount McKinley precisely, you still have to do it by hand [Glassner, 1989, p. 99].

The French mathematician Benoit Mandelbrot developed **fractals** as a geometric way to express seemingly irregular "non-geometric-looking" forms such as trees, coastlines, and clouds by noticing that they exhibited, at many levels of detail, patterns of **self-**

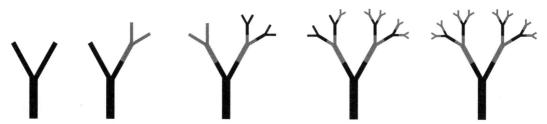

Figure 7.30 Four iterations of a fractal tree created with simple subdivision and self-similar replacement. The starting shape (left) is scaled and used to replace half of each branch. This process is repeated. (Alternating shades of gray are used to make the replacements clearer.)

similarity: The structure of a small section resembles the structure of the whole object [Mandelbrot, 1988]. The large-scale structure of a very regular-looking tree can be abstracted to a trunk and two main branches, for example. The form can then be subdivided into smaller portions, such as the individual branches. Smaller limbs can be created by replacing each branch with a new branch that has two smaller branches growing from it. Further subdivision and replacement continue to add to the tree (see Fig. 7.30). If this process is carried on indefinitely, a treelike form is created with infinitely many levels of increasingly smaller scale, self-similar detail. Mandelbrot describes such forms as being, spatially, somewhere between dimensions. The tree form has a 2D area that cannot be precisely measured (because the process of subdivision and replacement goes on indefinitely), but it's not 3D because it doesn't go outside the 2D coordinate system. He described the peculiar extra dimensionality as a **fractal dimension,** somewhere between 2D and 3D (the exact fraction depending on how the shape is constructed).

Rigorous, infinite self-similarity is required for a true fractal, but with computer graphics a few rounds, or **iterations,** of substantially self-similar forms can create a variety of realistic-looking plants and trees. Self-similarity with a randomization twist is used in the creation of plants and especially of rocks and mountains and other landscape elements. To make a mountain, for instance, the artist can randomly raise or lower vertices on a flat plane, pulling or pushing the surface of a plane. Each mountain or valley created in this manner is then subdivided into individual polygons, each of which is replaced with more polygons that have been randomly altered to create smaller scale dips and peaks. After only a few iterations of this process, surprisingly realistic terrains can be created (see Fig. 7.31). Random changes often are supplemented with creation rules based on actual ground formations.

GRAMMARS AND GRAFTALS   Another approach to natural form creation uses nongeo-metrical graph rules to calculate strings of expressions or *words* that can be represented by geometric entities such as branches and leaves. However, the forms produced by these rules or grammars are not as strictly self-similar as fractal forms. Alvy Ray Smith introduced plant forms such as **graftals,** a combination of *graph* and *fractal* [Smith,

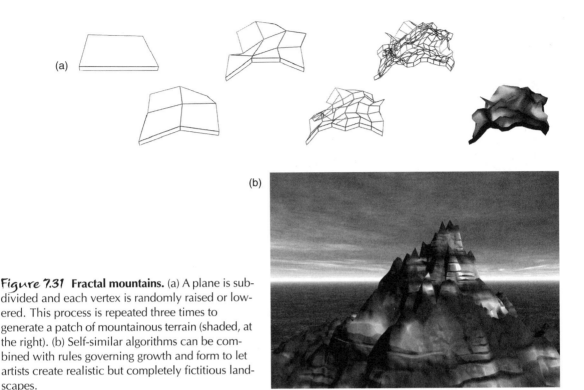

(a)

(b)

Figure 7.31 Fractal mountains. (a) A plane is subdivided and each vertex is randomly raised or lowered. This process is repeated three times to generate a patch of mountainous terrain (shaded, at the right). (b) Self-similar algorithms can be combined with rules governing growth and form to let artists create realistic but completely fictitious landscapes.

1984]. Based on grammars for modeling biological forms developed by Aristid Lindenmayer [Lindenmayer, 1968], graftals are created by starting with an initial structure and iteratively replacing portions of it with exact or varied copies of itself or new elements. In Fig. 7.32(a), the self-similar growth began with a single straight-line segment (first iteration). In the second iteration, the line segment was replaced according to the replacement rule by a line segment with two branches. In the third iteration, each line segment in the form was again replaced by a line segment with two small branches growing from it. In the fifth iteration, this process has been repeated two more times. In Fig. 7.32(b), the beginning form was a plain branch that was augmented by three flowering branches and two sets of leaves. In the second iteration, the flowering branches (plain branches with flowers and stems) were added—twice at the end of the top line segment of the plain branch and once at the end of its bottom line segment; leaves were added at the midpoints of the two line segments. In the third iteration, this process was repeated for each flowering branch: The single flower was removed, three new flowering branches were added, and leaves were added at the midpoints of the branch. By the fifth iteration, angles for sprouting and orienting leaves and flowers have

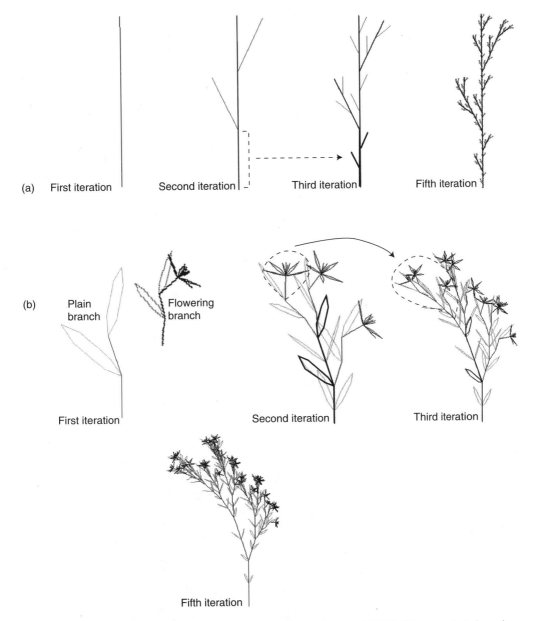

(a)　First iteration　　Second iteration　　Third iteration　　Fifth iteration

(b)　Plain branch　　Flowering branch

First iteration　　Second iteration　　Third iteration

Fifth iteration

Figure 7.32　Plants grown with Lindenmayer System software. (a) This 2D example is based on a replacement rule: Each line segment in the form is replaced with a line segment of the same length, growing shorter lines from points one-third and two-thirds of the way along the line. (b) The development of a shrub with leaves and flowers in 3D.

been varied systematically so that parts of the bush appear in front of others and at a number of different angles to the viewer. Each repetition was drawn at a smaller scale to accommodate the additional branches and flowers.

Fractals, grammars, and graftals can make a convincing plant or mountain from instances of a few simple geometric forms. Unlike a natural form modeled by hand (which might have thousands of geometric shapes), these methods require little storage space. They are both visually effective and technically efficient.

Growth simulations can create more complex plants than most grammar systems by incorporating numerous rules of biological growth deduced from the study of actual plants. With such systems, artists and designers can create plants that grow and bloom in response to light and the passage of time and that resemble specific real-life plant forms, as illustrated in Fig. 7.33 [Deussen et al., 1998]. Although most applications of this type generate realistic-looking objects and landscapes, the same principles and methods can be used to generate forms that look natural but do not represent any real-world 3D objects.

Like Renaissance naturalists who considered drawing plants to be part of studying them, today's algorithmic artists pursue knowledge of the rules governing the observable world. The uses of their knowledge often cross the boundaries of art, science, and science fiction.

Figure 7.33 Bernd Lintermann, *Stream*, 1998. Algorithmically-generated plants combined with more complex rules governing growth and distribution. (a) Individual plant samples. (b) Many instances of each type of plant, composed into a landscape. *(Courtesy of Bernd Lintermann)*

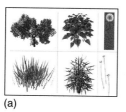

(a)

(b)

7.6.2 GENETIC AND EVOLUTIONARY ART OR ARTIFICIAL LIFE

When you make your own images of plant life, you might model several different trees, adjusting by hand the different parameters, such as branch width and leaf shape, many times before creating a suitable result. Tiring of performing exactly this process, Karl Sims, then an artist-in-residence at Thinking Machines in Cambridge, Massachusetts, designed a program that would automatically vary or *mutate* different plant parameters or *genes* in a group of plants. The artist could then select the best one, and random mutations of that choice would make up the next group of plants from which to choose. Such a **genetic art** program involves the use of a process of aesthetic selection to "breed" forms to the user's liking.

In Sims' "Genetic Images" show at the Centre Georges Pompidou, users were faced with abstract forms shown on 16 monitors controlled by a Thinking Machines Connection Machine. Viewers of the piece influenced its ongoing creation by standing in front of their favorite pieces. Their positions were recorded and used to determine which images were chosen to breed the next round of choices. In a manner reminiscent of the debates of the early days of computer art, when artists frequently generated a number of images algorithmically and then chose the successful ones, Sims asked:

> Can this interactive evolution of images be considered a creative process? The participants are just repeatedly choosing among groups of 16 images presented to them. However, after only five selections, the users choose one out of over a million possible paths. This is a large enough number of paths that users with different tastes usually produce quite different results.

The use of processes that mimic Darwinian natural selection—with aesthetic value as the criterion of "fitness"—calls into question not only the role of the artist, but that of all designers:

> We have difficulty believing that we ourselves were not designed by a god, but arose by accident via natural evolution. Similarly, we may also find it difficult to believe that artificial evolution can compete with our design abilities, and perhaps surpass even them [Sims, 1993].

The relationship of genetic art to larger philosophical, religious, and biological issues is explored further in **evolutionary art,** in which the evolution of genetically selected forms are based on rules and behaviors of biology. Artist Jon McCormack used artificial selection processes to create TURBULENCE, an interactive laser-disk installation showing a strange phantasmagoric "interactive museum of unnatural history" (see Fig. 7.34). The viewers control TURBULENCE via touch screen, and the animations are projected onto a wall. Strange specimen jars line the edges of the room. The work comments on the growing proportion of "made" objects in people's lives and landscapes and the taming of the "wild" in nature. The beauty of the generated forms inspires feelings of appreciation for nature and at the same time a sense of excitement at the imaginary worlds that technology can now help produce.

McCormack generates a complex emotional response in participants by presenting the destruction of natural places as the catalyst for new aesthetics made possible through

Figure 7.34 Jon McCormack, stills from *TURBULENCE: An Interactive Museum of Unnatural History*, 1994. *(Courtesy of Jon McCormack, produced in association with the Australian Film Commission. Copyright 1994 Jon McCormack)*

technology. He reflected, "I am sad for this loss of 'real' landscape, and naturally, most people will be. But the less anthropocentric view holds that sadness, morality, pride and beauty are only human concepts. Nature, 'red in tooth and claw' continues on: automatic, oblivious and inevitable" [McCormack, 1994]. The artist continued:

> All the time the speed of computers, their complexity, and that of their software—is getting better. The full version of this work took over 3 years to complete, much of the time spent waiting on the machine to complete its calculations. In a few years time what took years will be possible in seconds. This does not discourage me. What is important is *process,* the exploration, the insight and the augmented awareness that ensue from travels into logical space [McCormack, 1994].

For artist William Latham, who coined the term *evolutionism,* and his collaborator, mathematician Stephen Todd, the ability of the computer to create biological forms and "breed" them provides an opportunity to use aesthetic creations to critique the world of genetic engineering and the profound ramifications of tampering with nature. Latham's work on the computer is an extension of formal systems of growth and change that he previously drew by hand. His 3D work consists of forms that are based on a combination of plant grammars, fractals, and biological rules but look more like alien beings than anything found on this planet. His eerily surrealistic creatures are aesthetically compelling illusions created with geometry and pixels that hint at the horrors of a modern Island of Dr. Moreau (see Fig. 7.35).

Latham started working with computers in 1989 in order to automate his traditional work, which was based on often tedious object mutation and composition rules that he invented. The computer allowed him to accelerate this process and extend it to 3D forms. Among his inspirations he cites simple growth patterns in nature, D'Arcy Thompson's book *On Growth and Form,* art-historical attempts to create systems and methods for form creation (including Russian Constructivism and Kenneth Martin's drawings based on random dice throws), and human–machine interactions depicted in science fiction TV shows such as "Star Trek" and the "Dr. Who" episodes featuring the Daleks.

Like earlier computer artists who work with algorithms, both Sims and Latham have described the process of choosing forms as a type of gardening. The artistic role of choice, as opposed to actual image creation, is highlighted by these methods. Gardeners do not personally create flowers and trees, but without them the garden cannot exist. Although an artist or designer who chooses among (perhaps random) changes to an image is doing something different from someone who intentionally creates each image mark, both can produce powerful works that express personal experience and comment on cultural issues.

7.6.3   Particle Systems

Natural-looking, self-similar forms fill a gap in solid object modeling programs, but other 3D phenomena still cannot be easily modeled with any of the approaches discussed so far. For example, smoke, fire, air bubbles, and the like are not really single, distinct objects like a chair or a tree or self-similar structures like a

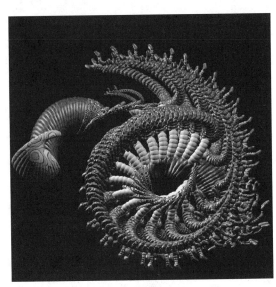

Figure 7.35 William Latham, *Mutation Y I 2nd Variant,* 1992 (Photographic print, 5′ × 5′). William Latham works with mathematician Stephen Todd to develop evolutionary forms and genetic algorithms for use as artistic tools. *(Courtesy of William Latham)*

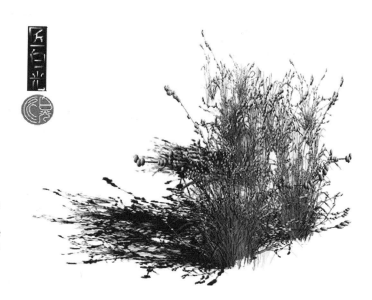

Figure 7.36 Alvy Ray Smith, *White Sands,* **1983** (created at Lucasfilm). "The flowering plants are graftals, the grasses are particle systems, the chop is my name and part of the piece." *(Courtesy of Alvy Ray Smith)*

Figure 7.37 Michael O'Rourke, *A la Recherche du Centre Exact: Union Square,* **1997** (Iris print on paper, 35″ × 43″). The artist built up the space in this piece by combining high-tech tools such as 3D graphics and particle systems with scans of traditional drawings done with pastel and charcoal. *(Courtesy of Michael O'Rourke)*

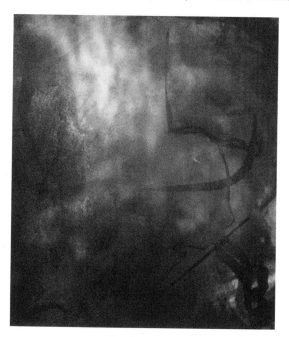

plant, but can be thought of as dispersed particulate matter. Such phenomena can be successfully represented with **particle systems,** or algorithmically controlled masses of individual shapes that are automatically created with hierarchies that can control movement of the entire system. Particle systems can be used to create natural forms such as plants and trees by defining the particles to look like branches, petals, or even parts of blades of grass (see Fig. 7.36).

Michael O'Rourke used particle systems to help create the atmospheric space and influence lighting choices in the work shown in Fig. 7.37. His use of particle systems is part of a desire to subvert the focus on objects and instead explore the space between them. He attempts to represent space with as few references to "things" as possible. (See Chapter 10, 2D and 3D Animation and Video, for a further discussion of particle systems in animation.)

7.7 Composition

We must begin with a large question: What is space? The existence and nature of space seems to be a truly basic, fundamental, and universal quality of reality; and if not of reality proper and entire, then, as Kant propounded, a necessary feature of our mind's operation in relation to it, and within it. Space and time, combined, appear to constitute a level of reality below which no more fundamental layers can be discerned, a field without natural parts, a universal attribute of Being that cannot be done away with, as much as Hume tried to do so [Benedikt, 1991, p. 125].

Michael Benedikt, *editor of* Cyberspace: First Steps

Representing and invoking space, whether realistic or fantastic or abstract, is essential to almost all visual art work. From the compressed, narrative, and iconic spaces of medieval painting to the theatrical space of Minimalistic sculpture and the linear perspective of the Renaissance and of photography, the representation of space has been an integral part of visual exploration and communication. In modern art work, spatial strategies have varied widely, from Cubism to collage to photography to Expressionist painting. In 3D graphics, the construction of space is severely constrained but effortless. An awareness of the strengths and weakness of spatial controls in 3D programs is important both for artists who desire to work in a realistic manner and for those who desire to subvert the standard spaces and work with them critically.

There are two main types of spatial composition in 3D computer graphics. First, 3D objects are arranged in the world to create a 3D scene. Second, points of view are chosen from which 2D images can be created for static works or animations.

The process of object modeling and scene composition in 3D modeling programs encourages viewing the world as an arrangement of separate, definable, and analyzable object-based constructions. This analytical way of thinking encourages certain types of composition and makes others nearly impossible. In many traditional 2D and 3D processes, from drawing to working with clay, single elements can be used to describe things other than discrete objects, blending forms and revealing connections among them. The structure of most 3D programs discourages such an approach.

Other strong influences on the compositional process include the automatic projective calculations performed by software, over which the user has little, if any, control. In particular, the perspective projection used is always linear, enforcing a Renaissance model of pictorial space. Figure 7.38 shows two different compositional approaches to creating artwork with 3D computer graphics. In the piece shown in Fig. 7.38(a), Matt Mullican took advantage of the emphasis of most 3D modelers on creating distinct, often hard-edged, geometric-looking objects in a space defined with linear perspective. In this virtual city, building shapes and colors are encoded according to a personal alphabet of symbols that the user can use to interpret the city. This piece is displayed on an interactive laser-disk system. In the piece shown in Fig. 7.38(b), Char Davies took advantage of the rendering capabilities of Softimage's high-end 3D software. The space that she created is ambiguously oriented and seems to envelop the viewer; it was based not on positioning distinct objects, but rather on controlling subtleties of color and of transparency.

(a)

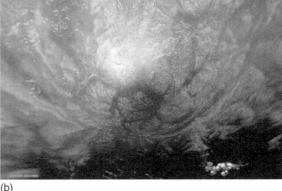
(b)

Figure 7.38 **Two different approaches to composing works with 3D systems.** (a) Matt Mullican, *Untitled*, 1989 (lightbox transparency, 36" x 48"). *(Courtesy of Digital Editions, Inc., Los Angeles.)* (b) In the 3D C G still image *Stream*, (1991), Char Davies placed 3D models in 3D virtual space and then moved the virtual camera point of view among them to capture the desired compositional framing. *(Courtesy of Char Davies)*

7.7.1 Placing Objects in the World or Scene

The artist's goals for the work influence a 3D composition. If the end product is to be a single "snapshot" taken from a predetermined point of view, the composition can be geared toward the impact of that one image. If the final production is an animation, the probable animation path or sequence of viewpoints and camera positions must be taken into consideration. If the end product is an explorable 3D world through which viewers may navigate in any way they choose, the composition must meet these much more general viewing needs.

The process of composing a final 3D scene involves the same types of operations as composing the individual objects but is usually a separate activity. In some 3D programs these two processes are even completed in different modules, and even within one program an artist may choose to model individual objects in separate files and then bring them later into a common 3D space. As objects often are modeled out of the context of the final compositions, the arranging and composing process can easily become excessively "object-based"—too like a 3D collage. Because of this separation, once the artist sees the objects composed in a 3D scene, redesigning some of them is often necessary.

7.7.2 Size and Scale

Like 2D object definitions, 3D object definitions can be visualized at any resolution. The file size is affected by the number and complexity of objects.

As with digital design and layout programs, size in unit measurements (e.g., millimeters or feet) is easily changed. If groups of objects are scaled relative to other objects

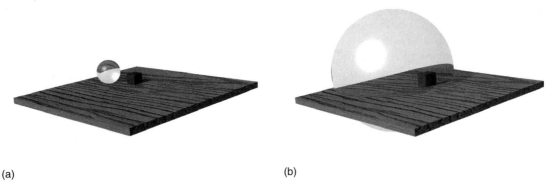

(a)   (b)

Figure 7.39 **Scaling in 3D can create unexpected results.**

or for printing at a range of sizes, however, the same compositional problems may arise as in 2D programs because object relationships can work well at one size but not at another. Some of the implications are analogous to those in 2D programs. For example, on a scaled-up object, textures created by texture mapping sometimes remain the same size and more tiles (repetitions of the texture map) are used to cover the object; the effect may not be what the artist originally intended. Also, simple shading methods, such as the simple fills available in 2D programs, tend to produce increasingly less realistic lighting effects as surface area is increased.

Scaling objects in a 3D program has more hazards than in 2D software in several respects. A change in relative scale of one object influences the composition considerations from all the infinite possible points of view, and the alteration from one viewpoint may not be obvious when the artist is considering the scene from another viewpoint. In a 3D space, predicting how scaling will affect an object's interaction with other nearby objects is difficult because, although its center point remains unchanged, its boundaries move to new locations, possibly obscuring other objects. In addition, when perspective is used, an object that is scaled up not only comes closer to the viewer but also gets larger relative to other objects; scaling a nearby object has a more pronounced effect than scaling an object that is far away. In Fig. 7.39, the scaled sphere completely engulfs the cube. (If the sphere were opaque the cube would be completely hidden.) Perspective accentuates the effect of scaling: The closer the sphere comes to the viewer, the more it disproportionately fills the screen.

Conclusion

3D programs represent a greater departure from traditional media than even digital painting, photoediting, and design programs. Traditional skills in sculpture or animation may not carry over and new ways of thinking about the creative process are called for. In 3D, most other types of graphics are brought together, making the usual distinctions between painting, photography, design, and sculpture less meaningful. Because there is no direct metaphorical counterpart to 3D programs in the traditional world, the anatomy of a 3D program is based more on the underlying concepts and functionality, making an understanding of those concepts even more useful.

The touch and composition options discussed in this chapter determine the experience of designing 3D worlds. Computer artists working in 3D soon learn to think in terms of primitives, profiles, and particles, and grow accustomed to bridging the 2D–to–3D gap by considering multiple views of their scenes. But creating the geometry is only the first step. Like a sculptor, the 3D artist works not only to define forms, but also to create surfaces that give the forms life and color. Like a stage set designer the 3D artist must set up lights to craft mood, and like a photographer the 3D artist must choose a point of view from which to present the work. These three processes—defining surfaces, lights, and camera positions—are covered in Chapter 8, Rendering 3D Worlds—3D Geometric Graphics II.

Suggested Readings

Bachelard, Gaston. *The Poetics of Space.* Beacon Press, 1969. (First published in French as *La Poétique de L'Espace,* by Presses Universitaires de France in 1958.) This incredible book will be of interest to most artists. Although it was not written with any thoughts about computers in mind, it suggests a huge number of possible modeling projects and methods of exploring personal spaces with 3D graphics by recreating the space of a person's real or imagined home.

Benedikt, Michael (ed.). *Cyberspace: First Steps.* The MIT Press, 1991. A thoughtful collection of essays on what cyberspace is, how we may work and play in it, and how it should be designed. Although published some time ago (in Web years), this book is still widely read and many of the ideas in it are just beginning to be realized. Includes essays on topics ranging from architecture to sociology to mathematical theory to corporate cyberspace to interface design.

Druckrey, Timothy (ed.). *Electronic Culture: Technology and Visual Representation.* Aperture Foundation, 1996. Includes Vannevar Bush's "As We May Think" in its valuable History section and many probing essays throughout. Requires some fortitude to make sense of both the theory and science vocabulary and references: not for beginners in either field. Good bibliography included.

Foley, James, Andries van Dam, Steven Feiner, and John Hughes. *Computer Graphics, Principles and Practice.* 2d ed. Addison-Wesley, 1996. The standard reference. Although tough going for beginners, this book is comprehensive and usually has the most thorough, correct, and detailed explanations of the principles underlying computer graphics. Known as "the Bible" among computer graphics researchers and programmers.

Glassner, Andrew S. *3D Computer Graphics, A User's Guide for Artists and Designers,* 2d ed. Design Press, 1989. A well-known graphics researcher, Glassner knows the field inside and out, having participated in forming parts of it personally while working at IBM, the New

York Institute of Technology (NYIT), and now Microsoft. He writes with clarity but assumes some knowledge of computing. If slightly technical language doesn't bother you and you want to deepen your knowledge of 3D graphics, this is an excellent resource. (If you've just read the 3D chapter in the present book, you now have the necessary background to enjoy Glassner.)

Kerlow, Isaac Victor. *The Art of 3-D Computer Animation and Imaging.* Van Nostrand Reinhold, 1996. Kerlow is a long-time computer artist, teacher (founder of Pratt's computer graphics program) and force in the computer art community. He is now at Disney. This book is based on many years of teaching graphics and is a practical resource for introductory courses and artists beginning to use 3D graphics. Comprehensive technically, it also includes practical advice for real-world use of 3D graphics, including general artistic concepts in traditional animation (such as story telling and story boarding) and lists of all Cinefex issue topics and SIGGRAPH Film/Video and Electronic Theater tapes. Amusing cartoons help bring concepts to life, and each chapter ends with quizzes.

Kerlow, Isaac Victor, and Judson Rosebush. *Computer Graphics for Designers and Artists.* 2d ed. Van Nostrand Reinhold, 1996. Kerlow's early book, with Rosebush, who is well respected in the world of computer science. Their book is written for artists but is technically sophisticated. The style is like hypertext "lexia," little tidbits and self-contained units of knowledge. Although there is an overall structure, the book is more of a reference than a narrative or high-level "how to," with explanations of most of the key terms in computer graphics, and illustrated with plenty of color images.

O'Rourke, Michael. *Three-Dimensional Computer Animation: Modeling, Rendering, and Animating with 3D Computer Graphics.* W. W. Norton, 1995. A clearly written and illustrated book that explains the technical concepts behind 3D modeling, rendering, and animation. Provides a level of detail of explanation rare in books for artists and designers but does not use jargon or assume a scientific or mathematical background.

SIGGRAPH Annual Conference Proceedings. Published each year as a special issue of ACM's *Computer Graphics* magazine. Along with the conference's *Visual Proceedings,* recommended in Chapter 2, the papers and panel discussion summaries in the general conference proceedings represent the widely acknowledged cutting edge in graphics research (from radiosity to morphing to plant growth algorithms). Most of the papers are too technical for artists with no background in the science of computer graphics to understand fully, but often the abstracts and parts of each paper are more accessible and will give artists a sense of future directions in graphics. A number of panels each year (with talks summarized or in full) are aimed at diverse non-technical audiences, including 2D and 3D artists, designers, and animators.

Exercises

1. *Art as model of reality.* Choose a relatively complex object and model it in different ways. You can do this on paper as well as on a computer with a 3D modeling program. Consider different goals for the model, such as an abstract visual art work, a recognizable but not realistic artwork (e.g., a caricature), a drawing for construction of an actual 3D object, and a 3D model to be used for training.

With StrataStudio Pro 2.5: Space precludes step-by-step instructions here for modeling a complex object. Try following instructions for building a model in your program's tutorials or use a pre-made model (most 3D software includes sample models). StudioPro includes a model of a ceiling fan, for example, that can be accessed through the Resource Palette from the Direct Imagination tab (drag the image into your document). It's already quite realistic.

Such a detailed model would not be necessary if the fan were viewed at a distance and did not have to be animated. A scene full of complex, detailed models will be slow to work with and to render. Using the ceiling fan model as a guide, create a simpler fan. For the base, create a cylinder with the Cylinder Tool on the main Tool Palette. (Pause with your cursor over any tool to see its name in the feedback area under the Button Bar.) For the blades, create a 2D, filled rounded rectangle with the filled side of the Rectangle Tool. Extrude it a bit by selecting it and clicking on the Extrude Tool (also in the main Tool Palette). Drag up a bit to extrude. Use the Move Tool to drag the blade next to the base. Check in Top and Right or Back views (use the drop-down menu on the upper left of the active window) to be sure they are properly aligned. Choose the Rotate Tool and move the center of rotation to the middle of the base by clicking and dragging from the blade to the base with the Command key (Mac) or Ctrl key (Windows). Use Edit: Replicate . . . to create three repetitions at 90 degrees to one another. Compare the very simple fan with the more detailed model. Add a few touches that correct for some of the crudeness of the simple model. For instance, try tapering the base and blades with the Modeling:Reshape option. You'll have to convert your primitive to a polygonal mesh or Bezier surface with the Convert button on the Button Bar.

2. *What is 3D?* Make a 2D traditional drawing of 3D objects. What visual cues indicate to you that the objects are really 3D? How can you transfer these cues to paper? What cues cannot be transferred? How many of these cues are represented in your 3D modeling program? How can you tell the difference between a drawing, photograph, computer model, and actual 3D objects?

With StrataStudio Pro 2.5: Draw a landscape from real life or a photograph and use conventional techniques to indicate depth and atmosphere, such as perspective and the use of blue in the distance. What techniques are you using to indicate that some objects are closer than others, or are they just larger? Or are they drawn differently, say, with heavier lines or more detail? Are there effects that you can see but cannot reproduce?

Now model the landscape roughly using simple extruded or lathed polygons for trees or houses or other object shapes. What cues are automatically supplied, such as shading and perspective rendering (move the eye icon at the top of the active window to change field of view)? Experiment with the Environment Palette (Windows: Show Environment Palette) Air and Ground options.

3. *What can be geometrically modeled?* Consider the objects around you at this very moment. Which can be accurately modeled with your current 3D modeling software? (Experiment—even simple objects can be impossible to model accurately.) Which render believably? What new techniques and/or effects would you need in order to create the objects that you cannot presently model or render realistically? What 2D postprocessing might help where 3D programs are lacking?

With StrataStudio Pro 2.5: Software and hardware limitations make it impossible to realistically model many complex objects, especially natural ones. Try modeling your hand. This classic exercise in observation and traditional rendering is great training on the computer as well. How can you represent the shapes of your fingers? Obviously plain cylinders won't do. Experiment with skinning cross sections. Draw your cross sections with the Bezier Pen Tool. Choose the Skin button from the Extensions Palette and click different cross sections in turn to see the skin automatically appear. Select a portion of your hand, say, a finger, and convert it to a Bezier surface. Reshape it to make the form more realistic. Use the Option key (Mac) or Alt key (Windows) to add new points if necessary. Texture mapping or work in a 2D program can be used to add skin textures and wrinkles.

4. *A new form of communication.* Human beings have never before had an abstract 3D form of communication—one that, like paper and pencil, does not depend much on physical substances. What types of ideas will benefit? Create a 3D message (to send to a friend) that you would not be able to convey easily with 2D drawings and for which building a physical 3D object(s) would not be practical.

> With StrataStudio Pro 2.5: Create a model of a dangerous underwater cave to familiarize explorers with its shape. First, create 2D polygon "ribs" to outline the contours of the terrain and then skin them. The more polygons per sample, the smoother the terrain will be. Add interesting textures from the Texture tab of the Resource Palette.

5. *Decomposition and hierarchy in modeling.* Make a drawing and 3D model of a relatively complex object (something with at least one moving part), using a hierarchy. How was the mental process of decomposition different in the 2D representation from in the 3D model? Consider the lines, colors and gestures that make up the drawing. In the model, consider the primitives and the operations used to shape and arrange them.

> With StrataStudio Pro 2.5: Bring up the Dining Chair model from the Direct Imagination Shapes options in the Resource Palette or model a similar chair. Try to find a similar chair in real life and make simple drawing of it. If such a chair isn't available, draw it from the screen. Note how, in a drawing, you can describe several objects at once with a single line, whereas in a model, you must make each object separately and position it.

6. *Mixing methods.* Most models require a mix of modeling methods. Because learning only one or two—and then depending on them, even when other methods would be better—is all too easy, this exercise requires that you experience different methods. Choose a simple object, scene, or abstract idea and model it at least four times, using primarily

1. primitives,
2. sweeps,
3. Boolean operations,
4. a digital clay approach, or
5. other means that your modeler offers.

What were the advantages and restrictions of the different methods?

> With StrataStudio Pro 2.5: Make the coffee mug of your dreams using several modeling methods. First, design the ideal mug on paper. Then make a model of it using 2D cross-sections and extrusions or lathing. Are you able to model all of its features this way? Use Boolean methods to create a new version and to make 3D textures on the outside by subtracting small shapes. Convert your extruded or lathed mug into a Bezier surface. What new possibilities does this open up? Finally, try out StudioPro's Metaballs features to make a truly

unique coffee mug. Create several elliptical shapes with the Sphere Tool from the Tool Palette. Shift-click to select them all. Choose Modeling: Metaball or click on the Metaball button on the Button Bar. A smooth surface will immediately form over the shapes. You can undo this action with Modeling: UnMetaball or the UnMetaball button.

7. *Planning hierarchy.* Much time can be saved by planning hierarchies in advance, on paper. Draw tree diagrams for a few objects (at least one of which should have simple moving parts). Experiment with different hierarchies before beginning to model. Make one or two of the models, referring to the tree diagrams. What changes do you still need to make?

This is mostly done on paper, so no application-specific exercise is given.

8. *Terraform your own world.* Use a 3D plant- or tree-growing program to create greenery for an imaginary dystopian world of the future. Integrate it with 3D models or with 2D digital images. Use particle systems to grow grasses and create atmospheric effects.

With StrataStudio Pro 2.5: StudioPro does not have a plant/tree-growing tool, but use the Hair options from the FX tab of the Resource Palette and the Wind option in the Air tab of the Environment palette to create mysterious other-worldly vegetation. Remember that Hair will not show up until you render.

CHAPTER 8

Rendering 3D Worlds— 3D Geometric Graphics II

Figure 8.1 Henrick Wann Jensen and Per H. Christensen, mental images GmbH & Co. KG, *Dusty Room Illuminated by Sunlight Through a Stained Glass Window,* 1998. Rendering, making a 2D image from 3D geometry, determines the look and feel of a work. Advances in rendering techniques have continually made possible new types of computer graphics, from wireframe images to flat-shaded shapes and smooth, volumetric-looking surfaces and photographic-like reflections calculated with a technique called ray tracing. Research into the physics of light–object interaction has led to even more sophisticated techniques, such as radiosity and radiance, that can accurately simulate the distribution of light energy in a modeled 3D space. For the image shown here, Jensen and Christensen used a combination of ray tracing, radiance, and volumetric photon maps to record the paths and destinations of individual photons in the scene. The scattering effects in the air are represented by 80,000 photons, the surfaces of the room with 220,000. The room itself is modeled with 2.3 million triangles.

Visually rich renderings using complex, physically based techniques used to take hours if not days to produce. Today, ray tracing in real time is a goal certain to be reached in the near future. Even the image shown here, which involved a great deal of mathematical calculation, was rendered in only 5 minutes, 27 seconds. [Jensen, 1998, pp. 311–320] *(Courtesy of Henrick Wann Jensen and Per H. Christensen, copyright 1998, mental images GmbH & Co. KG)*

8.1 Introduction

Imagine a world in which the most common building material is Tupperware™ and everything that cannot be manufactured with Tupperware is painted with solid matte colors. This scenario is not science fiction but the world entered every day by users of 3D graphics programs. Default rendering modes tend to make everything look like dull plastic. Such a world can be adequate for feedback during the creation of forms, but few artists would be happy if they couldn't eventually alter surfaces and draw on their knowledge of real-world surface qualities. Fortunately, most programs offer a range of premade "materials" and ways of defining one's own custom materials.

The factors that make up a **material** in a 3D program are combinations of surface properties and mappings of images and other information onto the surface. Surface properties determine how the surface absorbs, reflects, or transmits light rays. (For the basic concepts essential to 3D graphics and program anatomy examples, see Chapter 7.)

8.2 Surface Properties

When white light shines on a surface, some frequencies of light usually are absorbed. The frequencies that reach your eyes through reflection or transmission cause you to sense different colors. When you choose a color for an object material, you are modeling an object that absorbs all frequencies of light except the one that produces the color chosen. Thus, as in real life, when you shine a green light on a red 3D modeled object you see a dark, mostly colorless form. (For a detailed discussion of color interactions, see Chapter 5.)

Complexity of Color in 3D Programs

Color pickers in 3D programs usually are not very sophisticated—often just red, green, and blue color sliders—and do not take advantage of 3D methods of displaying color spaces (see Chapter 5 for detailed explanations of these concepts).

Like real-world objects, a 3D computer graphics model almost never appears to be a single color. Although a single gray is assigned to the vase in Fig. 8.2, even the simply shaded vase material in Fig. 8.2(a) has gradients of gray values. In Fig. 8.2(b), a glass material was used, and the final colors of the vase depend more on reflections and shadows from surrounding objects and lights than on the original color. Textures can also introduce color variations.

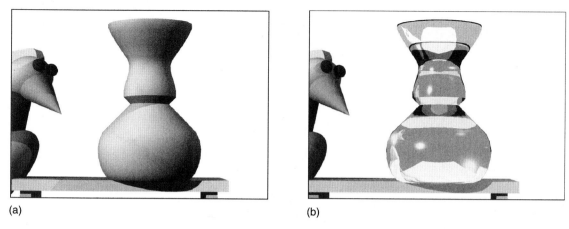

(a)   (b)

Figure 8.2 The final color of a 3D object is difficult to predict. (a) Plastic vase. (b) Glass vase.

Before learning about the different surface reflection characteristics, you should become familiar with the concept of a *surface normal*. The **surface normal** simply is the outward-facing direction of the surface (see Fig. 8.3); it is defined by a perpendicular line pointing outward from the surface. The length of this line or **vector** (a line with a direction) is always 1 unit. The concept of the surface normal is used extensively in computer graphics. For example, in this chapter I use the surface normal to compare angles between a surface and the direction of incoming light.

Figure 8.3 Examples of a surface normal.

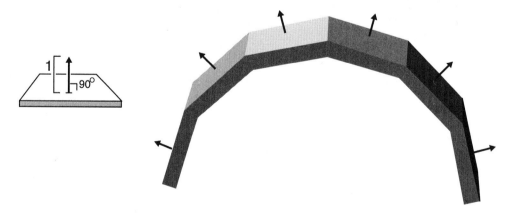

8.2.1 Surface Reflection Properties

There are two main types of surface reflection: diffuse and specular.

Diffuse, or dull/matte, **reflection.** The key characteristic of a diffuse material is that its brightness depends only on the angle of the light shining on it, not on the viewer's position (see Fig. 8.4). Most cotton and wool fabrics are diffuse reflectors. Their uneven, randomly aligned fibers scatter light in all directions so that the brightness is similar from any viewing angle.

Specular, or mirrorlike **reflection.** The key characteristic of a specular material is that it acts like a mirror, reflecting light only in a direction equal and opposite to the direction of the light shining on it. Only a perfect mirror exhibits solely specular properties; most reflective objects, such as polished metal, shiny plastic, or shiny apples, reflect light at a small range of angles opposite to the incoming light and are also partially diffuse. Specular reflections, also called **highlights,** are viewer-dependent; that is, the viewer must be at the right position—at an angle nearly opposite to that of the incoming light—to see them (see Figs. 8.5 and 8.6).

The color of a highlight depends on the type of material. For example, specular reflections from plastic are the same color as the incoming light (e.g., a white light shining on a red plastic ball causes a white highlight). However, specular reflections from metal are the color of the metal. These two types of reflectance, diffuse and specular, can create the range of effects summarized in Fig. 8.7. In each case, the length of rays indicates intensity. In *diffuse reflection,* light bounces off equally in all directions. In *specular reflection,* light bounces off only at an angle equal and opposite to that of the incoming light. In *specular reflection on a nonperfect reflector,* a specular highlight is evident over a small angle and loses its coherence. In a *combination* of *diffuse and specular reflection,* diffuse and specular components are additive.

8.2.2 Surface Transmission Properties

Light that is not reflected can be either absorbed or transmitted. Light that is transmitted illuminates whatever lies behind the object, creating the effect of **transparency.** If a surface is made 100% transparent, however, it becomes invisible.

Figure 8.4 **Viewing a diffuse table top.**

30% black

30% black

30% black

Figure 8.5 Specular reflection in action.

Figure 8.6 Viewing a specular table top. If the table has a mirrored top, the person seeing the specular highlight sees a recognizable reflection of the flashlight. As the table is slightly rough, the person just sees a bright spot that is 20% black.

When light passes through different media it is bent. Called **refracted light,** it makes objects in water, for example, appear larger below the waterline and at an angle to the parts of the object above the water line. Some materials refract the light more than others: Air has a refraction index of about 1, water of 1.3, and diamond of 2.4. (See Section 8.5.5 for a further discussion of transparency and refraction.)

8.2.3 Texture

In addition to the light absorption, reflection, and transmission properties of materials, artists can also give materials texture effects by using 2D images. The surfaces of most real-world objects, such as wood, are not a solid flat color but have a great deal of variation arising from inherent color differences in the material and the effects of light. **Texture mapping** lets artists apply 2D paint-type images to 3D objects. The effect is like wrapping the texture image around the object, but this analogy is somewhat misleading because texture mapping is much more flexible than that. In fact, the texture can be stretched or tiled over the entire model, and it also can be scaled and rotated (see Fig. 8.8).

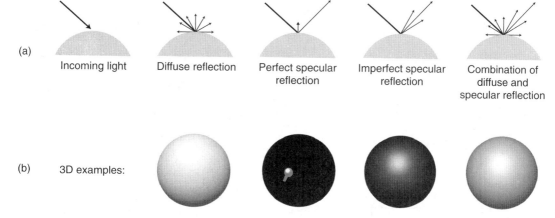

(a) Incoming light   Diffuse reflection   Perfect specular reflection   Imperfect specular reflection   Combination of diffuse and specular reflection

(b) 3D examples:

Figure 8.7 Ways in which light can bounce off of a surface. (a) Reflection properties for a 2D surface. (b) The same reflection properties for a 3D surface: a single light is positioned to the upper left of the viewer.

Texture mapping can go well beyond simulating physical materials—for instance, by using photographic or abstract images. You could map your best friend's face onto a bouncing ball, create patterns for wallpaper, or design a label for a soup can. A 2D house facade image can turn a simple polygon into part of a village. Texture maps are crucial for adding detail in games and other multimedia productions in which speed is of the essence because response time decreases as more polygons are drawn on the screen. As illustrated in Fig. 8.9, Any Channel's game engine uses texture mapping in place of geometric modeling to provide suggestive detail and create a richer visual environment than can be rendered in real time with polygons.

Texture map

Figure 8.8 Different ways to use a texture map. The artist can angle and scale texture mapping and choose separate settings for the tops and bottoms of shapes such as these cylinders.

Figure 8.9 Use of texture mapping to provide visual detail while preserving rendering rates. This screen grab from Any Channel's real time Any World engine uses texture maps to avoid modeling tiny details like computer displays and keyboard buttons. Despite the apparent complexity of the environment, there are only 156 visible polygons. *(Courtesy of Any Channel, Inc.)*

3D Painting

So-called **3D painting** is an application of texture mapping that lets an artist paint on the objects in a 3D world. To achieve the effect shown in Fig. 8.10, the artist uses a digital painting interface. The artist's hand-drawn marks are used to create a 2D texture map that is automatically applied to the 3D object. This process occurs behind the scenes, so the effect is that of painting directly on the 3D surface. The sensation of painting directly onto the 3D shape integrates these types of touch much more successfully than creating a texture map in a separate application, importing it, relating it to a 3D object, and then waiting for a rendering process to make it appear.

Figure 8.10 3D painting. The artist can draw directly on the 3D object.

Solid textures (usually) are procedural textures that are defined for a 3D volume rather than a 2D plane. The effect suggests a solid block of material, rather than a surface. If a solid marble textured cube were cut into, the new surface would show the cuts into the grain (see Fig. 8.11).

Close observation shows that in the real world almost all material textures have 3D qualities. For example, wood grain is not completely flat like Formica™; it has tiny variations of surface depth that catch the light in more complex ways than can be generated by simple texture mapping.

The detailed modulations of light and shadow that real 3D textures create are

Figure 8.11 Solid marble and wood textures.

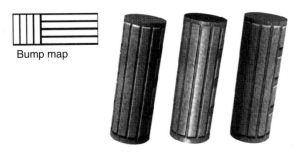

Bump map

Figure 8.12 Bump mapping. Here the same bump map is lit from three different directions. Note that the objects' silhouettes are not affected.

caused by many small surface angle changes. **Bump mapping** simulates this effect, not by actually modulating the surface, but by redefining the angles of the surface normals to simulate light hitting a surface that has been displaced up or down. When the object is rendered, the texture appears to have 3D qualities. Although a texture map could include shadows and reflections, such predetermined shadings probably would be inconsistent with the lighting in the scene. Because the relief-type shading created by a bump map is calculated with tilted surface normals, shadow and highlighting effects will change with chang-

ing light source positions (see Fig. 8.12). Because the geometry of the surface is not actually affected, the silhouette of the object is still composed of flat lines and curves.

Sometimes you really need the surface to be modulated, as when a smooth silhouette would be too unrealistic. **Displacement mapping** literally displaces the surface, changing the geometry of the object.

A 2D image can be used as a map of almost any surface parameter, including **transparency mapping,** where lighter image colors imply more surface transparency and darker colors more opaqueness (or vice versa). Other mappings could involve the use of a 2D image to control specularity or refraction.

The more parameters that a 3D graphics program offers for editing materials, the greater is the range of materials that the artist can create, both realistic and imaginary. No single program offers a way to make all types of materials (and not all materials can currently be simulated), but a wide range of materials can be created with various programs—at least the artist is no longer restricted to a world that looks like plastic.

8.3 WORKING WITH LIGHTS

The most dramatic visual transformation of a shot occurs in final lighting. It is here that the lighting crew paints the mood and ambiance of a shot using every imaginable lighting-source that a live-action filmmaking crew might use—including the sun and the moon. "Except we can make our sun come out whenever we want it to," says Toy Story lighting supervisor Galyn Susman. Nor does the lighting crew have to contend with heavy equipment, power plugs or gels. Everything is controlled with a computerized menu system.

"We have key-lights, back-light and rim lights," adds lighting supervisor Sharon Calahan. "We can put our shadows anywhere we want them, and we even have the ability to isolate lights to shine only on a particular character or object. In one shot, we have five lights shining just on Mr. Potato Head's ear."

"We've never done lighting like this before," says supervising technical director Bill Reeves. "The typical computer graphics scene uses diffuse, office light or has spotlights bouncing everywhere. We have dramatic moody lights in Sid's room, lens flares, flashlights and bright sun. In one sequence we have a rainstorm with dark gray skies. A few shots later, light streams through the window."
[See Fig. 8.13.]

Toy Story *production notes*

Figure 8.13 Frame from the movie *Toy Story*. (© Disney Enterprises, Inc.)

A 3D computer scene may show daylight, moonlight, or a city full of neon, but like a photographer's studio or an indoor film set, all the lights are chosen and positioned by the artist. Without lighting, the most artistically stunning 3D geometry could not be appreciated—the viewer would see only a black screen. Several types of lights are used in 3D programs, although all only roughly approximate the properties of real lights (see Fig. 8.14).

- **Ambient light** shines equally brightly on all surfaces to make all objects visible but does not appear to come from any specific direction. Ambient light mimics the brightness caused by interobject reflections (often too difficult to model in detail). By itself, ambient light usually is not very exciting.
- **Point sources** emit light from a single point equally in all directions. Point light sources immediately affect a composition by creating light and dark areas. They often become part of the composition themselves, as they imply a source at a certain location: Point sources in a scene usually are placed inside lamps or other objects that would be expected to emit light.
- When point sources are restricted so that light from some angles is blocked, the effect is like that of a **spotlight.** Spotlights can mimic many types of lamps and add drama to a scene. A variety of spotlight effects can be created by blocking part of a

Figure 8.14 Light types.

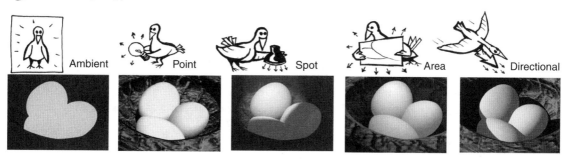

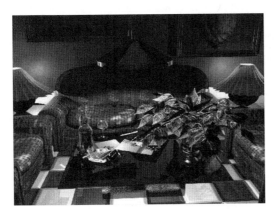

Figure 8.15 The influence of lighting choices on many aspects of a composition. In *Living Room* by Diego Velasco (1994), lighting sets the mood and plays an important role in the composition: The coffee table and sofa edges are relatively brightly lit and provide the focus, while the wall behind them fades to darkness. *(Courtesy of Diego Velasco)*

point source with hand-modeled surfaces. Usually the light's intensity diminishes with distance.

- **Area sources** emit light from an entire surface rather than a single point. Area sources can represent real-world lighting (e.g., fluorescent panels) better than point sources, but they still do not take into account many factors that characterize real lights, such as variations in color and intensity of light leaving the surface at different angles. They also are more difficult to use because they require a lot of calculation. Many commercial programs do not offer them. In any case, when a light is far enough away, its area becomes unimportant.

- **Directional,** or **remote, lights** simulate light sources so far away that their light rays seem to come from a single direction. This type of light may not have a specific location. It illuminates all objects in the scene with light from the same angle, shining parallel rays on it. A good example is the sun: Although its surface area is enormous, it is so far away that light coming from different parts of its surface does not influence how objects are lit on the earth. These lights are useful for modeling such distant light sources because they require less processing power (only one direction has to be calculated).

Lights can vary in *type, intensity, color,* and *location* (or *direction*). Diego Velasco utilized all these factors in the work shown in Fig. 8.15 to control aspects of the composition. To create the realistic shadows that structure this composition, Velasco placed lights inside the modeled lamps. The end-table lamps have point lights inside them, and the overhead lamp a directional light. Warm tints added to the lights' colors (slightly darkening the image) enhance the cozy feeling.

8.4 VIRTUAL CAMERAS AND POINTS OF VIEW

Early critics of photography claimed that it involved no artistic skills because the photographer only captured things that were there anyway. Anyone, they argued, could capture the same image as a professional by just standing in the right spot. These critics underestimated the difficulty of choosing that right spot and adjusting the camera to get the desired image. The same is true of 3D modeling. The decisions you make in composing a **virtual,** or **synthetic, photograph** of the final scene (choosing a point

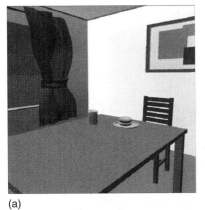

(a)

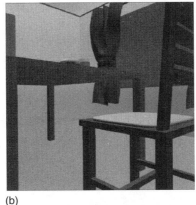

(b)

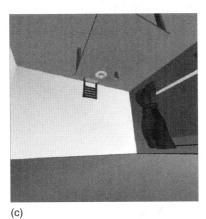

(c)

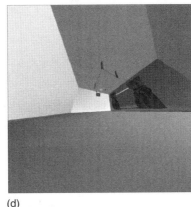

(d)

Figure 8.16 Point of view series, *The Hamburger Room*, 1995. (a) Adult's point of view. (b) Dog's point of view. (c) Fly's point of view. (d) An "extreme" fly's or perhaps alien creature's point of view. Note that all six sides of the room are visible. *(Courtesy of Jeff Beall and the Brown University Computer Graphics Group)*

of view, framing, etc.) can have just as much impact as the decisions you made during the 3D geometric composition process. For example, a single model was used to create all four images shown in Fig. 8.16, but the different points of view suggest distinctively different viewers and narratives.

Like a real camera, a **virtual camera** makes a picture based on the position of a **film plane,** or **picture plane,** relative to the scene. How much of the scene can be drawn on the picture plane depends on how much of it lies within the **view volume,** a volume in space determined by the eye of the viewer (the *viewpoint*) and a cross section that is the picture plane. The view volume does not extend to infinity but ends with a back **clipping plane** (see Fig. 8.17). (A front clipping plane often is used also.) By adjusting the parameters of the view volume, the artist can simulate many aspects of a real camera, including the

- **point of view,** which is the location of the camera in the scene;
- **direction of view,** which is the direction in which the camera is pointed;

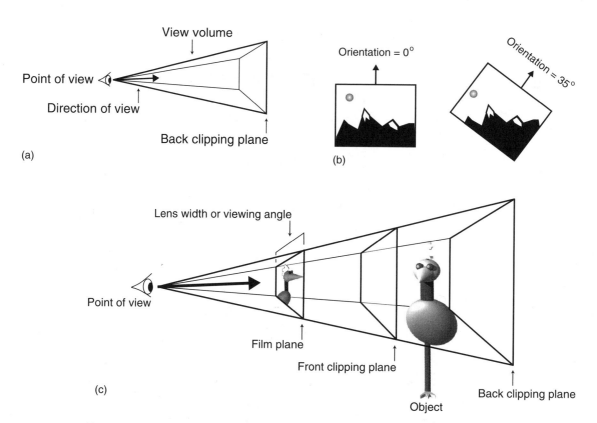

Figure 8.17 Parameters of the virtual camera. (a) Basic components of the virtual camera. (b) Two views of the same scene with different orientations. (c) A bird object inside the view volume and projected onto the film plane.

- **lens width,** or **viewing angle,** which is based on the distance between the point of view and the picture plane;
- **angle,** or **orientation,** of the camera, which is the angle or rotation of the view volume, usually expressed in terms of which way is "up" for the camera; and
- **focal length,** which is simulated by blurring the image in front of or behind a predetermined distance along the view volume.

A real camera always creates a *perspective projection*. In a **perspective projection,** a single point of view is represented, objects grow smaller as they recede in the distance, and parallel lines that are not parallel to the film plane converge at vanishing points (see Fig. 8.18a). A virtual camera usually offers a choice of perspective or *parallel projection*. In a **parallel projection,** all lines and planes parallel to each other on the 3D objects

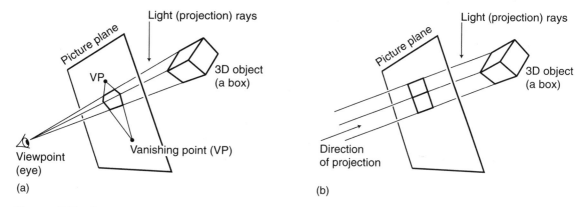

Figure 8.18 The two main types of projection: (a) perspective and (b) parallel.

remain parallel in the projection, and objects do not grow smaller if moved farther away (see Fig. 8.18b). In some programs, the virtual camera can create images like those made with a view camera, in which the camera film plane and lens can be tilted independently. Although perspective projection offers a more effective illusion of 3D space, parallel projection can be a better choice when measurements of accurate object dimensions are important—for instance, in architectural and mechanical drawing. Parallel projection is extremely useful during the modeling process because it is easier to judge relative object alignment accurately in a parallel view.

Parallel projections are called **orthographic projections** when they are along principal axes of the object, showing the principal faces of the object (e.g., the front, top, and side views shown in Fig. 8.19). Views that are not along one the major axes of the object are called **axonometric,** or off-axis, views. An **oblique projection** is created when the direction of projection is not perpendicular to the picture plane. A view camera uses a perspective oblique projection, and technical illustrators often use parallel oblique drawings—but oblique projections are not available in most of today's 3D modelers.

The construction and representation of space are essential in almost all visual artwork, and therefore you need to be aware of the spatial restrictions imposed by 3D programs and their effects on your work. Three-dimensional programs enforce either a diagrammatic, technical type of space—parallel projection—or a photographic, Renaissance type of linear perspective. In addition, the use of virtual cameras involves only one set of parameters at a time, enforcing a single viewpoint and single type of projection. You can make works with complex spatial identities by using a digital paint program to combine and possibly alter various renderings of a 3D scene made with different camera viewpoints, orientations, and projection methods.

(a) Perspective

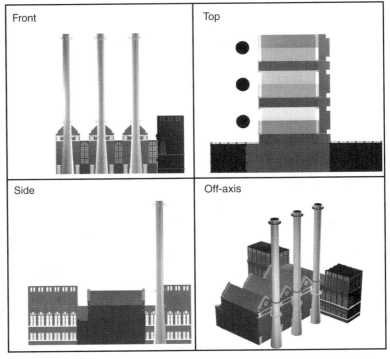

(b) Parallel views

Figure 8.19 Perspective versus parallel projection. (a) The perspective projection illusion of 3D space. (b) The parallel projections are less illusionistic but more useful to architects and others involved in a building's actual construction because measurements can be scaled directly from the drawings. Parallel views were used extensively during the construction of this model to align the different parts.

8.5 Rendering

The question that pops into artists' heads when they first render a complex 3D scene is, Why on earth is this taking so long!?! Although artists use rapid rendering techniques for feedback while creating a work, the more complex methods required to make the final images can take anywhere from several seconds to minutes, hours, or even days. The length of time needed depends on the machine used, the complexity of the model, and the rendering method.

The answer to the question posed is that, in addition to the rasterization process—sampling geometry to get discrete values—rendering a 3D scene involves the often extraordinarily complex tasks of transforming 3D primitives so that they are positioned correctly in the final scene, removing surfaces that should not be rendered, and calculating lighting effects. Artists have no control over projection methods, aside from choosing perspective or parallel projection. However, they do have some choice of materials and lighting methods that can dramatically affect the nature of the final image and the time that elapses before they see it.

In the series of pieces in the installation "The Constructed Forest" (see Fig. 8.20a), MANUAL used 3D modeling and rendering to explore the visual differences between constructed spatial elements and natural forest landscapes. The lighting and shading chosen to render the 3D-modeled portion (the palette) are relatively simple and produce an object that looks computer-generated, constructed in an analytical and technological sense. The wood texture map that wraps around the edges of the objects like a Formica veneer and the plastic feeling caused by the way the highlights are rendered impart the aesthetics of early computer graphics and make it clear that realism is not

Figure 8.20 Rendering in the work of two artists. (a) MANUAL (Suzanne Bloom/Ed Hill), detail from *The Constructed Forest ("This is the End—Let's Go On"—El Lissitsky)*, 1993. *(Courtesy of Ed Hill and Suzanne Bloom)* (b) Yoichiro Kawaguchi, *COACERVATER: Artificial Life Creation*, 1994. *(Courtesy of Yoichiro Kawaguchi)*

(a)

(b)

the goal. The smoothness of the object and the simplicity of the geometry contribute to the effect of a self-aware symbol rather than a simulated photograph in a style matching the photographic background. In Kawaguchi's *Artificial Life* series (see Fig. 8.20b), the rendering is more involved, in keeping with the subject matter of the work. The form, generated with genetic algorithms, is curved and appears topologically complex. The surfaces are not smooth but irregular and mapped with a complex texture map that is detailed in some sections and dispersed in others. Reflections from many light sources suggest wet plastic and organic substances. Complex and lurid coloring adds to the unfamiliar shapes to make this view of "artificial life" even more unfamiliar and alien.

Rendering is an extreme example of global touch. It affects how everything looks—indeed, how light behaves in the scene—and yet the entire final "painting" of a scene takes place without any influence of the artist's hand. Having pressed the Render button, the artist loses all control until the process has finished. Interactive rendering would let artists make adjustments and change variables during the rendering process, so as to treat some objects differently from others. I am unaware of any plans to make such interactive rendering available in commercial products.

(Because the artist has no interactive control, there is no separate "touch" section in this chapter.)

8.5.1 WIREFRAME

The simplest and fastest way to draw 3D objects is not to take lighting into account at all. The alternative is simply to draw the objects' structural components—the vertices and connecting lines—called **wireframe rendering,** in which the structure of the object is visually represented but the surface is not drawn (see Fig. 8.21).

Spatial coherence (the ability to discern the outside of an object from its inside) can be improved by drawing only those lines and vertices that would be visible if the object had an opaque surface, producing a **hidden–line wireframe rendering.** Wireframe rendering is most commonly used to provide a fast working or preview mode, but it can also be used to show the structure of objects without introducing extraneous information about surface properties. Interior elements of a complex object can be revealed by drawing outer parts of the model in wireframe. No lighting or shading calculations are necessary for pure wireframe, so it is a very fast way to preview a scene. Hidden-line wireframe images can take somewhat longer to render.

In addition, many artists have found wireframe's structural aesthetic appealing and purposely use wireframe as the final rendering method for 3D objects in their work, as in Fig. 8.22. In this piece, Toni Dove and Michael Mackenzie used wireframe models to set an aesthetic tone: The initial space was a wireframe model based on a prison drawing by Piranese and wireframe models were used in several sections of this interactive mystery narrative. The space created by the wireframe prison structure has a structural yet delicate appearance, and the white lines on a black background make the building

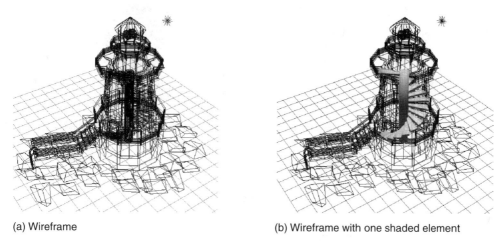

(a) Wireframe   (b) Wireframe with one shaded element

Figure 8.21 Wireframe rendering of a lighthouse. (a) Wireframe without shading. (b) Shading of individual elements to help isolate them when the wireframe becomes too complex.

strangely insubstantial. The clothing of the animated characters was created in a digital photoediting program by collaging elements of old-fashioned women's underwear. The corsets and other garments, such as skirt hoops and bustles, echo the wireframe motif. (See Chapter 11, Multimedia and Interactivity, for further discussion of this work.)

Despite all the technology involved, however, a handmade line drawing usually is much easier to read than a computer-generated wireframe rendering, since the artist can easily vary the line weights. Some programs offer a similar type of drawing aid, a type of depth cueing in which lines closer to the viewer are brighter than those in the distance (again see Fig. 8.22).

8.5.2 Modeling Light Interaction with Surfaces

In setting up the rendering process, the artist literally chooses how "light" will act in a scene. At one end of the spectrum, the goal is to produce needed results quickly enough to keep the program responsive and enjoyable to use. Such methods are designed for speed and do not attempt to imitate real light–object interaction or to provide photographic realism. At the other end of the spectrum are techniques that attempt to simulate the actual physics of light–object interaction by taking into account all the light energy in a scene and representing physical interactions at all levels down to reflection, refraction, and even diffraction of light at the object's surface. Renderings with this level of complexity presently take minutes or even hours for a single image.

Figure 8.22 Toni Dove and Michael Mackenzie, *The Coroner's Dream,* **1993** (still from interactive virtual-reality installation *Archeology of a Mother Tongue*). *(Courtesy of Toni Dove)*

Faster machines and special 3D graphics hardware acceleration already make possible rendering smoothly shaded objects in real time and animating them in various multimedia products, including, perhaps most noticeably, video games. In the near future, inexpensive 3D graphics hardware will let artists work with fully rendered (shaded, textured, and shadowed) scenes in real time.

8.5.3 Lighting Models

A **lighting model** is not a geometric object but a behavioral model of the way that light interacts with objects. Most lighting models are what are called *hacks:* simplifications and approximations that do a reasonable job but aren't physically based.

LAMBERTIAN OR DIFFUSE LIGHTING   A simple model of the behavior of light says only that light illuminates an object in direct proportion to its angle with the surface normal. Lambert's law of **diffuse lighting** states that the amount of light reflected from a surface depends on the angle between the incoming light and the surfaces (see Fig. 8.4). This lighting method is sufficient for simple diffuse material definitions.

PHONG LIGHTING   A slightly more complex model called **Phong lighting** takes into account the angle of the viewer, as well as that of the incoming light. This model is used to render specular reflections (see Fig. 8.6).

8.5.4   SHADING MODELS

Models such as Lambertian or Phong lighting are used to calculate the effect of light at any given point on an object's surface. Ideally, a lighting calculation would be performed for every point on the object's surface, but lighting calculations usually require too much processing power for this approach to be practical. In these situations, a **shading model** is used to generate color values for an entire surface (typically a small triangle) on the basis of just a few lighting calculations at selected points (e.g., the vertices of triangles in a polygonal mesh).

FLAT SHADING   In **flat shading,** lighting is calculated once for each polygon (usually by using a simple Lambertian lighting model), then the entire polygon is colored with that value. The result is a model that looks faceted because each polygonal face is distinctly shaded, usually differently from its neighbor. As with wireframe rendering, flat shading can be used to reveal structural aspects of objects and can also be effective aesthetically because of the faceted results.

Flat shading has some usually undesirable characteristics, however. In the rendering of curved shapes that are approximated and drawn as polygonal meshes, flat shading makes depicting a convincingly curved surface practically impossible for two reasons: (1) the surface is represented by a number of flat polygons that can only approximate an ideally smoothly curved form; and (2) an optical effect known as **Mach banding** intrudes (see Fig. 8.23). This artifact of the visual system increases the perception of contrast near areas of sharply defined value change. Because of this effect, increasing the polygonal resolution of the object can actually accentuate the perceived faceting of the surface, making it look corrugated instead of smoother.

GOURAUD SHADING   Henri Gouraud found a clever solution to the faceting problem in 1971 by averaging lighting values to create smooth gradients between them. With **Gouraud shading,** a polygonal cylinder or sphere looks curved (see Fig. 8.24). However, there are two main problems with Gouraud shading: The first is that specular reflections can rarely be recorded (and when they are, they are spread and averaged too much to be convincing). The second is that at the object boundaries, where there is nothing to average, the polygonal boundary lines are always clearly evident. Figure 8.16 is an entirely Gouraud-shaded scene.

Figure 8.23 Mach banding.
(a) The scalloped look of this gray-scale ladder is due to Mach banding. (b) Mach banding contributes to the difficulty of using flat shading for curved surfaces. Although increasing the number of facets improves the object's silhouette, it also accentuates the scalloped look of each facet, contributing to the corrugated look of the rightmost cylinder.

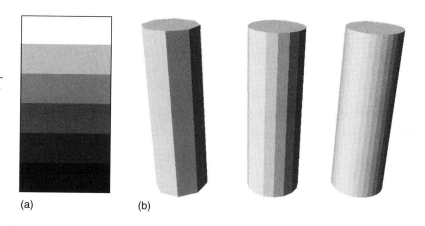

(a) (b)

PHONG SHADING   In 1975 Phong Bui-Tuong solved the specular problem with a shading method, now called **Phong shading,** that averages the surface normals instead of the lighting values (see Fig. 8.25). (See Chapter 10, 2D and 3D Animation and Video, for further discussion of the type of weighted averaging he used: *interpolation*.) Lighting calculations are then made for each point of the surface as if for a rounded form. With this artificial surface information, the lighting model can use the angles between the light, surface, and viewer to render specular highlights convincingly.

Most 3D graphics hardware now contain Phong lighting and shading, but Lambertian lighting and Gouraud shading are still the standard for fast screen feedback because

Figure 8.24 Flat versus Gouraud shading. In both the (a) flat-shaded cylinder and (b) the Gouraud-shaded cylinder, lighting values are calculated at the center of each polygon (the small circles represent percentages of black). The flat-shaded polygons are shaded with a single color, making the polygons visibly distinct. The Gouraud-shaded cylinder is shaded with averages of the grays from each calculation point, making a smooth graduation.

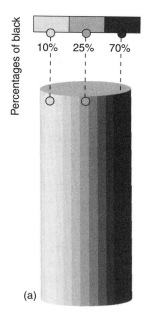

(a) (b)

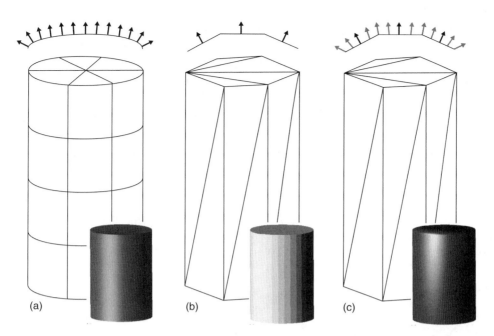

Figure 8.25 Surface normals in shading. (a) Surface normals along a real curved surface. (b) Surface normals along a polygonal approximation of a curved surface. (c) Phong shading: polygonal surface normals averaged with a weighted average to simulate surface direction changes of a real curved surface.

so many fewer lighting calculations are needed. Thus specular reflections may not show up in your image until you specifically choose a rendering method that takes viewer position into account (such as Phong lighting and shading).

8.5.5 GLOBAL RENDERING METHODS

The methods discussed so far are **local lighting models,** which render each object as if it were the only one in a scene. **Global lighting models** take into account light interactions between objects such as interobject reflection and shadows. The most popular global method used in today's programs is recursive ray tracing.

RECURSIVE RAY TRACING **Recursive ray tracing** works by considering the paths of light rays as they bounce around a scene illuminating objects. The light rays leave areas of shadow, create interobject reflections, and reveal transparencies. Tracing the path of every one of the infinitely many light rays sent by a light source into a scene is impossible, so ray tracing considers only those rays that will eventually reach the eye. In order to determine which rays those are, ray tracing works in reverse—**eye rays** are traced from the viewer's eye into the scene.

In **simple ray tracing** (by itself a local lighting method), an eye ray is sent into the scene for each pixel needed to make up the final image. If one of the rays intersects an object in the scene, the object's surface color at the point of intersection is calculated with any of the lighting models previously described. The resulting value is used to define the color of the pixel location through which the ray was sent (see Fig. 8.26).

Recursive ray tracing introduces a global factor by tracking the eye ray farther. The goal is to discover the effect of other objects on the color value at the initial point of ray–object intersection by asking such questions as: Are other objects (or parts of the object's own surface) casting shadows at that point? Are other objects reflected in the

Figure 8.26 Simple ray tracing. (a) Rendered view of a scene showing the eye, lights, and objects. (b) Eye rays are traced from the viewpoint through every pixel location into the scene. If a ray intersects an object, its lighting value at that point is calculated and contributes to the screen image. If a ray does not intersect an object, that pixel of the image remains white (or is set to some other background color). (c) Rendered image as seen from the position of the eye.

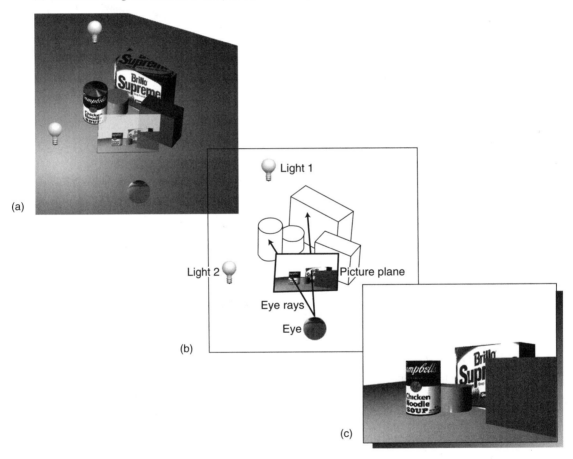

initial object's surface? And, if the initial object is at all transparent, are other objects visible through it? Figure 8.27 shows how an eye ray can be used to spawn additional rays in order to answer these questions.

To assess the effect of shadows, **shadow rays** are traced from the eye ray–object intersection point toward all the scene's light sources to ascertain if any objects are blocking the lights' paths (see Fig. 8.28). If a light source is blocked, that light does not contribute to the object's color value at the intersection point.

If the object is specularly reflective, a **reflection ray** is projected outward at an angle equal and opposite to the angle formed by the

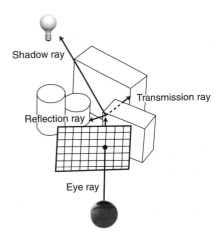

Figure 8.27 An eye ray spawning additional rays to determine reflections, shadows, and transparency.

Figure 8.28 Ray-traced shadows. Shadow rays are sent out toward all the light sources in the scene. If a shadow ray hits another surface on its way to a light source, that light does not contribute to the color value of the object at the original eye ray intersection. If no other light reaches that point either, it is completely in shadow.

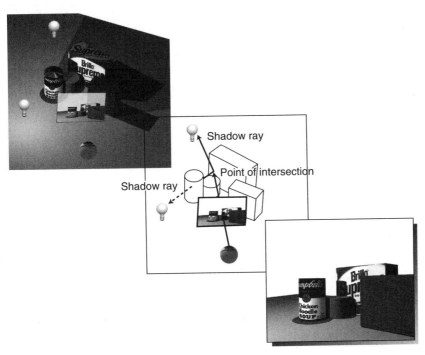

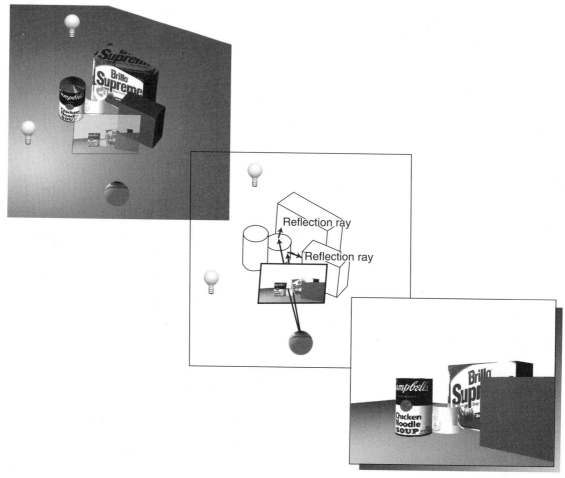

Figure 8.29 Ray-traced reflections. A reflected ray is sent out at an angle equal and opposite to the angle between the eye ray and the object surface. If the reflected ray hits another surface, that surface is reflected in the original object. The reflective properties of the shiny untextured cylinder are revealed by reflection rays showing both the soup can and the Brillo box.

eye ray and the object surface. If the reflection ray intersects an object, the color value of the object at that intersection point contributes to the specular reflection at the initial eye ray–object intersection point (see Fig. 8.29). Since diffuse surfaces reflect light in all directions, a very large number of additional rays must be sent out. Because of the huge number of calculations involved, diffuse ray tracing is not available in most rendering packages.

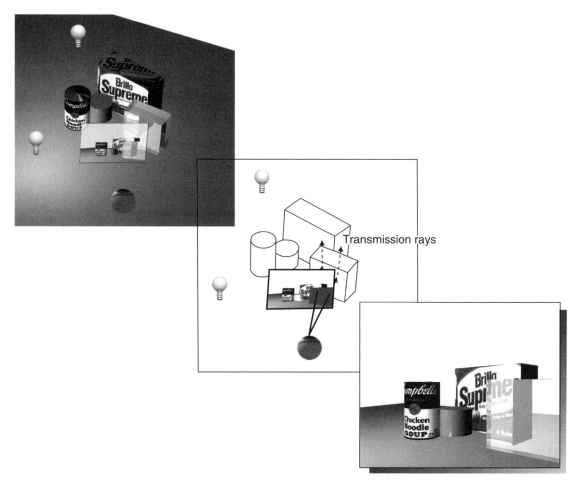

Figure 8.30 Ray-traced transparency and refraction. The cuboid closest to the eye is transparent and has a large index of refraction. The eye ray is transmitted through the cuboid and the cuboid's transparent and refractive qualities are visible after rendering with transmission rays.

If transparency and refraction are desired, the eye ray is sent on as a **transmitted ray** through the object (at a new angle if refraction is used) to determine which objects are partially visible (see Fig. 8.30).

Each reflected and transmitted ray can then spawn its own shadow, reflection, and transmission rays (see Fig. 8.31). When all the rays to be sent out have been calculated, the unwinding part of *recursive* ray tracing begins: The light paths traced so far are run backward to the initial point of intersection. The values of the interactions along the way are added to produce the final pixel value.

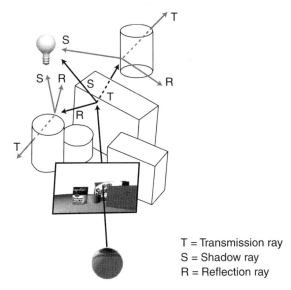

T = Transmission ray
S = Shadow ray
R = Reflection ray

Figure 8.31 Spawning additional rays from each reflection and transmission ray.

The recursive process can, in principle, go on until all transmission and reflection rays fail to intersect any objects. Thus ray tracing can be extremely slow because the number of rays grows exponentially: 5 recursions involve calculating 96 rays, but 20 recursions involve calculating more than 3 million rays. Fortunately, the improvements in quality fall off quickly with the number of ray bounces because each time light strikes an object, part of its energy is absorbed; the additional rays are therefore much less important than the first few. Figure 8.32(a) illustrates the effect of sending only one group of rays from the initial eye ray–object intersection point. Figure 8.32(b) shows what happens when three ray bounces are made after initial intersection. Note the increased detail in the refraction of light within the glass base and the large sphere, and in general, brighter reflections and better contrast. As depicted in Fig. 8.32(c), six bounces produce little quality enhancement over three bounces, although again the rendering of the glass base is improved. In general, the more transparent and mirrorlike objects there are in the scene, the more additional bounces will improve the effect.

Ray tracing can produce complex and convincing renderings of highly reflective or transparent surfaces such as glass and metal with shadows and refraction, and is great for simulating mirrored surfaces. Although the results can look like photography, ray tracing is still an extremely oversimplified simulation of light interaction among objects in a 3D space. Diffuse light interactions among objects are not calculated, for instance, and even light effects that are calculated are not necessarily correct; shadows' rays are always sent directly toward light sources, for instance, and do not take refraction into account. The hard-edged look associated with ray tracing can be softened somewhat with techniques that send out groups of rays "jiggled" a bit from the original trajectory. But for some types of objects, such as those with soft edges, and some types of light, such as subtle diffuse setups, ray tracing is likely to give unsatisfactory results.

The mysterious underwater scene shown in Fig. 8.33 was recursively ray-traced so that the central "life form" reflects its surroundings, giving a glimpse of the environment behind the picture plane. The distortions also emphasize the creature's curved 3D shape. Note how the hard edges and sharply defined reflections contrast with the underwater feeling suggested by the rest of the composition and the title.

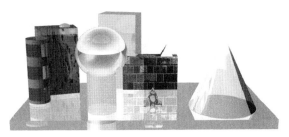

One ray bounce

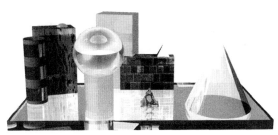

Three ray bounces

Six ray bounces

Figure 8.32 The effects of one, three, and six ray bounces.

Figure 8.33 Yoichiro Kawaguchi, _Ocean_, 1986 (frame from film). _(Courtesy of Yoichiro Kawaguchi)_

Environment Mapping

For times when ray tracing is just too demanding, a mirrored surface can be faked with a technique called **environment mapping.** Environment mapping creates mirrorlike effects by rendering the scene from the point of view of a mirrorlike object and then using the 2D rendered results as a texture map for the surface (see Fig. 8.34). The environment-mapped surface does not need to be planar.

Figure 8.34 Faking reflection with environment mapping. (a) Scene with cylinder, cube and "mirror." (b) Camera set up behind mirror. (c) Scene rendered from camera/mirror view. (d) Mirror-view image used as a texture map for mirror object's surface.

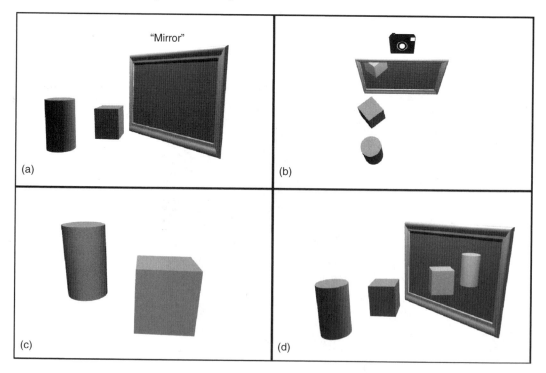

RADIOSITY   **Radiosity** is a global lighting model that incorporates more of the known physics of light–surface interaction than do the methods previously described. Based on thermal engineering models, radiosity tracks how all the light energy in a scene at any given time is being transferred among the scene's lights and objects. Each surface, including those of the lights themselves, is first broken into regular patches. Then **form factors** are calculated for each patch; they describe the percentage of emitted or reflected light that reach it from every other patch. The final amount of light coming from any specific patch is the amount of light that it naturally emits (if it is a light source), plus a percentage of the light reaching it from every other patch. Not surprisingly, a colossal number of calculations are needed to quantify the cumulative effects of emitted and reflected light for every surface in a scene (see Fig. 8.35).

After the form factors have been calculated and the lighting equations run, the objects are shaded with a diffuse shading model. In the diffuse, specular, and ray-traced non-radiosity models previously covered, an ambient factor is always added to account for global interobject light reflections. Radiosity calculates these effects explicitly, so an additional ambient term is not needed.

Although radiosity rendering can keep an entire network of computers (known as a **rendering farm**) occupied at night, once the calculations have been completed, the scene can be viewed interactively, in its fully rendered splendor, from any point of view. Because they depend on diffuse shading, radiosity renderings do not need to be updated with changes in viewing angle. This feature makes radiosity a perfect choice for architectural walkthroughs and other 3D environments in which objects do not move.

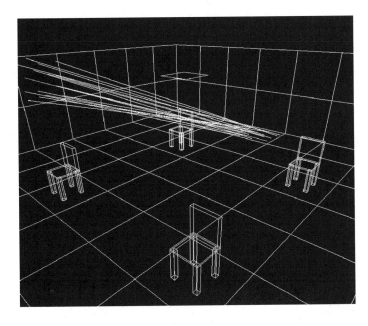

Figure 8.35 Snapshot of a radiosity rendering in progress. *(Courtesy of Andrew Willmott, Carnegie Mellon University)*

(a)   (b)

Figure 8.36 Radiosity rendering example. (a) A photograph of the Corbusier chapel in
Ronchamps, France. (b) A radiosity rendering of the chapel.   *(Modeling by Keith Howie and Paul
Boudreau, rendering by John Wallace and Eric Haines of 3D/EYE, Ithaca, NY. Courtesy of the Cornell Pro-
gram in Computer Graphics)*

An immediately noticeable result of radiosity is the appearance of **color bleeding,**
or the diffuse reflections of one surface in another. Color bleeding gives images visual
complexity and interest as well as heightened realism. Radiosity provides some beautiful lighting qualities that are not usually possible with ray tracing, including soft, modulated shadows that give images a look and feel not usually associated with computer
graphics. As illustrated in Fig. 8.36, radiosity rendering can help create a room filled
with light, including interobject color bleeding, soft shadows, and nuanced lighting of
the walls. Note, however, the lack of any reflections or specular highlights. Because
viewer position is not taken into account, specular and transparent or translucent surfaces cannot be rendered with radiosity. To achieve images with complex colors and
transitions, as well as the reflective qualities of ray tracing, a combination radiosity–ray
tracing technique can be used.

Although some rendering methods can produce plausible images (i.e., images that
look like photographs), the problem of creating an image from modeled objects that
matches a real-life scene or photo is far from being solved. According to Peter Shirley,
a computer scientist at the University of Utah:

> We can render smooth, plastic and metal surfaces, but many biological materials, like
> human skin, are not fully understood. The variations in reflectance due to freckles,
> skin moisture and oil, etc. are very complex and subtle. If we use a geometric data set
> of the right complexity we'll be overwhelmed trying to render it. The same goes for
> many types of cloth and also for man-made materials like mirrored sunglasses with
> rainbow reflections caused by thin-film interference. These are all difficult problems
> and though research is progressing, results are not yet integrated into any commercial
> production systems [Shirley, 1997].

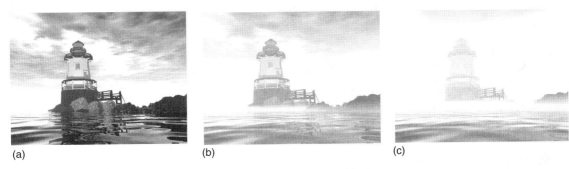

(a)   (b)   (c)

Figure 8.37 Depth cueing. (a) No fog. (b) Some fog. (c) A lot of fog.

8.5.6 Depth Cueing and Other Special Effects

Because even sophisticated rendering techniques such as radiosity cannot replicate the experience of viewing objects in the real world, many real-life visual effects are accomplished not with lighting and shading models but with special effects incorporated into the rendering process. Depth cues (visual effects that signal a change in 3D depth) can be introduced into the rendering process in this way. Atmospheric **color shifting** can be incorporated into lighting models by adding an attenuation factor that reduces color saturation and possibly also shifts colors toward blue as the distance of objects from the viewer increases. Other options that can be invoked during rendering include **fog,** which reduces color saturation and can be set to become opaque and white at user-determined distances (see Fig. 8.37).

Some programs have methods for **polygon painting** that let artists color specific polygons on an object's surface. These methods can make surface detail creation much easier and do not decrease rendering speed by adding polygons. It may be too time-consuming or just impossible, however, to achieve a desired color effect with 3D methods. Once an image has been rendered, it can be opened in a painting or photoediting program and worked on with all the color tools available in 2D raster programs. Such **post-processing** can give artists a more hands-on, local touch than is possible with most 3D programs. Note, however, that any touch-up applies to the rendered image, not the 3D source: Renderings from different points of view must be touched up individually.

8.6 Effect of Photorealistic 3D Graphics on "Visual Truth"

With rendering techniques such as radiosity and ray tracing and effects such as fog, computer-based models today can be so realistic that a viewer cannot determine whether the resulting 2D image is a real or synthetic photograph, as many saw in movies such as

Figure 8.38 Raptors in the kitchen in *Jurassic Park*. These raptors were created on a computer and composited with real footage to create a realistic, action-filled scene. *(Copyright 1993 by Universal Studios, Inc. Courtesy of Universal Studios Publishing Rights, a division of Universal Studios Licensing, Inc. and of Industrial Light & Magic. All rights reserved)*

Jurassic Park (see Fig. 8.38). Thus a modern critical approach to visual truth must take into account not only 2D digital imaging and photoediting techniques but also 3D synthetic modeling and rendering. The representation of reality provided by 3D computer graphics affects the interpretation of both 2D and 3D traditional art works. The reality ascribed to traditional photography is challenged not only by the computer's ability to alter captured data from the real world, but also by its ability to construct artificial worlds and create realistic visual data from them. With virtual photographs of 3D computer models indistinguishable from those based on the real-world objects, the language of realism can be used as an aesthetic tool in a much wider range of art-making methods than previously possible. At the same time, however, the authority of this visual language is further weakened by its disassociation with direct capture of real-world information.

8.6.1 NONREALISTIC RENDERING

Nonrealistic, or **nonphotorealistic, rendering** does not attempt to model the physics of light or simulate a photographic image. Instead, different nonrealistic methods use rules that produce either an aesthetically pleasing—or in some other way useful—drawing. Nonrealistic renderings are often designed to simulate the look of traditional tools such as paint, pencil, or pen and ink. The four images in Fig. 8.39 were made from the same model. The painterly rendering was achieved with a combination of classical rendering techniques, particle systems, and predefined brush images [Meier, 1996].

"In many applications—from architectural design, to medical texts, to industrial maintenance and repair manuals—a stylized illustration is often more effective than photorealism" [Winkenbach, 1996, p. 469]. This statement applies to other types of art work as well. In Fig. 8.40, a 3D model was rendered as a pen and ink drawing. Both the hat and cane were created with spline-based 3D models. The hat ribbon was modeled as a separate surface. Note the variation in the treatment of shadow areas: the curved shadow projected by the hat on its brim and the cross-hatching to indicate shadow on the curved portion of the cane. Although 2D raster images can be redrawn in different styles, effects such as these shadow treatments would not be possible without information from a 3D model [Winkenbach, 1996].

Figure 8.39 Four styles of painterly rendered fruit. *(Courtesy of Barbara Meier)*

8.6.2 INVERSE AND IMAGE-BASED RENDERING

Synthetic images offer incredible flexibility: They can be looked at from any point of view and easily altered. On the other hand, synthetic images are time-consuming to produce and often lack the richness that is easily produced by cameras and film. If images of an object or place can be captured, it may make more sense to try to extract the geometry from the image, or perform **inverse rendering,** combining the richness of real photographic information with some of the advantages of a 3D model. Depth can be extracted by comparing various images of an object—but only in certain highly restricted situations. The more general problem remains an important research area.

Image–based rendering involves the use of 3D information about a scene to make 2D images of it seem more like a real 3D environment. And even without any 3D depth information, a 2D image can be warped to make it seem more 3D. Apple's QuickTime VR popularized this approach by letting artists "stitch" together a sequence of images to make panoramic views. This multi-viewpoint image is then warped automatically, depending on the

Figure 8.40 Hat and cane. *(Copyright Georges Winkenbach, Inklination, Inc., courtesy of David Salesin, University of Washington and Inklination, Inc.)*

Figure 8.41 A perspective view created from a panoramic image with QuickTime VR. (a) The area bounded by the rectangle is interactively warped to provide (b) a new view into the scene [Chen, 1995]. *(QuickTime VR Image Copyright Apple Computer, Inc., 1995. Used with permission. Apple®, the Apple logo, and QuickTime are trademarks of Apple Computer, Inc., registered in the United States and other countries. All rights reserved.)*

user's "position" to create a sense of panning and zooming in a 3D space (see Fig. 8.41). Other methods include collecting a large number of texture maps from many views of a real object and then doing a view-dependent texture mapping onto a 3D model. Morphing also has been used to create new views of a 3D object based on 2D pictures.

Conclusion

Access to powerful 3D graphics programs has until recently been restricted to artists working in institutions with high-end graphics workstations and software support. As a result, most computer art shows, with the exception of those such as SIGGRAPH that naturally focus on the technical high end, have few if any complex 3D works in them. That is about to change.

Three-dimensional graphics is about to become commodified: The software is becoming more powerful, easier to use, and cheaper, and 3D graphics chips are becoming a standard feature of personal computers. Just as 2D raster graphics evolved from a high-priced research area to become part of off-the-shelf computers programs in the 1980s, so 3D graphics is emerging as a practical tool for artists of the late 1990s and beyond.

This chapter and Chapter 7 covered the creation and rendering of scenes. It is only natural, however, to want more from a model than a single picture from a single point of view. As discussed in Chapter 10, 2D and 3D Animation and Video, 3D animation takes advantage of 3D information already created to generate animated sequences— for example, letting a viewer "fly through" a 3D space.

One consequence of the emergence of 3D graphics into the mainstream will be its incorporation into multimedia programs, discussed in Chapter 11, Multimedia and Interactivity. Today, artists usually must rasterize a 3D model and use its 2D picture in multimedia, but soon artists will be able to import 3D objects directly into programs combining different types of images with sound, text, and interactivity. Already 3D graphics can be created for the World Wide Web with a descriptive language called Virtual Reality Modeling Language (VRML). This capability is discussed in Chapter 12, The World Wide Web.

The *Star Trek Holodeck* is not about to become reality. In the near future, however, artists with personal computers will routinely be able to create realistic, animated, interactive and visually expressive 3D worlds.

Suggested Readings

See the Suggested Readings at the end of Chapter 7.

Exercises

1. *Seeing the light.* Set up a still life with interesting lighting. Make a painting or drawing and a computer model of it. How did you handle light differently in your painting and your 3D model? What are the advantages and disadvantages of each method? When creating the movie *Aladdin,* Disney's animators turned off the hardware lighting of their SGIs, claiming that, if they wanted a highlight in a specific place, they would put it there. What do you think of this comment? How does automated lighting both enhance and restrict your control over light?

With StrataStudio Pro 2.5: Experiment with StudioPro's lighting options to try to make your still life scene look like the real thing, or like your drawing or painting of it. Keep in mind that rendering options will affect the results of the lighting, so you'll want to try out different rendering settings as well. Direct lights are controlled in the Environment palette, from the Light tab. Click on the small circle to swing the light. Point Light and Spot Light tools can be found in the main Tool palette. Select a light in your scene and look at the Object Properties palette in the Object tab to adjust the light's color and various effects. Double-click on the light to see the scene from the light's point of view.

2. *Light show.* In a series of still images or an animation, use lighting to tell a story. The model or models may be simple or complex, but they cannot move and the camera view must stay the same. How can lighting suggest emotion, drama, and narrative? How can it be used to reveal form and meaning through types of lights, brightness, color, and positioning? Suggested topic: the opening sequence of a TV sci-fi serial.

With StrataStudio Pro 2.5: Flashing police car lights can be used to evoke a number of reactions. Choose the Spot Light tool from the main Tool palette and create two spot lights. Arrange them back to back. Adjust the throw and aim of the lights by manipulating the virtual ray and circumference. Select a red gel for one light and blue gel for the other. Bring up the intensity to 100%. Set the directional light in the Light tab of the Environment palette to 20–40% intensity so that the spot lights are clearly visible. Create a simple wall with the Cube tool to test them.

Group the two back-to-back spot lights with Modeling: Group. Open the Project Window with Windows: Show Project Window. Drag the red Cut-out Point marker to 60 seconds. Drag the Current Time marker to 30 seconds. Rotate the lights 180 degrees by selecting them and using the Object Properties palette (Transformation tab). Drag the Current Time marker to 60 seconds and rotate the lights 360 degrees. Play back the animation with the small cassette-style controls in the upper left of the Project Window. If the lights are working well (i.e., rotating on the wall like a police light), then choose Rendering:Render . . . and render "all frames" instead of the default "current frame." When the rendering is complete the movie will appear on the screen in StudioPro's movie player.

3. *Points of view.* Using the same premise as in Exercise 2 but with points of view, create series of images or an animation in which objects and lights are fixed and only the camera moves. Use camera parameters such as position, orientation, focus, and lens width to create moods, expectations, a sense of the viewer's personality, and so on. Suggested topic: For a scene built around a personal memory (e.g., a room when you were a child) use point of view to convey the impression of the space from a child's perspective and then from an adult's.

With StrataStudio Pro 2.5: Open a scene you have already created. Place a new camera using the Camera Object tool in the main Tool palette. Adjust its viewpoint with the standard Move and Rotate tools. Double-click on the camera to see the world from the camera's point of view. Animate the camera by moving the Current Time Marker and repositioning the camera, just as with the lights in the previous exercise. Experiment with the camera's parameters. You can adjust the camera position and field of view in the main window or use the controls in the camera window to pan, zoom (dolly), move the viewpoint up and down (boom), rotate the camera in an arc, and rotate it around the x, y, and z axes (with pitch, yaw, and roll). Click on the buttons and wait. The longer the mouse is held down, the faster the motion will be.

4. *Style.* How can well-known art styles such as Minimalism, Abstract Expressionism, or Impressionism be accommodated by a 3D modeling/rendering program? Create a

3D model/rendering in the spirit of a previous art movement. What constraints are there on style owing to the nature of 3D modeling? What freedoms are there? What methods are analogous to the hand gesture, if any? What method resembles photography, sculpture?

> With StrataStudio Pro 2.5: Try using wireframe rendering, especially hidden line, to simulate the look of an engraving. Flat shading can be used to create a scene that looks as if it were constructed out of cardboard. Flat shading on rounded surfaces will look like corrugated cardboard if the resolution is set high enough. Gouraud shading can suggest plastic or painted wood. Try making a Jean Arp-style "wood" collage with Gouraud shading (the Shaded option). Use radiosity to create an atmospheric Minimalist sculpture lit dramatically in a gallery space. Set up a Renaissance-style landscape that suggests depth with perspective and bluish dispersed light in the distance, rendering the scene with ray tracing or raydiosity. Which provides the most painterly effects?

5. *2D meets 3D in texture mapping.* Go back to an earlier work that you did in 2D (or use another art work or found image). Make the work "3D" by basing a simple 3D environment on it and then using the entire image or pieces of it as texture maps. How does the result change your sense of space of the 2D image? Take synthetic photographs of the 3D piece to create new spatial compositions in 2D.

> With StrataStudio Pro 2.5: If your work is realistic, start by creating a rough 3D approximation of the 2D scene. If your work is more abstract, creatively decide which parts should be mapped to what type of objects and where. Bring your image's textures into the current StudioPro scene by clicking on the New menu in the Resource palette and choosing Surface Texture. Click on the Expert arrow in the lower left corner to see all of the options. Load in a small section of your 2D image (saved as a separate file) by clicking on the Map button. Load the same file into the bump map area. In the loading dialog box, choose Invert to reverse the values of the bump map image. Test out your texture by rendering the scene. (Make sure that Show Textures is checked in the Edit:Preferences Windows tab.) Adjust the effect of your texture by adding different types of maps; for example, opacity maps can create the effect of holes in your objects and produce striking results. Use the Texture tab in the Object Properties palette to change how the texture is mapped onto an object. Use Modeling: Edit Placement to bring up special texture placement tools in the main Tool palette to move, rotate, and scale the texture. Alternatively, try the Fit Texture button on the button bar to ensure that the texture is centered on the object and covers it entirely.

6. *Rendering methods are drawing styles.* Render an object or objects in a variety of ways (e.g., wireframe, flat shaded, Gouraud, Phong, or ray-traced) and bring all the images into a paint program. (Render with alpha channels if possible to make compositing easier.) Combine these images in a single 2D piece to create a work that features different ways of looking at the same thing. (A realistic rendering of a vase could be on a table, a flat-shaded image could be a book illustration, and a wireframe image could be a technical drawing on a desk.) Suggested themes: technology, X-ray vision, inner structure, apocalypse, or dreaming.

> See suggestions for rendering choices in Exercises 1–4. No additional application-specific features are involved.

7. *The pursuit of realism.* Set up a still life and model it. Take a photograph of it and compare the rendered model with the photograph. What are the differences? When would these differences matter in an art piece? Pay particular attention to subtle differences in shadows, reflections, and interobject color bleeding, as well as the overall feeling. What is the difference between creating a plausible image and a realistic one?

With StrataStudio Pro 2.5: Set up a still life that contains a mix of natural and manufactured objects. The first challenge is to create convincing geometry. A block of wood or a tin can is easy to model; an apple, with its subtle irregularities and glossy skin, will be harder. Use textures to improve on the plain geometry. Finally, try different rendering styles. Ray tracing is great for reflective objects, but may not represent the overall atmosphere they are in correctly. In addition, reflective objects in the real still life will reflect objects in the surrounding room. To add this feature to your model, take a picture of the room and load it as a Reflect Background in the Environment palette. Shadows can be difficult to simulate convincingly. Try lowering the intensity of the directional lights and increasing the light source radius of spot or point lights to create soft shadows.

Gallery Plate 7 **Charles Csuri, *John Glenn,* 1998** (Interactive VRML piece). *(Courtesy of Charles Csuri)*

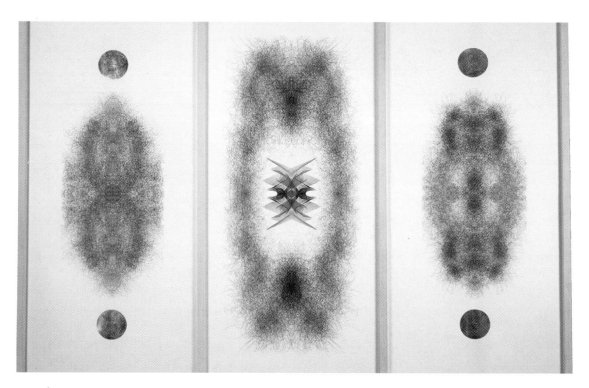

Gallery Plate 8   **Roman Verostko, center triptych of *Epigenesis: The Growth of Form,* 1997**   (9′ × 6′ section of 40′ × 6′ mural installed at the Frey Science and Engineering Center, University of St. Thomas, St. Paul Campus).   *(Courtesy of Roman Verostko)*

Gallery Plate 9 MANUAL (**Suzanne Bloom and Ed Hill**), *The Elegaic Tradition*, **1998** (from the Arcadian Landscape series, Lambda print). *(Courtesy of Suzanne Bloom and Ed Hill)*

(b)

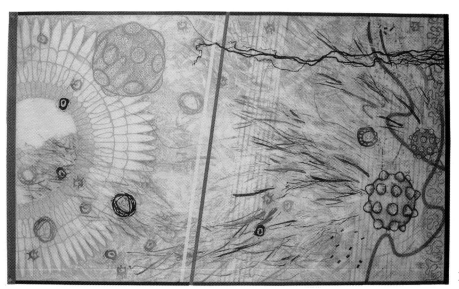

(a)

Gallery Plate 10 **Lane Hall and Lisa Moline, (a)** *Pollen* **and (b)** *Spawn,* **1995** (from the Woodland Goiter Series; computer graphics and woodcut on Japanese paper, 65" x 40"). *(Courtesy of Lane Hall and Lisa Moline)*

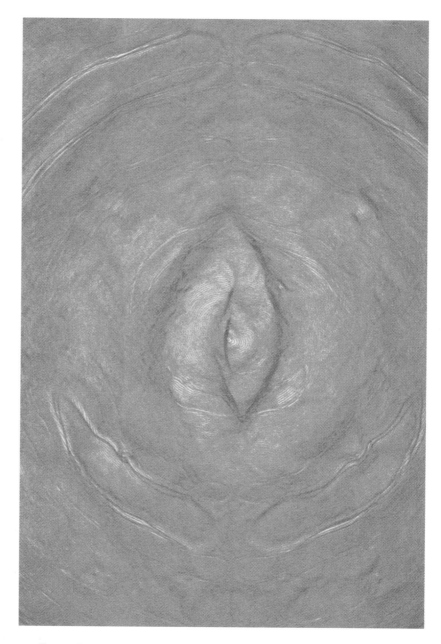

Gallery Plate 11   Jean-Pierre Hébert, *Polyphemus* (detail), 1997. *(Courtesy of Jean-Pierre Hébert)*

Gallery Plate 12 Richard Rosenblum, *Hysteria*, 1998. *(Courtesy of Richard Rosenblum)*

Gallery Plate 13 **Anne Morgan Spalter, *Shape Factory*, 1997.** *(Courtesy of Anne Morgan Spalter)*

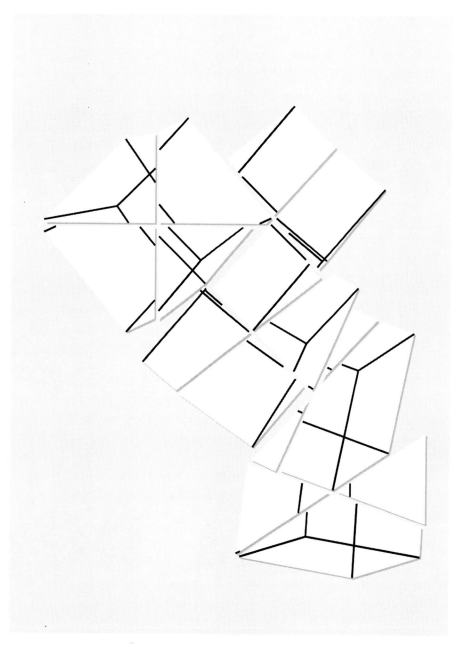

Gallery Plate 14   **Manfred Mohr, *p306/p350B*, 1980–94** (acrylic on canvas, 180 × 150cm). *(Courtesy of Manfred Mohr)*

Gallery Plate 15   **Annabel Safire, *Hell's Fury*, 1998.** *(Courtesy of Annabel Safire)*

Gallery Plate 16   **Emily Cheng,** *Blue Circle Lohan,* **1998.** *(Courtesy of Emily Cheng)*

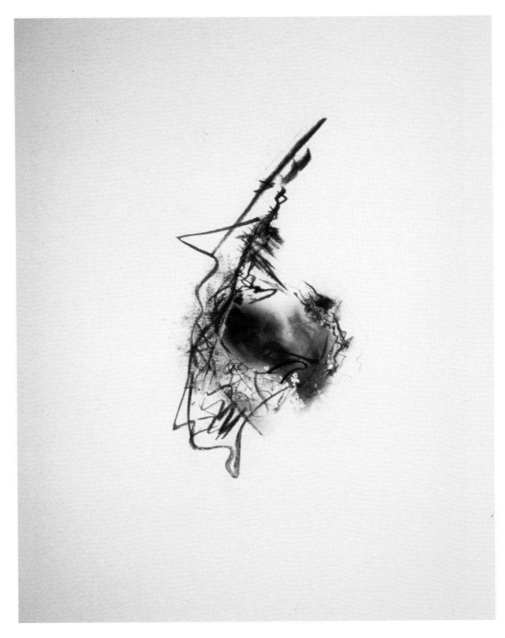

Gallery Plate 17 **Michael O'Rourke,** **_Petites Recherches #9,_ 1997** (Iris print, hand-drawn charcoal, pastel, and pencil, 19″ × 24″). *(Courtesy of Michael O'Rourke)*

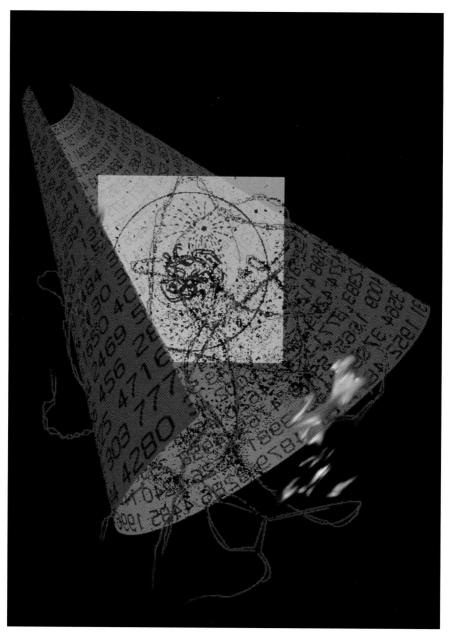

Gallery Plate 18 **Kathleen Ruíz, _Enumerated Repository,_ 1991** (photo-projection, 4' x 6'). _(Courtesy of Kathleen Ruíz and The Sandra Gering Gallery)_

Gallery Plate 19   **Cynthia Beth Rubin, *Two Layers of Memory*, 1998** (size variable).
(Courtesy of Cynthia Beth Rubin)

Gallery Plate 20 **Yoichiro Kawaguchi, *Evolver*, 1998.** *(Courtesy of Yoichiro Kawaguchi)*

Color Plates

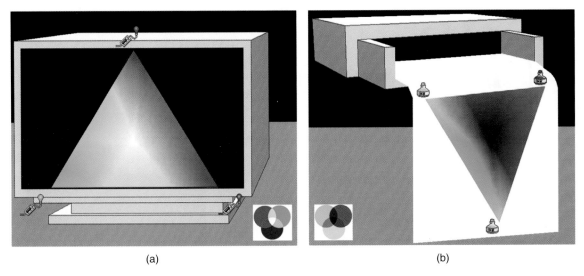

(a)

(b)

Color Plate 1   Additive and subtractive mixing. (a) All possible combinations of fully bright red, green, and blue lights mixed additively from the corners of the triangle toward white in the center. (b) All possible combinations of cyan, magenta, and yellow inks mixed subtractively from the corners of the triangle toward black in the center.

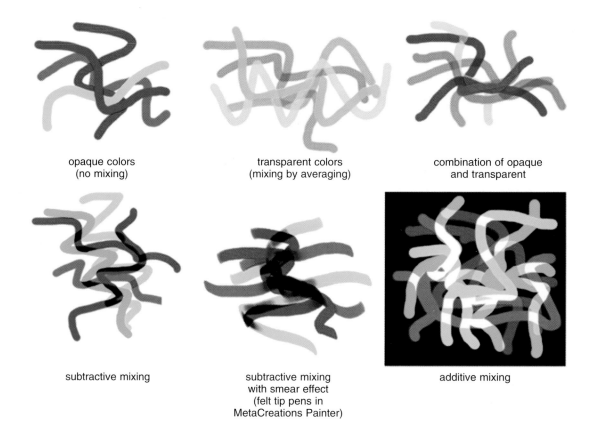

opaque colors
(no mixing)

transparent colors
(mixing by averaging)

combination of opaque
and transparent

subtractive mixing

subtractive mixing
with smear effect
(felt tip pens in
MetaCreations Painter)

additive mixing

Color Plate 2 **Mixing techniques.** One advantage of the computer is the ability to use several mixing techniques, additive, subtractive, and other types, all in the same work. These techniques contribute greatly to the touch and feel of a work.

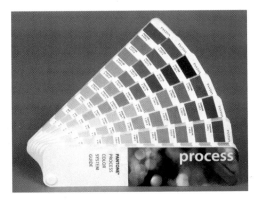

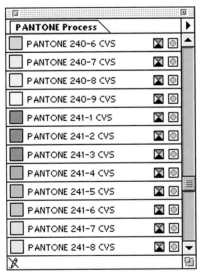

Color Plate 3 **Color-matching systems.**
Color naming and printed reference swatches ensure consistent color matching.

Color Plate 4 **Slices of 3D color space used in a 2D color picker.** (a) One of the color-picking modes in Adobe Photoshop shows slices of the RGB cube. The user can move the slice through the cube by changing a slider bar to the immediate right of the slice. (b) In another view, the slice is seen inside a 3D RGB cube. Moving the slice toward the cyan vertex, for instance, is accomplished by dragging it in the 3D program or moving the slider bar toward the top in the 2D picker.

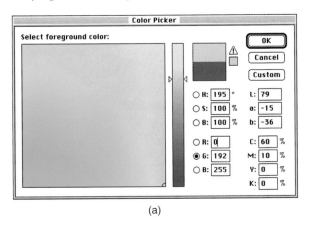

(a)

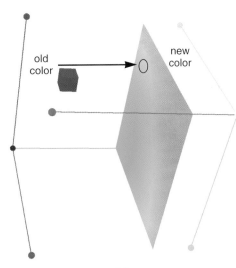

(b)

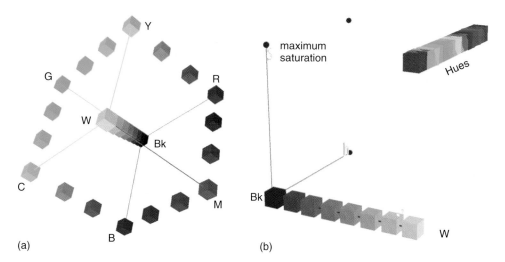

(a)

(b)

Color Plate 5 **RGB and HSV cubes.** (a) The RGB cube has fully saturated colors along the edges connecting the RGB vertices to CMY. Grays run through the center diagonally between the black and the white vertices. Note that the top of the HSV cone can be seen as a projection along the white–black diagonal of the RGB cube. (b) The HSV cube has maximally saturated colors along the hue axis, with saturation and value at their maximum value. Grays run along the value axis and have no hue or saturation components.

Color Plate 6 **Use of a double-hexcone color space in a 2D color picker.** (a) In a double-hexcone HLS space, the white vertex is pulled up to create a cone symmetrical to the one formed by the black vertex.

(b) MetaCreations Painter uses a circle from the middle of an HSL space with a cross section of the space showing the area between a given hue and the white and black extremes of the double hexcone. (Painter is a registered trademark of MetaCreations. These materials copyrighted 1998.)

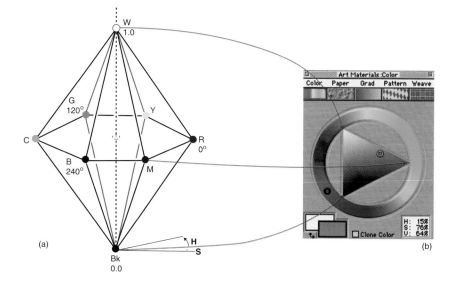

(a)

(b)

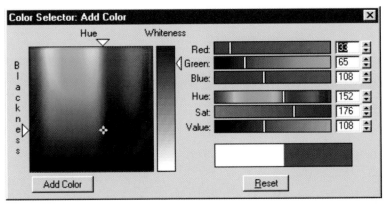

(a)

(b)

Color Plate 7   **HWB versus HSV.** (a) A color picker using an HWB space (from Kinetix 3D Studio Max). *(Courtesy of Kinetix/Autodesk, Inc.)* (b) A color picker using an HSV space (from Adobe Photoshop). The same color is chosen in both pickers, but to make the color whiter in the HSV space, a user must both desaturate and brighten it. In the HWB space, a user simply slides toward white with the whiteness slider.

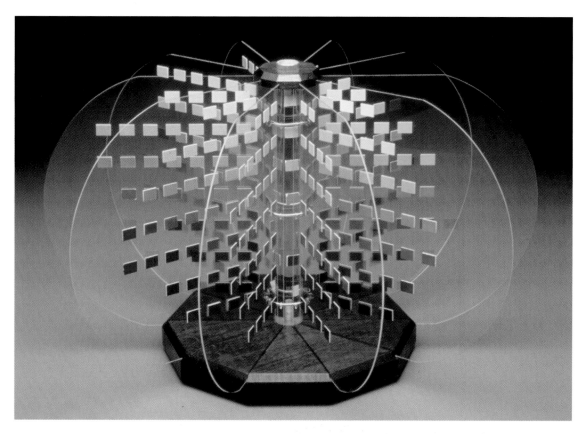

Color Plate 8 **Slices though the Munsell color space.** The swatches are arrayed at perceptually determined brightness positions, but the shape of this space lacks the geometric convenience of a cube or hexcone. *(Photo provided courtesy of GretagMacbeth)*

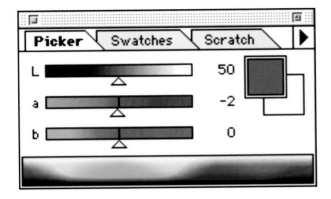

Color Plate 9
Photoshop's CIELab picker. The L channel is brightness or luminosity, the a channel is a red–green axis, and the b channel is a yellow–blue one.

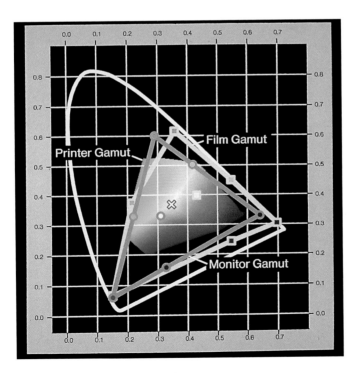

Color Plate 10 **The CIE chromaticity diagram used for color gamut comparisons.**
(Courtesy of M. Stone)

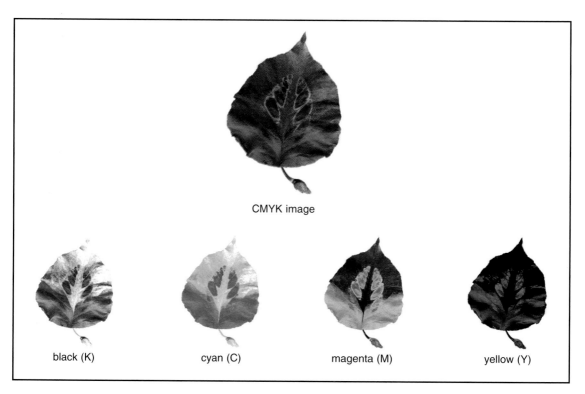

CMYK image

black (K)   cyan (C)   magenta (M)   yellow (Y)

Color Plate 11   **Color channels or separations for a CMYK image.**

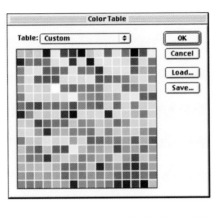

(a)

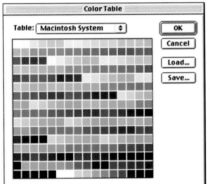

(b)

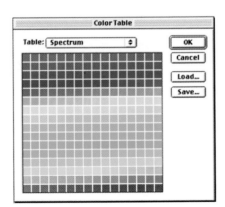

(c)

Color Plate 12 **Three views of Delft.** (a) An adaptive clut that best matches the colors of the original image. (b) A Macintosh system palette clut. (c) A vivid clut inappropriate to the image. Jan Vermeer, *View of Delft,* after the fire, c. 1658. *(Courtesy of Erich Lessing/Art Resource, NY)*

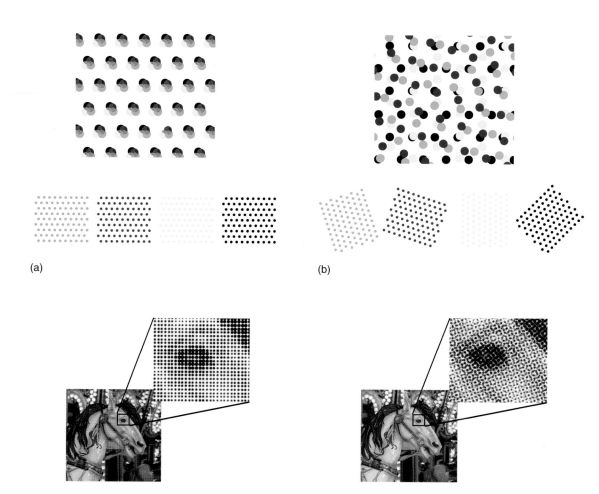

Color Plate 13 **Screen angles for process color printing.** (a) Screens all at the same angle (0°). (b) Screens at standard angles.

Gallery

Gallery Plate 1 Jennifer Steinkamp, *Balconette* **"New Voices," 1994** (Allen Memorial Art Museum, Oberlin, OH). *(Courtesy of Jennifer Steinkamp)*

Gallery Plate 2 **Michele Turre, *If Things Were Different,* 1997** (from the *Tree Fix* series, quadtoned ink-jet transfer print on Arches Aquarelle paper, 11″ × 13.75″). *(Courtesy of Michele Turre)*

Gallery Plate 3 **James Faure Walker, *Lost in Aesthetics, Shopping, and Kitchen Distractions,* 1996–97** (composite ink-jet print). *(Courtesy of James Faure Walker)*

Gallery Plate 4 **Joan Truckenbrod, *Icon Perpetrators,* 1997** (limited edition Iris print, 30″ × 32″).
(Courtesy of Joan Truckenbrod)

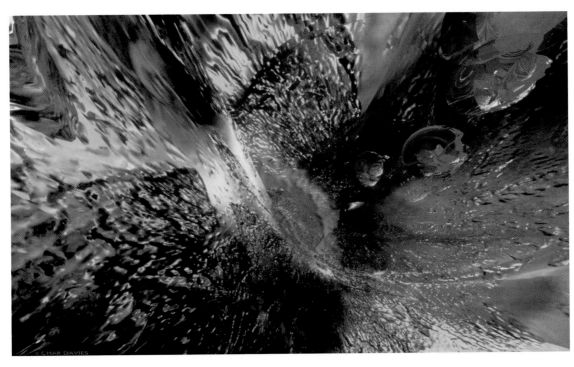

Gallery Plate 5 **Char Davies,** *Drowning* **(Rapture), 1991** (3D Computer Graphics Still). *(Courtesy of Char Davies)*

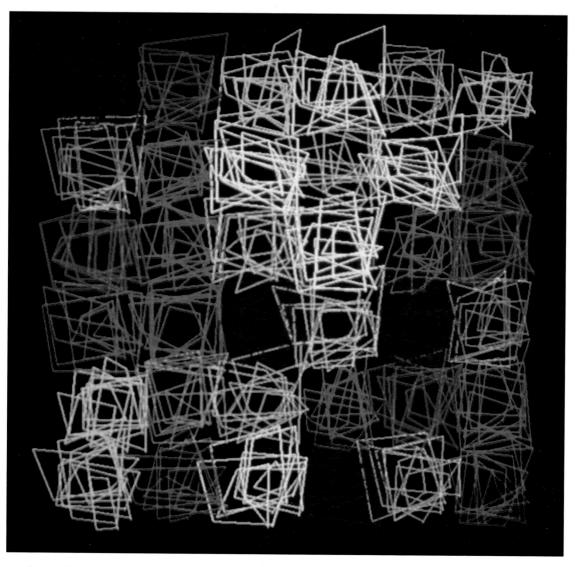

Gallery Plate 6 **Vera Molnar, *Dialog Between Emotion and Method*, 1986.** *(Courtesy of Vera Molnar)*

Gallery Plate 21 Annette Weintraub, *Waiting,* **1996** (tiled and laminated phaser prints, 31″ × 47″). *(Courtesy of Annette Weintraub)*

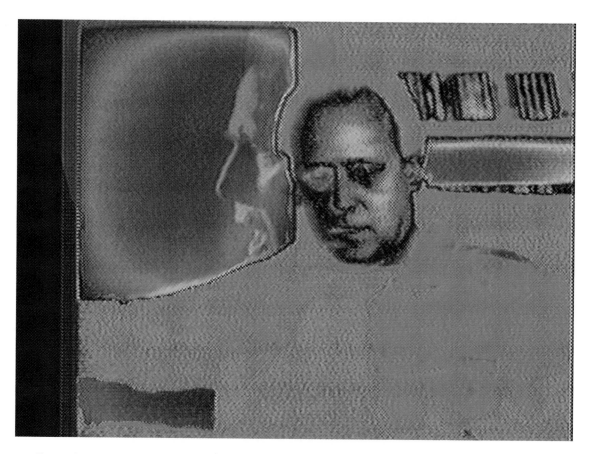

Gallery Plate 22   **Michael Wright, *Soul*, 1998.** *(Courtesy of Michael Wright)*

CHAPTER 9

3D Input
and Output

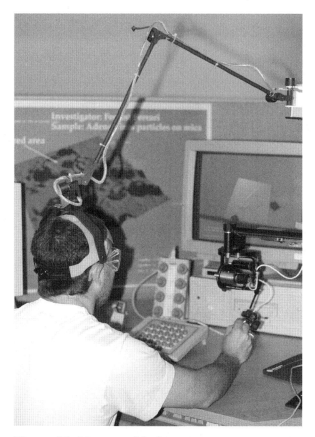

Figure 9.1 *"Connected."* This scientist is using a variety of devices to work with 3D information. In addition to a standard mouse, keyboard, and extra keypads, there are dials, a force-feedback arm, a mechanical head tracker, and, hidden, a digital scanning electron microscope that is creating the screen image.

9.1 Introduction

Three-dimensional computer graphics presents both input and output challenges. The 2D mouse and screen typical of most computer setups restrict artists to working with 3D information by making 2D motions (or typing in numbers and directions on a keyboard) and viewing the world through a series of 2D snapshots. These limitations contribute to many of the problems encountered in creating and arranging objects (see Chapter 7).

Some of the problems inherent in working with 3D forms can be solved by using input and output devices designed especially for 3D work. Input devices include 3D versions of mice and trackballs and systems that rely on the user's head motion to coordinate changing views into the 3D world. Display systems that feed a different image to each eye can make a user feel immersed in a *virtual reality.* Another way of making 3D data truly 3D is to use *3D printers,* machines that use computer data to manufacture real objects.

9.1.1 ACCESS TO EQUIPMENT

Three-dimensional graphics software and hardware have evolved from an esoteric Unix workstation feature to a commodity item for personal computers. However, many interesting 3D input and output devices are still designed only for high-end systems. The majority of the devices described in this chapter are expensive and sometimes not even available to the general public. The limited availability of such tools thus brings up issues of access similar to those faced by early computer artists, who had to be affiliated with large institutions in order to use a computer at all. As in the 1960s and 1970s, gaining access through an institution often means being employed there in some capacity, say as a programmer, engineer, or designer. Even if a university or company is enlightened enough to share its equipment with artists through artist-in-residence or other types of programs, artists still must adjust to the culture of that institution, which is often quite different from that of the art world or a design firm. Although access to high-end and experimental systems will remain difficult as long as R&D in the field continue to race forward, access to some of the devices described here is bound to become easier, like access to computers in general, in the not-too-distant future.

9.2 3D INPUT

Three-dimensional input devices give users control over motion in three dimensions, most often by allowing the user to move the device in all three dimensions, thus translating gestures into appropriate motions on the screen. Difficulties arise, however, in this move from the more abstract 2D world of the mouse or tablet into a 3D environment: arms can easily become fatigued, it is hard to hold one's arm still enough, and force feedback can actually be dangerous. No single device, like the mouse, has emerged as a 3D standard and most 3D programs do not have built-in support for any specific 3D input devices. As 3D becomes commonplace, however, demand for practical, effective 3D input devices should drive improvements and lower costs. Already several games have experimented with 3D joysticks, force-feedback devices, and gloves, with some success.

9.2.1 3D Mice and Trackballs

Three-dimensional mice and trackballs let artists use 3D gestures that can be directly associated with actions such as moving and turning an object. These devices usually offer a full six **degrees of freedom** (DOF)—translation and rotation around all three axes—so that the user can move and rotate an object freely in 3D space.

A **3D mouse** looks something like its 2D counterpart but uses sonar (or other cordless mechanisms, such as electromagnetic tracking) to track the mouse as it moves in 3D space. In a sonar-based 3D mouse, inaudible sonar transmissions from three sources in front of the mouse are received by three microphones inside the mouse itself (see Fig. 9.2). The different time lapses between transmission and reception are used to calculate the position and rotation of the mouse. However, the range of movement is limited because the mouse only works within range of the transmitters. Buttons on a 3D mouse can be programmed to select, zoom, or perform other functions.

Unfortunately, most 3D mice are not very accurate because of noise interference and because our hands and arms are not well suited for holding objects completely still in the air. The problem grows worse during longer sessions—as with a light pen, gesturing with the arm extended for long periods of time is physically exhausting. In addition, the transitions between picking up the mouse and positioning it and putting it down to use another device become tedious. For specific functions in 3D modeling, however, a 3D, 6DOF device can reduce working time by enabling the user to complete in one gesture operations that might otherwise take several steps, such as selecting and rotating an object.

A **3D trackball,** or spaceball, responds to pressure—pushing, pulling, and twisting—but the ball does not actually move. In fact, it is perhaps best thought of as a joystick that responds to pressure (see Fig. 9.3).

9.2.2 Joysticks

Interestingly, computer games offer much more varied input devices than are generally available in business or the arts. **Joysticks** have been coupled with games for

Figure 9.2 Logitech's 3D flymouse.

Sonar sources

Mouse/receiver

decades and are still widely used in them to control space ships and fly through landscapes. Buttons on the joystick base or handle often fire weaponry and perform other non-navigational actions (see Fig. 9.4). Some joysticks control only 2D motions, but more and more games require 3D navigation. Many joysticks have been adapted to 3D motion needs with incorporation of a twisting option for moving in a third dimension (see Fig. 9.5).

It might be interesting to exploit the joystick's speed and throttle capabilities in art creation. Unfortunately, most commercial joysticks are designed for use with specific game platforms, lack accuracy, and would require additional programming for use in other systems and programs.

Figure 9.3 3D Trackball.

Figure 9.5 Double joystick, custom-made at the University of North Carolina at Chapel Hill. These double joysticks spring back to an upright position and can be twisted to control an extra dimension. A linear slider at the back is used to adjust other parameters, such as scale.

Figure 9.4 Game joystick.

9.2.3 Gloves

A sensor-filled **glove** would seem a wonderful input device, one particularly suited to artists. What better input mechanism could there be than the hand itself? Unfortunately, gloves have proved difficult to use. Mechanisms for recording finger position and tracking the hand in space with the accuracy necessary for art production are expensive (in the $10,000 to $20,000 range). They also require attention and preparation not usually associated with an input device; to get the most from a glove it must be custom-fit and calibrated for a specific hand. As with the 3D mouse, the difficulty of holding the hand completely still in space and the noise inherent in most tracking mechanisms make fine-tuned gestures and visual feedback difficult to achieve.

Gloves work by sensing changes in finger angle, registered by flexible sensors in the glove, and by tracking the movement of the hand, usually with sonic or electromagnetic systems (see Fig. 9.6). Ultrasonic systems require two transmitters on the glove and three receivers in the room. Electromagnetic systems transmit a signal from a single source that, as with cordless tablets, induces a current in a receiver on the glove, from which the hand's position and rotation are deduced. Some gloves also provide haptic feedback: Small devices near the fingertips vibrate and create an inaudible buzzing sensation when the user contacts a virtual object.

Although not accurate enough for much fine-tuned work, gloves do have advantages, especially in virtual environments where redirecting your attention to a mouse or keyboard may be impractical. In virtual environments, gloves usually are used to perform predefined gestural motions or still-hand positions called **postures.** (A standard posture in

Figure 9.6 Glove examples.
(a) and (b) The Virtual Technologies CyberGlove uses fiber optics to register finger-bending; a tracker can be added. (c) This glove is for a video game.

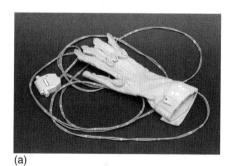

(a)

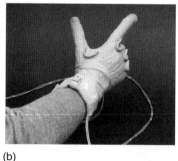

(b)

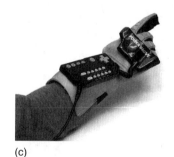

(c)

virtual environments, for example, is extending the index finger to mean fly or go ahead.) Gloves are also useful for capturing hand motion for real-time animation performances.

Toni Dove used a glove as the main interface device for her VR piece *Archeology of the Mother Tongue*. The user receives visual feedback about hand position from a model of the glove presented on-screen (refer to Fig. 11.4).

> The glove was used to work interactively once models were built and we were testing behaviors. I find that the best way to get a feel for how a piece will work interactively is to use the actual interface as much as possible while in development. Different interfaces can have a very different look and feel that will significantly alter the way a piece behaves and the way its content is absorbed [Dove, 1996].

9.2.4 DIALS

Usually arrayed on a dial box, **dials** can be programmed to control 3D properties such as *xyz* location, rotation, and scaling, or factors such as surface quality and color (see Fig. 9.7). Although dials do not tap the muscles and hand skills familiar from analog art making, they are intuitive, highly accurate, and often pleasant to use. The hand and arm do not become tired as they do with devices moved in 3D space.

In addition, dials can be relative or absolute: Their range can be infinite—the dial turns as many times as the user desires in either direction—or bounded—the dial turns only a certain number of degrees. Bounded dials are commonly used for absolute functions, and unbounded dials are typically used for relative motions and adjustments. Dials were popular on earlier graphics workstations, and are still sold for many Unix workstations but rarely for Macs or PCs.

9.2.5 FORCE-FEEDBACK DEVICES

Force-feedback devices are expensive and still experimental. Some commercial models do exist, such as SensAble Devices' Phantom arm, a force-feedback device that can be guided with the fingertip or a penlike attachment (see Fig. 9.8). No commercial art packages are designed to work with such devices, so custom programming is always necessary.

Figure 9.7 Dials.

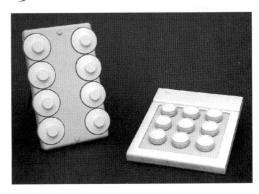

The sense of interacting with tangible forms that force-feedback devices offer can completely change the experience of using a computer. Bumping into and feeling the weight and texture of virtual 3D objects brings a sense of reality that no amount of visual sophistication can match. Interaction that involves physical sensations calls on parts of the body and mind that are not easily accessed through sight alone.

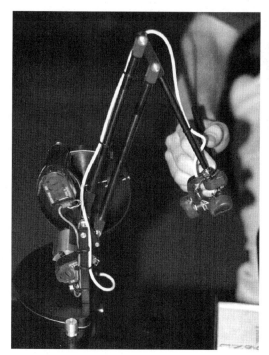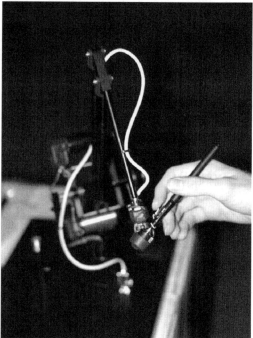

Figure 9.8 **The Phantom arm.**

Unfortunately, high-quality force-feedback devices usually require great technical expertise and patience to use and are also currently too expensive for most artists. (The Phantom arm costs about $20,000.) They can also be dangerous. The user of the Phantom arm in Fig. 9.8 is wearing protective goggles and is stepping on a pedal that keeps electricity flowing to the device: If pressure on the pedal is released, the power is cut. These precautions are necessary because a force strong enough to stop a moving hand in space is also strong enough to do damage if anything goes wrong. A force-feedback device such as the arm shown in Fig. 9.9 can rip off the user's arm or knock a user unconscious. Industry needs for such devices and their usefulness in virtual reality should drive the production of increasingly easy-to-use, less dangerous and less expensive force-feedback options.

9.2.6 HEAD AND BODY TRACKING

Virtual environments (discussed in more detail in Section 9.4.1) demand 3D input in order to determine users' positions in the virtual space. A **tracker** often is used to record the position and angle of a user's head, letting the computer automatically adjust the point of view. Trackers also are used with gloves and other devices. Tracking sensors can use sonar, like the 3D mice described in Section 9.2.1, or magnetic receivers and transmitters. In both cases, range of motion is limited and accuracy can be affected by noise (in the case of sonar) and metallic objects (in the case of magnetic tracking).

At the Computer Graphics Lab at the University of North Carolina at Chapel Hill, researchers have implemented a different approach based on optical tracking that lets a virtual reality user wander over much larger areas and eliminates sonic and electromagnetic interference. The ceiling of the tracking area is embedded with light-emitting diodes (LEDs) in a grid pattern, and the head-mounted display contains six cameras that observe the LEDs from six different angles. Data from the cameras are analyzed to deduce the changing position and rotation of the user's head, as shown in Fig. 9.10a. However, this setup is heavy and cumbersome. In a new research model, shown in Fig. 9.10b, all six cameras pointing toward the ceiling have been condensed into a golfball-sized device called the *hi-ball tracker*.

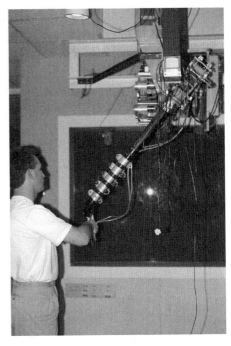

Figure 9.9 An Argonne Laboratory force-feedback arm at the University of North Carolina at Chapel Hill.

Bodily gestures or motions can be tracked by placing multiple sensors on or in the moving object and gathering location data over time. Such tracking points can also be used to control images on the screen and can be mapped to a 3D model, a technique often used to script complex animations. Polhemus, a leading manufacturer of 3D tracking devices, offers tracking options that support varying numbers of transceivers and receivers for tracking several objects at a time or many points on a single object. Such trackers range in price from under $1000 to many thousands of dollars, depending on accuracy, range, and number of positions recorded.

As an alternative to sensors, video cameras equipped with pattern-recognition software can be used to track moving forms. Although this method frees the user from heavy gear and can provide a wide range of movement, it does not yet provide the same accuracy as fixed-point tracking. With a combination of tracking and hand-held devices, the entire body can be used to draw, paint, work in 3D worlds, and generate animations.

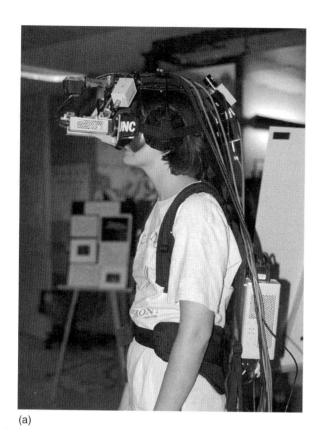

(a)

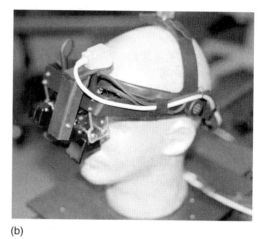

(b)

Figure 9.10 LED tracking systems.

PUPPETS   Traditional **puppets** and movable models long have been a mainstay in special effects for film. Now the puppet concept can also be used to determine the motion of 3D computer-generated creatures. In *Jurassic Park,* for instance, the motion of mechanical dinosaur models was used at times to animate the movements of the 3D modeled creatures. With motion sensors built into the joints of the mechanical model, artists could work with a real 3D entity, rather than having to program complex movements or position a computer-based model (see Fig. 9.11).

EYE TRACKING   Computer users commonly look in the direction they would like the cursor to go. **Eye-tracking systems** follow the user's gaze and update the cursor automatically. Affordable commodity eye-tracking systems for artists do not yet exist, but eye tracking has great potential as an input device for artists and many other types of computer users. Current systems track light reflected off the cornea or use sensors placed on the skin to measure muscle impulses. Both methods limit the head's range of motion and may require the user to wear a head mask; neither provides accuracy or ease of use comparable with more standard input devices.

Figure 9.11 **Digital Input Device (D.I.D.) designer Craig Hayes** (with raptor D.I.D. puppet used in *Jurassic Park,* 1992–93). The D.I.D. contained encoders at all pivot points to control the motion of a computer model. *(Courtesy of Tippet Studio)*

OTHER SENSES   Any information that can be translated into digital form can be used as input—temperature, vibrations, light, viscosity, and possibly even smells. Music and other audio data can control aspects of Opcode's MAX multimedia authoring software, for instance, and disc jockeys working live events frequently use music to control lighting effects. For most artists, however, the input realm is limited to what can be purchased for a reasonable price and does not require extensive technical expertise or programming skills.

9.2.7 3D DIGITIZATION

Capturing 3D information about objects directly, rather than modeling objects from scratch, is often desirable. As in creating pixel values in 2D with a scanner or digital camera, the artist can use a 3D capture device to record location coordinates and sometimes the associated color values. Such devices range from relatively inexpensive digitizing setups (well under $1000) to specialized machines costing many thousands of dollars. At the low end, an artist can use a device such as Digimax's Impulse, a mechanical digitizer for relatively small objects, to input point positions along a 3D form. The price escalates with increased accuracy and flexibility and more powerful software. Even without any digitizing equipment, an artist can measure the relative position of selected points on a 3D object and input the coordinates into a 3D modeling program to create profiles or primitives.

A 3D scanning unit from Cyberware called Cyberscan can create 3D modeled portraits by combining positional and image-scanning techniques. The Cyberscan (see Fig. 9.12) uses a laser-beam arm to sample locations on a person's head (somewhat like a dentist's panoramic X-ray machine). The 360° pass records the surface features and

(a)

(b)

Figure 9.12 Cyberware's Cyberscan 3D input device. (a) The Cyberscan device rotates in a full circle around the subject, using a laser beam to measure positions. (b) A 3D model with photographic texture map is the result.

color values of the head at the same time. The result is a 3D surface model, created to fit the position samples, with a texture map of the head wrapped around it to create a "3D photograph."

9.3 3D Output

9.3.1 Stereo Viewing

People perceive depth because the overlapping views seen by their two eyes are from slightly different perspectives; the disparity in viewpoint provides cues that the mind interprets as 3D depth, giving human beings **stereo vision.** The sense of space suggested by the two views is further reinforced by the changing relationships of near and far objects when people turn their heads, a phenomenon known as **parallax.**

When you work with a 3D program on the computer, however, you see only one version of any given view and therefore must gain any impression of depth only from 2D cues such as overlapping and perspective. Also, moving your head does not make objects in the scene move relative to one another—you see only a foreshortened version of the flat image.

A monitor or printer can create two slightly different views of a scene that, when viewed together properly, create a sense of depth. The different views are called a **stereo pair,** and the successful fusion in the mind of the two flat images into a single image with depth is called **stereopsis.** Stereo pairs can be viewed in various ways.

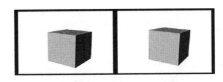

Figure 9.13 Stereo pair and viewer. Although stereo pairs, such as the cubes shown, can be fused in the mind with the unaided eye, a viewer that focuses the eyes properly makes the process much easier.

They can be positioned side by side on the computer screen (or printed and viewed side by side) and merged by focusing on a distant point in between them; doing this takes practice, and some people cannot do it at all. Three-dimensional viewers can help by presenting each eye with a different view through lenses that force the eyes to focus away from the image (see Fig. 9.13).

Another method puts one image on top of the other. Color-filtered stereo pairs are drawn on the same screen in different colors, say, red and blue. When a person views them with glasses having a red gel for one eye and a blue gel for the other, each eye receives only the image intended for it. However, when the images are distinguished by colors, the usable palette of each image is reduced. To achieve full-color stereopsis for 3D movies and other projection needs, the two images can be superimposed with different polarizations. Glasses with polarizing filters set at different angles show each eye the proper image, and special projectors are used with a screen that preserves the polarization.

Artists can easily make their own stereo pairs by rendering a 3D scene from slightly different points of view. For distant objects, the virtual camera can simply be panned; for closeups, it must also be rotated to ensure that it stays aimed at the same place. Some programs create stereo pairs automatically. Many can also create random-dot stereograms, which are images that look like collections of random dots or flat patterns but reveal a 3D structure when the eye is focused well behind the image.

Three-dimensional displays can be achieved on a single monitor by using red and blue superimposed images. Another method cycles the two images rapidly on the screen. The user views the screen with a pair of glasses containing rapidly cycling LCD

Figure 9.14 Single-display stereo viewing techniques.
An artist using shutter glasses and a 3D mouse.

shutters that temporarily block each eye's view. Synchronizing the screen cycling and shutter speed yields a 3D image with depth (see Fig. 9.14). With a tracker, stereo pairs generated in real time from 3D scene data let viewers move their heads to get a better sense of the objects and their relationships to one another.

Artist Rick Gibson uses red and blue views to create 3D images of his work. Viewers of his work in a gallery setting or over the World Wide Web (http://www.express.ca/rigibson) need to wear red and blue glasses (see Fig. 9.15).

9.4 VIRTUAL REALITY

When a display is close enough to the viewer, or otherwise surrounds the viewer, the difference between "right here" and "behind the screen" can merge and the viewer can effectively step into the virtual world of the computer image. Although so-called **virtual reality** (VR) is in a sense merely a display option, the experiential difference between viewing flat images on a small monitor a few feet away and being visually

Figure 9.15 Rick Gibson, *3-Deep*, 1996. Although these images look blurry without glasses, viewing them (in color) through red and blue gels offers another dimension to computer output. *(Courtesy of Rick Gibson)*

immersed in a synthetic space is so striking that virtual reality has become a field in itself, with its own uses, equipment, and design challenges.

9.4.1 STEPPING INTO THE SCREEN—3D VIEWING AND VIRTUAL WORLDS

Ivan Sutherland, creator of the first graphics system (see Chapter 1), realized that the nature of the display was important in the design process. In the mid to late 1960s he worked on another revolutionary concept, a head–mounted set of tiny screens that he called "the ultimate display" (see Fig. 9.16). This variant of screen-based viewing let viewers enter the space of the computer and examine an object on a qualitatively different level. The world created by computer graphics had depth; furthermore, it was not bounded by a small rectangle but appeared in any direction the viewer chose to look.

Sutherland's world was a fully **immersive virtual reality:** Only the computer image was visible to the user. Options that combine computer-generated stereopsis with portions of the real environment are called **augmented,** or **enhanced, reality.**

Virtual reality viewing devices typically depend on small LCD or CRT displays that are brought close to the eyes. These may be incorporated into a helmet for a **head–mounted display** (HMD), as in Sutherland's system, or into a free-standing device called a **binocular omni-orientation monitor** (BOOM) that the viewer can look into and easily disengage from (see Fig. 9.17). In the future, it may be possible to view virtual environments through lightweight glasses that can be easily flipped up for real-world vision. Figure 9.18 shows the view through an HMD created by Henry Fuchs and his research group at the University of North Carolina at Chapel Hill. Although it does not yet have flip-up glasses, it can selectively compose real-world information with the computer stereo display to create an augmented reality. Fuchs favors such augmented environments over fully immersive ones because "when we put on goggles or an HMD, we interact with a different world that often has absolutely nothing to do with our real world and right now the intersections are usually not

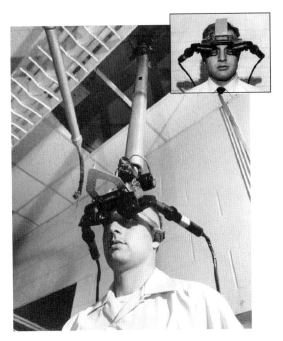

Fiɡure 9.16 Ivan Sutherland's Ultimate Display, **1968.** *(Courtesy of Ivan Sutherland)*

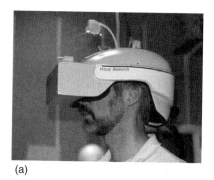

(a)

(b)

Figure 9.17 Virtual reality viewing devices. (a) Virtual Research Flight Helmet. (b) A Fake Space BOOM. The viewing mount is counterbalanced and provides motion and rotation in any direction around the base.

helpful—we move out of the tracking area or we bump into a real wall that is not depicted in our virtual environment" [Fuchs, 1997].

Most VR equipment is cumbersome and designed for single users. Equipment-free or unencumbered multiuser virtual reality viewing has inspired different approaches to bringing the audience inside a computer image. A pioneer in this area, Myron Krueger has developed a framework called VIDEOPLACE that uses video feed-back and computer projection to give users an immersive, interactive experience. In an ongoing series of art projects, Krueger has used his ever-improving setup to explore the potential of what he terms "artificial reality" as an art form. In CRITTER, for example, a user stands on a special platform and is recorded by a camera connected to a computer. The computer merges a single-colored silhouette of the user's image with an image of an animated, somewhat artificially intelligent creature (the critter), and projects the combined image on a wall in front of the user. The effect is one of directly interacting with a virtual creature (see Fig. 9.19).

> CRITTER'S general behavior is to cavort with you, chasing your image around the screen. If you hold out a hand, CRITTER will float down and land on it. If you stand still, CRITTER'S ambition is to climb up your silhouette until it reaches the top of your head, where it does a jig in celebration. . . . After seeing thousands of people trying to capture CRITTER with their hands, we made it sense when it is surrounded, search pathetically for an exit, and explode if there's no escape. Happily, reincarnation is instantaneous. [Krueger, 1991, p. 46]

Figure 9.18 HMDs of the future. Physicians can see computer visualizations in context with augmented reality HMDs that composite video and computer displays. Here an ultrasound test is viewed in real time inside a woman's body by merging video of her breast with digital ultrasound data. Artists could use this technology to combine their computer imagery with real-world input. *(Image courtesy of the University of North Carolina, Department of Computer Science)*

Figure 9.19 Myron Krueger, a sequence from *CRITTER*, 1984 (created with VIDEOPLACE). *(Courtesy of Myron Krueger)*

Figure 9.20 Unencumbered multiuser VR in a CAVE *(Courtesy of Pyramid Systems, Inc.)*

Another unencumbered virtual environment is the CAVE Automatic Virtual Environment. (CAVE is a self-referential acronym; the environment is simply referred to as a CAVE.) A CAVE is a room with a 3D environment rear-projected onto several walls and viewed through stereo glasses (see Fig. 9.20). Several users can work in a CAVE together, although only one person is tracked and can see the perspective calculated from her point of view. Others see a slightly oblique perspective.

Equipment for virtual reality is expensive and demanding of both personnel and processing power. As a result, few artists have had the opportunity to experiment with virtual environments. The Banff Center in Canada sponsors artist residencies and makes available high-end VR displays, input devices, and workstations. Toni Dove was an artist–leader of a team that developed the VR piece shown in Figs. 8.22 and 11.4. Although her piece was designed with VR displays, the impracticality of providing a VR viewing environment led her to show the work in other places as an installation incorporating the virtual world as projected video. Char Davies, whose work is displayed in Figs. 10.41 and 11.21, has access to high-powered computers and virtual reality equipment through her corporate affiliation as Director of Visual Research at SoftImage (now owned by Avid).

PHILOSOPHICAL ISSUES   The expectation of cheaper and far more realistic 3D environments has spurred debate about technologically produced environments competing with real ones. If a virtual environment can be created that is indistinguishable from a real environment, with objects that look, feel, and behave like objects in the real world, is the viewer having a "real" experience? If the virtual environment can be made to seem as authentic as the real environment, which is the model of which? It might be possible, in the distant future, to make the virtual environment a more compelling place to be than the real one (some might say that computer video games have already achieved this dubious goal).

Social theorist Jean Baudrillard has become famous in part for his widely read essay "The Precession of Simulacra," which begins with a reference to a Borges tale in which "cartographers of the Empire draw up a map so detailed that it ends up exactly covering the territory" [Baudrillard, 1983, p. 1]. He claims that media-induced "maps" are becoming reality and that reality is disintegrating beneath them—that we live in a *simulacrum*. As a familiar example, he cites the Lascaux caves, home of the earliest visual art on the planet. The caves, threatened by tourism, were closed off to prevent further decay. A reproduction of the caves was built nearby and that is what visitors now enter.

Benjamin Britton has taken the simulacrum a step further by creating a computer-based virtual Lascaux (see Fig. 9.21) which lets viewers enter a fully immersive 3D Lascaux replica. In a talk given to the Union of Prehistoric and Protohistoric Scientists, Britton points out that

> The viewers think, "Yes, that's really what it is like! It looks like that!" And so the reconstruction has really made history in the mind of those viewers, and that history is added to associated facts about the site proffered by other researchers. All these facts give meaning to the site for viewers, and viewers come to think they are learning the truth.

> The reconstructionist must ask, "What does this site mean?" With the lightest of touch, the reconstructionist must acknowledge that the fingerprints of subjective interpretation will be left on the model; and the scientist—now an artist—should make the fingerprints sing. . . . Instead of focusing your thoughts on photo montage, 3-D models and new technology, look within, look up, and recognize that your personal purpose is no different than that of your audience. By presuming to tell the story of the ancients, you are undertaking more of a responsibility than mere efforts at relative accuracy can sustain. You are, in fact, creating reality by building real experiences for people who will be affected and touched by your work. You are mythologizing, and you will need to be aware of that fact to undertake this work appropriately [Britton, 1996].

Figure 9.21 Benjamin Britton, still from *Lascaux*, 1995 (interactive installation). The Lascaux project calls into question the goals of historical reconstruction and the responsibility of artists and scientists involved in recreating the past for present-day viewing and interaction. The compelling nature of a good reconstruction implies responsibility and awareness on the part of its creator. *(Courtesy of Benjamin Britton)*

Perhaps in the future, tourists will view the Lascaux caves from the comfort of their homes and Baudrillard's descriptions of the force of modern media realities will be vindicated: "Simulation is no longer that of a territory, a referential being or a substance. It is the generation by models of a real without origin or reality: a hyperreal. The territory no longer precedes the map, nor survives it. Henceforth it is the map that precedes the territory" [Baudrillard, 1983, p. 2]. Inside the simulacrum, the concept of representation loses its meaning. "The age of simulation . . . begins with a liquidation of all referentials. . . . It is rather a question of substituting signs of the real for the real itself, that is, an operation to deter every real process by its operational double, a metastable, programmatic, perfect descriptive machine which provides all the signs of the real and short-circuits all its vicissitudes" [Baudrillard, 1983, p. 4]. Virtual reality rides at theme parks that whirl the visitor away on an experience that causes them to scream and experience real fear and real adrenaline already fulfill many of Baudrillard's criteria.

Scientific researchers do not feel that the technology is moving fast enough, however, for the deeper philosophical issues raised to be of much concern in the area of virtual reality. Henry Fuchs says:

> We should all live so long that we can't tell the difference [between the real worlds and virtual ones]. Look at audio, for example: we can walk around with a Walkman on but we don't usually have a problem separating the headphones' sound from real-world sound. It can be dangerous, but it's not a big philosophical issue. I don't think we'll have any problem telling the difference because the technology simply isn't that good and won't be for the foreseeable future.

> I'm much more worried that VR presentations will turn out not to be feasible and useful for a wide range of applications: that, like space travel, although the idea is good, the technology may turn out to be too daunting and our momentum may flag. Success may depend on technology landing in the right places, as laser technology did for audio. It depends a great deal on presentation quality—visual input and output. Most people have given up on HMDs, for instance. DARPA [Defense Advanced Research Projects Agency] isn't funding them anymore. Doubts are whether they will ever have wide enough fields of view or high enough resolution [Fuchs, 1997].

The quest for visually realistic virtual worlds is only one approach. Pattie Maes and Bruce Blumberg, professors at the MIT Lab, have discovered that visual realism is not necessarily compelling at all. What users of virtual environments seem to desire most is interesting character responses to user input and realistic dialog. The ALIVE system allows them to do just that. According to Maes, "ALIVE is a virtual-reality system where people can interact with virtual creatures without being constrained by headsets, goggles, or special sensing equipment. The system is based on a magic mirror metaphor: a person in the ALIVE space sees their own image on a large-screen TV as if in a mirror. Autonomous, animated characters join the user's own image in the reflected world" [Maes, 1995]. (See Figure 9.22.)

Figure 9.22 The Artificial Life Interactive Video Environment (ALIVE). *(Courtesy of Christopher R. Wren and the MIT Media Laboratory)*

9.5 3D Printing

"Automated fabrication ... has the potential to have an even more fundamental impact on society and society's economics than even automated computation. ..."

Marshall Burns, founder of Ennex Fabrication Technologies and author of Automated Fabrication: Improving Productivity in Manufacturing

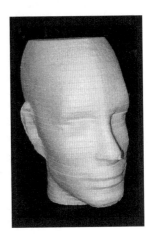

Figure 9.23 Layered Styrofoam™ head.

Imagine creating a 3D model on the computer and then printing it out—in 3D (see Fig. 9.23). That is the visionary goal for some automatic fabrication devices created for the world of computer-aided design and manufacturing (CAD/CAM).

Just as computer color printing used to be prohibitively expensive, today's 3D printing machines cost tens to hundreds of thousands of dollars. But with decreasing prices and new technologies, 3D printers could be standard peripherals for design companies and educational institutions in the near future. (As with high-end color printing, service bureaus can already create 3D output from your digital file for a fee.) The desktop publishing revolution may be succeeded by a desktop manufacturing revolution, with even broader implications.

The term **automatic fabrication** includes all automated processes for fabricating solid 3D objects from raw materials [Burns, 1993]. The types of machines most useful for artists are often those designed for **rapid prototyping** (RP), or the rapid creation of a part that may not have the accuracy or durability necessary in final applications. (Note that *rapid* is a relative term here; although simple shapes can be made in a few hours, large or complex shapes can easily take more than 20 hours to create.)

Automated fabrication machines are relatively small, safe, and straightforward to operate compared with the more traditional machines used for CAD/CAM (see Fig. 9.24). Such **computer-numerical-control** (CNC) machines are expensive behemoths designed to sculpt metal and plastic parts for industrial purposes, from automobile parts to molds for plastic cutlery. These manufacturing machines require the assistance of specialized designers and technicians throughout design and manufacturing. Not only do the machines require skilled oversight during use, but the objects must be designed with the capabilities of specific types of machines in mind. In comparison, RP machines can create an object of virtually any geometric shape.

Rapid prototyping machines use additive, layering technologies rather than subtractive processes that remove sections of material, such as milling. The additive approach usually cannot create parts that can replace solid metals (although research is underway to let these machines create metal parts). However, this approach eliminates many of the challenges inherent in designing for traditional manufacturing machines, such as having to know what forms are manufacturable and determining how to position pieces on the machine. The main technologies for automated fabrication are stereolithography (stacking and laser cutting), robotically guided extrusion, laser sintering,

(a) (b)

Fiɡure 9.24 A high-end NC milling station versus a rapid prototyping machine.
(a) The computer control panel of the Cincinnati Micron 5-axis milling machine is as
large as (b) the entire Stratasys Fused Deposition Modeling rapid prototyping
machine—and a lot more complicated to master.

**Fiɡure 9.25 Michael Rees, *Ajna Spine
2.22*, 1998** (stereolithography, 19″ × 5″
× 6″). *(Courtesy of Michael Rees)*

and droplet deposition on powder. Variations and other technologies exist and more are being created as demand rises.

Pioneered by 3D Systems, **stereolithography** involves the use of lasers to solidify layers of clear or colored resin. The result is a solid, layered model made of epoxy. Results are amber-colored, lightweight and translucent, and quite strong. Artist Michael Rees draws on a combination of eastern spiritual ideas, such as chakras, and western technologies, such as CAT scans, computer modeling, and RP technologies, to create his surrealistic anatomies. Their forms speak clearly of human body interiors, but their compositions are other-worldly and provocative (see Fig. 9.25).

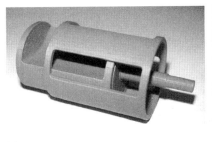

(a)

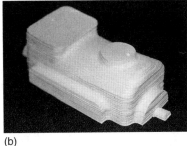

(b)

Figure 9.26 Models made with Laminated Object Manufacturing. (a) A valve for a two-stroke diesel engine (plasticized layers). (b) A locomotive created from layered paper.

Helisys' **Laminated Object Manufacturing** (LOM) is an example of stacking and laser cutting. Instead of hardening a resin to create solid material for each layer, LOM starts with solid layers of material, most often plain butcher paper, and then cuts away the unnecessary areas (see Fig. 9.26). Heat is used to fuse the layers.

Stratasys' **Fused Deposition Modeling** (FDM) is a robotically guided extrusion machine. It extrudes a plastic or other material through a nozzle, putting it down in layers where the object should be solid and cross-hatching looser areas or using a different substance for areas that will be removed later (see Fig. 9.27). When plastic is used, the result is matte and opaque. Wax can also be used in FDM, and most other RP technologies, for investment casting. Although the machines are now available for educational institutions for less than $40,000, media costs are a continuing expense: A gallon of the plastic material costs more than $500.

Selective Laser Sintering (SLS) from the Desktop-Publishing Corporation is a laser sintering process. The process consists of sintering (fusing into a solid) cross sections of an object from a layer of powder. Michael Rees's sintered sculptures blend the aesthetic qualities of the materials with elegant compositions and delicate forms, but like wayward experiments in genetics, the new anatomies have an aura of the freakish. The result is both sublime and disturbing (see Fig. 9.28). In addition to offering high speed and low cost, the SLS process can be used

Figure 9.27 Fused Deposition Modeling: An intake manifold for an SAE race car. The four interwoven pieces are created as separate shapes, one of which is shown to the right of the assembly. During modeling the interior is filled with cross-hatched plastic material that later must be removed (inset). Rubber and wax can also be used in FDM machines.

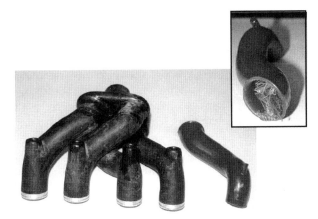

Figure 9.28 Michael Rees, *Ajna Spine 5,*
1998 (selective laser sintering, Duraform
material, 18″ × 6″ × 6″). *(Courtesy of Michael
Rees)*

with a wide range of materials from metal powders and glass to nylon. Machines with multiple nozzles can apply different materials to different parts of a model.

The latest technology is Z Corporation's **3-D Printing,** a form of droplet deposition on powder developed at MIT. This printing process involves the use of an ink-jet technology to apply an adhesive or binder to a layer of powder. The result is fragile if not dipped in wax or, for more demanding needs, impregnated with resin.

One of the barriers to the use of RP by artists and designers is that these machines require 3D model information that includes surface thickness. Most commercial modeling programs for Macs and PCs define only abstract surfaces (with no thickness information). Computer-aided design programs or high-end modelers such as Form-Z and Alias|Wavefront can specify surface thickness and export the standard file type for RP machines, stl (for *stereolithography*), a triangular mesh format.

Three-dimensional printing may bring us from the information age to a new age in which humankind "acquires untold powers to manipulate the properties of *matter* in much the same way that computers manipulate *information*" [Burns, 1993, p. 292]. Automated fabricators can produce parts on demand, making environments such as space stations and lunar habitats easier to envision. On the moon, and in the home, you may soon be able simply to select designs from a catalog and press a Fabricate button instead of going to the store or, in the case of space exploration, bringing spare parts along. Some RP machines can work with food-grade cornstarch and other edible materials, conjuring visions of the Star Trek replicator in sculptors' studios creating a meal on demand. Farther into the future, these types of machines may be able to work at the atomic level, taking raw materials and building virtually anything from them. In addition to solving most recycling problems, such technology suggests a mind-boggling array of potential new economic structures, legal issues, and creative endeavors.

In the present, automated fabrication technology is already a way not merely to visualize but to make 3D objects. And, unlike computer printing, which is often disappointing when compared with traditional 2D media, the materials used with 3D printing technologies have compelling aesthetic properties of their own.

Conclusion

Many 3D input and output devices are not yet available commercially, but this situation will surely change. In the meantime adventurous artists can experiment with existing options and even work with programmers to customize the more esoteric devices for use with personal computers and standard graphics applications.

As artists and designers more routinely experience 3D worlds through physical touch and use of their entire bodies, the nature of creative computer work will evolve, and immersive spaces and 3D printing will offer new ways to experience 3D forms.

Suggested Readings

Artists and designers interested in 3D input and output devices and their implications should consult the interface design readings in Chapter 11, Multimedia and Interactivity. In addition, general books on computer graphics often include sections on both 2D and 3D input and output devices (for example, *Computer Graphics for Designers and Artists,* by Isaac Victor Kerlow and Judson Rosebush).

Baudrillard, Jean. *Simulations.* Semiotext(e), 1983. Includes the now-famous essay entitled "The Precession of Simulacra" that calls into question the continued healthy existence of reality in the face of often media-induced alternate worlds, from the concrete, such as the copy of the Lascaux caves, to the abstract, such as Americans' "belief" in Disneyworld.

Burns, Marshall. *Automated Fabrication: Improving Productivity in Manufacturing.* Ennex Corporation, 1998 reprinting. Engaging and thorough coverage of automated fabrication techniques, from the standard types of CNC machining to the latest in additive RP options. Contains technical information but is written in plain English. The extraordinary implications of automated fabrication technology are also considered. Previously published by Prentice Hall (1993), a revised edition is expected to be released shortly. In the meantime the book is offered at a discount in Xerox form through Ennex Corporation and can be ordered over the Web at http://www.Ennex.com/service/publications/book.htm.

Dodsworth, Clark (ed.). *Digital Illusion: Entertaining the Future with High Technology.* Addison Wesley Longman, 1998. A valuable resource that contains chapters by leaders in numerous areas of computing. The book includes historical, theoretical, and practical information for understanding and creating compelling experiences with the latest technology. From government research labs to theme parks to discussions of narrative, this book not only details the hardware and software technologies, but also addresses issues of design and content, as well as viable business models, for "digital illusion." Although some chapters are more technical than others, the book was written for a general audience.

Krueger, Myron W. *Artificial Reality II.* Addison Wesley Longman, 1991. An overview of the field of "artificial reality." Historical and technical information is conveyed in the context of personal accounts of Krueger's varied research, including detailed descriptions of his well-known VIDEOPLACE project which became a framework for many art projects. An inspirational combination of art and science.

Prototyping Technology International. A lushly produced trade journal aimed at industry but with examples of RP technology that will inspire artists too.

Exercise

Most of the devices described in this chapter are as yet inaccessible to individual artists and students. Most 3D worlds will be accessed with a mouse or joystick for some time to come. Readers are strongly encouraged to experiment with any 3D input and output options available to them, but no specific exercises are included for this chapter.

CHAPTER 10

2D and 3D Animation and Video

Figure 10.1 Jon McCormack, *Four Imaginary Walls*, 1991 (interactive computer installation controlled by the weather). *(Copyright 1991 Jon McCormack)*

With *Four Imaginary Walls,* we watch the weather in a way denied to us by weather indicators of the past. A flag or leaves being blown around are good indicators of wind but give little indication of heat. The effects of the real wind, temperature and light create a sculpture made from virtual objects. These objects are referred to as 'virtual' because they could never exist in our reality. Their physics, mass, shape, colour, energy and behavior are described within the computer software. No two objects have exactly the same properties. The objects themselves are cubic in shape and become more energetic as the temperature increases. They are extremely light and are attracted to each other when at close distances. They have knowledge of their environment and of each other. They are contained within a limited space by four imaginary walls which are not visible to the viewer—only their physical properties can be felt.

The work presents itself at a number of levels. In its simplest form it reflects on the way physical forces and properties affect structure and form. Beyond this, it explores the notions of containment and the increasingly blurred relation between nature and machine. An analogous situation to that enacted here is the example of the crash of the financial markets of 1987. In that situation, the computers, which again had been programmed to respond to the prevailing "weather conditions" of Wall Street, reacted in the only way they "knew." The "viewing public," which included everyone from stockbrokers to the President, could only watch. The "masters" had already done the thinking and the creating, and in a cruel irony of history, repeated through a machine an exact replica of the collective human reactions which caused the financial crash of sixty years earlier [Richards, 1991].

10.1 Introduction

Time flies; but remember, you are the navigator.

Anonymous

"Computer-generated animation" is not computer-generated any more than a novel written with a word processor is computer-generated [Barzel, 1997].

Ronen Barzel, *animation scientist at Pixar and author of* Physically–Based Modeling for Computer Graphics: A Structured Approach, *Academic Press, 1992.*

The artist entering the world of computer animation and video-oriented motion graphics is faced with a wide range of tools and an associated range of technical and theoretical issues. The languages of film and animation, the history of video art, and advanced techniques in 3D graphics (e.g., inverse kinematics) may all merge in a single production.

Many books have been written on traditional and computer-based animation. In this chapter I discuss traditional animation, film, or video only when they relate to creating motion on the computer. The basic concepts outlined here should give you a sense of the animation options available and enough understanding of their structures to aid more detailed learning of any particular animation or video-effects application. The principles are the same whether the artist's aesthetic strategies come from cinema, photography, animation, video, or from within the emerging visual language of computer art itself.

Animated graphics are used in virtually all time-based media work, from TV ads and video to Hollywood movies, educational software, games, and, of course, art work. Different computer animation packages are designed for everything from helping animators work with hand-drawn figures to animating still graphics imported from other programs to editing and compositing film, video, and premade animation footage. When specialized for use with film or video, 2D animation programs are often called **motion graphics** or **video editing and special-effects programs. Three-dimensional animation programs** render and record sequences of images of a 3D scene, capturing the motion of objects and changing lights and camera views. I use the term **time-based programs** to refer to all the varieties of programs that let artists, animators, and videographers control visual elements over time.

Computer art works that change over time have been created since the earliest days of computer graphics (see Chapter 1). Like many other forms of visual computing, computer animation used to be prohibitively expensive and time-consuming. Dramatic improvements in hardware speed and the release of easy-to-use software have made the computer increasingly affordable and practical for 2D and 3D animation and video work.

10.2 Concepts

What makes an animation work? How can a sequence of still images magically create the appearance of motion? And how can the computer help to create such image sequences? The computer offers new and powerful methods for automatically creating pieces of an animation, but throughout the process the vision and creativity of the animator remain paramount.

10.2.1 The Illusion of Motion

Computer animation programs, like traditional animation, video, and filmmaking, depend on the illusion of motion that can be created by a sequence of slowly changing still images. This illusion is made possible by two physiological phenomena:

1. **Persistence of vision.** Images seen by the eye remain imaged in the brain for a fraction of a second after the actual image stimulus has disappeared. If still frames are shown sequentially at an appropriate rate, each succeeding image replaces the previous image without any noticeable blank space between them.
2. **Visual closure.** This mind–eye phenomenon fills the spaces between visual stimuli.

Changing the images gradually from frame to frame completes the illusion of continuous motion (Fig. 10.2).

Figure 10.2 **Eadweard Muybridge, *Athlete Running, High Leap,* 1879.** In his classic photographs, Muybridge revealed isolated components of motion, leading to enhanced understanding of human and animal movement. He showed the work with his motion-picture projector, the Zoopraxiscope, a device that used persistence of vision to create the illusion of motion from a sequence of still images. *(Courtesy of the Stanford University Museum of Art, Stanford Family Collections, 13932.103)*

| Keyframe 1 | Inbetween frame | Keyframe 2 | Keyframe 3 |

Figure 10.3 Keyframes and inbetween frames. A traditional animation example showing keyframes and an inbetween frame.

10.2.2 KEYFRAMES

The extent to which an image changes from one frame to the next and methods for controlling such changes are obviously important in sustaining the illusion of motion. A common strategy for planning and executing a series of changing images is to use **keyframes** that describe the extremes of an object's motion. In traditional animation houses, an animator draws the keyframes and assistants and "inbetweeners" draw the **inbetween frames** (Fig. 10.3). However, even with acetate cels (pieces of celluloid on which parts of characters or objects are drawn) to layer images and reuse stationary components, this is an extremely time-consuming task that requires skill and patience. Even a five-minute animation, for instance, has

5 minutes $\times$ 60 seconds/minute $\times$ 24 frames/second = 7200 frames!

A feature-length film contains more than one hundred thousand frames. Although keyframes and **pencil tests** (sequences drawn with outlines and not yet filled in with colors) provide some feedback before each frame is created in full detail, the traditional process requires careful advance planning because last-minute changes can be prohibitively expensive.

10.2.3 INBETWEENING

CREATING NEW FRAMES WITH INBETWEENING   The computer can dramatically expedite simple animation processes by producing inbetween frames automatically. In some cases automatic inbetweening is all that is needed—for instance, for flying logos and moving

Figure 10.4 Three keyframes. Three keyframes representing a ball on the ground, at its highest point, and back on the ground.

type. For more complicated animations (say, parts of a character), however, automated inbetweening tends to produce a mechanical feeling. Hollywood moviemaking generally uses inbetween frames only every other frame or so. Artists must use inbetweening carefully, and the more they understand about its options and limitations, the more helpful the computer will be as an animation aid.

In the simple scene shown in Fig. 10.4, the goal is to animate a ball thrown in the air—starting at ground level, rising into the air while moving sideways, and returning to the ground. The three keyframes needed are the ball's beginning and end positions and its highest point.

Now, instead of drawing the intermediate frames by hand, you can choose to **inbetween** these frames automatically. The simplest way to calculate the ball's positions in the inbetween frames is with linear interpolation. **Linear interpolation** allows you to calculate new positions at equal intervals along a straight line, as shown in Fig. 10.5. Linear inbetweening uses the positions calculated with linear interpolation to position the object in the inbetween frames (here the ball's center is placed at the interpolated positions). You determine the number of positions calculated and thus the number of frames created.

Figure 10.5 Inbetweening with linear interpolation. Linear interpolation creates inbetween frames at equal intervals along straight lines. The ball moves at a constant speed. Ticks indicate the locations of inbetween frames at regular time intervals (determined by the number of frames per second chosen by the user).

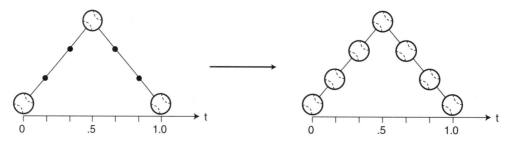

The Wild Wild World of Linear Interpolation

An interpolation is a rule for creating new information from information that is already known. Interpolation is used in virtually every type of computer graphics—from digital painting and photoediting to digital design and layout to 3D animation and multimedia—to calculate new values for parameters representing anything from color and lighting to image position. For example, to create a color gradient, you can choose two colors and ask the computer to interpolate smoothly between them, drawing a nicely shaded gradient from one to the other. Similarly, in shading a 3D form, the 3D program can calculate lighting at only a few points and then, using interpolation, fill in the rest of the surface colors to create a volumetric-looking object (using an interpolation of colors for Gouraud shading and of surface normals for Phong shading; see Section 8.5.4).

Linearly interpolating between two values (whether they are points in space or colors or rotation angles) simply means using a straight line as the "rule" for creating new values (see Fig. 10.6). You can also calculate new values by using other rules that are curves rather than straight lines (see the discussion of nonlinear interpolation in this section).

Interpolation can be used for any object transformation or change in appearance, including rotation, scaling, and shearing, as well as color, transparency, and even shape (see Fig. 10.7). Interpolation can also be used to calculate inbetween frames for a filter or automated image-creation algorithm. Karl Sims uses interpolation in his custom software to bend and swirl images over time, creating the sense of liquidity. In the piece shown in Fig. 10.8, he used 2D interpolations to dissolve the physicality of the 3D forms. He described it as follows: "The piece depicts the upcoming struggle between the virtual and physical sides of ourselves. As technology brings us the age of virtual worlds, our existence as individuals becomes less and less dependent on our physical being" [Sims in Capasso, 1994].

Morphing (discussed in Section 2.6) also involves the use of interpolation.

Figure 10.6 Interpolating between two points with a line. (a) Known: One loop causes a nausea factor of 2, and five loops cause a nausea factor of 4. Unknown: What is the nausea factor of three loops? (b) Using a straight line to interpolate between the two known values yields a nausea factor of 3 for three loops.

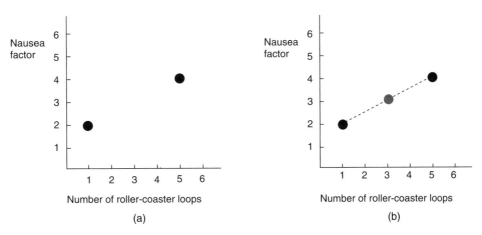

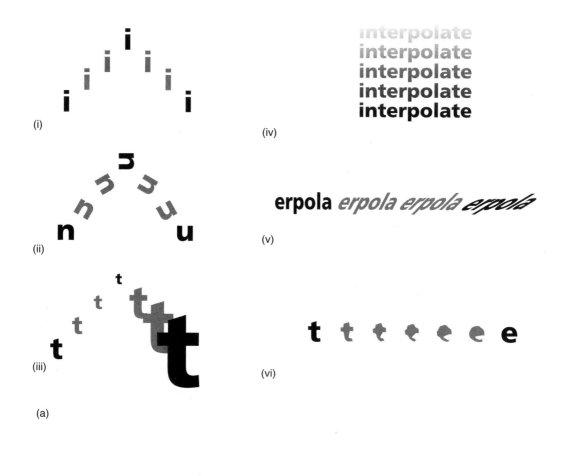

(i)

(ii)

(iii)

(a)

(iv)

(v)

(vi)

(b)

Figure 10.7 Interpolation of object transformations. (a) 2D interpolation (darker frames are key-frames). Parameters interpolated: (i) position; (ii) position and rotation; (iii) position and scale; (iv) color (white to black); (v) position and shear; (vi) position and shape. (b) 3D interpolation: both position and rotation are interpolated.

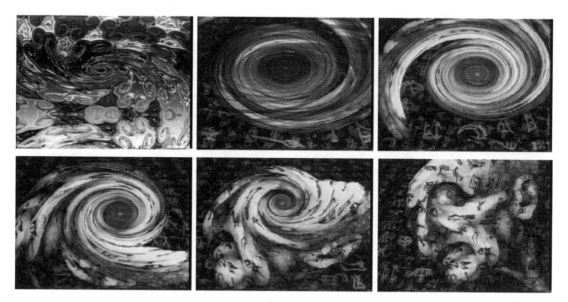

Figure 10.8 Karl Sims, *Liquid Selves,* music by Peter Gabriel and John Paul Jones, 1992. *(Courtesy of Karl Sims)*

The linear inbetweening previously shown in Fig. 10.5 does not produce a realistic animation of a ball moving through the air. One way to improve the realism and subtlety of this animation is to use a nonlinear, or curved, path in calculating inbetween frames (see Fig. 10.9). In this method, called **nonlinear interpolation,** the curves used for nonlinear interpolation usually are the familiar spline curves used in 2D and

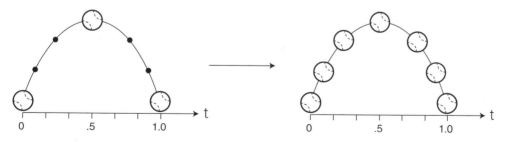

Figure 10.9 **Inbetweening with nonlinear interpolation.** Nonlinear interpolation can create equally spaced inbetween frames along curved paths. The ball still moves at a constant speed. (Note that the three keyframes used here and in Fig. 10.10 are the same as in Fig. 10.4.)

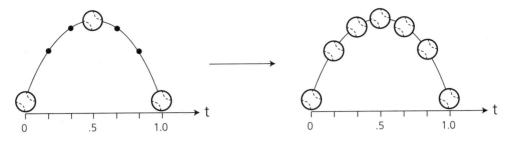

Figure 10.10 Inbetweening with nonlinear interpolation and easing. The ball changes speed as it approaches and leaves keyframes, so the dots indicating calculations made at equal time intervals are no longer equidistant along the path.

3D geometric drawing and modeling software (see Chapters 4 and 7). Using curves in defining motion paths and other types of object transformations greatly expands the usefulness and realism of automated inbetweening. After all, few objects move naturally in a straight line.

Note that, although the spatial path is a curve rather than a line, the calculations still are based on the assumption that the object covers equal distances in equal units of time. But few real-world objects can leap into motion from complete stillness or come to a full stop instantaneously. Even greater realism, flexibility, and expressiveness can be achieved by a *nonlinear interpolation of time* called **easing** that allows objects to *accelerate* or *decelerate* as they move between keyframes. This effect is produced by calculating the inbetween frames at unequal intervals along the path, concentrating greater numbers of inbetween frames near the keyframes to create deceleration and expanding the distance between inbetween frames to create acceleration (see Fig. 10.10).

MOTION PATHS   In many 2D and virtually all 3D animation programs, objects can be animated over editable user-defined **motion paths** made up of lines or curves (usually splines) (see Fig. 10.11). Motion paths can be changed to accommodate new needs, and also are essential for camera work. Objects can be aligned with an associated path, and changes necessary to maintain the alignment occur automatically.

10.2.4 MOTION BLUR

Motion blur occurs in film because the camera shutter is open long enough during each frame to register the impression of objects in motion. Although an individual

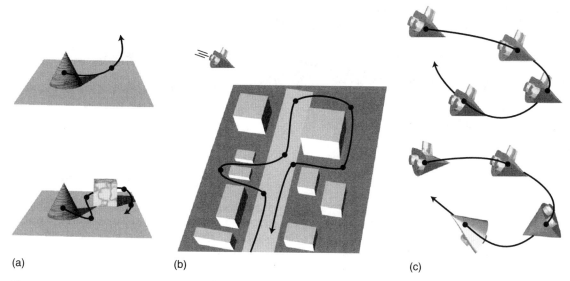

(a)   (b)   (c)

Figure 10.11 Motion paths. (a) On top, the motion path for a cone is a simple curve. Below, a cube is added to the scene and the cone must fly around it; the motion path is easily rerouted. (b) The motion path determines the path of a camera in a flythrough animation of a city. (c) In the top sketch the space ship is not aligned with its path. Although the path itself may be realistic, the way the ship flies along it is not. When the ship is aligned, as in the bottom sketch, its motion along the path is much more convincing.

movie frame seems slightly out of focus because of this motion, the effect of a sequence of them played back at 24 frames per second is vivid and sharp.[1] When an object is moving fast enough, motion blurring becomes noticeable even during playback and helps emphasize the relative speeds of objects being filmed (see Fig. 10.12). Traditional animators indicate motion blur by hand (see Fig. 10.13).

Simulated motion blur can bring visual works made on a computer closer to film in feeling and aesthetic language. Motion blur can also accentuate the sense of speed and distance in both 2D and 3D animation by making nearby objects blurrier than those in the distance. Motion blur can be added to static works to create a sense of motion that may or may not be realistic (see Fig. 10.14).

[1] Actually, although only 24 different frames are used, film is displayed at 48 or sometimes 72 frames per second by double- or triple-flashing each frame. Otherwise the images would flicker (hence the old term **flicks**).

Figure 10.12 Motion blur. The faster an object is moving, the more it becomes a ghostly streak rather than a recognizable figure.

10.2.5 REAL-TIME RECORDING

Inbetweening requires the use of a few hand-based, user-determined changes to generate additional frames. Another approach, called **real-time recording,** relies on the use of local-touch methods, capturing frames as the artist paints on the screen, moves objects around, or flies through a 3D world. The real-time creation of lines and colors on the screen becomes the animation. Because real-time recording directly captures complex motions of the hand, artists can create animations that would be difficult if not impossible to generate with inbetweening.

Real-time recording can be achieved by taking a picture of the screen at regular intervals during the drawing process and storing each snapshot as a separate frame, or by recording instructions for replicating the artist's actions. The artist can then view, create, and edit animated marks by playing back these real-time animations. Some

Figure 10.13 Motion blur in a comic strip.

Figure 10.14 Motion blur applied in a static program. Motion blur applied to the leftmost carousel image in Fig. 10.12.

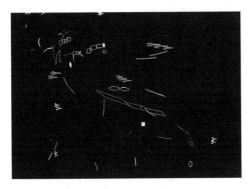

Figure 10.15 **Scott Sona Snibbe,** *Motion Phone,* **1990–1996** (stills from movies). A user begins with a blank canvas and palettes of colors and shapes. When the user starts drawing on the canvas, the speed and location of the marks are entered into a digital animation loop. By pressing on the keyboard or a graphics tablet, the user can change the shape, size, and color of the marks simultaneously. As the user continues to draw, new marks are added into the same animation loop, creating sequentially layered multiple rhythms of form and color. *(Courtesy of Scott Sona Snibbe)*

programs also let artists adjust keyframes in real time (as the animation is playing), automatically recomputing the inbetween frames as necessary.

Artist Scott Snibbe used real-time recording as an essential aspect of his *Motion Phone.* The *Motion Phone* in Fig. 10.15 is an ongoing project in which interactive animation is based directly on the motion of a user-controlled input device such as a mouse or tablet and stylus. The aesthetics of the work are inspired by abstract films produced in the 1920s, themselves inspired by the paintings of such artists as Wassily Kandinsky and Paul Klee. Snibbe considers the *Motion Phone* to be "an 'instrument' that brings spontaneous creation to abstract animation in both composition and performance." Snibbe further writes:

> An animator, using this tool, can create and develop themes the same way a composer does in front of a piano. A performer can then perform the developed themes of the composer with slight variation, or, like a jazz musician, improvise on the themes of the work. Once a performer has mastered the use of the *Motion Phone* as an instrument, it is natural to seek out others with whom to perform duets, quartets or even symphonies.

> Users of the *Motion Phone* can collaborate over a network to create animation on the same shared plane. Each individual can zoom in and out of the shared world to an arbitrary degree. With this capability, improvisations and visual conversations can take place in many locations and scales at once. One can zoom out and have a god's-eye view of the complexity of many different animations. One can also zoom in on what appears to be a single dot and find a complex abstract dance in progress [Snibbe, 1995].

Real-time, interactive animation creation is still unusual in the computer world. The real-time performance aspects of the *Motion Phone,* along with its responsiveness and rhythmic layering, make it decidedly different in process and results from most current computer-animated art work. However, that may change—Adobe AfterEffects now offers a motion sketch plug-in designed by Snibbe.

10.2.6 MORPHING

Ours is a crisis of cutting and joining, a crisis of editing; we have passed beyond the crisis of montage. This is a crisis of representation rather than of construction [Virilio, 1991, p. 112].

Morphing is a popular, often dramatic technique that combines the use of keyframes and interpolation to make one image seem magically to metamorphose into another. It improves on the standard special effect of *fading* from one image to another to indicate a transformation or transition of some sort. The drawback of using a fade to show a change from one situation to another is that, although the beginning and end images may be perfectly clear (see Fig. 10.16a and c), those near the middle are usually confusing and do not sustain a believable transition (see Fig. 10.16b).

In morphing, the important features of each image are warped as the fade progresses so that their locations sustain the illusion that one object is changing into another. First, important position points (or lines in some morphing programs) on the two images are indicated by the artist in the beginning and end keyframes. The morphing program then interpolates intermediate positions and uses them to warp the images so that the dissolving and resolving features create convincing composites (see Fig. 10.17). High-quality morphing requires the artist to choose a large number of points or lines and then align them on the beginning and end images. Even with great attention to detail within a morph program, the artist usually must touch up morphs in a digital painting or photoediting program to make them completely seamless.

Figure 10.18 shows a morph between the images shown in Fig. 10.16. Images (a) and (c) are warped as well as faded to create a new image (b) with characteristics of both the start and end images.

Figure 10.16 The problem with fades. In this vacation sequence (a) a plane fades into (c) a man on vacation. (b) In the intermediate image, the two forms are easily distinguishable.

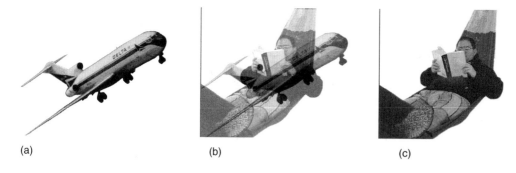

(a)   (b)   (c)

Start Imag

Morph Ima
51

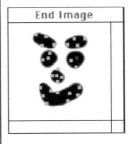
End Image

Figure 10.17 Choosing morph points or lines. Morph points or lines pin down the motions of key parts of the image. For faces, some of these points lie along the eyebrows, eyes, nose, mouth, and contours of the cheeks and chin.

Morphing is frequently used in TV advertisements and movies to show the transformation of old products into new and better products and to create characters with extraordinary capabilities, such as the form-changing antagonist in *Terminator 2*. Morphing is still just beginning to be explored as an aesthetic tool in animated artwork, however. Although it can easily create sequences that are merely tacky, it also has great potential for investigating connections among people, objects, and places—and even abstract visual arrangements. Because any object in an image can become any other object, morphing can suggest visual connections that otherwise might not be pursued. Seeing one object literally become another has an effect that the beginning and end images alone cannot possibly convey.

Cynthia Beth Rubin uses morphing to explore images and establish a type of space distinctly different from the Renaissance perspective space found in much computer art based on either digitized photographs or 3D modeling (see Fig. 10.19). Through 2D compositing and morphing, Rubin combines and integrates images from her own past and from Jewish history, creating a psychological space of memory and reflection that

Figure 10.18 Morphing. Now the middle image is part of a seamless visual transition bewteen the plane and vacation images.

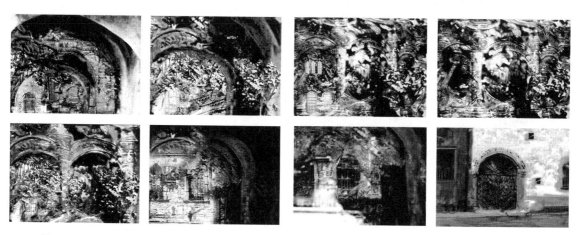

Figure 10.19 Cynthia Beth Rubin, sequence from *Inherited Memories*, 1997. Rubin's technique involves not just morphing from one source to another, but also using compositing and morphing iteratively to create a smoothly flowing sequence. *(Courtesy of Cynthia Beth Rubin)*

spans many centuries and national borders. In her animated works, images intermingle, pulsing and twisting to lead the viewer on a voyage composed entirely of photographs and appropriated images, but brought to life in a personal and painterly fashion.

> Morphing software has the potential to return us to the art of careful observation that was once part of drawing, and at the same time keep us within the medium of the computer. To use morphing software, artists have to look. To make the eyes of a Native American mask, for example, morph into the eyes of a Chinese mask, [one] must observe the forms in each of these sources, and notice the differences in relative size and form. When a bark painting from Somalia with a diamond pattern is morphed to an Indonesian batik with circular patterns, it requires studying the symmetry of each pattern, looking at the spaces between repeating forms, and carefully examining the patterns themselves [Rubin, 1995].

Trained as a painter, Rubin also values the morphing process because it demands close investigation of imagery, even when that imagery originated elsewhere. She asserts: "This is a better dialogue with the source than just simply copying it. This is a process of getting inside the image, and pushing it around until the appropriator begins to feel the decision-making process of the original artist" [Rubin, 1993]. She adds: "Often the initial morph from one of my complex images to another creates confusing transitional passages. I export intermediate frames from a morph sequence, work on them in a painting program, and then remorph them within the original images. By repeating this process I am able to achieve a consistent image flow with unexpected subtle changes that would be impossible with one level of morphing alone" [Rubin, 1997].

In a series of works using still frames from morphing sequences, Joseph Santarromana merged his face with the faces of icons of popular culture, such as Marilyn Monroe and Ferdinand Marcos (see Fig. 10.20), as well as the Unabomber sketch, Homer Simpson, and Ronald McDonald. For Santarromana, morphing provides a new way to pursue the issues of identity and its formation that are the basis for his work. The power of morphing became evident when Santarromana first started using the software to morph himself with friends and art world figures. He found that some people, even fellow artists and photographers, were made uncomfortable by having their images combined with those of other people and felt viscerally that they were somehow made vulnerable, even violated by this process.

Whether realized in video, installations, or on the computer, Santarromana's art draws on the pain and conflicts of his childhood experiences as a Filipino growing up in a region of the Midwest with a strong Ku Klux Klan presence. The struggle to form his own identity there made Santarromana acutely aware of the struggles of many people to create an identity for themselves and the role that media images can play in the process. His images do not pass judgment or become simplified political statements but instead offer themselves for contemplation. The textures and artifacts created by the morphing process and the drama of the portraits make them visually intriguing, and, despite their serious inspiration, the concept and images themselves are often humorous and playful.

Figure 10.20 Joseph Santarromana, art works done with morphing: (a) *M. M. & J. S.,* 1996 (#144, 34″ × 34″, Iris ink-jet print); (b) *Ferdinand M. & Joseph S.,* 1994 (#126, Icon series, Cibachrome print, 30″ × 30″). (a) In the Marylin Monroe morph, the glamour of the Hollywood star, the production techniques of Warhol, and Santarromana's face are forcibly combined through modern computer technology. (b) In the Ferdinand Marcos morph, the two identities have an eerie coexistence as a recognizable and yet somehow distorted image, like a Marcos from an alternate universe. *(Collection of Rebbecca and Alexander Stewart)*

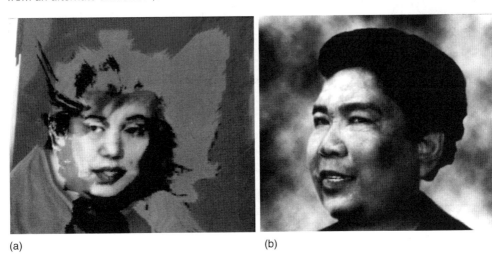

(a) (b)

10.3 Anatomy of an Animation Program

There are two main types of animation program interface: those that provide a series of **cels** or frame-like drawing areas to work in, and those that also offer a visible **timeline** for controlling animation processes. Some 2D animation programs do not have timelines, but virtually all 3D geometric animation programs do. Most timeline-based programs provide the following components. Animation programs that do not use a timeline probably contain a subset of these features.

> *Stage or composition area.* In this area of the screen, motion, animation, compositing, and effects are previewed and final playback can take place (see Fig. 10.21).

Figure 10.21 Basic elements of 2D and 3D animation programs. (a) The 2D stage or composition area of Macromedia Director. In this interactive multimedia authoring program, animations are set up and played back in the same screen area. *(Portions copyright 1998 Macromedia, Inc. Used with permission)*

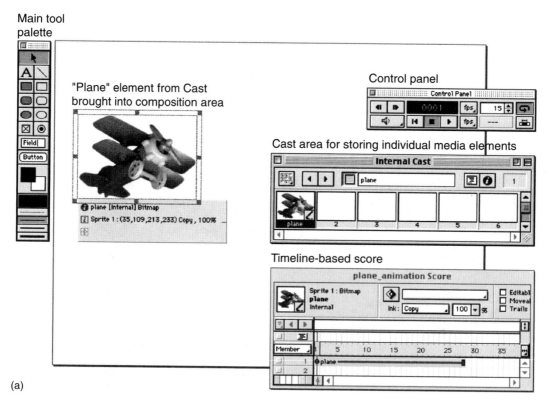

(a)

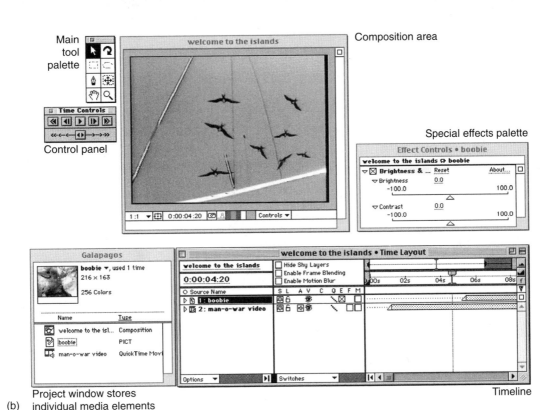

Figure 10.21 (Continued) (b) Composition area and auxiliary palettes in Adobe's AfterEffects® video compositing program. Sequences can be previewed within AfterEffects, but final movies must be rendered for real-time playback and high-quality special effects. *(Courtesy Adobe Systems Incorporated)*

Tool palette. A main tool palette is available in some animation programs (see Fig. 10.21b and c), but most of the tools and controls are contained in auxiliary palettes. A main tool palette may contain tools for moving images, magnifying a window, and other similar functions that apply to all parts of the program. The main area for controlling animated works often is a timeline window.

Auxiliary palettes and windows. Auxiliary palettes often play a major role and sometimes control entire program components. In general, you should look for palettes or program modules that help with the creation and editing of the objects and images to be animated, provide a visual way of storing and organizing the characters and footage used, and have controls for moving through a playback—usually drawn to resemble tape deck buttons (see Fig. 10.21a and 10.21b).

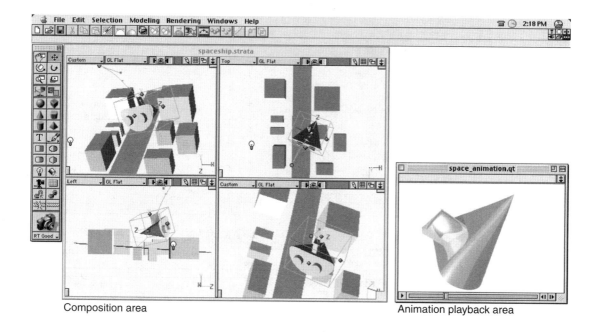

Composition area

Animation playback area

(c)　Timeline

Figure 10.21 *(Continued)* (c) 3D composition area of the modeling, rendering, and animation package Strata StudioPro. As in most 3D environments, animations are set up on a 3D stage, but for high quality, versions must be rendered and played back as a sequence of 2D images.

THE TIMELINE　The timeline area is often the main control area. A number of timelines are depicted in Fig. 10.21. Called by various names such as *time-layout window,* *dope sheet,* or *score,* the timeline framework lets the artist script, edit, and control the timing and other parameters of animation objects. The horizontal axis usually is divided into either frames or seconds and the vertical axis into rows or tracks for arranging the different images (or other media) over time (see Fig. 10.22). With a timeline, artists can view a time-based work spatially (and all at once) and control both spatial and temporal aspects of the composition.

Timeline

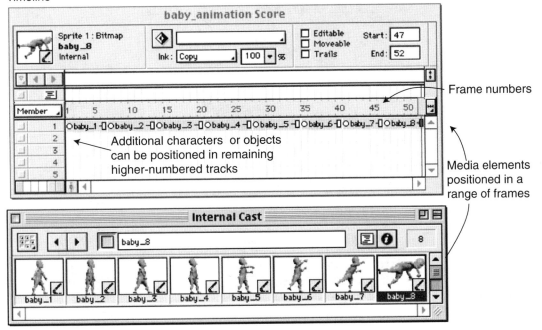

Frame numbers

Media elements positioned in a range of frames

Media storage area

Figure 10.22 Timeline example. In this time layout (Score) from Macromedia Director, the motion of different animation elements is displayed with special notation. Frame numbers running along the top and numbered tracks on the right help organize and coordinate images and other media. *(Portions copyright 1998 Macromedia, Inc. Used with permission)*

Tracks often are used like layers in drawing programs; each track has a stacking order. Tracks in a 3D animation can include not only the animated objects but also cameras and lights (see Fig. 10.23).

RENDERING VERSUS REAL-TIME PLAYBACK   Animation program interfaces are affected by the paradigm used for creating and playing the finished results. Some animation programs finish an animation or movie by rendering it as a sequence of static 2D frames, either directly onto video or film or to a file (most 3D animation programs fall into this category). Others create and render each frame in real time whenever the work is viewed. All interactive programs with animation capabilities, such as Macromedia Director, fall into the second category: The frames cannot be rendered in advance because their ordering and content may change with each viewing. Such

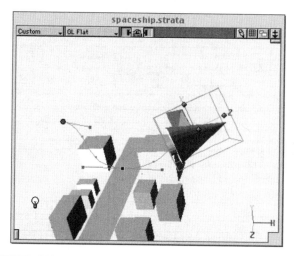

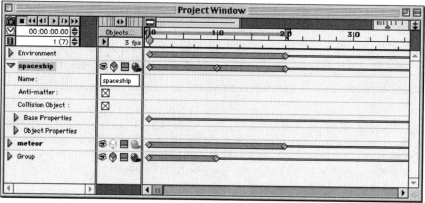

Figure 10.23 Timeline in a 3D program (Strata StudioPro). As in 2D programs, the tracks of the timeline are used for individual objects, such as the spaceship, and the horizontal axis is either frames or seconds. Individual lights and cameras can also be worked within the timeline (here the spotlight is named "meteor").

programs can play back their own creations and usually offer playback-only modules that can be obtained at no cost.

Rendered image sequences can easily take up a great deal of storage space (typically several megabytes or more). Instructions for animating and rendering images can be stored in much smaller files, often less than a megabyte (not including source images). Programs that render the final movie to a file can offer many more sophisticated rendering effects because the time needed to render each frame is not constrained.

10.4 Composition

As in previous chapters, the compositional issues discussed in this section are those of spatial composition, but now with the added complexity of compositions that change over time. However, animations involve many other types of composition, such as the narrative issues of plot line and characterization. Many texts have already been written on traditional approaches to such issues. For discussions of new forms of narrative engendered by the computer, such as hypertext and, in general, interactive multimedia, see the suggested readings for Chapter 11, Multimedia and Animation, and Chapter 12, The World Wide Web.

(There is no separate touch section in this chapter. I described the automated methods for creating new marks in Section 10.2, and hand-drawn animation on the computer depends directly on the types of touch already described in Chapters 2 and 4.)

10.4.1 Motion and Space

Today we must begin to recognize that the systems and instruments of measurement are less chronometric than cinemetric. The standard for measuring the space traveled through is no longer the time of passage but rather the speed, the distance-speed, which has become the measure and the privileged dimension of space as of time [Virilio, 1991, p. 58].

Animated works imply motion and *motion implies space* (see Fig. 10.24). Motion cues based on this rule and other observations from real-world experience can be used in animated art to evoke a sense of 3D space, even when all the images are created in 2D

Figure 10.24 Rate × time implies distance. In a landscape seen through the window of a moving car (right to left), objects closer to the car cross the field of view faster that those in the distance. The relative speeds of the objects are interpreted as different spatial depths in the mind of the viewer. For example, the tree starts on the far right and by the third frame is at the far left. However, the barn moves over only about a third of the view in that same time, and the sun does not move at all.

programs. This space can be coherent and illusionistic or can be constructed without consistent reference to spatial depth and structure.

In 2D animation programs, both spatial cues and motion cues must be developed by the artist, but in 3D programs spatial cues usually are generated automatically (see Sections 10.4.4 and 10.5.3). Although 2D animation requires more planning and greater knowledge of static and motion-based spatial cueing conventions, it can also provide greater freedom and encourage greater variation of these conventions.

10.4.2 DIGITAL VIDEO

The relationship between time and space is mediated by the technology used to record and present it. Different graphics concepts, such as 2D and 3D or sample- or geometry-based graphics, lead to different ways of approaching issues of space. In **digital video** applications, artists can work with video clips (i.e., sequences of captured, sample-based 2D images) that can be cut up and rearranged in time. Unlike traditional video editing, which requires fast forwarding or rewinding to reach a desired frame, digital video is *nonlinear:* The artist can simply click any place in a clip (or reach it by typing in time codes) to make it the current frame.

Sigrid Hackenberg finely controls timing in her video work to change the viewer's perception of the space portrayed. Hackenberg's larger-than-life self-portrait series, featuring head, mouth, eyes, hands, feet, and full body pieces, was directly affected by the use of a digital video editing system (see Fig. 10.25). The nonlinear editor gave Hackenberg, who was trained as a painter, total control over her video work, freeing her from expensive studio rental sessions and letting her experiment with hue, chroma, and brightness. She says that "it is now more like a moving painting but with content from photography and cinema. I use little movement and focus instead on subtle changes in speed, using double screens and dissolves" [Hackenberg, 1996]. "Sigrid Hackenberg [pushes] the notion of self-portraiture as the image of the artist evolves and changes in

Figure 10.25 Sigrid Hackenberg, *Self-Portrait, Hands,* **1994** (projected image: 7' × 10'). *(Courtesy of Sigrid Hackenberg)*

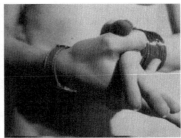

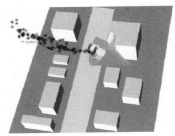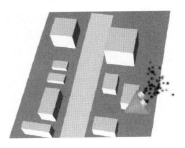

Figure 10.26 **Painting in time and applying automated effects.** A polluting spaceship is depicted with the help of a particle system trail drawn in real time by the artist.

front of the viewer. Hackenberg's video becomes hauntingly beautiful through her editing techniques, in which she expands time to approximately ½ real time speed, and consequently creates sexually and psychologically charged images" [Karlin, 1995].

The intersection between video and the computer brings into video production not only a new tool—the nonlinear digital editing system—but also new aesthetics and new ties to other art disciplines. True, an artist can use a digital video system to create exactly the same type of work as when using analog video. But as soon as the video information is digitized it takes on a new relationship with other digitized data and can be worked with in new ways. For example, it can be combined with other media types (see Chapter 11, Multimedia and Interactivity), processed through various filters and effects (see Chapter 2), and created and distributed by more than one artist in more than one place (see Chapter 12, The World Wide Web).

In turn, video brings to computer art its own distinctive aesthetic strategies, narratives, and logic. The sometimes slow-moving, exploratory, self-reflexive nature of much video art, for instance, obviously has influenced a number of Web-based works. "Videotapes are boring if you demand that they be something else. But they're not judged boring by comparison with paintings or sculpture, they're judged boring in comparison with television, which for the last twenty years has set the standard of video time" [Antin, 1986, p. 155].

Video can be combined with other types of touch, such as digital painting. Painting modules in video effects programs and specialized software such as Strata Media-Paint let videographers and animators paint over movies as they play. Effects range from **rotoscoping** (painting in effects by hand, frame by frame, as was done to create the light sabres in *Star Wars*) to controlling the position and other aspects of automated processes such as particle systems and filters that act over time (see Fig. 10.26).

10.4.3 COMPOSITING OVER TIME

Relative motion across the screen is not the only factor in creating an illusion of space for 2D animations. How the images layer, or composite, can dramatically affect the final visual message of an animated work. Mattes or masks (the two terms have become virtually interchangeable in the computer graphics world) and compositing effects are powerful ways of composing moving objects on the screen and creating the illusion of 3D and "2½ D" or relief-style spaces. Many interesting visual effects can be created by assigning different composition rules for overlapping graphics. One object can pass over another with a set degree of transparency, a specified color can be made transparent, or one object can cause the other to change colors in overlap areas (see Fig. 10.27). Such compositing operations are the same as those used in 2D raster programs (transparency, darkening, lightening, etc.) (see Chapter 2). Depending on the program, compositing effects are applied to each graphic individually or to entire layers.

An alpha channel can be used to create editable mattes or protected areas of an image (see Chapter 2) that can be controlled as separate objects to create moving areas

Figure 10.27 **Different compositing methods create a range of visual effects and a variety of different spatial cues about object relationships.** (a) In this animation of a spaceship flying over a background, the white rectangle around the ship makes it look 2D. (b) The color white is "dropped out" and the areas around the ship become transparent, making it look more 3D. (c) The image is drawn only where it is darker than the background. The ship now flies below a surface of cut-out shapes. (d) Light areas of the ship become transparent, giving it a ghostly appearance.

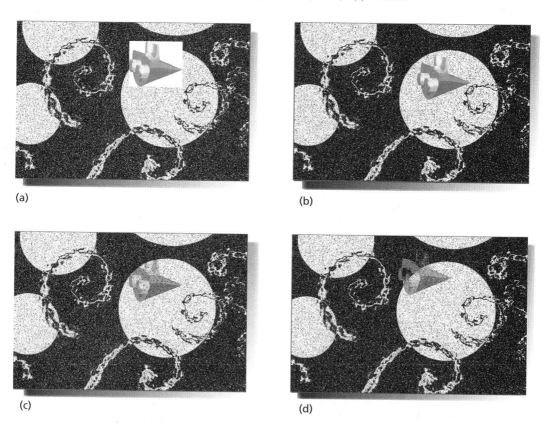

(a)

(b)

(c)

(d)

of transparency. Transparent areas in a moving image can be difficult to outline for each frame by hand; instead the computer can make a chosen color transparent or "drop out" a color, also called **chromakeying.** However, the color to be discarded must not appear anywhere else in the image, or see-through holes will result. Traditionally, **blue screens,** or bright blue or green backdrops, have been used to shoot scenes that will later be composited with different backgrounds. Effects that employ compositing methods serve not only to organize images in time, but also to integrate them in the highly constrained space suggested by 2D object and layer-stacking order. For instance, an object in a lower layer may slowly become visible as an upper layer object becomes transparent or acts as a partial mask. In Fig. 10.28, for example, color keying, compositing effects, and a changing matte shape are all important aspects of the composition.

The different approaches to orchestrating elements in 2D and 3D animation programs can be combined. Two-dimensional hand-drawn animations or 3D animation

Figure 10.28 Composing with layer or sprite interactions and masks. Several composition effects in Adobe After Effects. (a) A color is dropped out to create a composite image. (b) A text layer is moved across a background layer. (c) A changing mask reveals a background image. *(Courtesy Adobe Systems, Inc.)*

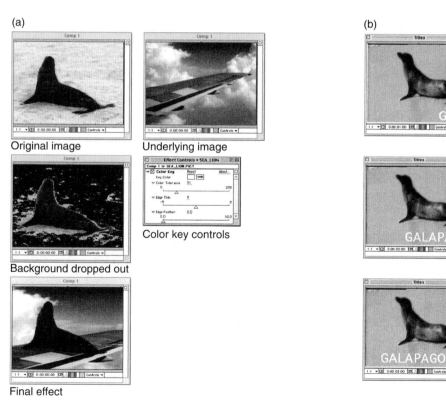

(a)

Original image

Underlying image

Background dropped out

Color key controls

Final effect

(b)

Mask creation area

 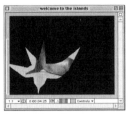 

(c)

Mask moving and changing shape to reveal the entire image

Figure 10.28 (Continued)

footage can be incorporated into a video composition. Video pieces and 2D animations can be projected onto surfaces in a 3D work, and 3D scenes can be used as backdrops to animated 2D characters. Both types of programs can be used to create sketches and storyboards for traditional animation or live action.

As shown in Fig. 10.29, Alex Rivera's *Papapapá* (*Potatofather*) presents a narrative of transformations by following the immigration of the artist's father and the historical

Figure 10.29 Alex Rivera, *Papapapá*, 1996 (video). In this sequence, the computer is used as a nonlinear editor and to apply text. Different images, related thematically but not physically, are placed one after another in rapid, transitionless cuts. In addition to photography, a 3D physical model of a man made of wires, a paper man (the artist's father, Augusto), a Pringles can, and a map are used as stop-motion animation props. Augusto, placed in the Pringles can by the wire-figure, is blasted off into space. *(Courtesy of Alex Rivera)*

Figure 10.30 Alex Rivera, *Papapapá*, 1996 (video). Blasted into orbit, Augusto lands in a "cyberbarrio" that integrates 3D computer models, 2D still and moving textures, and live video footage. Here he meets a 3D Pringles character, and TV sequences (often with rolling static) are displayed on large screens throughout the space. After the 3D adventure ends, the viewer is returned to straight video footage of a man buying potatoes in an American grocery store. *(Courtesy of Alex Rivera)*

importation of potatoes. "The stories of these two disparate immigrants, the potato, and my pop, converge as Augusto Rivera becomes a Peruvian couch potato, sitting on the American sofa, eating potato chips and watching Spanish language television" [Rivera, 1997]. The story continues in Fig. 10.30, ending with a scene from real life. "Rivera shows that what is referred to as 'cyberspace' is a space long inhabited by immigrants who find themselves distanced and not really a part of their new world" [Salas, 1995].

10.4.4 POINTS OF VIEW

In both 2D and 3D animations, a storyboard or other planning device is generally used to plan the sequence of different points of view in a piece. The point of view is easy to identify in a 3D program because it is defined by positioning a physical camera object. It can easily be experimented with simply by adjusting the camera and reshooting a desired sequence.

In a strictly 2D program, however, points of view must be carefully structured in advance because they determine how certain objects are drawn and animated, which objects to set in motion when, how objects should move relative to one another, and what is visible or hidden as objects move past one another. This conceptual design process is the same as in traditional animation: Is the story or sequence seen from a character's point of view? How far apart are the characters? Is the camera moving or still? Is the scene itself in motion? Are both moving at the same time? Where do you want to focus the viewer's attention? Such choices can be difficult to orchestrate correctly. And since, as in a 2D program these choices depend entirely on the point of view chosen,

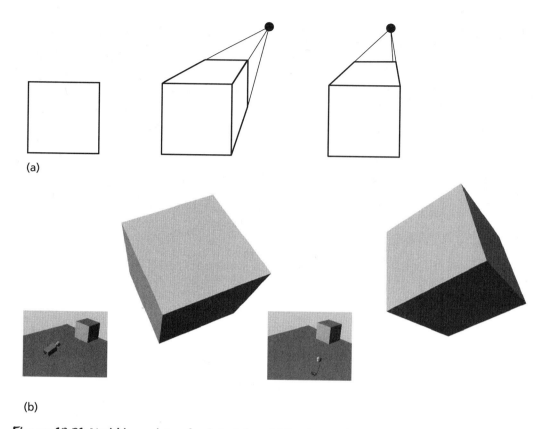

(b)

Figure 10.31 Vanishing point and point of view. (a) To change the point of view in a 2D program, the artist must place a new vanishing point, recalculate the perspective, and redraw the objects. (b) In a 3D program, the artist can simply adjust the camera to generate another view of a 3D object.

reshooting the animation from another point of view can entail redesigning the appearance and motion of each element.

In contrast, in 3D programs, choosing a camera, or viewpoint, determines in part how the objects move relative to one another. The different approaches to using points of view as a compositional tool in 2D and 3D animation programs are analogous to depicting a structure in perspective. In a 3D program, the artist changes the camera position, and the software automatically creates a new drawing. Although the artist has not had to make the new image pixel by pixel (or path by path), neither can the artist change it that way. In a 2D program, the artist must redraw the building "by hand" to see another side of it but directly controls the appearance of the drawing by choosing the vanishing point(s) (see Fig. 10.31).

Design Space Versus Display Space

In 3D programs, the artist designs and observes the motion of the objects from many angles and with different cameras before "filming" them for a final cut. The distinction between the working space and the final production space has been described by Alvy Ray Smith as a distinction between a **design space** and a **display space.** With animated 3D works, the design space is the 3D world seen on the screen. The display space is a sequence of 2D images representing a necessarily restricted view of that world. In addition to providing a different spatial experience, the final product often is presented in a different medium, such as video or film.

In traditional 2D animation, the separation of design and display space is apparent not only in the generation of separate cels for layering motions, but also in the use of the **animation camera.** Analogies to this important tool in traditional animation also exist in 2D computer animations: Translating or rotating a frame can simulate panning and rotating the ani-

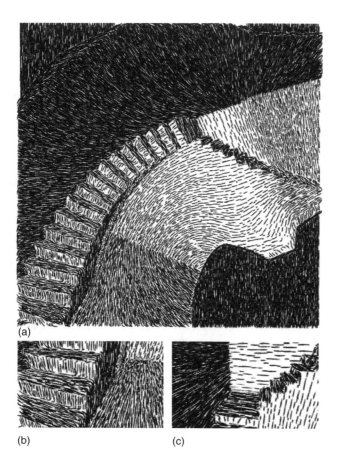

(a)

(b)   (c)

Figure 10.32 A distorted-looking design space used to create a spatially convincing display space. (a) This distorted 2D image is designed to create a convincing animated sequence from the point of view of someone walking up a flight of stairs. The 2D composition was generated automatically by a 3D program and rendered with pen and ink rendering style. (b) and (c) These two frames can be found within the image in (a). Finding (b) is easy, but finding (c) is a bit trickier. *(Courtesy of Daniel Wood, Adam Finkelstein, John Hughes, Craig Thayer, and David Salesin)*

mation camera, scaling can simulate zooming, blurring can simulate depth of field, and moving between layers can suggest 3D motion parallax.

Skillful and creative camera motions allow a 2D image to be the basis for what looks like a film or animation of a 3D world. In a technique known as a **filmograph,** a single still image is panned and zoomed through a small viewing window to create an animated journey through the scene.

Even more dramatic examples of the separation of design from display space are the complex **multiperspective panoramas** that animation studios sometimes use to create convincing "3D" shots (see Fig. 10.32) [Wood, 1997]. These images look bizarrely distorted but when "revealed just a little at a time through a small, moving window . . . the resulting animation provides a surprisingly compelling 3D effect" [Wood, 1997, pp. 243–250]. Creating these panoramas is difficult, but new computer methods may help the artist partially automate the process: A 3D computer graphics scene, resembling the space desired by an animator, is used to generate automatically a composition for a multiperspective panorama (and specifications for viewing it) that can be used as a guide for painting the actual image. In addition to automating part of the process, this technique makes possible combining 2D multiperspective panoramas with live action and 3D computer graphics effects.

10.4.5 Transitions

As in traditional animation and video, **transitions** such as *dissolves, fades,* and *wipes* can soften a sudden change between camera angles or different scenes. In computer-based work, complex transitions can be used just as easily as simple ones. Many programs contain a large selection of transitions (see Fig. 10.33), and elaborate transitional effects at first may seem quite compelling. However, a fancy transition used for its own sake becomes more like an animation segment or a *special effect* in its own right, and often is distracting.

The most common transitional effects mimic traditional dissolves and wipes. **Dissolves**, or **fades,** replace one image with another by replacing the pixels in a random-looking overall pattern. The user can control the size of the areas being replaced (from single pixels to larger, blocky-looking areas), the speed with which one image dissolves into another, and other factors. **Wipes** include traditional effects such as wiping from left to right (or in other directions), which makes one image appear to slide atop another, or more complex wipes, as when the halves of an image split down the middle to reveal a new image beneath (often called *barn doors*), or when one image replaces

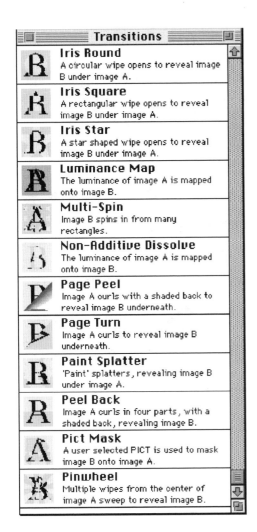

Transitions

Iris Round
A circular wipe opens to reveal image B under image A.

Iris Square
A rectangular wipe opens to reveal image B under image A.

Iris Star
A star shaped wipe opens to reveal image B under image A.

Luminance Map
The luminance of image A is mapped onto image B.

Multi-Spin
Image B spins in from many rectangles.

Non-Additive Dissolve
The luminance of image A is mapped onto image B.

Page Peel
Image A curls with a shaded back to reveal image B underneath.

Page Turn
Image A curls to reveal image B underneath.

Paint Splatter
'Paint' splatters, revealing image B under image A.

Peel Back
Image A curls in four parts, with a shaded back, revealing image B.

Pict Mask
A user selected PICT is used to mask image B onto image A.

Pinwheel
Multiple wipes from the center of image A sweep to reveal image B.

Figure 10.33 A portion of the Adobe Premiere® menu of transition effects.
(Courtesy of Adobe Systems, Inc.)

another through an intermediate checkerboard pattern in which the two images are interwoven. Because people are used to seeing them in TV and movies, these transitions usually are not even noticed but work subconsciously to smooth view and scene changes.

Another class of transitions, perhaps more accurately called effects, provides much more noticeable intermediate steps. These include page turning—one image seems to peel off from an underlying one—to transitions that become short cuts in and of themselves—as when an image is folded up into a 3D cube that spins to reveal a new image that is then unfolded onto the screen. In Fig. 10.34 a transition from one scene to another is handled with a range of transitions and effects.

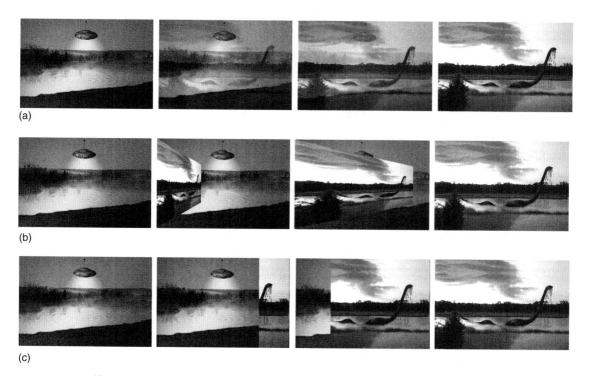

(a)

(b)

(c)

Figure 10.34 Transition examples. (a) Dissolve. (b) Spin in. (c) Wipe.

10.4.6 Object Interaction

So far, the discussion of the relative movement of objects has addressed keyframing, interpolation, and calculated image interactions due to matting and other image composition effects. Many of the most effective animation techniques, however, depend on the interactions of objects. They affect the viewer's understanding of the space in which the objects and characters are interacting, often either explicitly supporting or refuting an established level of visual realism. When the coyote paints a fake highway on a rock wall in an effort to fool the road runner into running full speed into a hard surface, we see a perspective landscape of the mountain valley, the brush bending against the rock, the paint dripping, and other visual cues that correspond with reality as we know it. When the road runner comes running up, the viewers expect him to crash into the rock face. Instead he runs right into the painting, which has mysteriously become a real highway (until the coyote tries to enter it, of course). The success of such stunts, from cartoons to surrealistic scenes in feature films, depends on establishing convincing object behaviors and interactions.

In 2D programs, almost all such interaction effects are created by hand, involving the use of keyframes that show the extreme positions of objects interacting, colliding and bouncing off one another, and falling as if affected by gravity. This process forces the artist to examine and understand the nature of the movement and interaction. It also enables the artist to vary that motion easily, as in traditional exaggeration techniques such as *squash and stretch, delayed timing,* and *preparatory gestures.* Some interactions, however, are extremely difficult to convey reliably in this manner, and others are just so complex that they are prohibitively time-consuming to design by hand.

Many object interactions, such as collisions (see Fig. 10.35) and the effects of gravity, can be automated in both 2D and 3D programs, although primarily in 3D. Like automatic spatial calculations, automated object behavior and interaction can be extraordinarily powerful and desirable tools. However, just as artists often want to vary the mathematically correct perspective of a 3D scene, automated interaction often works best as an initial structure that artists can refine by hand.

Figure 10.35 Collision detection. (a) 3D objects, if not otherwise instructed, follow their preset animation paths and simply pass through one another. (b) Collision detection automatically changes the path of an object when it meets a surface, simulating a real-life collision. Here the ball is programmed to bounce off of other objects.

(a)

(b)

10.5 Concepts in 3D Animation

The 3D animator is in some senses a videographer, shooting action that takes place in the 3D world of the computer. Setting up the animation itself, however, usually is not at all like directing live characters or shooting physical models. As in 2D animation, the animator often uses keyframes, but, because of the added complexity of 3D graphics, needs to keyframe and interpolate many more object properties. In addition to the extra dimension in moving, rotating, and scaling objects, the animator must take surface qualities and lighting into account. Fortunately, more types of motion can be automated in 3D than in 2D programs.

The coordination of object and camera motion is based on the same conceptual framework as 2D animation: keyframes and interpolation along motion paths. With these tools, the animator can have a camera zoom in on a scene, track a specific object, and move along a motion path. The animator also can animate lights by changing their position, intensity, color, or other parameters.

10.5.1 2D Versus 3D Animated Work

As with 2D programs, the animator can explicitly control over time most of the operations that go into making a 3D model in the first place (e.g., creating objects, repositioning them, changing their attributes, positioning lights, and working with cameras) with 3D animation programs. Many of the concepts behind such controls are the same as for 2D programs (e.g., keyframing, interpolation, and motion blur). The following concepts, however, are based on capabilities that usually appear only in 3D program environments. Three-dimensional computer animation is a vital and growing field that is often heavily technical in nature, and the following descriptions cover only its most basic aspects.

10.5.2 Using Hierarchy

The **hierarchical structure** used to build a static 3D object is important for modeling and even more crucial for animation. If an object's hierarchy has been poorly conceived in the modeling phase, animating the object correctly will be difficult, if not impossible. When the animator is positioning objects for keyframes, for instance, a correct and useful hierarchy permits easy movement of the entire object and positioning it in a range of natural poses that are consistent with the object's design (see Fig. 10.36). When the model's constraints are correct, not only is setting up keyframes much easier, but inbetween frames also are guaranteed to represent possible positions. Hierarchy also is the basis for many of the most sophisticated and frequently used types of automation in 3D graphics, such as inverse kinematics, discussed in the next section.

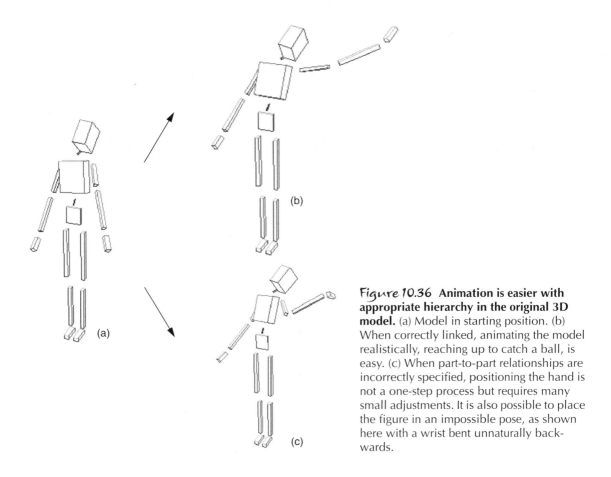

Figure 10.36 Animation is easier with appropriate hierarchy in the original 3D model. (a) Model in starting position. (b) When correctly linked, animating the model realistically, reaching up to catch a ball, is easy. (c) When part-to-part relationships are incorrectly specified, positioning the hand is not a one-step process but requires many small adjustments. It is also possible to place the figure in an impossible pose, as shown here with a wrist bent unnaturally backwards.

10.5.3 AUTOMATED MOTION

FORWARD KINEMATICS   In some cases, using specific key-frame positions is not the easiest way to specify object motions. **Forward kinematics,** usually simply called **kinematics,** are rules for motion based on a geometry of rigid objects connected with constrained joints that can be used to create an animation sequence without keyframing. Given a beginning position for an object and a rule for its motion, such as "move in this direction at this speed," you can calculate new positions according to kinematics for any number of additional frames. If planes in an animation are supposed to fly at a certain speed, for instance, you can use kinematics to control them. This process cannot take into account the effect of your object's motion on the rest of the model, but it may be sufficient in modeling the motion of individual elements that do not interact with one another. Kinematics is particularly useful for setting up parts of an animation in which an

When 3D Models Meet
the embarassing social consequences of lacking inverse kinematics

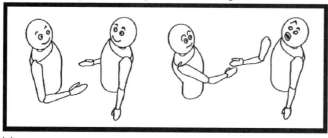

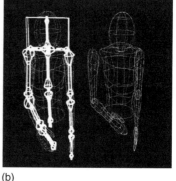

(a)

(b)

Figure 10.37 Inverse kinematics. (a) Two models meet to shake hands. Everything seems fine. But the model at the right lacks IK, and when its hand is moved forward, its entire arm rigidly follows, detaching from its body. The model at the left, however, has IK and the movement of its hand causes the rest of its arm to move in a natural manner. (b) A wireframe view of the two models shows that the one on the left has an IK skeleton but that the one on the right lacks any such relationships between its different parts.

object's final location is less important than how it gets there. For hierarchical models, kinematics alone often does not produce natural motions. The movement of a person's hand, say, can be defined kinematically, but as a hand rarely moves in isolation from the wrist, lower arm, and even upper arm, the movement probably will not look realistic.

INVERSE KINEMATICS   In forward kinematics, the end position and rotation of the object are not known; only its motion is known. In **inverse kinematics** (IK), a desired final position and rotation are achieved by creating movement within given constraints (e.g, hierarchical links). Inverse kinematics is more complex than forward kinematics because a given final position typically can be achieved through any of infinitely many different movements. Inverse kinematics systems must solve many equations at once and weigh possible scenarios by trying to achieve some goal such as minimal overall motion.

Consider a modeled figure with joints connecting the hand to the lower arm and the lower arm to the upper arm. Without inverse kinematics, if the artist repositions the hand it will move, but the lower and upper arm will not change positions in a natural way (see Fig. 10.37). This solution is only one of the many that are possible with inverse kinematics. Three-dimensional animation software considers not just the model's links or skeleton structure, but also preset constraints for achieving the best motion paths, such as finding the solution that involves the least overall motion.

Inverse kinematics uses an iterative process to take advantage of the constraints and hierarchy of the model. In order to move the hand, for instance, the 3D program must first consider the effect of the hand's motion on the lower arm, the lower arm's influence on the upper arm, and so on. In animating a running 3D figure, the use of links and inverse kinematics can ensure that every frame represents a physically possible position.

FORWARD AND INVERSE DYNAMICS   **Dynamics** are rules of motion based on laws of physics, such as $f = ma$ (force = mass $\times$ acceleration), used to add **physically based behavior** to an animation (refer back to Fig. 10.1). In an animation using forward dynamics and a gravity factor, the motion of a dropped object depends on the acceleration of gravity. Unlike kinematics, dynamics calculations are based on the ever-changing positions and motions of the objects in the animation and thus cannot be calculated for any frame before the calculations for all previous frames have been completed. In Fig. 10.38, a metal sphere with a given weight and friction with the floor and con-

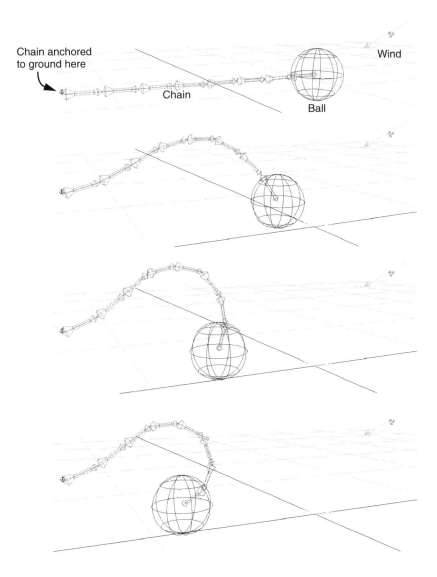

Chain anchored
to ground here

Chain

Wind

Ball

Figure 10.38 Dynamics and inverse kinematics. Animation of a ball and chain affected by wind.

nected to the floor by a chain is pushed by a wind. Although dynamics is used to calculate the position of the ball, inverse kinematics is used to calculate the changing position of the chain. Even this somewhat complicated animation ignores various factors, such as an expected rotation of the ball, the wind's effect on the chain, and the friction between links of the chain.

Inverse dynamics is used to figure out the forces necessary for a model to arrive at a desired location. It also is based on physical laws such as $f = ma$, but here they are used to calculate the force necessary for an object to reach a given position at a given time. As with inverse kinematics, solutions for inverse dynamics may be far from obvious and some limiting condition must be used; for instance, the force needed to get the object to the right place at the right time along the shortest possible path could be calculated.

BEHAVIORAL MODELING AND ANIMATION   Although the behaviors of many real-world systems cannot be adequately represented by forward and inverse kinematics and dynamics, they still can be animated with a computer by using more advanced behavioral animation rules. In fact, "Behavioral modeling blurs the distinction between modeling and animation" [Barzel, 1997]. The laws of physics can be applied to animations of objects colliding and to such complex phenomena as the tearing of fabric, animal movement and reactions, or complex machinery. Like the modeling of light and materials, much modeling of object behaviors attempts to simulate real-world phenomena (see Fig. 10.39).

Automation can also go beyond simulating mechanical operations and draw on **artificial intelligence** to produce 3D objects that display emotional behaviors and can be programmed with personality traits such as a desire to follow other objects around and interact with them. Effects such as bird flocking and fish schooling (see Fig. 10.40) are more common examples than are characters with developed personalities. Automated and artificially intelligent behavior is even more important in interactive animations (see Chapter 11, Multimedia and Interactivity), in which artists can create visual pieces that are not composed of prescribed frames.

Figure 10.39 Gene Greger and David Breen, *End of the Season*, 1993. The draping behavior of the cloth is simulated with a particle-based model utilizing empirical mechanical data from real samples of woven cloth. *(Courtesy of David Breen)*

Figure 10.40 **Rhythm & Hues,** *Business School* **(created for Andersen Consulting), 1995.** A pun on "school," this 3D animation coordinates schooling fish to form a larger fish, their former predator. *(Courtesy of Andersen Consulting and Young and Rubicam Advertising)*

PARTICLE SYSTEMS   I briefly discussed **particle systems** for simulating difficult-to-model phenomena such as smoke, fire, vapor, and explosions in Chapter 6. Because 3D modeling programs focus mainly on solids and surfaces, the user tends to think in terms of distinct, well-defined objects—the space between and inside those objects is largely untouchable. Particle systems offer a way of animating this space and providing different types of marks.

Char Davies uses particle systems in her immersive virtual-reality piece *Osmose.* She strives to create a sense of organic form and structure to support participants' explorations of the relationships between self and the world. Participants leave their familiar surroundings and constraints and enter one of a dozen virtual worlds based on elements of nature, including a forest, leaf, pond, abyss, cloud, and subterranean earth, as shown in Fig. 10.41. (See the discussion of the Osmose interface in Chapter 11, Multimedia and Interactivity.)

A particle system is an algorithmically controlled mass of small solid shapes that are automatically created and linked to simulate movement of a single, often nebulous, phenomenon. The artist can choose the shape of the particles, the rate of creation and extinction, the direction of travel, the density of the system, and other such parameters. Particle systems can create realistic simulations of visual events such as moving flames, clouds, water droplets, explosions, and others that are impossible to model in other ways.

Like other features of computer graphics programs, particle systems and flocking behaviors can be used to simulate real-world phenomena and add realism to a model or animation. The artist also can use them abstractly by choosing particle shapes and behaviors that encourage expressive visual effects unrelated to real phenomena.

10.5.4 MOTION CAPTURE

An alternative approach to deriving 3D motion synthetically is to sample it from real-world objects and living things. In **motion capture,** sensors are attached to relevant points of a moving object to track moving figures and record their motion. Motion

Figure 10.41 Char Davies, *Osmose*, 1995. (a) *Pond,* real-time frame captures from the immersive virtual environment. (b) *Subterranean Earth,* real-time frame capture. Throughout *Osmose,* space is experienced by the immersed participant as being bodily enveloping. This spatial sensibility, along with use of particle systems and an ambiguous, semi-abstract visual aesthetic, contributes greatly to the evocative power of the work. *(Courtesy of Char Davies and Softimage, Inc.)*

(a)

(b)

Figure 10.42 Motion capture.
Motion sensors placed at key locations of a person (or animal or moving object) can be used to animate a 3D model.

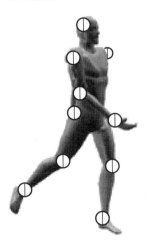

recorded in this way is associated with parts of a 3D model, which are made to move accordingly. Motion capture can rapidly bring subtle, difficult-to-simulate movements into a 3D animation, such as animals running and human facial expressions. Because motion capture does not require the complex calculations of techniques such as IK, it can also be used to support real-time interaction with 3D characters in a scenario in which a live actor's motion controls a 3D model (see Fig. 10.42).

Motion capture sometimes provides speed of production and realism at the expense of art. In animation, artists rarely draw motions by slavishly copying real-world phenomena, and usually must skillfully exaggerate or subsequently filter or tweak by hand motion-captured acting for it to become inspiring animation. This process often is made difficult by the large amounts and unwieldy formatting of the data captured. Motion capture is also limited to the motions that can be performed in the real world.

Conclusion

> *Cinematographic and videographic techniques—the artisanal invention of dissolves, feedback, slow-motion and time-lapse, zoom, live and delayed broadcast—now appear to have been pre-monitory signs, symptoms of a derealization of sensory appearances [Virilio, 1991, p. 111].*

Does the computer change perception of time and space? Certainly computer technology has changed methods of communication and has sped up many processes and activities. This social change has progressed in parallel with technical changes in the way that motion is evoked in time-based art work. The vertiginous rapid cutting of MTV—a high-intensity barrage of visual material that many viewers find impossible to process—reflects a need for speed and compression of information that is both spurred on and satisfied by new digital technologies. Nonlinear digital editing encourages complexly interwoven materials, numerous cuts, jumps, and transitional effects. Artists who consciously work against this torrent serve to reveal its presence in people's daily lives even more sharply.

The technology of frame creation, from linear inbetweening to morphing to 3D automated movement, makes things both easier and harder for artists who are using the computer. True, they can now achieve certain previously tedious effects at the press of a button, but when they use automated techniques without an understanding of the underlying concepts, they can all too easily become mired in complex technical problems or produce lifeless animations. Artists must balance the convenience and power of these automated processes against traditional hands-on control over the exact motion and appearance of images, volumes, and characters.

The ease with which motion can be created on the computer or added to still images remains a thrill, even when the artist is working through the night to finish a project. (Like a gourmet meal, the design process takes an extraordinary amount of time compared with the display process.) The animation or "bringing to life" of fictional characters, abstract relationships between color and form, and entire 3D worlds is a magical process.

Suggested Readings

Many of the books in the suggested readings for Chapters 7 and 8 also cover animation (see Kerlow, *The Art of 3-D Computer Animation and Imaging;* O'Rourke, *Three-Dimensional Computer Animation: Modeling, Rendering, and Animating with 3D Computer Graphics;* and Foley, et al., *Computer Graphics, Principles and Practice.*)

In addition, the *SIGGRAPH Annual Conference Proceedings* mentioned in the suggested readings for Chapters 7 and 8 contain papers, panel topics, and elements of the art show that involve animation. Each year the *SIGGRAPH Electronic Theater* presents a selection of ground-breaking examples of time-based computer work. Tapes are available from ACM SIGGRAPH.

Several books on theory from previous recommended readings contain writings relevant to time-based computer work; see Druckrey (ed.), *Electronic Culture: Technology and Visual Representation;* Benedikt (ed.), *Cyberspace: First Steps;* Lovejoy, *Postmodern Currents: Art and Artists in the Age of Electronic Media.*

Virilio, Paul. *Lost Dimension.* Semiotext(e), 1991. A text with cultlike status among theorists and computer artists. Virilio's writing style borders on the incomprehensible but when decipherable reveals a technological nexus of many disciplines. The subject matter is, roughly speaking, how technology has changed culture by altering people's perceptions of space and time.

Hanhardt, John G. (ed.). *Video Culture, A Critical Investigation.* Visual Studies Workshop Press, 1986. Includes essays on theory and practice, video and television, and film and video: differences and futures.

Exercises

1. *Motion discipline.* Create a short piece with a sequence of still images of your own design. At any point in the piece, introduce some motion into one of these images. What retroactive effect does the motion have on the experience of viewing previous still frames? On the frames that follow this motion? Suggested film viewing: Chris Marker's *La Jetée* (inspiration for Terry Gilliam's more recent film, *12 Monkeys*).

> With Macromedia Director 6.5: Use a program such as Adobe Photoshop or MetaCreations Painter to prepare a sequence of still images (start with 10). These can come from digital camera input, scanned images, or can be created on the computer. Make all the images the same size (same pixel dimensions, resolution, and color-depth). Use the File:Import . . . dialog box to bring the files into Director. Drag the files from the Cast Window into the Score window, arranging them sequentially. Each should take up about 40 frames. Use the Control Panel to play your movie. The changes from one image to the next are abrupt. Experiment with transitions: Click on the first frame of one of your images in the Score and choose Modify:Frame:Transition. . . . After designing the transitions, select the last image in the cast, choose copy, and click in the next Cast space. Paste the image. Double-click on the copy of your final image in the cast to bring it up in Director's painting program. Choose View:Onion Skin and let the previous image become partly visible. Modify one part of the image slightly. Select the whole image (Edit:Select All), copy it, create a new cast member using the small black "+" button in the upper left of the paint area, and paste. Continue the modification. (Repeat this step several times if necessary to complete the animation.) Play your movie using the Control Panel. Adjust the timing as necessary.

2. *Mining a single image.* Find or make an image that has undeveloped humorous potential. Using two or three of the frame-creation techniques discussed in this chapter (e.g., hand-drawn frames, linear and nonlinear inbetweening, morphing, or filmograph), create a short narrative by using elements of the image, with parts of the image as a backdrop.

> With Macromedia Director 6.5: For artists and designers who don't have access to a video camera, the filmograph technique can turn a still image into a motion picture. Begin with a

detailed image depicting a landscape or interior. Import the image and drag it into the Score, stretching it to cover several hundred frames. Set the Stage size to be much smaller than the entire image using Modify:Movie:Properties . . . . To animate the image, first create a new keyframe by option-clicking (Mac) or Alt-clicking (PC) on the first keyframe (it looks like a small, unfilled circle) and dragging it. (Repeat to create additional keyframes.) Next, click on the new keyframe and move the image on the Stage. Click the next keyframe and move the image somewhere else. Play back the movie to get a sense of the effect, which should resemble panning over the scene. Try resetting the scale in Modify:Sprite: Properties to simulate zooming in and out of parts of the landscape or interior. Use these simulated camera motions to create a narrative movie from the single image.

3. *Sense of touch and style in interpolation.* Using several of the interpolation methods described in this chapter, create short animations in which the methods used give the pieces different feelings and even different meanings. Do the positioning of frames and the interpolation methods play a similar role to hand-drawn gestures in a still piece, for instance by giving the piece a sense of style or personal touch? Explain.

With Macromedia Director 6.5: Set up several keyframes for a small sprite, say a balloon that will fly through the air. Design part of the balloon's flight with basic linear interpolation. Add further parts of the flight, experimenting with curvature and easing in Modify:Sprite:Tweening.

4. *Well-defined space.* Use one or more of the motion techniques discussed in Section 10.4 (e.g., velocity relationships, perspective techniques such as converging parallel lines, scale, mist/color change, layering, and element orchestration) to create a realistic space. How does the nature of the space convey your artistic intentions? (This exercise can be in done in 2D or 3D.)

With Macromedia Director 6.5: Design pieces of a landscape in Director's painting program or import them from another application. Arrange the pieces in the Score with the closer ones in higher-numbered channels. The overlapping effect immediately gives some sense of space. Now animate the sprites in accordance with the rules in Section 10.4 to create convincing spatial relationships through motion. Use keyframes to pace the movement of each sprite. Use the paint program within Director to add a bluish cast to images in the distance.

5. *IK special.* Create a simple creature in a 3D program. Experiment with different IK setups to give the model a personality when it is animated. For example, unlikely parts could be linked to make the model move in unexpected ways.

With Strata Studio Pro 2.5: Begin by creating an IK chain in a new document. Use the Bones tool in the Extensions Palette to click and drag out a bone. Click on the end of the first bone and drag to create a second bone. Repeat to create several bones. Draw some additional bones from various bone endpoints to form branches or arms. Using the primitives tools from the main Tool palette, create geometry around each bone. Your creature can look like a known animal or plant or can be from outer space. Use different views to be sure the body parts are aligned over individual bones. Choose Modeling:Reshape to bring up special IK tools in the main Tool palette. Open the Project Window and move the Cut-out Point marker to 30 seconds. Drag the Current Time marker to 15 seconds. Use the Resolve Tool from the main Tool palette to drag the end of the last bone. The entire creature should move in accordance with its bone structure. Play back the animation with the cassette-style buttons in the upper left of the Project Window. Continue refining the geometry and animation.

CHAPTER 11

Multimedia and Interactivity

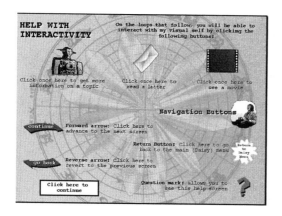

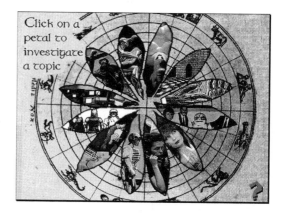

Figure 11.1 **Christine Tamblyn, *She Loves It, She Loves It Not: Women and Technology,* 1993.** This interactive CD-ROM is both an art piece and an instructional work exploring the relationships between women and technology. The user chooses from categories such as Power, Interactivity, Representation, and Communication, all arranged in a daisy-petal display (upper right). Each category contains images, text, video clips, and sound. "The visual aesthetic of the piece has a hand-made collaged look . . . deliberately [avoiding] the slick sterility of much computer art. Its content combines aspects of an academic essay or documentary film with a poetic series of associated links between graphics, film, text, and sound elements" [Tamblyn, 1994, p. 163]. *(Courtesy of the Estate of Christine Tamblyn)*

11.1 INTRODUCTION

Making art work with more than one medium is not a novel concept: Theater, opera, movies, mixed-media art work, and much performance art have long routinely coordinated a variety of media. **Computer-based multimedia** (or simply **multimedia**) is a broad term that describes several types of computer work, but only one medium—the digital data handled by the computer. Here *multi* refers to the various types of data and input and output that are combined into a single creation. Although graphics (including 2D and 3D, stills, animation and video), text, and sound/music are all common in multimedia, other types of data and devices are also used. They include motion sensing (a user's body motions become part of a piece), force feedback, voice and handwriting recognition, and output or feedback via printers or other devices controlled by the computer. Although the different media used in computer-based multimedia may not be physical, the field involves many of the same aesthetic challenges that more traditional multimedia productions offer, from coordinating complex integration of images, sound, and verbal material to working with teams of people and worrying about funding and distribution.

In this chapter I describe basic concepts and issues in multimedia and the **authoring tools,** or **environments,** used to create multimedia works. I introduce the terminology and working processes of these often complex programs and discuss the aesthetic and theoretical issues raised by several multimedia artists. My focus is on works that draw from the principles of computer graphics and thus are chiefly visual in nature.

Just as desktop publishing tools were once the domain of graphic artists and professional typesetters, computer-based multimedia used to be primarily the prerogative of film studios and other organizations that could afford powerful workstations and expert personnel. With the influx of cheaper and more powerful personal computers and multimedia software that nonprogrammers can easily use has come *desktop multimedia*.

Multimedia computers are relatively powerful personal desktop or laptop computers with additional components that make multimedia creations easier to produce and use. These components may include a large, fast internal hard drive, CD-ROM drive, additional RAM, acceleration cards for image display and for common 3D graphics operations (simple shading, texture mapping, and basic geometric transformations), a sound card, stereo speakers, and a video capture and conversion card (for digitizing video footage and recording onto video tape). Hardware **codec** (compression and decompression) devices make using long video or animation segments more feasible. All of these components (except the video conversion card, which is not used for playback) are helpful in both creating and experiencing multimedia works.

11.1.1 INTERACTIVITY

> *In its present form, equipment like television or film does not serve communication but prevents it. It allows no reciprocal action between transmitter and receiver; technically speaking, it reduces feedback to the lowest point compatible with the system [Enzensberger, 1986, p. 98].*
>
> Hans Magnus Enzensberger, poet and cultural critic

Interactive multimedia lets users communicate with the work. It not only engages their visual or aural attention but demands of them some type of action—for example different navigational choices or information used to modify images or characters. The term *interactive* usually implies a level of user decision making well beyond that of traditional media. Readers of a book, for example, make navigational choices by turning pages or using an index, but users of an interactive work have more powerful and flexible navigational options and can even influence characters, plot lines, and visual aspects of a work.

The potential for interactive TV and radio mentioned in the preceding quote is still largely unexplored, although products and services merging the TV and the computer are slowly becoming a reality. Instead, interactive computer-based art work had its artistic beginnings in the happenings of the 1960s, including performance art and groups such as Fluxus, and in kinetic mechanical and electronic sculptures that respond to viewer movement and sound. Theories of interactivity owe their start to these movements and to literary critics such as Roland Barthes who sought to involve the reader of a text as a cocreator of its meaning. That is, the reader could deconstruct a text in terms of the cultural influences upon it, experiencing it as one part of a larger, interconnected body of material (and often expanding its meaning beyond what the original author may have conceived).

Avant-Garde and Postmodern artists and theorists also set the stage for interactive multimedia by working against closure and the notion of "art objects." Although the theory was largely abstract, it became a reality with the advent of **hypertext,** which is interactive text that lets readers add their own comments and follow different narrative pathways. All these endeavors seek to break the unwritten assumption that art involves a viewer who passively contemplates a "masterpiece," made in a different place and often a different time by someone with whom the viewer has not communicated and probably never will.

Hypertext

The structure of much interactive multimedia is based on both technical and theoretical work on hypertext. Theodor Nelson felt that traditional methods of writing ignore the way the mind really worked, which is by association and linking [Nelson, 1974, p. 45]. He coined the term *hypertext* in the 1960s, and said that, as illustrated in Fig. 11.2, "Hypertext is non-sequential writing. It is no good to use, though, unless we can go instantly in a choice of directions from a given point. This of course can only mean on computer display screens" [Nelson, 1974, p. 47]. The concept had been envisioned in 1945 when Vannevar Bush (a noted scientist and President Franklin D. Roosevelt's science advisor) published his seminal article "As We May Think" in the *Atlantic Monthly* (it was subsequently reprinted in *Life*). This piece influenced a generation of researchers in both the sciences and the humanities. However, hypertext's conceptual history goes back even farther: to footnotes, indices, tables of contents, and annotation in general.

Bush proposed a machine that he called a *Memex* that would assist the mind in dealing with what we now call "information overload." In "As We May Think," he wrote, "The summation of human experience is being expanded at a prodigious rate, and the means we use for threading through the consequent maze to the momentarily important item is the same as was used in the days of square-rigged ships" [Bush, 1945, in Druckrey, 1996, p. 30]. Bush

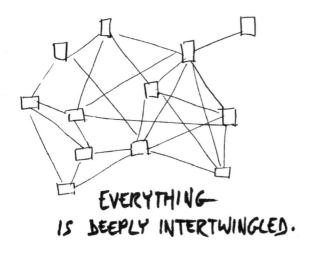

EVERYTHING IS DEEPLY INTERTWINGLED.

Figure 11.2 Everything is deeply intertwingled. *(Courtesy of Ted Nelson)*

conceived the Memex to be a mechanical, microfilm-based, desklike device that not only could take in and store information for easy retrieval, but would let the user

- create *associative links* between texts,
- form a *web* of trails through large quantities of material,
- *save* these trails for use by the same reader, or others, and
- *record* personal comments about the original texts; these additions would in turn be recorded and could be interlinked.

In the 1960s, Douglas Engelbart, working at the Stanford Research Institute, built a fully hypertextual system called Augment/NLS that he considered not merely a technical feat but a social one—a new way of working with information that would "augment the human intellect." A large public demonstration of the Augment/NLS system in 1968 showed hypertext in action, as well as fully operational remote computing, telecollaboration, and the first appearance of a device Engelbart called a "mouse." This demonstration influenced many young researchers in computer science, including Theodor Nelson and Andries van Dam, whose pioneering work together in hypertext at Brown University had started in the early 1960s.

Literary theorists such as Michel Foucault and Roland Barthes, writing largely in ignorance of these technologies, had already begun to describe literature as a system of interconnected texts. Bush introduced the now common terms *link, associative linking, web,* and *trail* to describe the Memex. Barthes discussed literature in terms of *links, nodes, networks, lexia* (blocks of text), and *paths.* Thus hypertext research has merged theoretical and technical concerns. Ongoing work is supported by a strong community of writers and scientists that organizes annual conferences, produces both fiction and nonfiction works, and has encouraged the birth of hypertext-specific publishing houses such as Eastgate Publishing.

As with many other forms of computer technology, hypertext tools were available for decades only on expensive workstations. Not until 1987, with Apple's free interactive design tool called HyperCard, did hypertext became familiar to the average computer user. Hyper-Card allowed even nonprogrammers to set up links among text, images, and sounds.

Today, the World Wide Web is the best-known example of a global hypertextual information resource. Many in the hypertext community, however, consider both HyperCard and especially the World Wide Web a minimal hypertext experience. Neither offers features such as structure beyond a sequence of cards or ad hoc connections between pages, the ability to link directly to objects (e.g., a particular button on a card), one-to-many links that let a user decide among several options, or conditional linking (e.g., a link that goes to one place if the reader has read most of the work, to another if the reader has not). Eastgate's Story-Space software has become the favorite of many hypertext authors because it has visual linking diagrams and supports branching to several options at once.

Bush said in 1945 that "the world has arrived at an age of cheap complex devices of great reliability; and something is bound to come of it" [Bush, 1945, in Druckrey, 1996, p. 31]. Taking the words *cheap* and *reliability* with a grain of salt, artists working today with complex interactive multimedia programs realize how far-sighted his vision was.

In the 1970s and early 1980s, creating interactive art work required programming skills; today, most interactive authoring tools offer ways for nonprogrammers to develop varied and interesting works. *Interactivity* is still an all-encompassing term, however. It is used to identify the simple-minded menu-choosing activity offered on an ATM machine and the more profound interaction made possible by, say, 3D physically based model behavior and artificial intelligence. Computer-based interaction holds potential for almost any type of multimedia production (because interactivity involves the user, it is a cornerstone of education and training software). Artists and designers can draw ideas from its current uses in fields as diverse as marketing and promotion, education, home banking, and video games.

11.1.2   THE RELATIONSHIP BETWEEN ARTIST AND AUDIENCE

In telephony manners are everything. While in commercial television manners are nothing. If you have a receiver you merely plug into the possibility of a signal, which may or may not be there and which you cannot modify except in the trivial manner of switching to nearly identical transmission or in a decisive but final manner by switching off. Choice is in the hands of the sender [Antin, 1986, p. 150].

David Antin, poet and critic

The computer is the great equalizer. Our imagery, what we appropriate from others, and what we draw into the computer ourselves, is all in there together. And, in some way which I do not completely understand, this liberates us to interact with sources as never before [Rubin, 1993, p. 78].

Cynthia Beth Rubin, computer artist

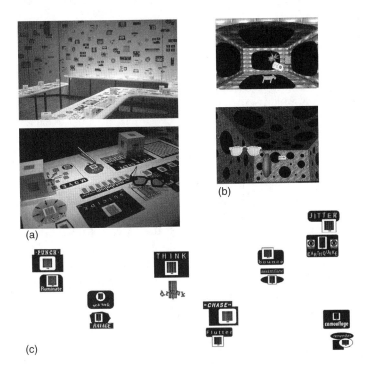

(a)

(b)

(c)

Figure 11.3 Perry Hoberman, *Bar Code Hotel*, 1994 (interactive installation). (a) Installation views. (b) Screen images. (c) Barcode examples. Although Hoberman and his collaborators designed the environments, the narrative that emerges depends on the actions of the users. *(Courtesy of Perry Hoberman)*

The computer's nature often compels collaborative work, and the complexity of interactive multimedia almost requires more than one person. The ease of collaboration extends so far, in fact, that works controlled and even formed by "viewers" are becoming more and more common. As illustrated in Perry Hoberman's *Bar Code Hotel* (Fig. 11.3), participants use bar code-reading wands to call up objects (by scanning in bar codes on cubes) and modify their behaviors, locations, and appearances by scanning in other bar codes on surfaces in the room. Besides controlling objects, certain bar codes affect and modify the environment in which the objects exist, even creating virtual earthquakes.

> *Bar Code Hotel* is an interactive installation for multiple participants (or guests). By covering an entire room with printed bar code symbols, an environment is created in which every surface becomes a responsive membrane, making up an immersive interface that can be used simultaneously by a number of people to control and respond to a projected real-time computer-generated stereoscopic three-dimensional world.

> Like any technology, bar code can be enlisted for other, less practical purposes. Misusing something that is normally in the service of control and authority holds the potential to reveal other, less constrictive scenarios. Of course, the ominous overtones of its intended use remain at least faintly audible.

> Bar code technology represents an early attempt to bridge the gap between the physical world and the computer. As such, it is the forerunner of present-day attempts to

allow computer comprehension of the world as it is (such as optical character recognition and artificial vision), as well as plans to embed digital information invisibly in the environment (ubiquitous computing and augmented reality) [Hoberman, 1994].

A theory of changing audience-author relationships emerged before the technology that now promotes it became popular. Starting in the 1960s, Roland Barthes—and soon afterwards Jacques Derrida, Michael Bakhtin, and Michel Foucault—all described systems of open texts on which the reader "acts" through a process of informed critical reading. These theories led to a clear understanding of the impact of hypertext. In "The Death of the Author," an essay that has become a standard reference for this topic, Barthes wrote that "a text is not a line of words releasing a single 'theological' meaning (the 'message' of the Author-God) but a multidimensional space in which a variety of writings, none of them original, blend and clash" [Barthes, 1977, p. 146].

Modernist artwork often assumed a fixed relationship between artist and audience, in which the artist produced the work and the audience passively observed it. In contrast, Postmodern artwork often encourages audience engagement, from events such as 1960s Fluxus happenings to today's performance art. Interactive artwork can blur the distinction between artist and audience to such an extent that often the terms seem to lack separate meaning. The *artist* may propose only the structure of the piece and the *audience* may actually create it. In this sense, the artist may be the creator of a conceptual artwork but not of a tangible one. Bonnie Mitchell structures and directs her collaborative Web works (illustrated later in Fig. 12.3), for example, but dozens of other artists create the actual images. Computer works resist closure by the initial creator and can easily remain an open and living part of a web of reference and incorporation.

For Foucault, this view of artwork (literature specifically) preceded the computer: "the frontiers of a book are never clean cut . . . it is caught up in a system of references to other books, other texts, other sentences: it is a node within a network . . .[a] network of references" [Foucault, 1976, p. 23]. Hypertext provided a testing ground for much literary theory; today, interactive multimedia and the World Wide Web offer an unprecedented venue for new relationships between artists and their audiences. Although the author–reader–spectator relationship has been a topic of theoretical writing for many years, never before have there existed the tools of creation and distribution necessary for large-scale experimentation.

An artist whose work lacks the authenticity of a unique production and who participates with viewers, rather than dictating to them, stands to lose much of the heroic genius status that is a hallmark of Modernism; the ego of the artist can be devoured by the nature of the medium and the networks. "Jean-François Lyotard, for example, rejects the Romantic paradigm of islanded self in favor of a model of the self as a node in an information network . . . 'no self is an island; each exists in a fabric of relations that is now more complex and mobile than ever before. Young or old, man or woman, rich or poor, a person is always located at 'nodal points' of specific communication circuits, however tiny these may be'" [Lyotard, 1984, p. 15; Landow, 1992, p. 73].

Technology may make dissolving the idea of individual authorship possible, but several forces work against that happening. One is that most countries' laws are written in terms of personal property. Rights of ownership and reproduction of a work with debatable authorship, and for which the term *copy* makes no sense, may be difficult to protect. Another reason, as George Landow points out, is that working with other people is not simply a matter of technology—it is difficult in its own right. The most common form of collaboration remains "the assembly-line or segmentation model of working together, according to which individual workers divide the overall task and work entirely independently" [Landow, 1992, p. 89]. New forms of artwork will have to take into account not just theory and technology but also the psychology of group interaction.

11.2 MULTIMEDIA CONCEPTS

The technical challenge in creating a multimedia piece is to integrate multiple data types. The artistic challenge is to combine the different media into a creative whole that is greater than the sum of its parts (see Fig. 11.4). Toni Dove's background in traditional multimedia and performance and collaborator Michael Mackenzie's skills as a playwright and director helped them conceptualize the interplay of sound, text, 2D images, and 3D spatial environments in this interactive piece. The combination of the media is a consciously constructed aspect of the aesthetic of the work. The creators used a variety of graphics—still images, video, and 3D models—and also interactive sound that changes depending not only on a user's location in the 3D world, but on how long the user has been there. The high-tech, cutting-edge aesthetic is complemented in the formal showing of the piece with a multimedia presentation (in the traditional sense) including a laser disk video and slides projected onto cloth-draped structures.

Figure 11.4 **Toni Dove and Michael Mackenzie,** *Archeology of a Mother Tongue,* **1993.** This scene from Dove's virtual reality installation shows a wireframe hand full of objects representing the short-term memory construct of one of the narrative's characters. The image includes video footage, painted areas, and 3D models. The user touches each object to enter it and hear a text describing the memory. Archeology of a Mother Tongue was produced at Banff Centre for the Arts. Three-dimensional design by Raonull Conover; programming by Graham Lindgren, Glen Frazer, John Harrison and Dorota Blaszczak. *(Courtesy of Toni Dove)*

11.2.1 Combining Data Types

The different types of data used in multimedia include static graphics, animated graphics, video clips, sound, and text. These different media are considered different **data types** because they usually come from different sources and are handled in different ways. A raster image, for instance, may come from a digital camera or a CD and is stored as a matrix of pixel values, whereas text may be typed in and is stored in standard codes for representing letters, numbers, and punctuation. Even a sequence of images for an animation is handled differently from individual still images. Geometric graphics, such as those created by digital design and 3D modeling programs, must often be rasterized before they can be used by multimedia software.

11.2.2 Coordination

In addition to the artistic problems of making different media work together, multimedia creators face many technical challenges over which they have varying levels of control. Coordinating incoming and outgoing information such as laser disks, CDs, video tape players, projection, and hard-copy text or images can require a great deal of experimentation. Within multimedia software, coordinating different types of data is partly up to the artist and partly determined by the capacities of the software and the machines on which it runs. For instance, different machines play time-based works at different speeds, so the frame rate usually cannot be guaranteed. A sound track developed on one machine may not be properly synchronized with animations when played on a different machine. Without video control that uses the standard Society of Motion Picture and Television Engineers (SMPTE) time coding, coordinating video clips with one another and with sound, text, or other images may be difficult. If a sound must be played, an animation run, and a video clip presented all at once, the program must decide which to handle first. In some programs, memory management features can help alleviate these problems, and the user may even be able to configure them somewhat. For example, a program may offer a choice of loading all time-based clips into memory when the multimedia piece is launched or of loading them only as needed for playback.

11.3 Anatomy of an Interactive Multimedia Program

Four basic structures are utilized to work with interactive multimedia: *timelines, stacks, flowcharts,* and *object-oriented environments.* All include simple, often visually based ways of designing interactivity, as well as more complex methods that involve the use of *scripting languages,* simplified programming languages that use English-like syntax.

Although the same program may be used to create and preview multimedia works, playback often requires a different mode or even a separate program. Many multimedia applications provide a *runtime version* called a **player** that can play back works but not create them. The runtime version takes up less disk space and RAM than the full program and usually can be obtained free of charge.

11.3.1 TIMELINES

Virtually all multimedia programs offer specific methods for controlling time and can create time-based works. The difference between multimedia programs and animation and video programs is that time controls in multimedia programs are used primarily to coordinate different media elements after they have been created elsewhere, rather than to create animations and edit video clips from scratch. The overlap between the programs described in Chapter 9 and those described here varies: Some multimedia applications provide no image-creation tools; others include full-blown paint programs and animation capabilities. In general, however, most media production is done before the elements are integrated in a multimedia program.

Timeline-based programs use the *timeline* analogy described in Chapter 10. Such programs are ideal for works that unfold in some natural way over time, such as multimedia movies. Because these programs often are designed to create noninteractive work also, they usually offer powerful tools for working with images, creating animations, and editing video. Movie clips and editable text can also be represented in the timeline. Media are placed in the timeline at a certain time or frame number, and, when that moment is reached during playback, the images appear and sounds emerge. Timeline-based programs can be thought of as nonlinear compositing and editing for multimedia.

These multimedia programs can go beyond the applications covered in Chapter 10 if the user adds interactivity. Because time is the most powerful logic in the piece, interactivity often largely consists of jumping nonlinearly from one frame to another. The Voyager Company's interactive version of the Beatles' *Hard Day's Night,* for instance, lets the user watch the film, stop it, return to an index and choose some other part of it to view (in addition to other features). More complex compositions can be constructed if the work is thought of as a number of separate sections that happen to be placed in the same timeline but are not inherently related to each other in time. This concept is used for many multimedia works because more than one mode or way of presenting information usually is involved. For example, in the *She Loves It, She Loves It Not: Women and Technology* piece previously shown in Fig. 11.1, the petals menu is placed in a certain frame, and each of the units it mentions (e.g., robots or power) takes up a certain group of frames elsewhere in the timeline. Clicking on different categories in the petals menu jumps the user to the appropriate place in the timeline, but the viewer does not perceive the jump as traveling through time.

Figure 11.5 shows a timeline-based version of a short multimedia work based on the Galápagos Islands. (Charles Darwin's visit to this isolated group of islands led to development of his theory of evolution. They are known for their often bizarre wildlife, some of it not found anywhere else on the planet.) *Virtual Galápagos* begins with a

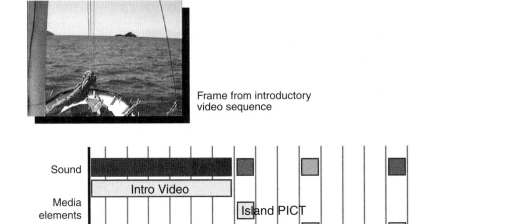

Frame from introductory video sequence

Figure 11.5 Timeline-based structure for *Virtual Galápagos.* In this diagrammatic timeline, the video clip is the only element that actually contains time-based information. The menus are still images that remain on the screen until the user makes some further choice by clicking a button.

video sequence of a boat approaching one of the islands. At the end of the sequence, the viewer sees a main menu featuring an image of the island (Island PICT) and three buttons, leading to three different subsidiary menus—one for birds, one for animals, and one for terrain (the Birds menu and the Animal menu are shown).

Because a timeline offers only a single level of hierarchy, complex branching and interaction can become difficult to visualize and control. Although the artist can work around these limitations, they nevertheless necessarily affect composition.

11.3.2 Flowchart Hierarchies

The structure of flowchart–style multimedia programs is based on an interconnected hierarchy that looks and acts like the flowchart used in designing computer programs or other complex sequential processes. The **flowchart** treats time not as a linear sequence of frames, but more like a waterfall that can be diverted into different channels if desired and sometimes even made to flow upstream. Different media elements are arranged in chart modules and appear when the program reaches that part of the

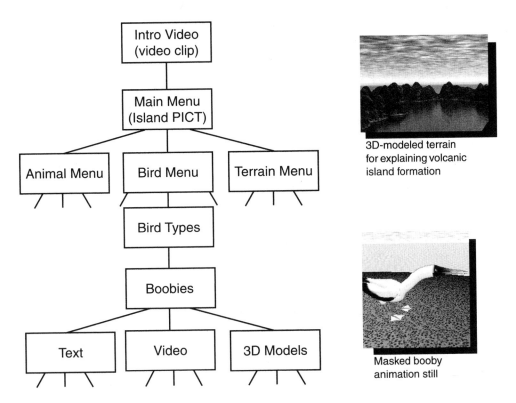

3D-modeled terrain
for explaining volcanic
island formation

Masked booby
animation still

Figure 11.6 Flowchart–based structure.

hierarchy. As the program progresses down the hierarchical chart, it displays images and movie clips and plays sounds. Interactive elements, including buttons and menus, can be added to give the user control over navigation. Figure 11.6 shows the Galápagos project in a flowchart structure. The user views the introductory video and then chooses to explore animals, birds, or terrain from a main menu. By choosing the Birds menu, for example, the user moves to a selection of bird types. Designing and understanding the navigational hierarchy in the flowchart approach is easier than in the time-based approach. However, time-based sequences, such as animations, usually cannot be designed within a flowchart–style program.

Flowchart–style programs are especially useful for highly structured works. One common type of application is training programs: The user can go from one training module to another, following a series of exercises to deeper levels of proficiency. For a simple multimedia training program, any type of program could be used, including those based on timelines. However, for a companywide training course for repairing a jet engine with thousands of parts and electrical and mechanical systems, a program with obvious hierarchy is desirable. Macromedia Authorware is an example of a popular flowchart–based multimedia program.

Artists and designers can combine the strengths of different structures by designing time-based sequences in a timeline-based multimedia program and then importing the material into a flowchart–based environment. Most multimedia designers sketch a flowchart when designing a hierarchy, even if that structure is not supported by their software (see Section 11.4.1).

11.3.3   STACKS/BOOKS AND CARDS/PAGES

Somewhere along the line Apple was a little afraid about telling people this was programming for the masses. They were afraid people would say, "Well, that's not for me." Programming clearly wasn't for normal people [D. Goodman, 1990, p. xxii].

D. Goodman, quoting Bill Atkinson, creator of HyperCard

Apple Computer advertised Bill Atkinson's HyperCard program in 1987 as a revolutionary new concept with the slogan "The Power of Association." Part of Apple's mission to empower personal computer users, HyperCard was a friendly environment that let nonprogramming users create their own applications with visual tools and simple scripting. The driving concept, which seemed extraordinary to many at the time, was to associate or link different pieces of data, say, a picture of a piano and text about the piano. You could easily design a program that let users click on a picture of a piano to bring up text describing the piano. Then if the users clicked on the text, they could travel to other links as well. The possibilities for organizing information and creating useful applications seemed endless and Apple hired "evangelists" to help promote the new tool.

Stack-based multimedia programs, such as HyperCard, IncWell SuperCard (formerly from Allegiant), and Asymetrix Toolbook, operate on a paradigm of **cards** or **pages,** which are spatial areas that can each contain different types of media. The cards are arranged in a linear hierarchy called a **stack** or **book.** Instead of advancing through time or along a branching hierarchy, the designer composes the work by arranging media in each card or page and creating connections between them. The designer puts graphic interaction tools such as buttons on the cards and then sets up interactions either by following prompts or writing short instructions such as "go next card" (see Fig. 11.7).

Figure 11.7 Stack- and card-based structure. The instruction "go next card" takes the user to the next card in the stack.

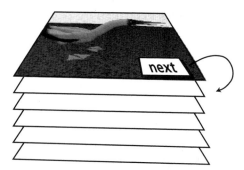

SCRIPTING LANGUAGES   HyperCard drew much of its power and flexibility from its built-in **scripting language,** HyperTalk. Phrases such as "go next card," "go prev card," and "beep" are examples of very simple uses of HyperTalk. To create more complex interaction or behavior, the designer writes longer **scripts** that can be anything from a single instruction to complex programming instructions that are several pages long.

Creating a complex interactive project usually requires knowledge of programming beyond the obvious statements mentioned here. Often multimedia producers hire a programmer to do complex scripting or augment a production's functionality by writing external commands in a less intuitive language such as C++.

Virtually all serious interactive multimedia programs contain scripting languages. For example, Macromedia Director's Lingo scripting language can be used to create complex interactive works.

Procedural and Object-Oriented Programming Paradigms

Interactive design *is* programming, even when the details are hidden. Artists and designers can make more informed decisions about software and design by understanding two of the main programming paradigms in use today.

Working in a **procedural mode** is like scripting a play: The characters and their lines or actions are all known in advance. You can leap from one place to another in the flow of events but the flow is always there (as in the time-based and flowchart–based approaches previously discussed).

Working in an **object-oriented mode** creates an environment that is more like hanging out at the mall: Characters are well developed but you don't know in advance exactly what they're going to say and how they'll interact with each other. The "characters" of an object-oriented program are called **objects,** and their "personalities" are built up by defining **attributes** or variables or parameters (e.g., color and size) and **behaviors** (e.g., blinking on and off when clicked). Not governed by a single flow that is sometime interrupted, objects can be designed independently from each other.

Because there is no obvious order for executing the instructions in an object-oriented program, in contrast to a timeline, how do you tell the objects when to act? You send them **messages.** When you click a "Quit button" object, for example, an "I've been clicked" message is sent to the button. The button responds to this message by sending a "quit" message to the application, causing it to close.

The object-oriented mode often better models the real world than the procedural mode. On the one hand, it lets you reuse work (objects from one program can be used in another) and can make programs easier to fix when something isn't working. On the other hand, it does not offer the same level of control over time as programs that support animation and have a timeline. And designing works with specific goals, such as training sequences, often is more difficult with this approach.

Most multimedia tools offer a mixture of these two paradigms. Timeline- and flow-chart–based programs have procedural structures but offer tools for creating buttons, fields, and other objects. Stack-based programs are more object-oriented—all their elements, from stacks to card to buttons, are objects that you can modify.

11.3.4 Object-Oriented Approaches

Object-oriented multimedia programs do not use a metaphor of a physical organizational structure such as a stack with layers or a flowchart. Instead, the focus is on creating interesting objects and their attributes, behaviors, and interactions with one another—and with user input.

For example, a bird in the *Virtual Galápagos* project can be considered an object with an appearance and behaviors, such as liking a certain type of berry (see Fig. 11.8). The bird can be designed to walk toward the berries whenever they are within a certain distance. How does it know the berries are there? The berries are also objects and send out a message stating that they are berries and giving their location. If a bird object is programmed to wander randomly around the island, it can be redirected to eat berries whenever it gets within a certain distance of a berry object. This scenario creates an animation that has no timeline-type control or simple flowchart hierarchy. Although the designer can't say exactly when, or even if, the bird will find every berry bush, when a number of birds and animals with different behaviors begin to wander throughout the island, infinitely many complex interactive scenarios can take place that would be impossible to script in advance with any other structure. The success of this type of multimedia work depends heavily on the appropriateness and depth of behavior and interaction given to each object.

11.3.5 Interfaces for Working with and Arranging Media

All multimedia programs can import and store a variety of media types (e.g., images, movies, sounds, and text), but the tools for editing and coordinating media vary widely. Most multimedia programs offer user-definable areas called **fields** that can contain fully editable text, into which artists can incorporate textual information and formatting directly from other sources. But, although most multimedia programs can import sounds and play them at a specific time or in response to a specific user action, sounds usually cannot be edited within a multimedia program (Opcode's MAX, geared toward interactive music composition, is an exception).

Keeping track of all the elements in a multimedia project—potentially hundreds of video clips and images, textual documents, and sounds and music—requires both

BIRD object (Blue-Footed Booby)

Attributes

appearance
an image file

walk style
an animation loop

fly style
an animation loop

song
a sound file

food preference
a text file

Behaviors

hunger
every 2 minutes an "I'm hungry"
message is generated for 1.5 minutes

eating
the "I'm hungry" message causes
eating behavior to begin. The bird
pursues any "food preference"
objects in the nearby environment.
When the bird reaches the food it
"eats" some of it (raises a fullness
counter and lowers a "remaining
food" counter in the food object)

walking
starts the walking animation loop and
translates the bird along the terrain to
the desired location (e.g., toward food)

flying
starts the flying animation loop and
translates the bird through the
air to the desired location (e.g., toward food)

singing
plays "song" sound file

Figure 11.8 Object-oriented approach.
In *Virtual Galápagos,* users can learn about
the islands and their inhabitants (as in the
previous examples) and can also choose different attributes (e.g., beak shape and size)
and can influence behaviors (e.g., making a
bird more aggressive). The birds and animals
are placed in an ongoing dynamic simulation
with varying food supplies to show Darwin's
concept of natural selection at work.

organization and appropriate software tools. Multimedia programs approach managing media elements in a variety of ways. Some maintain visual or textual listings of elements, and many offer timelines that show which media elements are present at which times. In Macromedia Director, for example, all elements are stored in a *Cast* and are represented by a grid of small thumbnail images (see Fig. 11.9). In many stack- and card-based programs, the images or text elements are pasted into individual cards and are not catalogued for reference elsewhere. In contrast, in object-oriented programs, textual lists of objects and their behaviors—and sometimes lists of images and other media elements—can be generated.

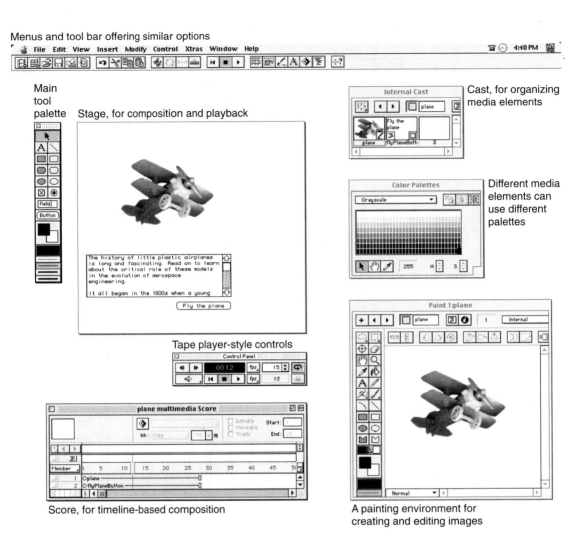

Menus and tool bar offering similar options

Main tool palette

Stage, for composition and playback

Cast, for organizing media elements

Different media elements can use different palettes

The history of little plastic airplanes is long and fascinating. Read on to learn about the critical role of these models in the evolution of aerospace engineering.

It all began in the 1800s when a young

Fly the plane

Tape player-style controls

Score, for timeline-based composition

A painting environment for creating and editing images

Figure 11.9 Multimedia program interfaces. (a) In Macromedia Director, a timeline-based multimedia program with some object-oriented additions, static visual elements can be edited in a paint window (lower right) and all the media elements (images, movie clips, sounds, buttons, text fields, etc.) are presented in a visual index (upper right). Tools for designing interactive elements are on the Main tool palette (top left), but complex interactivity must be scripted. All media elements in the final work must be arranged in a timeline (bottom left). *(Portions copyright 1998 Macromedia, Inc. Used with permission)*

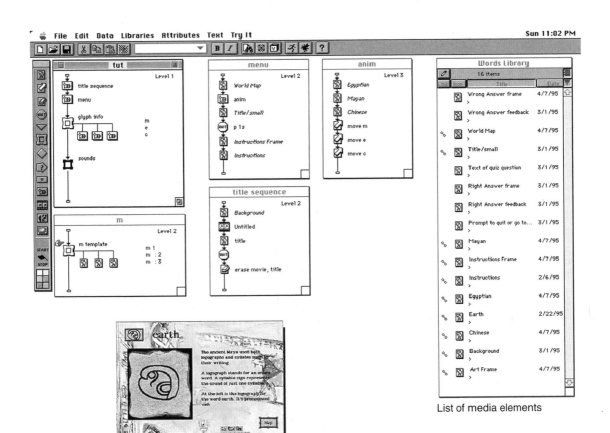

Scaled-down view of the end result

List of media elements

Figure 11.9 *(Continued)* (b) In Macromedia Authorware, projects are developed with the flowchart paradigm. Media elements and behaviors are shown as icons and arranged in hierarchies. Here the main hierarchy (upper left) contains many subhierarchies (shown in the similar windows to its right). The artist builds the program by stringing together media, timers, motion controls, and navigational choices. *(Portions copyright 1998 Macromedia, Inc. Used with permission)*

In addition to the final images used in a multimedia production (often 8-bit color images with resolution set for on-screen viewing), artists usually save high-resolution, full-color versions for future editing or revisions. Other source material, even if not used in the final project, may be saved for future versions or the creation of related works.

11.4 CREATING MULTIMEDIA

(There is no touch section in this chapter—the creation of media elements and the different type of touch associated with each approach are covered in Chapters 2, 4, 7, and 8.)

Main tool palette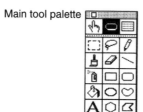

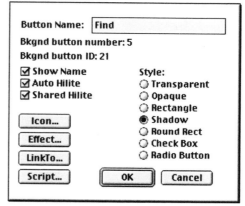

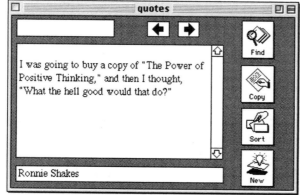

A text field is used to hold a different quote on each card

Double-clicking on a button brings up this dialog box, used to set the button's name and link destination

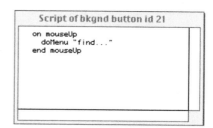

More complex actions can be designed with a script. Here the button is programmed to perform the same function as the "Find..." menu

Figure 11.9 (Continued) (c) This card- and stack-style program, Apple's HyperCard, includes simple painting tools and interactive elements such as buttons and text fields. Links can be designed entirely through the visual interface. Static art work created outside the program can be pasted onto a card, and sounds and movie clips can be called up in scripts. *(HyperCard 2.1 Copyright 1987-1991, 1993 Apple Computer, Inc. Apple®, the Apple logo and HyperCard are registered trademarks of Apple Computer, Inc. Used with permission. All rights reserved)*

11.4.1 PLANNING

Like animation and 3D modeling, multimedia works of any complexity benefit enormously from planning with the use of storyboards or other organizational methods.

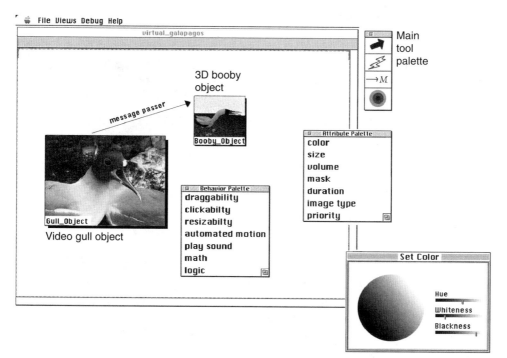

Figure 11.9 (Continued) (d) In the fictional object-oriented authoring tool Objectif, behavior and attribute palettes offer control over many of the most common features needed for multimedia objects. By dragging items from the palettes into object images on the screen, the artist can design objects rapidly. Double-clicking on either the gull or booby objects, for example, would reveal a motion behavior complete with motion path and speed, instructions for playing a sound file, file type information, including duration of animated sequences and rate of play, and priority settings for receiving messages. The visual "message passer" arrow can be double-clicked to reveal any messages sent from and to objects. This program also offers structural views of object hierarchies and of media layers used in a given scene.

Individual artists may not need a great deal of preparation, but, for a complex multimedia work involving a team of people, planning is essential.

Nancy Buchanan did all the work herself in *Developing: Some Snapshots and Home Movies* (see Fig. 11.10), which grew from a collection of materials and experiences. The artist has a background in painting, performance art, and video and now often uses the computer to combine media. This process is supported not by detailed planning and storyboards, but by the collection and intuitive integration over a period of time (sometimes years) of materials relating to themes such as the Gulf War, the Savings and Loan crisis, and in *Developing: Some Snapshots and Home Movies*, real estate development. Viewing and interacting with this work is structured to resemble flipping through a notebook, an "interactive journal," following the artist's associations. In fact,

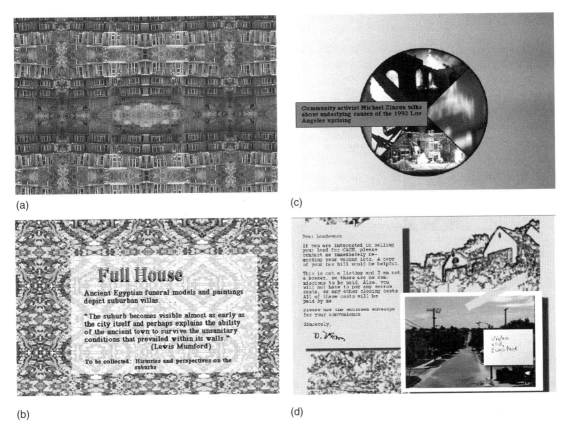

(a)

(b)

(c)

(d)

Figure 11.10 Nancy Buchanan, *Developing: Some Snapshots and Home Movies,* 1995. The screen shots show (a) pictures manipulated in a paint program, (b) a quote about suburbs set against manipulated housing images, (c) an interactive wheel for accessing stories about burning buildings, and (d) a scanned letter and postcard relating to land purchase. *(Courtesy of the artist)*

one of the things Buchanan likes about desktop multimedia is the flexibility that lets her dismantle and reassemble her works, depending on the context in which they are shown. When *Developing* was shown in 1994 in Riverside, California, Buchanan designed a section of it to deal specifically with Riverside, tailoring it to the local audience. She extends the flexibility of her work's forms even further by noting that "any HyperCard user is able to modify [her] work or disassemble it to make pieces of their own" [Buchanan, 1993, p. 427].

A large-scale commercial multimedia project, however, usually requires several months of strategizing, scheduling, storyboarding, designing, prototyping, and user testing. In addition to the organizational functions included in the authoring software

Figure 11.11 Storyboard. From left to right: Opening shot of boat approaching the island, Main menu, Birds menu, and Boobies menu.

used, multimedia producers often use separate database programs to keep track not only of file names and types but also such information as source, resolution, version number, licensing status, and associated costs.

Of the stages mentioned, **storyboarding** is the most crucial for most artistic projects. Multimedia works can easily become quite complex and, like 3D models, involve a type of construction that is not easily changed. Even sketchy hand-drawn plans can save huge amounts of time and energy. Storyboards should convey an idea of the flow of the work from the user's viewpoint. What main screens or scenes will compose the work? What choices will users have at each screen? Which media will be involved? If the work is object-oriented, what will be the main objects? Where in the course of the work will the objects appear and what will be the interface for using them? Figure 11.11 shows part of the storyboard for *Virtual Galápagos*.

Interaction also should be storyboarded. It can be done more abstractly, with a flowchart based on the storyboard (see Fig. 11.6). Designing the interaction, in essence, is designing a computer program and, as in programming, a good design saves untold numbers of hours later on.

When designing interaction in object-oriented authoring tools, the artist may find that fully diagramming the potential flows of events may be impossible. Instead, the artist can consider the main objects, the types of messages they send and where they send them, and the objects they receive messages from. For example, in the *Virtual Galápagos* object-oriented segment previously shown in Fig. 11.8, the Bird object can receive messages from plant life to know what type of food is available, and the plant life receives a message from the bird to know when it is eaten. Almost all possible message trails can be tracked on paper to eliminate design problems before the interaction scripting begins.

In multimedia projects involving many people or complex projects undertaken by a few people, more detailed planning is beneficial. Commercial production houses plan each screen and interaction completely in advance. For artists, this approach may lack spontaneity. The best approach depends on the needs of the creator, the nature of the work, and the purpose for which the work is being created.

11.4.2 CREATING, GATHERING, AND ORGANIZING MATERIALS

Media elements can be images created in paint-type programs, animation segments created in 2D or 3D animation programs, text written in a word processor, and sound digitized from traditional performances or created on the computer. The content of a multimedia creation can be digitized from any type of visual or audio material, searched for and downloaded from the Internet, or purchased from sound-effects libraries or film footage and stock photo bureaus.

Most media must be specially prepared for a multimedia environment. Multimedia programs rarely accept images saved in a paint program's native format, for instance, but instead require standard image-file formats such as PICT or TIFF. Sound also must often be converted into a format that the multimedia program can read. The resolution of sounds and images often must be reduced for practical purposes. For example, because most multimedia creations are viewed on-screen, a resolution greater than that of the screen (72 dpi for most Macs and PCs) merely wastes storage space and slows the display. If a piece is created for wide distribution, color depth often must be tailored to a lowest common denominator, which usually means reducing the images' color palettes to 256 colors and often using standard palettes as well (see Chapter 5). For multimedia works with large numbers of images, a program that can automatically *batch process* a set of images, such as Equilibrium DeBabelizer, can be extremely useful.

MULTIMEDIA DATABASES   Applications designed to store, arrange, and coordinate media are naturally related to **databases**—collections of information that can be interrogated by a user. As an art form, the database has grown in popularity, from Muntadas' project *The File Room,* a Web site about censored books (at http://fileroom. aa.uic.edu/fileroom.html), to works of Buchanan such as *The Peace Stack,* which grew out of her frustration at the apparent agenda of much prime-time media coverage of the Gulf War. As Buchanan culled articles from various different sources, she built up a database of viewpoints that contradicted the mainstream narrative of a simple war with a happy ending.

Natalie Bookchin applied the database idea to the entire scope of daily life in her *Databank of the Everyday* (see Fig. 11.12). This interactive CD-ROM contains a cross-indexed hypertextual collection of words with associated images and video clips of everyday actions such as scratching and shaving. Basing its form on the "loop" used in programming and the structures common to all databases (ways of storing and retrieving information), the work is without narrative pathways or intended "results." The *Databank* was designed to:

> Champion the loop as a new form of digital story telling; there is no true beginning or
> end, only a series of loops with their endless repetitions, halted only by a user's selec-

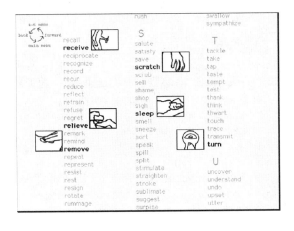
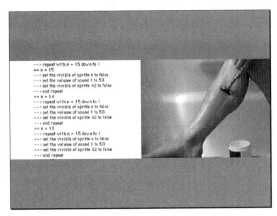

Figure 11.12 Natalie Bookchin, *Databank of the Everyday,* **1996** (interactive CD-ROM). *(Courtesy of Natalie Bookchin)*

tion or a power shortage. *Databank of the Everyday* takes as its subject the real everyday use of computers in our culture: storage, transmission, dissemination, and filtration of bodies of information. The work reflects on what media—from photography to computers—have always attempted to do: represent the truth of life and organize it into well-defined lists and categories [Bookchin, 1996, p. 36].

11.4.3 TEAMS

Only in recent art history has the individual artist played a significant role. In medieval times, artists did not even sign their paintings, and even in the Renaissance, which produced many artists who are now household names, works were frequently produced by "studios" with a master and apprentices. The idea of a single person creating a work to suit personal expressive needs from beginning to end and autographing it conspicuously is an invention of the Romantic era. The Modernist notion of the genius artist who creates entirely from within was dismantled somewhat by Postmodernist realizations that works are fed by many sources in the artist's culture. Computer-based multimedia art continues to confirm this theory by bringing together a diversity of media already in circulation and requiring teams of artists to work together.

Although art forms involving teams and collaboration have existed for many hundreds of years (e.g., theater, opera, and more recently animation and film), the tendency still persists, perhaps driven somewhat by practical convenience, to want to identify a work with a specific individual. Although hundreds of people work on any major Hollywood movie, the audience is aware only of the main actors and actresses and the director, and sometimes the producer. Can you name one famous editor? And yet editing can make or break a movie, as can camera work, casting, and many of the jobs listed in the credits that follow a major film. The relationship between the Modernist need to create art stars and the Postmodernist insistence on interconnection, interinfluence, and collaborative, audience-driven works remains an uneasy one.

These issues often come to the fore in multimedia productions. In a large project (and even most small ones), the creation of different media components requires time, energy, and expertise beyond the range of any one individual. Like film, multimedia work often is undertaken by a team that includes a producer as well as the creators of the actual materials. A musician may create the sound track while a graphic artist designs screen layouts. A 3D artist may create models that are animated by an animator and rendered by yet a third person. A video artist can shoot and edit video, but a digital video specialist may be in charge of digitizing the video and adding special effects. In addition, programmers often substantially influence a work by extending the capabilities of the multimedia application, especially for advanced animation and interactivity. With customized menu and icon control, interactive multimedia designers also become software designers. Because users' expectations for the quality and ease of use of most software are high, creative development work benefits from the support of software engineers and interface designers. The final team thus may include not only the artistic creators, but also computer scientists and interface specialists, as well as people in charge of dissemination and support.

Christine Tamblyn created *She Loves It, She Loves It Not: Women and Technology* (Fig. 11.1) with assistants but did not consider it a collaborative effort. Toni Dove's multimedia virtual reality piece *Archeology of a Mother Tongue* (Fig. 11.4), however, required coordinated collaboration between the visual production, narrative, sound, and programming. The tendency to create multimedia works requiring extensive collaboration may be influenced by an artist's former training. "In many ways the culture of art-making has motivated the directions taken in technologically driven art. More often, those moving from photography to computer technology employ means that they personally control, whereas video and installation artists who have worked collaboratively with artisans and technicians often continue to create monumental works demanding vast resources" [Earle, 1994].

Because Dove's work used custom hardware and software, no simple scripting language was available. In fact, the challenges of programming the 3D world and integrating the video and sound occupied three professional programmers. Of this relationship Dove has said, "It's both very interesting and frustrating [to work with a programmer]. Sometimes it can be like eating with a fourteen-foot fork because you want to do things and you have to do it through this conduit in order to make the behaviors happen. It's a collaboration with another person's ideas and with a whole set of possibilities inherent in a programming language" [Dove, 1995, p. 267].

Desktop multimedia programs are offering more and more sophisticated and yet easier-to-use features that give individual artists a great deal of power and control. Dove says that "most of the multimedia places I've worked at are chaotic and crazy. There are endless amounts of files in different places and people keep renaming them and they end up someplace else" [Dove, 1995, p. 274]. She has responded to this situation by deciding to master a set of tools that she can utilize directly and to contract out tasks requiring expertise that she lacks. She believes that this commitment is necessary, not only to have more control over her multimedia computer works, but also to use the medium better by understanding what a certain program or set of programs can do for her. Of one program she is currently investigating, she says, "If I don't understand how it works, what's easy, what's difficult, what it does most effectively, then I'm working in a dark room with the lights off" [Dove, 1995, p. 275].

For artists with traditional training in fields such as painting and sculpture, teamwork can be difficult to adjust to. In an art world that seeks recognizable names, a project to which five or six people make substantial contributions usually becomes identified with a single person, most often the director or producer (terms that are much better defined in film production than they are yet for multimedia art works).

11.5 COMPOSITION

The compositional structure of interactive art works, multimedia or not, is not visual, spatial composition *per se,* although a narrative structure and its navigational possibilities often can be visualized. Many other factors, arising both from programmed actions and user input, can control how interactive works are seen.

11.5.1 A FRAMEWORK FOR FORMS OF INTERACTIVE MULTIMEDIA

Interactive multimedia offers a new way of making art but so far lacks firmly established forms, such as "sonnet," "prose poem," and "haiku," that help people create and interpret written works. An unpublished framework helpful in organizing the range of interactive composition was developed by user interface designer Daniel Robbins while working in Brown University's Computer Graphics Group. Robbins' taxonomy of composition types is based on combinations of three key forms: books, games, and playgrounds (see Fig. 11.13). A *book* delivers specific, predetermined content that can be absorbed in a number of ways, often through linear or branching paths, over any length of time. A *game* may or may

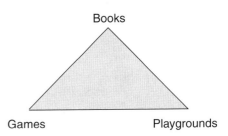

Figure 11.13 Robbins' taxonomy for interactive works.

not impart content but always has a goal, usually one that must be reached under time pressure. A *playground* has no goal and does not come to an end when a certain amount of preset information is attained. Each form can have varying levels of interactivity, from simple navigational choices that lead the participant through the piece to opportunities for changing its content.

Many CD-ROM products are closest to the book vertex of this pyramid: They use interactive navigational tools to present traditional information forms, such as movies and texts. In such works, the user clicks a button to advance through the piece's pages or to go backward to view earlier sections. Usually a table of contents, history, or other navigational structure is available that lets the user navigate nonlinearly, search for specific locations, or be guided by a suggested sequence of choices. The content is fixed, but interactivity lets the artist offer the participant a variety of ways to experience that content.

Navigation does not have to remain linear, however, and as the possibilities for traversing the content in different ways increase, the web of different viewings or readings of the work becomes more and more complex, often dramatically so. The interest and meaning of an interactive art work can come to lie as much or more in the structure of this web and the different readings or viewings possible than in the underlying content. In Robert Kendell's hypertext work "A Life Set for Two" [Kendell, 1996], the fixed pathways created by predefined links are only the starting place for dynamic floating links and variable text areas. Instead of following one of many preset paths through the work, a book-length poem, the user follows links that become available depending on user-chosen settings, the amount of text already read, and other factors. When the user reaches a section of text, variations on specific phrases are chosen by the program to create continuity of context. The experience of navigating the work is thus an integral part of its meaning and helps to construct the sensation of exploring an individual's memories and thought processes. "A Life Set for Two" would lie in between the book and playground vertices of the taxonomy shown in Fig. 11.13: Much of the content is fixed, and a narrative structure is enforced, but the piece also responds to the user's choices, altering the branching structure and even the words themselves.

As a work contains less narrative form and allows even deeper interaction, it moves toward the playground vertex. Here users may be able to add their own text to a piece and explore interactive 3D simulations that involve the use of object behaviors.

Most of today's interactive authoring tools consider only a 2D space. Although artists can bring in images or animations from 3D programs, the tools for controlling and interacting with objects have remained almost exclusively 2D. This situation is changing as hardware capable of handling real-time 3D interaction becomes more affordable and widespread. Figure 11.14a shows the initial state of an interactive 3D project, the *Creature Construction Kit*, designed to teach students about logical operators such as NOT, AND, and OR by letting them set up test situations that change objects' behaviors. The tool box contains logical operators, sensors (in this case eyes), and actuators (here rocket thrusters) for designing a robot. A simple robot can be constructed initially from only an eye and a thruster (see Fig. 11.14b). When the eye sees an object, the thruster fires; as soon as the object is out of visual range of the eye, the thruster ceases firing (see Fig. 11.14c). To construct a robot that can successfully track a moving

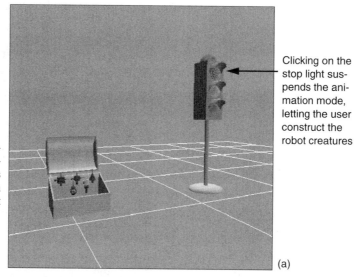

The toolbox contains logical operators represented as physical pieces of a construction set

Clicking on the stop light suspends the animation mode, letting the user construct the robot creatures

(a)

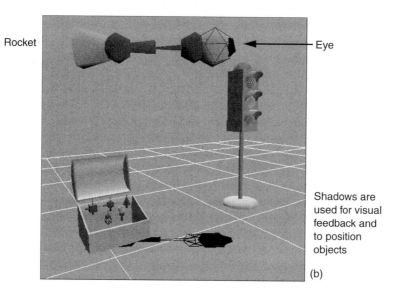

Rocket

Eye

Shadows are used for visual feedback and to position objects

(b)

Figure 11.14 *Creature Construction Kit,* **Brown University Computer Graphics Group, 1993.**
(a) The toolbox stores the sensors, actuators, and logical operators. Robots can be constructed when the light is red, and they animate when the light is set to green. (b) A robot consisting of an eye and single rocket thruster.

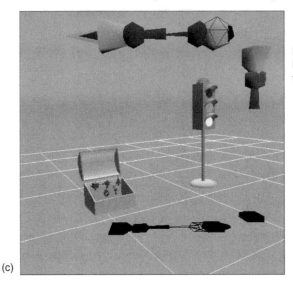

New object
introduced into
the scene.

(c)

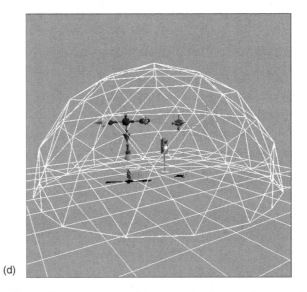

(d)

Figure 11.14 *(Continued)* (c) The eye sees an object and the thruster fires, moving the robot ahead. As soon as the object is out of visual range, the thruster ceases firing. (d) The user can view the scene from any angle, and the robots can animate anywhere in the hemisphere shown.

object, the user must add thrusters at different angles with logical operators that allow the robot to steer toward objects and keep them in view (see Fig. 11.14d). Unlike most computer-based instructional environments, the *Creature Construction Set* is entirely 3D; users work with the objects in a 3D space and can view the situation from any angle (see again Fig. 11.14d). The animation mode, accessed by clicking the green light, puts the user-defined object behaviors into effect.

Currently, there are few easy-to-use tools for nonprogrammers who would like build interactive 3D worlds with object behaviors and interactions, but such tools are expected to emerge soon. (The use of 3D models on the World Wide Web may jump-start this type of application; see the discussions of Virtual Reality Modeling Language (VRML) and Java3D in Chapter 12.) Simulations can be experienced today primarily in games. Many video-style computer games contain simple 3D worlds and offer ever-increasing levels of user interaction, such as id software's Doom and Quake. Some games (mostly 2D) simulate complex real-life systems, namely Maxis Inc.'s SimCity, SimPlanet, and SimAnt.

An art piece can be designed to lie anywhere in the book–game–playground pyramid. Near the book vertex, an online text could allow users to navigate to areas of interest and perhaps add their own comments. A game component could provide motivation by giving positive feedback or communicating a sense of urgency. A playground could provide online image- or sound-creation tools and let users interact with premade images or situations.

Dove's virtual-reality piece (Fig. 11.4) is certainly closest to the playground vertex. It provides a responsive 3D environment that the viewer explores freely, but because it contains a textual narrative it also has some aspects of a book. Buchanan's information-driven works and Tamblyn's *Women and Technology* CD-ROM allow access to fixed content through predetermined navigational paths and have no time pressure or action goals. Thus they are closer to the book vertex.

11.5.2 INTERACTIVE SPACE

What does composition mean for interactive multimedia? In addition to the spatial composition of each screen (or other surface) and the time-based compositing for video and animation segments, there is also the way in which the interactive structure uses space. Does it set up a 3D world through which the viewer can navigate? A virtual book through which the viewer leafs? Multimedia can combine different spatial experiences, perhaps offering a visual map as well as a textual reference or list-based ways of accessing information. In the *Databank of the Everyday* (Fig. 11.12) the viewer can look at alphabetical lists or categories with images, or click a full-figure image. Exploring the material through the figure is a different experience and suggests different connections from navigating through the alphabet.

George Legrady's *Slippery Traces: The Postcard Trail* (see Fig. 11.15) is:

A non-linear narrative in which the viewer navigates through a maze of about 200 interconnected postcards that cover a range of topics such as nature, geography,

Figure 11.15 George Legrady, *Slippery Traces: The Postcard Trail,* 1995, Interactive Digital Media Installation Project. As viewers navigate through the images, following their interests and desires, a database algorithm keeps track of each move, weaving a second-level story based on the sequence of choices. Viewers may choose to see this statistical analysis or metaphoric trace (situated beneath the postcard image) as it is constantly updated. (*Production Team: George Legrady (concept, design, and project and creative director), Rosemary Comella (consultant and technical and creative production), Wolfgang Munch (software development). CD-ROM version published in artinfact 3, 1996, by ZKM-Center for Art and Media Karlsruhe.*)

colonialism, the future, work, urban environments, technology, race, gender, the supernatural, kitsch, etc. Each postcard contains approximately five hot spots or links, each of which, when selected by the viewer, leads to a different image. The hot spot links to other images are based on literal, semiotic, psychoanalytic, metaphoric or other connections [Legrady, 1995b].

The sense of selecting an area and then blowing it up or otherwise activating it to reveal more information was inspired by a scene in the movie *Blade Runner.* In that scene a photograph is subjected to scrutiny through a series of spatial selections and enlargements, an example of a technology that "penetrates the photographic image, disrupting the spatial boundaries of the traditional photograph by moving and turning around within it. [The protagonist] forces the image to reveal to him what he is looking for (he re-invents the image to match his desire)—a subject (the woman's face)" [Legrady, 1995b].

The spatial composition of each card is deconstructed in terms of the hot spots, and the space of the entire project is a complex one of location, travel, and images designed for tourists. Moving from or through one image into another establishes a third dimension in the mind of the viewer, that of the interconnections between the individual cards. This part of the composition is customized in real time by the audience, changing with each viewing and each viewer. Part of the inspiration for this compositional strategy comes from Alain Robbe-Grillet's *Last Year at Marienbad* and its use of a shuffling of time and space where past, present, here, and there are woven together. In essence, the interactive operational mode gives the viewer the opportunity to develop the narrative.

11.5.3 User Interface Design

The convention of a window onto a small part of a fixed event is becoming one of a door leading into a world of sequenced, multi-sensorial events, consisting of temporally and spatially dynamic experiential constructions that the observer is free to enter or leave at will [Weibel, 1996, pp. 347–348].

Peter Weibel, artist and theorist

Only in restaurants or department stores are we faced with a closed list of alternatives. The interface of an interactive cinema cannot restrict itself to a model of choice, though this does not mean that choice is entirely banned. Response is the operative concept [Weinbren, 1995].

Grahame Weinbren, artist and theorist

User interface design is an integral part of interactive multimedia design. In fact, it often is one of the most important parts and can be crucial to the success of the work. For example, Perry Hoberman has the following to say about his work shown in Fig. 11.16: "A unique, interactive, multi-participant installation, the CATHARTIC USER INTERFACE 1.0 SYSTEM will allow users to QUICKLY and EFFECTIVELY work through whatever CONFLICTING EMOTIONS they harbor concerning the BENEVOLENT YET PERNICIOUS influences of COMPUTER TECHNOL-OGY on their lives. By pitching MOUSE-SHAPED BALLS at the KEYS of COUNTLESS WALL-MOUNTED COMPUTER KEYBOARDS, CUI participants will be able to trigger a VAST ARRAY of MULTIMEDIA MATERIALS dealing with THE MORE TROUBLING and PROBLEMATIC ASPECTS of TECHNOLOGY" [Hoberman, 1995].

Interaction design—how a user communicates with your piece and how your piece responds to the user—is part of user interface design. When designing interactive

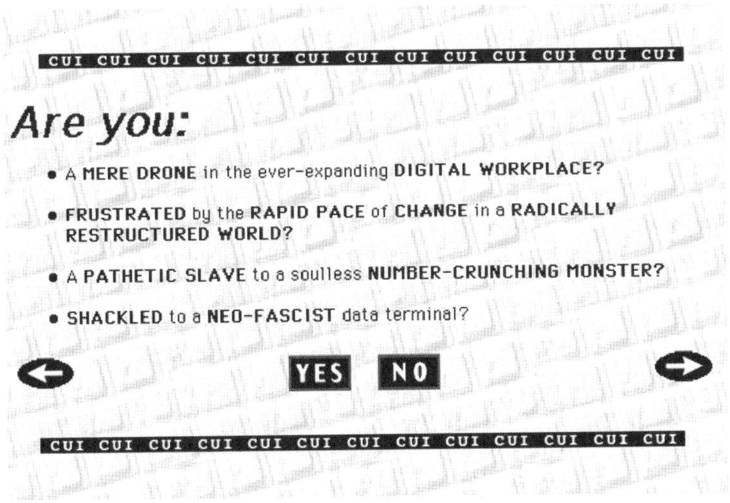

Figure 11.16 Perry Hoberman, *Cathartic User Interface*, 1995 (installation). This screen grab from Hoberman's Web site *Call for Participation* resonates with many artists and others who are faced with difficult-to-use interfaces. *(Courtesy of Perry Hoberman)*

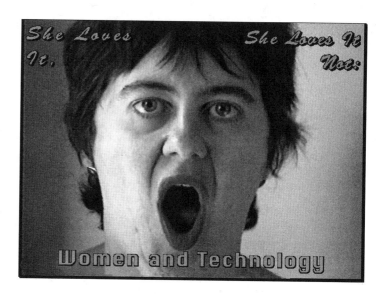

Figure 11.17 Christine Tamblyn, *She Loves It, She Loves It Not: Women and Technology,* **1993** (interactive CD-ROM). In this opening screen for the CD-ROM (also discussed in Fig. 11.1), the user is instructed by voice to click Christine's mouth to enter the piece. This interface design forces users to contemplate the female body and their expectation of neutral navigational devices and makes them suddenly conscious of the interface. It also injects a sense of humor. *(Courtesy of the Estate of Christine Tamblyn)*

works, the artist must either team up with an interface designer or by default become one. A work that is hard to use probably will fail to communicate its message (unless that *is* its message). Because interface design usually is taught only as part of computer science or advanced multimedia design, only a few basic guidelines are covered here.

Interface guidelines found in books and articles are written to help programmers create easy-to-use interfaces that do not call attention to themselves. For art work, the intent may be the opposite. If the piece is about the medium and in particular about the interface methods with which users communicate with the computer, the artist must work with critical awareness of interface elements. A dialogue box that forces the user to pick between two distasteful choices or a menu bar without a quit option can be used to call attention to the highly standardized forms and expectations at work in most applications (see Fig. 11.17). Christine Tamblyn consciously tries to rethink current interfaces, which she considers to have a "violent and aggressive character" that mirrors "the militaristic male pyramid with its rigid chain of command" [Tamblyn, 1994, p. 163]. She thus uses the body, multisensory experiences (combining image with sound and text) and a circular menu system (the petals in Fig. 11.1) in her interface.

You need to be aware of the conventions for "good" interface design, even if you choose to subvert them. In fact, a sound knowledge of interface design techniques is the best place to look for ways to use common interface assumptions creatively.

The interfaces used in most multimedia and personal computer software are graphic user interfaces (GUIs). Two-dimensional WIMP (windows, icons, mice, and pointers) interface design, in particular, has evolved to include many helpful rules and standards. The visual aspects accessible to the designer of an interactive program are mainly screen design, the design and use of buttons or hot areas, custom menus, custom dialog boxes, and sometimes custom auxiliary palettes. Cursor appearance can also be changed and animated.

Some of the most important guiding principles for effective interfaces are the following.

- *Strive for consistency and stability.* Don't surprise the user. A menu that performs a certain function at one time should not perform a different function at another time. Clicking a button that says "next" should always move the user ahead in the same way and at the same level of hierarchy.

- *Use consistent and meaningful metaphors to guide the user.* A piece that looks like a book and shows pages turning already gives the user information about how to navigate and what to expect. An interface metaphor can guide a user but can also constrain and mislead: Unnecessary details and excess realism can often detract from a metaphor's usefulness. The metaphor should lead to interface options that are easily identifiable and yet are not obtrusive. Interaction precedents, such as using VCR-type forward, back, stop, and play buttons, can also make using a multimedia work feel more intuitive. Figure 11.18 shows an interface design that does not follow these guidelines. In a CD-ROM produced by a government research lab, the opening screen offers users a slider bar from which to pick one of an unknown number of topics. This demonstrates an incorrect use of an easily identifiable metaphor and common interaction device, the slider. Sliders should be used to adjust continuous (or at least related) qualities, such as volume or game levels, not to make choices from a list of topics and credits and help options. Instead of revealing information and guiding the user, this interface choice hides information and is bound to cause frustration.

- *Make functionality obvious.* Users shouldn't have to wonder how to move onward or quit your interactive work (unless you want them to). You can guide their actions by making some choices more obvious and inviting than others. Think about screen design much as you would think about any surface design project. Although designing for paper and for the screen are not the same, many basic rules

Figure 11.18 What's wrong with this picture?

apply to both. Clear color use and typography, for instance, can make a work much easier and more pleasant to experience. Information that the user needs should stand out, and secondary information should be less conspicuous.

- **KISS (keep it simple, stupid).** Providing many additional features or navigational methods is often tempting. Most of the best, most pleasant, and most effective programs and interfaces, however, offer straightforward methods for communicating with the computer. Users who must pull down several menus, click many dialog boxes and decipher inscrutable icons soon become disenchanted. This guideline is especially important for works that are designed to be used only once for a short period of time—for example, a work displayed in a gallery with which users may spend only 5 or 10 minutes.
- **Test, test, test.** This guideline is by far the most important. A user interface that makes sense with your work and can be used easily is a success, no matter what rules were broken. An interface that consistently baffles viewers and causes them to miss the point of your work or just walk away from it is a failure, even if every rule is adhered to.

    Ease of use can be determined only through testing: challenges for a tester should include completing specific tasks and should take into account the steps the user goes through to accomplish the set goals. These tasks will help reveal whether you have designed an interface sensitive to the user's needs versus those of the machine. Encourage the test subject to talk out loud while working with the program. It is important not to influence the test results by interacting with the test subject and giving encouragement or hints. Staying silent is difficult, and many user interface designers recommend literally sitting on your hands to keep from pointing at the screen or grabbing the mouse away from the test subject (although users should be helped if they become too frustrated).

Three-dimensional spaces pose additional challenges. Because users typically interact with 3D objects by using a 2D mouse and screen, many actions are difficult to carry out reliably. Navigation and object interaction need interfaces that give the user control without being so complex and visually cumbersome that they detract from the experience of the work.

A simple gestural interface is used in Broderbund's MYST adventure game, in which 2D images of a 3D world create the feeling of a richly detailed 3D space (see Fig. 11.19). Users can navigate and interact with objects without ever using a standard button or dialog box. To move around, the user simply clicks with the mouse in the right, left or center of the screen: The right and left click cause the view to shift as if the viewer had turned right or left, and the middle click moves the viewer farther into the current space. This interface reinforces the sensation of being in a mythical 3D land and eliminates the flat 2D feel of buttons.

The 2D images in MYST are chosen in advance, not produced on the fly, and the camera is highly constrained. However, in some 3D environments—most notably games—a user may be able to control the camera and view a 3D space from any angle desired. Such freedom can easily be disorienting, though, so camera views usually are

Figure 11.19 MYST. No controls are visible, but once users discover that mouse clicks move them through the landscape (e.g., clicking left to go left or in the middle to move straight ahead), the interface feels intuitive and contributes to the sense of exploring a 3D space. *(Copyright Broderbund Software, Inc. and Cyan, Inc. Myst is a registered trademark of Cyan, Inc. All rights reserved)*

at least partially constrained to prevent users from flipping upside down or becoming motion-sick.

Many interfaces for navigation of spatial works, such as those used in MYST, strive to be transparent, not calling attention to themselves and instead letting the user focus on the 3D illusion. Many games meet this interface challenge by using keyboard commands for navigation, weapon firing, and the like. Keyboard commands or input from other devices such as joysticks or multibutton mice reduce screen clutter and may be essential in works where fast response is necessary and clicking screen icons would be prohibitively slow.

Grahame Weinbren, in his interactive work *Sonata,* used transparent interfaces for moving not through space, but through time and narrative. In this complex piece of interactive cinema, viewers navigate through a narrative that operates on many levels and through different points of view. The three images shown in Fig. 11.20a are from one part of the *Sonata* narrative, based on "The Kreutzer Sonata" by Tolstoy. In this story, a man who suspects his wife of having an affair with a violinist flies into a jealous rage upon hearing them play the Beethoven sonata together. In his passion he loses control and stabs her to death. The user controls which character is displayed on how much of the projection screen by pointing through the disassembled touch screen shown in Fig. 11.20b, interrupting its infrared beams. "The tension between the activity in the two spaces portrayed, and the fact that the more you see of one room the less you see of the other, motivates the viewer to constantly change the scene arrangement, and kindles a sense of tension similar to that attributed to the protagonist. This is a kind of expression that can only be accomplished by means of interactivity, which connects the viewer with the jealous rage felt by the protagonist in a way that is not possible within the confines of the traditional cinema" [Weinbren, 1997]. The sonata provides the soundtrack in this section.

(a)

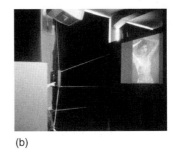

(b)

Figure 11.20 Grahame Weinbren, *Sonata,* 1993 (interactive installation). *(Courtesy of Grahame Weinbren)*

Timothy Druckrey describes the interface in more detail:

> The viewer navigates around the narrative using a unique interface. The four compass directions of the screen—up, down, left, right—each represent a different temporal direction. Right and left move us forward and backward in time respectively, down renders expansions of the present, and up, the introduction of material outside time. Thus, for example, touching the right side of the screen moves the narrative forward more quickly. . . . The left side of the screen reverses the direction of time. However, when we go back through events, as in remembering or retelling them, the events are necessarily seen in a different light. . . . So when the viewer activates "reverse time," a new view of events is revealed [Druckrey, 1993, p. 172].

Both MYST's spatial navigation and Weinbren's temporal model draw the viewer–user into the piece by eliminating potentially distracting interface screen elements. Such gesture-based navigation leads naturally to interface design for truly immersive virtual worlds in which the standard 2D WIMP interface tools simply do not work; people can't enter virtual reality with a keyboard and mouse. Gestural interfaces and voice-based input are being investigated for such situations.

In *Osmose,* Char Davies met the difficult challenge of virtual-reality interface design with one of the most aesthetically integral art work interfaces that I've seen. In an interface that is at once central to the meaning of the piece and yet deeply intuitive and in many ways transparent, Davies created a 3D world that is navigated with a head-mounted display and real-time motion tracking based on breathing and balance (see Fig. 11.21). According to the Web site overview of the work:

> In contrast to conventional VR interface techniques such as joysticks or gloves which are based on direct linear manipulation, Osmose incorporates the subtle, intuitive processes of breathing and balance as the primary means of navigating within the virtual world. By breathing in, the immersant is able to float upward, by breathing out, to fall,

(a)

Figure 11.21 The Osmose interface, 1995. The Osmose interface was informed by Char Davies' experiences of deep sea scuba-diving. There is also a correlation with meditation practices that, by focusing on breath, seek to bring the mind and body into a state in which the boundaries between inner and outer osmotically dissolve. (a) Immersant using the Osmose interface. The computer tracks breath and balance to create an illusion of floating: breathing in to rise, out to fall, and leaning to change direction. (b) The Clearing, real-time frame capture from the immersive virtual Environment *Osmose* (1995). *(Courtesy of Char Davies and Softimage Inc.)*

(b)

and by subtly altering the body's centre of balance, to change direction, a method inspired by the scuba diving practice of buoyancy control. The experience of being spatially-enveloped, of floating rather than flying or driving is key. Whereas in conventional VR, the body is reduced to little more than a probing hand and roving eye, immersion in Osmose depends on the body's most essential living act, that of breath—not only to navigate, but more importantly—to attain a particular state-of-being within the virtual world [Softimage, 1995].

As artists continue to explore the concepts and potentials of interactive multimedia, interfaces will continue to move beyond the menus and buttons of early GUI design, tapping into the body's natural ability to move and speak.

Conclusion

Interactive multimedia remains a largely uncharted territory that beckons to many artists. It brings together aesthetic and theoretical issues from various fields of endeavor, including theater, cinema, video, creative and critical writing, and performance art. In some senses it also reunites users and programmers through visual programming or simplified scripting languages, adding issues of program structure and interface design to the mix.

A multimedia work can be approached on any scale, from a personal project in which a single artist explores a topic in new ways to a large-scale production with a cast of dozens or even hundreds of people. As computers continue to become more powerful and cheaper, with increased speed and storage and memory, multimedia will become more and more a standard means of communication rather than an exception.

Although authoring tools have improved and new tools continue to be created, there is still no easy way for nonprogrammers to create complex programs. Visual programming, though more intuitive for many, can easily become overwhelmingly complex. The input and output devices available are also limited, although they are being improved.

Multimedia is an exciting and dynamic field, with aesthetic forms and exhibition and distribution venues still in their infancy. It is bound to affect not only the professional art world but also the way that art is taught—the physical tools for photography, animation, video production, and programming are now united in a single studio-in-a-box.

Suggested Readings

Baecker, Ronald, William Buxton, and Jonathan Grudin. *Readings in Human–Computer Interaction: Toward the Year 2000.* 2d ed. Morgan Kaufman, 1995. An excellent, comprehensive series of essays, aimed primarily at the technical reader. It may be hard going for artists but is worth working through relevant topics, especially for artists involved in interface and systems design.

Brinson, J. Dianne, and Mark F. Radcliffe. *The Multimedia Law Handbook, A Practical Guide for Developers and Publishers.* Ladera Press, 1994. A practical guide for artists, producers, publishers and others who need to understand the often complex legal issues involved in multimedia productions. This detailed text also includes sample contracts, informative case studies, and copies of the Copyright Office forms (in addition to other resources). Sample chapters can be read at http://www.eff.org/pub/CAF/law/multimedia-handbook.

Druckrey, Timothy (ed.). *Electronic Culture: Technology and Visual Representation.* Aperture Foundation, 1996. Includes Vannevar Bush's "As We May Think" in its valuable History section and many probing essays throughout. Requires some fortitude to make sense of both the theory and science vocabulary and references: It's not for beginners in either field. A good bibliography is included.

Landow, George P. *HyperText 2.0: The Convergence of Contemporary Critical Theory and Technology.* John Hopkins University Press, 1997. One of the seminal books written on HyperText (another being Jay David Bolter's *The Writing Space: The Computer, HyperText and the History of Writing*). Includes history, theory, and examples with an emphasis on educational applications.

Laurel, Brenda (ed.). *The Art of Human–Computer Interface Design.* Addison Wesley Longman 1990. This collection of essays has become a classic. Written by a wide range of practitioners, the book expands the reader's understanding of the field and offers many useful real-life applications. It is for beginners and advanced interface designers alike.

Lopuck, Lisa. *Designing Multimedia: a Visual Guide to Multimedia and Online Graphic Design.* Peachpit Press, 1996. A lush book with lots of truly useful information. It provides a great overview of multimedia production. It can be read all at once by beginners and then used as a reference by beginning and intermediate users wondering about specific topics such as color palette conversion and the pros and cons of aliased graphics in interactive works.

Mullet, Kevin, and Darrell Sano. *Designing Visual Interfaces.* Prentice-Hall, 1995. A book that is itself beautifully designed. It succeeds in making its suggestions deeply felt, through the writing, the many visual examples, and the organization. Although practice and experimentation are crucial for interface design, this book can help prevent many lost hours and can spark creative, effective design solutions.

Norman, Donald. *The Psychology of Everyday Things.* Basic Books, 1988. (Reissued as *The Design of Everyday Things* in 1990.) A now cult book written by a cognitive psychologist about industrial design in general but immediately applicable to computers. It answers the question posed by the author in his preface, "How come I can work a multi-million-dollar computer installation, but not my home refrigerator?"

Exercises

1. *Paradigm and project.* Create a general storyboard for a simple multimedia piece about the secret life of plants. (You may want to refer to the Stevie Wonder movie and album of the same name.) Be creative! Identify the situation, characters, and other relevant parts of the work. Now refine the storyboard, creating three versions, one for each of the book–game–playground paradigms discussed in this chapter. How do the options available and the paradigms used affect the design of the work? Do different approaches give you different ideas? If so, describe them. Which would you choose for a sci-fi game based on subduing aggressive plants from other planets? Which for a training system for gardeners? Which for an interactive multimedia music video featuring a dead flowers theme?

An application-specific exercise is not appropriate because storyboarding is done chiefly on paper.

2. "Are you looking at me?" Create an interactive multimedia piece in which interaction is the main artistic component and media play a secondary role.

With Macromedia Director 6.5: A lot of different interactions can be set up in Director without learning Lingo, the Director's scripting language (although reading the first chapter of the Learning Lingo manual will help). For your piece, experiment with Director's behaviors. Bring up the Behaviors Library with Extras: Behavior Library and bring up the Behavior Inspector with Window: Inspectors: Behaviors. Click any behavior in the Behavior Library to see it described in the Behavior Inspector. Add interactivity to sprites in your piece by dragging behaviors onto them. For example, drag the "System Beep" behavior onto a sprite to make it beep when clicked. Some behaviors require additional information. For example, the Go To/Play Number frame behavior will ask you for a specific frame number to go to. Sometimes it's easier to use markers rather than frame numbers for navigation. To create a marker, just click the white bar above the frames in the Score. Click the text "new marker" next to the marker to edit its name. Now you can use the Go To/Play Marker behavior. Try making a piece with just these simple standard behaviors and the sound behavior Play Member.

3. *Compare and contrast.* Critique the interfaces of two software programs with which you are familiar. What functionality is hidden? What causes frustration? What types of work does the interface encourage? How do they reflect the value or goals of the company creating the software? How do the primary markets for the programs affect their use by other groups—for example, the use of CAD programs or corporate presentation programs by artists?

An application-specific exercise is not appropriate; the critiquing is better as a discussion activity or a short written piece.

4. *Multimedia memory.* Our memories are often multisensory, multimedia phenomena. Make a multimedia memory come alive with a combination of graphics, text and sound. How can the play of media types help to draw the viewer/user into the experience?

With Macromedia Director 6.5: Think of words or phrases that contribute to your memory. Bring up the Text Window with Windows: Text and begin typing and formatting. Use the + button to create separate new text areas. Each of these text sprites will be stored in the Cast. You can drag them onto Stage as needed throughout your piece. You can import text saved as .RTF (for example, from Microsoft Word). Each page or column of text becomes a separate Cast member. Fields are useful for large blocks of text, text that can be changed while your piece is playing, and text that will be manipulated by Lingo. Choose the Field button on the Tool palette and click and drag on the Stage to create a field.

Create images of the memory in Director or use Import . . . to bring in images created elsewhere (most major file types are supported). You can also import QuickTime, AVI, or other Director movies. Three-dimensional animations will help provide variety.

Add sounds with simple behaviors or by importing AIFF or WAV files (or Mac system sounds). Imported sounds will be placed in the Cast. You can drag them to the Stage, which will place them in the next available sound channel. You may have to extend the sound sprite in the score to hear the entire sound play. Select the Looped checkbox in the Cast Member Properties dialog box to repeat the sound. You can record your own sounds and edit them in a program such as Macromedia SoundEdit 16. Many sounds can be downloaded from the Web. As with images, remember that most music is copyrighted.

Work on arranging and integrating these different media types to convey the sensation of your memory.

5. *Unexpected interface.* Design a user interface that calls attention to assumptions and expectations about human–computer interaction. Violate as many of the guidelines given in this chapter as possible. For example, use dialog boxes that offer only illogical or repugnant choices, hide the quit button, use colors that cause nausea, or tie important events to unlikely variables such as any leftward mouse movement. How can such strategies be used to convey ideas and make your art work more interesting? When will such strategies backfire? Explain.

With Macromedia Director 6.5: Director provides many user interface support tools. Make buttons using Insert: Control: Custom Button. . . . Your choice for button state images need not be at all standard. Use behaviors to give your buttons and sprites interesting functionality. You can also apply behaviors to frames, and they will begin when you enter the frame. For example, the Hold on Current frame behavior keeps the movie looping on a single frame until you take some action.

CHAPTER 12

The World Wide Web

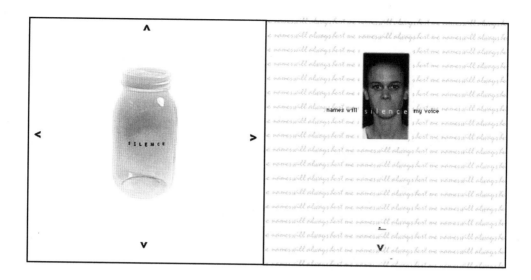

A daunting 68 percent of the messages posted by men made use of an adversarial style in which the poster distanced himself from, criticized, and/or ridiculed other participants, often while promoting their own importance.

Susan Herring
Gender Differences in Computer-Mediated Communication: Bringing Familiar Baggage to the New Frontier
© 1994

v

Figure 12.1 Stephanie Cunningham, *Silence*, 1996. This interactive Web piece investigates the derogatory words used online to describe women. Quotes from research on the subject supplement the artist's words and images. Viewers can add their own words and experiences. *(Courtesy of Stephanie Cunningham)*

12.1 Introduction

> *"Time" has ceased, "space" has vanished. We now live in a global village . . . a simultaneous happening [McLuhan, 1967, p. 63].*
> Marshall McLuhan, thinker, educator, and writer

Artists and designers are exploring new forms of art creation and distribution on the global network of computers called the *Internet* and the multimedia environment called the *World Wide Web* (WWW), or simply the *Web*. In this chapter I include a short history of both, describe the concepts that make them possible, and discuss a range of artistic uses for them.

Because of the dynamic nature of the Web and the relative slowness of writing and publishing a traditional book, only well-established Web addresses are given here. The Web site supporting the book (including this chapter) provides a set of annotated links to art sites, including galleries, individual artists and designers, and written material (see http://www.tba.com).

12.1.1   A Brief History of the Internet and The Web

A few decades ago, the idea of connecting millions of computers of all different types from all over the world was the stuff of science fiction. The idea that a non-scientist would be able to sit down at a computer and play a 3D game with people on the other side of the planet was not expected to become a reality. But it has.

Today, unlimited use of the Internet in the United States costs less than cable TV. To understand why, you have to look back to 1966, when a scientist named Bob Taylor was working at the Advanced Research Projects Agency (ARPA). He was in charge of overseeing the nascent field of computer research. In this role, Taylor had to work on many different machines and communicate with researchers who also had different types of machine. "It became obvious," he said years later, "that we ought to find a way to connect all these different machines" [Hafner, 1996, p. 13]. In particular, he wanted to find a way to share the country's scarce computing resources:

> Why not try tying them altogether? By building a system of electronic links between machines, researchers doing similar work in different parts of the country could share resources and results more easily. Instead of spreading a half-dozen expensive mainframes across the country to support advanced graphics research, ARPA could concentrate resources in one or two places and build a way for everyone to get at them [Hafner, 1996, pp. 41–42].

Thus the ARPANET was born in the late 1960s as a way to consolidate computing resources; at its first large public demonstration in 1972, it had 29 nodes. Soon other networks emerged, and, because they all used something called Internet Protocol (discussed in Section 2.1), they often were referred to collectively as the **Internet.** In 1985, the National Science Foundation (NSF) created a high-speed *backbone,* NSF-NET, which provided crucial infrastructure for the Internet, allowing regional networks to tap into the larger, faster network that supported research institutions.

The ARPANET was never conceived of as military infrastructure; its distributed design was intended solely to provide speed and reliability for research use. However, "the mainstream press . . . picked up the grim myth of a nuclear survival scenario and . . . presented it as an established truth." In fact, the project "embodied the most peaceful intentions—that researchers might share computer resources. . . ARPANET and its progeny, the Internet, had nothing to do with supporting or surviving war" [Hafner, 1996, p. 10].

The Internet provided a means of textual communication, **e-mail** (electronic mail), and a way to transfer files, but lacked easy-to-use navigational tools and any way to show images. The Web eliminated these restrictions and made the Internet accessible to the most naive of computer users. A collection of hyperlinked multimedia data stored on machines throughout the Internet, the World Wide Web is based on work done in the early 1990s by Tim Berners-Lee at the European Laboratory for Particle Physics (CERN), based in Switzerland. Inspired by a need to save limited travel funds, it was at first strictly textual and used by physicists to share research data. In 1993, the National Center for Supercomputing Applications (NCSA), at the University of Illinois at Urbana–Champaign, released Mosaic, a free program with a graphic user interface for exploring the information of the Web. Soon commercial companies such as Netscape Communications were formed to make competing programs. The number of Web servers continues to rise dramatically (see Fig. 12.2).

Documents on the Web can contain not just text and text-based links between documents, but also 2D and 3D graphics, animations, and sounds. Artists and designers are taking advantage of this new medium and its potentially huge audience to showcase their work, create work online, and explore new forms of collaborative interactive art creation. Figure 12.3 shows a sequence of images from *ChainReaction,* an ongoing Web project designed by Bonnie Mitchell, that involves digital image manipulation and networked integration of the visual environment. In this project, artists contribute "starter images" and then other artists view them and choose an image to work on further. The new derivative pieces are added to the site, and the process continues. The piece takes advantage of the geographically dispersed nature of the Internet and the multimedia capabilities of the Web to make artists aware of both individual choice and connectedness in creative pursuits.

Figure 12.2 **Almost 2.5 million servers—and growing every day.** *(Courtesy of Robert H Zakon, Hobbes' Internet Timeline ©1998 Robert H Zakon)*

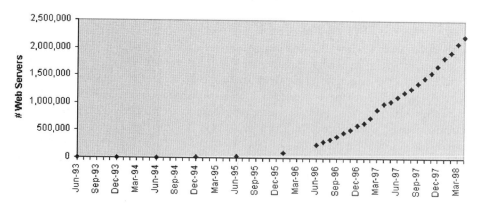

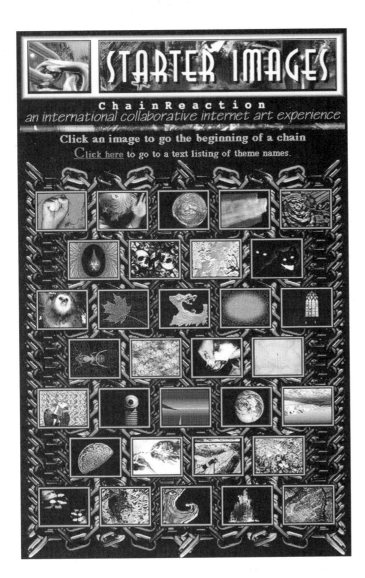

Figure 12.3 Bonnie Mitchell, *Chain Reaction*, 1995. Participants from around the world collaborated with SIGGRAPH and ISEA attendees in 1995 to create a nonlinear progression of digital images. Each of the 32 groups of starter images encompasses an expanding structure that allows 64 images (six generations) to evolve from the starter image. The entire Chain Reaction project has the potential to contain more than 2048 images. *(Courtesy of Bonnie Mitchell, Bowling Green State University Computer Art)*

12.2 CONCEPTS

The network of machines and connections that makes up the Internet and supports the Web is organized differently from the local networks that you may have experienced in a school or company. These differences are important for the present and potential future uses of the Web as an artistic platform.

12.2.1 The Internet Protocol

In **local area networks** (LANs), data flows in a predictable way along preset routes, and the transfer of a great deal of information from one computer to another may tie up the entire network. Such weaknesses of standard networks led to the idea of a distributed network that did not have predefined routes for data flow. Such networks were made possible by the development of a **network protocol** (a set of conventions for sending information) called **Internet Protocol,** or IP. This special protocol is not dependent on any type of preset configuration; instead, it breaks up files into standard-sized chunks of data called **packets** and sends them by whatever route of interconnections is most efficient at that moment. When all the packets have arrived at the destination machine, they are reassembled into a single file.

12.2.2 No Central Control

Internet Protocol created a network that can run without any centralized administration, which is a key feature in its growth. **Internet Service Providers** (ISPs) provide access for individuals for a monthly fee (usually $10–$20/month). Individual artists and designers have access to the same general body of Internet information as a corporate employee, and the information they publish on the Internet is just as accessible as that of IBM or General Motors. (Internal corporate documents can be shared via a secure **intranet** that uses the Internet's infrastructure but is not generally accessible.) As use of the Internet continues to grow, there is no guarantee that it will continue to function well and some experts even believe that it will collapse under its own weight as more and more people "get connected" and start sending everything from e-mail to video.

Because it has is no central management, so far the Internet and its collections of data have been largely unregulated and uncensored. More information about issues of governance and jurisdiction can be found on Web sites such as that of the Electronic Frontier Foundation, an organization working to ensure that the principles embodied in the Constitution and Bill of Rights are protected as new communications technologies emerge (http://www.eff.org/).

Although there is no centralized administration, the Internet is not free. Originally supported by the government (which still funds some portions of it), the Internet is now paid for mainly by its users. Most large sections of high-speed computers and linkages, the **backbones,** are now owned and run by corporations. These companies charge other companies and ISPs, which in turn charge customers for Internet access. Companies and institutions such as universities usually pay a large flat yearly fee that covers use by all employees or institution members.

12.2.3 Device Independence

The IP is **device-independent**; that is, it can be implemented with computers running virtually any operating system, including Microsoft Windows, the Macintosh OS, or some flavor of UNIX. Thus anyone's art and design work can be enjoyed by millions of people without different versions having to be designed for different machine types or individual setups.

12.2.4 WEB BROWSERS

The Internet's decentralized structure, device independence, and increasing reach (nobody knows exactly how many people use the Internet, but estimates range from 30 to 40 million) make it a perfect platform for the World Wide Web. Although the term *the Web* is used in many ways, it usually refers to the body of interlinked multimedia documents made available through the use of special software known as **Web servers** and viewed with programs called **Web browsers.** Web server software is used by Web site owners to publish information, on request, in a language appropriate for the browsers. The browser software is used to view Web documents; it understands the language of Web servers and can usually handle multimedia document elements such as images and sounds. Browsers use **Uniform Resource Locators** (URLs) to navigate to a particular server and then download the requested Web document, or **page,** for display and use. The most popular Web browsers are Netscape's Navigator (often just called "Netscape") and Microsoft's Internet Explorer (often just called "IE"). Both companies offer versions of their programs at no cost.

Web browsers provide two powerful features that are of great importance to many computer artists and designers. The first is **hyperlinks**—live links between one Web document and another by which users can navigate the Web. The second is multimedia: A Web browser can show both images and text and can also play back animation, sounds, and even full-fledged interactive multimedia documents. In time, all the types of programs discussed in this book, including 3D and full multimedia productions, probably will be available over the Web.

In a distributed network, items can be difficult to locate. **Search engines** let users find sites by topic categories or search for text within enormous indices of some proportion of all the text on the Internet.

12.2.5 BANDWIDTH

The Internet's combination of an easily accessible decentralized network, simple graphic user interface, multimedia capabilities, and live hypertext-style links from both text and images has created a new communications tool that is poised for significant impact on industry, education, and the arts. True multimedia art work, however, is presently hampered by the limited **bandwidth,** the number of bits of data transmitted per second, and compression methods available for sending data among machines connected to the Internet. A fast connection, on a T–1 line, for instance, is 1.54 Mb (megabits or 1000 bits)/second. Someone using a 28.8-, 48.8-, or 56-baud modem (*baud* is a measure of signal frequency often used interchangeably with bits-per-second, although for most modems the number of bits-per-second transmitted is several times greater than the baud rate) is receiving data much more slowly. Many modems connect at only 14.4 or even 9.6 baud (slower speeds, such as 2.4 baud, are not recommended for Web use). Files larger than a few dozen KB start to take noticeable time to download and, even on very fast systems, large graphics can cause significant frustration. Multimedia projects of the type described in Chapter 11 can easily take up hundreds of megabytes of disk space, so Web artists and designers must currently work within quite severe constraints that affect both functional and aesthetic choices.

IMAGE COMPRESSION   Image formats for the Web use *compression* techniques to make files smaller. The most basic type of compression, **run-length encoding** (RLE), reduces file size by storing rows of same-colored pixels as a single color plus a number, indicating the number of pixels in the row. For images with large areas of flat color, RLE is very effective, but for those with a lot of color variation this type of compression may not be adequate. A benefit of RLE and the common Web format GIF is that they are **lossless**; that is, they keep all the image information intact. Other methods, such as **JPEG** (developed by the Joint Photographic Experts Group), are **lossy**; that is, they sacrifice some image fidelity. The JPEG method involves the use of sophisticated averaging of similarly colored pixels. Data is irretrievably lost in the process, but the user can choose the balance between file size and image quality (the greater the compression, the lower the quality). New compression methods, such as those based on fractals and wavelets, may offer Web users much more dramatic compression in the future.

12.2.6   FORMS OF INTERNET-BASED INTERACTIVITY

> *In an interactive computer game designed to represent a world inspired by the television series* Star Trek: The Next Generation, *over a thousand players spend up to 80 hours a week participating in intergalactic explorations and wars. They create characters who have casual and romantic sex, who fall in love and get married, who attend rituals and celebrations. "This is more real than my real life," says a character who turns out to be a man playing a woman who is pretending to be a man. In this game, the rules of social interaction are built not received [Turkle, 1996, p. 354].*
> Sherry Turkle, sociologist, psychologist, and writer

The far-reaching nature of the Internet, severe constraints on file size, and the ease of using links (they take up virtually no storage space) have made interactivity one of the main features of many interesting Web art works. In addition to hypertext linking capabilities, one-way interaction is provided by **forms** that let a user send data to a Web site. Real-time **chat sessions** let users type messages in a shared space (see http://urth.acsu.buffalo.edu/irc/WWW/ircdocs.html for more information about Internet Relay Chat (IRC)). MUDs (Multi-User Dungeons, or Dimensions or Domains) and MOOs (MUDs, Object-Oriented), like the *Star Trek* group, are programs that let people engage in multiuser online games and other forums. These initially text-based shared environments are being adapted to integrate 3D graphics and other multimedia capabilities into their interactive environments.

The anonymity of the Internet immediately raises philosophical and sociological issues. A *New Yorker* cartoon taped to many Net users' doors for years shows one dog introducing another to the Internet by saying, "On the Internet nobody knows you're a dog." This medium lets people interact without knowledge of gender, age, race, economic status, or physical appearance. Who can question its relevance to Postmodern issues of representation, especially regarding gender and culturally based biases?

12.2.7 HELPERS AND PLUG-INS

The interactive and multimedia capabilities of Web browsers are quickly expanding thanks to **helpers,** or applications launched from within a browser to play video or sound or perform other functions, and **plug-ins,** which seamlessly add extra functionality. Plug-ins are available to interpret different image formats, play sound and video, use Postscript graphics, navigate and interact with 3D worlds, and much more.

A plug-in of great relevance to multimedia producers is Macromedia's Shockwave for Macromedia Director, which lets Web designers incorporate interactive multimedia pieces made with Director or Authorware directly into a Web page. (Other multimedia authoring tools will certainly offer similar plug-ins.) Web page visitors using such a plug-in experience animation, sound, and interactivity limited only by the need to keep files as small as possible (Macromedia's list of the best Shockwave sites and other Shockwave info can be found at http://www.macromedia.com/shockwave/).

12.2.8 JAVA

Sun Microsystems' **Java** is a programming language that can be used to write special applications for the Web called **applets.** Instead of downloading, storing, opening and running these applications from your hard drive, as with applications developed in most other programming languages, you can use Java applets directly on a Web page. Java dramatically extends the Web's capabilities from simple graphics and interaction based on links to a realm limited only by the creativity and programming skills of the applet creator (and, of course, the usual need to keep files small). Java is similar to the C++ programming language but contains enhancements and restrictions specific to the Web. One of the most important of these restrictions prevents applets from changing any information on a user's hard drive, a limitation designed to prevent inadvertent or deliberate damage.

Although Java requires programming, visual programming environments such as Symantec Visual Cafe for Java can simplify creation of Java applets. Multimedia authoring tools are also trying to make Java more accessible. Macromedia Director lets users use Java within Lingo scripts and automatically creates simple Java applets with a "Save as Java . . ." feature.

12.2.9 JAVASCRIPT

JavaScript, a scripting language for the Web developed by Netscape, is not a full-fledged programming language like Java (although some of its features and syntax resemble Java). You can't build a stand-alone application or applet with JavaScript. Instead Javascripts are embedded in a page's HTML, making it more interactive, creating mouse

Figure 12.4 Vivian Selbo, *Vertical Blanking Interval,* 1996. (a) *Vertical Blanking Interval* has a cryptic opening screen on which tiled media images and text flash. Clicking on this visual index involves the user in a bizarre and often humorous dialog (b) and (c) with images, text, and Java-Script alert message boxes that call attention to the software infrastructure of the site. In a similar vein, the user is shown analyses of Internet server statistics. *(Courtesy of Vivian Selbo)*

rollover events, for instance. It also makes the page more responsive to user input—for example, checking a form to be sure that a user has filled in each field. JavaScript can help artists without programming backgrounds enhance their Web pages and increase the level of interactivity. Vivian Selbo's project *Vertical Blanking Interval* (see Fig. 12.4) "investigates the gap between signals: the space between the keyboard and the chair, between need and desire, the net and tv, push and pull, flattery and innuendo" [Ada Web, 1996].

12.3 COMPOSITION

(The Web offers no new types of touch for creating visual materials—in fact, only some aspects of the touches discussed in previous chapters are available. The anatomy of a Web page creation program is discussed in Section 12.3.2.)

12.3.1 Hypertext Markup Language (HTML)

The primary way of controlling the composition of a Web page is with **HyperText Markup Language** (HTML), a set of special **tags** (see Fig. 12.5) used to indicate the structure of a Web page. The tags define, for example, which text is a heading, which text is the main body paragraphs, and which text is, say, a bulleted list. The tags themselves do not determine what the text will look like to a viewer. Each browser interprets the tags and displays the text according to its preset definitions. Thus artists' and designers' works are automatically formatted on the receiving end for the available screen space, fonts, and other capabilities of the receiving machine and its browser software.

12.3.2 Web Page Design and Layout

Relatively clear-cut graphic limitations have forced some interesting solutions. Designers often are compelled to simplify their graphics, work with fewer colors, and recast their messages in stripped-down form. The present limitations of Web graphics and multimedia controls are counteracted, however, by the extraordinary potential for linking documents and communicating interactively with audiences scattered throughout the world.

Figure 12.5 Tags structure a document but do not fully determine its appearance. (a) All HTML tags are enclosed in angle brackets (< >) and come in pairs that enclose the affected text. Thus <h1> indicates that the text following will be formatted according to the browser's h1 instructions. The closing tag </h1> indicates that the formatting should stop. The tags and text on the left created the text on the right in my browser. (b) Someone else could set the default text to, say, Helvetica instead of Times New Roman and could alter the default font sizes.

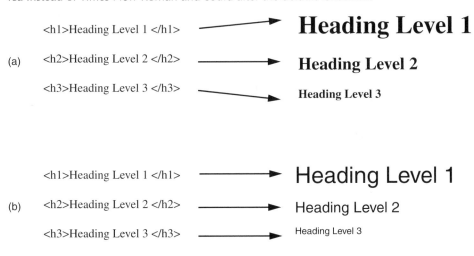

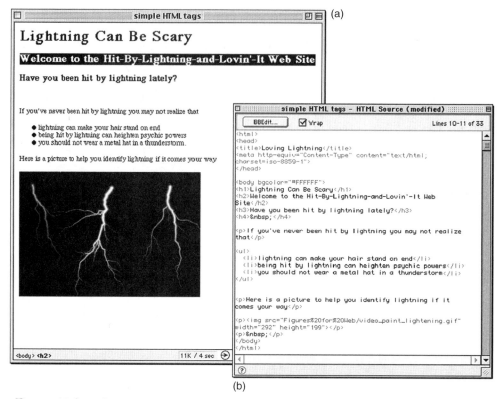

Figure 12.6 Authoring tools for the Web. In programs such as Macromedia Dreamweaver, used here, designers can (a) type and format text just as they would in a word processor and (b) view the HTML in a separate window. (Formatting choices are, of course, limited to those that can be represented by HTML tags.) The process also works in reverse in Dreamweaver: A designer can type in HTML tags by hand and immediately view the effect in the browser-style window. When the designer selects text in either window, the corresponding section of the document is selected in the other. *(Portions copyright 1998 Macromedia, Inc. Used with permission)*

The layout of a Web page is constrained by the choices available in HTML's system of formatting instructions. The HTML tags are used to structure Web documents and to create links with other Web documents. Because these markup tags began as a way to indicate document structure rather than nuances of appearance, their capabilities will seem limited to artists and designers familiar with even the most basic design and layout programs. Additional tags (beyond those supported by official HTML release specifications) sometimes are made available by companies for use with their browsers, but there is no guarantee that other companies' browsers can make sense of them.

Although today's serious Web artists and designers must still learn HTML, software programs such as Adobe PageMill, Microsoft FrontPage, and Macromedia Dreamweaver already use graphic user interfaces resembling page-layout programs to arrange text and images for Web pages (see Fig. 12.6). Many page-layout programs and word processors already have or will soon have HTML conversion options to convert documents to Web formats automatically.

The present options for HTML-based formatting include several levels of headings, one type of body text, image placement at the center, right, or left of the page, rudimentary text and image alignment, and tables for organizing text and images. Text cannot easily be run around or over images, and the fonts usually are determined by the end-user's browser, not by the document's creator; **style sheets** give the creator of the page much more control over the fonts and formatting but are not yet handled well by all browsers. **Frames** divide the page into independently navigable sections. In *LOVE*, Group Z used frames innovatively to create a multilevel composition with borders and to vary the layout of different sequences (see Fig. 12.7). "LOVE consists of 7 series of 7

Figure 12.7 GroupZ, Belgium, *LOVE*, 1995. (a) Opening screen. (b) From the third series, by Michaël Samyn, "'Forever young' shows pictures, drawings, quotes from letters and other souvenirs of (girl)friends he had in [his teen years]" [GroupZ, 1995]. (c) "'The Love List' is actually not a series but a single page that appears seven times in LOVE. It is a list of names of people who love each other and you are hereby invited to add your own love to it. It is sort of like an old tree in which you can carve your name and the name of the one you love" [GroupZ, 1995]. *(Courtesy of Michaël Samyn for Zoper!)*

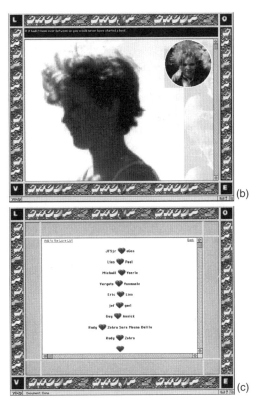
(b)

(c)

(a)

pages. They are linked together in an interface that lets you navigate from page to page in 5 directions. From almost every page you can reach 5 other pages. And yet it is not easy to reach all 49 of them. Like in real life, LOVE sometimes stops when you don't expect it to" [Group Z, 1995].

Regularly revised, HTML provides new capabilities, third-party tags, and plugs-ins that push the limits of Web page design almost daily. One of the few certainties about the Web is that it will continue to evolve rapidly.

12.3.3 LINKS

Although the graphic and layout capabilities available on the Web pale in comparison to regular graphics and publishing software, the ease of creating links and the huge body of data that can be accessed are stupendous. Unlike an image, a link takes up very little storage space. A work can thus have complex linking and even external interaction scripts and still be responsive, even over a slow connection.

The structure of links and the actions required by the user (usually clicking with a mouse) are, not surprisingly, often a crucial part of the experience of a Web piece. For instance, in the ad319 piece *Body, Space, Memory* (see Fig. 12.8), clicking on both images and text sets up an analogy between clicking to penetrate farther into the Web and clicking into the physical space of a body and the conceptual space of associations set up by the artists. The form and the thoughts intermingle in a way peculiar to this electronic medium. In the Heartbeat section, the user repeatedly clicks a small spherical-looking "heart-rock," and the repetitiveness of the clicking sets up a rhythm that guides the sensation of viewing this part of the piece. The graphics are extremely simple, and the interactive linking capabilities are fully exploited.

Treating links as a touch can lead to art works in which the linking structure, not the linked content, is the art. New forms of art work that are described in terms of their linking structures have begun to emerge. The *Mola Web,* for instance, is a collaborative World Wide Web piece that makes the Web's hypertext capabilities its main aesthetic focus. The piece consists of written works and a graphic in the style of a mola textile (a Panamanian layered reverse appliqué, often very complex). Every part of this image, which serves as an entry point into the piece (see Fig. 12.9), is linked to portions of the text and every word is a link. The perceptual space created by traveling the links is made visual through the Web browser convention of assigning different colors to linked words and changing the color after the user has explored a link. As the user reads with a combination of linear scanning and hyperlink jumps, a colored pattern emerges. At first it is composed predominantly of unexplored link colors, gradually turning to the linked color as more of the piece is visited.

12.4 THE WEB AS DATABASE

In some senses, the Web is an enormous multimedia database, and the challenge in using hypertext navigation and search engines is to find the information desired. However, the ease with which images can be copied from and placed on the Web does not

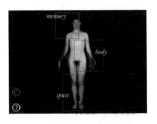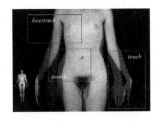

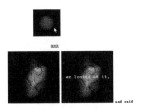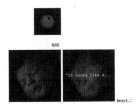

Figure 12.8 Ad319, *Body, Space, Memory*, 1995. A selection of screens generated by entering the Body Space and repeatedly clicking the "heart-rock." *(Courtesy of Ad319: Nan Goggin, Robb Springfield, Joseph Squier, and Kathleen Chmelewski)*

mean that doing so is legal! Copyright laws apply to the Web just as they do to traditional media (see the copyright sidebar in Chapter 2).

The ability to form a collection of text and images that is explored through hypertext linking and searching has led to many Web art projects that draw on the database format, accessing or amassing links or data. In 1994, Antonio Muntadas created *The File Room,* an archive about censorship, to which users can add new examples, and it has been growing ever since (http:// fileroom.aaup.uic.edu/FileRoom/documents/homepage.html).

David Blair's art project *WAXweb* has pushed the multimedia database limits of the Web. Originally a movie entitled *Wax, or the Invention of Television Among the Bees, WAXweb,* first launched in February 1994, consisted of more than 2000 pages of hypertext,

Figure 12.9 Carolyn Guyer, Michael Joyce, Nigel Kerr, Nancy Lin, and Suze Schweitzer, *Mola Web,* 1995. Based on layered mola textiles from Panama, this map provides the entry point into the *Mola Web.* Clicking on any portion of the map brings the user to a text section or image that is in turn fully linked. This site also links to external Web sites, such as the site URouLette, which lands the user at a randomly selected Web site anywhere in the world. *(Courtesy of Michael Joyce)*

available to both Web and MOO users. Web users still have access to the hypermedia portions of the document. They contain the entire film embedded as 4800 color stills, 560 mpeg video clips, 3D components created with VRML (discussed in Section 12.6.1), and 2200 AIFF audio clips, including the soundtrack in English, French, German, and Japanese. (Options for users to add links and content to the Web site may be reinstated.) The text of the film's voiceovers can be displayed in the user's language of choice. Figure 12.10 shows several *WAXweb* screens. By exploring associative links among movie clips and visual forms, the user can experience the movie as a hypermedia event.

12.5 EXTENSIBLE MARKUP LANGUAGE (XML)

Structural tags, links, and databaselike functionality will become both easier to create and more powerful through the **Extensible Markup Language** (XML), a tagging language similar to HTML. Both XML and HTML come from the same parent standard, the **Standard Generalized Markup Language** (SGML), a relatively complex ISO standard originally devised for structured textual documents and later extended to hypermedia. XML can be considered a simplified subset of SGML.

In XML you can create your own tags and then define, in a separate style sheet document, how they should influence the appearance of your text. For example, you could create a <cliff> tag to indicate paragraphs that could be used as an overview of a long book. Later, when you wanted to prepare your overview, finding those paragraphs would be easy. You could also make those paragraphs stand out by defining a different font for them.

(a)

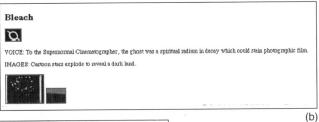

(b)

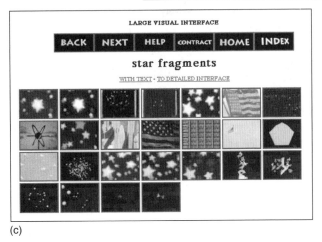

(c)

Figure 12.10 David Blair, *WAXweb*, 1994. . . (based on the movie by David Blair). (a) The narrative begins. A user can continue to read the story line or link through one of the images. The last paragraph of text explains that the protagonist believes that the dead can be made visible through photography. The bottom, right-most image is clicked, bringing the user to a page of associations. (b) The first association, Bleach. The images are of cartoon stars, and clicking the stars brings the user to (c) a selection of frames in the movie in which stars appear. Each star's image provides another navigational opportunity. *(Courtesy of David Blair)*

In addition to increasing dramatically the options for a document's structure, XML provides linking options that give the Web much more sophisticated hypertext capabilities, including one-to-many and many-to-one linkages and the ability to store link structures separately from the underlying content. Link sets for a Web site (or covering many sites) could be developed and exchanged. Site creators could create different paths for different audiences, such as novice, advanced, and disabled users. The XML structuring also makes linking to any aspect of a page easy, from a general URL to specific paragraphs to text strings. For example, an artist could create a Web piece comprising a set of links over a number of sites, linking to every instance of the string "lamp shade."

12.6 3D on the Web

> Cyberspace is a completely spatialized visualization of all information in global information systems, along pathways provided by present and future communications networks, enabling full copresence and interaction of multiple users, allowing input and output from and to the full human sensorium, permitting simulations of real and virtual realities, remote data collection and control through telepresence, and total integration and intercommunication with a full range of intelligent products and environment in real space [Novak, 1991, p. 225].
>
> Marcos Novak, architect, artist, composer, and theorist

William Gibson coined the term **cyberspace** in his 1984 science fiction novel *Neuromancer* [Gibson, 1984], describing it as a virtual realm of 3D visualizations of information structures contained in the world's interconnected computers. This vision of a hyperreal matrix fueled much subsequent science fiction and has influenced how both artists and scientists think about virtual reality. Another sci-fi novel, Neal Stephenson's *Snow Crash* [Stephenson, 1993], describes a **metaverse** in which the characters have **avatars,** or 3D representations of themselves that they design. The metaverse is an entire social world in which people meet and interact through their avatars. In both visions, the virtual realm is not just textual or made up of 2D still or moving images but is a 3D virtual world in which people, information, and places are compellingly represented.

12.6.1 Virtual Reality Modeling Language (VRML)

One of the first steps toward realizing some of the visual dimensional richness of the shared spaces described by visionary writers is the **Virtual Reality Modeling Language** (VRML, pronounced verm-el). Through VRML, many of the technical and theoretical issues described in Chapters 7 and 8 begin to merge with the concerns of the Internet and the Web.

This language describes polygonal forms and simple interactions and behaviors that can be understood by browser plug-ins. Instead of downloading actual 3D models, the browser downloads the textual VRML descriptions of geometric shapes, light sources, and textures, which the browsing machine then renders. Although limited in complexity (and of necessity usually small in file size), VRML models can be used to create interesting 3D worlds that are navigable via hyperlinks that can be associated with any of the polygonal facets of the model. The *WAXweb* creation has VRML sections in which users not only can explore the 3D graphics of the original movie, but also add new VRML models to its interactive database.

Victoria Vesna used database functions, interactive forms input, and VRML in *BODIES, INCorporated*. In this piece, users select body attributes by filling out a questionnaire. Future versions of the piece will enable users to interact with one another's virtual bodies in a communal 3D VRML world (see Fig. 12.11).

Figure 12.11 Victoria Vesna, *BODIES, INCorporated*, begun 1996. (a) Visitors to the Web site can order a body by using a primarily multiple-choice form (body-part texture selection portion). (b) Heads shown with sample textures. (c) Visual feedback is provided during the body-construction process in a VRML browser. *(Courtesy of Victoria Vesna, Nathan Freitas: VRML programming, Robert Nideffer: interface design)*

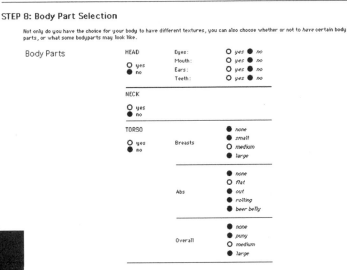

STEP 8: Body Part Selection

Not only do you have the choice for your body to have different textures, you can also choose whether or not to *have* certain body parts, or what some bodyparts may look *like.*

Body Parts

HEAD	Eyes:	○ yes ● no
○ yes	Mouth:	○ yes ● no
● no	Ears:	○ yes ● no
	Teeth:	○ yes ● no

NECK
○ yes
● no

TORSO		
○ yes	Breasts	● none
● no		● small
		○ medium
		● large

		● none
		○ flat
Abs		● out
		● rolling
		● beer belly

		● none
		● puny
Overall		○ medium
		● large

(a)

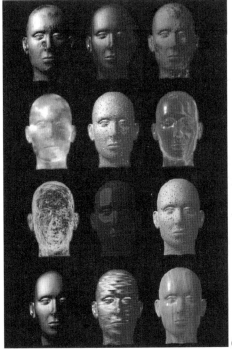

(b)

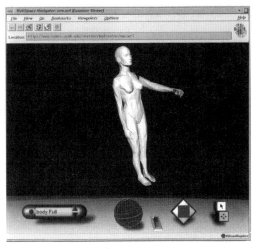

(c)

Vesna created this site to explore perceptions of physical and virtual, public and private, and individual and collective space. For example, she draws attention to assumptions about the nature of virtual worlds by requiring participants to sign a series of contracts spelling out the responsibility of a cyberbody owner, including an obligation to protect the body from duplication or theft. Once a body has been created, it cannot simply be deleted. Instead, the body's owner must enter another site, *Necropolis© INCorporated,* and there endure a public and visually detailed death based on real murders or accidents.

12.6.2 JAVA 3D

Whereas VRML is primarily a description language, with some behavior and interaction control, **Java3D** works with Java and is a full programming environment for creating 3D applets. Still unclear is the degree to which Java3D and VRML will work together. If the major corporations and institutions involved do not settle on a 3D standard for the Web, the widespread use of 3D in Web sites surely will be slowed. In addition, 3D applets and 3D sections of Web sites may work only from single platforms or browsers.

12.6.3 COLLABORATION

Several large-scale collaborative works have been underway, some for years, at the SITO site (http://www.sito.org/). In a collaborative process known as *gridding,* one participant creates the center square, say, of the grid and others create adjacent squares, always taking into account the need to merge with and react to the neighboring squares. Usually a grid is considered complete when all the squares have been designed and joined. In an infinite grid, however, layers are added on top of older squares. A viewer can view squares from random layers or choose a set of custom squares to make up a grid image. *HyGrid,* a current project based on gridding but utilizing more complex rules, contains more than 300 images, all linked along visually navigable paths pursued by clicking the images (see Fig. 12.12).

The nature of the gridding projects does not distinguish among trained artists, designers, and the general public. Everyone is invited to work on the project and the goal is the sense of community and enjoyment of participation as much as the creation of a finished product. In this sense, although the grids have documentation, the artwork resembles a performance piece more than a painting. Hundreds of people can work anonymously on such projects, with the roles of creator, owner, and audience becoming intermingled.

12.7 DISPLAY AND DISTRIBUTION

While cultural myth actively claims that art is a human universal—transcending its historical moment and the other conditions of its making, and above all the class of its makers and patrons—and that it is the highest of spiritual and metaphysical truth, high art is patently

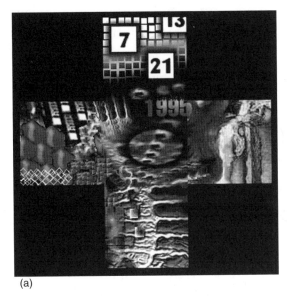

(a)

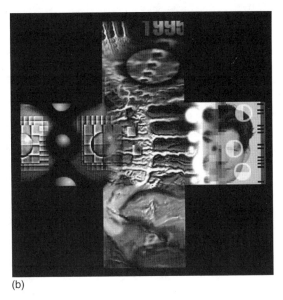

(b)

Figure 12.12 **Ed Stastny,** *HyGrid,* **begun 1995,** (a collaborative Web project). (a) The center square was created by Ed Stastny; contributors (clockwise from the top) were Jon Van Oast, Bob Anderson, Ranjit Bhatnagar, and Robin Fercoq. (b) Clicking the bottom square brings the viewer to a new grid based on that square; new contributors (clockwise from the right) were Jon Van Oast, Bob Anderson, and Ed Stastny. *(Courtesy of Ed Stastny)*

> *exclusionary in its appeal, culturally relative in its concerns, and indissolubly wedded to big money and "upper class" life in general [Rosler, 1994].*
> *Martha Rosler, artist and critic*

Will the Internet and the Web succeed where other avant-garde uses of technology have failed? Will art be made by and consumed by "the masses" without the intervention of high-art institutions? The potential certainly exists, but today the Web remains a demographically restricted phenomenon. According to Andrew Kantor:

> Zona Research's report, "Internet and Intranet: 1996 Market, Opportunities, and Trends," notes that, regardless of terms like "global" and "worldwide," the Internet is neither. "Our research indicates that aside from the educational community, the vast majority of all Internet and Intranet activity is occurring in North America and other English-speaking regions," said Clay Ryder, senior industry analyst at Zona. "We see a direct correlation between the deregulation of the telecommunications infrastructure of a region and the growth of Internet and Intranet use within that region" [Kantor, 1996].

Although it is too soon to tell, the exponential growth of online Web sites, artist and designer home pages, and online discussion and resources all point to a new way of viewing and distributing art that easily bypasses museums, galleries, and social cliques.

It is said that "the power of the press belongs to those who own one." With the advent of personal computers and public worldwide networks, many artists and designers will control a far-reaching means of distribution.

Both individual artists and designers and more traditional galleries and design houses are likely to thrive on the Web. Obviously, Web-based works will be seen on the Web, but other types of work can also be shared over the Web, bringing more works to more people. New audiences may develop for art work—people who could not or would not travel to view work in a gallery or museum or might feel uncomfortable doing so. An expanded audience for art and an expanded sense of engagement created by interactive, participatory works have the potential to change the exclusive community of art production, viewing, and ownership into a much more inclusive one.

12.7.1 ARTIST PORTFOLIOS

I don't have to wait anymore for a gallery to call me up or to get permission from a location. I just put [my outdoor sculptures] on the Web for people to see. In a way it doesn't matter whether or not they were ever really installed. . . . I was just in Italy, for instance, and I shot all kinds of sites. I'm going to put up a piece in Venice. I went to Cambodia, to Angkor Wat where there's a 1 mile long reflecting pool and I'm going to put up a piece there too [Kornfeld, 1998].
Douglas Kornfeld, sculptor and computer artist

This chapter has been concerned primarily with the World Wide Web as a new art-making tool and generator of new art forms. However, the Web also is an extraordinary means of exhibiting, marketing, and distributing almost any type of art work. Both computer artists and designers and those using traditional media can present selections of their work on the Web, either as a temporary show or as a résumé/portfolio. Personal Web pages with art work and supporting information let artists and designers show their work without having to be associated with a gallery or a design firm. Viewers are usually encouraged to respond to art work online, and artists and designers often include their email addresses in their information. (Searching for *images* and *fine art* turns up many interesting sites.)

12.7.2 TRADITIONAL MUSEUMS AND GALLERIES ON THE WEB

Many museums and galleries now offer online counterparts to shows and collections (check out http://www.yahoo.com/Arts/Museums_and_Galleries/or search for the name of your favorite art institution). For electronic art work, a Web site can sometimes offer the same quality as a gallery space. For traditional artwork, the reproduction quality can approach that of color prints but will never, of course, match viewing the work in person. The Web provides rapid and inexpensive access to works in faraway places. In addition, online works often are annotated and interlinked in attractive and instructive ways. The National Museum of American Art in Washington, DC (http://www.nmaa.si.edu/) has a Web showing of "Metropolitan Lives: The Ashcan Artists and Their New York." In addition to images of the paintings and text discussing the Ashcan school, viewers can see QuickTime movies, including clips from archival films showing New York City in the early 1900s. The Los Angeles County Museum of Art hosts shows with online elements that include video clips of artist interviews (http://lacma.org/).

More and more museums are supporting both traditional art work online and Web-based work. The Dia Center for the Arts in New York City (http://www.diacenter.org/) has always featured innovative work and naturally began to support and show artists using the Web. The Whitney Museum of American Art, also in New York City, has made a commitment to showing work created with this new tool (http://www.echonyc.com/~whitney/).

12.7.3　Web-Based Galleries

Artists who put their work on the Web can reach a potentially enormous audience. But how will anyone even know that a particular artist's work is available? Unless the artist is already so well known that people can be expected to search for the artist's name, simply establishing a site may not attract are very large audience. **Online galleries** play the important role of establishing high-quality sites to which viewers will return again and again. Curators are just as necessary on the Web as in traditional forums, if not more so. The @art gallery at http://www.art.uiuc.edu/@art/gallery.html, for example, has exhibited electronic work by many well-known artists. Affiliated with the School of Art and Design at the University of Illinois at Urbana–Champaign, this Web site is the creation of faculty members Nan Goggin and Joseph Squier. They seek to encourage artists' involvement in ever-expanding communities and to provide a high-quality virtual gallery that attracts serious artists and art lovers. Another well-known Web site is the ada gallery at http://www.adaweb.com/basics.html, which is run by artists Ainatte Inbal, Cherise Fong, Andrea Scott, Vivian Selbo, Matteo Ames, and Benjamin Weil.

Conclusion

The World Wide Web changes every day. The vision of a communal, graphic, interactive 3D cyberspace often is clearly articulated, but actually the Web is still quite limited—and some say that WWW should stand for Wild Wild West. The Web is technology in the making and its users routinely cope with the unstable versions of software and hardware that only small groups of testers formerly encountered. Web sites that disappear without a trace, software that crashes, and programs that are incomplete are typical annoyances and a certain level of chaos prevails.

Despite the rudimentary reality of the Web today, its promise is great and its progress is rapid. For artists and designers, the Web is presently best for creating works based on social interaction and communities rather than for exchanging high-resolution, full-color imagery or lengthy video content. Although the bandwidth is severely limited for most users and the design tools are poor compared to desktop publishing programs, the Web offers unprecedented opportunities for interaction among people around the world, as well as access to an ever-growing worldwide database of interconnected information.

Many of the limitations that define the Web today will disappear, and more and more art programs will have built-in Web features, easing the transition from desktop computer-based to Web-based art. MetaCreations Painter already has Web formatting and compression options along with network capabilities that let artists and designers in remote locations work together on a single image. In the not-so-distant future, the Web may be able to support work created with all the types of software discussed in this book and may well be an integral part of the art world, essential to many types of art creation and enjoyment.

Suggested Readings

Benedikt, Michael (ed.). *Cyberspace: First Steps.* The MIT Press, 1991. A thoughtful collection of essays on what cyberspace is, how we may work and play in it, and how it should be designed. Although relatively old, this book is still widely read, and many of the ideas in it are just beginning to be realized. Essay topics range from architecture to sociology to mathematical theory to corporate cyberspace to interface design.

Damer, Bruce. *Avatars!: Exploring and Building Virtual Worlds on the Internet.* Peachpit Press, 1998. Presents the making of avatars and experiences in virtual worlds in an accessible and practical manner. The book includes a CD and has an accompanying Web site to help readers get started making their own avatars and traveling to virtual lands. Detailed descriptions of several virtual communities on the Web will help readers feel right at home in cyberspace.

Gibson, William. *Neuromancer.* Ace Books, 1984 (and sequels *Count Zero,* Ace Books, 1987, and *Mona Lisa Overdrive,* Ace Books, 1988). Jack into the matrix with Gibson and the slick writing of this cyberpunk science fiction genre. This series has certainly influenced many people's views of technology (although Gibson claims to have written *Neuromancer* on a typewriter). Also check out his book of short stories, *Burning Chrome,* Ace Books, 1982.

Graham, Ian S. *HTML Sourcebook, A Complete Guide to HTML 3.0,* 2d ed. John Wiley & Sons, 1996. A comprehensive reference, useful to have on hand after learning the basics.

Lemay, Laura. *Teach Yourself Web Publishing with HTML 3.2 in a Week,* 3d ed. Sams.net Publishing, 1996. For artists and designers who want to explore HTML in depth. This book provides a detailed tutorial and requires no technical background.

Stephenson, Neal. *Snow Crash.* Spectra, 1993. Welcome to the metaverse and a world run by the Mafia, consisting almost entirely of strip malls. If you enjoy Gibson and Stephenson, also check out Bruce Sterling.

Weinman, Lynda. *Deconstructing Web Graphics.* New Riders, 1996. Case studies of high-profile Web sites showing how Web designers and programmers face the many challenges of Web site creation and utilize the forces shaping this new field, from HTML to Java.

Weinman, Lynda. *Designing Web Graphics, 2.* New Riders, 1997. A rewrite of the excellent *Designing Web Graphics* (1996). It contains lots of practical information about getting graphics onto the Web. A CD–ROM provides helpful tips and software. See also Weinman's Web page at http://www.earthlink.net/~lyndaw. Written in an engaging style, tattered versions are found in many artists' and designers' studios.

For more Web information: New books on the Web come out every day. Browse your local store in person. Also, try Web searches for tutorials and documentation on HTML or other Web topics. There is a great deal of current information online that is free.

Exercises

1. *Art of the link.* Create a Web piece in which the linking structure is the essence of the piece.

> With Macromedia Dreamweaver 1.2: Type your text directly into a new Dreamweaver document or copy and paste text from elsewhere. (Many programs will save text as HTML, and the text can be opened from within Dreamweaver.) Add images by using the small icon of the mountain and sun or Insert: Image. Select Window: HTML to see the HTML that you are generating (you can also edit the HTML directly in this window). Create a second page and save it in the same directory as the first. To create a link from a text area, select the text and type in the desired destination page in the Link area of the Properties window. To create a link to particular places within a page, place the cursor at the desired location and select Insert: Anchor. Name the anchor. To link to an anchor on the same page, select an area of text and type #<anchor name> in the Link area. To link to an anchor on a different page, type <page URL>#<anchor name> in the Link area. To create a link from an image, select the image and type a link destination in the Properties window Link area.

2. *Viewing art on the Web, pros and cons.* Compare the pros and cons of viewing art work on the Web versus in a museum or gallery versus in reproduction in art books. In particular, think about your own work. How do you want people to see it? Interact with it? Who is the audience and what is the best way to reach them? How can computer technology and networks help?

> With any browser: Go to www.yahoo.com and select Arts & Humanities and then Artists. Explore some of the categories to see what types of things are online. Also visit at least one gallery that specializes in Web-based art work, such as the @art gallery at http://gertrude. art.uiuc.edu/@art/gallery.html.

3. *Web conversion.* Convert a piece that you have already created (whether with the computer or traditional media) to a Web piece. In what ways should the piece be changed to accommodate the limitations and advantages of the Web?

> With Macromedia Dreamweaver 1.2: Import an image that you have already worked on as a 2D piece. Select the image, and choose Map from the Properties window. You are now in the image map editor, which lets you select different portions of the image and create links from them. The result is a single image that you can use to link to any number of other places. Check the HTML window to see how the links are described. Use image mapping to create a Web piece based on your original image, spread (in sections or with variations) over several Web pages.

4. *Holiday from self.* Take part in an online game or chat session in which you represent yourself as someone other than who you are. You can change your age, sex, race, and so on. How do these changes make you feel? Does doing so represent freedom or discomfort? In what ways do you choose to be who you are in everyday life?

An application-specific exercise is not appropriate.

5. *Your own Web-based art form.* Bonnie Mitchell's pieces are about new structures and forms made possible by the computer and networks. After looking at her virtual worlds Web site at http://creativity.syr.edu/~worlds/, design a new art form for networked computer artists and designers. Specify the rules and constraints. (For example, in Mitchell's work each new image must be based on an old one and fit into the preset map.) What might constitute a good or bad example of your new genre? Who would be the participants and who the likely audience (these may overlap)?

For beginning students, this exercise is best done on paper.

Conclusion

Figure 1 **Douglas Kornfeld's studio.** Catalogue cover for "The Computer in the Studio" show at the DeCordova Museum and Sculpture Park and the Computer Museums, Lincoln and Boston, Massachusetts, 1994. *(Copyright Willard Traub, Photographer)*

Speed and the Lost Dimension

Speed is the essence of the computer's power over symbols. You can add by hand and do symbolic algebra by hand, but you can't do digital imaging or 3D modeling by hand. The brute-force methods used to process millions and millions of tiny pieces of information about color, height, width, and depth become elegant when accelerated. This capability also makes the medium a fitting one for Postmodernist production in which patient handcrafting is supplanted by the instant photographic image and composing of premade materials.

No longer sublimated, speed is now recognized as that which gives form to images—to images of consciousness, such as mental or ocular images, and to our consciousness of optic or opto-electronic images. If speed is now the shortest route between two points, the necessarily reductive character of all scientific and sensible representation becomes a reality effect of acceleration, an optic effect of the speed of propagation. This speed is metabolic in the example of ocular and mental images, and technological in the case of the form-images of photographic and cinematographic representation, of the virtual images of infography, and of the representations of optic lasers [Virilio, 1991, p. 117].

Without a place in time or space, collapsed into a nonspatial world of encoded instruction, computer art lives most of its life in Virilio's "lost dimension." In this dimensionless territory, concepts of space and time have been eroded through jet flight, 24-hour television, digital communication, and global networks. On the computer, the history of a work, and the evidence of the artist's hand and testimony to the process of creation (and often also of exchange afterwards) are erased as soon as they are made. A digital work has no evident history. The artist can choose to capture the history, in minute detail if desired, by recording every stroke and decision made, but that must be done consciously and independently. From the bits themselves, someone else cannot determine how long a piece was worked on, how many versions it went through, how old it is, or how many hands it has passed through.

THE ROLE OF ECONOMICS

Not only computer-based art work, but the computing medium itself is an obvious product of the cultures that create it. Computers and software are created for markets that are determined not by artists but by technology-driven businesses such as aerospace and the military. Eventually, the software trickles down to larger markets and becomes commodified: Military flight simulators become games, customized CAD programs lead to off-the-shelf CAD and drawing software, Hollywood special effects houses produce commercial versions of custom software, such as Pixar's Renderman, and so on.

When using graphics software, you should ask yourself, For whom was this program developed? This question is important because it determines what the software lets you do and tries to make you do; what it makes easy and what it makes prohibitively difficult. A program designed primarily for manipulating photographs might support only limited tools for freehand drawing and emphasize instead effects such as lens flares or motion blurs. A program designed for drafting may offer and encourage accuracy and numerical input but discourage intuitive gestures; or a line might be easy to measure but hard to process randomly for interesting visual results.

Because artists represent a small market, their needs often are not considered by the companies creating the hardware and software on which artists are coming to depend. As new art forms develop, artists must continue to communicate with software companies so that their voices contribute to the directions R&D take. This medium is in flux and still young. Much can be done to improve it and shape it.

On the one hand, helping to form a medium is exciting; on the other hand, constant change in a medium can make developing a style and body of work difficult, and the user of that medium must constantly learn new skills. The pace of change appears to be accelerating, not slowing down, owing in part to the Internet as a distribution mechanism. Artists (and computer users in general) must cope not only with programs that change faster, but also with those that do not work as well as the users might hope. Because the medium is far from stable, it offers unusual possibilities and inevitable frustrations.

> Software is market-driven: often it doesn't work well not because people are lazy or stupid, but because it's hard to create and because product cycles (the amount of time it takes to get a new product out of the door) are getting shorter and shorter. In the automobile industry, the product cycle is tied to the yearly rollout; in computer software, getting there first counts for a lot, and this forces companies to come out with new products faster and faster. Software can be anything you want it to be, but most of the time fierce commercial pressure leads to immature releases and less than perfect software. This news is both good and bad because, while there's less discipline, there is also more creativity [van Dam, 1997].

The Nature of the Medium

> *Matter must continue its natural life when modified by the hand of the sculptor. . . . Matter should not be used merely to suit the purpose of the artist, it must not be subjected to a preconceived idea and to a preconceived form; both must come from within matter and not be forced upon it from without [Brancusi, 1923].*
>
> *Constantin Brancusi, pioneer of abstract sculpture*

The artist's usual expectations for attaining technical skill and the usual assumptions about the rate of change of a medium are overthrown by the computer. The computer stands alone as an art-making tool that lacks an intrinsic material nature. As the computer's capabilities vary with the programs written for it, new ways of working with images on the computer appear with a rapidity unprecedented in the history of art. A graphics program that you have come to know and love can become obsolete in a matter of months. The tools of creation are routinely bought and sold. You will have little, if any, control over the features put into programs in the first place and how they evolve.

The push for "newer and better," rarely relevant to traditional art materials, dominates the computer world as hardware and software companies compete to make computers faster and let software developers strive for ever more ambitious goals. As a result, unless you program your own art software or decide not to upgrade equipment, mastering even a single software package is practically impossible. The chance to use a new, more powerful 3D modeler, a faster computer, or entirely new software and hardware such as voice-recognition or virtual-reality devices can be almost irresistible. This impulse often is encouraged by juries and curators looking for art made with the latest technologies to include in high-profile computer art shows.

You should be aware that the choices available in software, unlike the capabilities inherent in a physical substance such as oil paint or marble or film, usually result from decisions made by other people, not from the inherent capabilities of the computer. Realizing this can help you focus better on choosing and mastering the specific capabilities important to your art work.

The temptation to believe that you will produce better, more interesting, more up-to-date work with new software and more features is always present, but there is no end to the number of features and new packages available, and the desire to explore fully the tools and capabilities at hand can sidetrack you from your artistic goals. You should not feel obliged to learn every feature of a program, nor should you be constrained by the lack of features in a program—other applications often can provide supplementary capabilities. Balancing the advantages of new tools against the time and energy necessary to learn them is a constant issue. Although it is exciting to be presented regularly with new capabilities and new ways of working, such an environment may turn out to be less conducive to thoughtful art-making than one that changes much more slowly.

LIMITS OF TECHNIQUE AND THEORY

Whether this condition of the availability of all traditions still permits an aesthetic theory at all, in the sense in which aesthetic theory existed from Kant to Adorno, is questionable, because a field must have a structure if it is to be the subject of scholarly or scientific understanding. Where the formal possibilities have become infinite, not only authentic creation but also its scholarly analysis become correspondingly difficult. Adorno's notion that late capitalistic society has become so irrational that it may well be that no theory can any longer plumb it applies perhaps with even greater force to post avant-gardiste art [Bürger, 1984].

Peter Bürger, literary critic and theorist

In this book I discuss the computer in the visual arts from both technical and theoretical perspectives. But technique and theory, of both art and computing, must be studied and then forgotten, not in the sense of no longer knowing about them, but in the sense of devoting no conscious effort to them while you are working. Although you can plan and analyze works intellectually before and after you make them, doing so during the actual process of creation tends to be counterproductive.

If the technical aspects are overwhelming, you can focus on a more familiar type of program or set of features or work with another artist who has a more technical background. If the theoretical ideas begin to transgress your sense of self and turn your art work into a philosophical exercise or journalism project rather than a process of personal artistic expression, you must step back. Knowledge of theory in today's art world, like the technical knowledge necessary for a deep understanding of computer graphics, can be a wonderful resource. But when theory stops being a source of inspiration and instead becomes ideological, you must remember that theories that deconstruct social interaction by identifying codes and heuristics are themselves a product of a culture's own assumptions.

Just as an image cannot be trusted as a document of reality, so words on a page, even these words, must not be accepted without reservation. Theories that were proclaimed with the certainty of revelation in the 1980s are now viewed with skepticism if not outright rejection by many art historians. Irving Sandler writes of the late 1980s, "Art theory had become, in a word, academic and indeed, it remained influential only in graduate art history programs in which unregenerate tenured ideologues taught that scholarship meant choosing and mastering a dogma; poking through works of art for evidence supporting it; and evaluating the work on the basis of the dogma" [Sandler, 1996, p. 546]. For young artists, the field can seem quite intimidating. In discussing what style or tradition or theory to choose from, Thomas Lawson claims, "It all boils down to a question of faith. Young artists concerned with pictures and picture-making, rather than sculpture and the lively arts, are faced with a bewildering choice" [Lawson, 1984, p. 153].

Perhaps a parable of sorts will help. In the fifth century B.C. the philosopher Xeno proposed several paradoxes in an attempt to show that motion does not really exist. In one he argued that an arrow shot at a tree could never reach it since it must first travel halfway to the tree, but before it can do that it must first travel halfway between the starting point and halfway point, and so on. Since another halfway point between the beginning and position last decided upon can always be calculated, the arrow must travel through infinitely many positions. Therefore, he concluded, it could never reach its target and in some sense must always be at rest. A mathematical way out of this paradox was not discovered until the seventeenth century with the invention of calculus and a rigorous theory of limits. But anyone, even in the fifth century B.C., could clearly demonstrate empirically, without the aid of philosophical theory or calculus, that arrows shot at trees did indeed reach them. Similarly, many of the claims of Postmodernism that were expected to lead to the end of Modernist art and in particular the end of painting, often are compelling to read but have had no apparent effect on either artists' desire to make images or the art market's willingness to support them.

Several important critics have questioned, in fact, whether the analytic, deconstructive process of Postmodernism, in revealing the infrastructure of artistic production, has not, in effect, exposed the plumbing and electrical conduits at the expense of making the house unlivable. With theory, as with the technical content in this book, you must learn to take what you need to go along your own chosen path. The essence of creativity is not to get stuck in any single outlook or dogmatic interpretation of meaning but to keep moving fluidly. The Taoist author Deng Ming-Dao writes, "Creativity does not mean the arbitrary making of something out of our cultural minds. Rather it is spontaneous movement in tandem with Tao, a movement that will generate life and not misery for others. One has reached the ultimate levels of creativity when one has mastered skill so thoroughly that it can be forgotten" [Ming-Dao, 1992, p. 68].

Do new technologies cause cultural shifts and inspire new theories? Or does the climate of thought determine which technologies are developed and used? The answer in the case of computer art is some of both. The situation is similar to the use of perspective in Renaissance Europe. In the sixteenth century, the climate of thought was changing rapidly, driven by the newly proclaimed power of individual, empirical observation. Perspective, invented by the Greeks nearly a millennium before and then forgotten, was an ideal technique to show that the individual's point of view mattered as it never had before. This combination of technique and theory helped to bring about one of the greatest periods of art the world has ever experienced.

Today you live in a climate of complex theories about the impact of everything from economics, technology, and mass media to cultural assumptions about gender, sexuality, appearance and, not least of all, the role of artists and the nature of creativity. The all-purpose universal computer has provided an extraordinary technical force that both inspires and reflects the needs of the various constituencies designing its hardware and software. As a technology, computer graphics sheds a particularly bright light on the issues raised in many recent theories of art and literature, such as loss of the original, the death of the author, the power of appropriation, the questioning of visual reality, the paradoxical combination of high-speed processes and tedious waiting, and the desire to create and experience art work outside traditional art institutions.

Will the confluence of late twentieth–century art theory and computer graphics technology yield a new Renaissance in the visual arts? The continued shaping of this revolutionary machine is up to you and countless other artists using it. Understanding the history of computers and computer art and the concepts presented in this book will help you make the most of this new medium and better fit the technical power of computer graphics to compelling theoretical ideas about art and to your own adventure of personal expression. As Hans Hoffman has said:

> There is in reality no such thing as modern art. Art is carried on up and down in immense cycles through centuries and civilizations. No choice is given us. Goethe says, "the wave that lifts us will finally swallow us." It is our destination and the destination of every culture [Hoffman, 1952].

Appendix A

Modern Art Periods

Figure A.1 Jackson Pollock, *Echo (Number 25), 1951* (enamel paint on canvas, 7′ 7⁷⁄₈″ × 7′ 2″. Pollock worked with a mark made by dripping paint rather than applying it with a brush or other tool. His dense compositions consume the canvas without reference to traditional composition, are spatial, and yet are impenetrable. His space was a space of paint. *(© 1999 Pollock-Krasner Foundation/Artists Rights Society (ARS), NY. Courtesy of The Museum of Modern Art, New York)*

Terms such as *Modernism* and *Postmodernism* are used throughout this book and in the discussion of art in general. To clarify their usage in this text and provide some context for readers unfamiliar with them, I briefly summarize here the essential points of Modernism, the Avant–Garde, Postmodernism, and Pluralism.

A.1 MODERNISM

Modernism includes movements such as abstract art, Constructivism, Abstract Expressionism, and, in many ways, Minimalism. Modernism, "as a chronological term, is often restricted to the period 1860–1930 or thereabouts, though it may extend it to postwar art or 'late' modernism" [Foster, 1984, p. 189]. For my purposes in this book, Modernist art includes the late Modernism of the 1950s and 1960s with the additional recognition that, as a style and a philosophy of art for art's sake, it remains popular today. The content of Modernist art work often is the formal language of art itself: color, tone, line, and form, as evidenced in different media and explored outside the context of realistic imagery. The purity of each medium is stressed, and the visual, verbal, and time-based media are kept strictly apart. Modernist art critics held that in large part art was autonomous and displayed universal qualities transcending the time, culture, and place in which it was made.

Painters such as Robert Motherwell, Piet Mondrian, and Lee Krasner, and sculptors such as Constantin Brancusi and Henry Moore are some of the better known creators of Modernist art work. A part of the Modernist movement was its focus on artist-heroes or "art stars" such Jackson Pollock (see Fig. A.1) or William de Kooning. Some (mostly European) movements within Modernism, such as Russian Constructivism and Suprematism and Italian Futurism, united exploration of form and color and other abstract concepts, including composition and motion, with political agendas. Other movements, such as Abstract Expressionism, were not overtly concerned with political issues, although this movement is now seen as a part of an individualist, humanist sensibility often associated with the United States. Most early computer art work had a Modernist bent to it, dealing as it did with procedures for creating and systematically experimenting with abstract forms, and even exploring the possibility of programming universal aesthetic qualities (see Chapter 1).

A.2   THE AVANT-GARDE AND POSTMODERNISM

The historical avant-garde movements were unable to destroy art as an institution; but they did destroy the possibility that a given school can present itself with the claim to universal validity [Bürger, 1984, p. 97].

Peter Bürger, literary critic and theorist

Many of the ideas central to Postmodern art were first brought to public attention by a movement known as the **Avant-Garde,** which flourished in European cities and in New York in the 1910s and 1920s. This historical avant-garde included Dadaists, Surrealists, and the seeds of Pop Art. Marcel Duchamp, a well-known Dadaist, experimented with almost every challenge to the art world later pursued by Postmodernist artists, challenging both accepted subject matter and media for art. He and other Dadaists exploited collage, invented the "found object" as art work (see Fig. A.2) and held impromptu events or "happenings." The Avant-Garde also attempted—most critics feel unsuccessfully—to make an often ephemeral art outside the context of art institutions, such as galleries and museums, that would appeal directly to the public. Duchamp is famous in part for submitting (under a pseudonym) a urinal as "found art" to a gallery show in New York City. Ironically, the comment made with this gesture was considered of such

Figure A.2 Marcel Duchamp, Bicycle Wheel, 1951 (third version, after lost original of 1913, 50 1/2" × 25 1/2" × 16 5/8"). One of Duchamp's "found art" assemblages that served to call into question the entire concept of fine art. *(© 1999 Artists Rights Society (ARS), NY/ADAGP, Paris/Estate of Marcel Duchamp. Courtesy of The Museum of Modern Art, New York)*

Figure A.3 Barbara Kruger, *Untitled (You Invest in the Divinity of the Masterpiece)*, 1982 (unique photostat 71 3/4" × 45 5/8"). (*Courtesy of The Museum of Modern Art, New York*)

importance that a version of the urinal was purchased by The Museum of Modern Art in New York City and subsequently has been widely reproduced in art texts.

Postmodernism is an all-encompassing term, with origins in architecture and literary theory, that is used to differentiate certain art practices from those of Modernism. It is particularly important for artists using the computer because many Postmodern ideas are directly relevant to the use of computer technology. Postmodernism began in the late 1960s, and there is debate about whether it continues to exist or officially perished in the early 1990s. Certainly its approaches are still well represented, if only among other ways of making art. In essence, Postmodernist art is the coexistence of several styles, often "appropriated" directly from sources throughout different times and cultures. It is characterized by art work that is pictorial and often deals directly with political, social, and gender issues and the effects of mass media on culture. It is less concerned with craft, uniqueness, tradition, masterpieces, specific media, and museum and gallery exhibition than with conceptual grounding, engagement in social change, critique of cultural assumptions, and awareness of multicultural viewpoints. Barbara Kruger used the quintessential postmodern medium of photography to appropriate a well-known section of Michelangelo's Sistine Chapel (see Fig. A.3) to make a statement about art: "We have psychological, social, and economic investments in seeing the Sistine Chapel as a work of Art" [Staniszewski, 1995, p. 40].

Postmodernist art critics do not believe in Modernism's autonomous qualities of art; instead, they argue that art can be understood only by investigating the social, political, and economic contexts in which it was made. Such investigations reveal assumptions implicit in a work (e.g., gender roles or race relations) and often are used to reveal meanings of which the artist may be unaware. Postmodernist approaches in many ways suggest that the art critic is inherently more influential in the interpretation and evaluation of art work than the artists themselves.

Appropriation, or the reuse of imagery and styles from other artists, time periods, and cultures, is prevalent in Postmodernist work because it evokes associations difficult to conjure up in a single traditional medium and because it submerges the issues of craft and style in the conceptual power of composition. In addition, the role of theory, from various disciplines but particularly literary theory, is greatly extended in Postmodernist art, and many artists are engaged in reading, writing, and creating art projects more closely allied with philosophy than with traditional art work.

A.3 Pluralism

Both Modernist and Postmodernist work thrive today, along with other approaches that include a wide range of media, conceptual content, and levels of craftsmanship. Not the least of these is the growing number of digital efforts and art forms based on them. Irving Sandler calls the present an era of **Pluralism** (more truly pluralistic than the period in the 1970s that bears the same name). In the absence of a strong-ism, artists are free to work in whatever way best suits them.

Computer technology not only plays an important role in different artistic styles but is linked, like photography, through its very nature with pluralistic interests outside the art world, including universities, research labs, the government, the military, and businesses, particularly those that produce software and hardware. Because of computer graphics, the use of visual work in a wide range of other disciplines is growing, and already the computer-based tools and methods for visual thinking in the arts, humanities, and sciences can no longer be easily distinguished. Thus you may be witnessing the beginning of an era in which definitions of art and distinctions among disciplines become less important as the means of communication become richer.

APPENDIX B

Computing
Theory

B.1 Symbolic Logic

Computers can seem unbelievably complex, intimidating, and above all mysterious. But several of the most important theories underlying them require no previous study of technology or computer science; they are concepts that anyone can understand. These theories deal with symbols and ways in which they can be combined (familiar ground for artists). More than a century ago, at the same time that Charles Babbage was designing his mechanical calculating machines (see Chapter 1), a brilliant Irish mathematician, George Boole, was working on an area of mathematics and philosophy called **symbolic logic,** an extension of algebraic relationships and notation to concepts that are not numeric.

In symbolic logic, symbols are assigned to different situations that are either true or false and then the symbols are used in more complex logical relationships. Let's replace "I am on a roller coaster" simply with "R," "I am feeling nauseous" with "N," and "It is pouring rain" with "P. " If I am feeling nauseous, then N is true; if I am in my office and not on a roller coaster, then R is false. These situations can be combined in different ways with logical relationships such as AND, NOT, and OR. For example, the situation N AND P is true only if I am nauseous and it is pouring rain. If either N or P is false, then N AND P is false. The situation N AND (NOT)P is true only if I am feeling nauseous and it is not pouring rain. The situation R OR P is true if either one or both of the situations "I am on a roller coaster" and "It is pouring rain" are true.

Claude Shannon, the founder of modern information theory, integrated symbolic algebra with computing when, as a graduate student at MIT, he showed that Boolean algebra could be applied to the problem of switching circuits. The true and false, or 0 and 1, of Boolean algebra remains the underlying basis of digital computing, in which millions of transistors are either on or off. This discovery showed how a machine could be used to work with symbolic logic.

B.2 The Universal Machine

But what would be the nature of such a machine? The idea of a device that could handle even the most complex symbolic logic problems with a series of simple steps is credited to Alan Turing, a British mathematical prodigy who was instrumental in decrypting German codes with his computing devices during World War II. In a groundbreaking paper written in 1936 (at the age of 24), "On Computable Numbers," Turing postulated a simple-minded machine that would read a potentially infinite tape having squares filled with 1s or 0s.[1] The machine would process the tape according to stored logical instructions one square at a time and could either leave the 1s and 0s alone or could overwrite a 1 with a 0 or a 0 with a 1.

---

[1]An identical theory was published at the same time by Emil L. Post, a professor at City College of New York, but Turing's eminence has resulted in his getting credit for this idea.

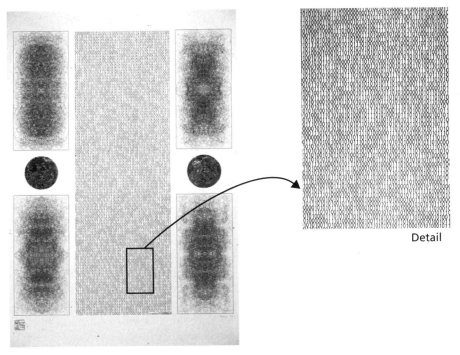

Detail

Figure B.1 Roman Verostko, *Illuminated Universal Turing Machine,* 1995, (44″ × 30″).

At first the usefulness of such a machine would appear to be severely limited by the set of stored instructions used to process the tape and the likelihood that different machines would have to be built for each conceived purpose. But Turing also postulated that there must exist a "universal Turing machine" that could do everything any specialized Turing machine could do.[2] The Turing machine was intended to show that complex problems could be solved by a series of simple operations. The modern computer is the realization of this concept. Computers are the world's first universal machines and have no predetermined function: Their purpose changes with the software run on them.

Figure B.1 shows a computer art piece by Roman Verostko that takes as its topic the universal Turing machine. "The rectangular area text is an algorithm for a Universal Turing Machine in a binary format (see detail). This version is quoted from Roger Penrose's *The Emperor's New Mind*. The circular gold-leafed glyphs are applied by hand,

---

[2]In fact, some things can be proven not to be computable. Gödel's Theorem deals with this discovery in depth, and Turing postulated the impossibility of a specialized Turing machine that could decide whether a Turing machine would calculate indefinitely or come to a halt.

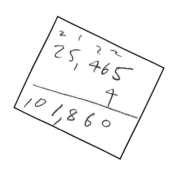

Figure B.2 Calculating in everyday life. A $10 calculator can solve this problem faster than you can type. By hand it takes a few seconds at least. When the problems get more complex, the disparity only grows larger.

as in medieval manuscripts. The text, which is the prototype logic for all computers, is illuminated like a holy scripture and presented as an authoritative text in our information-age culture" [Verostko, 1995].

The elegance of Turing's theory derives in part from its simplicity. In fact, everything done by a Turing machine can, in principle, be done by hand. The computer simply reads in symbols, applies rules to them, and writes symbols back out. The magic comes with the speed at which a computer works and its ability to store programs and other information and control other devices. In the early days of computing, extraordinarily rapid numeric computation directly influenced wartime efforts in cryptography, weapons building, and missile trajectory calculations (see Chapter 1). Now this extraordinary ability to accelerate symbolic processes is applied in almost all areas of thought. Think of using a calculator: Quick—what's 25,465 times 4? (See Fig. B.2.) Such problems require only a few instructions for a computer and today's personal computers are rated in terms of MIPS, or millions of instructions per second.

URL List

@art, URL	http://www.art.uiuc.edu/@art/gallery.html @art, an electronic art gallery affiliated with the School of Art and Design, the University of Illinois at Urbana-Champaign
ad319, URL	http://gertrude.art.uiuc.edu/ad319/bsm/bsm.html ad319's Web project, *Body, Space, Memory*
Adaweb, URL	http://www.adaweb.com/home.html The adaweb Web Gallery
Ars Electronia, URL	http://www.aec.at/ Ars Electronica
Buxton, URL	http://www.dgp.toronto.edu/people/BillBuxton/billbuxton.html Bill Buxton's home page
Copyright, URL1	http://lcweb.loc.gov/copyright/ The Library of Congress US Copyright Office Web site
Copyright, URL2	http://www.law.cornell.edu/uscode/17 Title 17 of the US Code—Copyrights
Copyright, URL3	http://www.eff.org/pub/CAF/law/multimedia-handbook A primer on intellectual property law for multimedia and Web developers, based on the *Multimedia Law and Business Handbook*
Cunningham, URL	http://gertrude.art.uiuc.edu/@art/cunning/opening.html Stephanie Cunningham's Web art piece *Silence*
Dia, URL	http://www.diacenter.org/ The Dia Center for the Arts
Digimarc, URL	http://www.digimarc.com/ The Digimarc Corporation, a company specializing in digital watermarking technology and smart image applications
EFF, URL	http://www.eff.org/ The Electronic Frontier Foundation, an organization devoted to protecting rights and promoting freedom on the electronic frontier
Ennex, URL	http://www.Ennex.com/service/publications/book.htm Ennex Corporation's page for ordering *Automated Fabrication, Improving Productivity in Manufacturing* by Marshall Burns, Ph.D.
Gibson, URL	http://www.express.ca/rigibson The three dimensional homepage of Rick Gibson in Vancouver, British Columbia
GroupZ, URL	http://www.adaweb.com/~GroupZ/LOVE/index.html Group Z's Web project, *Love*

Hygrid, URL	http://www.sito.org/synergy/hygrid/
	Hygrid, one of SITO's collaborative art projects
IRC, URL	http://urth.acsu.buffalo.edu/irc/WWW/ircdocs.html
	A page of links to Internet Relay Chat resources
ISEA, URL	The Inter-Society for the Electronic Arts
Kornfeld, URL1	http://www.tiac.net/users/dkawaka/Deeringpark.html
	An installation in Deering Oaks Park, Portland, ME by artist Douglas Kornfeld
Kornfeld, URL2	http://www.tiac.net/users/dkawaka/FW.html
	An installation at the Fuller Museum of Art in Brockton, MA by artist Douglas Kornfeld, front wall
Kornfeld, URL3	http://www.tiac.net/users/dkawaka/rtwl.html
	An installation at the Fuller Museum of Art in Brockton, MA by artist Douglas Kornfeld, right wall
Kornfeld, URL4	http://www.tiac.net/users/dkawaka/merri.html
	A digital proposal for an installation on Merrimac Street, Boston, MA by artist Douglas Kornfeld
LACMA, URL	http://lacma.org/
	The Los Angeles County Museum of Art
Mitchell, URL	http://creativity.bgsu.edu/collaboration/
	Bonnie Mitchell's Web projects. Includes ChainArt 1992, Digital Journey 1993, Diversive Paths 1994, ChainReaction 1995, and As Worlds Collide 1997/98
MolaWeb, URL	http://iberia.vassar.edu/Mola
	The Mola Web project by Michael Joyce, Nigel Kerr, Nancy Lin, and Suze Schweitzer
Muntadas, URL	http://fileroom.aa.uic.edu/fileroom.html
	Antonio Muntadas' The File Room, a Web project on censorship that includes lists of censored books
NLM, URL1	http://wwwetb.nlm.nih.gov/monograp/ergo/
	The National Library of Medicine's Guidelines for Designing Effective and Healthy Learning Environments for Interactive Technologies
NLM, URL2	http://www.nlm.nih.gov/research/visible/visible_human.html
	The National Library of Medicine Visual Human Project. Transverse CT, MRI, and cryosection images of representative male and female cadavers at one millimeter intervals
NMAA, URL	http://www.nmaa.si.edu/
	The National Museum of American Art
Ransom, URL	http://www.forgotten.com/models
	Ransom Interactive's model sets
Selbo, URL	http://adaweb.com/project/selbo/
	Vivian Selbo's Web project, *Vertical Blanking Interval*
Shockwave, URL	http://www.macromedia.com/shockwave
	Macromedia's Shockwave site
SIGGRAPH, URL	http://www.siggraph.org
	The ACM Special Interest Group on Computer Graphics
SITO, URL	http://www.sito.org/
	The SITO site for collaborative art projects
Smith, URL	http://www.research.microsoft.com/~Alvy/
	Alvy Ray Smith's home page at Microsoft Research

Vesna, URL	http://arts.ucsb.edu/bodiesinc
	Victoria Vesna's *Bodies, Inc.* Web project
WAXWEB, URL	http://bug.village.virginia.edu/
	David Blair's WAXWEB, the first online movie
Weinman, URL	http://www.lynda.com/
	Author Lynda Weinman's Web site
Whitney, URL	http://www.echonyc.com/~whitney/
	The Whitney Museum of American Art
Yahoo!, URL	http://dir.yahoo.com/Arts/Museums__Galleries__and_Centers/
	The Yahoo! search site's list of Art Museums, Galleries, and Centers
Zakon, URL	http://www.isoc.org/zakon/Internet/History/HIT.html
	Robert H Zakon's Internet timeline

References/Bibliography

Ada Web, 1996	http://adaweb.com/nota/messages/read_vbi.html
Albers, 1987	Josef Albers. *Interaction of Color.* New Haven: Yale University Press, 1987.
Antin, 1986	David Antin. "Video: The Distinctive Features of the Medium." In *Video Culture, A Critical Investigation,* John G. Hanhardt (ed.). Layton, UT, G.M. Smith, Peregrine Smith Books, in association with Visual Studies Workshop Press, 1986, p. 155.
Bachelard, 1969	Gaston Bachelard. *The Poetics of Space.* Boston: Beacon Press, 1969. (First published in French as *La Poétique de l'Espace,* Presses Universitaires de France, 1958.)
Baecker, 1995	Ronald Baecker, William Buxton, and Jonathan Grudin. *Readings in Human–Computer Interaction: Toward the Year 2000,* Morgan Kaufman, 2nd ed., 1995.
Barthes, 1977	Roland Barthes. "The Death of the Author." In *Image–Text–Music.* Trans. Stephen Heath. Hill and Wang, 1977.
Barzel, 1997	Ronen Barzel. Personal communication, December 1997.
Baudrillard, 1983	Jean Baudrillard. *Simulations.* New York, Semiotext(e), 1983.
Benedikt, 1991	Michael Benedikt (ed.). *Cyberspace: First Steps.* Cambridge, MA: MIT Press, 1991.
Benjamin, 1968	Walter Benjamin. "The Work of Art in the Age of Mechanical Reproduction." In *Illuminations, Essays, and Reflections,* Hannah Arendt (ed.). Harcourt Brace Jovanovich, 1968.
Bense, 1965	Max Bense. *Aesthetica: Einführung in die neue Aesthetik.* Agis-Verlag, 1965.
Blatner, 1993	David Blatner and Steve Roth. *Real World Scanning and Halftones.* Peachpit Press, 1993.
Blum, 1966	Herman Blum. *The Loom Has a Brain: The Wonderful World of the Weaver's Art.* Littleton, NH: Courier Printing Co., 1966.
Bolter, 1991	J. David Bolter. *Writing Space: The Computer, Hypertext, and the History of Writing.* Hillsdale, NJ: L. Erlbaum Associates, 1991.
Bookchin, 1996	Natalie Bookchin. Statement in *Visual Proceedings, SIGGRAPH '96.*
Brancusi, 1923.	Constantin Brancusi. Quoted in "Constantin Brancusi: A Summary of Many Conversations." *The Arts,* Vol. 4, No. 1 (1923), pp. 16–17; reprinted in Bach 1987, pp. 316–31.
Brinson, 1994	J. Dianne Brinson and Mark F. Radcliffe. *The Multimedia Law Handbook, A Practical Guide for Developers and Publishers.* Ladera Press, 1994.
Britton, 1996	Benjamin Britton. From a talk given to the Union of Prehistoric and Protohistoric Scientists, Forli, Italy, September 1996.
Bruno, 1995	Michael H. Bruno (ed.). *Pocket Pal, A Graphics Arts Production Handbook,* 16th ed. International Paper Company, 1995.
Buchanan, 1993	Nancy Buchanan. *Leonardo,* Vol. 26, No. 5, pp. 423–429.
Bunch, 1993	Bryan Bunch and Alexander Hellemans. *The Timetables of Technology.* New York, Simon and Schuster, 1993, p. 237.

Burns, 1998   Marshall Burns. *Automated Fabrication: Improving Productivity in Manufacturing.* Los Angeles: Ennex Corporation, 1993.

Bush, 1945   Vannevar Bush. "As We May Think." In [Druckrey, 1996].

Bürger, 1984   Peter Bürger. *Theory of the Avant-Garde.* Trans. Michael Shaw. Minneapolis: University of Minnesota Press, 1984. (Translation of *Theorie der Avantgarde,* 2d ed. Suhrkamp Verlag, 1980.)

Buxton, 1986   William Buxton. "There's More to Interaction Than Meets the Eye: Some Issues in Manual Input." In [Norman, 1986], pp. 319–337.

Capasso, 1994   Nicholas Capasso and Brian Wallace. Catalog for "The Computer in the Studio." DeCordova Museum and Sculpture Park, Lincoln, MA and The Computer Museum, Boston, 1994.

Carlbom, 1978   Ingrid Carlbom and Joseph Paciorek. "Planar Geometric Projections and Viewing Transformations." *Computing Surveys,* Vol. 10, No. 4 (1978), pp. 465–502.

Chen, 1995   Shenchang Eric Chen. "Quicktime VR—An Image-Based Approach to Virtual Environment Navigation." Apple Computer, Inc., *Computer Graphics, Proceedings of SIGGRAPH '95,* p. 38.

Cone, 1996   Jon Cone. Personal communication, April 12, 1996.

Cost, 1997   Frank Cost. *Pocket Guide to Digital Printing.* Albany, NY: Delmar Publishers, 1997.

Damer, 1998   Bruce Damer. *Avatars!: Exploring and Building Virtual Worlds on the Internet.* Berkeley, CA: Peachpit Press, 1998.

Davis, 1994   Philip J. Davis. "Mathematics and Art: Cold Calipers Against Warm Flesh?" In *Mathematics Education and Philosophy: An International Perspective,* Paul Ernest (ed.). Washington, DC: Falmer Press, 1994, pp. 165–183.

Deussen, 1998   Oliver Deussen, Pat Hanrahan, Bernd Lintermann, Radomír Měch, Matt Pharr, and Przemyslaw Prusinkiewicz. "Realistic Modeling and Rendering of Plant Ecosystems." *Computer Graphics, Proceedings of SIGGRAPH '97,* pp. 275–286.

Dodsworth, 1998   Clark Dodsworth (ed.). *Digital Illusion: Entertaining the Future with High Technology.* Reading, MA: Addison-Wesley, 1998.

Dove, 1995   Pamela Jennings. Interview with Toni Dove in *Felix: A Journal of Media Arts and Communication,* Vol 2, No. 1 (1995).

Dove, 1996   Toni Dove. Personal communication, July 3, 1996.

Druckrey, 1993   Timothy Druckrey (ed.). *Iterations: The New Image.* Cambridge, MA: MIT Press, 1993. (Based on the show at Montage 93, Rochester, NY and the International Center of Photography in New York City in late 1993 and early 1994.)

Druckrey, 1996   Timothy Druckrey (ed.). *Electronic Culture: Technology and Visual Representation.* New York: Aperture, 1996.

Durbeck, 1988   Robert C. Durbeck and Sol Sherr (eds.). *Output Hardcopy Devices.* Boston: Academic Press, 1988.

Earle, 1994   Edward W. Earle. Essay for the "DIGITAL DIGRESSIONS: Art at the End of the Millennium" show at the University of California, Riverside (UCR), California Museum of Photography, 1994. This essay can be read at http://cmp1.ucr.edu/essays/edward_earle/ millenium/09_new_art.html

Enzensberger, 1986   Hans Magnus Enzensberger. "Constituents of a Theory of the Media." In John G. Hanhardt (ed.), *Video Culture, A Critical Investigation.* Layton, UT, G.M. Smith, Peregrine Smith Books, in association with Visual Studies Workshop Press, 1986, p. 98.

Fetter, c. 1971   William A. Fetter. "Computer Graphics at Boeing." Seattle: Boeing Company, c. 1971.

Flam, 1994   Faye Flam. *Science,* Vol. 265, August 12, 1994.

Flash, 1993   *Flash* magazine editors. *Underground Guide to Laser Printers.* Berkeley, CA: Peachpit Press, 1993.

Foley, 1996   James Foley, Andries van Dam, Steven Feiner, and John Hughes. *Computer Graphics, Principles and Practice.* 2d ed. Reading, MA: Addison-Wesley, 1996.

Foster, 1984   Hal Foster. "Re: Post." In Brian Wallis (ed.), *Art After Modernism.* New York: The New Museum of Contemporary Art, 1984.

Foucault, 1976   Michel Foucault. *The Archeology of Knowledge.* Trans. A. M. Sheridan Smith. New York: Harper Colophon, 1976.

Franke, 1985   Herbert W. Franke. *Computer Graphics–Computer Art,* 2d. ed. Berlin: Springer-Verlag, 1985.

Fuchs, 1997   Henry Fuchs. Personal communication, May 1997.

Galyean, 1991   Tinsley A. Galyean and John F. Hughes. "Sculpting: An Interactive Volumetric Modeling Technique." *Computer Graphics, Proceedings of SIGGRAPH '91,* 1991.

Gerritsen, 1988   Frans Gerritsen. *Evolution in Color.* Shiffer, 1988.

Gibson, 1994   William Gibson. *Neuromancer.* Ace Books, 1984 (and sequels, *Count Zero,* New York, Ace Books, 1987 and *Mona Lisa Overdrive,* New York: Ace Books, 1988).

Glassner, 1989   Andrew S. Glassner. *3D Computer Graphics,* 2d ed. New York: Design Books, 1989.

Goodman, 1987   Cynthia Goodman. *Digital Visions: Computers and Art.* New York: Harry N. Abrams, 1987. (Written to accompany the 1987 "Computers and Art" show at the Everson Museum of Art, Syracuse, NY)

Goodman, 1990   Danny Goodman. *The Complete Hypercard 2.0 Handbook.* New York: Bantam Computer Books, 1990.

Gore, 1996   Al Gore. "The Technology Challenge: How Can America Spark Private Innovation?" Speech by the Vice President for the 50th anniversary of ENIAC, University of Pennsylvania, Philadelphia, 1996.

Graham, 1996   Ian S. Graham. *HTML Sourcebook, A Complete Guide to HTML 3.0,* 2d ed. New York: Wiley Computer Publishing, 1996.

Grimm, 1995   Cindy M. Grimm and John F. Hughes. "Modeling Surfaces of Arbitrary Topology Using Manifolds." *Computer Graphics, Proceedings of SIGGRAPH '95,* 1995.

GroupZ, 1995   Michaël Samyn. http://www.adaweb.com/~GroupZ/LOVE/index.html

Hackenberg, 1996   Sigrid Hackenberg. Personal communication, December 1996.

Hafner, 1996   Katie Hafner and Matthew Lyon. *Where the Wizards Stay Up Late: The Origins of the Internet.* New York: Simon and Schuster, 1996.

Hall and Moline, 1996   Lane Hall and Lisa Moline. Personal communication, June 14, 1996.

Hanhardt, 1986   John G. Hanhardt (ed.). *Video Culture, A Critical Investigation.* Layton, UT, G.M. Smith, Peregrine Smith Books, in association with Visual Studies Workshop Press, 1986.

Harraway, 1991   Donna J. Haraway. *Simians, Cyborgs, and Women: The Reinvention of Nature.* New York: Routledge, 1991.

Herndon, 1994   K. P. Herndon and T. Meyer. "3D Widgets for Exploratory Scientific Visualization." *Proceedings of UIST '94,* ACM SIGGRAPH, 1994.

Hoberman, 1994   Perry Hoberman. Bar Code Hotel Web site at http://www.portola.com/PEOPLE/PERRY/BarCodeHotel/

Hoberman, 1995   Perry Hoberman. Cathartic User Interface (CUI) Web site at http://www.portola.com/PEOPLE/PERRY/cui/index.html

Hoffman, 1952	Hans Hoffman. Statement in *Hans Hoffman* exhibition catalog. New York: Kootz Gallery, 1952; Cynthia Goodman. *Hans Hoffman.* New York: Whitney Museum of American Art, 1990, p. 175.
Hofstadter, 1989	Douglas R. Hofstadter. *Gödel, Escher, Bach: An Eternal Golden Braid.* New York: Basic Books, 1979.
Holcomb, 1996	Michael Holcomb. Personal communication, July 3, 1996.
Hughes, 1997	John F. Hughes. Personal communication, 1997.
Itten, 1974	Johannes Itten. *The Art of Color: The Subjective Experience and Objective Rationale of Color.* Trans. Ernst van Haagen. New York: Van Nostrand Reinhold, 1974. First published in 1961. Also a smaller version, *The Elements of Color: A Treatise on the Color System of Johannes Itten Based on His Book the Art of Colo*r, New York: Van Nostrand Reinhold, 1970.
Jennings, 1990	Karla Jennings. *The Devouring Fungus: Tales of the Computer Age.* New York: W. W. Norton, 1990.
Jensen, 1998	Henrik Wann Jensen and Per H. Christensen. "Efficient Simulation of Light Transport in Scenes with Participating Media Using Photon Maps." *Computer Graphics, Proceedings of SIGGRAPH '98,* pp. 311–320.
Kandinsky, 1947	Wassily Kandinsky. *Point and Line to Plane.* Bloomfield Hills, MI: Cranbrook Press, 1947.
Kantor, 1996	Andrew Kantor and Michael Neubarth. "Off the Charts: The Internet 1996." *Internet World,* Vol. 7, No. 12 (1996) http://www.iw.com/1996/12/charts.html
Karlin, 1995	Oliver Karlin. Exhibition essay for a one-person show by Sigrid Hackenberg at the Roger Merians Gallery, New York City, 1995.
Keiner, 1994	Marion Keiner, Thomas Kutz, and Mihai Nadin. *Manfred Mohr.* Zürich: Waser Verlag, 1994.
Kendell, 1996	Robert Kendell. *A Life Set for Two.* Eastgate Systems, 1996.
Kerlow, 1996a	Isaac Victor Kerlow and Judson Rosebush. *Computer Graphics for Designers and Artists,* 2d ed. New York: Van Nostrand Reinhold, 1996.
Kerlow, 1996b	Isaac Victor Kerlow. *The Art of 3-D Computer Animation and Imaging.* New York: Van Nostrand Reinhold, 1996.
Knowlton, 1998	Ken Knowlton. Personal communication, May, 1998.
Kornfeld, 1995	Douglas Kornfeld. Artist's Statement, 1995.
Kornfeld, 1997	Douglas Kornfeld. Artist's Statement, 1997.
Kornfeld, 1998	Douglas Kornfeld. Personal communication, June 1, 1998.
Krauss, 1984	Rosalind Krauss. "The Originality of the Avant-Garde: A Postmodern Repetition." In *Art After Modernism,* Brian Wallis (ed.). New York: The New Museum of Contemporary Art, 1984.
Krueger, 1991	Myron W. Krueger. *Artificial Reality II.* Reading, MA: Addison-Wesley, 1991.
Landow, 1992	George P. Landow. *Hypertext: The Convergence of Contemporary Critical Theory and Technology.* Baltimore, MD: The John Hopkins University Press, 1997.
Landow, 1997	George P. Landow. *Hypertext 2.0: The Convergence of Contemporary Critical Theory and Technology.* Revised, amplified edition of [Landow, 1992].
Laurel, 1980	Brenda Laurel. "On Dramatic Interaction." In [Druckrey, 1993].
Laurel, 1990	Brenda Laurel (ed.). *The Art of Human–Computer Interface Design.* Reading, MA: Addison-Wesley, 1990.
Laurel, 1993	Brenda Laurel. *Computers as Theatre.* Reading, MA: Addison-Wesley, 1993.

Lawson, 1984	Thomas Lawson. "Last Exit: Painting." In *Art After Modernism,* Brian Wallis (ed.). New York: The New Museum of Contemporary Art, 1984.
Lazowska, 1996	Ed Lazowska. "A Half Century of Exponential Progress in Information Technology: Who, What, When, Where, Why, and How." University of Washington Annual Faculty Lecture, Seattle, 1996.
Leavitt, 1976	Ruth Leavitt (ed.). *Artist and Computer.* New York: Harmony Books, 1976.
Legrady, 1995	George Legrady. "Image, Language, and Belief in Synthesis." In *Critical Issues in Electronic Media,* Simon Penny (ed.). Albany: State University of New York Press, 1995a.
Legrady, 1995b	George Legrady. Essay on "Slippery Traces" at http://www.c3.hu/butterfly/Legrady/project1.html
Lemay, 1996	Laura Lemay. *Teach Yourself Web Publishing with HTML 3.2 in a Week,* 3d ed. Sams.net, 1996.
Lindenmayer, 1968	Aristid Lindenmayer. "Mathematical Models for Cellular Interactions in Development, Parts I and II." *Journal of Theoretical Biology,* Vol. 18 (1968), pp. 280–315.
Lopuck, 1996	Lisa Lopuck. *Designing Multimedia: A Visual Guide to Multimedia and Online Graphic Design.* Berkeley, CA, Peachpit Press, 1996.
Lovejoy, 1989, 1997	Margot Lovejoy. *Postmodern Currents: Art and Artists in the Age of Electronic Media.* New Jersey: Simon & Schuster, 1989 and 1997 (2d ed.).
Lyotard, 1984	Jean-François Lyotard. *The Postmodern Condition: A Report on Knowledge.* Trans. Geoff Bennington and Brian Massumi. Minneapolis: University of Minnesota Press, 1984.
Maes, 1995	Pattie Maes. "Artificial Life Meets Entertainment: Interacting with Lifelike Autonomous Agents." Special Issue on New Horizons of Commercial and Industrial AI, *Communications of the ACM,* Vol. 38, No. 11, pp. 108–114, ACM Press, November 1995.
Mandelbrot, 1988	Benoit Mandelbrot. *Fractal Geometry of Nature.* San Francisco: W. H. Freeman & Co., 1988.
MANUAL, 1998	MANUAL (Ed Hill and Suzanne Bloom). Personal communication, May 8, 1998.
Marcus, 1992	Aaron Marcus. *Graphic Design for Electronic Documents and User Interfaces.* Reading, MA, Addison-Wesley, 1992.
McCormack, 1994	Jon McCormack. Artist's statement for TURBULENCE, 1994.
McLuhan, 1964	Marshall McLuhan. *Understanding Media: The Extensions of Man.* New York: McGraw-Hill, 1964.
McLuhan, 1967	Marshall McLuhan and Quentin Fiore. *The Medium is the Massage.* New York: Bantam Books, 1967.
Meier, 1996	Barbara J. Meier. "Painterly Rendering for Animation." *Computer Graphics, Proceedings of SIGGRAPH '96.*
Ming-Dao, 1992	Deng Ming-Dao. *365 Tao Daily Meditations.* San Francisco: Harper, 1992.
Mitchell, 1992	William J. Mitchell. *The Reconfigured Eye, Visual Truth in the Post-Photographic Era.* Cambridge, MA: MIT Press, 1992.
Mitchell, 1995a	William J. Mitchell. *City of Bits: Space, Place, and the Infobahn.* Cambridge, MA: MIT Press, 1995.
Mitchell, 1995b	William J. Mitchell and Malcolm McCullough. *Digital Design Media,* 2d ed. New York: Van Nostrand Reinhold, 1995.
Mohr, 1997	Manfred Mohr. Personal communication, December 19, 1997.
Moline, 1996	Lisa Moline. Personal communication, July 4, 1996.
Mullet, 1995	Kevin Mullet and Darrell Sano. *Designing Visual Interfaces: Communication Oriented Techniques.* Englewood Cliffs, NJ: SunSoft Press, 1995.

Nake, 1974   Frieder Nake. *Ästhetik als Informationsverarbeitung.* New York: Springer-Verlag, Wein, 1974.

Nees, 1995   Georg Nees. *Formel, Farbe, Form: Computerasthetik für Medien und Design.* Berlin: Springer-Verlag, Heidelberg, 1995.

Negroponte, 1996   Nicholas Negroponte. *Being Digital.* New York: Knopf, 1996.

Nelson, 1974   Theodor H. Nelson. *Dream Machines.* 1974a. (*Dream Machines* and *Computer Lib* [Nelson, 1974b] are bound together, back to back, in the same book. You can read *Dream Machines* starting in one direction and *Computer Lib* starting in the other. They meet in the middle.)

Noll, 1966   A. Michael Noll. "Human or Machine: A Subjective Comparison of Piet Mondrian's 'Composition with Lines' and a Computer-Generated Picture." *The Psychological Record,* 16, No. 1, pp. 1–10, 1966.

Noll, 1972   A. Michael Noll. "The Effect of Artistic Thinking on Aesthetic Preferences for Pseudo-Random Computer-Generated Patterns." *The Psychological Record,* 22, No. 4, pp. 449–462, 1972.

Noll, 1994   A. Michael Noll. "The Beginnings of Computer Art in the United States: A Memoir." *Leonardo,* Cambridge, MA: MIT Press, Vol. 27, No. 1, pp. 39–44, 1994.

Norman, 1986   Donald Norman and Stephen Draper (eds.). *User-Centered System Design: New Perspectives on Human–Computer Interaction.* Hillsdale, NJ: Lawrence Erlbaum Associates, 1986.

Norman, 1990   Donald Norman. *The Design of Everyday Things.* (Originally published as *The Psychology of Everyday Things* by Basic Books in 1988.)

Norman, 1990   Richard B. Norman. *Electronic Color, The Art of Color Applied to Graphic Computing.* Van Nostrand Reinhold, 1990.

Novak, 1991   Marcos Novak. "Liquid Architectures in Cyberspace." In [Benedikt, 1991].

NSF, 1997   National Science Foundation. "Science and Engineering Bachelor's Degrees Awarded to Women Increase Overall, but Decline in Several Fields." Washington, D.C.: NSF 97-326, November 7, 1997.

O'Rourke, 1995   Michael O'Rourke. *Three-Dimensional Computer Animation: Modeling, Rendering, and Animating with 3D Computer Graphics.* New York: W. W. Norton & Co., 1995.

Palfreman, 1991   Jon Palfreman and Doron Swade. *The Dream Machine: Exploring the Computer Age.* Boston: WGBH Television, and London: BBC Books, 1991. Also a PBS Television series in five parts and the companion book *The Machine That Changed the World.*

Popper, 1993   Frank Popper. *Art of the Electronic Age.* New York: Harry N. Abrams, 1993.

Poynton, 1996   Charles Poynton. *A Technical Introduction to Digital Video.* New York: John Wiley & Sons, 1996.

Poynton, 1998   Charles Poynton. "'Black Level' and 'Picture.'" http://www.inforamp.net/~poynton/notes/black_and_picture/index.html (part of Poynton's Gamma FAQ at http://www.inforamp.net/~poynton/GammaFAQ.html), 1998.

Prusinkiewicz, 1990 Przemyslaw Prusinkiewicz and Aristid Lindenmayer. *The Algorithmic Beauty of Plants.* New York: Springer-Verlag, 1990.

Rees, 1998a   Michael Rees. Quoted in an interview with Bill Jones in *ARTBYTE,* Vol. 1, No. 1, 1998.

Rees, 1998b   Michael Rees. Personal communication, May 12, 1998.

Reichardt, 1968   Jasia Reichardt (ed.). *Cybernetic Serendipity.* A *Studio International* special issue. Catalog for "Cybernetic Serendipity," held at the Institute of Contemporary Arts, London, 1968.

Reit, 1981   Seymore V. Reit. *The Day They Stole the Mona Lisa.* New York: Summit Books, 1981.

Richards, 1991	Noel Richards and Jon McCormack. "Four Imaginary Walls: Jon McCormack." 1991. Catalog essay for Australian Perspecta 1991, a biennial exhibition of Australian Art at the Art Gallery of New South Wales.
Rivera, 1997	Alex Rivera. Personal communication, January 1997.
Rose, 1989	Frank Rose. *West of Eden: The End of Innocence at Apple Computer.* New York: Viking Penguin, 1989.
Rosler, 1994	Martha Rosler. "Lookers, Buyers, Dealer, and Makers: Thoughts on an Audience." In *Art After Modernism, Rethinking Representation,* Brian Wallis and Marcia Tucker (eds.). New York: The New Museum of Contemporary Art, 1994.
Rubin, 1993	Cynthia Beth Rubin. "Quoting & Appropriation, Whose Work Is It?" *Media Information Australia,* No. 69, August 1993.
Rubin, 1995	Cynthia Beth Rubin. "Cultural Transformations: Morphing Sensibility." *Computer Graphics,* August 1995.
Rubin, 1997	Cynthia Beth Rubin. Personal communication, February 1997.
Rubin, 1968	William S. Rubin. *Dada, Surrealism, and Their Heritage.* New York: Museum of Modern Art, 1968.
Ruíz, 1996	Kathleen Ruíz. Personal communication, 1996.
Saff, 1978	Donald Saff and Deli Sacilotto. *Printmaking, History, and Process.* New York: Holt, Rinehart, and Winston, 1978.
Salas, 1995	Fred Salas. The First Annual Border Film Festival, 1995.
Sandler, 1996	Irving Sandler. *Art of the Postmodern Era: From the Late 1960s to the Early 1990s.* New York: Icon Editions, an imprint of HarperCollins, 1996.
Savage, 1986	John E. Savage, Susan Magidson, and Alex M. Stein. *The Mystical Machine.* Reading, MA: Addison-Wesley, 1986.
Schwartz, 1992	Lillian Schwartz with Laurens R. Schwartz. *The Computer Artist's Handbook: Concepts, Techniques, and Applications.* New York: W. W. Norton, 1992.
Sherr, 1988	Sol Sherr (ed.). *Input Devices.* Boston: Academic Press, 1988.
Shirley, 1997	Peter Shirley. Personal communication, April 29, 1997.
Sims, 1993	Karl Sims. Artist's Statement for "Genetic Images" at the Centre Georges Pompidou, Paris, 1993.
Sims, 1994	Karl Sims. "Evolving Virtual Creatures." *Computer Graphics, Proceedings of SIGGRAPH '94.*
Smith, 1978	Alvy Ray Smith. *Paint.* New York: New York Institute of Technology, Technical Memo No. 7, 1978.
Smith, 1984	Alvy Ray Smith. "Plants, Fractals, and Formal Languages." *Computer Graphics, Proceedings of SIGGRAPH '84.*
Smith, 1995a	Alvy Ray Smith. Personal communication, April 25, 1995.
Smith, 1995b	Alvy Ray Smith. "A Pixel is *Not* a Little Square! A Pixel is *Not* a Little Square! A Pixel is *Not* a Little Square!" Microsoft Technical Memo No. 6, 1995.
Smith, 1996a	Alvy Ray Smith. Acceptance speech for a Technical Academy Award for "pioneering inventions in digital image compositing." Received with Ed Catmull, Tom Porter, and Tom Duff, 1996.
Smith, 1996b	Alvy Ray Smith and Eric Ray Lyons. "HWB—A More Intuitive Hue-Based Color Model." *Journal of Graphics Tools,* Vol. 1, No. 1 (1996), 3–17.

Snibbe, 1996	Scott Sona Snibbe. Essay on the Motion Phone, at http://www.snibbe.com/scott/mphone/about1.html
Softimage, 1995	Softimage web site overview of Osmose at http://www.softimage.com/Projects/Osmose/
Solomon-Godeau, 1984	Abigail Solomon-Godeau. "After Art Photography." In *Art After Modernism,* Brian Wallis (ed.). New York: The New Museum of Contemporary Art, 1984.
Sontag, 1973	Susan Sontag. *On Photography.* New York: Dell Publishing Co., 1973.
Staniszewski, 1995	Mary Ann Staniszewski. *Believing is Seeing: Creating the Culture of Art.* New York: Penguin Books, 1995, p. 154.
Stephenson, 1993	Neal Stephenson. *Snow Crash.* Spectra, 1993.
Strong, 1990	William S. Strong. *The Copyright Book,* 3d ed. Cambridge, MA: MIT Press, 1990.
Sutherland, 1963	Ivan E. Sutherland. *Sketchpad, A Man-Machine Graphical Communication System.* Garland, 1980 (published version of Sutherland's 1963 MIT doctoral dissertation).
Swirnoff, 1992	Lois Swirnoff. *Dimensional Color.* New York: Van Nostrand Reinhold, 1992.
Tamblyn, 1994	Christine Tamblyn. *ISEA 94 Proceedings,* 1994.
Tamblyn, 1997	Christine Tamblyn. Personal communication, 1997.
Truckenbrod, 1997	Joan Truckenbrod. Personal communication, 1997.
Tufte, 1983	Edward R. Tufte. *The Visual Display of Quantitative Information.* Cheshire, CT: Graphics Press, 1983.
Tufte, 1990	Edward R. Tufte. *Envisioning Information.* Cheshire, CT: Graphics Press, 1990.
Tufte, 1997	Edward R. Tufte. *Visual Explanations: Images and Quantities, Evidence and Narrative.* Cheshire, CT: Graphics Press, 1997.
Turkle, 1996	Sherry Turkle. "Constructions and Reconstructions of the Self in Virtual Reality." In [Druckrey, 1996].
Turre, 1998	Michele Turre. Personal communication, May 26, 1998.
U.S., 1975	*Twentieth Century Music Corp.* v. *Aiken,* 422 U.S. 151, 156 (1975).
U.S., 1787	U.S. Constitution, ARTICLE I, SECTION 8, CLAUSE 8.
U.S. Code, 1976	U.S. Code, Title 17, Copyright Act, enacted 1947, revised in its entirety 1976.
U.S., 1995	Working Group on Intellectual Property Rights. "Intellectual Property and the National Information Infrastructure." Washington, D.C.: U.S. Government Printing Office, September 1995.
USA	*Circular 22: How to Investigate the Copyright Status of a Work.* Washington, D.C.: U.S. Government Printing Office; and *Circular 1: Copyright Basics.* Washington, D.C., U.S. Government Printing Office.
van Dam, 1994	Andries van Dam. Personal communication, 1994.
van Dam, 1997	Andries van Dam. Personal communication, August, 1997.
Verostko, 1995	Roman Verostko. Web site at http://www.mcad.edu/home/faculty/verostko/Gallery.html
Verostko, 1997a	Roman Verostko. Web site at http://www.mcad.edu/home/faculty/verostko/mural.html
Verostko, 1997b	Roman Verostko. Personal communication, January 7, 1997.
Virilio, 1991	Paul Virilio. *The Lost Dimension.* New York: Semiotext(e), 1991.
Walker, 1995	James Faure Walker. Personal Notes from his SIGGRAPH '95 Artist's Sketch presentation: "Still Video and the Painterly Poem."
Walker, 1996	James Faure Walker. Artist's statement for show at the Mariani Gallery, Greeley, CO, 1996.

| Wallis, 1994 | Brian Wallis and Marcia Tucker (eds.). *Art After Modernism, Rethinking Representation.* New York: The New Museum of Contemporary Art, 1994. |

Wallis, 1994 — Brian Wallis and Marcia Tucker (eds.). *Art After Modernism, Rethinking Representation.* New York: The New Museum of Contemporary Art, 1994.

Weibel, 1996 — Peter Weibel. "The World as Interface." In [Druckrey, 1996].

Weinbren, 1995 — Grahame Weinbren. *Millennium Film Journal,* No. 28 (Spring, 1995).

Weinbren, 1997 — Grahame Weinbren. "The Digital Revolution is a Revolution of Random Access" in *TELEPOLIS,* an online magazine at http://www.heise.de/tp/english/default.html, Verlag Heinz Heise, Hannover, Germany, February 17, 1997.

Weinman, 1996 — Lynda Weinman. *Deconstructing Web Graphics.* Indianapolis: New Riders, 1996.

Weinman, 1997 — Lynda Weinman. *Designing Web Graphics, 2.* Indianapolis: New Riders, 1997.

Weintraub, 1995 — Annette Weintraub. Personal communication, 1995.

Whitaker, 1994 — Jerry Whitaker. *Electronic Displays, Technology, Design, and Applications.* New York: McGraw-Hill, 1994.

Winkenbach, 1996 — George Winkenbach and David H. Salesin. "Rendering Parametric Surfaces in Pen and Ink." *Computer Graphics, Proceedings of SIGGRAPH '96.*

Winkler, 1998 — Todd Winkler. *Composing Interactive Music: Techniques and Ideas Using MAX.* Cambridge, MA: MIT Press, 1998.

Wood, 1997 — Daniel Wood, Adam Finkelstein, John Hughes, Craig Thayer, and David Salesin. "Multiperspective Panoramas for Cel Animation." *Computer Graphics, Proceedings of SIGGRAPH '97.*

Zeleznik, 1996 — Robert C. Zeleznik, Kenneth P. Herndon, and John F. Hughes. "SKETCH: An Interface for Sketching 3D Scenes." In *Computer Graphics, Proceedings of SIGGRAPH '96.*

Zeleznik, 1997 — Robert C. Zeleznik. Personal communication, February 1997.

Index

2D,
animation; 323-368
3D compared with; 358
fractals positioned between 3D and; 240
geometric graphics; 117-157
images; 37-86
texture mapping use of; 262
raster graphics; 37-86
tools, positioning 3D objects with, difficulties with; 231
video; 323-368
2X rule for image resolution; 97, 189
3D,
animation; 221-222, 323-368
2D compared with; 358
concepts; 358-365
lighting and surface quality concerns; 358
motion capture use; 363-365
particle systems use; 363
positioning objects in scenes; 250
programs; 325-(def)
CAD, keyboard use for numerical input in; 90
color,
complexity; 259-(sb)
components; 259
composition; 249
controls, widgets; 221-(def)
digitization; 307-308
forms,
comparison of methods for creating; 230-(sb)
generation of, as global touch; 240-248
fractals positioned between 2D and; 240
geometric graphics; 211-256, 257-296
concepts; 214-219
geometry; 214-(def)
input/output; 297-322
interactive multimedia, *Creature Construction Kit*; 396
Java; 432
modeling; 215-(def)
advantages over physical models; 213
algorithmic form generation; 240-248
characteristics compared with 2D; 216-217

hierarchy in; 234-237
making a 3D geometric model; 217-218
surface thickness information required by 3D fabrication machines; 320
multimedia tools, WWW as stimulant to development of; 399
objects,
assembling; 231-239
Boolean operations on; 226-227
positioning with 2D tools, difficulties with; 231
on the Web; 430
output; 297-322
painting; 264-(def), 264-(sb)
primitives; 221-(def), 221-222
printing; 317-320
Printing, as automated fabrication process; 320-(def)
programs,
anatomy of; 219
common interface features; 219-221
raster graphics, volume visualization and; 218-(sb)
rendering; 215-(def)
sample-based programs, volume visualization and; 218-(sb)
scanning; 307-308
sculpting; 228-230, 228-(def)
textures, complexity of; 265
touch, building blocks for; 221-230
video; 323-368
viewing, virtual worlds and; 311-316
worlds, positioning objects in; 250
6DOF (degrees of freedom); 300-(def)

A

absolute mode; 94-(def, sb)
Abstract Expressionism,
as Modernism component; 448
ACM (Association for Computing Machinery); 30, 253-(sr)
ad319; 426, 427-(fg), 427-(url)
additive,
color mixing; cp-1, cp-2, 110, 161-163

br = bibliography, def = definitions, fg = figure, fn = footnote, sb = sidebar, sr = suggested reading, url = URL list, cp = color plate, gp = gallery plate. For specific art works, see *art works;* for specific individuals, see *people.*

br = bibliography, def = definitions, fg = figure, fn = footnote, sb = sidebar, sr = suggested reading, url = URL list,
cp = color plate, gp = gallery plate. For specific art works, see *art works;* for specific individuals, see *people.*

br = bibliography, def = definitions, fg = figure, fn = footnote, sb = sidebar, sr = suggested reading, url = URL list, cp = color plate, gp = gallery plate. For specific art works, see *art works;* for specific individuals, see *people.*

br = bibliography, def = definitions, fg = figure, fn = footnote, sb = sidebar, sr = suggested reading, url = URL list, cp = color plate, gp = gallery plate. For specific art works, see *art works;* for specific individuals, see *people.*

br = bibliography, def = definitions, fg = figure, fn = footnote, sb = sidebar, sr = suggested reading, url = URL list, cp = color plate, gp = gallery plate. For specific art works, see *art works;* for specific individuals, see *people.*

br = bibliography, def = definitions, fg = figure, fn = footnote, sb = sidebar, sr = suggested reading, url = URL list, cp = color plate, gp = gallery plate. For specific art works, see *art works;* for specific individuals, see *people.*

subtractive vs. additive; 161-163
transparency, tool shape and; 51-52
palettes; 176-177, 176-(def)
  images as; 176
pickers; cp-6
  HSB, HSL, and HSV spaces as; 171
  limitations of in 3D programs; 259-(sb)
  RGB cube used for; 170
primary; 163-164, 163-(def)
printers, laser; 194
range of possible, CIE space used for comparing;
  175
relative nature of; 160-(fg)
sampling, input device considerations; 95-104
selection,
  color space used in; 173
  in geometry-based programs; 151
separations; 169-(def), 175-(def)
shifting; 289-(def)
spaces; cp-4, cp-7, cp-8, cp-9, cp-10, 163-(def),
  169-175, 169-(def)
  CIE; 173-175
  designing your own; 173
  HSL; 170-171
  HSV; 170-171
  HWB; 171-172
  perceptually-based; 172
  RGB cube; 170
  using; 173
tint, in HWB color space; 172-(def)
touch separate from, in geometric programs; 136
unreliability, as disadvantage of ink-jet printers; 196
water-based,
  ink-jet printer use; 196
  wax-based inks compared with; 199
wax-based, water-based inks compared with; 199
Colossus; 11
compositing; 80-(def), 347-(def)
  over time; 347-351
composition; 69-(def), 231-(def)
  3D, object creation operation; 231-233
  aesthetics of, scaling impact on; 150
  area, of animation programs; 340
  color, color space use for structuring; 173
  controlling both spatial and temporal aspects of,
    timeline use for; 343
  in geometric graphics; 145-148
  issues, of scaling and size in 3D objects; 250-251
  master-instance hierarchies influence on; 238
  multimedia,
    interactive use of space; 399

  production use; 395-408
  taxonomy of types; 395
in raster graphics; 69-82
relative scaling impact on; 78
rules, animation impact of combining different; 348
of simple shapes, alternatives to in 3D object construction; 226
spatial,
  in 3D worlds; 249
  in *Slippery Traces: The Postcard Trail*; 400
  time-based change impact on; 345
strategies; 70-71
in time-based media; 345-357
tools,
  3D viewpoint; 352
  accuracy as, in geometric programs; 150-151
  color as; 249
  color as, in geometry-based programs; 151
  in geometric programs; 144-151
  managing objects as, in geometric programs; 146
  point of view as; 249
  size and scale as, in geometric programs; 148-150
  transparency as; 249
Web-based; 422-426
compression; 420-(def)
  codec (compression and decompression); 371-(def)
  image; 420
  JPEG; 420-(def)
  RLE; 420-(def)
computer-numerical-control (CNC); 317-(def)
concepts,
  animation; 326
    3D; 358-365
  color; 159-179, 160-177
  computer graphics,
    geometric graphics, 2D; 117-157
    geometric graphics, 3D modeling; 211-256
    geometric graphics, 3D rendering; 257-296
    image processing, 2D; 37-86
    modeling, 2D; 117-157
    modeling, 3D; 211-256
    raster graphics; 37-86
    rendering, 2D; 117-157
    rendering, 3D; 257-296
  digital design and layout programs; 121-126
  geometric graphics,
    2D; 117-157
    3D modeling; 211-256
    3D rendering; 257-296
  hypertext; 372-374-(sb)
  image processing, 2D; 37-86

br = bibliography, def = definitions, fg = figure, fn = footnote, sb = sidebar, sr = suggested reading, url = URL list,
cp = color plate, gp = gallery plate. For specific art works, see *art works;* for specific individuals, see *people.*

br = bibliography, def = definitions, fg = figure, fn = footnote, sb = sidebar, sr = suggested reading, url = URL list, cp = color plate, gp = gallery plate. For specific art works, see *art works;* for specific individuals, see *people.*

br = bibliography, def = definitions, fg = figure, fn = footnote, sb = sidebar, sr = suggested reading, url = URL list, cp = color plate, gp = gallery plate. For specific art works, see *art works;* for specific individuals, see *people.*

br = bibliography, def = definitions, fg = figure, fn = footnote, sb = sidebar, sr = suggested reading, url = URL list,
cp = color plate, gp = gallery plate. For specific art works, see *art works;* for specific individuals, see *people.*

br = bibliography, def = definitions, fg = figure, fn = footnote, sb = sidebar, sr = suggested reading, url = URL list, cp = color plate, gp = gallery plate. For specific art works, see *art works;* for specific individuals, see *people.*

br = bibliography, def = definitions, fg = figure, fn = footnote, sb = sidebar, sr = suggested reading, url = URL list,
cp = color plate, gp = gallery plate. For specific art works, see *art works;* for specific individuals, see *people.*

br = bibliography, def = definitions, fg = figure, fn = footnote, sb = sidebar, sr = suggested reading, url = URL list, cp = color plate, gp = gallery plate. For specific art works, see *art works;* for specific individuals, see *people.*

line(s) *(continued)*
    polyline; 131-(def)
    in raster graphics; 122-(fg)
    width; 150
linear,
    elements; 121-(def), 135
    interpolation; 328-(def), 329-334-(sb)
    perspective; 271-(def)
link(s),
    as artistic tool; 426
    as associative; 373
    Roland Barthes use; 373
    Vannevar Bush use; 373
liquid-crystal displays (LCDs); 112-(def)
literary theory,
    computer graphics synergy with; 30
    hypertext impact; 373
    Postmodern; 376
lithographic transfers,
    creating from photocopies and laser printouts; 205
local,
    area networks (LANs); , 418-(def), 418
    rendering; 276-279
    touch; 49-52, 51-(def), 52-(fg), 65-67, 91, 128-133,
        134-135, 135, 334
locking,
    as extreme form of joint; 237
    layers; 148
LOD (level of detail); 216
lofting; 223-(def), 230-(sb)
LOM (Laminated Object Manufacturing);
        319-(def)
lossless; 420-(def)
lossy; 420-(def)
low,
    contrast; 56-(def, sb)
    frequency; 56-(def, sb)
    pass; 56-(def, sb)
lpi (lines per inch); 187-(def)
luminance; 174-(def)

M

Mach banding; 44, 277-(def)
manufacturing,
    automated fabrication tools; 319-(def)
    computer-aided; 229, 317-320
    desktop; 317-320
    numerical controls; 8
    precision; 213
mapping,
    bump; 266-(def)
    displacement; 266-(def)
    environment; 286-(def)
    texture; 251, 262-(def), 264-(sb), 266, 320
    tonal; 53-55, 53-(def), 165
    transparency; 266-(def)
markup languages,
    HTML; 423-(def)
    SGML; 428-(def)
    XML; 428-(def)
masking,
    in geometric graphics; 129
    in raster graphics; 65-(def)
    selection and; 65-67
    shadow mask; 112-(def)
master-instance hierarchy; 238-(def), 238-239
material(s); 259-(def)
    archival; 204
    artist; 106-107
    creating; 392-393
    diffuse reflection impact; 261
    gathering; 392-393
    organizing; 392-393
mathematics,
    of biological evolutionary art; 246-247
    Boolean algebra; 139-(fn)
    calculus; 132-(fn)
    of complex forms; 216
    convolution; 57-(def)
    fractals; 240
    Grace Murray Hopper; 9
    interpolation; 137-(def), 278-(def), 328-332, 336,
        358
    iterations; 241-(def)
    linear interpolation; 328-(def), 329-334-(sb)
    randomization; 241
    symbolic logic; 454, 454-(def)
    theoretical; 213
    topologies; 229
medicine,
    3D sample-based programs use in; 218
    augmented reality in; 313-(fg)
    scanning data; 106
mesh,
    polygonal; 226, 230-(sb)
    triangular; 320
mini-computer; 5-(def)
Minimalism; 448
mirror images; 61
mixing of colors; cp-1, cp-2, 164-165
    additive; 110, 161-163
    color-mixing space; 163-(def)

br = bibliography, def = definitions, fg = figure, fn = footnote, sb = sidebar, sr = suggested reading, url = URL list, cp = color plate, gp = gallery plate. For specific art works, see *art works;* for specific individuals, see *people.*

multimedia *(continued)*
    data types; 378
    databases; 392-393
    environment; 371-(def)
    interactive; 370-377, 371-(def), 372, 378-387,
        395-399
    materials; 392-393
    navigation in; 396
    non-interactive; 371
    productions; 388-392
    program interfaces; 384-387
    programs; 378-387
    user interface design in; 401-408
Munsell system; cp-8, 172
mutation,
    in genetic art programs; 245-(def)
    Mutation Y 1 2nd Variant; 247-(fg)
    in texture generation; 63-(fg)

N

National Science Foundation (NSF); 415,
    466-(br)
National Television System Committee (NTSC);
    175
networks,
    distributed; 418
    Internet; 415-416, 417-422
    LANs (local area networks); 418
    Portable Network Graphics (PNG) image file for-
        mat; 166
networks *(continued)*
    Roland Barthes use; 373
    self as node in; 376
NLE (nonlinear editor); 104-(def)
noise; 58, 300, 302
nonlinear; 346-(def)
    digital editing system; 347
    editor (NLE); 104-(def)
    interpolation; 331-(def)
    RGB monitors; 165
nonrealistic rendering; 290, 290-(def)
NPR (non-photorealistic rendering); 232-(sb)
NSF (National Science Foundation); 415,
    466-(br)
NTSC (National Television System Committee);
    175
numerical,
    calculation; 150
    controls; 8, 317-(def)
    input; 90, 135

NURB (non-uniform rational B-spline);
    131-(def), 226-(def)
Nyquist rate; 98-(def)

O

object(s); 119-(def), 251, 383-(def)
    3D; 226-227, 231-239
    abstract; 235-237 (def)
    behavior; 356
    changes to; 234
    composition with; 145-148
    in geometric graphics; 122
    geometry and; 153
    interaction; 356-357
    interiors; 218
    managing; 146
    object-oriented programming (OOP); 119, 378,
        383-384-(sb)
    paint object; 151-(def)
    positioning; 250
    relationships; 150
    representations; 225-(sb)
    space between; 248
    transformations; 329
oblique,
    projection; 271-(def)
off-axis,
    view; 271-(def)
"On Growth and Form", (D'Arcy Thompson);
    247
OOP (object-oriented programming),
    as interactive multimedia structure; 378
    mode; 383-(def)
    object-based programs unrelated to; 119
    as paradigm; 383-384-(sb)
operations,
    3D; 222-(def), 223-(def), 230, 231, 319
    Boolean; 139, 226-227
    digital clay; 228-230
    with no counterpart in traditional art-making; 238
order (stacking),
    in geometric programs; 145-(def)
    impact on illusion of depth; 145
    relative; 147
    of tracks; 343
orientation; 270-(def)
orthographic projection, 271-(def)
oscillons,
    Ben F. Laposky's name for his artwork; 14
output,
    3D; 297-322

---

br = bibliography, def = definitions, fg = figure, fn = footnote, sb = sidebar, sr = suggested reading, url = URL list,
cp = color plate, gp = gallery plate. For specific art works, see *art works;* for specific individuals, see *people.*

computer displays; 110–115
decisions about; 110
digital video; 346–347
displays; 87–116
introduction to; 109–110
large-scale; 113
photoprintmaking use of; 205
printers; 181–210
printing; 317–320
projection systems; 112–115
service bureaus; 207–208

P

page,
as composition tool; 144–(def)
description language; 125
as multimedia structure; 382–(def), 382–383
turning; 355–(def)
Web; 419–(def), 423–426

painting(s),
3D; 264–(def), 264–(sb)
cave; 82, 314
digital; 37–86
paint object; 65–(def), 151–(def)
painterly brush strokes with paths; 135
polygon; 289–(def)

PAL broadcast gamut,
CRT gamut vs.; 175

palette(s),
auxiliary; 221, 341
color; 176–177, 176–(def)
eight-bit; 176
main tool; 126
in painting and photoediting programs; 48–(def)
tool; 220–(def), 341

Pantone color system; 168, 169–(def)
parallax; 308–(def)
parallel projection; 270–(def)
PARC (Xerox Palo Alto Research Center);
26

part-to-part relationship,
hierarchy use to model; 234
importance for correct movement; 359–(fg)

particle systems,
3D animation use; 363–(def)
modeling; 247–248, 248–(def)

partitive mixing; 161–(def)
patches, spline; 229–(def)
paths; 128–(def)
color application to; 151
drawing with; 134

dynamic nature of; 135
filling; 136–(fg)
interior region of; 128
motion; 332–(def)
painterly brush strokes with; 135
Roland Barthes use; 373
subtracting; 139
tool; 151–(def)

patterns,
building up; 197
in fills; 150
moire; 98–(def), 98
pattern-recognition software; 305

pedabytes; 75–(def)
pencil tests,
in animation; 327–(def)

people,
Adams, Ansel; 240
Aiken, Howard; 12
Albers, Josef; 80, 160, 178–(sr), 461–(br)
animation; 365–(sr)
Antin, David; 374, 461–(br)
Atanasoff, John V.; 11
Atkinson, Bill; 27, 382
Babbage, Charles; 9, 11
Bachelard, Gaston; 252–(sr), 461–(br)
Baecker, Ronald; 408, 461–(br)
Bakhtin, Michael; 376
Bangert, Colette; 10
Barthes, Roland; 67, 372, 373, 376, 461–(br)
Bartz, Carol; 31
Barzel, Ronen; 325, 362, 461–(br)
Baudrillard, Jean; 314, 315, 321–(sr), 461–(br)
Beall, Jeff; 269–(fg)
Benedikt, Michael; 249, 252–(sr), 436–(sr), 461–(br)
Benjamin, Walter; 183, 461–(br)
Bense, Max; 21, 461–(br)
Berger, Charles; 67, 205
Berners-Lee, Tim; 416
Bezier, Pierre; 132
Blair, David; 427, 429–(fg)
  [WAXweb, URL]; 459–(url)
Blatner, David; 208–(sr), 461–(br)
Bloom, Suzanne; gp-9, 40–(fg), 273–(fg)
  [MANUAL, 1998]; 39, 465–(br)
Blum, Herman; 8, 461–(br)
Bohr, Niels; 215
Bolter, Jay David; 461–(br)
Bookchin, Natalie; 393, 393–(fg), 461–(br)
Boole, George; 139, 454
Brancusi, Constantin; 442, 449, 461–(br)

br = bibliography, def = definitions, fg = figure, fn = footnote, sb = sidebar, sr = suggested reading, url = URL list, cp = color plate, gp = gallery plate. For specific art works, see *art works;* for specific individuals, see *people.*

br = bibliography, def = definitions, fg = figure, fn = footnote, sb = sidebar, sr = suggested reading, url = URL list, cp = color plate, gp = gallery plate. For specific art works, see *art works;* for specific individuals, see *people.*

br = bibliography, def = definitions, fg = figure, fn = footnote, sb = sidebar, sr = suggested reading, url = URL list, cp = color plate, gp = gallery plate. For specific art works, see *art works;* for specific individuals, see *people.*

performance art; 335, 372, 376
persistence,
    of vision; 326-(def)
perspective; 251
    alternative; 144
    changes in; 352
    linear; 271-(def)
    multiperspective panoramas; 354-(def)
    projection; 251, 270-(def)
    as tool for conveying a feeling of space; 146
Phong lighting; 277-(def)
Phong shading; 278-(def), 329
PhotoGrade; 191-(def)
photography,
    computer art integration, in 1970s and 1980s; 29
    digital editing; 37-86, 48-49
    image processing impact on; 39-42
    originality issues compared with computer art;
        183-184
    photoetching; 204
    photolithography; 204
    photoprintmaking; 205

br = bibliography, def = definitions, fg = figure, fn = footnote, sb = sidebar, sr = suggested reading, url = URL list,
cp = color plate, gp = gallery plate. For specific art works, see *art works;* for specific individuals, see *people.*

br = bibliography, def = definitions, fg = figure, fn = footnote, sb = sidebar, sr = suggested reading, url = URL list,
cp = color plate, gp = gallery plate. For specific art works, see *art works;* for specific individuals, see *people.*

br = bibliography, def = definitions, fg = figure, fn = footnote, sb = sidebar, sr = suggested reading, url = URL list, cp = color plate, gp = gallery plate. For specific art works, see *art works;* for specific individuals, see *people.*

br = bibliography, def = definitions, fg = figure, fn = footnote, sb = sidebar, sr = suggested reading, url = URL list, cp = color plate, gp = gallery plate. For specific art works, see *art works;* for specific individuals, see *people.*

sculptures,
> 3D; 228-230, 228-(def)
> compared with other methods for creating 3D shapes; 230-(sb)
> computer; 23-(fg)
> computer-controlled; 23
> *Forest City Sculpture Festival*; 119-(fg)
> input; 104-(fg)
> kinetic; 372
> Michael O'Rourke; 224
> organic; 318
> solid texture; 265-(fg)
> volumetric; 218-(def), 218, 228

search engines; 419-(def)

selection; 65-(def)
> of colors; 151, 173
> component; 231
> Darwinian; 245
> in geometry-based programs; 122
> masking and; 65
> mouse advantages for; 91
> in paint vs layout programs; 123-(fg)
> paths; 120
> tools; 151
> vertices as selectable points on linear elements; 128

Selective Laser Sintering (SLS),
> as automated fabrication tool; 319-(def)

self-similarity,
> in fractals; 241
> as fractals characteristic; 240-(def)

separations,
> color; 175-(def)

servers,
> Web; 419-(def)

service bureaus; 207-(def)
> services provided by; 207-208

SGML (Standard Generalized Markup Language); 428-(def)

shade,
> in HWB color space; 172-(def)

shading,
> 3D forms; 329
> complex; 123
> flat; 277-(def)
> Gouraud; 277-(def), 329
> methods; 251
> models; 277-279, 277-(def)
> Phong; 278-(def), 329

shadow(s),
> as 3D color component; 259

> mask; 112-(def)
> rays; 281-(def)
> as tool for conveying a feeling of space; 146

sharpening,
> blurring compared with; 59
> filters; 59-(def)

shearing,
> object; 330-(fg)

SIGCIVA (Special Interest Group for Computers in the Visual Arts); 30

SIGGRAPH (ACM); 30, 253-(sr), 365-(sr)

signal processing,
> vocabulary; 56-(sb)

simulacrum; 314-(def)

simulation,
> in 3D multimedia; 399
> accuracy; 383
> flight; 213
> genetic; 245
> growth; 244-(def)
> of real-world phenomena; 363
> texture mapping use; 262

sintering; 319-(def)
> Selective Laser Sintering use; 319

six degrees of freedom (DOF); 300-(def)

size,
> 3D objects; 250-251
> change; 148
> file; 72-(def), 73, 75-(sb), 148
> image; 72
> printer paper; 193-194
> scale and; 148-150

SKETCH; 232-233-(sb), 233-(fg)

Sketchpad, (Ivan Sutherland); 25-(fg), 238

sliders; 237-(def), 403

SLS (selective laser sintering); 319-(def)

SMPTE (Society of Motion Picture and Television Engineers); 378

Society of Motion Picture and Television Engineers (SMPTE); 378

solid(s),
> modeling; 211-256, 218-(sb)
> solid-ink printers; 198-(def)
> textures; 265-(def)

sonar,
> 3D mouse use; 300
> body tracking use; 305
> tracking; 302

space(s),
> 2D, transparency used to enhance; 80

---

br = bibliography, def = definitions, fg = figure, fn = footnote, sb = sidebar, sr = suggested reading, url = URL list, cp = color plate, gp = gallery plate. For specific art works, see *art works;* for specific individuals, see *people.*

br = bibliography, def = definitions, fg = figure, fn = footnote, sb = sidebar, sr = suggested reading, url = URL list, cp = color plate, gp = gallery plate. For specific art works, see *art works;* for specific individuals, see *people.*

br = bibliography, def = definitions, fg = figure, fn = footnote, sb = sidebar, sr = suggested reading, url = URL list,
cp = color plate, gp = gallery plate. For specific art works, see *art works;* for specific individuals, see *people.*

br = bibliography, def = definitions, fg = figure, fn = footnote, sb = sidebar, sr = suggested reading, url = URL list, cp = color plate, gp = gallery plate. For specific art works, see *art works;* for specific individuals, see *people*.

498 INDEX

br = bibliography, def = definitions, fg = figure, fn = footnote, sb = sidebar, sr = suggested reading, url = URL list, cp = color plate, gp = gallery plate. For specific art works, see *art works;* for specific individuals, see *people.*

br = bibliography, def = definitions, fg = figure, fn = footnote, sb = sidebar, sr = suggested reading, url = URL list,
cp = color plate, gp = gallery plate. For specific art works, see *art works;* for specific individuals, see *people.*